BOLLINGEN SERIES XVIII

GLADYS A. REICHARD

NAVAHO RELIGION

A STUDY OF SYMBOLISM

BOLLINGEN SERIES XVIII

PRINCETON UNIVERSITY PRESS

Published by Princeton University Press, 41 William Street,
Princeton, New Jersey 08540

In the United Kingdom, Princeton University Press, Oxford

THIS IS NUMBER XVIII IN A SERIES OF WORKS SPONSORED BY
BOLLINGEN FOUNDATION

Library of Congress Card No. 63-14455
ISBN 0-691-01906-1
First Princeton/Bollingen Paperback printing, 1974
First Princeton/Bollingen printing in the Mythos series, 1990

Princeton University Press books are printed on acid-free paper,
and meet the guidelines for permanence and durability of the Com-
mittee on Production Guidelines for Book Longevity of the Council
on Library Resources

10 9 8 7 6 5 4 3 2 1

*Printed in the United States of America by Princeton University Press,
Princeton, New Jersey*

TO

ROMAN HUBBELL

FOR INCALCULABLE AID AND ENCOURAGEMENT

CONTENTS

PART TWO

SYMBOLISM

PART THREE

RITUAL

CHARTS

xi

FIGURES

FOREWORD TO THE
SECOND EDITION

In writing *Navaho Religion*, Gladys Reichard undertook a stupendous task, at which she was eminently successful. She set out to expound all the manifold elements—some, to the uninitiated observer, large, and some small, but all, to Navaho thinking, important—that make up a complex and apparently disorderly ceremonial system, to classify and explain the symbolism, and, in her Concordances, to reduce most of the diverse elements at least tentatively to order.

The Navaho religion is based on a central core of doctrine and philosophy which the author sketched understandingly in her Introduction. This embodies broad ideas that one recognizes immediately as part of the reservoir of universal religious thinking. The ordinary Navaho probably has but an incomplete grasp of these ideas, as the ordinary member of the Christian or other religion is uncertain when it comes to concepts of the same sort. The reservoir is in the mind of mankind, but by no means all mankind draws from it. Where the ideas are expressed in symbols, these serve one believer as doorways into the inner courts of understanding, another rather as doors at which thinking stops in favor of literal acceptance. Among a preliterate people with an individually independent and entirely unorganized priesthood, such as the Navahos, even the priests will vary enormously in depth of thought and in interpretation.

At what stage in the development of their religion the

lofty central elements came into the thinking of the Navahos we do not know and cannot profitably speculate. These elements serve now to inform and bind together what strikes the observer as an almost infinite elaboration of ceremonies, of divisions within groupings of ceremonies, of rites and acts, and a symbolism that extends from high art forms to the inner significance of apparently casual gestures, single words, the most ordinary objects. From one point of view, Navaho religion offers lofty doctrines that have affected the religious thinking of more than one sophisticated non-Indian, from another, a notable aesthetic richness, and from a third, mere complexity. It has something of the quality of a great river delta, in which the single broad current proliferates in an elaborate pattern of streams, branches, and intersecting rivulets. From ground level these seem a mere tangle, but if one attains a suitable vantage point, one sees that they are in fact parts of a pattern, that they fall into a natural order governed by such basic laws as gravity, even though the factor of chance is also present.

No student knows Navaho religion whole, as he might, for instance, know Roman Catholicism. The most learned and intellectual Navaho priest—what we lamely call a "singer" or "medicine man"—knows a major chant, perhaps two or more related ones and their branches, he has observed many others, and there may be some whose performance he has never attended or whose name he hardly knows. Washington Matthews, who in the 1880's first gave us a glimpse of the riches of Navaho ceremonial and its attendant art and literature, was best acquainted with the Night Chant. Reichard's entry was through the Shooting Chant. (Incidentally, I earnestly hope that her arguments for retaining the well established term "Chant" in preference to the meaningless but currently fashionable "Way" will prevail.)

As Reichard pointed out, the increasing number of written studies and attempts at classification enabled her to set in tentative order far more of the ceremonial material than she could have mastered of her own knowledge. We may speculate on what all this complex would become were it to survive not only until it was all written down, but until Navaho singers and theologians had become equipped to exploit fully the written word. Unfortunately, it is most unlikely that this interesting development will ever come to pass.

To the writing of this book Gladys Reichard brought unusual equipment. She was a trained anthropologist who had spent more than thirty years in study of the Navahos. She did not merely visit them; she lived with them and even mastered their art of weaving, after no little exasperation. Similarly, she did not only observe and study the ceremonies, she participated in them. Her books *Dezba* and *Spider Woman* amply testify to the warm, human understanding and affection that informed her studies. An able writer, aesthetically sensitive, she had the quality that enables some students to penetrate to the full values and beauties of an alien belief and ceremonial, as many anthropologists never do, and to communicate her findings.

This book does not touch upon the historical background of Navaho culture nor the provenience of the various parts of the ceremonial. Had it done so with anything like completeness, the product would have been so expanded as to be unmanageable; yet certain of the matters Reichard treats of would be made more comprehensible by some brief reference to pertinent history, in so far as we know it. The average student of Navaho ethnology has at least a general idea of this context, but some statement of it may be of benefit to readers who take up this book out of general interest in the study of religion or other universal topics.

Around the eleventh century of our era, people of Athapascan stock began filtering into the American Southwest from an original homeland in western Canada and Alaska.

Their descendants, the Navahos and the various Apache tribes of our Southwest, sometimes referred to all together as the "Apacheans," despite great diversity, display common physical and cultural characteristics that allow us to think of those original immigrants as united by more than closely related languages. Their southward drift may have been no more than the automatic filling of vacuums, the movement of hunters into undisturbed territories; it may have been caused in part by the pressure of stronger peoples, such as a westward drive of Algonquians spearheaded by what became later the tribe we now know as the Blackfeet. The Athapascans possessed a simple culture, materially very simple, not highly developed in any respect. If we may judge by their descendants, the cultural configuration included an important, durable element of individualism, a love of personal—or at least familial—freedom. They were not disorganized but unorganized, and they preferred to be that way. They grouped themselves in small bands. Units larger than the family were changeable, loosely controlled, easily dissolved. Some of them moved southward over the High Plains, skirting the Rockies, some must have come down between the cordilleran ranges, crossing the Plateau and Basin Areas, to end by settling in the Southwest. The Navaho migration legends mentioned by Reichard raise the possibility that some might have come down along the West Coast and then turned eastward to join the main body. The process of immigration continued, under the pressure of the later Plains tribes, until the early eighteenth century. It deposited in the territories claimed by Spain the various groups that the Spanish, taking over a Zuñi name, termed generically "Apaches."

As they moved along, the Athapascans were exposed to a variety of influences, which we can detect in the recent cultures. Once inside the Southwest, the migrants made further contacts with one or more of the differing ancient cultures of that area. What anthropologists tend to overlook is that the Apacheans were not only on the receiving end; they brought contributions of importance from the north. Here we need more comparative data. It is characteristic that the major northern contribution is not in material things, but in the imaginative realm of myth and tale.

From the time of their settlement in the Southwest, inevitably the various Apachean groups underwent continuing changes. They became increasingly differentiated. In religion, they retained certain important common elements, and they received certain new elements in common as well as others that set them apart from each other quite sharply. Of all these groups, the Navahos underwent the most striking cultural change, drawing heavily from the Pueblos but adapting the Pueblo elements to a totally different, in fact, antagonistic, configuration. The probability is that Navaho culture never did stop changing. When it might have become stabilized, the advent of the Spanish gave this energetic people a whole new warehouse from which to borrow—or steal.

The religion and ceremonial must have been undergoing similar constant change. It still is, now under the degenerative influences of intense contact with white men. Rites and chants developed, mythology evolved into a manifestation of true art. Among the Navahos, it is quite apparent, there was a great flowering which, in material culture, seems to have been at its crest from the period of the adoption of large-scale farming and the subsequent growth of this group into a numerically large people, which probably occurred close to the beginning of historic times and up to the end of the nineteenth century, after which the art of weaving declined. Presumably it was during this same period of creativity that the myths and prayers were perfected and, with the ceremonies, so luxuriantly elaborated.

Up to their final subjugation in 1868, the Navaho people was not a tribe as we understand the word. It was a group of

Apacheans speaking a single branch of the language, using a single culture, and recognizing itself as one people, but without a unifying political organization. This sense of unity continued despite a continuing increase in numbers and an expansion over ever wider territory, until, after 1870, the power of the North American white man made the Navahos into a tribe.

It is not at all surprising, then, that the ceremonies are so many or that there are such differences of opinion about them and so many apparent conflicts. It is remarkable only that we find as much agreement as we do. In many widely scattered settlements the people were fusing the borrowed elements and those that were originally Northern Athapascan into one religion and upon this letting play a newly released creativity. There existed no central authority, no court of last resort. Of course, contradictions developed that can only be rationalized or waved away. The end product was a single religious and ceremonial system, containing local differences, but so much a unity that any Navaho from any part of the wide Navaho country can comfortably take part in any observance anywhere within it: this is the best argument I know of that anarchy may be a workable system.

Above I remarked that the Navahos adapted the many elements they borrowed from the Pueblos to their own very different cultural configuration. This thought is worth following a little further. We have no historical record and virtually no archaeological trace of the Navahos as nomads. The hunting and gathering people who traveled, during we know not what span of time, from Canada to New Mexico obviously experienced a fairly extended period of nomadism; but when we first know of the Navahos, about 1625, they are anchored to the large planted fields (in Tewa, *navahu*) from which they received their Spanish name, *los Apaches de Nabajú*. Even at the height of their herding, earlier in the present century, they were nomadic only in that they shifted between a summer and a winter range, both definitely established; and, before their conquest in 1864, their fields and orchards were what most impressed white observers.

The general Apachean insistence on individuality was not affected even by the important change to farming. At the peak of their agriculture, be it noted, the Navahos also attained the peak of their raiding. Their insistence on reshaping whatever they borrowed to fit a loosely organized, democratic, untrammeled way of life is one of the most striking characteristics of an unusual people. They had ceased to be nomads, but they would not give up mobility. The history of Neolithic man throughout the world centers upon the formation of villages, the elaboration of social and material culture, the centralization of authority, in response to the shift to dependence upon crops and herds as sources of food. The Navahos made that shift, they were craftsmen, they had everything that should have led to a firmly ordered village life, but they did not form villages and they limited their material possessions to what could be packed up in an hour and transported wherever one chose. This condition is only now really changing; until very recently the ordinary well-to-do Navaho family could load everything it owned into a wagon or two and be off whenever it chose. Its travel would be slowed by its sheep, and it might have to send back later for its store of corn, but everything else could be transported with ease. They refused to be possession-bound. This trait may also bear upon their love of jewelry, worn massively by both sexes, as a form of concentrated, transportable wealth.

The Pueblo culture is exactly the opposite—a culture of stability, copious possessions, and permanent housing in quasi-urban villages. From the Pueblos the Navahos borrowed wholesale, taking everything except what was really important. In many Navaho myths we find clearly reflected the wonder felt by a simple, impoverished, wandering people upon first encountering the elaborate mode of life, the comforts and riches, of the Pueblos.

In a modern Hopi village of four or five hundred people,

almost as many elaborate and handsome masks may be housed in usable condition, as well as a great variety of paraphernalia, properties, and quantities of ceremonial garments. (Hopis, in discussing their aboriginal riches, usually mention the garments as in the same value class as jewelry.) These handsome, often impressive, articles are loaded with symbolism. In accord with his basic pattern, your Navaho must reduce his ceremonial equipment to what is readily portable. A well-equipped singer can bring all his paraphernalia on the back of his saddle. It fits the pattern that the Pueblo element the Navahos have developed to the highest point, far beyond Pueblo imaginings, is one which requires no more than the grinding stone to be found in every hogan and the simplest raw materials, plus memory and skill, the hand and the brain: namely, the now world-famous sandpaintings. Whatever has to be carried about is reduced, simplified, as Navaho masks are vastly simpler than Pueblo. The permanent equipment is supplemented by what can be made for the occasion, be it a major sandpainting or a knotted string. In this situation, it is readily understandable how it came about that the Navahos enriched their comparatively simple equipment with the most lavish attribution of symbolism.

The historical dimension has much to add to our thinking about the central divine group of Changing Woman, Whiteshell Woman, and the twin warriors, Monster Slayer and Child-of-the-water. What we know of these gods leaves us with many unanswered questions and a feeling of a mystery as yet unpenetrated, which history and comparative material have not as yet resolved, but do make more apparent. In Concordance A, Reichard devoted far more space to Changing Woman than to any other deity. It is evident that she found a special quality in this goddess, with which I thoroughly agree, and which I would describe as even more than the essential womanliness Reichard mentions: Changing Woman is the nearest thing to what we would consider a truly good, lofty divine being.

Reichard writes (pp. 406-7):

> Changing Woman . . . is the most fascinating of many appealing characters conjured up by the Navaho imagination. . . . Changing Woman is Woman with a sphinxlike quality. . . . She is the mystery of reproduction, of life springing from nothing, of the last hope of the world, a riddle perpetually solved and perennially springing up anew, literally expressed in Navaho: ". . . here the one who is named Changing Woman, the one who is named Whiteshell Woman, here her name is pretty close to the [real] names of every one of the girls."*

In this brief and sympathetic statement is contained one of the unsolved problems, Whiteshell Woman. She and Changing Woman are sometimes two, sometimes one. In some accounts, Monster Slayer and Child-of-the-water were born to Changing Woman, by the Sun's direct rays or from Sun indirectly through water; in others, the first is Changing Woman's son, the second Whiteshell Woman's. In either case the children are twins, and most of the epic would go just as well had the second goddess never been introduced. The creation of the world, the emergence of mankind, and the setting of the world in order by the twins (or by Monster Slayer) form one grand epic cycle. At the end of it, Whiteshell Woman is disposed of in a way that seems little more than a bit of literary tidying up. Her child (if he be hers, or if there be any difference between being hers and being Changing Woman's), Child-of-the-water, also has a quality of superfluousness. He plays a brave part in the slaying of Big Monster and takes the first scalp; after that, the authors of the story do not seem quite to know what to do with him.

---

*I do not understand the last part of the quotation, which is apparently from one of Reichard's informants. Women's names almost always refer to war and have no resemblance to those of these goddesses.

He sits at home and watches a life token while his brother goes forth to battle—like a woman, one feels. Of course, by then he has been established in the Navaho pantheon, and parts are found for him, but he is never, or rarely, essential.

He sits like a woman—among the western Apaches he *is* a woman, daughter of the great goddess and mother of Monster Slayer, when he is not a ridiculous uncle. The Jicarilla cycle and treatment of Child-of-the-water differ from the Navaho only in detail. The Chiricahua Apaches make him the hero and give Monster Slayer (Killer of Enemies) a secondary role, and a thoroughly inferior, even silly one. Killer of Enemies is referred to as a brother but is definitely not a twin. The Mescalero Apaches follow the Chiricahua pattern in some versions, and in at least one they eliminate Child-of-the-water entirely.

Let us look to the north, to the Athapascans between the Algonquian barrier along the Canadian border and the Eskimos of the Arctic coast. Here we find no awe-inspiring gods or goddesses, but tales of a monster slayer and monsters. of the earth conceived of as anthropomorphic and female, and suggestions of a similar concept of the moon. The observation that both the earth and the moon appear to age and to be renewed, although in quite different cycles, is so universal as to be banal. These various items, and several others with a familiar ring to Navaho students, occur in the north in a body of somewhat disconnected stories. The people who migrated into the Southwest and encountered the concept of the organized myth-cycle produced far more inspired mythmakers who wove these and matter from many other sources into an epic. Reichard related Changing Woman to the earth, probably correctly, but we cannot say she *is* the earth, even though on a lofty level of thinking she personifies it. It seems likely, then, that Whiteshell Woman was related originally to the moon but lost that connection when the present idea of the Moon-bearer was taken over.

Casting doubt on this idea, however, is the lack of a concept of two goddesses among the other Apacheans.

Among them, Whiteshell Woman disappears—or does she? For all but the Navahos and Jicarillas, the great goddess, mother or grandmother of the hero god, if anything explicitly greater even than Changing Woman, is White-painted Woman. In the languages of these tribes, the word for "white-painted" just misses being a homophone for the Navaho "changing." Thus, in Chiricahua (transliterating Hoijer's recording into Reichard's orthography), "white-painted" is nádlè·cé, and in Mescalero nádlè·cń, while the Navaho "changing" is nádle·hé.

We have here a very close phonetic resemblance between two names, a fairly close conceptual resemblance between White-painted Woman and Whiteshell Woman (the names do not sound at all alike), and a possible confusion between ancient concepts of earth and moon. The possibilities lead one's thoughts in a spiral. This goddess or these goddesses, in turn, are the source of a culture hero who is also very much of a creator, and who may be one god, or one of two brothers, or nephew to a surplus uncle of dubious character, or twins.

These divinities form a major, core element of Apachean religion. What we know about them presents a historically tantalizing puzzle. They also hint at a mystery in the religious sense, a symbolization of concepts lying, so far as research has revealed up to now, below the level of verbalization employed by modern believers. One thing is clear: somewhere along the line the idea of twins or pairs came into Apachean thinking but never was comfortably assimilated. I think it unlikely that the idea of twin heroes came from the wretched little Pueblo war gods, rather, as P. E. Goddard has suggested, it is the pathetically appealing Stricken Twins who derive from that source. In the present state of our knowledge, one could speculate indefinitely, and to no good purpose, about this apparently intrusive element. I dwell upon this curious complex of changes and apparent confusion within a set of key concepts because it bears upon the symbolization of numerous ideas of prime importance.

Reichard, a woman, has stated more clearly than others Changing Woman's quality as "Woman . . . the mystery of reproduction." It is Sun who fertilizes her, but a thoughtful man can see in Monster Slayer the Man, the setter in order and the shaper, even though not the original creator, the imposer of law upon a world in which, until then, his own monstrous kin ran wild and mankind could not survive. We can see him and his mother as complements, under whatever name they go, and note with interest that in this case the functional male is not the breeder. The parallel cases known to me usually involve Christian influence, which I do not think can be found here.

The initial historical notes in this foreword were set down as a brief statement of context for readers not familiar with Navaho studies. From there I have gone on to what, when *Navaho Religion* first appeared, I hoped to discuss with Gladys Reichard when next I saw her. Circumstances prevented that discussion, and now it cannot occur, so I add certain observations as a way of sprinkling a bit of pollen in tribute to her great work.

Oliver La Farge

PREFACE

The materials on which *Navaho Religion: A Study of Symbolism* is based are varied. With the aid of grants from the Southwest Society and the Council for Research in the Social Sciences, of Columbia University, here gratefully acknowledged, I spent, since 1930, eight summers and parts of two winters on the Navaho reservation, learning the language and participating in the daily and the ceremonial life. I planned the field project as a result of studying and retranslating Gray Eyes' dictation of the Male Shooting Chant Holy, recorded in text by Father Berard Haile in 1924 and given me by the Southwest Society in 1928. Red Point's family settlement at White Sands, six miles south of Ganado, Arizona, was my headquarters. There I witnessed performances of the Male Shooting Chant Holy given by Red Point, two of which were sung over me. After Red Point's death, in 1936, Jim Smith became my instructor, especially for the Male Shooting Chant Evil; together we made phonographic records of the prayers and songs.

Red Mustache of Kinlichee instructed me in the Big Star and Endurance chants, and dictated the myths. Others from whose knowledge I benefited were Black Mustache, Red Point's close friend, of Klagito; Boy Chanter of Salaine, two chanters from the neighborhood of Rough Rock, a Shooting Chanter from Keam's Canyon, Yellow Lefty from the vicinity of Tuba City, and another chanter whose name I did not learn. All these singers of the Male Shooting Chant Holy had acquired their knowledge directly or indirectly from Gray Eyes, having been themselves his pupils or having learned from one of his students.

In 1937, tłắ·h,* of Newcomb, New Mexico, dictated to me *The Story of the Navajo Hail Chant*, and took me to chant and other rite performances in the vicinity of his home. The late Hastin Gani, father-in-law of Jim Smith, both of Beautiful Valley, knew many chants; he specialized in the Beauty Chant. I visited his family and saw him often, and got much information and many explanations from him. To the expert performances of the Feather and Wind chants, sung by Feather Chanter of White Cone and the late Wind Singer of Ganado, I owe perspective; to Rain Singer of Ganado, careful details of divination and the Rain Ceremony.

When Dr. Elsie Clews Parsons edited Stephen's *Hopi Journal* she found his Navaho notes, which were particularly valuable since they had been taken so early as 1883–85. In 1924, Red Point painted in watercolors forty-eight sandpaintings of the Shooting chants and dictated their explanations for the late John Frederick Huckel. A selection from the Huckel Collection, which is now at the Colorado Springs Fine Arts Center, was published in my *Navajo Medicine Man* (1939). From this collection, which contains sixty-three other paintings, and from the manuscript which accompanies them, I learned much, since they contain details not elsewhere available.

Sandpaintings of the Navajo Shooting Chant resulted from collaboration with Franc J. Newcomb, who collected the eighty sandpaintings of the Bush Collection, at Columbia University.

I am as greatly indebted to the uncopyrighted works listed

---

*For a note on Navaho language, see page xxxi.

in the bibliography as to those for which permission to quote has been granted—by Harvard University, The Linguistic Society of America, the University of Chicago, and Miss Mary C. Wheelwright.

In addition to the persons and institutions mentioned above, many friends, white and Indian, have contributed vastly to my comfort and pleasure, as well as to my work. Of many excellent interpreters, Adolph Bitanny was primarily responsible for the illumination shed upon the intricacies of the Navaho language.

I am especially grateful to Barnard College and Dean Virginia Gildersleeve for extra time during which to pursue the work; to Dr. L. C. Wyman and Dr. Clyde Kluckhohn for discussions of incalculable value; to Dr. Roman Jakobson, Dr. Claude Lévi-Strauss, and the late Dr. Clark Wissler for suggestions in preparing the manuscript; and to Dr. H. S. Colton, of the Museum of Northern Arizona, and his entire staff for putting all their facilities at my disposal.

Others who have helped me in innumerable ways are Mrs. Roman Hubbell, Mrs. Barbara Goodman, Mr. and Mrs. Lloyd Ambrose, Mr. and Mrs. Horace Boardman, Mr. and Mrs. John Simm, and Mr. and Mrs. Fred Wilson. In assuring all of my deep gratitude and appreciation, I take sole responsibility for the conclusions reached and for errors of fact or interpretation which may have crept into the work.

GLADYS A. REICHARD

Barnard College,
Columbia University.

NOTE ON THE NAVAHO LANGUAGE

Since the Navaho language is very different from English, and particularly since the religion has a highly specialized idiom, I sometimes use Navaho words, chiefly when I can find no satisfactory English equivalent. They appear in a phonetic typography, which has no capital letters, even for proper names (such as co and be'γotcidí) and words that begin a sentence.

In this as in all my earlier publications, I have consistently held to the same phonetic system. I have accepted the Sapir-Hoijer descriptions of the sounds (see Bibliography) according to the system Sapir and Hoijer were using when I started my work in 1930 (they have since changed the characters). A brief explanation of those I use follows:

The vowels—a, e, i, and o (there is no u)—are pure, with continental European values; they are very short. There are several vowel modifications, all as important as the vowels themselves: −˙ (superior dot after the vowel) indicates lengthening of the vowel; ˛ (cedilla under the vowel) indicates nasalization of the vowel, as, for example, in French 'enfant' (in Navaho phonetics, ạfạ). Pitch is grammatically important in Navaho. If the vowel or syllabic n has no diacritical mark for pitch, it is neutral in tone; if it has an acute accent (−́), it is high; an inverted circumflex (−̌) indicates a rising tone; a circumflex (−̂) indicates a falling tone.

The following consonants have approximately the same values as in English: h, k, kw, l, m, n, s, t, ts, w, y, z.

The symbols b, d, and g differ from English in being unaspirated; English speakers often hear them as p, t, or k.

j is a voiced spirant, like j in French ' je.' c is the voiceless form of j, pronounced as sh in English ' show.' dj is the corresponding voiced affricative, pronounced as j in ' judge.' tc is the voiceless affricative pronounced as ch in ' church.'

As I have said, s and z have the same phonetic values as in English: that is, z is voiced, as in ' zone '; s is voiceless, as in ' so.' dz is the voiced affricative, as in ' adze '; ts is its voiceless counterpart, as in ' bits.' In Navaho, dz and ts may occur initially or intervocalically.

There are five sounds in the l-series: l is the voiced lateral as in ' law '; ł is the voiceless lateral approximately as in English ' play.' The voiced affricative dl, its voiceless counterpart tł, and the glottalized affricative tł do not occur in English. Examples in Navaho are dloh, ' laughter '; tłah, ' salve '; and tłoh, ' hay, grass.'

The sound represented by the Greek gamma (γ) is a velar voiced spirant, approximating r in German ' Garten ' (as pronounced in Berlin). γw is its labialized form, which before a, e, and i, particularly when intervocalic, may be heard as w. x is the voiceless spirant, approximating ch in German ' ich '; xw is its labialized form, as in Navaho xwi·h, ' satisfaction.'

$\stackrel{\perp}{}$ is the glottal stop, as in Navaho 'e'e'a·h, ' west.' It is similar to the sound heard for the ' tt ' in the New York City dialect pronunciation of ' bottle.'

ṁ, ṅ, ṭ, k̇, tṡ, tċ, tł, and ẏ are glottalized forms of the sounds described above—none occurs in English or the best known European languages.

(For a comment on the spellings 'Navaho' and 'Navajo,' see page 749.)

INTRODUCTION

The Navaho, largest and most colorful Indian tribe in the
United States, is superficially the best known. Its members
wear costumes derived from old Spain and the cowboy
tradition, and they travel on horseback or in covered wagons
more frequently than in pickups, trucks, or sedans. They
crowd to the 'squaw dance,' where, within a mile of high-
way or railroad, their eerie singing and strange rites carry
the ordinary white person miles from reality and back
uncounted years into what he considers the prehistoric
past. Occasionally he can watch a sandpainting being made
and used for its original purpose; more often he sees repro-
ductions which have for him an exotic appeal.

Navaho Religion: A Study of Symbolism tries to demonstrate that there is much more to the dance, song, and sandpainting than the primitiveness that meets the casual eye;
that there is a religious system which has for years enabled
the Navaho to retain their identity in a rapidly changing
world. Its aim is to show how and why these people are pre-
occupied with ritual, and further, how the principles of their
system differ so radically from our own as to be almost
incomprehensible to whites, even after considerable study.

The 'squaw dance' is only one of many ceremonies performed to protect Navaho society, its means of subsistence
and acquisition, its medicine, and above all, its peace of
mind. Song, dance, and sandpainting are each only one of
numerous parts necessary to the ceremony, which is actually
a complicated charm. To it Dr. Washington Matthews gave

the name ' chant,' since long and elaborate prayers chanted or intoned are still another ritualistic requirement. Other recorders, especially in the last fifteen years, have called the ceremonies ' ways,' translating literally a Navaho postposition. For instance, Night Chant has become Night Way or Nightway; Mountain Chant, Mountainway or Mountain Top Way; the War Ceremony [1] has become Enemy Way. In my opinion, the change has added to the terminology but little to the understanding of Navaho ceremonialism, and I am content to use the old term ' chant.' Since no English word is adequate to describe the religious complex, explanation and interpretation must be substituted.

A Navaho ceremony, whatever it may be called, is a combination of many elements—ritualistic items such as the medicine bundle with its sacred contents; prayersticks, made of carefully selected wood and feathers, precious stones, tobacco, water collected from sacred places, a tiny piece of cotton string; song, with its lyrical and musical complexities; sandpaintings, with intricate color, directional, and impressionistic symbols; prayer, with stress on order and rhythmic unity; plants, with supernatural qualities defined and personified; body and figure painting; sweating and emetic, with purificatory functions; vigil, with emphasis on concentration and summary. But it is the selection of these and other elements and their orderly combination into a unit that makes the chant or ceremony effective. Few of these details were unknown when I started my work, but the reasons for their selection and their meaning as a whole had been only vaguely realized. This analysis has shown that the interpretation is based on an interlocking system of associations.

A ceremony may last from one to nine nights—the Navaho count by nights—and the intervening days. The first night of a typical nine-night ceremony consists of an hour or two of singing, which accompanies a simple ritualistic performance. The early morning hours of the first four days are taken up with sweat-emetic rites, composed of numerous and intricate ritualistic acts whose purpose is to drive out evil and purify the patient and all other participants. Several hours of the early afternoon of each day are devoted to the preparation of prayersticks, over which a responsive prayer is intoned by chanter and patient. The prayersticks are then placed at designated points—under a rock, near an arroyo, under a tree at the south, in a branch of a pine tree at the west—where the gods must see them. The prayersticks carry a compulsive invitation to the deities to attend the ceremony. If the sticks are made properly and deposited according to deific decree, and if the prayer is repeated without a mistake, the gods cannot refuse to come. The two main emphases of the first four days are on exorcising possible evil and on invoking the deities.

At pre-dawn of the fifth day the contents of the chanter's bundle—all items sacred to the chant, though odd and nondescript to the white man—are laid out on a mound which forms an altar a few yards from the door of the dwelling in which the ceremony is held. As each piece of ritualistic property is placed, the chanter utters the appropriate sentence of a prayer and the patient, as a symbol, takes hold of the property. The altar is there to announce the preparation of a sandpainting inside the house, to inform the gods that they are expected, to warn persons not concerned that they should stay away. One painting is made on each day of the second group of four days. A simple painting may be finished by one or two painters in half an hour; an elaborate one may require from three to forty assistants working eight or ten hours. When the painting is finished, the patient sits on it, while the chanter applies sand from the various figures of the painting to specified parts of the patient's body, and performs other ritualistic acts. All this is to identify the patient with the deities represented in the painting. The rite lasts about half an hour on each of the fifth, sixth, and seventh days, and from an hour to two and a half hours on the eighth, the last, day. A part of the sand-painting ritual of the eighth day is the body or figure painting, which serves to identify the patient with the deific helpers. Early on this day a final rite, combining exorcism and the attraction of good powers, is the bath. The patient, with the aid of relatives, shampoos his hair and washes his body in suds made from yucca (soapweed) root and dries himself with coarse, ceremonially ground corn meal.

On each intervening night, that is, on nights two to eight, the singing resembles that of the first night, becoming longer as the ceremony progresses. Just as the sandpainting of each day is representative of a group made up of numerous paintings—Thunders, Snakes, Holy People, Arrow People, and the like—so on each night certain groups of songs are chosen from a vast number known to the chanter. He designates and starts the song; the chorus of laymen assisting him carries it on. If they do not know it, the chanter sings until they learn it or until it is finished. Generally each rite becomes longer and more elaborate as the chant proceeds.

The eighth day is called ' The Day.' It is often a very busy one what with the bath, sandpainting, body or figure painting, and preparation for the ninth night. On this, ' The Night,' the singing lasts from late evening until dawn, the purpose being to summarize all the purification, invocation, attraction of power, and identification of the entire ceremony. Song-groups representative of all the rites are included. The night becomes a vigil, theoretically for all present in the ceremonial dwelling, practically for those most concerned. To show he is in sympathy with the entire effort put forth in the chant, the patient concentrates on all the songs and the few ritualistic acts. Since power is to the Navaho like a wave in a pool, always effective though becoming weaker the farther it radiates from chanter and patient, each person in attendance derives benefit from what is done in proportion to his proximity to the ritual.

The Navaho has always been recognized as an individualist. Since his inherited membership in a clan and a clan group imposes upon him rigid restrictions, as well as obligations to a great many people, and his acquiescence in his religious system requires the strictest sort of discipline, one may well inquire wherein his individualism lies. To answer, one must understand the ramifications of the socio-religious system.

Doubtless the most important factor is that he does not feel bound. He retains his individualistic attitude because of the system rather than in spite of it. Since his membership in a clan and clan-group and an additional relationship to his father's clan and clan-group make it possible for him to consider a great many persons obligated to him, he emphasizes his privileges rather than his duties, which, in the opinion of an outsider, may be quite onerous. The elaborate ceremonies are possible only if assets are accumulated—sheep, horses, cash, labor, transport, and, above all, willingness to provide. If Tall Navaho decides to have a Mountain Chant sung, he calls upon Shorty to donate a sheep and invites him to attend the performance. Shorty considers the request an honor, for has he not upon several occasions borrowed small sums from Tall Navaho which he has not yet returned? But if in the course of the winter, eight other ambitious relatives, some of whom Shorty hardly knows, request contributions, he may become a bit chagrined at the drain on his resources; though he may grumble, he does not assert his individuality and refuse, nor does he feel that his individualism has been violated. If he cannot give a sheep, he can at least promise to help with the singing, and his wife will aid with the cooking and even contribute some flour and baking powder.

When Tall Navaho's wife enters the hogan or ceremonial enclosure, unmindful of ritualistic requirements other than knowing that women sit at the north side of the hogan, she may stalk casually to the right of the fire, since that is the shortest way to the place she is bound for. The chanter or someone else will say, "Go around the fire," meaning ' move in a clockwise direction.' She reverses, goes the roundabout way, and takes her place. She does not interpret the request as depriving her of her individuality any more than Shorty does if the chanter tells him to wind a string around a withe in a clockwise direction when he has unthinkingly started to wind it counterclockwise. The homogeneity of belief interprets dogma as protecting individualism rather than impinging upon it.

From approximately eight thousand in 1868 the Navaho population has grown to more than fifty thousand. This small tribe, adapted to a pastoral life, occupies more than 25,000 square miles of land, most of which is accessible only with difficulty. Consequently, the residence groups of two, three, or at the most twelve houses and from three to fifty inhabitants are, properly speaking, mere settlements; they rarely attain, even in irrigated districts, the character of villages. Of necessity, therefore, Tall Navaho, Shorty, and their sisters have had to learn to act independently from earliest childhood. In fact, there are many times when inability to do so may be fatal, either to the person or to his herd—the right-minded Navaho puts the flock ahead of himself since it represents the bulk of the family's resources. Theoretically, a Navaho female, child or adult, should never be left entirely alone. Actually every individual spends many hours alone.

I consider solitude the basic reason for Navaho development of and insistence upon self-reliance. The right to come to one's own conclusion is respected, though the decision itself may be 'talked down' in a family or local council. The individual is persuaded; he is not high-pressured into a judgment contrary to his own.

It is no wonder then that loneliness has become a mythical and religious symbol, that from loneliness stem some of the greatest powers the Navaho conceive. The co-operation that extends from the individual, on the one hand to family and all residential relationships, and on the other to clan members, father's clan relatives, clan-group members, and finally, to strangers, seems to be due to the fight against loneliness. I believe that the Navaho derived his clan organization from observations of some tribe or tribes he met in the past, rather than that he himself originated it. However encountered, the clan organization was adopted, emphasizing help as a primary ideal which gives the lonely individual security in his broad and often unfriendly terrain. I am an alien, but Navaho social theory included me as a responsibility, and the persons practicing it unconsciously were able to give me the feeling of security they themselves had achieved. This, in brief, is an explanation of the privilege a Navaho individual values in his personal subordination to his group, and an explanation of his extreme pleasure in any group activity, be it harvesting, building a dam, or attending a council meeting, rodeo, ceremony, or Christmas party.

There is another limitation to which the Navaho submits—

the finality of an older person's decision. The judgment of a grandparent has priority over that of a parent, that of an older sibling over that of a younger, even if it be that of a twin only twenty minutes older. The principle, though verbally unformulated, is thoroughly binding in practice. Once during a grave crisis in the relations of members of the family of Red Point (hereafter abbreviated RP), my judgment, reluctantly given, was accepted as final. Surprised as I was at the whole affair, I was even more astonished to learn that my decision was so important because I was the senior of the group at the time. "We have no older relative to consult," the quarreling man and woman explained after requesting and acting upon my advice. They considered this lack such a calamity that the family soon after made a liaison with another large family living four miles away, although the clan and other ascertainable relationships were very tenuous. RP's children gained an ' older sister ' in the person of the sixty-year-old mother of the second family, and the arrangement has since been quite satisfactory.

A good Navaho is, therefore, an individual who can and may make his own decisions, but he is most stable if he has social corroboration. To this end he must develop fortitude, particularly to endure the often exorbitant demands of his physical environment, a major requirement of the economic life and the religious dogma. Ideally, the ' good ' individual should be industrious, dependable, tractable, skillful, good-humored. He should be able to live with others without friction, for social relations are a part of the universal scheme which demands harmony for right living. If he has certain of these qualities he may be expected to obtain wealth, which will help to make him respected. If, however, his skill and management make him wealthy too quickly, particularly if he gains property through stinginess or refuses to help his kin, he may be accused of chicanery, or worse, of practicing sorcery, especially if one of his skills is chanting.

These qualities are the ideal; but, oddly enough, the prototype in several biographical descriptions of successful medicine men is a youth who has, of all the good qualities, primarily intelligence but who, until he starts his professional training, is the Navaho idea of a wastrel. He assumes no responsibility. He resists the admonition to marry and settle down. He may work, but he is sometimes lazy, at best unsteady. He is a rover, traveling widely, becoming a professional visitor, usually at a home where there is a desirable girl or a bevy of attractive women. Just as soon as marriage, which involves a tie, is hinted at, he mounts his horse and moves on. He does not invest such property as he may gain, but spends it in dissipation, particularly gambling, although he may gain by the same means. An old man, reformed, boasts of youthful philanderings and tolerates those of his grandson or nephew, but does not condone their irresponsibility for the results of their dalliance.

To even the most thoughtless youth the chants and ceremonies have a great appeal, and crowds of young men are a common sight at any religious gathering. There are various reasons for their attendance: at a ceremony, companionship and feasting are to be enjoyed; there may even be racing and other sports; the young men may spontaneously start a rodeo. Going to the ' sings,' as they are often called, makes a good excuse for roaming. There is still more to it, however. Often a chanter needs something that requires sustained effort; he must have an herb that grows fifty miles away. It is not unusual for an apparently undisciplined young man to volunteer to go for it on horseback and to bring it back on time. Many delight to act as chanter's assistant. They gather wood ritualistically for the sacred fire, sort out tiny bits of jewels for the prayerstick offerings, patiently bunch twigs of blue spruce and Douglas fir to be tied with careful knots to ceremonial articles. Most young men enjoy making sandpaintings.

In the ceremonial hogan there is good, informative talk; ritual preparation and its accomplishment give pleasure. No phase of Navaho religion is doleful. Reverence means keeping things in order, not pulling a long face. Few rites demand silence. When it occurs, as during a prayer, it is to allow concentration rather than to emphasize decorum. In addition, singing seems to have tremendous appeal for the Navaho youth. If a young man is not able to attend the sandpainting rites or to take part in any of the eight-day activities, he will, nevertheless, exert himself to be present at the Vigil, which, according to white standards, is devoid of action, monotonous, in fact often boring. I have never met a Navaho who thought so. I have attended many a night's singing, staying from beginning to end. Often the women give evidence of weariness, some sleep for short intervals, but many men seem to get more and more interested as the night advances. They sing more vigorously as new groups of songs are introduced, much as if they are progressively stimulated by their own efforts. Since the songs carry symbolically the plot of what the Navaho believes to be the original adventures of the chant hero, it is likely that the singers follow the development as carefully as we follow a good drama. They know what is going to happen, anticipate the familiar, and take pleasure in identifying themselves with it. Finally, with the dawn and the end of the series, comes a feeling of elation at the accomplishment of a long, detailed, but joyous task. It seems to me important that the most profane youth, though he may assert that young people do not believe these things any more, derives great comfort from the whole experience. Even the most sophisticated Navaho is occasionally sung over, but he may have the sing at an isolated spot so as to escape criticism and the accusation of being ' superstitious.'

All this inescapable tradition accounts for the development of the Navaho chanter, who is no ordinary individual. He differs from the youth untrained in ceremonial lore and the youth who has not settled down, in that he has knowledge and, in acquiring it, has accepted responsibility for the welfare of his fellowmen. Not only is he charged, through correct performance of a ceremony, with the well-being of the patient he sings over, but he must risk the danger that his knowledge, weakened by error, may harm him. Nevertheless, the intelligent youth, grown older, though he may have been a waster, may be persuaded to take up the chanting profession. To do so, one must have wealth, for a novice must pay his teacher for all he learns. Of course, he gets paid for singing after his training is complete. When he becomes an independent singer he gives a fee to his instructor after each performance—a sort of voluntary royalty. Sometimes an older chanter accepts from a younger relative a mere token payment, kinship being a substitute for property. On the other hand, wealthy old men who are not learned may furnish the means for a young man to take the proper chant training. As in most societies, old men are more likely to have wealth than young ones.

A chant may be learned in several ways. Once a novice has decided upon the profession, he or his intermediary makes an agreement with an older man who is an expert, and pays a fee, the amount being unstipulated and voluntary. If the novice has time, he may go to live with the chanter for some months, even a year, studying intensively. Concentrating on the songs, prayers, and ritualistic acts, he will assist whenever his teacher chants; the chanter will explain details and their reasons to his pupil. When judged competent, the novice is sung over to initiate him, fix his knowledge, and protect him from the danger of possessing chant power. From this time on he is considered a singer and may be requested to sing. RP spent months at Gray Eyes' home learning the Shooting Chant; tłá·h left home to devote years to the various types of the Night Chant, meanwhile giving up all other activities.

Some men cannot arrange to specialize in this way. They take up their training piecemeal, making it a point to attend every performance the teacher gives, asking questions and getting help from him more informally whenever possible. Such men earn their way as they go, saving to pay for a ceremony to bless a set of equipment now and then. There is no time limit on learning; chanting is a lifetime interest. Jim Smith (JS) had sung the Male Shooting Chant Evil and the Male Shooting Chant Holy for a long time before he acquired the wide boards and bundle prayersticks at the ceremony described in Concordance C of this work. He had to borrow these important items before he got his own. He is a popular chanter, regards his knowledge with assurance, and doggedly persists in filling in the gaps. He knows the Night Chant but has never been able to have the masks dedicated for himself and has never sung it.

I do not mean to indicate that all chanters are male. Most are—all my instructors were—but there are respected women chanters. Although all the Shooting Chant[2] singers I encountered trace their knowledge to Gray Eyes, many considered his sister a final arbiter in disputes.[3] A woman was famed for singing the Night Chant, considered by the Navaho as the highest achievement, and several sing the Female Shooting Chant and have taught it to other women. Unfortunately, I have never known a woman chanter. There were some mild complaints about my not being a Navaho and about my using pencil and paper; but I never heard any objection on the ground that I am a woman to my presence at a ceremony or my ambition to learn. A wife is more likely to help her husband acquire knowledge than to set herself up as a chanter.

Usually men who take up chanting are approaching middle age and those who have arrived are elderly or old. However, one of my instructors was called Boy Chanter because he had learned the Shooting Chant well enough to sing it by the time he was twenty-six.

Although Navaho singers act independently and are not organized into a priesthood, those who sing the same chant often discuss differences. Their deliberations serve as a check on the individual who may inadvertently make a mistake, and may also bring out distinctions in teaching. Often a discussion shows that one instructor advocated details or an 'arrangement of one kind, whereas another emphasized something different. Most of the discussions seem trivial to whites, but to the chanters they are of paramount importance, and they attest to the Navaho insistence on individual opinion.

From my sample of more than a dozen chanters, none may be chosen as representative or typical; each differs in important respects from the others. RP was energetic, active, dominating. tłá·h was energetic, ambitious, self-confident, gentle but firm; he sought no personal glory. Hastin Gani (HG) was patient, somewhat phlegmatic and easy-going, and not in the least aggressive; he practiced numerous ceremonies—his specialty was the Female Beauty Chant. Red Mustache (RM), like RP, was for many years undisciplined. After much persuasion his maternal uncle prevailed upon him to marry and learn to sing. As an old man he emphasized his reform and his subsequent contentment with the course he had chosen, adding with pride that for some thirty years he had been faithful to his wife. JS differs from them all in having always been a solid, dependable, obliging, unerring, but unimaginative citizen. He is purposeful and steady, rarely gets excited even when all others about him lose their heads.

Yet all the chanters I know have much in common. All are friendly and gracious if properly approached. All value the power inherent in knowledge. Possession of esoteric information commands respect and predisposes chanters to communicate more. In this they follow tradition. An old man of the Mountain Chant myth admonishes his discouraged sons, unsuccessful in the hunt: "You kill nothing because you know nothing. If you had knowledge you would succeed." [4] All chanters share the same assumptions: the conviction that dogma is final and everlasting, a common belief in the universal order, assurance that man has or may obtain power to fit into the world securely and smoothly, and faith in their own power to correct error when it becomes necessary to reduce the friction generated by ignorance in the universal machine. These ideals hold them together, but the chanters reserve the right to be themselves, to criticize and even, after discussion, to continue to differ. In many respects chanters differ from lay Navaho chiefly in the high specialization attained by rigorous training and in their more marked idealism.

When asked about the satisfactions of a chanting life my acquaintances, all except tłá·h, mentioned first economic security. They could hardly be expected to formulate certain other rewards that are apparent to an outsider who has observed them in action over a period of years: Ritualistic power increases their influence in the community. Less tangible, and impossible to separate from other aspects, is the singer's aesthetic reward from his profession. The conviction of having done the right thing, of having been put back into order after straying, is the great satisfaction the Navaho derives from religious practice. The difference between the greater and the lesser chanter is the degree to which the sacredness of the charm that is his chant pervades his life. The most ordinary Navaho may have no interest in causes or meanings, but trusts in punctilious ritualistic performance; the chanter is recompensed even more by his erudition since he knows the reason for each detail.

The body of Navaho mythology is to Navaho chanters what the Bible is to our theologians. The singer discussing his belief, as well as the layman asked a direct question, resorts for his answer to myth, which he considers final. It is therefore almost impossible to separate mythology or mythical concept completely from reality or practice. Because nearly every Navaho has some faith in his ceremonies, whether he knows the significance or not, and because he cites myth for his reasons, I consider the myth material a major contribution to the analysis and interpretation of the religion. Though in some of its concepts it may seem childlike, it is never childish, and its very childlikeness is sometimes merely evidence of a deep realization of spiritual things. Consequently, Navaho chant mythology should no more be relegated solely to the realm of children than our Bible.

The mythology has two aspects, the secular and the sacred. In certain ways, especially in the plots, both aspects have material common to many American Indian tribes. Among the secular myths, some of the Navaho coyote tales, for example, can hardly be distinguished from those of a number of other tribes; and when they can be, it is because the narrative style is characteristically Navaho. The sacred myths, which account for particular ceremonies, are distinctive in the way the plot assists the development of ceremonial detail, and in the intentional though implicit explanations of the parts and the whole. As in the determination of the chant, so in the myth, differentiation depends upon selection.

PART ONE
DOGMA

CHAPTER 1

NAVAHO CATEGORIES

NAVAHO DOGMA is based upon a cosmogony that tries to
account for everything in the universe by relating it to
man and his activities. It assumes that even before man
existed, the purpose for his appearance on the earth and his
use of all nature's apparatus was formulated—by whom, no
one knows. To the Navaho religion means ritual. Each ceremony has its own myth, a long account of deific decrees, from
which it derives its authority. In it human activities are so
co-ordinated with supernatural adventures and ritualistic
explanations that the myth plot aids the chanter's memory.
After the scene has been set and the plot developed, most
legends become purely descriptive of the sacred properties
and the accompanying ritual. The implied explanations must
be elucidated by the chanter.

Mythological decree is just as real—that is, ' circumstantial '—to a Navaho as his dinner. Morgan, in his study of
dreams about human wolves, bases some of his most important conclusions on a differentiation between circumstantial
and imaginary or mythological evidence.[1] My experience con-
vinces me that evidence cannot be separated in this way.
When any subject is discussed, whether a Navaho is ostensibly indifferent to religion or a fervent believer, at some point
his only recourse is to tradition, especially when cause or
purpose is involved.

The song, the myth, the material properties, the ritualistic
acts, the rites that make up the ceremonies are held together

3

by an elaborate system of symbolism, a sum total of numerous associations. Various phases of nature, life, and human activity have a place in this system. Before the symbolism, which is in a sense exotic, can be understood, some of the basic Navaho beliefs must be examined.

One reason for the confusion is that the white man has gone about interpreting Navaho religion as if it were the same as his. Details that define Navaho beliefs, though perpetually surprising in their originality, are not confusing once the principles are grasped. The chant may sound like a jumble of diverse elements; places are introduced, gods characterized, ideals formulated by verbal, musical, and material symbols. Properties demand a wide knowledge of plants, animals, minerals. Tangible and intangible elements are interwoven in the sand- and figure-painting, dance and pantomime, accompanied by songs, drums, and rattles. A good chanter so integrates the innumerable details as to give an impression of a smooth sequence. As we probe deeper we come to comprehend in some degree how the co-ordination is brought about, but we are likely to conclude falsely that the whole thing is merely a feat of memory, not a system at all.

In Navaho religion no one thing has more absolute significance than another. We may speak of ' high gods ' as members of an elaborate pantheon, but Changing Woman or Sun is no more important at a particular moment than the humble roadrunner or a grain of corn. In the entire conceivable span of time the ' great gods ' may perhaps dominate, for their power spreads over all space and time. Since, however, for the most part the ceremony is concerned with the specific moment, omnipotence and omnipresence are subordinate ideas, if indeed they exist as absolutes.

Although Navaho dogma stresses the dichotomy of good and evil, it does not set one off against the other. It rather

4

emphasizes one quality or element in a being which in different circumstances may be the opposite. Sun, though ' great ' and a ' god,' is not unexceptionally good. He seems always to have aimed to make the world fit for man's habitation. Why then did he father the monsters, the terrible creatures that long hindered the realization of this very purpose? The answer to this and other similar inconsistencies is that what is wholly good is merely an abstraction, a goal that man as an individual never attains. Everything except the concept itself may have some evil in it, but is classified as good if good prevails qualitatively or quantitatively. Similarly, few things are wholly bad; nearly everything can be brought under control, and when it is, the evil effect is eliminated. Thus evil may be transformed into good; things predominantly evil, such as snake, lightning, thunder, coyote, may even be invoked. If they have been the cause of misfortune or illness, they alone can correct it. Like cures like. Examples of good turned to evil are less common, yet when Changing-bear-maiden's lore, which was essentially good, was combined with the power of Coyote, which was innocent of control, it became evil. Good then in Navaho dogma is control. Evil is that which is ritually not under control. And supernatural power is not absolute but relative, depending upon the degree of control to which it is subjected. In short, definition depends upon emphasis, not upon exclusion.

For this reason such words as ' always,' ' never,' ' most important ' are out of place in describing supernatural ideas, because no category is exclusive—all overlap or include exceptions. The classes of deity illustrate the monistic principle. The characterization of First Woman in some settings puts her in a class wholly evil, yet she, like Sun, seems to have had the vision of a world made for man, and

5

the purpose of bringing it into being. When she withdrew from that world she said she would bring colds and similar afflictions, thereby allying herself with evil, yet the part she played in the creation and training of Changing Woman was totally good.[2]

To illustrate further the position of a being in more than one category let us consider the chanter. Though by effort and training he may get control of supernatural power, he is not a success until he *is* that power. Before taking up the singer's course he is human; while learning to sing he identifies himself with the mythological heroes who experienced dangerous adventures in order to gain the power of the chant; as he intones their names and uses their symbols he becomes successively the Persuadable, the Undependable, even the Unpersuadable Deities; and as he uses the properties that stand for them he may become the Helper of Deity, of man, and even of the evil powers. According to a basic principle of Navaho ritual, identification, the chanter incorporates within himself the entire complex of godly notions and even has the power to make others like himself, that is, like gods. He is a center that receives power from all proper sources and distributes it to all worthy subscribers.

The Navaho, though apparently specific, may actually be generalizing. They often give particular reasons for belief or ritual that may be identical with those given at other times to explain other things. For example, to the question what would happen if a man looked at his mother-in-law, the invariable answer is: "He wouldn't feel good. He would go crazy and act like a moth at the fire." This seems a distinctive enough punishment until we learn that the same fate is in store for anyone who breaks an incest rule, who sees a ghost, or wittingly desecrates a sacred object.[3] It is indeed a general penalty for breaking familiar taboos.

Again we may be misled into jumping to conclusions concerning the character of certain supernaturals or their functions when we read for the first time that someone, let us say Coyote, "will have charge of dark cloud, heavy rain, dark mist, gentle rain, and vegetation of all kinds." It seems a lot when we consider how thoroughly Coyote is despised. Then we find that, at a time when his power was requested and he obdurately refused, the gods offered to put him in charge of darkness, daylight, heavy rain, gentle rain, corn, vegetation of all kinds, thunder, and the rainbow, and he accepted.[4] This list is not too different from the first, and at least concerns the same individual. Continuing the analysis of mythology we find that Frog, who was beaten in a race by Rainboy, was recompensed for the loss of his body by the return of his feet, legs, and gait, and by being put in charge of ' dark cloud, heavy (male) rain, dark mist, gentle rain, and holiness wherever they may be '; and further, that Rainboy, after initiation, was put in charge of ' heavy and gentle rain, snow, and ice.' [5] By this time we may well ask, "Who *is* in charge of rain?," for Changing Woman too has charge of female rain and vegetation of all kinds.[6] We must, therefore, conclude that despite the precise specification, these promises are stereotyped, signifying, "We shall give you our best if you will help us"; in other words, they are actually a rationalization or systemization. No particular being is in charge of rain, because one is dependent upon another.

The confusion of analogical thought should constantly be kept in mind when a classification is being studied. When the Navaho says two things, which turn out to be very different, are the ' same,' ' similar,' he is not avoiding the truth, but construing the words with meaning entirely different from ours. The primary meaning of ' alike ' in Navaho is ' used for the same purpose,' ' having the same function '

7

—analogous rather than homologous. Consequently, things may be ' alike ' when they are symbolically associated or complementary.

Several characteristics of the Navaho language frequently cause misunderstanding. Words may be bipolar; that is, a word may have a meaning obvious in a particular context, and in another setting the opposite. An element that means ' up ' may also mean ' down '; one that at times means ' on ' or ' upon ' may mean ' off ' or ' off from on '; ' from (there) ' frequently means ' to here, hither.' Hence, good may sometimes be evil and vice versa.

Another linguistic habit, of considering a whole, all, or any one of its parts as the ' same,' affects classification. For example, djic* means ' medicine bundle as a container,' ' medicine bundle with all its contents,' ' contents of medicine bundle,' or a ' separate item of a medicine bundle.' The chanter knows perfectly well that the hide or muslin wrapper is not the ' same ' as the bull-roarer, that the ' wide board ' differs greatly from the talking prayersticks or from the otterskin collar, yet in certain circumstances each is djic. He is acutely aware of the context and, therefore, of ' sameness ' and ' difference,' whereas his questioner is unable to determine the meaning because he is ignorant of the cultural context.

Aware of diversity in interpretation, the conscientious investigator does not take as final a Navaho's statement that another prayerstick, another rite, another song, is the same as the one he has seen or heard. By attending the second day's performance as well as the first and, subsequently, the third and fourth, he gets his most valuable data. Compiling

---

*See p. xxxi for a note on the Navaho language. In this work, the Navaho phonetics are printed in the same typography as the text. In accordance with phonetic practice, capital letters are not used.

the details day by day is very different from comparing elements from various chants only, although eventually we must do that too.

The following examples are given in some detail in an attempt to make the reader realize that a revamping of assumptions is essential if Navaho categories are to be compared with our own. On the day Wyman saw the sandpainting illustrated in *An Introduction to Navaho Chant Practice*, Figure 23, he asked what painting would be used the next day. "Just like this, only blue," was the reply. The next day the painting was that of Figure 24 of the same work, a picture much more complicated and with many different features; even similar details in the second painting were colored differently from those in the first.[7] Both had the same function, but the second elaborated on the themes of the first.

In the field of ethnobotany, Wyman corroborates my conclusion. Defining the terms ' Navaho family ' and ' Navaho genus ' he writes: "The Navajo think of plants as falling into large categories according to their use (purpose or method). . . . They regard the species in a category as being definitely related in some way, although the same species may sometimes belong to more than one category. In a few instances, these groups do contain a number of species from the same botanical family, although this is because they have similar morphological or pharmacological properties. . . . A Navajo [botanical] family may be named for the ceremonial in which the constituent species are used; the etiological factor held responsible for the disease treated with the herbs; the disease or disease group itself . . . ; the supposed pharmacological effect of the herbs; the method of preparation for use; the method of administration. Family names may be combinations of these factors."[8]

9

Much attention has been devoted to classifying Navaho ceremonies, but it is difficult to reconcile such statements from informants and texts as: "The Shooting Chant is the same as the Hail Chant. . . . Everything [in the Hail and Water chants] is exactly the same. . . . Our paintings, prayer-sticks, tobacco pouches, bundle properties, our rattles are alike." [9]

A superficial glance at the myth or any part of the ritual of the Shooting, Hail, or Water chants shows marked differences in the elements specifically mentioned. The purpose, however, is the same; afflictions caused by lightning, hail, and water are felt to be so similar and the association among the symbols of the three chants so close that one may be substituted for another.

The chant name is another case in point. The choice is arbitrary; one item of an associated group is just as likely to be selected as another. The places, times, functions, and origins from which chant names may be chosen are infinite. The name selected for a particular chant may combine many associations, either of the chant symbols or of symbols representing a cross section of the dogma.

' Shooting Chant ' is a short form of na'atoe', ' concerning-the-shooting-of-objects-that-move-in-zigzags.' Lightning, snake, arrow, or indeed any one of many other names might have been chosen; all indicate what the chant stresses. Hail stands for things injured by cold storms. Most storms are accompanied by lightning and wind, but summer storms with hail are less usual, as are winter storms accompanied by lightning. Consequently, a chant is differentiated from the Shooting and the Wind chants, by its distinctive symbols related to hail; at the same time these symbols are associated with the main symbols of the other chants. Unlike the Shooting, Hail, Wind, and Water chants, the Bead Chant gets its

10

name from the major conflict of the explanatory myth, whose purpose was to obtain valuable ornaments symbolized by the word ' bead '; the Endurance Chant from its chief episode, a race between the powers of evil, represented by Changing-bear-maiden, and the power of good, symbolized by Youngest Brother.

What for many years has been called the Mountain Chant is named for the dwelling place of the many spirits the chant invokes, summarized by Bear, Snake, and Porcupine. The Night Chant, which supersedes all others, is named for the time during which a major performance, the dance of the masked gods, is held. Another common name for the Night Chant, Grandfather-of-the-gods (γé'i· bitcei·), refers to Talking God, leader of the dance.

The freedom of association illustrated by sandpaintings and chant names indicates the existing confusion similar to that which accompanies an attempt to classify disease, and is comparable with that which arose in classifying plants. Since the ideal is well-being, one of the most frequently encountered irregularities is bad health. Causes of disease are fixed by analogy; medically and ritualistically determined causes coincide only by accident. A ceremony may be recommended to drive away fear, to cure symptoms—colds, fever, sore throat, fatigue, itching, lameness, rheumatism—and, since disharmony may show up in ways other than illness, the same ceremony may be held to attract the good offices of animals, rain, and the protective gods. Although disease is included, it is by no means the chant's exclusive purpose; affinity with our medical terms, if there is any, is fortuitous. The ceremonies should, therefore, be classified on magical-associational, rather than medical, principles.

The Bead Chant is said to be sung for skin irritations, yet RP sang it for a young man who had some serious abdominal

11

trouble and no itching. According to Kluckhohn and Wyman, the Bead, Eagle, Feather, Wind, and Awl chants were sung for head affections. The Night Chant is supposed to be especially effective as a cure for insanity, deafness, and paralysis; the Mountain and Hand Trembling chants purport to cure mental uneasiness and nervousness—ailments not further defined. The Shooting Chant is armor against diseases caused by snakes, lightning, and arrows, but the Wind Chant features snakes as extensively; it protects against their power and the harm of storms.

A few mythical examples illustrate the ease with which the Navaho make comparisons by selecting similars and minimizing contrasts:

A wandering clan, People-of-the-large-yucca-place, affiliated with the dził náxodiłni˙ because their red arrow holders, similar to shawl straps, looked much alike.[10]

The People-of-base-of-the-mountain, finding that they had headdresses, bows, arrows, and arrow cases similar to those of the tańe˙szahni˙, concluded that they were 'close' relatives. These two clans have since been so intimately affiliated that their members may not intermarry.[11]

When the People-of-water's-edge met the People-of-the-mud-place, they noticed that their names had much the same meaning and that their headdresses and accouterments were alike. They therefore became great friends, but not so ' close ' that their members could not intermarry.[12]

Traditionally the Navaho were willing to make clan affinities on the basis of comparable traits; today they readily accept friendship and co-operation by pointing out analogies.

CHAPTER 2

WORLD VIEW

The Universe

As EXPLAINED in Chapter 1, the Navaho reason from mythological precedent. Myth must be viewed as teleological; cosmogony is purposeful though sometimes the custom or object explained is not even known until its mythical creation. Unless this paradox is accepted, the materials cannot seem other than ridiculous. The religions to which we are accustomed are recognized as beliefs rather than as proved theorems, but even our scientists keep their science separate from their religion. If we are tolerant of a religion not our own we understand it better, and we should try to realize that the Navaho does not make everything clear because he does not feel any need for consistency. The chanter, accustomed to concentrate upon the chant he knows or owns, has little perspective on the ritual as a whole. When inconsistencies are pointed out, analogy and the system of associations afford easy explanation.

Among the primary mythical concepts are ideas about time and space. If something happened once, it may happen again. If there is life and activity in this world, there must have been similar worlds elsewhere, below and above. Man and his experience must be identified with events in earlier— that is, mythological—times and in the lower worlds. Hence time and place are symbols of recapitulation. There is belief in progress from the lower worlds to this, so far the best, because it is man's world. Progress is not evolutionary in the developmental sense. There is no belief in the physical relationship of man to the primordial creatures. Rather, progress is measured by intellectual criteria. Once the beings gained knowledge, there was no need to worry about their bodies; they were supernaturally transformed. Knowledge was acquired and increased through difficult experience and the struggle to learn nature's laws, with help from the supernaturals. Consequently, one who knows how to keep things in order has the key to life's problems. Thus progress should not be measured by moral standards any more than by biological evolution.

Since for eons man has been advancing toward oneness with the universe, he identifies himself with all its parts. This world may be considered a functioning central world; others, left behind but remembered in myth, are underneath; there are others above. The number of worlds is hypothetical, there being little agreement about it; myth furnishes details of four underworlds, of the sky immediately above, and of one still higher, Land-beyond-the-sky.

The worlds are thought of as superimposed hemispheres, each supported by pillars made of precious stones—four of whiteshell at the east, four of turquoise at the south, four of abalone at the west, four of redstone at the north.[1] Called Those-who-stand-under-the-sky, they are regarded as deities. The space between the hemispheres is filled with stars. Each higher hemisphere is larger than the one below, since the characteristics of the lower were imitated and added to, and the whole was magically enlarged. Each time the vaguely defined creatures had to move out of an earlier world one took along a token quantity of soil from every sacred place in it; in the world they were entering the soil was placed in the same relative place it had occupied below; then a supernatural being blew on and stretched it. The lower worlds

14

were small and moved rapidly, making the inhabitants dizzy. Although motion was a phase of life, it became bearable only in this world, which was so large in proportion to the inhabitants that its rotation was not unpleasant.[2]

In each of the lower worlds a color predominated and affected the inhabitants. In the first, the red world, were twelve kinds of black insects, including bats; in the second, the blue world, there were blue birds—swallows and jays; in the third, the yellow world, grasshoppers; in the fourth, there were beings from all the preceding worlds and the ancient pueblo people.[3] This world has all colors regularly placed in the world quadrants—white (or black) at the east, blue at the south, yellow at the west, and black (or white) at the north.

In the lower worlds color took the place of light. Not until the people reached this world and concerned themselves with creating sun and moon did they formally differentiate color and light (Chapter 15).

The sky pillars are connecting links between the worlds as well as supports of each world. One other, the reed of emergence, more frequently mentioned in myth, is a major place symbol in ritual.[4] The reed grew rapidly enough to save the people; it was commodious enough to hold many of them and, in some unexplained way, they were able to climb it. The sky of the world left behind (the under part of the world being approached) was so hard and smooth where the reed met it that the refugees could find no opening in it. One of the winds showed them a vulnerable spot and there was always some ' person ' with the power and physical strength to peck a hole through. The Place-of-emergence therefore became a local symbol of escape. Called ' Center-of-the-earth,' its location in this world is so much disputed that it should not be considered as fixed. There has been no exodus from this world to the sky nor is any predicted, hence there is no way, at least for an ordinary person, to get to the sky. Rainboy, guided by the gods, went on four conveyances; The Twins traveled past dangers and over mountains as if they were points on the earth, but ultimately reached Sun's home in the sky; they returned to earth by climbing down the Hole-of-emergence, formed of cliffs made of precious stones. Presumably a theoretical passage, reed, or column leads from this world to the world above it.

In characterizing their forebears the Navaho ascribe to them sentience and a cognizance of human problems. From the earliest conceivable times there was a roving, growing population whose overwhelming need was food. The wanderers had no social institutions and had to learn to recognize them among the people into whose territory they intruded. As they were addicted to sorcery, they were antisocial; they offended strangers by wife-stealing and other sexual offenses. However, upon arriving in a new world the primordial ancestors of the Navaho made vows to co-operate with the natives; as they learned more and more they kept their promises longer and longer. At each pause in the upward migration they accepted more social curbs—some were learned from the old residents, some were commands of their own leaders. The leitmotiv of the earlier worlds—confusion, uncertainty, error—led to evil, witchcraft, and death. Each subsequent step in the emergence changed the emphasis until now, in this world, stability, knowledge, and co-operation are ideals, the chrysalis of ignorance having been shed in the lower worlds.

The metamorphosis was brought about only because among the original beings there were some gods who advised, coerced, and guided them. The provenience of these deities— the First Pair, Coyote, the prototype of Talking God, and

Black God—is nowhere accounted for; they appear and use their powers for escape and transformation whenever the myth requires a prestidigitator.

As one might expect, the origin and transformation of the present Navaho world are more fully described than any of the nether regions; it will be discussed below (pages 19–25). Two higher realms of the universe are depicted in broad lines, and conceivably there are other worlds above those. The sky is a world just like this one; in it Sun, Moon, and stars are visible to us as they move through the space between the world hemispheres. Above the stratum into which we look, the heavenly bodies have their homes, living much like the people here on earth. The better-known Thunders also live in the sky realm.

The Land-beyond-the-sky is inhabited by extra-powerful storm elements—Winter, Pink and Spotted Thunders, Big Winds, and Whirlwinds. They run a school for novices learning the ritual of the Male Shooting, Hail, Water, and Feather chants; the pupils are conducted thither and back by other gods.

Though previously they had been content with color, First Man and First Woman, when they arrived in this world, wanted light as well, probably because the world was large and many places existed far from the mountains that had previously furnished illumination. After due consideration the First Pair made the sun of a large turquoise disk surrounded by red rain, lightning, and various kinds of snakes. It was heated with fire kindled by Black God's fire drill. From a piece of rock crystal the First Pair made the moon, bordering it with whiteshell, forked lightning, and sacred waters; it is slightly warmed by rock crystal's light.[5]

Among the supernatural company there were two men, one old, one younger, who had risen unexpectedly from a spring. For a long time the two had merely accompanied the people, not performing any unusual deeds, but endearing themselves to the travelers. They had planted the reed through which the beings of the fourth world escaped to the fifth. When First Man and First Woman had finished making the sun and decided to place it in East Wind's country, they appointed the young man, who until then had no name, as the sun-bearer. Moving to the east with the orb, he became Sun. They put the old man in charge of moon and gave him the name Moon-bearer or Moon.[6]

One version of the creation myth shows concern to account for Sun's position among the spheres. After the disk had been lighted by dint of great effort, it became too hot and burned the people because the sky and earth were too close together. First Man and First Woman raised the orb a short distance, but it was still dangerously hot. They then made two poles of turquoise and two of whiteshell, which they gave to Those-who-stand-under-the-sky (Sky Pillars). The latter pried the sky far enough from the earth to prevent burning, but the heat was insufferable. Finally, they decided to stretch the world and, by blowing hard, expanded it until the temperature was comfortable for the inhabitants.

Sun's permanent home, a major symbol of the Male Shooting Chant Sun's House branch, is at the eastern quarter of the sky. In it is a rattle that warns of his return. When it sounds the fourth time, Sun arrives home, takes off the sun, and hangs it on a peg on the wall—on earth the sun sets. Formerly he moved from east to west and back in a day, pausing at the center of the sky (noon) to eat his lunch. Since Changing Woman has lived in the west, he stops there and rests at evening. On dark, stormy days he stays at home and sends out his lightnings, which may do mischief.[7] Sun thus carries out his daily schedule.

His seasonal journey begins at the winter solstice; he climbs the southernmost sky pillar and, as the season advances, reaches the northernmost; he retraces the route, spending an equal number of days at each pole.[8] On the rare occasions when he becomes angry he hides his light partly or completely; the earth experiences a solar eclipse which presages misfortune. The Navaho believed the influenza epidemic of 1918 was caused by the solar eclipse of June 8.

This World

The fullest version of the cosmogony considers this one the fifth world. Cicada, the first person to come up into it from the fourth world, won it from the Grebes. The non-human creatures emerged to find themselves on a lake surrounded by high cliffs, from which spread a plateau. They had great difficulty in discovering a way out of the lake. At length Blue Body, a god who was with them, threw four stones he had brought with him to the north, south, east, and west. These stones split the cliffs and when the water flowed off in four directions, a part of the lake bottom was found to be connected with the mainland. As the mud was too deep for traffic, Smooth Wind was invoked; he blew and dried out the mud so that the people could disperse.[9]

Traditionally the Navaho tribe has always been on the move. They love to travel, yet feel a deep attachment to their present habitat. They have an extraordinary interest in geography. The number of place names in myth and ritual is legion. Some correspond to the names of identifiable places, others seem to be mythical or ritualistic symbols referring to localities in the lower worlds (pages 152ff.).

The earth, very different from what it is now, had to be transformed. Essential parts, as well as the earth itself, are called ' our mother.' "These [the sacred] mountains are our father and our mother. We came from them; we depend upon them. Between the large mountains are small ones which we made ourselves. Each mountain is a person. The water courses are their veins and arteries. The water in them is their life as our blood is to our bodies." [10] In the Wheelwright collection there is a sandpainting of the earth; mountains are depicted as parts of her body and streams as blood vessels. Each mountain has an ' inner form ' (bi· yistí'n), something which gives it life, perhaps makes it sentient (cp. *Pollen ball*, Concordance B).

Many physiographical features were planned by First Man, who made a model of the earth from the soil brought in small pouches from the lower worlds. Seven or more mountains are mentioned in the myths, but attempts to identify them with actual elevations are more or less futile. One mountain of ritualistic importance lies in each of the cardinal directions forming the mythical boundaries of the Navaho territory. There is agreement about the location of the southern mountain, Mt. Taylor (tsodził), and the western, Mt. Humphreys (doko'osłí'd). The eastern mountain, sisnádjini· (sisna·djiní), [11] ' Black-belted-one,' and the northern, dibéntsah, ' Mountain sheep,' are variously identified (*Mountains*, Concordance A). Other mountains between these have ceremonial significance.

tćô'l'į'į (untranslatable) is not satisfactorily identified with any present-day mountain. It is Changing Woman's place symbol because on it she was found as a baby and there she lived until the monsters had been conquered. [12] It is said to lie somewhat east of dził náxodiłi·, ' Mountain-which-customarily-turns '; it is sometimes considered as the center of the world. ' Upper-mountain-ridge ' ('akidahne·sta·ni·), also near the center, is associated with evil. [13]

Chart I (insert) summarizes the mythical origin of the

CHART I

CREATION OF THE EARTH

Direction	Color	Mountain	Fastened by	Covered by
east	white	sisnádjini˙	lightning	daylight dawn
south	blue	Mt. Taylor	great stone knife	blue sky blue-horizon-light
west	yellow	Mt. Humphreys	sunbeam	yellow cloud yellow evening light
north	black	dibéntsah	rainbow	darkness
center		dził˙náxodiłi˙	sunbeam	mirage
center		'ak˙i dahne˙st'á˙ni˙	mirage stone	
east of center		tc'ô˙l'í'í	rain-streamer	rainbow heat
ridge running north and south		noxoziłi˙		
'way over on west side'				
prairie				

(continued on next page)

Jewel Symbol	Bird Symbol	Vegetation Symbol	Sound Symbol	Part of Earth's Body
whiteshell whiteshell with belt of dark cloud	pigeon white thunder	spotted white corn	thunder in young eagle's mouth	
turquoise	bluebird blue swallows	blue corn		
abalone	yellow warbler	black yellow corn		
jet various	blackbird cornbeetle	red, white, blue variegated corn	thunder four times	
various mirage soft goods	bluebird			
	grasshopper	all kinds		
various				heart
flint				skull
				breast
				pericardis and diaphragm

CHART I (continued)

Peopled by	Moved by	Extra Gifts	Tutelary
Rock Crystal Boy Rock Crystal Girl Whiteshell Boy Whiteshell Girl Dawn Boy Dawn Girl	spotted wind	white lightning dark cloud male rain white corn	xaˑctc'é''óγan
Boy-who-carries- one-turquoise Girl-who-carries- one-corn-kernel Turquoise Boy Turquoise Girl	blue wind	dark mist female rain wild animals	Black God
White Corn Boy Yellow Corn Girl Evening Light Boy Abalone Girl	black wind (?)	dark cloud male rain yellow corn wild animals	Talking God
Pollen Boy Cornbeetle Girl Darkness Boy Darkness Girl	yellow wind	dark mist vegetation of all kinds animals of all kinds rare game	Monster Slayer
Soft Goods Boy Soft Goods Girl		dark cloud male rain goods of all kinds pollen	Talking God
Mirage Stone Boy Carnelian Girl		dark cloud male rain	
Jewels Boy Jewels Girl			

mountains and the associated symbols. The mountains are fastened and covered with elements that represent natural phenomena; their colors are associated with the precious stones; they have bird, plant, and sound symbols; they are inhabited by Holy People. The mountains represent parts of the earth's body—heart, skull, breast, and internal organs—and, like the body of an earth person, they have the power of motion, given them by the Winds. Other gifts have been bestowed upon them. For example, sisnádjini· was fastened by a bolt of lightning and covered with daylight, and additional gifts of white lightning, dark cloud, male rain, and white corn made it symbolically even more complete.

Changing Woman, when she sent her people eastward, gave a different description of the world, which by this time was habitable. Some details correspond amazingly well with the terrain between the Pacific Ocean and Wheeler Peak in the Taos Mountains, and north as far as the San Juan River.[14]

Changing Woman, so named because she renews her youth as the seasons progress, was created and trained to bring forth twin sons, who freed the earth from the monsters. Old, gray-haired, wrinkled, and bent in the winter, she gradually transforms herself to a young and beautiful woman.[15] Restoration to youth is the pattern of the earth, something for which the Navaho lives, for he reasons that what happens to the earth may also happen to him. Regaining strength after disease due to contact with strangers, attack by evil or offended powers, or loss of ritualistic purity is interpreted as rejuvenation like that of Mother Earth.

Although Changing Woman's sons overcame the monsters one by one, it was impossible to obliterate their carcasses. Consequently, the Navaho country is still littered with unburied remnants of their bodies. Big Monster, for example, is thought to have lived near Mt. Taylor. After killing him, The Twins cut off his head and threw it far to the east, where it now stands as Cabezon (Spanish ' head ') Peak. The blood of Big Monster flowed in a great stream down the valley until stopped by the flint club of Monster Slayer. It coagulated and may be seen now as the lava formation in the vicinity of McCarty's Wash. Another time The Twins raised a storm to kill other monsters whose heads may still be seen as volcanic peaks around the base of Mt. Taylor.[16]

Similarly, Cliff Monster, who lived at Winged Rock, turned into lava rock when overcome by Monster Slayer. This spectacular rock, which resembles a winged creature poised, is called Shiprock by the whites. The long lava dike at the southwest is said to be the blood of the Cliff Monster.

Besides accounting for the peculiarities of places, the cosmogony teaches that the earth should not be injured. As each monster fell, the earth shook, causing earthquakes. Mountains were weak and ill because the bodies of enemies had been left unburied on the surface of the earth. They should be disposed of in an orderly manner. The death of the monsters and their fall, as well as enemy corpses, impaired the vitality of the earth; its devitalization communicated itself to the people; hence they became ailing. If the earth is placated, as it may be by revenge and compensation, people's indispositions may be cured. Because the monsters were enemy prototypes, offerings and prayers should be made to the earth when victors rejoice over a defeated enemy.[17]

Vegetation is considered the ' dress ' of the earth and the mountains, a gift bestowed at creation, a function of Changing Woman's annual rejuvenation. The Navaho have a sentimental attitude toward plants, which they treat with incredible respect (Chapter 8). However, in contrast to the

numerous etiologies of corn, accounts of the origin of particular plants are few. In some myths corn is considered primeval,
for First Man had some in the first world. Other myths
account for it as the gift of a god or a neighboring people.
Whatever its origin, its value is constantly emphasized.
According to one myth, Talking God gave corn to Whiteshell Woman and her sister, Turquoise Woman, saying,
"There is no better thing than this in the world, for it is the
gift of life." Later, when he visited them again and they
told him they still had it, he said, "That is good, for corn is
your symbol of fertility and life." [18]

Each animal has a place in the universal scheme. The rare
game animals (dini')—deer, antelope, elk, and mountain
sheep—are especially valued ritualistically, even though
today they are so scarce that many children have never seen
one.[19] Throughout mythology and ritual, vegetable and flesh
food are felt to belong together. Contrary to many remarks
in the literature on Navaho ritual, there is no such thing as a
corn or a game ritual, since one involves, if only implicitly,
the other. When Changing Woman placed on the forehead
of Monster Slayer a black stick which grew and symbolized
deer antlers, he felt three kinds of seeds in his hand.[20] The
story of the contest with Deer Owner is pointed up so as to
contrast and eventually associate the advantages of meat
and vegetables as a diet, for the hero who overcame him
traded knowledge of agriculture for the release of the rare
game animals.

The hunting animals carried packs of corn on their backs,
for they had charge of the corn-growing rite of the Fire
Dance.[21]

Mountain sheep, as valued game animals, play a major
role in mythology and ritual. Many characteristics of the

Hunchback God are like those of the mountain sheep. If Hunchback God is not actually the animal, he at least had supernatural control over it, and the hump on his back, like those of the hunting animals, is made of clouds containing seeds of all types of vegetation.[22]

The complementation of corn by game is brought out by Talking God, who, in the myth of the Night Chant, instructs the hero: "Never give corn to eat of its own substance. If you give it, corn will thereafter ever eat corn until all the land is destroyed. Then men will starve and have to eat one another, and thus destroy their own race. Give corn flesh to eat. For like reasons corn must be fed to the masks in the ceremonies. Should meat be fed to them, men would, thereafter, eat men."[23] The masks of sacred buckskin represent game animals. According to tradition punishment was inevitable if the injunction was disobeyed.

Once, many years ago, when the ceremony of the corn was taking place and a young virgin was grinding meat to feed the corn, a wicked woman went out from the lodge and fed corn to the corn hanging on the poles of the drying frame. That year the people starved and men ate the flesh of other men.[24]

Since time is relative and, ritualistically speaking, past, present, and future are interchangeable, the cosmogony would be expected to include some prediction of the world's fate. Stevenson's informant believed that this world had already been destroyed five times, by whirlwind, hail, smallpox, coughing, and the slaughter of the monsters.[25] One of Stephen's informants mentioned destruction by fire, whirlwind, and flood, and predicted that after four more creations and their disappearance the Navaho would be annihilated. A second informant said the first lied. The world had been destroyed four times, he admitted, but added that two years before (in 1883) the time had been up for the final destruction. From then on, therefore, he said, the world must last.[26]

The chanter tłá·h believed that a people different from the Navaho would succeed them. He thought the whites were the successors and for this reason was not only willing to teach them the fundamentals of Navaho belief but also deeply concerned that they should learn accurately.

CHAPTER 3

THE NATURE OF MAN

Man's Origin

FIRST MAN and First Woman existed in the lowest mythological world. From the beginning their purpose was to arrange conditions suitable for the Navaho to people the earth. The First Pair had some human traits: they could think and talk; they knew something about sex; they had some inkling of the difference between good and evil. Their knowledge was imperfect because incomplete and, therefore, uncontrolled; they thought that the universe was undeveloped rather than chaotic. A notion of conscious creation, ability to glimpse the future, and the will to control it set First Man and First Woman apart as supernatural beings.

Although the First Pair were the primary cause of the disasters in the lower worlds, they formulated a scheme to overcome the results of ignorance. It included the miraculous appearance of Changing Woman as a baby in a cradleboard, her careful training, the sanctioned mating with Sun, the birth of The Twins, and the acquisition of ritual power which enabled them to subdue the monsters. Did First Man place the wonderful baby on the mountaintop for himself to discover? Was it another of the supernatural deeds of Sun, who had already fathered the monsters? Did the baby appear through the efforts of both First Man and Sun? Or were First Man and Sun different manifestations of the same power? If First Man was the promoter, he was nonplused by his own creation and was matching his power against that of Sun. If Sun originated the plan, he was knowingly storing up sorrow for himself, for he loved his terrible children and did not want to do away with them; or perhaps he thought his new wife and her remarkable children would compensate for his grief. Most likely the baby and her protection of man were brought about by the co-operation of First Man and Sun. Myth leaves many other questions unanswered. Why should the First Pair or Sun want human beings on the earth? Why should they care about human welfare once man had appeared? Man is the mythmaker. His interest is in man, whose development he explains. First Man and Sun can be made to contribute to his motives. Mythmakers are not concerned with logic.

The account of the emergence is further confused by references to insects, grasshoppers, swallows, and creatures which, though described as non-human, are credited with many human attributes. Diverse origins are suggested for the human form, but all by association are probably one and the same.

Several versions ascribe human beings to a supernatural transformation of corn which existed primordially with First Man. Sun was said to be corn's father, Lightning its mother. According to one version, the results of the transformation were persons called First Man and First Woman, who are also referred to as ' our ancestors.'[1] From this account we may conclude that First Man and First Woman not only *had* corn in the early worlds but also *were* corn and came to symbolize transformation into human form.

One origin is attributed to the transformation of turquoise and whiteshell images by deific ceremonial. Since, however, the jewels were laid beside corn ears, the significance is in the association between corn and precious stones rather than in the gems themselves. According to Navaho interpretation, the two would be ' the same ' (Chapter 1).

Changing Woman is said to have created human beings by rubbing pieces of her epidermis from various parts of her body. As she held the skin in her hand it changed to six groups of people, who subsequently founded some of the Navaho clans. In one version of the story the skin became shell, which in turn became people.[2]

In some myths the origin of man is secondary to the origin of clans. One division of the Navaho, which settled on the San Juan River and traces its ancestry back to Whiteshell Woman, is thought to have been transformed from corn; the division that came from the West to join the people of the East originated in Changing Woman's epidermis. The people from Rumbling Mountain were considered holy because "they had no tradition of their recent creation, and were supposed to have escaped the fury of the alien gods by some miraculous protection." The progenitors of one clan, Big Water People, are supposed to have come up out of the water.[3]

The conclusion to which Navaho tradition forces us is that man is so closely related to deity that it is impossible to draw a sharp line between the human and the supernatural. The substances from which the transformation took place—corn, precious stones, and Changing Woman's epidermis—are not, according to Navaho reasoning, necessarily different, because the association of corn, whiteshell, and epidermis makes them one.

Theory of Reproduction

The remarks of Stephen's informant indicate the emphasis on reproduction:

"We do not have grass enough. Even if we had grass enough, the land is not broad enough. My people work both night and day, the men and women creating children, my flocks and herds making young. The Americans are always clamoring for more land; so are my people. I long for enough land to stretch my limbs. From here [Keam's Canyon] you can see the San Francisco Mountains at the west. By riding a short distance to the north you can see Navaho Mountain, a short way to the south are the White Mountains [sic], and at the east is Mt. Taylor. Remember what a small patch of ground this really is. Think how much effort will be made this very night to increase the number of children, lambs, colts. We do not have enough land."[4]

The ritualistic teachings stress male and female as a basic form of symbolism; the notion is that only by pairing can any entity be complete.

Mythology suggests that light and water are essential for conception. Sun stands for heat as well as light; water symbolizes semen. When Changing Woman first became mature she had not learned about sexual intercourse, but, in trying to satisfy her desire, let the sun shine into her vagina; at noon when Sun stopped to feed his horse she went to a spring and let water drip into her.[5]

In the account of the birth of the monsters light and water are again indicated:

A girl who was carefully watched, having gone alone in the direction of the sunrise, used a smooth pebble from the river to cleanse herself after defecating. She placed the warm stone [6] in her genitals and raised her skirt so as to examine herself. At this moment Sun rose and sent a ray into her. She must have been menstruating when this happened, for she became pregnant.[7]

In this case the pebble, being from the river, may have stood for water, or menstrual fluid may be its equivalent.

Stevenson records that Talking God and xa·ctčé·'óγan were created from corn by Changing Woman and her sister. When Changing Woman placed an ear of white corn, and her sister an ear of yellow corn, on the mountain where the fogs meet, ' the corn conceived, the white corn giving birth to

Talking God, the yellow to xa·ctčé·'óγan.' [8] Sun's presence is implied, since he is believed to rest periodically on mountain tops, which figure frequently in creation.

It is said that the warmth and moisture of the Buffalo's body makes plants grow and produce pollen. [9]

From these examples it seems that water represents Sun's semen, a fluid which, if warmed or lighted, may cause generation. Throughout Navaho mythology an attempt to protect girls from being struck by sunlight is stressed. There seems to be some feeling that virginity has ritualistic value, which in some individuals should be preserved (Chapter 8). Since virgins are few, the mythical references to girls ' not struck by sunlight ' must point to an effort to keep them pure. Kept hidden inside a house with only a very small opening, they were shielded from Sun's seductive wiles. Pueblo girls similarly protected were desirable to the Navaho. [10]

The function of Sun and water in generation and the Navaho belief that two fathers are responsible for twins explain the agreement about the fatherhood of The Twins or War Gods. Matthews summarizes their character: "From their mythic associations I would assume that Monster Slayer is the god of light, with its associated heat, while Child-of-the-water is the god of darkness, with its associated moisture." [11] I do not know from what evidence Matthews inferred this. I do not consider that the myths alone justify it, but it must be more than coincidence that both he and I came to the same conclusion independently. [12]

When First Man and First Woman were fumbling with creation, which included customs and institutions as well as material things, First Woman set herself up as a leader in matters of sex. She had already been punished for unsanctioned intercourse and decreed that women should henceforth recognize and approve of sexual relations. She made

30

male and female genitalia so that one sex should attract the other—the penis of turquoise, the vagina of whiteshell. After treating them ritualistically, she laid them side by side and blew over them medicine (infusion), which was to cause pregnancy. She went further and determined the degree of desire—great for men, much less for women. Intercourse was to leave the penis weak, the vagina strong.[13]

Sexual indulgence was a preoccupation of the inhabitants of the lower worlds; it led to the floods which necessitated the emergence. First Man taunted his wife with being interested in sex alone. His rebuke gave rise to a quarrel in which she said that women could get along without men. To prove the challenge the men moved across the river and destroyed the rafts that had carried them. As years went by, the women became weaker; they needed the men's strength to produce food, and they became maddened with desire. As a result of self-abuse they gave birth to the monsters that later destroyed men. The men too practiced perversion, but from their excesses no evil survived. After many had died and great suffering had ensued, the women yielded and begged the men to take them back. They did so, and all agreed that henceforth man should be the leader in matters of sex since he belonged to the stronger sex.[14]

The separation of the sexes with its consequences proved that neither is complete without the other, that sexual needs must be allowed expression but should be controlled. World harmony demands woman's potential, as well as man's kinetic, energy.

Specific roles

Man's Constitution

The Navaho conception of man includes careful definition of his spiritual as well as his anatomical makeup. The body is composed of skin, flesh, bones, and internal organs—all

31

considered as layers, each tissue carefully fitted to those next it. Nevertheless, between the layers are interstices ('atałah) through which ghosts may travel. They enter the body where there are whorls—for instance, at the finger tips and hair spirals—as frequently as through orifices—mouth, nose, ears.

Navaho knowledge of anatomy is good, of physiology very poor. Most parts of the body, even internal organs, have names. One category which shows ignorance of function is the division of blood vessels—those of the head and limbs ('atšo·s) and those of the trunk, including the jugular ('aɣá·z). Since ritual is a means of cure, anatomy must be considered, but since cure is primarily concerned with spirit, and there are various expressions of man's spiritual being, they must be understood in order to interpret Navaho belief and the function of religion.

I have previously discussed the possibility of determining essential concepts of being and their relative importance by analyzing prayers in which a people asks for what it most desires.[15] The Navaho calls upon his gods to restore not only his head, his breast, his finger tips, his limbs, and his body but also the tip of his tongue, his voice and sound, his breath, his power of motion, and his mind. To express such ideas, he has at his command a great many words which, unless properly translated, make the prayers seem ridiculous. Many of these words have very specific connotations which cannot be casually rendered by single English words. For instance, a word for 'soul' was indispensable for teaching Christian doctrine. A word meaning 'that which stands within' was adapted to the missionaries' need for explaining the spiritual, the undying part of man. Actually, this word refers to a belief that in the chest of a man there is an image, a symbol of turquoise, which, if it remains upright, will make him strong. It is a part of only those who have undergone certain ceremonies and therefore is not inherent or immortal, but rather something ritualistically added to defend body and spirit (Chapter 12, *Agate; Pollen ball*, Concordance B).

The Navaho has little idea of personal immortality. Rather, the individual becomes universal; at death the person is left behind with the body. However, somewhat more specific concepts define the relation between body and spirit and demonstrate how the complete man functions. A group of words refers to ' breath ': 'ayol means ' wind, breath, blowing '; 'ayi, ' a single puff of breath '; 'aγi' includes a notion of sound and means ' manifestation of life.' Breath is one test of life:

You must never leave the deer's windpipe whole, but split it down the center. As soon as it is split, the deer is dead; otherwise it is alive.[16]

Related to words connoting breath are those which include or emphasize sound: 'adzi, ' any kind of sound emitted by a living being '; 'i·né", ' sound characteristic of a living being ' —for instance, the sheep's baa, the cow's moo. More closely related to dogma is 'ájí, ' manifestation by breath and sound of the life and power of a being, that which keeps one power-ful, that which one is plus what he has secured through ritual.' This word indicates identification with many powers in the ritualistic act called ' breathing in.' Still another term, 'ají·h, means the ' evil, poisonous, injurious element of breath accompanied by angry sound,' as the roar of an attacking bull; a person may be killed simply by contact with this type of breath. [17]

One must be very careful not to inhale the breath of a dying deer (one has killed). This would make one sweat and one would be sick at once.[18]

Closely related to breath and sound, in fact, a combination

of the two, is voice, speech, or language. The 'word'—that is, the formulation of sounds into organized speech—is of great ritualistic value, and in order to be complete, man must control language. The better his control and the more extensive his knowledge, the greater his well-being (Introduction, Chapter 16). In prayer, therefore, man requests, "My voice restore for me. . . . May the pollen of Wind's child govern the tip of my speech." With a clear voice, with control at the tip of the speech—that is, the mouth—a person is insured against error.

Man may breathe and speak, his organs may function well, but without the power of motion ('agá·l) he is incomplete, useless. Therefore he prays, "My gait restore for me."

All parts of man's body and spirit are co-ordinated by 'mind, will power, volition, reason, awareness' ('áni', 'ánį'). A summarizing phrase occurs frequently in prayer: "My mind restore for me."

Mind keeps body and spirit in adjustment. When the body is complete with organs, breath, sound, voice, and the power of motion, it is said to have 'i·nái, 'life, the quality of being alive.' A universal expression of life, 'i·na', refers to the relation between simply being alive, aliveness, and all phases of nature, culture, and experience; it may be extended to mean 'outlook on life, career, philosophy.'

The 'name' ('áji'), an important manifestation of being, is ritualistically acquired.[19]

Normal adjustment of the body parts gives a person 'atse·, 'strength, firmness, physical dependability.' Add to these attributes power derived from supernatural experience and he is 'strong, enduring, powerful, capable of controlling good and warding off evil' ('adzi·l).

There are two words for 'personality' in Navaho: xaya', 'ability, behavior,' excludes physical characteristics; xayá

is the sum of physical and mental traits plus talen[?] [ritual]
demeanor.   [sorcery]
                                                     [breath again.]

One purpose of ritual is to extend the personality s[?]
bring it into harmonious relation with the powers
universe. The opposite of this endeavor, actually a[?]
aspect of it, is to keep a man from contact with evil. S[?]
the most exaggerated form of evil, depends upon direc[?]
tact with a person or some part of his body. Theref[?]
should take care of waste matter in such a way that
will have access to it. An evilly disposed person may
perspiration, dead skin, phlegm, tears, urine, excr[?]
menstrual blood, combings, or nail parings ('atcxi˙n) i[?]
a way as to bring about the death of the person to whom they
once belonged (Chapter 6).

Personal possessions ('antcxǫ̧'ǫ̧) may also be subject to
sorcery, depending on how far a man extends his identity.
Individuals differ as to how far they carry identification of
person and possessions, but where the line is drawn determines how much of a man's property is destroyed at his
death.[20] Clothes have absorbed perspiration, dirt, and skin
scales; a man may become one with his favorite horse and
even with his silver ornaments or saddle; a person absorbs
consciously and unconsciously the power of every element of
the chant symbolized by the bead token. He becomes a part
of it and therefore it must be a part of him. A possession that
is the extension of his personality when he is alive may include
also the extension of his evil, tč·í˙ndi˙, after he dies. Hence,
instead of being harmed, it may harm. For these reasons girls
who have worked in the laundry at school may be ' sung
over ' when they return home. They have breathed steam
containing the perspiration of a foreigner; this may become
dangerous if the stranger dies. Potential harm from this
source may be averted by the War Ceremony.[21]

35

Myth illustrates what was considered necessary to life and soundness:

When Talking God transformed corn ears, which he placed between buckskins, into people, Wind entered between the covers and gave the newly created man and woman the breath of life. He entered at the heads and came out at the ends of the fingers and toes, and to this day we may see his trail at the tip of every human finger. Rock Crystal Boy furnished them with minds and Cornbeetle Girl gave them voices.[22]

Rainboy, hero of the Hail Chant, was completely destroyed, blasted into bits, scattered in every direction by the wrath of Winter Thunder. The description of the reassembling of his body by the gods illustrates some of the problems of body construction:

The Thunder People gathered Rainboy's bones and flesh and placed them between sacred buckskins; when White Wind was laid under the top cover, Rainboy began to move, but he could not get up. Pink Thunder put Little Wind under the cover. It entered Rainboy's ear; he could hear, he had life at the tips of his fingers and everywhere Wind had gone, but still could not get up. Talking God then put Rain's Son under the cover. He supplied moisture—tears, saliva, and nasal mucus. Rainboy tried in vain to get up. Talking God put collected pollen under the cover and it turned into toenails, fingernails, body hair, and perspiration, yet Rainboy could not stand upright. Insects of all kinds were called to help. Some found small portions of Rainboy's blood and brought it back, but not until they found the curve of his upper lip could his restoration be complete.[23]

In the myth of the Flint Chant, Holy Boy was destroyed by Winter Thunder and similarly reconstituted. Spider People restored his nerves and blood vessels, Winds caused his nerves to function, and Sun made him wink.[24]

Whenever, in a myth, the essentials of life are suggested, they are selected from the many available concepts. Never are all mentioned; seldom is the choice the same in two

Nature's creation of man

myths or even twice in the same myth, and each new legend is likely to include at least one not previously recorded. Taken all together they give a psychosomatic picture of man's constitution. When any part gets out of balance, treatment emphasizes the mental rather than the physical (cp. Chapter 7).

Life Cycle

Man's life cycle is called a ' walk ' through time. He travels a ' trail ' repeatedly symbolized in sandpainting and ritual.[25] A major purpose of the ritual is to carry him safely and pleasantly along this road from birth to dissolution. The following life periods are recognized:

Male	Female	Period
'áni·d na·γái		just born, newly arrived
'aγwé" ('awé")		babyhood
'acki·	'até·d	weaning to adolescence
diné·	tc'iké·	adolescence
xasti·n	'asdzá·ní	early married life
xastoi, xastxoi	'asdzá"	advanced maturity
	xa'asti	very old age, beginning of disintegration

The spirits of children and women are believed to be naturally weaker than those of men;[26] therefore children from their very birth are brought into contact with ritual. Infants have not learned responsibility for their own well-being or for that of others. Education, which may be ceremonial repetition, aims to give them a sense of obligation. Children learn physical control very young; it is not unusual to see a year-old handling a butcher knife or a pair of scissors. As soon as they can walk, children learn to differentiate men's and women's activities by imitating and helping their parents. From the moment of its birth a child is treated as an adult, but it is not expected to do more than its age warrants. The child is allowed to try any activity it may want to take part in and must submit to every ritual requirement. Although an infant cannot sprinkle pollen or blow ashes, its mother or someone who ' stands for it ' does so, once for herself, once for the baby. If the mother subjects herself to a chant or ceremony, the baby must be included. Because she nurses and cares for the baby, it may be expected to be harmed or benefited in the same way; therefore it must be made immune to the evil, susceptible to the good, of the chant. The child's mother may be the sponsor only if she has had the chant in question or a closely related one sung for her, or if she is a co-patient with the baby. She may put the child in the hands of a woman who qualifies or who with it goes through the rites that will assure it of protection because of the power being sought.

In religion, the child must conform. Though a baby cries, screams, and wriggles, chanter and sponsor follow through, gently but firmly insisting on carrying out every ritualistic detail. Later they may laugh at the spectacle a baby has made of itself. Ceremonial demands are relentlessly though casually met with a rigor that has not been emphasized in discussions of Navaho training. Religion thus aids the adult in discipline; belief in supernatural punishment is inculcated in the cradle.

If persistently corrected, the child's mistakes are not serious, and until it learns better, the responsibility for proper ritualistic behavior rests on the adult relatives.

During the period from babyhood to adolescence there is little difference in the ritualistic treatment of male and female children. At adolescence, however, there is a definite change. The girl, because there is physical evidence of her maturity, becomes a tribal symbol of fecundity at her adolescence ceremony, and from then on a symbol of the power of reproduction.

No particular moment marks the transition from boyhood to manhood. When the Navaho were even more mobile than they are now, the boy had to be trained for activities which took him away from home—hunting, war, and trading. Young boys then submitted to rigorous physical training for their self-protection (Chapter 6). Nowadays there is little formal training; consequently the boy's life goal is but vaguely defined. Knowledge must be ripened by experience, which takes time to acquire. Youth is tried and repeatedly teased, ridicule being a major form of discipline.

Gradually, by a subtle process difficult to define, the young man grows into a position of responsibility in the various social groups—first his own family, clan, clan group, and, after marriage, his wife's groups. If he can be relied upon, he may be referred to as xasti·n; later, as he accumulates knowledge, he is xastoi, ' one who has authority.' After marriage the woman may be 'asdzá·ní or asdzá·', the latter a more respectful term. Respect is a matter of individual opinion, the word with which an older person is referred to depending primarily on the speaker's opinion of his knowledge and accomplishment. Otherwise age is not necessarily fruitful. There are many old men who have not fulfilled their obligations or at best have done so halfheartedly; some have not earned the title xastoi, which implies knowledge and wisdom. Numerous complaints are made about them, though care is taken lest the grumbler become a victim of sorcery.

When a person is referred to as xa'asti, ' extremely old,' he has lost his competence and perhaps some of his faculties. Even then, though he is physically weak, his spiritual power (bíjí) may be strong and communicable and his power for evil (biji·h) feared. Such an old person should, therefore, be treated with the patience shown a child. If suspected of witchcraft, he may receive an overabundance of attention.

39

Treatment aims to prevent antagonism. At the same time the persons who lavish care upon him try to get rid of him, urging him to visit another family who, as soon as they decently can, pass him on to still another.

Opinion about the ideal life span differs. Some say it is 102 years, reckoned from the number of counters in the moccasin game. Others say it is seventy years, doubtless a white man's idea, and still others consider it the age at which some very old man is said to have died. Those who have not gone to school do not know their ages; at best, age can be ascertained only approximately by reference to some outstanding event. The very old tell how big they were when they went to or returned from Fort Sumner (1863–68), or perhaps they were born during the journey back. Younger persons reckon their age from the influenza epidemic of 1918; still others from local happenings which may sometimes be dated by the trader or some other white man.

Death and the Dead

The phobia of the dead is well-known, but the attitude toward death has hardly been analyzed. Normally the Navaho staves off death as long as possible, relying upon religious formula to keep him safe. He admits that death is inevitable and is not nearly as afraid of it as he is of the dead. Long distances between habitations, sudden severe storms, rising streams, as well as the exigencies of handling stock, have kept him constantly aware of emergencies.

Bravery, even foolhardiness, is the norm; cowardice is deplored. A well-trained Navaho depends upon his physical. prowess reinforced by songs, prayers, and formulas. When circumstances get too much for his resources, he is inclined to be fatalistic rather than terror-stricken. He becomes of necessity a good loser.

Indifference about the afterlife doubtless reflects the ethical system, which holds that man suffers here on earth, if at all, but need not expect punishment after death; the individual spirit may be lost in the cosmos. Man can better his life here on earth by ceremonial control; he cannot change his ultimate destiny.

There seem to be cases of 'willing to die.' The Navaho tell of persons who, apparently in excellent health, say, "I'm not going to live long," give up customary activities, and within a few days die. These accounts have been corroborated by white men who knew the individuals personally. So far such cases have never been investigated by our medical men; warnings of disease and the Navaho definition of symptoms differ so much from ours that diagnoses are very difficult (Chapter 6). Dr. A. A. Brill told me that he had made autopsies on whites who were said to have 'willed to die' and found no ascertainable reason for their demise. The reports of such deaths among the Navaho are sensational rather than numerous and, if they occur at all, are doubtless exceptional.[27]

In lack of interest in death and the afterlife, Navaho mythology differs from that of neighboring and related tribes. There are only a few references to these subjects in the large body of recorded myth. Since sorcery, fear of the dead, and ignorance are characteristic of the underworlds, the first experience of death is appropriately assigned to an early world.

When the first person, a hermaphrodite (referred to by Matthews as 'she'), died, no one knew what had become of her breath. Some men searched far and wide for it; eventually they came to the Place-of-emergence, looked down through the hole, and saw the deceased combing her hair. They returned, reported to their companions, "She is not dead, but in that world there is no provision for increase. Those who die continue to live without change." Four days later

41

the men died. Since that time people have feared to look upon the dead, have avoided places where the spirits of the dead may be, and are nervous about ghosts (tćĭˑndiˑ).

Another story accounts for death after the pre-human beings had reached this world. Soon after their emergence, they tried to find out whether they would live forever or die. Someone threw a hide-scraper into the water and said, "If it sinks we perish; if it floats we live." It floated and all were glad, but Coyote came along and said, "Let me divine your fate." Pronouncing the the same words, he threw a stone into the water. It sank. The people became angry with him, but he rationalized (with customary Navaho acceptance of the inevitable): "If we all live and continue to increase as we have done in the past, the earth will be too small to hold us, and there will be no room for the cornfields. It is better that each of us should live but a limited time on this earth, then leave and make room for the children." The people realized the wisdom of his words and resigned themselves.[28]

These explanations seem to indicate that the Navaho look upon death as failure to grow, and upon the land of the dead as static, although they do not emphasize stagnation.

I have not been able to confirm the explanation that property is destroyed because the deceased needs it in the afterlife. Such an idea is not consistent with my informants' belief that one loses personal identity at death and becomes an indefinable part of the universal whole. Yet Stephen writes, "They [Navaho] destroy or bury property so the dead may 'cut a swell' in the underground world."[29]

One of Hoijer's informants volunteered, in an account of mortuary customs:

"If he [the deceased] had horses, they club the horses to death at the door of the hogan. His best saddle, saddle blanket, bridle—on all of these they hammer [to destroy them]. Only in this way will they be of use to [the deceased], they say. . . . If these belongings were not destroyed, then some Navaho wandering about would pick them up. Being hammered in that way, no one will bother them. They are called the ghost's belongings. . . .

42

"In this way a Navaho burial is well done. When it is done so [the deceased] is pleased with it. Right among us his spirit wanders about. For that reason, his belongings and the horse he will ride are buried with him. If this is not done, he comes back for his belongings, they say." [30]

My informants say, "We give to the dead to show respect, to indicate that they were loved by those who survive."

Destiny

The Navaho of my acquaintance often speculate about the fate of the dead. I have discussed the matter with many individuals, laymen as well as chanters. From none have I got even an intimation of a belief in an afterlife or afterworld. Most laymen thought there was nothing. The chanters stressed the idea of harmony and of tčí'ndi'; all repudiated the idea of a *personal* immortality. Though the direct opposite of Wyman's findings, I think their opinion conforms with mythological teachings and interests already cited. Those of Wyman's informants who thought the afterworld resembled this one gave a description very much like that of many American Indians,[31] at least those of the Plains and Plateau regions. My information leads me to contrast the Navaho to these other tribes. For example, the Apache have made much of the afterworld in myth and given a good picture of it; this seems remarkable in view of the few references in Navaho myth.

After I had written the brief summary "Human Nature as Conceived by the Navajo Indians,"[32] I received a long criticism from Adolph Bitanny (AB). His remarks corroborate what I have said here, but he adds one point I have not emphasized and one I had not considered at all. I quote from his letter:

"In Navaho a man has three forms of hereafter amounting to concepts similar to immortality. First there is what I call prolongation of man, which can be stated as a biological continuation—that is, parents to offsprings. This is pretty much conceived in plant and animal kingdom. The second concept is the physical hereafter; that is, when a body or a living entity dies—that is, ceases living—it disintegrates and harmonizes with the elements of the earth. This concept is elemental in that it's a return from animistic [living] entity to the element that makes up the universe. This concept has oftentimes played havoc with many a Navaho mind because some will say that a spirit does derive from the body upon death to become partially imbibed with other living entities. You hear many of the Navaho say that the after-death-spirit dwells here or there or is manifested in various animals like coyotes, bears, snakes, etc. The third concept or tenet represents a form of hereafter which I call intangible. This is manifested in terms of memory in the minds of the community in which the former body moved or lived. The memory of habits, traits, personality, temperaments, deed (bad or good) lives in the minds of the community in a form of stories about him. This method of thinking appears to be very clearly expressed in all ceremonies of purification."

The ' rightness ' of biological continuation is well brought out by Navaho love and treatment of children and also by disdain for the childless, who are held to have failed in completing their life role. In his ' second concept ' AB includes sa'ą na·γái bike xójó·n and tčí·ndi·; he touches upon an afterlife when he says, ". . . spirit dwells here and there," becoming explicit with examples of what we might call transmigration, confined, however, to the perpetuation of evil through sorcery, since one phase of witchcraft deals with the transformation of men into harmful animals.

Comparison with other Indian religions, including those of neighbors of the Navaho, brings out an astonishing lack of correlation between two customs, avoidance of the dead and avoidance of speaking of the dead. The Zuni, for example, though they do not like the dead and consider death an inconvenient interruption of normal affairs, do not have the unrea-

44

soning terror of the dead the Navaho have, yet the Zuni do
not like to mention the deceased's name or to talk about him;
they try to put him out of their thoughts so as to get life's
activities back into the normal course. In contrast, the
Navaho delight in talking about the life, good deeds, and
accomplishments of the deceased. They are pleased when a
child is said to resemble the recently dead or when an outsider reminds them of an event concerning him. The family
I know best and other Navaho of my acquaintance demonstrated by their behavior AB's reference to memory as a
form of spirit perpetuation.

Consideration of the nature of the universe, the world, and
man, and the nature of time and space, creation, growth,
motion, order, control, and the life cycle includes all these
and other Navaho concepts expressed in terms quite impossible to translate into English. The synthesis of all the
beliefs detailed above and of those concerning the attitudes
and experiences of man is expressed by sa'ą na·γái, usually
followed by biķe xójó·n. Various explanations are given for
these phrases, which constitute the benediction (climax) of
many prayers or songs. xójó·ní means 'perfection so far as
it is attainable by man,' the end toward which not only
man but also supernaturals and time and motion, institutions, and behavior strive. Perhaps it is the utmost achievement in order.

The remoteness of the concept of sa'ą na·γái from any concept in Christianity doubtless accounts for difficulties of
getting a word to approximate 'soul' and Navaho refusal
to accept the Christian idea of afterlife. If man, like every
other conceivable thing, becomes sa'ą na·γái, he must lose
not only his body but even his individuality—the very
antithesis of Christian teaching. Christianity strives for
future personal survival and resurrection by trial on earth;

45

Navaho religion, accepting the body and all personal short-comings, emphasizes the opportunities of the present and tries to amalgamate them into a unity of experience and being with the past and future.

Various kinds of information support this conclusion. For years sa'ą na·γái was translated ' in-old-age-walking,' and it is sometimes felt that sa'ą na·γái bike xójó·n is a single inseparable concept, the whole thing to be construed ' in-old-age-walking-the-trail-of-beauty.' Linguistically this translation is incorrect, bike xójó·n having been recorded and not phonetically differentiated from bike xójó·n (bike, 'according-to-it,' ritualistically, ' by decree of ').

I discussed the concept exhaustively with tłá·h, who said that chanters are seriously concerned with the meaning and that there are two main schools of thought. The one that interprets it ' according-to-old-age-may-it-be-perfect ' relies upon a false etymology of sá, ' old age,' made not only by whites but also by some Navaho. The other school argues that sa'ą (or są'ą) is desirable; old age, though inevitable, is to be put off. It is, of course, better to become old gracefully than to die young, but belief in Changing Woman's rejuvenation may delay old age. As the seasons advance she becomes old, it is true, but she has the power to reverse the process, becoming young again by degrees, as two children, deifically ' borrowed ' from the original cornfield, testified:

"When we went in, our grandmother lay curled up, nearly killed with old age. She got up and walked with a cane of whiteshell to a room at the east. She came out again somewhat stronger. Then, supported by a cane of turquoise, she went into the south room. She came back walking unaided. She went next into a room at the west. She came out a young woman. She went into the north room and returned, a young girl so beautiful that we bowed our heads in wonder." [33]

This bit of the myth accurately describes the Navaho

belief in the final ideal. tłǎ·h therefore accepted the conclusions of the second school of thought in considering są'ą as 'harmonious or desirable destiny' or even 'restoration-to-youth.' The singer of the Rain Ceremony said, "są'ą na·γái is from the bottom of the earth. Sunrise and sunset have it. It is the power of renewal for everything every six months through Sun." For these and for linguistic reasons, I have accepted this dictum, translating the phrases 'according-to-the-ideal may-restoration-be-achieved.' I say 'phrases' advisedly because, according to Goddard, a song is assigned to each.

When Mirage Talking God blessed the house at Changing Woman's puberty rite, he sang two songs. At the end she inquired, "Why do you sing thus? Two old men are lacking. With what am I going to reach my destiny? According to what decree will things be perfect?" Talking God therefore added the songs about sa'ą na·γái and biḱe xójó·n.[34]

Like a passage in the Shooting Chant, this reference to two old men leads one to suppose that these ideals were personified and symbolized in song. In an assembly of the Holy Ones the chants were ordained and the rules laid down. Duties and powers, among them the songs, were assigned various creatures. "The monsters will be among your songs which, because of them, will be strengthened, respected, and feared," the gods told Holy Young Man from Rumbling Mountain when he was put in charge of the Shooting Chant. "Among all other chants we make, your songs will be included to strengthen them. And your songs, Sky Man and Earth Woman, will bring them all without exception, and yours, Restoration-to-youth and According-to-perfection, will always be at the end."

Father Berard gives still another explanation. The song phrase są'ą na·γái bitłah refers to the symbolism of ritualistic tallows of the War Ceremony. He says it is equivalent to naxosdzá·n biká'' tłah na·stcí·n, 'collected tallows on the surface of the earth,' that is, tallows from the game animals. "są'ą na·γái is supposed to be the inner form of the earth, which at times stretches itself, then takes another position. This change in position accounts for changed conditions on the earth's surface. . . . On the surface of the earth we find beauty or happiness (bike xójó'n) in plants, water, trees, and mountains. Therefore są'ą na·γái and bike xójó'n, 'the inner form of the earth and its outer surface,' are usually combined in song and prayer." [35]

Since są'ą na·γái, according to tłǎ·h and others of my informants, includes everything, we may expect to find it expressed by various symbols. Perhaps that is the only way in which an abstraction of this kind can be explained. The explanation of Father Berard's informant is an attempt at personification; that of Goddard's seems to be of persons. As concepts the two phrases are a projection into the future, since characters such as First Man and First Woman and others belong to the past.

Even more difficult is the concept behind tčî·ndi· (tčî·di·), which expresses the residue that man has been unable to bring into the universal harmony, for, despite the efforts of the gods, man, and nature, some evils refuse to be woven into the pattern of well-being. Perhaps the best rendering would be 'potentiality for evil.' Wyman has discussed tčî·ndi·, mistakenly translated as 'devil' or, somewhat better, 'ghost.' [36] Nothing in the Navaho idea corresponds to any notion of 'devil'; the interpretation may be dismissed. 'Ghost' means something more tangible than tčî·ndi·. It has been accepted because it so often refers to the dead; it may in fact mean 'the contamination of the dead.'

The dead body, the house where the person dies, things in contact with the body are tčî·ndi·—that is, full of dreaded power, potentiality for evil. When evils are listed for the purpose of exorcism, tćî·ndi· often take first place. Informants say they are more prevalent and come closer to man at night than in the daytime. Ghosts are inexorable; they cannot be persuaded to become helpful to man. tćî·ndi· exist and the best man can do is to drive them off or avoid them. By providing himself, as it were, with a thick coating of positive power—prayer, song, the strength of the gods—and by arming himself with things feared by tćî·ndi·—flint points, ashes, soot, ghost 'medicine'—he may at least keep evil at bay.

On the road of life to his final destiny, which will make man one with the universe, he is concerned with maintaining harmony with all things, with subsistence and the orderly replenishment of his own kind. Since nothing in the universe is endowed with omnipotence, dangers, evils, and mistakes still exist; by himself man cannot annihilate error. Consequently, all beings in the sky, on the earth, in the waters, under the earth, and in the subterranean waters either aid him or must be overcome by superior power. Man may hope to obtain such power by proper manipulation, that is, by magical techniques. He is aided by earth elements—plants, animals, rocks, waters, mountains.

The supernaturals are greater than man. They brought him into being and designated, through long suffering and teaching of one object lesson after another, the control man should exert over himself and his natural surroundings. Through them he learned what was good and what was harmful, and how evils and dangers could be converted to good. None of these powers is purely good; some are almost wholly evil. Invocation and propitiation of the gods and the forces of nature are useless unless one is in rapport with his fellow-men. Proper behavior was defined by the gods along with life-giving and life-preserving principles.

49

CHAPTER 4

PANTHEON: CHARACTERISTICS OF SUPERNATURALS

A T VARIOUS points in man's walk through life all the courage and endurance he summons may fail; he then invokes the superior power of the supernaturals. Dogma does not try to account for the origin of the deities. They simply were, without birth or creation, or they were transformed from something that already existed.

There are three Navaho names for deity—γé'i', xa·ctčé·, and diγini·—but, as is usually the case with Navaho categories, they are not exclusive. γé'i· is used both for those who help man and those who harm man. Talking God, for instance, whose name is xa·ctčé·łtihí, and γé'i·tsoh, Big Monster, are both classed as γé'i·.

Some, but not nearly all, the Holy People have names with xa·ctčé·, a part of a noun compound that seems to mean ' god ' or ' favorable power.' When asked the difference between Holy People and γé'i·, JS said γé'i· were seen in masked impersonations, but his explanation does not account for First Man, First Woman, Coyote, Big Fly, Thunder, and others who are not masked so far as my material goes, though they are sometimes included as γé'i·. Further investigation indicates that the class γé'i· includes all beings whose power supersedes that of man, whereas xa·ctčé· includes only beings whose characteristics belong more emphatically to the class I call ' persuadable '; that is, they are easy to invoke and have no primordial meanness or evil intention.

Contrasted to xa·ctčé· (but also included in γé'i·) are

na·γé"—specifically, 'monsters,' generally, 'evils, dangers, whatever is hostile to man.' These are well described in myth, but because tradition emphasizes their subjection rather than their contribution to man's well-being, they do not appear in the assemblies of the gods. The symbols that represent them in the rituals exorcise rather than invoke them.

The Holy People—diγini·, 'the-particular-ones-who-are-holy'; diγin dine'é, 'holy group or groups'—are by no means always well disposed toward man, but they may be on man's side on a particular occasion. Sun, Changing Woman, Talking God, Monster Slayer, Thunders, and Winds are among the many deities referred to as Holy People. When Sun generated the monsters, he was not favoring man, yet he begot The Twins to save man. Talking God similarly seemed for endless days against rather than for the Stricken Twins, yet eventually he caused their triumph. Monster Slayer was originally human but, through trial, error, and divine dispensation, became holy. His failures are attributed to ignorance, not to evil intention. Destructive rather than constructive powers are more commonly ascribed to Thunders, Wind, and Snakes, yet with great effort they may be persuaded to aid man. 'Holy' seems therefore to describe a mood or attitude of the gods rather than a particular class.

It may include also those whose power is relatively insignificant yet upon occasion indispensable, those I have called 'helpers, aides, or mentors.' If Chipmunk, one of the least of earth's creatures, has the particular power to aid in overcoming a cosmic monster, she is as important at the moment she is needed as Sun's child with all his god-given weapons. For with all the power of his revered mother and his dashing father, he would fail if, thinking Burrowing Monster was dead, he had no way of proving it and got caught when the monster revived. A little everyday person who, even when the monster lived, took a run out to the end of the horn, could easily make the test. Examples of the importance of the apparently insignificant are numerous in story and chant, for in the Navaho conception of order or destiny, the least as well as the greatest is accounted for. Occasionally, too, the ' great ones ' perform some invaluable but ordinarily insignificant function, instead of exhibiting the extraordinary powers of which they are capable.

I have tried in vain to arrange the supernatural beings in chronological sequence and in the order of their importance. If we consider only the texts that acquaint us with the Shooting Chant and the War Ceremony, we might say that Sun was the deity above all others; furthermore, we would know almost nothing about the gods called xa·ctčé·. Matthews, who worked intensively on the Night Chant and assembled more information about xa·ctčé· than is found in all the other available chant myths put together, was led to conclude: "Much is said about the sun god in the Origin Legend and in other legends of the tribe. In these tales he appears as a god of the greatest powers; yet his cultus today is not so important as that of other gods. He is not appealed to so frequently as some others are."

This statement could not be corroborated by the Shooting Chant, in which prayers, songs, sandpainting, and symbols of Sun are so numerous as to indicate a sun cult. Matthews' further remark, "Sun is never personified in any of the rites of the Night Chant and never represented in the dry-paintings," [1] is also astonishing to the student of the Shooting Chant—or would be, did he not realize that each chant is so organized that one power or group of powers may be the focus of emphasis in one, quite secondary in another. Furthermore, powers of such great significance in one chant as to set the key may in another be subject to taboo. Snakes of various kinds are so ubiquitous in the Shooting and Wind chants as to be a major theme. From the Hail Chant—in many respects closely related to the other two—Snake is excluded.

If Matthews had started with the Hail Chant instead of recording the Night Chant first, he would of necessity have concluded that Thunders were important deities, that snakes were shunned almost completely; moreover, there would have been only minor indications that the gods he defines as ' major ' existed at all. Their role in the Hail Chant, while not exactly minor, is, to say the least, casual.

Though their traits are implicit and references to them scattered, many of the gods are well characterized. The total impression of each god can be ascertained only from the associations that form the basis of the ritual. Some deities are described by myth or ritual and symbolized by masks or sandpaintings. Often, however, the power a being controls is brought out by a description of its home, a seemingly casual reference to its demands for a prayerstick, or an action—for instance, the alacrity with which it accepts an offering or its hesitancy in assenting to a plea for aid. I have collected much of the scattered information under the name of the deity in Concordance A, and from it made the following classification of gods, which is intended to be suggestive rather than definitive:

Persuadable deities (P)
Undependable deities (U)
Helpers of deity and man (H)
Intermediaries between man and deity (I)
Unpersuadable deities (UP)
Dangers considered as deities (D)
Beings between good and evil (B)

One condition frequently referred to in the myths, and by implication in the chants, is the possibility that any god may be duplicated. The Stricken Twins, seeking help, wander from one god to another having the same name but living in different places. There are many references to Talking God and xa·ctčé·'óγan, both of whom sometimes travel in groups. Usually one Talking God is not distinguished from another; in one version of Changing Woman's development the deity in charge of her puberty ceremony was called Mirage Talking God.

I have discussed the question of 'multiple selves' in *Navajo Medicine Man*.[2] Since time and space may be telescoped or expanded, a god here today may easily have been here yesterday and, if here yesterday, he may have been here also a hundred or a thousand years ago. If it is a spirit able to appear miraculously when needed, there is no reason why there should not be a group of four spirits, four times as helpful, or why four identical spirits cannot be in different places at the same time. Once the imagination has conjured up the original figure, multiplication is simple enough. A deity who can move on a sunbeam, rainbow, or streak of lightning may as easily be in four places at one time.

In Gray Eyes' story of the Shooting Chant, the new permanent home Changing Woman helped to prepare for Monster Slayer is described with the added explanation: "There [beyond Mt. Taylor] his father was preparing a home for him. His mother, although she was staying here [at tčô·l'į'į], was helping Sun get it ready and knew all about it" —which suggests that Changing Woman may be another manifestation of Sun's 'Sky Wife' (cp. Chapter 5).

If a rock crystal is desperately needed, Rock Crystal Man appears and offers advice or a token of power which may be greatly increased if a group of his own kind accompanies him; hence, there may be four or sixteen Rock Crystal People. The appearance of the same god in different guises is somewhat more difficult to understand. The protagonists of the different chant myths, the wonderful boys who enlist with greater or less difficulty the sympathy and protection of the gods, seem to be representative of Monster Slayer, if not actually he in person. When arrayed in armor, he is Monster Slayer; without it, he is Holy Man; in another situation he is Reared-in-the-earth. Place makes a difference, and when four gods instead of the usual pair are needed, four may turn up. Child-of-the-water, who is also Holy Boy, may be Changing Grandchild. There is less evidence, except their extraordinary behavior and experiences, that other leading men of the drama represent the great warrior or his peaceful counterpart. Some Navaho chanters see remote connections between similar symbols from which they generalize; others are too literal-minded to comprehend any connection between the symbols. For the latter, each detail by itself is as stated; there is no need to assume a relationship to anything else. Father Berard has at last tacitly accepted the theory of multiple selves and Maud Oakes' informant corroborates it.[3]

In enumerating the gods and explaining the difficulty of distinguishing exactly between γé'i', xa·ctćé', and other groups, I mentioned the question of rank, pointing out that superiority or inferiority depends upon the situation. Many chant myths follow a certain pattern: a youth, for one reason or another, cuts himself adrift from his family, enters upon a series of adventures, experiences terrifying enough to break the hardiest, which make him for some time an associate of deity. Eventually he leaves the earth to join the gods, whereupon he himself becomes divine. Many legends end with the disappearance of the hero; none tells which god he became or what his permanent human-deific position is. It is generally understood that Monster Slayer and Child-of-the-water are the War Gods, having been transformed from earthly beings. They are γé'i·, at least in the sense that they are impersonated by masked dancers, but are perhaps in a class by themselves.

The names of the gods and their position in the ceremonial lodge are often carefully noted. Differences in the roll call of deities at a gathering and in the position occupied by one at different times show the absence of a hierarchy and the capacity of one deity to be in different places at the same time:

When the Stricken Twins reached the assembly of gods at Broad Rock in Canyon de Chelly, many γé'i· were present. xa·ctćé''óγan led the meeting and asked each of the following gods in turn if he had shown the Stricken Twins the way to their home: Monster Slayer, Child-of-the-water, Shooting God, Fringed Mouth, Hunchback God, Male God, Female God, Red God, Black God, Talking God, then Superior God, Whistling God, xa·ctćé·dó·di·, and Water Sprinkler.[4]

Monster Slayer and Child-of-the-water are intermediaries; Fringed Mouth, Hunchback God, Black God, Talking God, and Water Sprinkler are masked gods in the Night Chant; Male God, Female God, Red God, Superior God, Whistling God, and xa·ctćé''dó·di· are so lightly sketched as to be unclassifiable.

After Rainboy was destroyed by Winter Thunder, Big Fly took the news to Dark Thunder, Chief of the Thunders. The Black, Blue, Yellow, and White Thunders, Whirlwinds and Winds of the same colors, Spotted Thunder, Pink Thunder, and be'γotcidí met to discuss what could be done. Talking God and xa·ctćé''óγan had a part in this council.[5]

To another assembly came ' all the Holy People ' (diγin dine'é): First Man, First Woman, Salt Woman, be'γotcidí, First Warrior, Black God, Changing Woman, Sun, and all the gods (γé'i·). Talking God and xa·ctćé''óγan were ready when Monster Slayer and Child-of-the-water were heard coming. All bowed their heads and put their hands on their knees as Talking God and his companion blessed the house.[6]

The importance of the War Gods is emphasized by their entrance, but the membership of the divine group and the reason for their order is not apparent.

After the Dark Thunder People had fought with the Winter Thunder group until there was great destruction on both sides, the Holy People met to see what could be done. To this meeting at the home of Dark Thunder came Changing Woman, Monster Slayer, Child-of-the-water, Bat, Big Fly, and Black God.

At this time two meetings were held simultaneously, one at the home of Dark Thunder and one at the home of Winter Thunder; the same deities were present at both. Although Changing Woman begged the ' great gods ' to carry the offer of peace to Winter Thunder, everyone was afraid until finally, after much coaxing, Bat, who occupied the humblest seat near the door, consented to go.

At the home of Winter Thunder, whither they had gone, Black God forced Winter Thunder to listen to a proposal. When they sat down to talk it over there were Winter Thunder, Duck, Mudhen, Big White Duck, Beaver, Big Snake, and so many allies that they had to stand outside the house.

Eventually an agreement was concluded by the Dark Thunder and the Winter Thunder groups. As they were about to leave for the fight, Talking God told them to get in line. This time there were Monster Slayer, Child-of-the-water, Changing Woman, Talking God, Big Fly, Pollen Boy, Cornbeetle Girl, the two Racing Gods and their grandmother, and the four Whirlwinds. All the Holy People, except be'γotcidí, came: Cloud People, Water People, Fog People, Moss People. The same deities assembled at Dark Thunder's and at Winter Thunder's house. Talking God laid down a wide rainbow for Dark Thunder's party and took his place at its head. The other people stood on it behind him and xa·ctčé''óγan stood at the rear; the whole assembly was made invisible by a dark cloud. The organization of Winter Thunder's party on a white rainbow was exactly the same: Talking God was in front, xa·ctčé''óγan at the rear, and all were hidden by a white fog.[7]

57

At another assembly for Rainboy's welfare the following participated (the places of some in the ceremonial hogan are designated): Changing Woman, Blue-whirlwind-maiden, Salt Woman, Turtledove Maiden, Talking God, Winter Thunder, Dark Thunder, Blue-male-god, Corn-female-god, xa·ctčé-'óγan, and many others. Changing-bear-maiden, Pinyon Jay, Female God, Gopher, and Thunder Girl brought in food offerings. The food was refused and the donors were expelled.[8]

On the last day, when the body painting was done, Big Snake and his group were told to get out. When they retired, First Man, First Woman, Salt Woman, Coyote, be'γotcidí, Black God, Water Sprinkler, Talking God, xa·ctčé·'óγan, Left-handed-whirlwind (the one that blows anti-sunwise), Wind People, and Frog with her many grandchildren came in. In the description of this assembly, each being sat at either the north or the south side of the house; his position indicated whether he was favorable (south) or opposed (north) to the patient. Coyote sat near the door so he could affiliate with either side, according to his whim.[9]

The omnipresence of the spirits may be a comfort to the Navaho who is under the direct protection of the gods, as evidenced by myth or the sandpictures that represent it:

As six gods escorted co from their home to his, they often saw the heads of the gods sticking out from roots of trees and stones, from springs and swamps.[10]

The supernatural endowments of deities, who are by no means perfect, are emphasized in essentially human terms. The most powerful beings are sometimes thwarted by a circumstance with which a man could easily cope.

Changing Woman, respected above all the gods, stubbornly refused to move to the new home made for her in the west. When forced, she remarked plaintively that she was afraid she might be lonely. Sun wept when asked to give the power necessary to kill the monsters. Talking God is helpless when his fellow gods fail to recognize him as the father of the Stricken Twins, their realization of his fatherhood being the only thing lacking (Chapter 8). Unfailing understanding of man's weaknesses, even when fancy takes its wildest flights, may be one reason the Navaho have no supreme god.

Belief in the close relation between man and the Holy People is demonstrated by the explanation of the origin of some of the clans. The progenitors of certain clans were called Holy People. Either the group had broken off from the main body of the tribe and had later rejoined it, or ' it had no history of recent origin.' [11]

Matthews attributes the reddish or yellowish hair of the masks to the fact that in mythological times friendly and alien gods (γé'i') both had yellow hair. My materials give other explanations for the red marks on masks and heads of sandpainting figures: they represent the treasured red bonnet Sun obtained through the exploits of his gambler son. The fair skin and light hair of be'γotcidí are emphasized in the myths—a probable explanation of tlǎ·h's belief that he is the white man's forerunner.

The next excerpts from myth illustrate the exactness with which some of the talents of the gods are described. The powers are carefully incorporated in prayersticks offered to invoke their aid in ritual.

The gods took charge of Self Teacher, who tried to get away from his home in an unseaworthy log, and made for him a model river conveyance. They tied the tree with rainbow ropes so it would not fall with too much force. Monster Slayer and Child-of-the-water cut it with their powerful stone knives and it fell to the north. Zigzag Lightning went through the fallen tree from butt to tip and Straight Lightning darted from tip to butt, hollowing it out even before the branches had been removed. The first hole was crooked; the second god made it straight, but it was still too small. The Winds—Black, Blue, Yellow, and White—entered it in succession, each enlarging it a bit until a man could sit in it. Talking God provided a bowl of food, a vessel of water, and a white cloud for bedding. The gods contributed everything necessary for Self Teacher's comfort, but the particular god who fulfilled each need is not mentioned.

Meanwhile six gods—four Hunchback Gods from Sheep-trail-extends-out, one xa·ctćé·'óγan from tséγihí, and one from tsétah—got Self Teacher's pet turkey ready for the journey. They attached ropes of zigzag lightning, rainray, straight lightning, and rainbow to the log, but their concerted effort was not enough to budge it when they tried to carry the log with the man inside it to the river. Then the six were called; two of the Hunchback Gods at each end crossed their poles under the log, while the two xa·ctćé·'óγan took their places at the center. They were then able to carry the log, though with some difficulty. As they proceeded, their strength failed and they were about to let it go when the Winds came to help them, Black Wind and Blue Wind in front, Yellow Wind and White Wind behind.

When Water Monster pulled the log containing Self Teacher down to the bottom of the river, Water Sprinkler with his magic jars was able to open the water so that the trail of Self Teacher could be found. However, he could not enter the house of Water Monster until the gods above had sent him a short rainbow. Even then, when he got into the innermost room Water Monster chased him out. He returned with Black God, who frightened Water Monster with his fire, finally making him yield. Water Sprinkler then extinguished the fire. As the troupe of gods left Water Monster's home, Frog told Self Teacher how to invoke Water Monster, Water Horse, Beaver, Otter, Big Fish, and himself, Frog, with prayersticks if these water people should ever give disease to man. At a falls in the San Juan River the log stuck again; the Water Fringed Mouths loosened it by raising it with a rope of zigzag lightning. When the whirling log finally came to the lake that was its destination, the gods standing at each side of the lake removed the end plugs of clouds with their poles—xa·ctćé·'óγan at the east, Talking God at the south, and one of the Hunchbacks at the west and north—thus freeing the hero.[12]

The gods were not always able to control one another or to predict the exact results of their endeavors. Rainboy of the Hail Chant, blown to bits after having been seduced by

Winter Thunder's wife, had to be restored by Winter Thunder. It was exceedingly difficult to persuade him and, though he had promised to be helpful, the gods knew that Winter Thunder would try to nullify their good offices if they allowed him to say, "May he weaken." They therefore persisted in repeating the counter-formula "May he be revived" so rapidly and loudly that Winter Thunder could not possibly get his evil words in.[13]

After the entire Hail Chant had been carried out in Rainboy's behalf and he had acquired all its power, he was expected to accept it. For a long time he, a humble earth youth, hesitated, keeping all the gods anxiously waiting for his one word of approval.[14]

A striking characteristic of the pantheon is its kinship organization. None of the kinship references is carried out as elaborately and consistently as that of any Navaho family or clan, but there is a strong tendency to relate one being to another. Sun is an idealized philanderer; almost any young earth maiden is his potential mate. The lot of such a girl was hard until she was rewarded by the supernatural achievement of her children; then her whole family shared their honor.[15]

Sun had one wife who seems to have been legitimate, permanent, typical; she kept house in the east for him. She was Dawn's daughter; her father is not mentioned. She bore Sun many children—all brothers and sisters of The Twins. Two, Dawn Boys, were models for the shaping of The Twins at Sun's house (cp. *Pressing*, Concordance B).[16] Changing Woman became Sun's second wife and eventually established a home in the west where he could rest.

Talking God is said to be the maternal grandfather of the gods (γé'i· bitcei·), a relationship that gives the Night Chant one of its names. Frequently an inferior addresses a deity as

'grandfather,' a term with great persuasive force that indicates the proper respect of a younger person toward an
elder.

If the Navaho pantheon were a closely knit family or clan
organization, it would be profitable to pursue the discussion
of the kinship of the Holy Ones much further, for we might
find evidence of a hierarchy. However, chanters corroborate
the casual and inconsistent kinship allusions in the literature
by their reluctance to carry the god relationship more than
two or three generations and by their confusion when conflicts are pointed out. Neither of the two reasonable explanations for the common use of kinship terms for the gods
presupposes hierarchy. One is the Navaho tendency to utilize
the persuasive power of kinship terms to the full. The people
simply carry into their mythology a cultural habit of which
it would be difficult to rid themselves. The second explanation is that the deific kin-terms are a holdover from a
mythological style prevailing in a large region, the northern
Plateau, from or through which the Navaho may be presumed to have come and whence many of the plots seem to
have derived.

CHAPTER 5

PANTHEON: TYPES OF SUPERNATURALS

Persuadable Deities

SOME OF the gods who play a major role in the chants analyzed may be called Persuadable Deities because their motives are good. Among them are Sun, Changing Woman, most of the xa·ctćé·, Racing Gods, and all their duplicates (Chapter 4). Some of these have many kinds of power; Gopher, Yellow Rat, Chipmunk, and other helpers have perhaps only one or at best few powers. First Man, First Woman, Salt Woman, be'γotcidí, and others might be included here as well as among the Undependable Deities, since they exerted a great deal of influence in creation and in guiding the universe so that man could extricate himself from uncontrolled forces, and are sometimes readily invoked —that is, their wishes are known; prayersticks offered to them with the proper prayers counteract their less favorable traits.

Undependable Deities

The Undependable Gods are persuadable only with difficulty because meanness or the desire to do mischief is a large part of their makeup. Consequently, First Man and First Woman may be put into this category also, although, as has just been said, they are sometimes amenable to man's requests for help. One can never be sure how they will respond, but proper handling may compel them to work for man's benefit, at least temporarily. Man may ultimately control their powers, but he may be obliged to resort to their somewhat doubtful methods.

First Man and First Woman have control of witchcraft. As they took their places in the cosmos after the world was made, they warned the Earth People that they might do harm by sending disease. When, therefore, the causes of man's grief are ascribed to their evil propensities, great effort must be put forth to gain their good will.

Helpers of Deity and Man

Innumerable beings assist deity, man, and even the evils. One type, which bridges the supernatural distance between man and god and plays a major role in instruction, I call ' mentor.' Mentors are few and, like the gods, each may be a different aspect of a single idea. Those most commonly mentioned in my material are Big Fly and Wind. They are said to ' sit on the ear ' of a person who needs instruction and to whisper answers to questions or forecast the future. Stephen records that First Man created a feather or a wing which he attached to his ear. Sapir's informant explains it as a little extension at the end of a down feather. Moved by Wind, this feather represents Sun's power. Big Fly, when a daytime mentor, may be symbolized as Wind's Child, or Sunbeam. Bat sometimes substitutes for Darkness; both are the night protectors corresponding with Big Fly and Sunbeam.[1]

Mentors are described as ever present, although invisible at assemblies. When, after four nights of discussion, no constructive plan has been achieved, a voice from near the door or from some concealed place in the ceiling gives a clue to the proper offering and the god to whom it should be presented. The suggestion is sometimes enigmatical, but furnishes enough information to be understood if the people concentrate. Eventually the voice appears, embodied as Big Fly, Wind, Bat, or Darkness, and explains itself as a guardian of the home of some powerful supernatural, all of whose secrets it knows.

The mentors differ from the gods in that they do not themselves require an offering or payment, but volunteer their aid. On the other hand, characters that serve as mentors do not always act in the same capacity; they may resemble Holy People, contribute rites or ritual, and accept payment. Talking God has been noted as a major deity, but he often serves as a mentor, and others serve in multiple roles.

Another type of helper is the messenger who reports news, announces a ceremony and invites people to sing, or goes on a tour of investigation. As the people moved from one world to another, messengers were dispatched to report on the size and condition of the earth. Black Hawk, Hummingbird, and One-who-walked-on-the-bottom-of-the-water were sent out by First Man; all reported water in every direction. Badger, moving upward into a new world, found mud; later Panther and Wolf inspected the world. Coyote's reports are clues to events, but are rarely accepted unless corroborated. Wind, Roadrunner, and Turkey, for instance, are reliable, and it is said that Turtledove always reports things carefully (cp. Chapter 4; *Racing Gods, Sunbeam, Shooting Star*, Concordance A).

After the hero of a chant has been treated, he should observe a period of restriction, usually four days, during which he absorbs the powers given him. In myth he often remains alone without food or shelter. When he gets hungry and longs for company, a helper—Beaver, Owl, Gopher— tells him that the gods neglected to impart a bit of vital knowledge, usually some detail as how to make incense, which they themselves fear.

65

A small class of helpers may be called fatalists. When something is badly needed and can be obtained only at great risk, someone makes the inevitable remark, "I may as well go. I have to die sometime." Usually the volunteer succeeds in accomplishing the mission.

To complete the category of helpers one should include all the animals—predatory animals representative of hunters, rare game animals that allow themselves to be caught for food, Beaver and Otter, Gila Monster, Birds, Rodents, Insects. Particularly notable among the insects is Spider, originator of spinning and weaving, who gave The Twins feathers to represent the thread of life and save them from peril. Like First Woman, she is sometimes dangerous, laying a trap for people and getting them into trouble. The roles of other insects are discussed elsewhere, but Pollen Boy and Corn-beetle Girl are to be noted as helpers, since they typify fertilization.

Besides the almost infinite number of helpers symbolized by animals of every kind, other groups personify abstract ideas (Chapter 3). Sky, Dawn, Evening Light, Mirage, Heat, Sun, Summer, Stars, as well as precious stones—whiteshell, turquoise, rock crystal, and jet—and even manufactured articles, such as flint arrowpoints, are called ' people ' and behave like persons.

Intermediaries Between Man and Deity

The line between the Holy People and Earth People is not sharply drawn, and in many respects the protagonist of the myth and ritual belongs to both, since he connects the human and divine. With few exceptions, he starts out as an Earth Person showing no special talent. Often disobedience involves him in supernatural affairs. As punishment for disregarding some admonition, he is led upon adventures. He meets a supernatural who directs him, gets into difficulties, and endures much suffering. Among his tribulations are long, dangerous journeys which take him to angry deities who say he must be punished but mean he must be taught. Each encounter yields some element of a ceremony which he brings back to his people. He cleanses his family so they will be able to deal with holy things and teaches someone, usually his brother, to sing the ritual. He stays long enough to supervise the brother's first performance, often over a sister, then disappears into the air, sometimes taking a relative with him. He promises to bless and watch over his family and bids them remember him whenever they see some natural phenomenon such as rainbow, rain, sunglow, or growth.

The difficulty of differentiating between Earth and Holy People is sometimes evidenced in the tales. Frequently it is said, "Earth People do not come here." When the Stricken Twins went to the Hopi, they were called ' Earth People.' An indication of inferiority, it implied that the Hopi may have considered themselves holy. However, after the twins had shown their power, the Hopi confessed that they were merely Earth People just like the twins.[2] Actually the Hopi were bluffing, and learned to their sorrow that the twins were supernatural.

The Twins, or War Gods, are the type heroes of the stories. Their exploits in overcoming the first and worst enemies of the earth are recounted in the myths of the Emergence, the Male Shooting Chant Holy, and the War Ceremony. In the account of the Shooting Chant the transition between Earth and Holy People is made when The Twins appear in two guises—their own, as Monster Slayer and Child-of-the-water, and as Holy Man and Holy Boy (Chapter 4).

After the major evils and dangers had been overcome, minor difficulties, inconveniences, and misunderstandings

remained. These were transformed into good in various ceremonies which have The Twins or one of their manifestations
as hero-teachers. The Stricken Twins of one version of the
Night Chant seem to be such a manifestation. Talking God
as their father behaves like Sun; their mother may be the
earthly counterpart of Changing Woman; and they are War
Gods who failed again and again, children who endure the
sorrows of Earth People and who, with little help, must prevail over the suspicion and snobbery of the gods. The adventures of the Stricken Twins contrast sharply with those of
The Twins on their journeys to Sun when success accompanied them in a kind of supernatural glow.

In the Hail Chant, Rainboy starts out as the unlucky
gambler. In the Shooting Chant his counterpart is Holy Boy.
So similar were the two that even the Holy People sometimes
took one for the other. Because Monster Slayer had charge
of corn, agriculture was possible, but life was very one-sided
without rare game, which was under the control of the
incestuous old sorcerer Deer Owner, from whom war power
alone could wrest it. In the legend of the Eagle Chant,
Monster Slayer overcame him and acquired the eagle-
trapping ritual. The same motive—raising vegetables and
conquering the gamekeeper—occurs in the Feather Chant,
where game is more highly stressed, and in the Night Chant,
which emphasizes the power of the gods.

In the Eagle Chant, Monster Slayer is the perfect lover; in
the Feather Chant, the hero is despised as a gambler and is so
ill-treated by his family that he leaves home. The stories
develop four aspects of the hero—the individual or twin
representation, the gambler, the visionary or whirling log,
and the eagle decoy. The hero of the Feather Chant combines
the gambler and the visionary types.

The Twelve Brothers of the Endurance Chant are almost

certainly duplicates of The Twins in their idealized domestic form. RM, who told the story, said explicitly that the Youngest Brother, the little one with power, was Monster Slayer.

The hero of the Big Star Chant was the son-in-law of the One-who-customarily-sees-the-fish, who, RM says, is the same as Monster Slayer.[3] I have found no reference to this young man's father-in-law, but presumably he belongs in the sorcerer class (cp. *Deer Owner*, Concordance A). Through the eagle decoy the hero gained entrance to Skyland, where he learned the secrets of the stars. The beggar or dirty boy of the Bead Chant, by making an eagle decoy, got the powers of the sky-flying creatures, including snakes.

The tales of the Visionary are quite similar in two versions, one belonging to a form of the Night Chant and one to the Feather Chant. Parts of these stories are almost identical; so close is their relation that the Feather Chant seems in some respects to be a branch of the Night Chant. The tales are differentiated, however, by the contrast in the aid given, evident in the motivation. In the Visionary or Whirling Log plot the gods volunteered their aid and everything went well for the hero, who was selected by the gods. In the Feather Chant version everything was hard for him; he had to guess and fumble before the gods would aid him.

One theme in the introduction to the myth of the Visionary I have found nowhere else. The boy was subjected to supernatural training because he had dreams and heard voices which later turned out to be prophecies. He understood the talk of birds who are enemies of man. His gift sets the story in motion. Later the tale becomes more a list of ceremonial detail than a drama with a well-integrated plot.[4]

In contrast to the Visionary hero is Reared-in-the-mountain of the Mountain Chant myth, who did not realize, until after many adventures, that he was chosen by the Holy

People. An ordinary Navaho youth who disobeyed his father's injunctions, he was captured by the Utes, symbolic of all Navaho enemies. Even this occurrence put him in the way of meeting supernatural beings and becoming an intermediary between them and the Earth People.

It is almost impossible to decide whether the protagonists of the tales are human or divine. The latter probably fits them better, for they miraculously disappeared from the earth, presumably to join the gods. When in the realm of the supernatural beings, they yearn for their human families; yet when they return to earth they so long for the company of the gods that they cannot stay. Their nostalgia for the earth and its people leaves them apparently suspended between earth and heaven.[5]

Unpersuadable Deities

The intermediaries between man and gods may err or disobey deific commands, but they are never contemptible, their lapses being due to ignorance. The monsters, Unpersuadable Deities, are essentially evil, the results of abnormal sexual indulgence in a lower world or of blood shed at their birth and not ritualistically disposed of because they were not acknowledged by their mothers. They appear as colors under rocks and at the base of cliffs and are usually called ' Those-who-talk-at-the-base-of-cliffs.'[6] They are also called γé'i·, but if the term ' holy ' is applied to them it refers to their maleficent power. They harm man instead of aiding him. Predacious monsters, they were conquered by the War' Gods. Lest they produce weakness in the earth, which must communicate itself to man, they must be remembered in ceremony by exorcistic rites.

The monsters have different names and descriptions in

different versions of the myths. Big Monster, called also Big-gray-monster and Big-lonely-monster, is the prototype. As he symbolizes all and was the hardest to deal with, his conquest set the pattern for the rest. Since the Navaho names do not always differentiate the Unpersuadable Deities from xa˙ctčé˙, those more easily persuaded, the following distinctions made by translation should be noted:

Big Monster	γé'i˙tsoh	Gray Monster	γé'i˙ łbahí
Big God	xa˙ctc'é˙tsoh	Gray God	xa˙ctc'é˙ łbahí

Dangers Conceived as Deities

Monsters and dangers have the same function—to strengthen The Twins' war power. In the legends of the Shooting Chant, Enemy Way, and War Prophylactic ceremonies, the dangers are encountered by The Twins on their first journey to their father; in some of the others they are lacking or come after certain monsters have been vanquished. Dangers are not as thoroughly personalized as monsters; they are rather described as natural phenomena which must be brought under control. That they are just as animistic is attested by the pollen-paintings of Oakes' Plates II and III, where the spirit of the danger is represented. The pictures of the Slipping (Sliding) Sands, Cutting Reeds, and Crushing Rocks illustrate a type of danger that destroyed Earth People just as the monsters did.[7]

The dangers are really mythological motives common to many North American tribes, but since the Navaho have utilized them in their ritualistic complex, they have become a type of symbol. The unravelers of the Shooting Chant, for instance, represent not only the thread of life given by Spider Woman to Monster Slayer for his protection but also the subjection of the Sliding Sands; Black God's fire drill stands

71

for not only the power of fire but also the episode of The Twins' encounter with the Cutting Reeds.

An interesting combination in painting that indicates the close relation between monster and danger is the picture of Hot Spring in Oakes' Plate IX.[8] Actually this represents The Twins overcoming Big Monster, but instead of the monster himself the painting shows the place he dominated, in terms of a danger that had to be removed.

Beings Between Good and Evil

Monster Slayer and his brother overcame the great monsters and dangers, then traveled throughout the world looking for other evils to subdue. At one time their mother, by means of a fierce storm, killed many minor evils, sometimes called ' gray gods,' and indicated that none was left. However, Wind told Monster Slayer about such creatures as Old Age, Cold, Poverty, Hunger, Sleep, Louse, Craving-for-meat, Desire, and Want. Without consulting his mother, he sought them in their dwellings, where he found them a disgusting lot. They had sore eyes, sticky eyebrows, and mucus running from their noses, but each gave a good reason why it should not be destroyed, and he was powerless before their words and gentle ways. For instance, Monster Slayer had no difficulty with Eye Killers when he cast salt into the fire made with his fire drill, but when Sleep passed a finger gently down over Monster Slayer's nose he simply fell asleep; he could not understand such a weapon.

His mother explained when he got home: "These you should not kill because they meet somewhere in between good and bad. Poverty and Hunger are somewhere between that which gives pleasure and that which gives pain. That is why they should not be destroyed. That is why we have these things today." [9]

Order of Monsters, Dangers, and Beings-in-between

In various versions of the war heroes' adventures the order of events differs. The sequence has significance just as have those of color, direction, and ritualistic acts (Part Three), a particular sequence belonging to each ceremony. The chanter enumerates the monsters and dangers automatically and casually according to the way they come in the ceremony he knows. He may know, but does not say, that the order differs for each setting; more commonly he does not know the order for ceremonies other than his own. I have indicated the order in Chart II (page 74).

Chart II, incorporating the results of an analysis of eight narratives, shows that the order of monsters can hardly be fortuitous, as Father Berard states.[10] For convenience the evils are numbered.

Note that the order 1, 2, 4 occurs in five versions, that 1, 2, 4, 6 occurs in three, and in one (BS) in reverse sequence, and that there are other less apparent regularities. One reason for the order of the evils is the plot, which sometimes depends upon it. Monster Slayer filled the colon of Burrowing Monster with its blood. In one version the blood-filled colon was merely a trophy and the episode of Burrowing Monster need not have a significant influence on the plot. In other versions, where the colon became a lure for Cliff Monster, the Burrowing Monster episode must come first.

I think that the order of episodes comprising the creation myth differs with the type of chant into which it leads. The monster story as an integral part of the Shooting Chant is obvious. Unfortunately, I do not know Gray Eyes' other lore. Slim Curley was the narrator of the Enemy Way legend, and myths of the Night and Flint chants as well. Jeff King, who dictated the tale of the War Prophylactic Ceremony, stresses

CHART II

ORDER OF MONSTERS, DANGERS, AND BEINGS-IN-BETWEEN

1 Big Monster
2 Burrowing Monster
  (Horned Monster)
3 Kicking Monster
4 Cliff (Winged) Monster
5 Tracking Bear
6 Eye Killers
7 Tracking Antelope
8 Traveling Rock
9 Gray Evils
10 Bony Bear
11 Water Monster
12 Frog People
13 Gray Gods (perhaps same as 9)
14 Syphilis People
15 Old Age
16 Cold
17 Poverty

18 Hunger
19 Big Fish
20 Sleep
21 Louse
22 Craving-for-meat
23 Big Centipede
24 Crushing Rocks
25 Cutting Reeds
26 Spreading Stream
27 Trapping Cactus
28 Rock Swallows
29 Changing-bear-maiden
30 Two Old-blind-men
31 Spider Woman
32 Slipping (Sliding) Sands
33 Tearing Cactus
34 Seething Sands
35 Water Bugs

ORDER OF OCCURRENCE

SC	EW	WP	Leg	BeC	NCM	NT	BS
31	26	15	24				
26	33	25	25				
24	32	24	33				
32	25		34				
25	24						
1	1	1	1	1	1	1	7
2	2	2	2	2	2	2	3
3	4	4	4	7	4	4	8
4	6	6	6	4	3	3	6
5	5	5	5	3	5	7	4
6	10	8	8	6	6	6	2
7	11		minor evils	8	23	18	1
8	12		15	5	24	20	19
9	13		16		25	22	20
	14		17		26	15	17
	8		18		27	17	18
					28	5	21
					29	30	22
					15		
					20		
					21		
					17		
					18		

For abbreviations, see note on opposite page.

its relation to the Beauty Chant; Matthews' informant of Version A was also a singer of the Beauty Chant. The sequence of monsters these men give is comparable with that of Curtis's account of the Beauty Chant. The chanter, tłá·h, to whom we owe the order of the Navaho Creation Myth, specialized in the Night and Hail chants, but knew others.

The initials BS designate the order given by RM, chanter of the Big Star Chant, and do not mean that the monster-subduing theme is necessarily a part of that chant; his sequence was an explanation of origins, not the formal narration of a myth.

RM knows only chants belonging to the evil side—Big Star, Endurance Chant, Female Mountain Chant Evil—a type in which reversal of the normal order is common. His knowledge seems, therefore, to account for the order he gave, diverging most widely from all the others, particularly for the unit 6–4–2–1, which, in turn, is the exact reverse of the order of the Enemy Way, War Prophylactic, and Legend accounts.

Gods as Sun Manifestations

The mutability of the gods, the very difficulty of keeping them in classes, leads me to conclude that a Sun cult is outstanding; that many, if not all, things go back to Sun, although I do not mean by this to indicate a belief in monotheism. If I were to carry my generalization so far it would not be to Sun, but to that ultimately inexplicable term, universal harmony or destiny, monism rather than any kind

---

The following abbreviations refer to the texts: SC, Male Shooting Chant Holy (Reichard ms. by Gray Eyes); EW, Enemy Way (by Slim Curley, Haile 1938b); WP, War Prophylactic Ceremony (Jeff King);[11] Leg, Origin Myth (Matthews 1897, Version A); BeC, Beauty Chant (Curtis); NCM, Navaho Creation Myth (tł'a·h);[12] NT, Navaho Texts (Charley Mitchell);[13] BS, Informal enumeration of monsters by RM.

of theism. Sun is an agent of that monism, a central deity who correlates the nether and celestial worlds with this one, who exists to assist man to his final destiny. Changing Woman may possibly be the female manifestation of Sun. First Man and First Woman seem to be respective manifestations of Sun and Changing Woman in the worlds below this. They, like Sun, had a vision of the earth and man; indistinct it was, to be sure, but they worked toward it with such insight as they possessed. During the period when the sexes were separated, normal practices were impossible— the men had little influence on the future; the women may have conceived as a result of self-abuse because the quill feather, elk antler, stone, and cactus were manifestations of Sun, to whom generation is ultimately ascribed (Chapter 3).

In several versions of the creation myth, First Man was the creator; he and his wife were co-leaders of the pre-human beings after the reconciliation of the sexes. In tłǎ·h's story of the Emergence, be'γotcidí accomplished nearly the same things as First Man in the other stories. be'γotcidí was light-skinned and red-haired, characteristics that may identify him with Sun. After Changing Woman and the people escorting her had arrived at the western ocean, they saw be'γotcidí walking toward them on the water; his hair was shiny and little rays of light sparkled from him. A young man helped the people out of the fourth world by making a great reed grow; later he was made the sun-bearer. When the people separated after the earth was created, Monster Slayer was made chief on the earth, and be'γotcidí in the sky, yet in other tales Sun is chief in the sky.

According to Matthews, be'γotcidí and Sun together created the animals. In the song commemorating the task, the patient or sponsor is identified with be'γotcidí and, as a child, with Sun.

Just as First Man is Sun's uncontrolled, undeveloped, but prescient prototype, so First Woman seems to be a rudimentary archetype of Changing Woman, with none of the idealism now attached to her. According to one version of the Emergence, the flood of the second world was caused by the illicit intercourse of First Woman and Sun. Sun had a wife in the sky who was fat and jealous. First Woman too was fat and jealous. Changing Woman had been in the sky preparing a home for Monster Slayer at the same time that she was on earth. In the underworlds the First Pair stood for life; in this world Sun and Changing Woman represent life. There is much to identify Changing Woman with the earth; First Woman in sandpainting is brown, ' the color of the earth.'[14] JS told me that Sun's sky wife was called be'γotcidí 'asdzá·n, ' be'γotcidí Woman.' In another place she is called Dawn Woman.

The relation between Changing Woman and Sun is developed by the characterization of their children, The Twins, who are endowed with the powers of both parents. A similar but more obscure connection through their children exists between Sun and be'γotcidí: one of Sun's offspring was a gambler who became so powerful that he won the wealth, even the persons, of all the people. Sun connived to defeat the gambler by pitting him against another son, Gambler's double. Gambler, defeated, returned to be'γotcidí, who was thought by some to be Moon Bearer, by others the god of the Americans or Mexicans. Both be'γotcidí and Sun possess great wealth, much of it in the form of domesticated animals.

Appearing as White Body and Yellow Body in the third world, Talking God and xa·ctčé·'óγan seem to be manifestations of Sun especially concerned with man's domestic affairs; these gods have many characteristics in common with Sun. Talking God's behavior toward the mother and the

77

Stricken Twins parallels Sun's mating with Changing Woman and the subsequent recognition of and concern for The Twins. The difference is in the function of the stories, that of the Stricken Twins to account for domestic tranquillity, wealth, and good health, that of The Twins to explain the conquest of earth's primordial enemies. The head feathers of Talking God are correlated with Dawn, one aspect of Sun in his relation to Sky; those of xa·ctčé·'óγan, with yellow evening light, another aspect of Sun and Sky. According to Stevenson, white corn was the son of Turquoise Woman and Sun, later transformed into Talking God. Talking God, like be'γotcidí, has charge of game.

First Man and be'γotcidí are the difficultly persuadable manifestations of Sun, who is not uniformly on man's side. Talking God and xa·ctčé·'óγan, kindly disposed toward man, are the contemporary manifestations of Sun in charge of subsistence—agriculture and flesh-producing animals.

Big Fly is a part of the Sun-Sky complex. In the first world First Man created a feather to be moved by Wind and to hint at Sun's power. Big Fly also stands for the skin at the tip of the tongue, that is, speech. Big Fly as Sun's day messenger may sometimes be identified with Talking God. Performing the same functions for the night are Bat and Darkness. All—Big Fly, Bat, and Darkness—have in common the ability to penetrate where ordinary beings cannot go and the power of feather or wing motion.

Sun manifestations in another series are Moon, Black Wind, and Yellow Wind. Winds personify motion, for Breeze, Zephyr, and Whirlwind act as mentors and are identified with feather, Big Fly, Bat, and Darkness. Winds, linked with Sun, Moon, and mentors, are well disposed to man, or at least easily persuadable. On the other hand, in the Hail and Wind chants their evil aspects come out; in company with Thunder and Hail they represent storm, bluster, anger, and uncontrolled impulse.

Coyote, exponent of irresponsibility and lack of direction, seems to be an uncontrolled aspect of either Sun himself or his child. Coyote, as a child of Sky, represents lust on earth, matching Sun's promiscuity as a celestial being; Coyote, however, observes no rules. Sun, though reluctant and protesting, assumes responsibility for his children; Coyote sates his desire and leaves confusion or worse behind him. Any good that Coyote accomplishes is fortuitous; Sun's good deeds, though forced, result in control. Coyote does all the daring things Sun would like to do—in fact, once did; Sun secretly gloats over them, but of necessity appears to disapprove.

Black God, feared even by Coyote but sometimes paired with him, is still another manifestation of Sun as Darkness or Sky. Outstanding in the drawing of Night is the Milky Way; the same symbol is painted on Black God's breast and arms. The offering acceptable to Black God in the War Ceremony was a tobacco pouch closely resembling Sun's. A prayerstick offering was presented to Black God, but after he had accepted it, he taught the people not to duplicate it but to make the rattlestick substitute—an exact duplication of the circumstances in which Sun gave his arrow to Earth People. If Night or Sky is a phase of Sun, if Black God's picture is a representation of Night Sky and Black God behaves like Sun, then Black God is a manifestation of Sun representing control of fire, flame, and heat.

CHAPTER 6

THEORY OF DISEASE

THE CAUSES of disease fall into two categories, definite and indefinite. Failure to observe some of the numerous restrictions that regulate the correct Navaho life is a relatively definite cause. If a person knew and heeded them all, he could exist only as a hidebound ascetic, hardly free to do much required by his daily life, or most of his time would be occupied in removing the harmful effects of broken taboos. Restrictions do not, however, weigh as heavily upon the ordinary person as might be assumed. Normally life goes on quietly and satisfactorily enough. A man may observe some of the most obvious restraints or he may not keep any. As long as nothing happens, he is not conscious of breaking them. As soon as misfortune becomes marked—lightning strikes his sheep, his crop is ruined by hail, his wife has a miscarriage and does not regain her strength, his child coughs—he considers what he might have done to offend the powers. As he thinks over his past, he has no difficulty in finding numerous lapses. Further thought makes the accumulation of neglect so impressive that he is impelled to seek the proper cure, a ceremony.

A sick Navaho may be the victim of bad dreams—of death, the dead, snakebite, tooth pulling, fire, lightning. There are some good dreams—of horses, sheep, cattle, wealth—which automatically bring good fortune. To dream of being killed was always bad and had to be counteracted in some way or other.[1]

Excess in any activity may bring on sickness. Too much

weaving or silversmithing, sexual indulgence, undue concentration, hoarding property may bring affliction.

Ignorance, either of the ceremonial law or of transgressing it, is a major source of ills. Experts who know the rules are diviners who may adduce definite grounds for a man's troubles. They recommend the chant to be tried; it often succeeds in straightening out a person's affairs. If, however, the reason for the affliction is not apparent, one may have to undergo a series of rituals until one that relieves is found.

Quite remote, but nevertheless dangerous, are the effects of the incompletely buried monsters, which, if not remembered by man, cause carrion eaters to feast upon the flesh of the dead, the sounds of enemies to enter the earth, debilitating it so that man gets fever, cold, and worms. The monsters symbolize enemies presumed to have techniques for the Navaho's undoing, which, being strange, are indefinite and therefore fearful. In the same class is the malevolence (ba'át'é) of the undependable deities, who must be won over to favor the sufferer.

Contact with the dead (tčí·ndi·) or anything remotely connected with them is another indefinite reason for disturbance. A house in which a person died may be burned; if not, a hole is torn through the north wall and the roof beams are allowed to fall in, indicating that the place should be avoided. A Navaho would risk freezing rather than seek shelter in such a house or lay a fire with wood from it. He may, however, inadvertently make his camp near an ancient ruin that gives no indication of being a place of the dead but has as bad an influence upon him as a newly made grave. No one can be sure a place is safe unless he knows its history.

When BWW was affected by ' weakness all over,' her illness was ascribed to the fact that unwittingly she had camped on an ancient trail that led to a deer impound. Deer were confused when driven into it to their death; it is reasonable to assume that BWW would become confused in such a place. Moreover, special ritualistic treatment was required to guard hunters. BWW, unprotected by hunting power, was a natural victim of circumstances of which she was completely ignorant. A locality may be unsafe even for the uninformed because it is believed to be the dwelling place of the gods.

Disease may be contracted because an individual is too weak to withstand the power of a chant, either in learning it or in having it sung for him. Even today Navaho cite as proof the case of Matthews who, while studying the Night Chant, suffered a paralytic stroke (cp. Chapter 7).

Worse than any source of evil so far mentioned is sorcery, since it is due to the intentional ill will of some man, powerful because he knows how to manipulate a vast amount of power, indefinite because its import is dubious and because only superior power turned against the sorcerer can counteract it; uncertain too because one can never be sure who the practitioner is.

With witchcraft power dogma links father-daughter incest —it is doubtful that cases are ever proved—robbing graves, and even rapid acquisition of wealth, especially if accompanied by unwillingness to share generously.

Doubt may, therefore, be advanced as the ultimate cause of man's troubles, uncertainty being interpreted in different ways depending upon the duration of an ailment. If it is cured by directing ritual to definite causes, the dogma is verified. If illness persists, dogma is not questioned, but rather man must continue to try out different combinations until he includes the proper causes.

RP formulated the theory of disease when he said, "Causes and mistakes you know about are not bad because you know what to do about them, but those you don't know—*they* are the ones that are dangerous." Gray Eyes' suggestion of the procedure was corroborated by my other informants: "If you try one sing and you don't get well, you have to try another, perhaps many. Sometimes after a man has had many big [elaborate] ceremonies, he does not get better. Then he tries a little [short, simple] sing and he gets well. That is because at first they didn't know the proper reason for his sickness."

The following cases illustrate various interpretations:

A girl was to have the Big Star Chant sung for her, but on the night it was to start she was taken to the hospital, where her disease was diagnosed as endemic, non-contagious meningitis. After five weeks, she was dismissed as cured. Upon her arrival home the family announced that the Big Star Chant would be sung. A diagnostician had declared that her illness was due to sorcery; she was the victim of witch-objects shot into her by an unnamed wizard or by ghosts. Although from the time she left the hospital she had seemed perfectly well, not until after the Big Star Chant and, several months later, the War Ceremony had been performed for her, did the Navaho consider her out of danger. Her disease was so severe and strange that it was ascribed to indefinite causes—effect of the dead, possible witchcraft, or even witch-objects shot by the dead—and to make certain of including other indeterminable causes, possible evil due to strangers, including white people who treated her at the hospital, the War Ceremony was performed for her.

MA's repeated illnesses show how her daughter solved the conflict between the Navaho and the white man's ideas of curing. MA was a grandmother, head of the family group I know best. When I first met her she was a little over sixty years old, wiry and energetic, though she continually coughed and occasionally complained of headache. Her husband, RP, had sung the Shooting Chant for her long before, and she had frequently been a patient or co-patient of other chants. Her symptoms grew more oppressive and, since RP was going to conduct a War Ceremony in the neighborhood, he decided that she should be one of the patients (bándá·'i·). She was born the year the Navaho returned from Ft. Sumner (1868) and, since her mother had suffered all the misery of the five-hundred-mile trek to Ft. Sumner and back and the five-year incarceration there, all kinds of enemy forces had had a chance to affect her.

During the last night of the War Ceremony one of the auditors, Little Singer, who had gone to sleep in a temporary roadway, was struck by an automobile and severely injured. This accident vitiated the whole effort; the ceremony was stopped and a council held to determine the reason for the untoward happening. Two groups carried on the discussion—one of conservative elders, one of middle-aged and younger men who were more progressive because they had attended school and worked for the Indian Service. During the afternoon they had put on a dance from the Night Chant as a feature of a program to dedicate a new government building half a mile from the place where the War Ceremony was held; the same visitors attended both affairs.

The orthodox elders contended that Little Singer's accident was due to performing in the summer (August) the Night Chant dance, which should be danced only when the ground is frozen; that the Navaho dance should not have been given at a white man's affair; and they went on to enumerate various ills that had befallen the Navaho because they were too much affected by white man's ideas. The progressives argued that the old men themselves danced at the Gallup Ceremonial every year in August; that they had known the dance was contemplated and had not forbidden it. They pointed out also that the Navaho owe sheep, silverwork, and automobiles to the white men and, if the Navaho were to be consistent, they would have to give them all up. The discussions lasted until early morning, when the council broke up without coming to a conclusion.

At dawn MA, who had previously only complained, was seized with violent chills, nausea, and head throbbing—' a knife was cutting into her side.' She was taken home and word came that Little Singer had died in the hospital—his being the fourth death there in a week. RP was prevailed upon to consult a doctor for his wife. He consented, but reluctantly, because he would have to go to the hospital, a place of the dead. It was the Fourth of July and no doctor was available. RP, much relieved, summoned a Flint chanter, who sang emergency rites over MA for four nights. Twice before when he had sung for her she had recovered. She improved now.

Her health, though better, was far from normal when, a few weeks later, word came that a Shooting Chant was to be sung near her home. As it was likely that she had failed to observe some of the restrictions when it had previously been sung for her by her husband, she became once more the one-sung-over. At first she seemed to gain strength but, after she got wet in a sudden hard storm, the pneumonia symptoms reappeared. By this time she was so weary she consented to go to the hospital; there she died.

After her death I had many talks with MC, her daughter. The doctor had said that although her mother had tuberculosis, it was not the cause of her death; she had succumbed to pneumonia. MC seemed to accept the doctor's explanation, but several years later explained to me the ' real ' cause of the succession of misfortunes that had befallen the family—the death of a grandchild several months before MA's demise, an accusation that RP was a wizard, his own death three years later, followed by that of CF, his oldest daughter, within a few months. The ' real ' cause was the following incident.

One night RP had returned home exhausted, discouraged, and frightened. While on the mountain gathering some plants for ceremonial use, he had lost a flint belonging to his medicine bundle. He searched for it diligently until dark, but failed to find it. He felt that this misfortune was too great for him to cope with. His spirit rallied, as we have seen, but he considered subsequent happenings inevitable in view of his carelessness in losing the flint arrowpoint.

The case of CM, CF's widower, further elucidates MC's reasoning and had happier results. A restriction calls for a survivor's continence for a reasonable period, preferably a year, after the death of a spouse. CM was sung over and freed from the contamination of his wife's death, but after a month took another wife. Eight months later, his cough grew worse; he lost his ambition and good spirits. It was necessary to consult a diagnostician, for obviously his condition was due to his disregard of a requirement. The Male Shooting Chant Evil was sung for him.

By this time MC was the oldest female in the family.

Although, as we have seen, she admitted the white doctor's explanation of her mother's death, she believed implicitly in the inevitability of her father's prediction of disaster. Her ability to reconcile two types of reasoning is further demonstrated by her attitude toward CM's second wife who, she thinks, has tuberculosis.

One rite of the Male Shooting Chant Evil includes drinking an infusion; the chanter drinks first from a bowl, next the patient drinks, then it is passed to the member of the audience sitting at the south side of the doorway. He drinks, and it is passed sunwise around the hut until the last person at the north side has drunk. Since men sit at the south, women at the north side of the ceremonial circle, women receive the bowl after the men. MC considered it particularly important that she and the younger women should drink some of the infusion, but she warned them not to drink if Mrs. CM drank first. On the first day Mrs. CM sat beside her husband so that she was the first woman to receive the infusion; whereupon MC's group of women merely pretended to drink when their turn came.

Their chagrin at missing the benefit of the rite was later evident from their resentful grumbling. The next day they entered the hogan early and sat so close to the patient that it would have been difficult for another person to squeeze in. Mrs. CM came in much later and took her place near the door. Later MC and her group smugly boasted of the success of their strategy.

MC has been to school and has worked for white people, doing things their way. Her home on the reservation is more like a Navaho's than a white man's, but she and her husband have more modern conveniences than the uneducated Navaho. When a member of her family is ill, she tries to get him to go to the doctor. Failing that, she recommends a sing; indeed she feels best satisfied if the person consults a physician *and* is sung over. She differs from most Navaho in seeking assistance before an illness has run too far.

I do not know why MC felt so strongly about drinking the infusion or why she picked out Mrs. CM as a germ-bearer.

Many of the audience had coughs, her own husband included, yet she had never been finicky before. The reason doubtless was psychological. Up to the time CM remarried, he had been a beloved member of the family group, in which there was little friction. Both MC and her niece, AD, resented a new wife because she had been substituted somewhat underhandedly after the death of her predecessor and without consultation with the family. Moreover, she was unpopular.

By their treatment of Mrs. CM, MC and AD disregarded the principle of harmony. They should have welcomed her at the sing and helped her all they could. They did not even invite her into the house, although there were few guests, nor did they offer to share their utensils. She camped a short distance from their dwelling and had to ask for everything she needed. They did not even notify her when the chanter was ready for the audience. In many years' sojourn with the family it was the only time I ever saw a guest so snubbed. On the other hand, no blame was attached to CM. He had erred; he was being sung over; he was doing the right thing.

The case of the girl with meningitis illustrates the viewpoint of the bewitched. Like the War Ceremony, the chant prescribed for her cure stresses exorcism. The case of a sorcerer came to my attention, but I did not know the individuals concerned.

A man with considerable learning came under suspicion because of his great prosperity. He had once pawned a bracelet someone recognized as having been buried with a rich girl's corpse. From that time proof of witchcraft was clear, for only a sorcerer can safely rob a grave. After some years he became ill; for a long time he did nothing. At length, without consulting a diagnostician, he had several chants sung for him, but kept getting worse. Reluctantly he went to a diviner who, without mentioning names, insinuated that the illness was the result of robbing the dead, meaning that sorcery had boomeranged. The man

87

confessed, had a chant sung for him to remove the power of witchcraft, and recovered. He was the witcher and the bewitched, the victim of his own power, which he was not strong enough to control.

Prophylaxis

White doctors and hospital personnel deplore the fact that the Navaho do not come for consultation until their condition is hopeless. Often, even if they mean to stick to their own methods, they wait a long time, hoping the illness will pass. The delay is contrary to Navaho belief, which seeks prevention. The numerous Blessing rites, carried out to avert untoward results, usually last one night and are frequently held for House Blessing, Girl's Adolescence, wedding, and purification, particularly of persons and objects that have been contaminated by the dead (Concordance C).

Blessing rites may be performed to protect chanters before they sing for the first time or to renew their power; more frequently, a chanter is initiated by becoming the patient of the chant he plans to sing. A full ceremony may also be carried out with the chanter as the one-sung-over to dedicate some portion of his ceremonial equipment. The Male Shooting Chant Holy Fire Dance branch, described in Concordance C, was sung because a singer was making mistakes, felt uncertain about his power, and wanted to renew it. JS was sung over in the Male Shooting Chant Holy Sandpainting branch to consecrate the talking prayersticks and ' wide boards' of his bundle.

Disease

Since the ascribed causes of disease have little connection with physiology, it is futile to try to separate symptom, disease, and cure. Furthermore, all three are approached emotionally; the mind's control over the body is stressed

(Chapter 3). Since, therefore, illness is fundamentally the same as disturbance—cosmic as well as human—it is not surprising to find references to confusion, bewilderment, frustration, futility (bóxóne·sdzâi·).

Frustration is symbolized by the circle of bewilderment. The Navaho fears encirclement, since evils that might be with him in the circle cannot get out and good cannot get in to him. He feels weak, lacks energy and ambition, and knows not where to turn. For this reason the incomplete circle is ritualistically favored; it allows the egress of evil and the entrance of good.

Orthodox weavers run one thread of a contrasting color through the border of a rug to let out the spirit of the rug as well as of the weaver. The encircling guardian of many sand-paintings is left open, usually at the east; in ceremony one quadrant of the hogan or ceremonial may be closed to all except the singer. In the War Ceremony it is the southeast; in a Flint rite I saw, the southwest.[2] One idea behind these customs is to concentrate such evils as may have accumulated in a limited space from which they may be driven and the mind freed.

Whenever there is a generalization such as the above, its opposite also must be reckoned with. Closed circles made of meal or pollen or perhaps merely described on the ground, hoops, and rings are frequently encountered in ritual. They represent a space so narrowed down that it is under control, an area from which evil has been driven and within which power has been concentrated. The series of hoops, commonly used in the exorcistic rites, exemplify this idea. The hoops are constructed by a ritual that puts power into them; the patient sits inside them until he absorbs the power (see *Circle, Hoops,* Concordance B; *Hoop transformation rite,* Concordance C).

Mythological incidents may be understood in the light of the concepts included in the closed and open circles.

When the Swallows and Spiders could no longer endure Coyote's contumely, they wove webs around him in every direction. Closed in with evils—his own and the bad wishes of the Spiders—he died.[3]

A Black God had been induced to attend the blackening of the War Ceremony patient; in fact, he had come to originate it. After plants were burned to form soot, Crow and Buzzard, couriers of evil, offered to kill the ghost of the enemy. Said Buzzard, "You see I used my feathers in trying to harm the person, but I did not succeed." Crow said something to the same effect and their feathers were burned and combined with the soot of the plants. Then Crow said, "The patient should not go there alone. I will accompany him. I myself will make the first attack on the enemy's ghost. I will crawl completely into the blackening material."[4]

At the same gathering, feathers, one of roadrunner (who was without fault of any kind) and one of turkey, were placed back to back. The inner surface of the feathers is concave; their juxtaposition in this way forms a hollow tube through which ghosts can find their way out.[5]

Mental disease has a somewhat quantitative connotation. If a person is simple or feeble-minded, he is said to ' have no sense ' (do"áxályą·dah) or to ' be twisted ' (di·gis). If there is so little control that he becomes rash, he is said to be ' moth-crazy ' ('a·ztċą), so out of his mind that he might jump into the fire. In Chapter 1, I noted this as a possible punishment for breaking taboos.

The Night Chant has many references to insanity and its cure. Since the gods invoked are tutelaries of the sacred mountains (Chart I, Chapter 2), it seems as if insanity may be ascribed to a cosmic, therefore inevitable, cause as well as to failure to heed restrictions.

Frustration illustrates the mental viewpoint, weakness (tséstí·ntsoh) the physical. The healthy, right-minded Navaho possesses strength, endurance, fortitude; he abhors weakness. In former times boys trained incessantly, exposing themselves to cold, heat, hunger, and thirst, and undergoing rigorous tests for endurance. If they did not, they were told that their systems would be full of ugly things which should be eliminated; they would be quick-tempered, weak-minded, unable to stand life's hardships, and would end up a disgrace to their families.[6] Characteristically, calmness and strong-mindedness are valued along with a sturdy system. Physical training parallels ritualistic pattern in the belief that weakness is due to ' ugly things ' that can and should be worked off by exertion.

Weakness may be caused by grief and by breathing the harmful parts (bitcxi'n) of strangers (Chapter 3).

Monster Slayer, after slaying Burrowing Monster, became weak, so weak that he fell over from smelling the waste (bitcxin) and steam from the monster's heart. When he tried to subdue Traveling Rock and thought he was dead, Monster Slayer stepped on one of its chips. His strength suddenly failed him; his breathing became labored and he trembled.[7]

Weakness is a result or symptom of other diseases more specifically [but not satisfactorily] described by Matthews. "Patients having these [the following] diseases are weak, stagger, and lose appetite; then they go to a sweat-house and take an emetic. If they have ' yellow [disease],' they vomit something yellow (bile?). If they have ' cooked blood ' disease, they vomit something like cooked blood. . . . ' Slime ' disease comes from drinking foul water full of green slime or little fish. ' Worms ' comes from eating worms, which you sometimes do without knowing it, but ' tapeworm ' comes from eating parched corn." Matthews remarks that the joints of the tapeworm (*Tænia solium*) resemble grains of corn. In this, as in other cases, diagnosis by analogy is clear.[8]

91

Fainting may be due to extreme weakness. One verb stem (-tsaʼł) refers to coma, fainting, unconsciousness, and dying, all physical manifestations of fear. Unconsciousness may be differentiated from death by the stem -tłił, which basically means ʻ stun.ʼ A person may become unconscious for various reasons; he is stunned by evil, often witch power. Helplessness may be induced by the Shock rite. An impersonator of an animal or god frightens a patient, who falls down unconscious, then revives him. Henceforth, the latter is not only immune to all danger from the deity impersonated—Bear, for example—but may even count upon him for protection.

Nervousness (naxoyiłná, xodiʼsnáʼʼ, xaxodisiʼ) is hardly to be differentiated, except in degree, from bewilderment, anxiety, or fear. Trembling is a form of nervousness, which might perhaps be a symptom, yet is ritualized as a power of the diviner and, like trance or shock, may be induced ("Diagnosis," page 99).

The First Pair, when they took up their places in the sky, threatened to send coughs, colds, and fever to Earth People. Whites introduced tuberculosis. Navaho are especially susceptible to pulmonary diseases; almost everyone coughs continually. Their manner of living is conducive to bronchial and lung troubles—frequent exposure to marked changes of temperature, sudden downpours, heavy snowstorms combine with low living standards and ignorance of sanitation to bring on and foster pulmonary diseases. Spitting is so habitual as to be a vice. During a ceremony there is not an inch of floor space in the hogan free from sputum. Everyone sits on the floor and becomes the potential carrier of the germs on it. The women particularly disseminate bacteria with their rippling cotton skirts, twelve or fifteen yards in fullness, and the Pendleton blankets laid on the floor and subsequently used as bedding.

The treatment of the Flint Chant differs with the kind of discharge from the mouth. If it is merely phlegm, one kind of rite is indicated; if there is blood as well, the rites are modified. Phlegm is attributed to Thunder, blood to Bear or Snake.[9]

Traditionally fever (tśí·s ni·dó·h, tśí·h ni·dó·h) is an effect of anxiety:

The old sorcerer of the War Ceremony myth, when his attempt to seize a captive was thwarted by his son-in-law, so grieved over the affair that his lips became parched and dark.[10]

After yielding to Talking God the first time, the girl who later became the mother of the Stricken Twins came home and her lips were parched as a result of her anxious thoughts.[11]

Paleness and dry skin are caused by an enemy ghost.[12]

As among whites, rheumatism includes a multitude of causes and effects. Arthritis, inflammatory rheumatism, lameness, limping, paralysis—all come under the same heading, although pain is usually connected with rheumatism.

The afflictions of the Stricken Twins of the Night Chant tale set the theme; one was suddenly lamed, the other blinded for no ostensible reason—their symptoms are not described. Since the sheep's Achilles tendon is mentioned as a cure, it seems that an injury of the leg tendons was assumed. In the story of the Visionary, explaining a branch of the Night Chant, the songs of Fringed Mouth are said to cure headache, sore eyes, and contraction of the leg tendons. After learning the ceremony, the Visionary's youngest brother cured a boy who had headache and was deaf in one ear, a girl whose mouth was crooked (lateral facial paralysis), and one whose hamstrings were hardened.[13]

When the Stricken Twins were taken by their father to the home of the Mountain Sheep gods, they saw, among other

DOGMA

things, on each of the four walls a large crystal which emitted
light, and with each stone there was a special charm or
remedy to cure disease: the stone of the east was a remedy
for blindness, that of the south a remedy for lameness, that
of the west a remedy for deafness, and that of the north a
remedy for the ' crooked face.' [14]

Another form of lameness (rheumatism) is called the
' warps ' (naltcí). Matthews describes it as a "gradually
increasing symmetrical, antero-posterior curvature of the
spine, which, when it reaches completion, after years of
progress, brings the knees in close proximity to the chest and
renders walking impossible. . . . The disease is not accompanied by abscesses or sinuses, and the general health of the
afflicted person is not seriously impaired. . . . The writer has
seen at least half a dozen sufferers in the pueblo of Zuni, all
adults and mostly males." Vertebrae excavated in the Southwest are evidence of this disease.[15]

In the Bead Chant story, lameness is associated with skin
disease, both having originated from feathers showered down
upon pueblo warriors by eaglets from their eyrie on a ledge
high above.[16]

Mistakes made in the Night Chant, by the patient or one
learning it, are believed to cause blindness, warping, crippling,
and ' twisted mouth,' which, according to Matthews, means
lateral facial paralysis (bizé'' xodi'ge'z).[17] Crawler, the extraordinary star of the film *The Mountain Chant*, directed by
Roman Hubbell in 1926, derived his name from paralysis of
the lower limbs. He gave up learning the Night Chant when
paralysis indicated his incapacity to withstand its power. His
disability did not prevent him from learning and successfully
practicing other major chants, among them the Mountain
Chant.

Deafness should be included with paralysis, blindness, and
the other afflictions mentioned, since the Night Chant is sup-

94

posed to cure it as well. Although Matthews was deaf for a long time before he became paralyzed—probably even before he started to learn the Night Chant—the Navaho considered that both were due to the same cause, learning the Night Chant.

The sanitary arrangements being what they are, it is not surprising that the Navaho are victims of skin disease; impetigo is the curse of young children. The attitude toward serious sores is the same as that with which we are familiar. At the Hogan School, when the interpreters were trying to work out an article about germs, RP told the following story:

Long ago fawns became scarce. There seemed to be plenty of deer, but fawns were not being born. The old men got together and tried to originate a masked ceremony to increase the supply. When the performers took off their masks, they had sores wherever fawn spots had been painted on their bodies. From that time on it was decreed that only those in the best of health should be allowed to wear masks.

The old men, experimenting with affairs too strong for their powers, made mistakes and were punished. With this little homily RP felt that he had disposed of everything essential to the germ idea—imitative magic is a panacea; if one of its applications fails, try another or give it up and yield to the inevitable.

Cancer (na'ldzid) and diabetes are said to be rare among the Navaho, doubtless because cases are not reported. Several instances of cancer came to my attention.

T's wife became ill with what the white doctor diagnosed as cancer of the breast. After both breasts had been removed, she improved. The Flint (Knife) Chant was sung to free her from the obvious evil of the surgeon's scalpel. I saw her nearly two years after the operation; she was again very ill. Her lungs were badly congested; she had a high fever; she coughed terribly and spat blood; she was so weak that she could not stand up, but nevertheless shampooed her hair in yucca suds brought in a basket to the place where she lay. She had been brought to the rite that was to reveal the next treatment to alleviate her persistent illness. Her family had already spent large sums on ceremonies performed for her.

T's wife was an expert who had woven some of the largest and most intricate sandpainting designs. Most Navaho attributed her illness to copying the sacred patterns, a risky matter at best, since it is forbidden to put sandpaintings into a permanent medium. RP ascribed her trouble to mistakes made by a singer of the Shooting Chant when he had sung over T's wife twelve years before. RP believed that singing the same chant now without error would ' straighten everything out.' T's family had, however, not consulted him and it was not good form for a chanter to give an opinion unless his advice was requested.

The diagnostician used the trembling method (see below) for his divination and prescribed the Female Shooting Chant, to be followed by the War Ceremony. After the Female Shooting Chant, T's wife recovered from the pneumonia to the point where she could walk about her home. After the War Ceremony she was said to be ' all right.' However, the cancer recurred and less than a year after her first attack, she contracted pneumonia again. By this time she had become too discouraged to undergo another ceremony and called in her white friend, the trader. He felt she was dying and suggested that a Catholic priest might comfort her. She allowed him to call a priest, who administered the last rites. She who had been an orthodox Navaho died a Catholic; she who was being eaten away by cancer died of pneumonia.

The following account was given me by a white woman who knew well all the individuals concerned. I can only testify to the good faith of all, and to the fact that my friend at no time considered the case from a folkloristic (superstitious) or mystical point of view. She simply cited it as a case the Navaho did not question and repeated the doctor's report.

Because of illness, a Shooting Chanter had for years been unable to practice. Various sings were performed over him, but he became steadily worse. Finally a trader's wife persuaded him to go to a doctor some sixty miles away. The doctor told his white friend that he had examined the chanter carefully, was convinced he was dying of cancer of the rectum, and that nothing could be done to save him. The Navaho was so ill he could not get home in a single trip and stopped off for some days with acquaintances along the way. At the last stop the Navaho with whom he stayed would not accept the doctor's verdict. He summoned a group of singers, who sang continuously for many days and nights until the patient showed signs of recovery. The singing was the Life form of the Mountain Chant (cp. Chapter 19).

The chanter stayed several months with his friend, then went home. Not only was he able once more to go about his ordinary affairs but he even took up his chanting profession, and when I heard the story had been carrying it on with vigor for some five years.

Up to the time the Shooting Chant was held for MC (1932) she had migraine headaches. They recurred often and with such severity that RP decided to do something about them, having concluded that they were due to the evil influence of lightning which, seventeen years before, had struck a building in which MC had been, though she was not obviously injured at the time. The Male Shooting Chant Sun's House Branch Red Inside phase was performed in all its elaboration, one rite only being omitted. Because AD, MC's niece, then twelve years old, suffered from headache, she was a co-patient. The first day of the chant, both patients had severe headache; MC could hardly go through it.

The same year RP sang the Male Shooting Chant Prayer-sticks branch over me to make it safe to work with the chant myth and to protect me in traveling. MC was my counselor and confidante through it all. I asked her if she got head-aches as frequently and as severely as she had before her sing; she said no, she was all right now. I complained about the rigor of the emetic, sweating, and the tedium of the chant, for I knew she had not enjoyed it either. She said, "That's the way AD was. She was mad all the time." But now she's sorry because she gets headache lots now." This was to say that AD had not really given herself up in spirit to the blessings of the chant, though formally she had done so—she had breathed in the sun.

I had a severe headache the second day of my own chant, but did not mention it. RP, when he rubbed the infusion on my hands and arms, remarked, "Your body is much cooler today. Yesterday you were hot, but the medicine is taking away your fever." Probably I had had none at any time, but on the day I was supposed to have improved, I certainly felt much worse than usual.

Since trachoma (' granulated eyelids ') is a prevalent contagious disease, ' eye trouble ' is a common complaint. In my experience its treatment is more or less incidental. A chant is not often given to treat it alone, but rather someone who has eye trouble becomes a co-patient with another being treated primarily for something else. A ball of collected tallows, an indispensable item of the chanter's medicine bundle, is rubbed over the eyes of all the patients; what is left is returned to the bundle for future use.

Blindness, partial or complete, is hardly differentiated from other eye troubles, although soreness of the eyes not accompanied by dimmed vision may be.

Sore eyes, headache, and pain in the bones are attributed to breaking ceremonial restrictions on sexual intercourse, or to intercourse too soon after childbirth.

Ear trouble, from earache to deafness, is related to headache; the two may be treated simultaneously.

Respiratory complaints are differentiated from cardiac ailments, but the latter are not distinguished from digestive disturbances. The Navaho name for acute indigestion is 'aɣas or 'aɣas naxaṅa', ' the aorta crawls about, moves, palpitates.' 'aɣas really means ' major artery '—aorta or spinal—but most people, especially the younger ones who know Navaho less well, take it to mean ' acute indigestion.'

One of my interpreters once had a cloth tied under her breasts so tightly she could hardly breathe, but she asked me to tighten it. She explained that she had a bad pain in her stomach which might move up to her heart and kill her. I drew the cloth as tight as possible and we went on with our affairs. The cloth must have fulfilled its function, for the next day the pain was gone.

Pain of the reproductive organs, especially menstrual and labor pains, are sometimes differentiated from those of the digestive system. More generally though, as in appendicitis, ' abdominal pains ' cover all. Since ' vomiting ' may be a symptom of an abdominal disease, it seems that the Navaho, like many whites, often do not distinguish stomach from intestinal affections, although they differentiate the organs, giving each a name.

Diseases of the genitourinary system are common, but little about them is understood. Even the best interpreters scarcely know the difference between the venereal diseases; ' sores and boils ' describes most of such complaints.

Diagnosis

The Navaho method of prescribing for sickness has been called diagnosis, though divination would be a far better word, since those who recommend treatment are seers or prognosticators. They may divine to locate lost persons and articles, stolen property, or water in a dry region, and to find one guilty of practicing sorcery. There are three ways of determining an illness—gazing at sun, moon, or star, listening, and trembling. Listening is nearly, if not quite, extinct; ' motion-in-the-hand ' indicates trembling induced by proper ritualistic circumstances. The diviner is seized with shaking, beginning usually with gentle tremors of arms or legs and gradually spreading until the whole body shakes violently. While in a trembling state, the seer loses himself.[18] Guided by his power, he sees a symbol of the ceremony purporting to cure the person for whom he is divining. Gazing may be accompanied by trembling; usually the diviner sees the chant symbol as an after-image of the heavenly body on which he is concentrating. I do not believe the Navaho differentiated very much among the three means of divination, all being interrelated; the emphasis on one or the other doubtless depended upon the diviner's power.

Whereas the singer owes his power to the possession of knowledge, the seer owes his to a supernatural gift with which he is born. A dog will not bite a person with the divine gift, but as dogs unless provoked do not often bite anyone, a seer must show some positive indication of his talent.[19] After his attention is supernaturally called to his gift, a man learns songs and ritualistic acts before he practices. Sometimes the talent is revealed at a performance of the Hand Trembling Chant. Power to divine is considered warranted only when the possessor is under ritualistic control; there are checks against unlimited demonstration of trembling, which may be interpreted as illness.

Wyman records the behavior of a woman who began to shake during a performance of a Hand Trembling Chant being sung for her. She was seized with an attack of trembling, beginning at the knees and hands and culminating in wide motions of the right arm. She made many parallel marks in the sand, pointed toward the south, and patted her body from feet to head. The trembling continued through several acts of the chant; when it subsided, the patient, who was not a seer, said that the trembling had revealed the cause of her illness. Eleven years before, she had been in a hogan when a young man, standing outside, had been struck by lightning and hurled into it. Wyman goes on to say, "Involuntary attacks of hand trembling by patients (and others) while attending Hand Trembling Way chants are not uncommon, and diagnosticians often have their first experience in this way." [20]

Wyman, Hill, Morgan, and Kluckhohn have published excellent accounts of the origin and functions of divination.[21] Wyman's descriptions and my own correspond more closely than Wyman's and Morgan's, though they both worked in approximately the same locality and I in one far distant. Wyman and Kluckhohn differentiate between seers, chanters, and curers. However, in the region where I worked there was considerable overlap, some chanters being seers as well, others, like RP, taking upon themselves the responsibility of prescribing the treatment.

Morgan and Wyman differ about the necessity of discussing the patient's illness. Morgan says: "The man with [the power of] motion-in-the-hand enters the hogan of the patient. Friends and relatives are present and the sickness is discussed. (These discussions are important in order to estimate their effect upon the prognosis.)" [22] Wyman records: "All my informants insisted that the diagnostician need not know anything about the case before beginning, and that he always goes to work without preliminary gathering of information. They seemed surprised when I suggested such a thing, saying that 'he does not need to,' since the information is supposed to come through supernatural means. On each occasion where I saw a man-with-motion-in-the-hand work, including one performance for myself, he started the ritual without preliminary discussion." [23] Despite this statement, Wyman brings himself into partial agreement with Morgan by the following: "In each instance, however, he had been around enough to gather casually about as much information as he could gather by further discussion." [24]

These statements explain the apparent success of divination. If a man's relatives discuss his case, it may be more by way of summarizing and organizing known facts than of consciously providing new clues. In a Navaho community almost nothing happens to an individual that is not carried by grapevine far from its original source. The diviner is a receiving station for gossip and focuses his attention on the least unusual happening; he has excellent powers of deduction and a good memory as well. He uses the well-known devices of fortunetellers and oracles the world over. He makes a generalization that might apply to anyone. When a facial expression or an exclamation indicates that he is on the right scent, he follows with greater detail, constantly sensitive to acquiescence or denial afforded by the least sign.[25] His chances of being right are better in a society like that of the Navaho, where life is less varied and belief in the religion more prevalent, than in ours, where skepticism is pronounced.

I have several times emphasized my impression that the sincerity of the chanters I knew was impeccable.[26] My experience with seers has been less fortunate. Their rites seemed to me trumped up and artificial; the diviner seemed to have an ax to grind. Usually the chanter recommended was a friend or relative of the diagnostician. Tozzer, however, states that although he had no doubt much humbug might be involved, he felt that the diviner he saw at work was sincere.[27]

As the patient, accepting the seer's decision, has a test of its rightness, the diviner's power can hardly be abused. Because of the effort and expense entailed by a long chant, the incumbent wants to be reasonably sure it will not be in vain. He may, therefore, have an essential trial rite performed. In the War Ceremony this may be the blackening; the Sun painting is often chosen as a test for the Shooting Chant; a sandpainting of the Bead Chant was tried for L. Detached rites may be performed also for those too ill to submit to the full chant, or for a person unfortunate enough to need a chant at a forbidden season—the Night Chant in summer, for example. Improvement of the patient's health after a test rite indicates the correct diagnosis, regression a false one.

The Navaho form of divination is a subject of tremendous interest which has been treated only descriptively; a great deal of work still needs to be done. Statistics on the number of times divination is tried, and on the efficacy or failure of prognostication, and particularly Navaho opinions on why they succeed or miscarry, would do much to illuminate the entire problem of the occult.

CHAPTER 7
THEORY OF CURING

Intrusion of Evil

THE FIRST step in curing is taken by finding out, by a review of past behavior or consultation with a seer, the particular evils responsible for illness. Bad things sent by malevolent spirits, or even the spirits themselves, may enter the body. A few examples of the evil beings, the way they operate and the means of their disintegration, demonstrate the ritualistic curing process and its explanations.

Turkey Buzzard was 'in full charge of wickedness' (bąhági·'íté). When the earth was still dominated by monsters, he sent Crow to search for human flesh, which was becoming scarce. The Twins shot at Crow; their arrows just grazed his feathers and sent him, much frightened, back to his chief. When Turkey Buzzard sent feathered arrows at the boys, they failed to reach the target because of the ' grinding sound of The Twins' flint armor,' and returned to their owner. Four times the arrows flew out and back, reporting to Turkey Buzzard, "In vain we tried to do what you ordered. Four times we encircled the armor at every point and failed to find an opening anywhere."

Turkey Buzzard then lost hope: "I used to be able to make a living, but now there is no way of life possible for me." At this point his disintegration began. He could not sleep at night; to relieve his incessant itching, he scratched himself until his ugly skin began to fall off. He scratched his head until he was completely bald (red), and coughed without ceasing. His condition was reported to First Man, who hardheartedly replied, "If he opposes the purpose for which the children were born, let him die in agony. Tell him that!"

When this decree was delivered, Turkey Buzzard replied, "Let it be as he says, but leave me at least my life. Had I any way of knowing this purpose? Now I know it, I am in favor of it, so let me live. Wherever Monsters are killed and decay, we, Crow and I, will be present as scavengers. And now my evil attitude will become one of responsibility. If I am restored I shall be dependable." Then the very flints that had contributed to his dissolution became the means of his restoration.[1]

The Twins, with weapons, song, and the power of their Sun father, attacked Big-monster-who-travels-alone. First they weakened his confidence by escaping the clubs he hurled at them. When Sun acted, the flint armor dropped away from the east side of the monster. At subsequent attacks the monster's armor and valuables disappeared from the south, west, and north sides. By this time he staggered helplessly and, as weapons were directed toward his heart, the life blood began to gush forth. He fell, causing the earth to tremble violently, and only after some time did he quiet down completely.[2]

In Coyote many aspects of evil power are embodied—he is active, with unlimited ability to interfere with people's affairs; his potentiality for turning up unexpectedly is enormous. He has a life principle that may be laid aside, so that any injury done to his body affects his life only temporarily and he may even recover from apparent death. He possesses an incredible fund of evil knowledge which man must match and, as he may appear in any form, he is the werewolf of Navaho witchcraft.

Coyote was allied with the First Pair as Crow was with Turkey Buzzard, in the capacity of spy. As First Man and First Woman went to their permanent home in the Northeast, where evil and danger originate, First Woman threatened, "When I think, something bad will happen. People will become ill. Coyote will know [and presumably carry out] all my thoughts."[3]

Some evils, fortunately few, the residue of unbelievable cruelty, refused to submit to any kind of control.

A chief, trying to prevent adultery, cut off noses, gouged out eyes, and unsexed men and women. Later he concluded that amends must be made for these deeds and set about it by originating a chant. Then, as uninvited guests, came people with venereal disease or without noses or eyes. They pronounced curses no ritual was ever found to counteract: "Harm shall come to you because of your eyes." "Noseless people will always exist. You will be deaf; your teeth will fall out." "We shall not accept any prayers or songs! Absolutely nothing will move us." "We shall be the rottenness that follows the noseless and one-eyed ones. We shall continue to kill from our home in the north." [4]

These brief incidents explain in microcosm the attack on evil with the purpose of forcing it to yield to good. Fear, the primary cause of illness, is established, confidence undermined. Fear may be combated by a power who will stand up to it, refuse to abandon courage. By turning inward, using one's own powers, one may find the strength to overcome evil. Turkey Buzzard feathered his arrow with his own wing feather, which subsequently became a ritualistic symbol of release. And when Crow contributed his part to the War Ceremony, saying, "My whole person, even my feathers, may be burned to blacken a person troubled by enemy ghosts," Buzzard agreed: "I, too, will give my feathers for this purpose. Vainly I tried to harm the person. The patient should not go out to meet the enemy's ghost alone. I will accompany him, being the first to attack the enemy's ghost. I shall crawl completely into the soot." [5] He meant that the soot used for the blackening would represent the area of protection contributed by the scavengers Buzzard and Crow. A defense may be impervious to evil, either because of its nature—for example, armor—or because of its attributes—for instance, the sound and light of flint. The circle of protection made by the sound of The Twins' flint armor repelled the greatest harm in Turkey Buzzard's repertoire. Big Monster succumbed as soon as there was even the slightest penetration of his armor.

Once error has been identified, it is important to admit it. By confessing their evil-mindedness, Crow and Turkey Buzzard put themselves in line for restoration. Confession may be a form of bravery; for example, heroes or chanters recount everything that happened to them, their mistakes and failures as well as their correct procedure and successes.

Indefinite evils such as ghosts are difficult to deal with because the chance of hitting upon the proper ones is small.

Black God explained his reason for helping in the War Ceremony: "It is certain, my grandchildren, that the monsters who formerly were powerful are gone. However, had I refused to perform this rite for you, their ghosts would have devoured you again, even worse than they did ordinarily. Their ghosts are now preparing to increase their former size. That is the reason people are not feeling well. How could conditions be good anywhere? The slaughter of the enemies at Taos was the climax of the bad state of the world. As it was not in the original plan, many enemy ghosts swarmed from there.

"Now the ghost of Big-monster-who-wanders-alone, that which used to be his life and ran out from within him, is planning once more to become their chief. Plans are even being made to transform the grass, soil, mountains, and water into ghosts. If such plans were successful, people who are to be born in the future would have no sense, but would be easily persuaded by these ghosts to break taboos. If then people went wild because they had not observed the ceremonial restrictions, the ghosts would rejoice. Furthermore, if people died, their ghosts would be allied with the original evils. If in the more distant future ghosts should tempt you to break taboos, perform the ceremony to ward them off. For these reasons I am entrusting to you that which I contribute to the ritual, so that it may be a means of defense, a hope to you for the future." [6]

Two men were on the warpath; one asked the other to blacken him for the War Ceremony. "For which enemies?"

the second man asked. "Since we have been at war twice now, it can be for bad things [gray ones] of any kind that affect you. Two places must be considered, Taos and Blue House, where evils [gray ones] of every description exist." [7]

There was, however, an attempt to limit the number of enemy ghosts.

Black God, on his way to the first War Ceremony, rested while the flying animals and the quadrupeds carried on a contest of boulder hurling. When they had finished, some rocks were left. These they laid in two piles on which they placed herbs ceremonially, remarking, "What a great number of enemy ghosts there are for Black God to oppose with his rite. There are two large piles of rocks and even some rocks left over. There are as many ghosts as there are stones." [8]

Purification

After the causes of illness have been determined and guilt admitted, ugly things must be expelled; hence numerous rites are directed toward purification. Rites may have certain acts that exorcise, as well as some that attract good. Cleanliness, coming before godliness, is almost synonymous with sanctity. People of one group are offensive to those of another because they smell bad: The gods bade the precursors of the Navaho who lived in the fourth world to cleanse themselves so that they, the gods, could communicate with them. Before being conducted into far and holy places by the gods, Earth People, who eventually became intermediaries between man and deity, had to bathe and sweat. After association with the Holy People, a hero, rejoining his earth family, is much offended by their odor and will not stay with them until they have been ceremonially cleansed. Warriors and hunters, returning from their quest, must rid themselves of the odor of danger.[9] Odor is, therefore, evidence of the profane just as purity is a symbol of sanctity.

Evils entering the body may be in the stomach, or they

may be in the form of arrows or witch weapons imbedded in the flesh. Both types may be exorcised at once by the sweat-emetic rites. Changing-bear-maiden treated herself by walking around a hot fire and taking the emetic to get rid of the many arrows shot into her body by the Swallow and Spider People. Son-in-law of One-who-customarily-sees-the-fish took the same treatment to force out witch objects injected by Ants, Bear, and Snake People.[10]

When I failed to vomit according to ritualistic requirements, RP admonished, "You must throw up, because if you don't, bad things will stay in you and make you sick."

When contemplating exposure to danger—hunting, war, contact with the supernatural as layman, learner, or chanter —a Navaho purifies himself by sweating. Many family settlements have a house where a sweatbath may be taken any time a group of people of the same sex sees fit; a sweatbath renews vigor, makes one feel fresh and confident, rids the mind of doubt as well as the body of accumulated dirt. The sweat-emetic rites are very complex, their function being similar to that of the ordinary sweatbath but with a more elaborate ritual. The pit sudorific is another form of sweat healing. It combines the elimination of evil by perspiring with the attraction of good from the green boughs and leaves laid over the heated earth on which the patient lies.

Hill, describing the training of young boys, includes purgatives as a means of expelling evil. Wyman and Harris have a brief note on a species of *Pentstemon* that was considered a cathartic.[11]

Fasting is a ceremonial necessity, hardly mentioned in mythology. Its purpose seems to be to make the patient susceptible to and retentive of the powers being invoked for him. Customarily, before being treated on a drypainting, the patient fasts; the interval between meals may vary greatly.

During most ceremonies he eats late at night, between nine and twelve, and not again until after the sandpainting rite is completed the next day. If the painting is small, the rite may be over early in the morning and fasting is scarcely detectable since some Navaho families do not eat much before ten in the morning; but if the painting is large, requiring much work, the patient may not eat until nearly sundown—a fast of fourteen to twenty hours. Matthews records abstention from food by patients and chanter of the Night Chant for twenty-four hours. The same rule is observed by those blackened in the War Ceremony, although at intervals small quantities of sacred mush may be taken.[12]

Ceremonial fasting is doubtless related to the old discipline to develop fortitude when boys and men, particularly warriors, competed in performing deeds requiring long abstinence from food or drink.

Bathing and shampooing the hair, incorporated in the rite termed ' the bath,' symbolizes a change from profane to sacred, from the strange and doubtful to the controlled. Body and hair are washed in suds of the *Yucca baccata;* the body, hairstring, jewelry, and clothing of the patient are subsequently rubbed with corn meal—white for males, yellow for females (*Bath*, Concordance C).

Not only the patient and his immediate vicinity but even an extended space to be occupied by deity should be cleaned. Consequently, all participants in the ceremony imitate him, though in varying degree. Some of the visitors at the ceremony sweat and take emetic with him; practically all attendants shampoo their hair. The ceremonial house is also purified. In my experience a new structure was not built every time a major chant was undertaken; an old hogan, carefully cleaned each time, was used again and again. Most belongings were removed from the house, but a few carefully chosen possessions were left to absorb the power of the chant. The earthen floor was neatly swept, the surface layer having been removed.

When Talking God began to help Self Teacher, he directed: "After four days you may expect me again. Have yourself and your house clean and in order for my coming. Have the floor and all around the house swept. Have the ashes taken out. Wash your body and hair with yucca suds the night before I arrive, and bid your niece also wash herself with yucca." [13]

Continence is a restrictive form of purification. A patient is supposed by regulation to refrain from sexual intercourse for four nights before a ceremony. In the Shooting Chant I participated in, no stress was laid on prior continence, but the rule was observed by both chanter and patient for four nights after the ceremony. Restrictions may be more or less stringent for other chants and perhaps in recent years the rule is less strictly applied than formerly (*Restrictions*, Concordance C).

Sexual intercourse was forbidden between the day a war party was decided upon and the day of departure, the interval being spent in preparation and purification, with much sweating and singing. Women were allowed to join a war party, but could not be leaders; the rule of continence was strictly enforced while they were away from home. Continence was required of the patient for the duration of the War Ceremony and four nights following. It was not required of the leaders, but moderation was encouraged.[14]

Other rites to bring about purification are the brushing rites—one type is a benedictory sequel to the sweat-emetic rite; another, the rite performed to brush evils out of the ceremonial space in the evil-chasing ceremonies. The sandpainting of these chants plays a dual role. After the rite is

111

finished, some of the sand is deposited at considerable distance from the ceremonial hogan; each day it is taken successively further so that the evil will not be likely to return. The idea is that the sand absorbs the evil. A part of it, on the other hand, is placed under the patient's bed so that he may absorb the good of the supernaturals represented by the sand.

Attraction of Good

The ritualistic process may be likened to a spiritual osmosis in which the evil in man and the good of deity penetrate the ceremonial membrane in both directions, the former being neutralized by the latter, but only if the exact conditions for the interpenetration are fulfilled. One condition is cleanliness, the ejection of evil so that the place it occupied may be attractive to good powers. The chanter's ultimate goal is to identify the patient with the supernaturals being invoked. He must become one with them by absorption, imitation, transformation, substitution, recapitulation, repetition, commemoration, and concentration.

The purpose of sandpaintings is to allow the patient to absorb the powers depicted, first by sitting on them, next by application of parts of deity to corresponding parts of the patient—foot to foot, knees to knees, hands to hands, head to head. In some chants parts of the drypainting may be slept on to give more time for absorption; sleep seems to aid the process. The chanter applies the bundle items to the body parts of the gods, then touches parts of the patient's body with his own—foot to foot, hand to hand, shoulder to shoulder in the ceremonial order—and finally with the bundle equipment; this is an elaborate rite of identification (*Application of bundle*, Concordance C). The powers, represented by the sandpainting, are conveyed indirectly by the chanter through the bundle equipment and his own body to the

112

patient's, all because the chanter has obtained power to do this by his knowledge.

An incident of the Hail Chant illustrates absorption through contact during sleep and the digestive process.

Rainboy, before starting to instruct his brother in the Hail Chant, brought clean, fine sand from the cornpatch and spread it neatly around the fire. He drew a line in the sand for each song, later erasing a line as his brother learned the corresponding song until all were gone. When all had been erased, Rainboy gathered the sand into a pile and put it under his brother's pillow. He kept tally also by shelling a kernel of corn from the ear and tossing it into a basket. When all the songs—447 altogether—had been learned, the corn was made into ' unseasoned gruel,' which the novice ate.[15]

Warriors customarily cut the bloodstained shirt of a victim into strips which they subsequently wore as bandoleers, in this way absorbing the power of the enemy brought under control.[16] Bandoleers frequently occur as a symbol, an associated form being the figure painting in which lightning is painted on the torso where the bandoleer would hang.

A person who has been subjected to a ceremony potentially possesses a great many powers to keep him safe. He facilitates the process of absorbing the powers represented by the paint, bandoleers, and head feathers in which he has been ceremonially dressed by observing four nights of restrictions during which he avoids activity and association with his fellows. Meanwhile, he is dangerous to others who have not been so treated. They must not come near him or touch dishes from which he eats; what is invaluable to him may harm those too weak to endure the newly acquired power.

A large part of every rite may be the exact imitation of a mythical scene or incident. For instance, in the Shooting Chant the ' pollen ball,' containing, among other things, a turquoise, is administered to the patient and set straight

113

within him by ritualistic acts. In this rite the chanter imitates Sun, who placed a turquoise ' man ' in his son's chest and performed the same acts so that it would remain upright and stand firm. This man was to make the youth ' invincible to any danger, however great ' (*Pollen ball*, Concordance B).

The Sun's House screen of the Shooting Chant is a replica of Sun's ' real ' house; prayersticks resemble those the gods prescribed in the mythical past. When The Twins visited their father in the sky, they were rubbed and shaped like their brothers, the Dawn children. Kneading, a common rite, seeks to imitate supernatural beauty and strength (*Pressing*, Concordance B).[17]

Identification is brought about by correspondence. When new bundle items are made, the old models belonging to the officiating chanter are always in evidence; the new one is repeatedly held near the old one so that every detail may match. The bundle contaminated by the death of its owner is purified at a ceremony in which each item is laid to correspond with that of the singer whose bundle has not been so tainted (*Rite for removing contamination of the dead*, Concordance C).

Transformation allows for miraculous results in myth and ritual. A common mythological theme is the transformation of the hero who eats food of strange people. Supernatural guardians give warnings to prevent irrevocable transformation. The mentor says, "If you eat that, you will never see your mother, father, sisters, or brothers again." Reared-in-the-mountain, hero of the Mountain Chant, was warned by Wind not to eat the food of Bushrat lest he become a rat.[18]

Transformation from eating strange food is unalterable only if the hero eats it without supernatural protection. Rainboy had to spend four nights near where the Fire Dance was held for him. He had no food, but was fed on the first night by Hummingbird, on the second by White Goose, on the third by White Owl. On the fourth night Rat Woman brought him food similar to that which Reared-in-the-mountain had refused. Three times Rainboy refused the food, but when Rat Woman finally made gruel of parched corn right before him, Whirlwind told him to eat it. Rat food would have transformed Rainboy into a rat, but food ceremonially controlled by Rat Woman was safe for a person who had been ritualistically treated.[19]

The touch of a coyote skin was sufficient to turn a hero into a starved, mangy, powerless coyote, and only ritual carefully carried out could restore even a divine being to his usual self. This theme is emphasized by a rite in the Male Shooting Chant Evil, Big Star, and Endurance chants and mentioned in the myth of the Bead Chant.[20] Some transformations are quite complicated, passing through more than one stage. Various body parts of Changing-bear-maiden became products useful to man—porcupine, pinyon nuts and cones, various chants—but they represent the remnants of a transformed evil.

Blowing is a common way of producing transformation.

Winter Thunder blew upon the materials which had been the Fire Dance corral for Rainboy's ceremony and turned them into rock.[21]

The Hunchback gods gave the Visionary of the Night Chant a mountain-sheep skin to put on; it did not fit. They blew upon it and it fell into place; he became a mountain sheep.[22]

Monster Slayer let Gopher take part of the hide of Burrowing Monster as a reward for his aid. When Gopher tried to put it on, he found it too large. As he tried to fit it to his body, Monster Slayer blew upon it and thereafter it was impossible to remove it.[23]

A great many ceremonial items are substitutes for the originals they represent. Sand is a substitute for clouds and other perishable materials on which the mythical protagonists saw the first sandpaintings drawn. Whenever an object is lacking for a ceremony, it may be represented in sand—a chanter who does not own a Sun's House screen may substitute a sandpainting for it; a Shooting Chanter once told me that the snake paintings of his chant were a substitute for real snakes which the Navaho previously used as the Hopi do in their Snake Dance. Sun withheld his ' real ' arrows of precious stones from Earth People, giving them only the bundle talking prayersticks as a substitute.[24]

Often a token quantity represents an unlimited amount. For example, the materials that compose prayersticks— reeds, tobacco, feathers, cotton string, jewels—are infinitesimal in amount though of immense importance. The tiny ' bead ' token of some chants is the symbol of the entire ceremony, a symbol so thoroughly identified with the owner that if the bead breaks, misfortune will befall him.

The chant is a recapitulation of scenes in the myth drama whose function is commemoration. Events of the lower world are remembered and certain episodes are acted out or represented in symbols to preserve the timelessness of power.

The sick Navaho identifies himself with the rejuvenation of Changing Woman when he recapitulates in the Shooting Chant the place, the circumstances, and the ritualistic details she experienced when she was restored to youth and beauty. He occupies a ritualistically determined position in the hogan blessed for the chant, takes hold of the bull-roarer offered by. the chanter as he is led step by step to the spot on the sandpainting predetermined by tradition.

The ancestors of the modern Navaho fought their way past warring alien tribes and, by continual fighting, established themselves in a large new terrain. Nowadays, though their battles for independence are rhetorical, their fear of non-Navaho ghosts has not abated. To counteract such alien influences, they recapitulate in the War Ceremony, circumstance for circumstance, act for act, and curse for curse, everything the war party deemed necessary to defeat the enemy. They ride upon his ghost, shoot at him, render themselves invisible—in short, re-enact the winning struggle and thereby attain virtue.

Remembrance of a power to whom man owes a cure puts him into a good state of mind; it is a manifestation of faith, indicating a willingness to seek a change, to put forth an effort for restoration. The intermediary demonstrates this feeling when he tells his human relatives to remember him.

After Rainboy had taught the Hail Chant to his older brother, who had sung it over their sister, he told his relatives to keep on singing. As they did so, he and the sister began to rise into the sky and gradually disappeared. Rainboy had admonished them just before this event, "Don't run away when it rains. If you do, I shall not think well of you." [25]

Reared-in-the-mountain, as he took similar leave of his younger brother, said, "When you see the showers pass and hear the thunder, know that I am in them. Remember me, too, when the harvest and the beautiful birds come and know that it is the order of your older brother." [26]

The Visionary of one myth of the Night Chant, co, said to his brother, a novice, "When summer comes, look for me in the storms and male rain and know that in them is your brother." [27]

Repetition carries the idea of recapitulation still further. If it is good to reproduce a scene and its circumstances, it is far better to do so many times; hence four or more, even twenty-three or forty-six, times seems not too often for repetition in prayer, song, or symbol. Of course some details —color, sex, accouterments—are modified, but the formulaic

117

repetition is preserved throughout. The events of a day are repeated four times in a five- or nine-day chant. Prayersticks, if properly made, are effective, but if their number is doubled, trebled, or multiplied even further they are better. The essential figures of a sandpainting, only one or two perhaps, may suffice, but it is far better to have a large number. Repetition is compulsive and authoritative.

When it had been decided that he who achieved revenge for the harm done Corn Man should be rewarded by getting two young and beautiful nieces as wives, Coyote carried the news abroad. People did not believe him, since he often reported falsely. He defended himself: "It is true. I have asked any number of times, therefore it is true." Even then the people demanded corroboration, although it is implied that had anyone else repeated the report as many times, it would have been believed.[28]

Concentration carries commemoration further. The purpose of the attentive demeanor most becoming to a patient, even to the point of passivity, is to make his mind receptive. Although he may not understand what is being done, he can co-operate with the chanter by paying strict attention. The long prayers must be said from beginning to end without skipping or repeating a word and without mistakes of any kind whatsoever. Prayers may take as long as one hundred minutes.[29] The gravest responsibility rests upon the chanter, who usually closes his eyes. The patient can help him and, of course, himself by responding accurately so as not to distract the chanter.

The value of concentration is demonstrated also by the vigil, either of a single night or particularly of the last night of a long ceremony. The songs previously sung, and some additional ones, are repeated by way of summarizing and sealing all that has been done. The patient, and, ideally, everyone in the hogan, should remain awake; by paying

118

attention to the song summary, one benefits from the entire performance even though one is present at this rite alone. Missing any part of the long series interrupts the flow of power, causing weakness.

In an incident of the Night Chant myth, inattention is deplored. The Visionary's brothers ridiculed the voices he claimed to hear. After some time, during which they were unsuccessful in the hunt, his brother-in-law began to think there might be some truth in his revelations and begged him to tell about them. The Visionary answered, "No, I will not speak as long as others sit by in scorn and show no desire to listen." [30]

Therapy

Whether any of the measures believed to be curative has actual therapeutic value is doubtful. Those that seem to be have a psychological rather than a physical effect, since they are hardly continued long enough or repeated often enough or at short enough intervals. Though massage is prescribed in some rites, it is often a mere temporary laying on of hands; if real pressure is applied, it is so momentary that it can have little effect on the circulation.

The Navaho hardly appreciate the value of sudden temperature changes; they rely on symbolism rather than on therapy. In the old days boys had to roll naked in the snow. RP, who had been trained in the school most orthodox in these matters, said, "Rolling in ordinary snow was not so bad, but when the snow was dry, *that* was really cold!"

Most Navaho think nothing of going from a warm hogan —the ordinary heated hogan is *very* warm—into a zero or sub-zero outdoor temperature. The patient, wet with perspiration, steps outside into the raw, blustery air with no more clothes than he had for the sweatbath—a skirt for the women, a G string for the men. Some, like MA and T's wife, get pneumonia and die. The Navaho do not see any connection between the weakness of the sick and the rigorous temperature changes; the cause of death is the evil the body was unable to throw off.

Some effort may be made to alleviate the shock of sudden change in the ceremonial bath. I have seen warm water supplied, a blanket warmed to throw over a wet head or body, but never has the patient been excused from going outside before his hair dried. It should be remembered, however, that the Navaho, hardened by his daily habits, can stand much more than a white man. The favorite chants, attracting large crowds, are held in winter when the attendants move to the place of assembly with the intention of staying at least one, more probably two or three nights. Since there is no shelter, each person brings his own bedding; for many, especially horsemen, there is only a Pendleton blanket between them and the frozen ground.

Wyman considers the temperature changes he experienced in Navaho treatment of his knee possibly beneficial.[31] The various heat treatments as well as other rites may have some psychological merit as counterirritants in assuaging pain, at least temporarily. Too little is known about the pharmacological properties of the herbs, the difficulty of making proper tests not yet having been surmounted. I took the emetic of the Shooting Chant, composed of fifteen herbs, in large quantities four successive days; I could observe no effects whatsoever. Kluckhohn and Wyman agree that the emetic does not seem to be effective.[32]

Differences in the ostensible efficacy of the emetic are a matter of faith. CF, who believed implicitly in the ritual, performed it conscientiously and got the expected results. TC does not enjoy the sweat-emetic rite any more than I do, but as the chanter's assistant, he often has to endure it. He suggested to me one day, "Just rub the medicine [emetic] on you. You don't have to drink much." I noticed then that he made considerable business of the rubbing part of the rite, drank almost none of the emetic, and did not vomit.

TC's expedient, as well as the selection of plants, shows that cures are ascribed to herbs by analogy. Weakness was overcome by herbs having strong odor. Certain ' medicines ' are said to be distasteful to the evil powers. Enemy ghosts fear *Aquilegia formosa* (xazéi·dá̜'í, ' chipmunk food ') and *Hierchloe odorata* (tɫoh nɫtci·n) because of their pungent smell. ' Chipmunk food ' has commemorative value in addition, because it recalls the aid given by Chipmunk to Monster Slayer when he slew Burrowing Monster.

Ghosts are also afraid of the specially prepared soot of the blackening rite, of the red ocher which belongs to Child-of-the-water, of the sparkling rock that represents bright or flashing light.

Dieting is completely unknown—perhaps understandably in a tribe that has never had more than the lowest subsistence standards—and loss of appetite is evidence of waning strength. Upon any and all occasions, infants and the ill are offered any available tidbit, however indigestible or inappropriate. The attitude toward diet is of a piece with that toward disease and curing. You must eat to be strong; you show strength to demonstrate you have it. Therefore you eat to show you are strong. When any connection between food consumption and strength is drawn, flesh food and corn, foods around which so much ritual is woven, are stressed. Wyman's informants said, "How could a person get strength without eating? Give him all he can eat, especially corn meal." [33]

The irreverent crowd, ridiculing the Racing God of the Mountain Chant myth, showed their belief in game as strength-giving when they taunted, "He is too weak and lazy to hunt. He lives on seeds and never tastes flesh." [34]

121

Properly combined, corn meal and rare game are good; they cannot be altered by chemical or any except supernatural change. They are good things with which to fill space left vacant by ejected bad things.

The following prescriptions show how causes and cures are grouped: Chiricahua Wind, Eagle, and Awl chants were prescribed for headache. The Eagle and Bead chants were supposed to cure head diseases, boils and sores, inflamed throat, swollen legs, itching, lack of appetite. and vomiting, since the diseases were thought to have been shaken from the feathers of mythical birds.

Warm infusions poured into the external meatus served as a remedy for earache. Wyman records: "Eye medicines are usually prepared by cold or warm infusions and used as eye washes or drops, and the whole head is often bathed to relieve headache and swelling about the eyes. Hole fumigation or the application of dry powder may be used. . . . Since eye diseases [along with other head disorders] may be treated by Plume Way [in which Game Way plants are used], eye medicines are among the plants used in these chants." [35]

Beauty Chant was recommended for snakebite, rheumatism, sore throat, and stomach, kidney, bladder, and abdominal trouble. Anuria and other kidney and bladder troubles are numerous. The Navaho cures are a repetition of the type regularly encountered: Shooting, Beauty, Red Ant, or Eagle chants for venereal diseases, hematuria, pelvic pain, bladder stones, as well as for anuria. It is almost certain that the relation between syphilis and arthritis and other bone-deforming affections is not recognized.

Diseases frequently traced to hand trembling and star gazing are tuberculosis, nervousness, and mental disease; paralysis of the arms to overdoing motion-in-the-hand; and impaired vision to excessive star gazing.

CHAPTER 8

ETHICS

Meaning

THE ETHICAL system is a function of social as well as religious organization. The family into which an individual is born determines his obligations and privileges. The extended family has a much larger membership than the simple unit in our society, since it is a subdivision of a clan—a social group that counts descent and inheritance in the maternal line. A person may, therefore, depend upon help from his mother's brothers rather than from his father, from his maternal grandparents rather than from both sides of the family; he may be called upon to aid his sisters and sisters' children rather than his own. Members of his own— that is, his mother's—clan are his closest relatives. Among them there is economic responsibility, which may be extended to members of two to five related clans, called the clan-group. Since relationship is traced through the female line, relatives of a family, clan, and clan-group address one another by reciprocal terms such as female parent-son, mother's father-daughter's child, mother's brother-sister's son, older brother-younger brother, older sister-younger sister. Kinship, with all the duties it entails, may even include strangers having the same clan name, whether or not any blood relationship can be traced.

For instance, a clan brother met for the first time could, if he chose to push a request so far, make a claim to be considered as seriously as one made by a blood brother. At whatever inconvenience, the claim would be satisfied or a very good reason for refusing would have to be given. Such obligations, inherent in the social structure, are compulsive; they include every kind of request individuals make of one another, but they are mainly economic..

A Navaho has a sentimental rather than economic duty to his father, members of his father's clan, and clan-group. If one is ill, one's immediate relatives decide upon the ceremony to be sung; they and the clan kinsmen expect to meet the expenses, although if necessary they may request contributions from members of the clan-group. Reciprocally, they must be helped—needs are stated directly to one another and an agreement is reached. On the other hand, one does not ask his father's clan relatives for such aid, nor does one make a definite bargain with them. They may, however, volunteer even a large donation to the enterprise.

Since the responsibilities are accepted without question, many ethical problems, which in our society are settled by individual moral judgment, hardly arise. With us questions of parental authority, support of the incompetent, distribution of wealth (including generosity and hospitality) have constantly to be solved anew. The Navaho can depend upon his social code to settle most of them; individual judgment plays a small role.

In Navaho life ethics is empirical rather than theoretical or theological; ethics includes actual as well as ideal behavior, etiquette and law, as well as religious restrictions. Since he seldom sees a white man who treats him as a brother, the Navaho does not comprehend the preacher's statement that all men are brothers, although he shares the ideal. Since the whites he knows scheme and cheat him whenever possible, their verbal reiterations that honesty is the best policy leave him unconvinced. He may not know that their belief in rugged individualism admits cutthroat competition while it consigns honesty to religion. Ostensibly the white man practices his religion on Sunday; the Navaho observes his daily.

The code tells a Navaho what he should or should not do, what the punishment is—not for the transgression, but for the correction of error. There are so many supernatural decrees that no one can possibly be acquainted with all. Each adult does what he can to find out what is correct and to teach his children. Many a Navaho never runs afoul of any rule, since he does not directly encounter supernatural displeasure. He may be well aware that something he contemplates doing is wrong. If he wants to do it very much, he will carry out the techniques for preventing ill effects; he will hardly decide not to do it. If, in spite of prophylactic rites, he becomes sick, he need not reform, nor does he think the measures taken have been ineffective; he submits to cleansing and more rigorous rites quite similar to those previously tried. Magical performances fail not because they are faulty but because the correct ones have not been combined.

The nearest Navaho approach to the concept of sin is ' being out of order, lacking control,' a definition that involves rationalization, not salving a bad conscience; confession of error, not a feeling of guilt; laying on of hands, not a plea for forgiveness; propitiation, not expiation; identification with deity, not humiliation of the offender; and in the end, a sense of human achievement, not of subservience to divinity.

Since goodness is so closely tied up with order and compulsion, it is also deeply concerned with property. The gods themselves, according to tradition, set a value on all knowledge comparable to a price on merchandise; consequently the Navaho dickers with the divinities as he does with the trader. Prayers, formulas, songs, song series, rites, and ceremonies all have material values that must be recognized as an element of ethical control. And since the order was established through uncounted years without the volition of any living individual, a Navaho can no more reject it or even part of it than he can a member of his body; all he can do is comply.

Conformance, following rules as unyielding as a mathematical formula, is unemotional; it is as inexorable as a machine, once the gears have been engaged. Property belongs to the ethical ideal, for whether a large quantity or only a token is offered, the deity must respond. The gods have as little choice about answering man's requests when properly formulated as man has in evoking them.

It may be difficult to learn the type of offering acceptable to a deity, to procure the unusual materials that compose the offering, and to discover the proper mode of presentation, but once all these things have been attended to, the deity must help man. The god shows his willingness to aid by addressing the petitioner by kin terms—' my daughter's son, my son's son.'

Comparable with the offering to deity is the advance payment made to the chanter. Having decided upon a ceremony, a person customarily sends an intermediary to the singer chosen, offering him an unstipulated, preferably large, amount—horses, sheep, silver, money, buckskin, buffalo robe, or other goods. The chanter will not necessarily refuse to sing if the payment is small. Like some of our doctors, he considers the patient's circumstances, accepting the best a poor man can offer. The arrangement is not, as might appear at first glance, purely economic, for both chanter and patient believe that the ceremony could not possibly be efficacious if nothing were paid.

Kinship may be a substitute for property in a transaction of this kind. Yet the patient believes he should pay something to validate the ceremony, even if the chanter is a close relative—father, maternal grandfather, or maternal uncle. Here, in the voluntary nature of the payment, in the patient's economic circumstances and in the value set upon kinship, are some of the few places where individual judgment enters into the system, and to this estimate strictly material considerations may be irrelevant.

With the initial payment offered the chanter it is expected that certain indispensable parts of the chant will be furnished—for instance, four sandpaintings. If the sum is inconsiderable, or if the sponsor does not provide abundant help, the paintings may be small and simple. If the payment is larger, they may be large and elaborate. The lesser ones will be effective; the greater ones more so. Various accessories may be included or omitted according to the monetary arrangements. It is better to have more rather than few rites, bétter to have detailed rather than simple rites performed, but if a man is not in a position to make a great show, the cheaper ceremony, if properly done, will cure him. A conscientious singer will not be careless or negligent just because the ceremony is less elaborate.

The Concept of Honor

Since property ideas and exchange are so important to the Navaho and to us, it is essential to consider the ideas that prevail about honor and honorable dealings. Mythology, because it is naïve, furnishes some of the most illuminating evidence about ethical ideals. The motivation of a story may subtly indicate an attitude with a basis so obvious in practice that it may escape notice. Even the plot itself, by what it includes, and particularly by what it omits, often yields an unexpected clarification of some point. A Navaho tale may start with the theme of the unmarried mother—often of twins—but the plot develops not as might be expected, to deplore illegitimacy, but to teach how bad it is to keep the father's identity a secret. Lying is condoned to the end that the tribe may gain supernatural power. If lying and cheating are themes, they result in punishment, not because they are bad ethics but because the one attempting the deception was unskillful. Poetic justice demands the acceptance of responsibility and skill in practicing techniques, rarely the exposure of a traitor or cheat.

The description of an enemy is often a clue to the ideas of honor held by the narrator or his group. The following excerpt from a long tale illustrates the Navaho interpretation of Hopi character:

The Stricken Twins, one crippled, one blind, having been instructed by the Navaho gods, who gave them a magic rat, worm, wind, and grasshopper, went to the Hopi at Awatobi to procure the luxuries necessary to pay the deities for the instruction which was to originate the Night Chant.

When the Hopi thought the boys were only pitiable visitors, there was no treatment contemptible enough for them. Each time the twins destroyed the crops—first with the supernatural rat; next, with the worm; again, with the wind; and a fourth time, with the grasshopper—the Hopi hypocritically treated them cordially until the twins removed the scourge. Within four days after the corn had been restored, the enemies renewed their atrocities, each time more severely, until finally they cursed the boys to their faces.

Each time the boys demanded a greater reward for removing the plague. When the Hopi elders offered the compensation for restoring the corn after the attack by wind, they spread three unwounded buckskins down. On one they piled paperbread and other articles of food; on the others, clothing, baskets, precious stones, feathers, pollen, and all the other treasures the boys asked for. "Yet they did not put the best they had on these buckskins, no more than we Navaho give away the best we have if we can help it."

For the restoration after the last attack by the grasshoppers, the boys held out longer and exacted more than promises because of the previous betrayals. And now, even though the chiefs were desperate, having exhausted all their resources, they promised everything the boys asked for. The boys said firmly, "If we help you this time, we want no more scraps or leavings of food, we want no secondhand clothes, we want no more inferior things; we must have the best of everything. First we must have four more fine large sacred buckskins, and we must have an abundance of other skins—doeskins, fawnskins, antelope skins, and furs. We must have fine necklaces, eardrops as long as a finger, besides turquoise of lesser size. We must have beads of all kinds. We must have fine necklaces containing shells of all kinds—the best from everybody's house. We must have five baskets made of jewels." These and other things enumerated had been demanded by the gods who sent the boys. The boys added emphatically, "All these things must be of the best. Now give us these and we will try to save what is left of your corn."

The Hopi found the demands exorbitant and were reluctant to comply, but in council the chief reassured them, even in his desperation, "Fear not to give them. When the boys have chased away the grasshoppers and restored the crops, we will kill them and get all our wealth back again."

The boys restored the fields and prayed for rain, then tied up the treasures with a band of lightning, thus making a very small parcel, and the Hopi chiefs watched them lest they get away with the treasures. The boys moved off on their magic rainbow and the Hopi pursued them. By means of their magic the twins made them follow until they were completely exhausted. When the last ones saw that the pursuit was vain, they cried out, "Farewell, my beautiful beads! Farewell, my precious necklace! Farewell, my rare turquoise basket! You are gone forever; I shall never see you again!" And, as they realized that their valuables were gone, they wept and wailed.

When the twins announced their victory and gave an inventory to the gods, xa·ctčé''óγan said at once, "We rejoice to hear that they have secured an abundance, and that everything they have is of the best. We must divide with our neighbors. Go out to all the other holy places and tell the people to come in." [1]

This is myth, but it reveals what is casually accepted. It lists the things gods and men, both Hopi and Navaho, consider most valuable. It weighs the value of a promise, and indicates that words, even if repeated four times, cannot always be believed. Among many interesting implications of this story, two statements especially reveal Navaho attitudes: "We do not give away the best we have if we can help it" and "We must divide with our neighbors." Just as the Navaho tale discloses the opinion of their Hopi neighbors, whom they never trusted, it shows that they understand the enemy's motives and implies that theirs may be the same. They are hardly teaching a moral or dealing with an ethical ideal; they are quite practically using a technique. The attitude of the Hopi toward goods, the words of farewell, the weeping and crying, are all illuminating. Property loss is played up more in the last scene of the excerpt than is a human casualty in any myth.

The ethical allusions are quite typical of the attitude toward cheating, lying, and stealing. The Navaho does not expect anyone to give up his best if he can help it, because he would not do so himself. This attitude differs from our own in that ideal and practice are the same; it is a realistic, rather than a sentimental, point of departure. The caution is also realistic and the consequent behavior dependable, whereas with us the ideal makes a demand upon the individual that is likely to meet with a hesitant and disappointing evasion. Only when the Hopi chief promises the best, then withholds' it or places it on the blanket with the mental reservation that by killing the bargainers he will get it back, do ethics enter. To the Navaho this is deception, chiefly because it amounts to cheating the gods, who know better tricks. If one expects to benefit from their service, one emulates them. The Hopi thought they were dealing with human beings like themselves, and only a preknowledge of divine ethical practice, which they did not possess, could beat their tricks.

In practice as well as in myth, the Navaho is frank in discussing property and exchange including withholding, fraud, sharp practice, and falsehood. It is ritualistically improper for a chanter to mention a definite sum as his payment for singing, but he may candidly enumerate the details to be included in the performance and those to be withheld.

Twenty-two items belong to the bundle of the Male Shooting Chant Holy. All should be set out on the sandpainting mound before the door at the east when a sandpainting is being laid inside. Said RP, "Some chanters do not put all twenty-two pieces out every time, if the people have not given very much calico. I always use them all, no matter how small the amount."

The statement illustrates the chanter's concern for those who aid him. The calico is the reward given those who help with the night singing; it is not a part of the chanter's fee.

The Navaho has great regard for circumstantial evidence and is not likely to lie when faced with it. Otherwise, when under suspicion, he has the ceremonial privilege of lying three times before answering a question that may involve him; the fourth time he is asked, he should tell the truth. Such change of evidence is surprising, not to say shocking, to the white man who has the patience to listen to questioning by a Navaho judge, and expects the Navaho defendant's first answer to be final.

Children are taught not to steal because they might be caught.[2] Young men, when questioned, said, "We are told not to steal, not because it is sinful but because if someone saw it, the thief would get a bad reputation in the community."

Old men said they knew of nothing in the religion that forbids stealing, but they would not steal an article unless they needed it. Asked if they would take anything from an unprotected car, they said they would unless they knew the owner. Hill remarks that being caught with stolen goods or in attempts at cheating are humorous situations [3] —they have no ethical connotation; they merely indicate the discomfiture of the culprit at getting caught.

One may wonder how property is protected; here again kinship obligations enter in. One would not steal from a kinsman; on the other hand, if the kinsman were not present to give permission, an article might be borrowed and he might be informed about its absence later or it might be returned before he discovered it was gone. If it was damaged when returned, he would hardly make a fuss no matter how he felt. And since everyone is related to nearly everyone else, the claim of kinship for borrowing may usually be pressed. The Navaho have a highly perfected system for guarding property, hardly detectable by the outsider. At a large gathering a small area, marked out by a wagon and its campfire or even by a pile of goods covered with a blanket or tarpaulin, is watched by one of the owning group, usually an old person. Anyone will tell on a pilferer. If there is no one to keep guard, all possessions are removed from the vehicles to the temporary camp where the night is spent, it being generally admitted that you would not expect to find anything not protected.

I cannot imagine, however, that anyone would steal food or supplies from a sheep-herder who had temporarily left his camp. His meager supplies, chiefly food, which may have to last him two or three weeks, have a certain immunity, for he is far from the source of supply; it would be dangerous for the sheep if he left them to get himself some food. No one would want to force him in desperation to kill one of the flock, and finally, everybody is a herder or puts himself so completely in the herder's place that depriving him of his scanty store would be the Navaho equivalent of taking candy from a baby.

The old men who said they knew of nothing in the religion that forbids theft might have gone on to say that there is a good deal to sanction dishonesty. All forms of deception are practiced by the gods or the heroes in their charge. Often they gain by trickery or ruse. The contest between the Stricken Twins and the Hopi illustrates the test of power, matching of wits. The deities also cheat one another.

There were footprints of little children before Changing Woman's door, but, when the monster asked her for the children, she said she had made the marks with her hand because she was lonely.[4]

Changing Woman not only denied that she knew who the father of her children was, but answered first that it might be anybody. When the question was repeated, she said it was Barrel Cactus; at the third question, she said it was Sitting Cactus. In other words, she lied three times. The fourth time, The Twins answered their own question, telling her that their father was Sun.[5]

There seems to be little difference between refusal to answer a question three times and making a false answer three times; both are ritualistic, probably the reason Changing Woman did not answer her Twins' question truthfully. In the first case she lied to protect her children.

Other deities constantly cheat and lie. The whole pattern of Sun's character is built upon deceit. He mates with girls without the knowledge of their parents or of his sky wife. He causes them to lead sneaking lives and to tell untruths. One of his favorite ruses is to create a duplicate who, endowed with Sun's powers, wins by cheating.

133

The mentors—Wind, Bat, Big Fly—are in a sense the personification of deception, for they whisper the answers to examination questions their protégés would otherwise fail. In this respect the mentors enable novices to deceive Sun himself.[6] When superior powers ask how Earth People knew the details of the offerings they demand, the People say they just knew, that no one told them, whereas in fact the mentors have instructed them.

The entire progress of the Stricken Twins as they visited one god after another was based on falsehoods. Talking God had deceived their mother. Whenever the boys asked a deity or a group of gods to help them, the gods answered that it was impossible because they knew nothing about curing the blind and the lame, yet each had some power for this purpose.

Human beings even prevaricated to the gods, who did not call their bluff. Our sense of proper justice would be to impress the liar with a feeling of guilt; the Navaho is interested in accounting for ritualistic instruction, and gods do not expect their protégés to be any more truthful than they themselves are. Indeed the gods may interpret trickery as courage; they may even aid in making a falsehood become a fact.

When Self Teacher invoked the help of Talking God for traveling in his whirling log, the god asked him if he had the eighteen sacred things to offer the gods. The hero answered that he had, although he owned nothing except the rags in which he was clad. The god thereupon gave him accurate instructions for his journey. Subsequently the youth went home and had his niece steal the required objects from the neighbors.[7]

Scavenger (of the Bead Chant) was betrayed by the pueblo people, who tried to make him get eagle feathers for them; for this betrayal they were duly punished—first by the itching diseases and later by the loss of their valuables, the dancing beads. The chief's wife had substituted imitations of these wonderful beads. By pretending that he was a stranger to his brother, to whom he had taught the chant and who had not yet paid him for the instruction, Scavenger showed up the deception and got the genuine ones. After taking the beads from their owners, the brother gave them to Scavenger to pay for the chant.[8]

It would be difficult to find a better example of playing both ends against the middle or of the intricacy of Navaho reasoning. Whenever wealth is connected with ritual, the association validates ownership.

Sex Morals

Even though the encouragement of reproduction is the primary purpose of Navaho ritual, sexual matters are closely related to sorcery and evil. Since there is often merely a hairline between good and bad, numerous regulations are to be expected. Just as the basis of honesty differs from ours, so also do attitudes about sex, and just as man's relation to his fellows and to deity concerns property, so too does sex concern both property and social structure. Polygyny is a recognized institution; since it is opposed to the white man's sense of morality, to him it appears to be promiscuity and a thing to be abolished. The Navaho looks upon marriage and fidelity, whether to one or several wives, as stabilizing forces —a man assumes responsibility for wife and children; he settles down. An old man, looked down upon in his community, was condemned not for having several wives but for neglecting his offspring.

Divorce, easy among the Navaho, is public acknowledgment of friction. The father, after leaving his wife's home, the normal place for him to live, may still help provide for his children. He may be pitied for losing the privilege of getting acquainted with them.

Sexual favors are a property rather than a concern of

religion. A good deal is made of chastity in some respects; virgin children are required to perform some rite in almost every ceremony.[9] Although the War Ceremony includes sexual exhibitionism, otherwise rare, the rattlestick, the leading symbol, must be carried by a female virgin.[10] I was told that since girls lose their virginity very young, it is hard to find a virgin who qualifies. During one performance I saw, two tiny girls took turns holding the rattlestick because it had been impossible to get a virgin old enough to stand up under the strain alone.

A virgin girl and boy are required to grind medicine for the Flint Chant, but, adds the informant casually, "If children lie about their virginity, the medicine gets wet. They are dismissed and new ones are chosen."[11] Apparently chastity is a ritualistic ideal though in daily life it is preached more than practiced. Girls should be guarded, but there are so many loopholes, due mainly to the Navaho environment, that the rule is indifferently kept. Mothers urge very young daughters to participate in the Girls' (Squaw) Dance, a socio-religious rite of the War Ceremony. The girl's mother receives the money the man pays her daughter. A young man may pay a girl to dance with him exclusively, and stealing away together at this time has public sanction.

In mythology a maiden's intercourse with deity is tolerated. Certainly First Man and First Woman gloated over the relation between Changing Woman and Sun, for it was part of their plan for society even before marriage had been instituted. Other girls seduced by Sun suffered, but their distress contributed to the ceremonial order. The story of the Stricken Twins brings out several notions about children born out of wedlock.

When Talking God, dressed in his beautiful garments, appeared to the girl of fourteen ' but not yet a woman,' she was bashful, hung her head, and rubbed her feet together as bashful virgins do when a man speaks to them. After some time he succeeded in getting an answer out of her and he kept courting her gently. "I have come to seek you in marriage, but I will not coax or persuade you against your wishes," he said at length. She replied, "I have never been married. We are not fitted for each other. You are too fine a man for me. You are dressed in beautiful clothes, while I am covered with rags. Then I fear my relatives will scold me if I marry without their consent and I fear to speak to them."

"You need tell no one about it," he suggested, "and I will not tell anyone. Such is the custom of my people. We wed in secret and tell no one."

After the first intercourse, she was filled with remorse and wept. She feared to face her parents lest they learn her secret and kill her. When she got home she was feverish with uneasiness. Her parents said nothing and she met Talking God three times more. When twin boys were born to her, her parents' concern, apparently the real reason for punishment, was to learn who the father was. They kept her from sleeping; they even threatened to kill her if she did not tell. She said she did not know and her brother interceded for her, saying perhaps her lover was one of the gods.

Since the family seemed to believe this, they were kind to the boys until their first disappearance and the strange experience which left one lame and the other blind. The family had no way of caring for two extra members who could not make a living, and the story goes on endlessly, showing the family sometimes overcome with pity for the twins and at others blaming the mother bitterly for their poverty and hard life. The reproach was that her lover was not known, not that she was unmarried.[12]

The problem of the unmarried girl with a child is economic and social rather than ethical. No payment has been made for the girl; the family has an extra person to support without the aid of a son-in-law. In myth, though the reward is long delayed, the ceremonial lore, a tribal asset, offsets the marriage requirements.

Adultery is intercourse with a married woman that is not

subsequently paid for, being considered a violation of a man's rights to his wife's person. Since fidelity is not uniformly expected, the payment is made to silence the husband's complaints or truculence. Its significance is economic rather than moral.

Seduction of a youth by the wife of a powerful being may be the motivation of a myth; calming the husband's spirit of revenge may be the reason for the origin of the myth.

Bat helped Rainboy of the Hail Chant to escape a beating by the townspeople, then turned him loose to live by his own skill. Rainboy was attracted to the home of Winter Thunder, whose wife seduced him. In revenge Winter Thunder destroyed him and the Hail Chant was devised to restore Rainboy. The whole purpose of the story seems to be to demonstrate the innocence of the hero, for he was lassoed by the woman with a supernatural rainbow. It took great effort on the part of many gods to render the extreme jealousy of Winter Thunder harmless.[13]

Beautiful wealthy women with a subtle smile are a decoy for innocent young men, but when the youths yield, they gain power and ritualistic lore through their subsequent suffering (*Decoy woman*, Concordance B).[14]

Adultery may be mentioned quite casually, but is not condoned; it usually reflects upon the husband, for it demonstrates his weakness.

The fourth chief of the Translucent Rock People was called the Unlucky One or the One-cheated-by-his-wife because his spouse was unfaithful.[15]

Women of Big Knee's settlement were unfaithful to their husbands. Big Knee had twelve wives and complained to their relatives about their behavior with other men. "He used to give much of his abundant harvests to the clans to which his wives belonged, but, in spite of his generosity, they were unfaithful to him." In vain the clansmen moralized with the women and finally told the chief he would have to settle the matter himself; they said they would approve of anything he did. He then shamefully mutilated one of his wives and she died. He cut off the ears of the next one he caught and she died. He cut the breasts off the third and she died. He amputated the nose of the fourth and she survived. He then decreed that cutting the nose should be the maximum punishment for infidelity—it disfigured but did not kill. Matthews remarks that in his day such severe punishment did not prevail among the Navaho, the maximum being a mild whipping.[16]

The tale continues with the revenge of the women, which closely parallels that of the War Ceremony legend; doubtless their spite is a reason adultery is today so lightly regarded.

The Navaho believe that all secrets, even those of sorcery, are divulged during sexual intercourse.

Deer Owner, the incestuous sorcerer who had his daughter for a wife, communicated to her his most cherished lore by means of which he kept rare game from Earth People and killed their gifted youths. When Self Teacher freed her from her father-husband's power, she taught her new lover the secrets that released the game and brought about Deer Owner's downfall.[17]

Changing-bear-maiden, unlike the normal Navaho girl, repulsed the advances of many suitors by pronouncing charms and formulas too strong for their power. Coyote overcame her resistance, having as an aim the acquisition of her lore as well as the satisfaction of his lust. As they indulged, they exchanged powers, teaching each other their most precious secrets, which had to be exorcised as evils by The Youngest Brother, who had heard the secrets whispered.[18]

The Endurance Chant tale points out the dangers of intercourse when trying to keep a secret, and at the same time condemns overindulgence. The chant so oddly referred to by Kluckhohn and Father Berard as ' Prostitution Way ' ('adjiłe·')[19] has a similar moral, or rather seeks to undo the effects of any kind of recklessness. It may be sung to encourage success in love, trading, and gambling, and to dissipate the evil results of uncontrolled lust. Except for sexual indulgence, none of the things for which it is prescribed has even a remote relation to prostitution, and the name is misleading on other grounds; it assumes that the Navaho institutionalize prostitution and class all recklessness with it. Therefore to call the chant Prostitution Way, besides being inaccurate, is insulting to the person it is sung over, since a married man may need it as well as one who contemplates a dangerous undertaking. 'Excess,' 'Recklessness,' or 'Rashness' Chant would more accurately suggest its meaning.

If prostitution is defined as payment for women's favors, the Girls' Dance and even the betrothal should be so classed. I do not accept this definition or classification. Occasionally a girl refuses to marry, lives alone, and has many male visitors, or a girl may move about from settlement to settlement, creating jealousy among the women, who say of her, "She has no mother." They do not mean that she is bereaved, but that she is responsible to no one; such a girl is, in Navaho eyes, a prostitute.

Several other customs regulate matters that in our moral code are classed with sex. The Navaho recognize and traditionally sanction the status of the transvestite (nádle·); the hermaphrodite is a frequent figure in their mythology. Its origin goes back to the third world, when the hermaphrodites learned all about the work of men and women and lived as women. They invented pottery, the gourd dipper, the metate, the hairbrush, the stirring sticks, and the water jar. Matthews places their origin in the fourth world and adds that they went with the men when the sexes separated. As the first hermaphrodite was also the first person to die and was seen at the place of emergence, such abnormal creatures are associated with death.[20]

Very little is known at first hand about the hermaphrodite

and transvestite, although they seem not to have been as rare in the past as they are today. Hill gives hearsay evidence about five, and recounts his own acquaintance with one. Another was tłǎ·h, frequently referred to in this work.[21] Hill does not record that, as a baby on the way back from Ft. Sumner, tłǎ·h was emasculated in an attack by the Utes, and later became a transvestite. When I knew him just before his death, he was very much like other men in appearance, voice, and manner. He wore male attire. He wove blankets—among the Navaho the women are weavers—but only with sand-painting designs, which were a part of his professional knowledge. I am pretty sure that had there been no rumors or whispers, no white person would have picked him out of a Navaho crowd as abnormal.

Hill describes the role of the sexually abnormal among the Navaho and gives a picture of Kinipai, who said she was a true hermaphrodite and wanted to be considered a female. He concludes that such children were regarded as fortunate, were treated as favorites, and that respect for them increased with time. They are said to bring riches, of which they have charge. tłǎ·h was exceedingly clever, and ability to achieve at both men's and women's work would certainly double a person's resources. His aptitude for his singing profession would have enriched him in any case.

Certain questions arise in connection with Hill's conclusions. Was the respect accorded such persons due to their abnormality? Was it because bisexualism belonged with the underworld, in both origin and its association with death and other forms of evil? Was transvestitism respected because it was unusual and therefore dangerous? Since abnormality, the lower worlds, death, and wealth belong in the class of things feared, it seems to me that the answer is positive. It should be pointed out, too, that Kinipai was eager to speak of her own sexual experiences and sorcery, yet was afraid to discuss dreams (Chapter 6). Hill suggests that tłắ·h rationalized the position of the hermaphrodite in the Navaho pantheon. Possibly he did, since he rationalized many phases of religion and was much more aware of consistency in our sense than any other Navaho I ever met.[22]

Animals and Plants

Prevailing attitudes about animals and plants are discussed as a concern of ethics, since they involve a curious aspect of humaneness and contribute also to the understanding of the contrast between daily behavior and ritualistic procedure.

The Navaho treatment of animals is a paradox. Although for years the tribe has depended upon domesticated animals for subsistence, the religion still emphasizes the rare game animals, which are almost as scarce in the Navaho environment as in ours. The belief that wild animals are helpers of human beings has not been laid aside now that game has been supplanted by the more easily obtainable sheep, goat, or steer. If a few, such as Bear and Snake, are difficult to persuade, the Navaho puts himself out a little more than usual so he will not incur their wrath. Yet for the domesticated animals upon which he depends for food he has little religious respect; to him they are property rather than sentient beings. The old-fashioned Navaho counts his wealth in horses, yet his best specimen is, according to white standards, a nag. He is interested in how many he has, which will win a race, how far his pet will carry him. He is not particularly concerned that most range horses are skin and bones, that his favorite horse is exhausted long before it arrives at its destination, or that the race may ruin the horse. He pushes it to the limit, never for a moment considering that the horse might suffer.

Better treated are sheep and goats, not because they are

respected like the wild animals but because sheep are the most direct source of satisfaction—they furnish the daily meal. They are despised because they have no sense—"they cannot take care of themselves." Sheep are a ceremonial substitute for rare game, but, unlike them, have no supernatural powers; each family has fetishes with prayers sacred to sheep and horses so that there may be rapid and easy increase, but the Navaho do not expect to get power from them, except indirectly through wealth.

The difference in the treatment of the horse and of the dog and cat is great; respect for the horse as property is one extreme, and contempt for a non-contributing, hence despised, form of life is the opposite. Most Navaho dogs are only incidentally or perhaps accidentally useful: some help with the sheep; some guard the house—if the viciousness of a pack of hungry dogs with tails between their legs can be called guardianship; some afford pleasure to adults and children alike. All the dog stories I have heard to the contrary notwithstanding, I have never seen a well-trained, reliable sheep dog. The dog is considered another, hardly a higher, form of coyote. In myth and dogma its place is despicable, for it has the undesirable characteristics of the coyote and little, if any, of its power. One need not fear the dog or cat; both reproduce so freely that the supply need not be fostered, as is the case with sheep.

An adult Navaho does not intercede for a dog tormented by children; he laughs with them at its agony and helplessness. He does not put a superfluous litter or a sick animal out of its misery. He may take it out into the desert where its chances of living are even poorer than at home. When asked why they thus prolong its suffering, a Navaho told me, "It has its life. You wouldn't deprive it of that. But if it can't take care of itself, you can't help that either."

143

In strange contrast is the attitude toward flowers. The Navaho do not cultivate flowers for their beauty; white people often find them unwilling to work in a flower garden. Yet descriptions of landscape show great appreciation of abundant wild flowers. Every plant is a symbol of vegetation without which neither man nor animals could exist. Flowers, therefore, are treated ceremonially. To pick them without taking them into ritual, to let them wither as cut flowers is quite out of order, even dangerous, there being no aesthetic compensation for the fear such sacrilege may engender.

PART TWO
SYMBOLISM

CHAPTER 9

THE NATURE OF SYMBOLISM

THE EXAMINATION of concepts has implied that there is a
system by means of which they are held together, a co-
ordination of series of symbols with special significance, so
projected as to fit into a comprehensive pattern. The pattern includes everything in the dogma and ritual; all the
diverse elements are combined in a unit, actually a philosophy
of life and preservation. By association the elements are
drawn into a whole, so subtly that many of the people concerned may be unaware of it. The scheme may be compared
with a language. The ordinary speaker, using it merely for
communication, is unconscious of its components—sounds,
grammatical forms expressing concepts, and, above all,
meanings. The linguist who analyzes the language finds
general principles and interpretations that apply not only to
the language under consideration but also to other tongues,
even to language in general. The speaker, who has never
thought about these matters, may even deny that general-
izations are possible.

Similarly, Navaho ritual is composed of symbols, each of
which may differ in kind as much as phonetics, psychological
concepts, and individual significations. Yet the whole is com-
prehended in varying degrees, even if only through feeling
and faith. Since the associations are inculcated by a lifetime
of continuous habituation, it is not to be expected that many,
if any, of the Navaho could formulate them; indeed, most
Navaho would be surprised to learn that anyone should want

147

to. A few chanters, the learned men of the tribe, realize that snakes, lightnings, arrows, flints, hoops, and precious stones are associated—' the same,' they would call them; many do not. The latter are content to depict in sandpainting Snake as a person of zigzag shape, to sing of zigzag lightning, to relate the incident of Arrow People in myth, and to cause flints to rattle in a basket, without mentally making any connection between them. The fact that they do not is no proof that the associations are not integrated.

I do not, therefore, consider my analysis of symbolism one any Navaho would or could make; I do not even maintain that any does. Many, however, have contributed verification to the scheme piece by piece, so to speak, as did Jeff King when he said that, though The Twins were only two, they were four (Chapter 4). I derived the system from detailed study of drypaintings, masks, prayersticks, and other tangible elements of rituals, combined with widely scattered remarks in the explanatory myths. In addition, by extensive comparisons and discussions, I investigated the meaning of many words that enter into religious concepts. Moreover, armed with mythological and linguistic information, I was able through my own participation in the rites to make inquiries about the function of items and procedure that would not otherwise have occurred to me, inquiries that elicited responses often as surprising to me as they may be to the reader.

As we have seen, the universe is conceived as a place for man, and all natural phenomena are interpreted as his allies or enemies. Gods are defined as human personifications, sometimes with only a single or minor power but one helpful to man. Man has had to discover techniques to manipulate the deities so as to divert their powers in his favor; even skills and cultural institutions—knowledge of hunting and agriculture, marriage, clan organization, co-operation with tribal and extra-tribal individuals, language—have a focus in the harmony into which all are inextricably combined. The chant or ceremony with its myth is a means of co-ordinating the various details of the dogma.

The symbolic details are not necessarily construed in exactly the same way, even in a given tale, and generally they differ from myth to myth. Nevertheless, when the interpretations change, a comparison of many myths yields associations ultimately valid. For instance, the transformation of corn ears into human beings indicates an obvious association between wind and breath, and cross references establish whorls—through whirlwinds—as elements of the associative group; hence the explanation that breath enters the body at the places where there are whorls. Since down is easily set in motion by wind or breath, down feathers and motion are further extensions of the group.

By identification, a symbol that stands for a power is the power. Hence to understand the symbol with its various meanings is to comprehend the power and the techniques required to invoke it. The symbols have many manifestations; even negation has become one, for it is as important to know what to omit and why as to know what to include. Knowledge, therefore, is power derived through a long and involved process of learning divulged by the myths. Step by step a hero attains divinity as he progresses from one adventure to another. The remark of the singer of the War Ceremony illustrates the transformation from divine personage to power and its control: "Black God would scarcely consider Monster Slayer a patient, but a power, which disease always fears."[1]

He who would control the various supernaturals must start with the aid of mentors, who give him foreknowledge; he must be willing to put forth effort and to profit by it; he must submit to tests which require great courage; and eventually, as a human being, he must identify himself with divinity. Later, becoming an intermediary—transformed from human hero to god, subsequently represented by the chanter—he must take over responsibility for his fellow men.

When Big Monster aimed his flint club at The Twins, Sun, their mentor, told them by exactly how much the club would miss the mark, so that they were able to avoid it each time. The Youngest Brother was warned not to allow Changing-bear-maiden to help him with even one finger out of the hole in which he was hidden, lest by so doing she condemn him to the powers of evil she herself had embraced through Coyote's diabolic offices. [2]

Just as the cause of illness may be vague, so the hero was exposed to uncertainty in handling numerous situations, but from each sprang some essential good, to be brought back and incorporated in the resulting chant. The wanderings of the Stricken Twins demonstrate the trial and error, the effort and perseverance necessary to the culmination of the Night Chant. The Stricken Twins put themselves into a position worthy of divine aid; they acceded to requirements no matter how difficult; they emerged from their tribulations to endow their fellow men with the greatest of the ceremonies.

A hero undergoes tests which give him power. Each test is a symbol to prove his strength. The frequently recurring smoking test is an excellent example. The entire complex of incidents that describe the journey of The Twins to the home of their father is an elaborate test of judgment and worth which does not end until the evils have been destroyed and their powers brought back to man.

Effort must be expended by all connected with a chant, since they emulate the deities who control it. The patient must submit to the ritual; whether or not he understands its details, he takes all the ritualistic acts on faith, even though he may occasionally rebel at the requirements (Chapter 6). The sponsor for the ceremony indicates his willingness to conform by producing the property necessary to its conclusion. Ritual often demands the rare or remote herbs, minerals, or animals, known to exist only in restricted and isolated spots. The water that goes into the so-called ' collected waters ' must be gathered after a pilgrimage to the top of the sacred mountains or to the oceans on each side of the continent (see *Rain Ceremony*, Concordance C). I took RP a bottle of water from the Hudson River, but there was doubt about its power since it had not been ritualistically obtained. It proved its worth because rain fell on the day it was first used, but it probably never functioned as powerfully as it would have had it been properly collected.

Laymen assist the chanter by going on long, tedious, or dangerous journeys to procure ceremonial properties. I once drove TC and an old man on a day and night journey of a hundred and thirty-five miles just to get a single pine twig that had only one bud—two or three buds are more common—and a few twigs of blue spruce. TC could not see from the ground how many buds the pine twig had. He climbed about twenty feet to the lowest branch of yellow pine, crawled out on various branches until he saw the required kind on another tree, then swung himself across from one branch to another. We all derived benefit from the quest—I because I furnished transportation, TC because, after exposing himself to danger, he got the right twig, the old man because he directed us.

The expenditure of care and time is well documented by myth. Often tasks are more difficult for gods and intermediaries than they are for man himself. When Talking God was conducting the hero of the Night Chant on a tour of the homes of the gods, other gods abducted him, thus delaying his progress.

The combination of symbols representing many kinds of power establishes the ceremony's success. The symbols may be isolated, even though each has most significance in its relation to others.

The following words express the ideas discussed in this section:

'adzi·l, ' complete power, natural and acquired, strength, endurance.'

'álí·l, ' power acquired through knowledge, control,' hence, ' magic ' and ' each or all items included in its acquisition and manifestation.'

yictcí·n, ' symbol, imitation, small likeness, representation of '; ' sample, token.'

bíxo·"ą̊·"i·, ' knowledge.'

Place and Position

Since supernatural occurrences must be recapitulated, it is important to set the stage for every rite; therefore place is an outstanding symbol. Names of mountains are constantly repeated in prayer, song, and myth. One of the most difficult of the hero's tests, a formal requirement of his instruction, was to name every holy place on the earth as he looked upon the panorama from a great height.[3] Sandpaintings have some representation of the setting where a supernatural event took place. If a painting has a linear arrangement of figures, the symbol is a bar upon which they stand; if the layout is circular, the place symbol—representing mountains, lakes, or other bodies of water, habitation, ladders leading from one kind of world to another—is at the center. Rainbow, Dawn, Blue Sky, Yellow-evening-light, Darkness are other representations of place and time which may be simultaneous or interchangeable.[4]

The care taken by the gods in choosing a site for a ceremony is emulated today when the Navaho discuss long and earnestly the most favorable place:

The gods had agreed to help the Stricken Twins by a ceremony held at House-where-they-move-about, but when the twins disregarded a restriction, the whole ceremony was called off. Much later the deities consented again to try a cure, discussing for an entire night a proper place for the chant. They argued that since the previous ceremony had been broken off at House-where-they-move-about, it must be a place of ill fortune, and they decided to have it at Broad Rock, where it was successful.[5]

As part of their instruction, heroes may be taken on long tours; they visit the deific homes and often, by merely being introduced to a god, receive great favors. The hero must remember every detail of the idealized home, and subsequently mention it repeatedly in song, prayer, and descriptions of ceremonial properties. The Sun's House screen, symbol of a branch of the Male Shooting Chant Holy, is an example of a place—Sun's home—selected as a chant theme (Chapter 19). A chanter gives his assistants the most careful instructions about placing the prayersticks, and they pay close attention, because place is of primary value in invoking the gods for whom the prayersticks are made (Chapter 18).

Just as purification differentiates the sacred from the profane, or marks the transition from the secular to the divine, place dictates a person's behavior in his own or in foreign territory. Things happen to him abroad which he can later control by remembrance and recapitulation at home, as the War Ceremony demonstrates. Its events are divided between those on (facing) enemy territory and those within the Navaho boundary. To indicate the change, the ' danger line ' was drawn, a mark over which the enemy feared to pass. Consisting of zigzag lightning, flash lightning, sunstreamer, and rainbow, it was supposed to deter the enemy from overtaking the victorious Navaho as they raced homeward with booty and captives. At the front the line's power was put to a more severe test; the Navaho depended upon it to stop the advancing foe. It is the theme of a song, "I make a mark, they cannot cross it." [6]

When Monster Slayer was preparing his men for the attack on Taos he ' talked out '—that is, excoriated the enemy in prayer—and, in addition, ' drew a line out there in the valley against the enemy, a line the enemy must not pass.' [7]

The protection of the line was demonstrated also when Monster Slayer made a mark with his club to prevent two pools of Big Monster's blood from meeting as they flowed over the land. Had they joined, the slaying would have been in vain. [8]

To illustrate the hold of place upon the Navaho, let us recall the Male Shooting Chant Evil, sung for CM to rid him of the results of breaking the continence restriction after his first wife's death (Chapter 6). CM had thoroughly identified himself with RP's home for several reasons: he had been happily married to RP's daughter for many years; he had no mother or close maternal relatives and, therefore, no home in the Navaho sense; his brother, TC, with whom he was very congenial, lived at RP's settlement with his wife, MC, another of RP's daughters; CM had learned much about ceremony from RP, whom he frequently assisted.

It would have been proper to have had the chant at the settlement of his second wife, Mrs. CM, particularly since her adopted father was a great singer, and her brother-in-law, who also lived there, was the officiating chanter. Moreover, RP's children were friendly to the members of Mrs. CM's family. Had the ceremony been held at Mrs. CM's home, RP's daughter and granddaughter would have had no right to dictate about it; they would have been guests instead of hosts, and the unfortunate situation described in Chapter 6 would not have arisen, or at least would not have been noticeable. Why then did CM choose to have the chant performed at RP's? ' Place ' seems to be the reason. RP's house had for years been a center of ceremonials—in Navaho eyes, a fortunate place. RP had endowed it with a spirit precious to the Navaho and sensed even by whites.[9] CM felt at home there; in fact, after his second marriage he sometimes returned to work with his brother for several weeks at a time. To him it seemed a more propitious setting for his undertaking than his second wife's home, the best substitute he had for his mother's; the feeling was thoroughly reciprocated by RP's children.

Place, representative of a power, must be distinguished from position, a symbol of magical manipulation. There is a spot in the lodge or its environs that patient, chanter, assistant, and each member of the audience should occupy; no other will do. Position was emphasized in the description of deity (Chapter 4), and just as persons have their places, so ceremonial items must be exactly placed, particularly in relation to one another. The chanter relentlessly insists upon such order.

Once tłá·h had a disagreement with another chanter about the order of prayersticks in a rite performed for tłá·h's nephew. Neither gave in and for days tłá·h voiced deep resentment because he considered the order a mistake which must inevitably have an untoward effect upon the patient, an effect tłá·h could see no way of preventing.

Each member of a family has a stipulated place within the hogan—the unmarried men at the south, the single women at the north; the bed of the senior married couple joins the male and female sides of the house at the west. In the ceremonial hogan (or shade) the men usually sit at the south, the women at the north; patient and chanter sit at the rear—that is, at the west side behind the fire. If there are variations on this plan, they are due to ritualistic requirements. For example, the patient of the Shooting Chant, male or female, sits alone at the south side of the hogan during the ' short singing ' of the first three nights.

Frequently, though not invariably, certain deities have characteristic stations with respect to others. Talking God, as a leader, had the front position when he traveled with a group on one of the supernatural conveyances. He stood on a rainbow at the front while xa·ctćé·'óγan stood at the back, and the accompanying group of Holy People, or the hero they conducted, stood between them. In the Night Chant, Talking God at the front was aided by Water Sprinkler at the rear, while Visionary, whom they were escorting, was between. When the gods took Self Teacher to the underwater world, Water Sprinkler guarded the front and Black God the back; thus protected, Self Teacher was led safely out from the home of Water Monster.[10]

Even the body position of deities may be distinctive. People in myth are told, for instance, that Black God, though so old he can scarcely walk, may be recognized by his upright sitting posture. They find him sitting with one leg hanging limply over his knee, a posture signifying aloofness, which must be overcome by the proper approach of those asking a favor (see *Ceremonial indifference*, Concordance B). The same pose is assumed in life by a Navaho whose feelings have been hurt; usually he takes up a position half sitting, half reclining in front of the fire, ' among the ashes,' a place ordinarily avoided. His position and attitude indicate that

156

some member of the family must guess at the offense under which he feels himself suffering and make restitution to bring him to a normal frame of mind and, incidentally, to his proper place in the family circle.[11]

In the House Blessing song of the Shooting Chant the following sequence is mentioned: east post, west post, south post, north post, outside layer of earth on the roof, the layer of bark that holds the layer of earth, the back of the interior, the center (symbol of the fireplace), and the place of the metate just north of the door.[12] The places indicated in prayer include those just named, but extend the locality somewhat. The singer asks blessings for the patient: from the hogan roof, through the inside of the house sunwise around the fire, and out the door to the immediate vicinity of the dwelling, where the gods protectingly encircle it, and farther to the plants, trees, and rocks. The space indicated is safe for the patient because it is circumscribed, but it is universally extended when the prayer includes Mountain Woman, Water Woman, various birds, and many distant sacred localities.

The sequence illustrates the role played by space in the attraction of good. The patient derives most from the chant because it is performed for him. A few persons may act as co-patients; they benefit proportionately as they participate in the rites. The chanter's assistants get a spiritual reward for their help; the audience, by participating in such activities as medicine drinking, pollen sprinkling, ashes blowing, and singing, and even by their very presence, gain blessings. The Navaho believe that every chant adds to the general well-being of the tribe. For this reason in a prosperous year much wealth is expended on elaborate chants, for singing is still the preferred investment. As the blessings of such chants spread, the more there are the more likely they are to fill the territory occupied by those who believe in them. Conversely, when

SYMBOLISM

times are bad, great efforts are made to hold as many ceremonies as possible, since they alone can change ill fortune
into good.

The attitude toward space is manifested also by the feeling
that persists about outsiders. One reason the Navaho do not
wish to teach their lore to strangers is that they ' will take it
outside of the tribe,' a reason too why formerly they did not
approve of sending their children to school. My case was
nicely rationalized: "She will always come back, so she will
not be taking it away."

Space is involved in exorcism as well as in attraction, but
in reverse. Whereas the attractive techniques of the Holy
chants aim to concentrate as much as possible of the good
within a territory, the manipulation of the Evil chants
attempts to disperse evil, the farther the better, the idea
being that the more space around each evil, the less its power.
As evil is driven out, good must be enticed to fill the space;
consequently, exorcism alone would not suffice. These principles are closely correlated with the concept that foreign
things, being distributed over large areas and subject to
techniques not under Navaho control, are most dangerous of
all. The tenets explain the fear of the indefinite and the
endeavor to narrow undefined causes to those whose control
is understood.

Time and Timing

From some viewpoints time is eternal, having no beginning
or end. Once an event has taken place, its effects may be
repeated at any future time; for instance, occurrences in the
underworlds still affect this world and man. MC was sung
over for illness contracted years after she had been in a place
contaminated by lightning; BWW became confused long
after the trail to the deer impound had lost its function

(though it had not been forgotten, Chapter 6); a person may suffer because of parental infringement of a restriction before his birth. A man who looks upon a bone of one of the ancient people subjects himself to attack from alien ghosts; moreover, if he should do so while his wife is pregnant, the child at any time during its life may be attacked by foreign ghosts.[13]

The experiences of the people in the nether worlds are concerned more with chronology than with lapse of time. We are told what happened, not how long it took. Myth may refer to a number of days, yet no statement is made as to how long a day lasted—it may have been years or only the period between sunrise and sunset. However, the explanation of Sun's daily and seasonal journeys (Chapter 2) shows an interest in the etiology of time, as did First Man when he created the world.

After making a miniature of the world, in which he imitated its present physiography, First Man drew a diagram on the ground to indicate the seasons. He divided it into halves—winter and summer—then into thirteen subdivisions, standing for the months, to which he gave names such as month of the slender wind (November), month of snow crust (January), month of the eaglets (February), month of shedding antlers (March), month of delicate leaves (April), month of enlarging seeds (August), month of maturing vegetation (September), and the like. To each he gave a ' soft feather '— that is, an indication of life and good fortune—and a heart. For example, the month of crusted snow had Morningstar for its soft feather and ice for its heart; month of large leaves had Wind for its heart, rain for its soft feather. The months were designated as times of reproduction and growth —when mountain sheep mate, when deer shed their antlers, when antelope drop their fawns, when fruits ripen.[14]

A major division of day and night fits the dogma—during

the day good may be expected; night is the time when ghosts, Coyote, and other evil powers hold sway. To receive Sun's blessing, many rites must be performed in daylight hours. Sandpaintings of the Holy chants should be laid and disposed of during sunlight hours. On the other hand, those of the exorcistic chants are made and used during the hours of darkness (Chapter 11, *Reversal*).

Although temporal duration is of little moment, timing is a major device of the ceremonial order. Timing is related to number, direction, song, offering, prayer, and all other elements that make up the chant, since, to be effective, each must come in at exactly the right time. Timing measures the number of nights of a chant's duration and determines the sequence of events. In addition, some events must occur simultaneously. Most frequently, ritualistic acts are accompanied by song; certain motions, passes, and gestures depend not only upon the song but upon its very wording. Foam for the bath is made from the yucca root to the accompaniment of song; pollens are sprinkled across the foam at a particular word of the song. In like manner, the pollen ball of the Shooting Chant is administered, the knots of the plant garment are cut as significant phrases are sung.

Materials from which ceremonial properties are made are considered as ' natural '—that is, ' neutral '—with a potentiality for good which, by ritualistic performance, may be enhanced so as to sanctify the resulting item, giving it active instead of merely potential power. To watch the laying of a sandpainting may be somewhat dangerous for the uninitiated who has not been sung over. A chanter has undergone many performances of the chant he knows—for his initiation, for the dedication of specific chant properties, for renewal of his power—and therefore need not fear it. Although the layman may not witness the preparation of objects used in the chant sung for him, the chanter should participate in almost every activity. There is, however, a time when even he must not witness the completion of the sandpainting preparation, a moment of sanctification when the painting becomes sacred —the instant when the encircling guardian of the sandpainting is started.

JS was sung over at a performance of the Sandpainting branch of the Male Shooting Chant Holy for the purpose of making and dedicating four wide boards and four talking prayersticks for his bundle. He helped with all the sandpaintings, but gathered up his blanket and cigarettes and went out just before the painters began to lay the encircling guardian. One day, however, they forgot that he was in the hogan—or perhaps did not know of the restriction—and started to work on the feet and skirt of the encircling rainbow while he was still putting the finishing touches on another figure. When he saw what had happened, he called out, grabbed his blanket, told the men to erase the figure and remake it. He did not return until it was finished.

The Hoop Transformation rite (Male Shooting Chant Evil) requires a representation of four mountains with an arrangement of hoops, sand designs, and feathers, all outside the hogan. Anyone may watch the construction of this feature; animals must be kept away from it. After each part has been set up, a trail of corn meal connects each part and leads into the hogan. When, to complete the whole, two eagle tail feathers are crossed on top of each mountain, the Hoop Transformation arrangement becomes sacred; the instant of placing the feathers becomes the moment of consecration.

Direction

The earliest witness of a Navaho ceremony noted direction as a symbolic device. Matthews discussed ' the laws of butts and tips ' at length and amply illustrated them in his later works.[15] These laws are constantly observed and I need merely summarize their significance. Plants, like other living

161

things, are ritualistically dealt with from base to tip, because
growth, and therefore life, is upward. The earth may be the
ultimate cause of all that is good—reproduction, vegetation,
and power of attainment—but it holds within it the evils
beaten into it at the War Ceremony. If the directional symbolism, which is relative, not fixed, is to represent growth,
the ritualistic act must be upward, but since the sky also
furnishes gifts, it must be included. Since rain falls, there
must be downward motions.[16]

The number of ritualistic directions may be interpreted in
several ways. They may be counted as five—east, south,
west, north, and up-and-down (in a single motion); as six—
the same with up and down counted separately; as seven—
the same as for six with the addition of ' around.' Perhaps
up and down may be considered a single direction as often as
two, being indicated by a single continuous motion of the
hand. Pollen sprinkling and other ritualistic acts may become
so perfunctory that the motions in all directions—east,
south, west, north, around, up, down—are so continuous as
to seem like one.

A quadrant as well as a line may indicate a direction: by
east the southeast quadrant may be meant; by south, the
southwest; by west, the northwest; and by north, the northeast. Since there are two ways of designating these directions
—a circle from east to north in sunwise direction and a cross
from east to west and south to north—the one may represent
the quadrant, the other the trail. The track of turkey approaching its master includes both the line and the quadrant
division of the circle, and the combination of the turkey track
with that of its master shows the cross line for the turkey, the
arc for the master.[17]

Circular space—the hogan or circular sandpainting—may
be divided into quadrants by imaginary lines or by crosses,

Greek and Maltese. When the arrangement of figures is linear, each retains its theoretical direction, although the onlooker may not be aware what it is. For instance, in a sandpainting of the Mountain Chant there are four figures of Long Bodies in a line. The northernmost (black) is said to belong to the north, the one under it (white) to the east, the next below (blue) to the south, and the bottom one (yellow) to the west. I mention the colors because they are differentiating, but directions and colors do not always have the same meaning in linear paintings (Chapter 13). For example, figures of a painting belonging to the Navaho Wind Chant in the Bush Collection are said to belong to the following directions: Snake at top (black) to the north, Snake next below (blue) to the west, Snake next (yellow) to the south, Snake at bottom (white) to the east.[18]

The subdivisions of the day are associated with directions— Dawn with the east, Day Sky with the south, Yellow-evening-light with the west, and Darkness or Night with the north.

The rule of the open circle (Chapter 6) affects the directional circuit. When a patient is told to make the ceremonial circuit and return to his original position, he is warned not to complete the turn when reversing. He is, of course, unavoidably moving anti-sunwise when returning. The following excerpts from myth describe the path:

When First Man saw the cloud that indicated a wonderful happening—the cradle with the baby who later became Changing Woman—he ascended the mountain over which it hung, first from the east side, then from the south, west, and north, each time having gone to the foot of the mountain before ascending in a new direction. To get the cradleboard he had to go east, but, instead of going from north to east, he returned without crossing his own path.[19]

The path First Man took when he discovered Changing Woman is exactly the same as the one she herself customarily traveled when walking about on the sacred mountains.[20]

In these settings two ritualistic requirements are at odds: one decrees that the circle be left open, the other that the circuit be sunwise. The open circle wins. The countermovement is defended on the ground that the turn is not completed; to finish it would bring the patient to a starting point within a circle smaller than the original one—he would be ' winding himself in.' To turn and with care avoid crossing the path brings one back to the start in an ever-widening circle, allowing space for the exit of evil, the entrance of good. Pallbearers in their journey to the grave and back move along such a path.[21] The double ceremonial circuit is therefore a satisfactory compromise, making the best of a conflicting situation and meeting adequately the major requirement of avoiding the circle of frustration (Chapter 6).

The following are examples of progress in counter-sunwise direction:

The circular brush windbreak used on the hunt was laid out symmetrically. It was marked first from east to south to west—that is, sunwise; then the leader returned to the east and marked another semicircle from east to north to west—that is, anti-sunwise.[22]

Black God in the first world became angry at the chiefs of the four directions and broke their water jars. The waters flowed from east to south and from north to west—that is, both sunwise and anti-sunwise.[23]

On the blue and pink prayersticks of the Shooting Chant, dedicated to the Winds, the lines are to run anti-sunwise. One of the Whirlwinds moves counter-sunwise.

Talking God sprinkled pollen toward the east and north over the suds prepared for Rainboy's bath.[24]

At some points in the Restoration Rite there is anti-sunwise movement (Concordance C).

All these examples have one feature in common: they refer to extraordinary dangers—hunting, lower worlds, Undependable Deities (Winds, Whirlwinds)—which require reversal. Rainboy was a patient in the Hail Chant because Winter Thunder, exceedingly difficult to persuade, wanted revenge. The Restoration rite seeks to bring one back from the land of the dead, where all things are the reverse of those we know here.

The other cases are not difficult to explain since they occur in the War Ceremony, which may almost be said to have reversal as a theme.

While the dangers of enemy slaying were being exorcised in the War Ceremony, the beneficiary told his nieces, the Corn Maidens, to choose any men they wished for husbands. The men were standing in a line with Monster Slayer at one end. The girls circled him in a sunwise direction, then crossed their own path and went around the next dancer in a counter-sunwise direction, and so alternating to the end of the line, always keeping their own path continuous.[25]

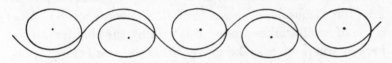

Fig. 1. Spiral path of dancers

The line of the dance was more complicated than any so far encountered, the sunwise and countersunwise circuits alternating as illustrated in Figure 1.

The Black Dancers of the War Ceremony are clowns who seem to break every rule. It is, therefore, not surprising to note that the mixture of mud and dung with which they are smeared is applied to one in a sunwise direction, to the next anti-sunwise, and so alternating until all have been treated.[26]

The observance of ceremonial direction applies to the handling of ritualistic property as well as to the motion of people. Knots, for example, must be tied in a particular direction so as to preserve the open quadrant lest ghosts interfere with the life of the person tying or for whom they are tied.

Sandpaintings that seem to lack an opening are sometimes explained by what appears to be clever rationalization. An odd composition is that of Scavenger in the Eagles' Nest.[27] Scavenger appears in the circle of the nest, but he is not really enclosed, for his head is over the circular lines at the east; incidentally, the design so produced is artistically effective.

The painting of White Coiled Mountain[28] seems to break the rules. If we trace the white snake from the head, it moves anti-sunwise. If, however, we start from the tail—as the Navaho tell us—the coiling is sunwise, but the tail starts out of the western instead of the eastern quadrant of the mountain it represents. Since it is coiled, it is thought of as projecting upward in a spiral, an effect that extends its power into the atmosphere above (*Spiral*, Concordance B). The circle of small snakes around it is said by the chanters to be broken wherever a snake moves after the one before it; all are obviously moving sunwise.

I have examined many sandpaintings in addition to those published. Few have exceptions to the rules of direction and, unfortunately, there are no explanatory data for these, or at best only indefinite suggestions.

Plate VI of Oakes and Campbell has two figures, War Gods, each within a colored frame, which is said to be "a rainbow of protection and strength." Plate XIII is also completely bordered by a rainbow, which the singer explains: "This painting is from Blessing Way, and is very holy. It is given, so that each man will have a personal blessing that has nothing to do with war" (cp. Chapter 19). Both paintings were executed in corn meal, powdered petals, and various pollens.[29]

A possible reason for complete enclosure is apparent in the notes given by the singer; since the pictures represent blessings only, there can be no evil about them. They are like the hoop-enclosed space referred to in Chapter 6, thoroughly circumscribed, protected.

One sometimes reads that the opening of a sandpainting is ' always ' at the east. It usually is, since the Navaho dwelling or ceremonial enclosure faces east. Medicine men strewing sand in a non-Navaho building have to decide upon an expedient set of directions. For example, the entrance to a museum or department store may be out of sight of the place where the painting is to be laid; east is arbitrarily determined and a prayer is offered to make the decision correct. On one occasion the chanter laid all the pictures on the floor of a warehouse just in front of the door, which opened to the south. He had, therefore, to choose whether the paintings should open at the east, which meant toward a wall, or at the direction corresponding with the entrance. His solution was simple: for the occasion, four days, he said the south would be east. The broken circle orientation superseded the absolute directional requirement.

After remarking the rarity of mirror symmetry, especially in the circular sandpaintings, I became acquainted with the paintings of *Navajo Medicine Man*, Plates I-X, laid out in mirror symmetry, requiring half the picture to be read sunwise, half anti-sunwise. The Bead Chant, to which these pictures belong, is concerned with eagles in a realm alien to the hero.[30] The chant is associated with eagle trapping; hence the central theme is exorcistic—hunting is a dangerous and uncertain undertaking. The symmetrical arrangement, involving two opposite directions, may therefore be tolerated.

In winding, sunwise motion is carefully adhered to by

167

bringing the string up toward the body of the winder with the end under, as in Figure 2.

Direction with respect to the body is also observed. The right side is considered normal; the left, awkward, difficult, but not necessarily harmful or unlucky. When Turquoise Boy was placed inside Monster Slayer's thorax, Black and Yellow Wind were called upon to set him properly on the left side. "For this reason the man's offering is placed on the left [south] side of the sandpainting, the woman's on the right or north side." [31] The man's body is oriented as he comes in the door facing the rear of the hogan. I would expect the orientation to be as he faces the door, since that is the ritualistic position of the patient during the time the rite takes

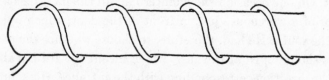

Fig. 2. Direction of winding

place. Instead, the patient's right and left are co-ordinated with his place in the house rather than with his position on the sandpainting.

Wristlets belonging to the figure-painting rite of the Male Shooting Chant Sandpainting branch were put first on the right wrist, then on the left.

The feet and shins of the patient are painted first on the left, then on the right in the figure-painting of the Shooting Chant.

Child-of-the-water in the belly of the fish cut his way out first on the left side, from which his head protruded, then on the right, from which his feet appeared. [32]

In the cincture rite, the knots of the strings were cut first from the front, then from the right side, the back, and finally the left side. [33]

Applications of ceremonial properties, such as the laying on of prayersticks, may be from the right foot up the side, across the body, and down the left side to the left foot, a body circuit representing ' around,' or the blessing brought by ' application ' to specific body parts—the soles of the feet, knees, palms of the hands, to the breast, the back, the shoulders, the face, the mouth, and the head.

When Rainboy was treated in the Hail Chant, the loops of the unravelers were pulled out first at the left, then at the right.[34]

Evil spirits customarily step left foot first.[35]

Body-part directions change sequence details in different chants and for different purposes. The order followed in the prayer for protection and dedication of power in Gray Eyes' version of the Shooting Chant mentions front, back, under, and above the body. The song to Monster Slayer of the War Ceremony mentions the same directions with respect to the body, and adds ' around,' these directions being preceded by emphasis on soles, toe tips, knee tips, palms, finger tips, tip of the body, tips of the shoulders, tip of the face, tip of the eyes, tip of the mouth, top of the head.[36] The purpose of this song is to identify the patient with Monster Slayer as the remains of the emetic are rubbed on his body. The ritualistic parts of the body are the same as in the blessing prayer, but ' tips ' are emphasized, the ' tip of the body ' instead of ' front and back ' because the war garb of Monster Slayer is of flint, symbolized by arrowpoints at various points of his body. Such symbols have value as identification, repetition, exaggeration.

Reversal of the rule from foot to head is explained by the following: "The prayers are like this: he [warrior] starts with the enemy's head and mentions all the different parts of his body down to the ground and ends his prayer in the ground. This is just the same as burying the man." [37]

When a sequence is given from bottom to top, the strongest color is usually at the bottom and the next strongest at the top. For instance, when the hoops of the Big Star Chant are laid flat, the twinkling (thorny) one is at the bottom; on that are white, yellow, and blue; black tops the pile. The hoops are arranged in the same sequence from south to north. Since the order in the sunwise circle is black, blue, yellow, white, and twinkling in the center, these linear arrangements from top to bottom represent the sunwise order from east to north and center last.

CHAPTER 10

SEX, DOMINANCE, AND SIZE

SINCE REPRODUCTION is a primary concern of Navaho religion, sex would be expected to be a major symbol. To understand it, the relative position of the sexes in the culture should be examined. Actually, there is little to limit what women may attain in any phase of Navaho culture.[1] Their status in the home, in the economic, social, even political life is equal to that of men. Theoretically they may reach the highest place in the religious life also, but very few women have become chanters (Introduction).

The ritualistic treatment of females contrasts somewhat with woman's high position in the tribe. The belief that the minds of women and children—the uninitiated—are weaker than those of men seems to explain, at least partly, the reason for certain sex restrictions, more numerous and more rigidly imposed upon women than men.[2]

It is often assumed that regulations against female participation in supernatural affairs are due to woman's functions—menstruation and childbearing—in many tribes believed to corrupt sacred things. Conversely, woman may be greatly feared because her sexual role puts her into extraordinary rapport with the supernatural. She may, therefore, have to observe restrictions so as not to endanger the male members of the tribe. Both these ideas—fear of woman's corrupting influence and wonder at her power—are prevalent in many North American tribes, but I have found no evidence that the Navaho subscribe to either.

The Navaho try to protect everyone against woman's physical weakness; once strengthened by ritual, a woman may undertake and withstand anything a man can. Her protection is quantitative rather than qualitative—she needs more than a man, but the character of the prophylactic or defensive measures is the same. I am constantly amazed that the Navaho never questioned why a woman should undertake the task I proposed—learning the religion. Never have I been excluded from any rite on the grounds of my sex, nor was my right to an interest in ritual ever challenged because I am a woman. As the particular cases illustrate, the reasons for restrictions were most often lack of supernatural armor, a shortcoming common to both sexes.

tłá·h's response to my request that he dictate the story of the Hail Chant is instructive. At first he demurred without saying why. Explaining that I had had the story of the Shooting Chant in my possession and had been sung over twice because I wanted to learn more about it, I showed him my bead, the token of the chant. Immediately his whole attitude changed: "You have the bead. This [the Hail Chant] will not harm you," and he was ready to begin dictation. Our interpreter, LT, was more vulnerable. She had no bead, no protection against the danger of mouthing sacred lore. She was in the class of a chanter's helper, who assumes no responsibility but does as he is told. tłá·h warned her against repeating some of the unusually sacred words—formula and curse, for instance—that I could say without harm.

Women are allowed to sing the Night Chant; consequently, they must own and handle the masks, its focal symbol. However, women as patients of or attendants at the Night Chant are enjoined against seeing the masks and, until they are completed, the sandpaintings. This chant is sometimes postponed until the female patient's menstruation ceases. A

menstruating woman was not allowed in the hogan of the
Rain Ceremony or in the place where prayersticks for the
Night Chant were being made. The reason for the latter
restriction is that the gods might reject the offerings.[3] Here,
as in other cases, the assumption of contamination may be
false. Whereas many North American Indian tribes treat the
pubescent girl as if she were tainted, the Navaho honor the
moment of her maturity. I have had no evidence that menstruation itself is considered corrupt; rather, its appearance is
regarded as the fulfillment of a promise, the attainment of
reproductive power. Menstrual fluid is another matter: it is
feared and avoided because it is body matter that may harm
not only the one who threw it off but also the one exposed to
it. It differs, however, from other forms of 'atcxi'n excrement, nail pairings, hair combings—in belonging exclusively
to woman; carelessly handled, it must, therefore, be extraor-
dinarily harmful to man or, ceremonially protected, unusually
beneficial (Chapters 3, 11).

Restrictions on pregnant women are to protect the unborn
child. It behooves parents to guard the child from dangers
that may beset it during gestation, though they may not
become apparent until the child grows up. The behavior of
the father as well as of the mother may affect the child. The
primary danger is in contact with a dead person or a symbol
of the dead.[4] Consequently, the War Ceremony is dangerous
to a pregnant woman, since its very purpose is to eliminate
by recapitulation enemy ghost power.

Stevenson cites an interesting case that concerns the effects
of ceremony upon an unborn child. The wife of the man
chosen to sing the Night Chant was pregnant and the people
who chose him doubted that he would officiate, for they said
his seeing the sandpainting might cause the child's death.
The singer himself was so sure of his power that he sang the

173

chant. He said he would shield the child by administering, shortly after its birth, a mixture in water of all the sands used in the painting.[5] The pregnancy was not believed to have any adverse effect on the patient or any participants of the chant. A male chanter (JS) told me that a woman chanter, even if pregnant, may sing her chant, for she will recite a particular prayer to protect her child. Since the reason most often given for restraining a woman from certain activities is security, it is practically certain that some such idea prevails also concerning the effect of menstrual fluid. Doubtless it is more powerful than other worn-out body material and may, therefore, be more weakening.

During the first days of my apprenticeship, I was told that because I was a woman I could not be present when a sandpainting was being made. Women did, however, go into the hogan while the painting was going on—to grind colored pigments, to take a message, to take food; later I learned that they had been sung over. They were under the protection of the paintings and for this reason were said to ' own ' them. Since those early days five paintings have been made for me, and, in regions where I am practically unknown, not only have I been allowed to enter the hogan while paintings were being made but have even been invited in.

On one such occasion, the most memorable in my experience, I ventured a criticism after the twenty-five or thirty sand strewers had examined a finished sandpainting[6] and had not detected a glaring mistake. When I called attention to it, the medicine men all shook my hand, thanking me. They assumed that I knew a great deal more than I really did and respected my apparent authority. The reaction was to knowledge, not to a man's or a woman's knowledge.

Restrictions directed against women are sometimes general —that is, enjoined upon both sexes; a male patient of the

Night Chant, unless a chanter, should not see the masks being prepared any more than a female, because no one should witness the preparations for the chant being sung for him. I have recorded merely the taboos I happened upon, but I think that if a special study were made, corresponding restrictions applying specifically to women would be found for men, and that the underlying reasons for both would be similar.

Few articles on restrictions discuss their opposite, prescriptions, which may amount to privilege and honor. Navaho ritual, true to the dogma that opposites must be included, prescribes honors in one activity and represses them in another. Women are barred from holding aggressive offices in the War Ceremony—that is, they may not conduct it; the stick receiver and the ashes strewer must be a man; women and children should no more hear talk about its proposed performance than in the old days they could listen when the men were planning a raid. Yet the person in charge of the rattlestick, the master symbol of the War Ceremony, should be a reliable female virgin; sometimes only a very small girl can fulfill the requirements (Chapter 8).[7]

The woman at the first blackening ceremony had to be coaxed and, upon consenting to be blackened, gained the privilege of representing Earth Woman, who had been put in charge of continuous growth and all things on the earth's surface.[8]

Women furnish the food for all ceremonies; bringing it into the ceremonial enclosure is one of their ritualistic duties. In the War Ceremony women of the patient's clan bring in many-colored yarns for the decoration of the rattlestick.[9]

Women prepare the drum tapper and the material for the cover of the pot drum, the making of which is an important rite of the War Ceremony.[10]

It is decreed that a man should grasp the pot drum firmly, whereas a woman should merely put her hand under it while the prayer is being said, and that the rattlestick should lie in the woman's hand or that she should merely touch it during the prayer. These differences in ritual are said to show she is not a warrior and carries no weapons.[11] They illustrate also the contrast between male and female ritualism.

Matthews early observed the Navaho distinction between that which is coarser, rougher, and more violent, called male (biką'), and that which is finer, weaker, and more gentle, called female (ba'á'd). As I have already shown, the terms include more than the literal differentiation of sex, since two deities of the same sex may be paired and perform the same kind of functions as do male and female in other cases.[12] Therefore, in ceremonial the underlying symbolism must be understood. It classifies potency, mobility, energy, bigness, and dominance as male; and generative capacity, passive power, endurance, smallness, and compliance as female.

The descriptions of the gods illustrate these characteristics: Sun is the ideal male, Changing Woman the ideal female, both sexually and ritualistically. Another type of pairing includes two members of the same sex: Sun and Moon, both male; and Monster Slayer and Child-of-the-water (cp. Chapter 4).

Matthews notes that in the Night Chant sandpaintings male divinities are represented with round and female with square heads. The choice is probably different in every chant, for even in the Night Chant a round-headed figure may represent a goddess.[13] JS gives additional rules for the Shooting Chant, but there are many exceptions. He says he represents ' people ' by round heads; when Snakes are ' just snakes ' he gives them diamond-shaped heads. When males and females both have square heads they are siblings, ' all of one kind, all belonging to one family '; when the male of a pair has a round head, the female a square one, they are married. JS adds that the head shape must be learned for each painting.

Examination of the published sandpaintings shows that none of these rules except the last was consistently followed.

All the snakes in Newcomb-Reichard, Plate III, and *Navajo Medicine Man*, Plates XIV and XVI, are ' people,' yet the Arrowsnakes have round heads. Perhaps there was a differentiation between dominant round heads and the secondary square heads, each group indicating a related family. However, when RP painted the picture corresponding with that of Newcomb-Reichard, Plate III, with twenty-four figures instead of twelve, all had round heads, although some figures were male and some female.

The prayersticks of the Night Chant carry out the theme of the round-square heads. The naturally circular ends of the sticks sufficiently represent the caplike male mask. Facets are cut on the female sticks to represent female masks.[14]

Holy Man, Holy Woman, Holy Boy, and Holy Girl all have square heads, and similarly, the heads of Dawn Boy, Blue Sky Man, Yellow-evening-light-girl, and Darkness Girl are all square in Newcomb-Reichard, Plate XVIII. The following are shown with square heads regardless of sex: Snake People, Corn People, Pollen Boy, Cornbeetle Girl, Buffalo and Medicine People, Thunders and Water Monsters, Arrow People, Scavenger.

All the flint-armored male figures are represented with round heads.[15]

There is some reason to believe that square-headed figures represent ' people ' or their intermediaries, whereas round heads stand for deity itself. This suggestion would account for the difference between snake forms and it would differentiate the Holy People from the flint-clad deities. Plate X in *Navajo Medicine Man* shows three male figures—Holy Man with a square head in the middle between two flint-armored round-headed figures which represent Monster Slayer and Child-of-the-water; Plate XX shows relatively the same arrangement. Interpreting round heads for deity and square heads for those less powerful may be a way of contrasting dominant and secondary motives.

If we bear in mind JS's rules and combine them with the rule of deity (dominant) and intermediary (secondary) power, we have the explanation of some cases, but we need the help of the chanter for others.

If the contrast is between deity and intermediary, the former is represented by round, the latter by square heads.

The rule would account for the square heads of the Holy People, invariable in my material, who represent man and god, and the round heads of the flint-clad boys, who represent divinity.

If the sex of the deity is to be expressed, the male may have a round, the female a square, head.

In *Navajo Medicine Man*, Plate XXII, the husbands of the Sky, Sun, Water, and Summer People have round heads, the wives square. But in Newcomb-Reichard, Plate XIX, these same people, acting as separate, probably family, groups, all have square heads. Perhaps these two pictures best illustrate the contrast between the divine and human; in the Dark-circle-of-branches form of the chant (*Navajo Medicine Man*, Pl. XXII) the figures are deities; on the other hand, separate parts of the picture in Newcomb-Reichard, Plate XIX, identify the patient with deity at each of the four-day emetic rites; hence the figures are intermediaries.

Pollen Boy and Cornbeetle Girl, both yellow, have round heads, whereas blue Cornbeetle Girl has a square head; here the sex of deity is differentiated. Pollen Boy and Pollen Girl in Newcomb-Reichard, Figure 10 and Plates IIB and XXII, have square heads. Plate IIB probably represents intermediary power; Plate XXII and Figure 10 may mean the same or they may indicate siblings.

The deities who owned the domesticated plants—white corn, blue bean, yellow squash, black tobacco—are described as male and all have round heads.[16]

The inhabitants of the Lodge-of-dew, called Long Bodies, all with square heads, are described as female. They were helpers of Reared-within-the-mountain of the Mountain Chant.[17]

When sex is not involved, the shape of the head may represent dominant or secondary power:

Sun and Moon as persons, or Sun-bearer and Moon-bearer, are represented in Wheelwright, *Navajo Creation Myth*, Set II, 1, to look like Monster Slayer and Child-of-the-water without armor. The Sun-bearer (black) has a round head, Moon-bearer (white) a square head. Both are male; here, as in Gray Eyes' myth, Moon is the maternal uncle of Sun.[18]

Bigness indicates an abstraction, a whole standing for its several parts—a large central cornstalk represents all corn, a huge Thunder (with small Thunders painted on it) all thunders. Length is a symbolic aspect of size. Sandpaintings gain power from the elongation of figures as well as by repetition. Jeff King explains the relative smallness of the Warrior Twins: "[They] are short and both of the same color, for they have not yet been given their names and have not much power."[19] Long prayersticks have greater power than short ones. A single long prayerstick rather than a number of small ones should accompany the Big Thunder painting just referred to.

CHAPTER 11

ALTERNATION, REVERSAL, AND NEGATION

O NE REASON for some changes in repeated sandpaintings is the stipulation that the chanter change colors or the color sequence in successive performances, a rule that accounts for some differences previously thought to be errors. Since the chanter's achievements have never been listed, there is no way of verifying color details. Although I saw a chant repeated more than once and knew the chanters who would have given me such a list, I was unaware of *alternation* at the time and missed the opportunity.

The main function of alternation, whether of colors or of ritualistic acts, is to prevent overdoing; a very slight change makes a rite ' different.' A chanter may paint Thunder's tail brown one time, black the next.[1]

According to the myth, the Shooting chanter should vary the figure painting: the first time black should be inside; the second time, white; the third, blue; and the fourth, yellow.

RP's sequences for the successive figure paintings of the Shooting Chant (with Blue Corn People sandpainting) were:[2]

1st b-w-u-y*   2nd y-b-w-u   3rd u-y-b-w   4th w-b-u-y

The first three series are in a regular succession, the last color being the first in each new sequence. That the fourth is not a mistake is attested by the fact that my two figure paintings were exactly like the first and fourth. RP had most

---

*The list of abbreviations will be found on page 745.

180

likely sung the chant twice, but he may even have sung it six or ten times during the year intervening between the two performances for me.

Alternation is by no means confined to color combinations. When RP sang over me, he asked if I wanted stripes or dots on my face as a part of the figure painting. When I chose stripes, he said, "Remember this and you can have dots next time." Unfortunately, I forgot and had stripes the second time as well as the first. The theory is that the two give more complete protection—stripes for Sun's House power, dots for hail (cp. *Figure painting*, Concordance C).

Alternation is an artifice of singing. The double sandpainting of the Shooting Chant is made to the accompaniment of two choruses singing alternately. Presumably this is the pattern also for the Hail Chant, where one group represents Winter Thunder's, the other, Black Thunder's party. The same device, alternation with symbolic significance, is emphasized in the War Ceremony. Two groups of performers, representing the Navaho victors and the enemy or vanquished, should sing alternately; the singing should neither overlap nor lapse for even a moment.[3]

In the Night Chant the position of the plants on the bath platform should alternate: once they should be arranged in the form of the Greek, the next time of the Maltese cross. The number of prayersticks also should alternate. If there are six once, there should be eight or ten the next time.[4]

. . .

Reversal is among the techniques of magical manipulation. Sanction of procedure otherwise forbidden stresses the importance of opposition and enhances compulsion. It has already been illustrated as applying to direction and explained as exorcistic rather than as attracting good. It is most common

181

in the Evil chants, but may characterize also rites of the Holy chants. Red inside, rather than in its customary position, outside, in the sandpaintings of the Red Inside phase of the Shooting Chant is an example of color change in a Holy chant with exorcistic emphasis.

Outline colors of the centers of two comparable pictures, one to attract good, the other to repel evil, are reversed (Chapter 19). The one with red inside is chosen when the chant theme includes the evil inherent at a place where Holy Man was changed into a coyote. It signifies in brief detail the change of Holy chant phases, selected if a person's illness is attributed to lightning or storm. The Hoop Transformation, a reversal rite (were-coyote motive), is employed when sorcery is suspected and is a major rite of the Evil chants.

The various phases of the Male Shooting Chant Evil are differentiated by reversal. Five large hoops are a part of the Hoop Transformation, one called ' jagged,' being made of a thorny wildrose withe. In the simpler form of the rite they are set up (from the hogan outward in a chosen direction) b-jagged-u-y-w, but if the Prayer on buckskin rite is included, the order is jagged-w-y-u-b, except for the jagged hoop, a reversed sequence.

To emphasize exorcism, the sunwise circuit is changed to anti-sunwise; the direction for body treatment, normally from foot to head, is reversed—a technique tantamount to annihilation; square knots, normal to the living, are tied as grannies for the dead; odd numbers characterize uncertain undertakings (exorcistic) in contrast with even numbers to indicate greater confidence (Chapter 7, "Attraction of Good"); sandpaintings are a part of night rather than daytime performance; even masked dancers, ordinarily limited to winter dancing, may appear in the Feather Chant in the summer. There may even be contrary interpretation of dreams.

Of hunters Hill records:

"Topics that dealt with blood and death, which under ordinary circumstances were avoided, were now [during hunting or hunting training] spoken of with the utmost freedom. The hunters were charged to keep their minds on killing and things pertaining to death. The demeanor, habitually gay, became dour, and no joking or levity of any kind was countenanced. Dreams of killing and defeat, which in ordinary circumstances were omens of disaster, were interpreted on a hunting trip as signs of good fortune. After meals, instead of the usual ' may it be pleasant,' the hunters recited some phrase connected with killing. Again, pollen was thrown into the fire, an act which, under ordinary circumstances, was one of the worst sacrileges a Navaho could commit." [5]

Order, the foundation of Navaho ritual, is reversed in Coyote's character. He threw the stars into the sky in a haphazard manner, he defied hunting rules, he vacillated between evil and good in the ceremonial assembly, he chose October, a changeable and uncertain month, to be his. Plants representing him in the rites are unselected, as are his arrow feathers, and his songs are not grouped in order. After the Bats had killed him, they ground up his skin with soil from undesignated places and scattered the mixture in every direction (*Coyote*, Concordance A).

Clowning is an exaggerated form of reversal. Commonly war raiding was carried on with the utmost circumspection and a minimum of noise. The Hard Flint boys acted like noisy rowdies just when the war party was ready to attack Taos; their behavior added the rite of the Black Dancers to the War Ceremony.[6] The Black Dancers perform daring practical jokes—grab people, undress them, and rub them with dung, or a piece of sheepskin smeared with menstrual blood, fearsome because it is generally considered even more dangerous than excrement. In the Night Chant, Water Sprinkler shocks (and entertains) the audience by reversing

183

everything the serious dancers take pains to do correctly.

Clowning, at least in the old days before the whites had much effect on Navaho morals and even perhaps today in isolated areas, reached a peak of obscenity in the Fire Dance event of the Mountain Chant and in the characterization of be'γotcidí.[7] Silly, obscene behavior is more than intentionally and obviously amusing. Its symbolism may best be understood by the attitude of the audience.[8] Almost everyone laughs at the antics of a clown in the dance space. Yet mingled with amusement is shock at the thought that anyone, even a god, dares to ridicule sacred things. And if the clown approaches too close, the smiles of the women and children quickly change to expressions of surprise tempered with fear. The reaction is similar to that of our own children at the circus. When the clown is at a distance a child laughs; addressed directly, he may cry or edge away. Masked impersonators are bogeys during the first years of the Navaho child's life, and woman may repeat the threat of deific visitation so often as to come to believe it.

. . .

A conscious *negation* is as significant as other symbols. Prescription is almost impossible without restriction, and evidence has already been given of the numerous restrictions the Navaho observe.

Watersnake should never enter into the Male Shooting Chant Holy because one of Sun's ' sky ' children was bitten by a water snake and cured by The Twins.[9] This negation is especially interesting from the viewpoint of the position and repetition of snake figures in the sandpainting. For aesthetic reasons, four kinds of snake, one for each quadrant, would be advantageous. Instead there are only three. Watersnake would make a good fourth, although other kinds might also be chosen. Perhaps one reason that three are prescribed is to give an odd number of snakes, since they are evil (Chapter 14).

Several passages of the Hail Chant myth reiterate that Big Snake should not participate in the chant in any way. So strongly did tłǎ·h feel the importance of this restriction that, when in the list of deities present at one of the assemblies Big Snake's name crept in—automatically, it seemed—he got up, hunted about the room until he found a copy of the *National Geographic* magazine, and pointed to a picture of a Chinese dragon which he said was Big Snake, entirely different from the ordinary Big Snake commonly referred to! [10]

To judge from the chant myths I myself have recorded, the negation is as significant a symbol as direction, sex, or color, and should always be ascertained. Each chant has at least one kind of strictly forbidden food; many chants have more. I was emphatically forbidden to eat fish after the Shooting Chant had been sung over me ' because the pollen ball I ate had fish blood in it,' symbolizing the capture of Child-of-the-water by fish.[11] MC was forbidden to eat animal entrails after her sing because they were a part of the mixed stew she had ceremonially eaten.

The myth of the Hail Chant, while it enumerates particular foods required by the chant, especially warns against eating corn dumplings during the chant, for to do so would cause hard times and damage to the crops by hail. The dumplings are synthesized as hail symbols. The Night Chant seems to have something in the way of a food display closely paralleling that of the Hail Chant, and restrictions are enumerated, especially about the preparation and cooking of food.[12]

That negation is an important symbol is evidenced by the care with which it is noted in texts:

The Hail Chant and the Shooting Chant formerly had three ' wide boards ' each and the Shooting Chant had two bull-roarers, but 'when the two chants met,' Hail gave Shooting one wide board, so that now Shooting has four and Hail only two. In exchange, Shooting gave up one of its bull-roarers, so that now each chant has one.[13]

The Bead Chant has no rattle because the original Bead chanter exchanged it for two prayersticks of the Awl Chant.[14]

In the Hail Chant myth the details of the Fire Dance are carefully enumerated. After teaching them all to Rainboy, Talking God told him not to use the Fire Dance form of the Hail Chant in the future.[15]

Similarly, the hero of the Bead Chant, after instructing his brother in the lore of the Fire Dance, decreed that it should henceforth be omitted.[16]

A hero of the Night Chant, made a special trip back to his home to show his younger brother a sand picture which he then said was never to be used.[17]

No prayerstick was to be offered to Long Bodies, who aided the hero of the Mountain Chant; a linear painting was to be substituted, never one with a cross arrangement.[18]

Holy Man showed the hero of the Mountain Chant how to stand holding the plumed arrows, but did not give him any.[19]

When Deer Owner's daughter showed the home of the game to her newly acquired husband, there were two prayersticks to represent deer, antelope, sheep, and fawn, and one for Talking God, but none for elk.[20]

Even the absence of elaboration is mentioned, indicating that the rite or chant in its complete form has neglected no essential symbol.

When people were created from corn for Whiteshell Woman, ' no songs were sung and no prayers were uttered during the rites, and the work was done in one day.' [21]

CHAPTER 12

COLOR AND PRECIOUS STONES

Color

COLOR, AN outstanding symbol of Navaho ceremonialism, is especially significant in combination, but first I discuss the more general aspects of each color in the order in which they most commonly occur. No color or sequence runs through a single chant consistently; none has the same meaning in every setting, nor does chance account for apparent exceptions to the rules; every detail is calculated. If there seems to be a variation, it is for cause.

White (łgai, łgaihígí˙) apparently differentiates the naturally sacred from the profane—black or red, for instance—which, through exorcism and ritual, must be transformed to acquire favorable power.

Myths explaining the earliest beginnings of creatures that later became manlike take for granted the existence of corn; man was created from a white ear (Chapter 3). In some versions the corn was of whiteshell, and the three—whiteness, corn, and shell—are associated, accounting for the quality whiteness; for a vegetable product and the staff of life; and for well-being, supernatural favor, and wealth.

White corn is associated with maleness, yellow with femaleness. In the Sun-Moon combination, Sun is blue, Moon is white. However, various attributes of Sun are white: he appeared to Changing Woman on a white horse; parts of his house were composed of whiteshell; a white rock stuck up out of the water at the east of his house; he directed The Twins

187

to descend from sky to earth at a white spot on a mountain.[1]

White garments are indicative of purification, readiness to undertake contact with divinity. Myths that have a description of the bath indicate that beautiful white clothes are supernaturally provided for the patient after he has washed in yucca suds. Such garments were furnished to Monster Slayer by Talking God; to Changing Woman at her nubility rite by First Woman. At present Changing Woman is believed to live in a home made of whiteshell in the western ocean (Pacific). When the sisters, Whiteshell Woman and Turquoise Woman, came to the home of Monster Slayer— represented in the Eagle Chant as the owner of corn—he made them purify themselves by bathing, then gave them white buckskin clothing.[2]

White is discussed first because it is the color of the east, and, frequently in the Shooting Chant, of dawn or daylight. Talking God, the tutelary of the east, wears white clothing, and the white eagle feathers of his headdress are spoken of as the rays of pre-dawn.[3]

According to Matthews, Talking God's is the only white mask[4] worn in the Night Chant, of which he is the leader. Yet in the Hail Chant we are told that the Winds borrowed the mask from Talking God and did not return it. For this reason the faces of the Wind in the Wind Chant are blue.[5]

It is said that white clay drives away enemy ghosts,[6] perhaps because day, in contrast with night, when ghosts dominate, brings back the possibility of self-protection.

When The Twins arrived for the first time at the home of their father, Sun, they were hidden in four curtains representing the times of day, the first being the white of dawn. Mountain-fallen-away and Rock-which-reached-through-the-sky had sky covers, one being dawn white. The homes of the Buffalo were partly made of dawn.[7]

The white line of the Shooting Chant figure painting represents flash lightning (xatso'oɫɣaˑɫ).

I shall later consider the position of white in the color sequence; it may occupy several of the cardinal directions at some time or other (Chapter 13). At Rumbling Mountain, white in the southern quadrant signifies the motion of the rocks. At the west of the center, from which Endless Snake emerges, white guards the mountain.[8]

In the double sandpainting, a white line is drawn around a black mountain representing foam on water. White dots on a black bar stand for seeds or foam; similar dots on the bodies of Sky, Sun, Water, and Summer People are seeds.[9]

Contrasting with the natural goodness of white in the preceding examples is its emphasis when applied to Winter Thunder. In the Shooting Chant paintings there is a Pink Thunder where a white one would be expected. JS explained the absence of the white one: "He is such a bad one that you don't put him in the sandpainting because he might come. You don't want him to come."

Winter Thunder, though white, is nevertheless depicted in the sandpaintings of the Hail Chant. He must be present because without him Rainboy could not be restored. The name of Winter Thunder, 'iˑñi' djiɫgai, is derived from the stem for ' white.' Meaning 'thunder is inherently white,' it signifies the rare winter thunder. Winter Thunder's home, all white, was decorated with snow rainbows. There was much valuable whiteshell and turquoise in the house and even his wife's attractive face was white. After Rainboy had lain with her, her husband struck him, a deed that could be requited only if Dark Thunder and his adherents overcame Winter Thunder in war. With difficulty it was learned that Winter Thunder's offering was a white prayerstick. To signify acceptance he smoked a whiteshell pipe, blowing smoke in all directions. Later, as his war party advanced toward Dark Thunder's territory, it was heralded by a white cloud.

Reflecting the ill nature of Winter Thunder are white rain and mist, which Hill remarks are omitted from prayers of the Rain Ceremony because they carry hail.[10]

Blue (do·tłij, do·tłijígí·) is discussed next because in the sunwise circuit it often occupies the southern quadrant. In fact, its position there is more consistent than that of white in the east.

There has long been a psychological question about the way primitive people regard blue and green. The point has been made that colors may be distinguished, yet not named. The Navaho differentiate the colors and have names for them, but Navaho blue, green, and yellow differ from ours in value. The ideal blue is the bright color of good turquoise; green is the color of certain mature plants—corn leaves, for instance. Immature succulent plants are usually described as shades of yellow. Green (yellowish) is named from water scum (tátłidi·).

When RP reproduced the sandpaintings in water colors, he substituted green for blue. I thought the reason was lack of blue paint, but even when given blue paint, he persisted in using green. Since his paintings are remarkably consistent and accurate when compared with others and with the mythical description, I assume his reason was to make a slight change to quiet doubts he may have had about the preservation of the pictures in a permanent medium—a well-known restriction.[11]

In the Day-Sky sequence—Dawn, Blue-day-sky, Yellow-evening-light, Darkness—blue signifies the bright blue sky of day and belongs to the south. I do not understand Matthews' remark that "blue is associated with zenith in myths but not in acts and sacrifices,"[12] since the Day-Sky sequence, which seems to be the god sequence as well, is common in the Night Chant.

Matthews records also that blue is the color of the south and is female. It is true that blue occurs most frequently at the south, but not always, and it is not by any means always female; in the Shooting Chant, for instance, it is male. Still another association noted by Matthews is black for the sky and blue for the earth. The bundle wands of the Night Chant represent the legendary fourth world—four black wands are placed at the north, four blue at the south of the lodge. The black doubtless designates Sky; blue, Earth.[13] In describing the center of a Shooting Chant sandpainting, RP said the water could be either black or blue, presumably black if for a male patient, blue if for a female. These are not the usual sex colors of the Shooting Chant, both being male, but probably represent Sky and Earth.[14]

The black Sky People in Newcomb-Reichard, Plate XXII, have blue eyes, whereas all the others—Sun, Water, and Summer People—have black eyes. Blue may be merely a contrast, though white is the more usual contrast to black.[15]

Blue sometimes stands for the earth shadow. Edged with pink, blue rises in the east and moves to the zenith to become darkness. This phenomenon is called naxode·ctłi·j, ' cosmic-streak-of-blue, earth shadow.'

An element readily noted in the sandpaintings is the so-called rainbow (ná·'tśí·lid); one not always properly differentiated is the sunray (cábitłó·l). These are really two symbols, each composed of a red and a blue line, but the first has a white outline which also separates the two colors. The sunray stands for the light rays emerging from a cloud when the sun is behind it; it is not the same as ' sunbeam ' (cáńdí·n), which is white and yellow.

In the picture Mountain-of-motion, which symbolizes the motion of various parts of the earth, blue at the west represents the motion of clouds. The painting that commemorates the rejuvenation of Changing Woman for the Shooting Chant shows blue deities, Water People, at the west. Rain water may be closely akin to clouds, but the motion of water in streams is represented by yellow.[16]

Just as white signifies the presence of, or the change to, holiness, so blue seems to represent the fructifying power of the earth, especially as demonstrated by the domesticated plants. The corn in Newcomb-Reichard, Plate III, is representative of all corn; hence it is large, having twelve ears, and blue, because it is of the earth in a painting for a female patient (for a male, it would be black).[17]

I shall have occasion to note that birds have significance within the chant complex. The bluebird (dóli·) is the bird of dawn, of promise, and of happiness. Talking God told the Visionary of the Night Chant that he would appear among the Navaho in the form of a bluebird. When blue is applied to other birds, no matter what their actual color, as it often is in prayer and song, it stands for happiness.[18] In a sandpainting, blue was sprinkled on magpie feathers to indicate their sheen (Chapter 15).

When The Twins made their second visit to Sun, he asked them to sit. There were three seats, one of whiteshell, one of turquoise, and one of redstone. Wind warned them not to sit on the white or blue seats, because they were seats of peace and The Twins had come as warriors. Monster Slayer, therefore, chose the red seat and Child-of-the-water was directed to stand. According to an episode of the War Ceremony legend, one of Sun's favorite horses was blue.[19]

One set of The Twins' theme colors, black for Monster Slayer, blue for Child-of-the-water, is perhaps the Sky-Earth sequence. In a rite of the last day of the Shooting Chant, the head feather is attached to the scalplock. According to the myth, there was a discussion about whose name should be mentioned when the head-feather bundle was fastened: "Monster Slayer's head feather was red when he overcame the monsters, Child-of-the-water's was blue. Therefore these will not do. The head feather of Changing Grandchild is yellow, so let his name be mentioned hereafter." [20]

Yellow (łtsoi, łtsoihígi˙) represents fructification, closely associated with pollen. Since ' real ' pollen (yellow) is gathered from cattail rush, it symbolizes more particularly, although not exclusively, the power of wild vegetation. In the sandpainting of the Night Chant the legs of the dancing figures are yellow to signify that they are knee-deep in pollen; the lower parts of the Buffalo bodies of Shooting Chant pictures are outlined in yellow to represent the power of reproduction and growth. Woman originated from a yellow corn ear; yellow corn meal is a female symbol of domesticated plants. The inexhaustible food bowl is yellow, symbolizing sustenance. [21]

In the Day-Sky sequence, yellow is the most consistent in position and meaning. At the west, it represents the yellow of sunset or evening light. xa˙ctćé˙óγan is a god of the west and sunset. Matthews and tłắ˙h describe his headdress as consisting of eagle plumes (white) and owl feathers (yellow). In the sandpainting all are white, representing the rays of yellow evening light corresponding with Talking God's pre-dawn rays. [22]

In the Sun-Wind sequence, consisting of Sun, Moon, Black Wind, and Yellow Wind, the position of yellow may seem confusing because Yellow Thunder and Yellow Snake are associated with Black Wind. On the other hand, Yellow

Wind is associated with Pink Thunder, Pink Snake with red-stone. The stripes put on the patient's face during the figure painting of the Shooting Chant refer to the Sun-Wind sequence, the name of Yellow Wind being mentioned as the yellow streak is drawn across the chin.[23]

In the Lightning-Rainbow sequence, consisting of zigzag lightning, flash lightning, sunray, and rainbow, the last (red-blue and white) is associated with yellow, and the yellow line of the figure painting of the Shooting Chant stands for rainbow.[24]

Yellow symbolizes the motion of streams or earth waters in the picture whose center depicts the motion of various cosmic forces.[25]

Black (łjin, łjinígí·), *dark* (diłxił), is a sinister color; it threatens and, since it confers invisibility, it also protects. It is paired with blue in the Day-Sky sequence; it is jet of the precious stones. One of the most puzzling questions of color symbolism is the position of black and white in the paintings; black is sometimes at the north—the accepted direction where evil and danger dwell—and sometimes at the east (Chapter 13).

In connection with direction, sex, color, place, and vegetation symbolism, black is paired with yellow or blue almost as often as it is with white. Black Wind is the power of Sun; with it are associated Yellow Thunder, Yellow Snake, and abalone. Sun gave Black Wind as a mentor to Monster Slayer, Blue Wind to Child-of-the-water. Later Big Fly was substituted. The Winds when acting as mentors match the boys they guard in color.[26]

Black Buffalo, whose name was Abalone Woman, had a house of dawn and darkness which was white and black. In this instance both types of pairing—black-yellow and black-white—are associated with the same person.[27]

Black has already been considered in connection with blue as representing Sky in the Sky-Earth sequence. Black Sky (yá diłxił) is to be distinguished from Darkness (tca·łxe·ł), the black element of the Day-Sky sequence.

The black-blue pair is found in the Mountain Chant where the home of mountain sheep consisted of two black and two blue rooms. The wood of the Dark-circle-of-branches represents the black and blue spruce, which first helped Reared-in-the-mountains. In the songs the black mountain is male; the blue, female. However, the hero of the chant was told by Wind to choose food from the black jar at one end and from the white at the other end of a row of jars in Bushrat's home.[28]

In the Shooting Chant, the Lightning-Rainbow sequence, black paired with white represents the male zigzag lightning; white, the straight female lightning.

An interesting use of black-blue symbolism is found in the Grinding Snake picture in *Navajo Medicine Man*, Plate XV. The black center represents a metate; the blue rectangle on it a mano. This picture is comparable with Plate IX of Newcomb-Reichard, which has a white metate. The explanation of these pictures is not entirely clear, but suggests a black-blue, black-white, and, possibly, blue-white metate-mano pairing.[29]

References to black are too numerous even to list, but the following are typical. Darkness was a blanket, one of the covers of each of The Twins' cradleboards; it later hid them from Sun's anger when they first came to his house in the sky. When the storm caused by Changing Woman threatened her house, her older son covered it with a black cloud staked to the ground with rainbows (black-yellow), with a black fog made fast with sunbeams (black-yellow), with a black cloud fastened with sheet lightning (black-white), and with a black fog secured by zigzag lightning (black-black).[30]

When Frog raced with Rainboy the second time, to confuse his opponent he threw down successively a dark cloud, a male (dark) rain, a dark fog, and a female rain. Rainboy lost his way in the darkness and ran in the wrong direction.[31]

Black God's entire costume is black, even though he is the fire god. He often got what he wanted by burning the home of the recalcitrant or harmful person, but when he went with Bat to offer the prayerstick to Winter Thunder he threw down his fire drill with great force and so much smoke filled the house that it became completely dark. Probably the striking of fire and darkness from the same implement, the fire drill, symbolizes a black-red color pair. Another event suggests such a pairing: it will be remembered that Winter Thunder indicated his willingness to meet Dark Thunder by white smoke and that a white cloud announced his war party; at the same time a dark cloud from which red light glowed indicated where Dark Thunder's warriors were.

Corresponding with Monster Slayer's blackened body is Child-of-the-water's, covered with red ocher. The bodies of Land Fringed Mouth gods are painted (longitudinally) half black, half red.[32]

Blackening ('ante·c) is one of the most reliable rites for frightening ghosts—ghosts of the Navaho dead in the one-night vigil, of foreigners in the War Ceremony. The main purpose is to disguise the patient, to conceal him from lurking evils. When so blackened, he may absorb the invincibility of Monster Slayer, who was painted black with a coal of dark sky.[33]

Blackness and invisibility have advantages for the exercise of good as well as evil power. A vegetation symbolism is described for the creation of the world. Coyote had tried to outrival First Man in making a miniature of the earth, a model over which they quarreled bitterly. Little Wind warned First Man that, unless he guessed the proper meaning of Coyote's plan, it would supersede his own. Since Coyote's was bound to be distorted, its permanence would be disastrous to man.

With Little Wind's prompting, First Man interpreted the five lines as follows:

Lines of	Color	To represent
turquoise	blue	green vegetation
abalone	yellow	mature vegetation
jet	black	vegetation with black leaves or horizontal stripes on the mountains
whiteshell	white	snow-covered mountains
rock crystal	crystalline	ice

Black as a vegetation color belongs to the yellow mountains of the West (San Francisco Peaks).[34]

Like the other colors, black has an abstract meaning, even if the meaning is expressed specifically. A symbol of all forms of an existing category of concepts, it denotes origin and summary: large black corn with twelve ears, painted for a male patient (corresponding with blue for a female), represents all the corn of the universe.[35]

The black Endless Snake (see *Never-ending-snake*, Concordance A) symbolizes all snakes, their origin and the inevitable struggle against evil. The great Black Thunder represents all thunders as well as their origin. The Place-of-emergence is depicted in black because it represents the origin of all things.[36]

Red (łtci·', łtcí·', łitci·'ígí·) is the color of danger, war, and sorcery as well as their safeguards. As such, it is paired with black.

In early times, when pre-human creatures were struggling

from the lower worlds and seeking in vain for an exit to a higher realm, they saw a red head sticking out of the sky and heard a voice telling them to fly to the west—it was Red Wind, who had twisted a passage through the sky like the tendril of a vine. Later, in the fourth world, the people came to a red water and were warned that it would hurt their feet if they tried to cross without a raft. Since rites of the Night Chant commemorate events of the fourth world, the requirement to deposit the prayerstick of Red God (xaˑctčéˑłtcíˑ) in red ground may refer to this episode.[37]

Before the earth had been made safe for humans, the gray monsters sent out messengers—red Crow (gâˑgiˑ), red Turkey Buzzard (djeˑcóˑ), red Woodhouse Bluejay (tšáńdílji'í), and Coyote—whenever they got wind of the existence of Earth People.[38]

According to tłắˑh's version of creation, Red Turtle, Red Thunder, Red Otter, and Red Water Monster were guardians of the third world.[39]

In the war legend there are many references to red. First Man gave a prayerstick, colored with blue paint and sparkling earth, symbols of peace and happiness, to Child-of-the-water to watch while his brother went on one dangerous mission after another. When the warrior got into serious trouble, the prayerstick turned red as blood.[40]

Red outlined the dark cloud that presaged the attack of Dark Thunder and his allies.[41]

After the attack on Taos, when two desirable girls had been captured and deprived of their valuables, Sun rose red and trembling, indicating to the warriors that the girls were his children. Revenge is implied, but it was averted by giving Sun the precious stones taken from the captives.[42]

When Gambler pitted his strength against the Pot Owners, he painted his face and the back of his head red so that the enemy could not tell which way he was facing. Monster Slayer's head feather was red when he slew; Child-of-the-water's was blue.[43] Red and blue seem to be the rainbow, rather than the armor or danger, pair of colors.

A nice contrast illustrating reverance is shown by two groups before they set out for the west. Changing Woman's group made ceremonial mush of whiteshell in the prescribed tall black pot, stirring it with ceremonial sticks. They ate, rubbed themselves with a little of the mush, and prayed as they ate. First Woman's group made their mush of redshell, grabbed the food, ate carelessly, and drank hot water. They represent heedless people who bring sickness and refuse to co-operate with the gods.[44]

Protection may be achieved by changing ordinary colors to red. The sandpaintings, Plates XIV (normal) and XVI (reddened) in *Navajo Medicine Man*, illustrate the difference; the red one is said to belong to the Male Shooting Chant Evil.[45] The position of red among the outline colors of the center illustrates another important symbolic use of color (Chapter 19).

Red ocher is used in many ceremonies, in especially large amounts in exorcistic forms. It is mixed with ordinary sheep tallow and a token quantity of sacred tallow provided by the chanter. The red salve is applied to face, hair, or other parts of the body as the rite requires. The entire body of the impersonator of Child-of-the-water may be covered with powdered red ocher (*Overshooting rite*, Concordance C).[46]

Other explanations of the occurrence of red are the following:

At the close of the Night Chant we see the red of the sunset because Child-of-the-water traveled on Darkness when he went to join his brother.[47]

After the moccasin game, in which the people gambled for night and day, Bear ran off in haste, having reversed his

199

moccasins. As he ran away, his fur looked red in the sunlight; this red is sometimes indicated in sandpaintings of Bear even today.[48]

Big Snake, who had aided in the contest with the famous gambler, was rewarded with a piece of redstone which he was to wear on his head, as he does in some sandpaintings.[49]

Red may signify flesh. Some skirt tassels of gods depicted in the sandpaintings are black and white with a small dot of red between them; this dot represents flesh, particularly of rare game, and is a symbol of plentiful meat.[50]

In the seventh act of the Hail Chant Fire Dance, Cedar Waxwings and Titmice came in with pine and spruce branches. As they held them around Rainboy, he disappeared and the branches became trees. On the tips of the twigs red spots could be seen; these were bits of Rainboy's flesh. The act commemorated his destruction by Winter Thunder and his eventual restoration.[51]

Red stands for blood as well as for flesh. Talking God explained the color of the red yarns tied to the rattlestick of the War Ceremony as he instructed Monster Slayer: "This [red] represents the blood that will flow on the soil." [52]

A gambler who visited the place where game was kept learned the hunting ritual. One of the songs contains the line, "Over there where the black bow and red-shafted arrows lie across each other, it is red with blood from the mouth of a male deer." [53]

Red is a dominant color of sorcery:

A female were-coyote had marks on her face like those of the figure painting of the Shooting and Hail chants; she was painted red around her shoulders and had white and yellow spiders painted on her arms. . . . The man who saw her saw also some sticks painted red projecting from her hide.

Some men intending to kill a Mexican by sorcery had a small red basket among their properties.

Sorcery medicine was made of dark red corn meal and the gall of various animals.[54]

Pink (disǫs) indicates the glint of copper, and stands for a reddish shimmering quality of light. For sandpaintings pink is made by mixing red, white, tan, and yellow sands, sometimes with a touch of black. Pink is quite common in some chants, the Shooting Chant in particular, where it depicts Thunder, Water Monster, Water Horse, Sky People, and Changing Grandchild. The featherlike appurtenance of Thunder's tail, which symbolizes reverberation, is pink.[55]

Pink Thunder is said to live in the Land-beyond-the-sky, and may represent the power of the celestial worlds.[56]

Serrated flint is represented as pink. Paired with yellow, it occurs most often as armor of the duplicate Twins.[57] Possibly pink indicates in some cases shimmering yellow, or perhaps sky shimmer as opposed to the shimmer of subterranean waters.

In discussing the paintings of the Bead Chant I remarked that pink and white—colors of eagles (and hawks)—were interchangeable, implying, as I at that time thought, that one could be substituted for the other and that the two perhaps stood for the same thing. I now believe that pink represents the attempt of an Earth Person to attain the power of a sky or deep-water being; that such power is perhaps more difficult to acquire than that of the white denizens of the same realms; at any rate, that pink and white are differentiated. It seems to me significant that pink Eagles attend Scavenger, hero of the Bead Chant, before he reaches the sky; afterward, the Eagles are white and he himself, having acquired the power of them all, has wings of every color, including pink and white.[58]

It is almost certain that pink is not another way of representing redstone. Pink is the outline color of the redstone arrow and stands opposite abalone (yellow), which has red as an outline color.[59] This and the pairing of yellow and red with Black and Yellow Winds suggest a close relation between yellow and pink, but what relation is not quite clear.

Gray (łbai, łbahígí·) is almost universally the color of evil, equivalent to our use of the word ' dirty ' in its moralizing sense, ' despicable.' The monsters are referred to generally as gray, but after the main ones had been destroyed, ' gray gods ' were said to exist, some of which were destroyed wholesale by a hail and wind storm. Big Monster, whom Coyote overcame in contending for Changing-bear-maiden, was called Big-gray-monster.[60]

After Monster Slayer had given some of the Cliff Monster feathers to Bat Woman as a reward, she went to a place where gray birds lived. They merely hopped about, for they had no wings; they were not to be trusted. Because Bat Woman disobeyed the hero's instructions, the feathers in her pack were changed to gray birds, then into birds of all colors which were no longer harmful.[61]

Monster Slayer came to the home of Deer Owner, one of the gray gods, or one of the Syphilis People. He found a pretty girl and was offered food. As he had been warned not to eat it, he took out a small quantity of his own gray food, which he mixed in his own yellow bowl with water from his own water jug.[62] This reference to gray food may be literal, for the corn meal of ceremonial gruel is gray, but in this case it may be that grayness, being evil, is also protection against evil.

Hill's informant particularly states, "These [clothes of hunters] had always to be grayish color, never red or black." [63]

Just as black and red protect against danger, so gray perhaps protects against primordial evils. Ashes rubbed on bodies of the War God impersonators before they shoot at the symbolic scalp ward off such evils (*Overshooting rite*,

Concordance C); pallbearers are similarly disguised or protected.

Brown (yictłij) means literally 'speckled, dim, gray.' In each chant there is a prescribed color for the faces of the deities. The symbolic color may or may not appear when the picture is complete since the faces may be covered with other colors. The designated face color for the Shooting Chant is brown, but for the Sun's House branch the colors of the Day-Sky cycle are so superimposed that the brown is not visible. Brown is considered the 'natural' color of 'persons' and of the earth.[64]

Beaver, Otter, Bat, and some other animals are represented in brown. The deities of some chants have strings hanging from their arms, the strings of the Shooting Chant being brown and yellow to represent otterskin. The chanter's collar of beaver or otterskin, depicted on the gods of the paintings, is brown.[65]

Sparkling, see Chapter 15.

Variegated ('ałta·s'ái) is a summary of all the colors. Literally it means 'projecting-in-every-direction.' In a sense it signifies purity, as white does when indicating a change from human to divine. When Talking God first prepared The Twins for their great deeds, he dressed Firstborn in white and Secondborn in clothes of all colors. White may here represent the power of Talking God; variegated, that of xa·ctčé''óγan, who is sometimes said to be clothed in all colors, although in the Night Chant he wears black.[66] Since some parts of the description of xa·ctčé''óγan—his association with yellow evening light and his yellow headdress, for example—connect him with yellow, there is some reason to believe that variegated and yellow are closely associated. The relation between abalone and yellow also contributes to this conclusion, which, however, does not mean that yellow and variegated are not distinguished.

Offerings, paint, feathers, corn ' of all kinds ' are often mentioned in the tales and are ceremonially very common. The clothes of Holy Woman and Holy Girl and the encircling guardian of the painting are varicolored in sandpaintings; several versions of Holy Woman and Holy Girl have been published; they are duplicated by others in private collections. Some were even made by the same chanter at different times--never is the variegation twice the same; the chanters say it need not be. The shape and relation of the different colored spaces differs in the Shooting and Hail chants.[67]

The term ' variegated ' occurs in prayers as a summary of all colors. In the Shooting Chant, Black Thunder is the chief of all thunders, but a guardian of Changing Woman's western home was a Varicolored Thunder, larger than the others; he was paired with Black Thunder at the north door. The representative of a group is probably variegated when peaceful, black when counteracting evil. The hogan blessing prayer refers to hogan covers of varicolored soft goods and to a floor of varicolored precious stones.[68]

Spotting has apparently at least two functions, one to summarize, the other to terrify. One phase of the Sun's House branch of the Male Shooting Chant is called bitši's 'oltłij, ' dotted body,' distinguished by the encircling sandpainting guardian, sometimes called Mirage. In the shape of a rainbow, the central part is composed of varicolored dots; the whole is then outlined. RP said that the guardian so described represented all the precious stones. When Talking God came for The Twins, he strung out a rainbow and motioned for them to step on it. On it he put white, black, blue, sparkling, and yellow medicine (herbs).[69] If this rainbow were depicted, the variegation would doubtless be a superimposition on the original colors, red-blue-white.

Water Sprinkler is said to be represented with a body sprinkled with powders of many colors.[70]

Badger, the fifth of the hunting animals in the Bead Chant, is depicted with a body spotted in all colors.[71]

An invocatory prayer for a prayerstick includes petitions to many deities, such as Corn, Mirage, Heat, Precious Stones (often varicolored in dots); the prayer concluded by mentioning varicolored horses from Sun's house in the east, varicolored sheep from Changing Woman's house in the west, varicolored fabrics from Moon's house in the east, and varicolored hard goods from Whiteshell Woman's house.[72]

Spotted Wind is mentioned as having aided in restoring strength to the heroes of the Shooting Chant. In the Hail Chant myth it was difficult to propitiate Spotted Thunder, but eventually he consented to sprinkle his medicine, cattail pollen, on the suds of Rainboy's bath and even to wash his hair. Spotted Thunder lived with Pink Thunder in the Land-beyond-the-sky where Shooting and Hail chant lore were taught to novices. Spotted Thunder's house was striped and guarded by a spotted, swastikalike arrangement of sticks. Spotted Thunder was said to be the ' head ' of the chants— Shooting, Hail, Water—and the chanter explains that Rainboy's "visit to him was just like a visit to the President at Washington."[73]

In an assembly of the Hail Chant, Wind People sitting on the south side had gourd rattles—dark, blue, yellow, pink, and spotted. Those on the north side had similar rattles, but the striped ones corresponded with the pink; dotted in all colors (do·γe·d), with the spotted (dactłij).[74]

Stephen enumerates the Winds that dried up the third world as the people emerged—Left-handed Wind, Striped Wind, Spotted Wind, and Shiny Wind.[75]

An incident of the Shooting Chant represented in sandpainting is the kidnaping of Holy Boy by the Thunders, who had ' real power '—Left-handed Thunder, Winter Thunder, Spotted Thunder, Left-handed Wind, and Spotted Wind.

Stripes have a terrifying effect.

When The Twins attacked Big Monster, he raised his face and they saw it was striped. The numerous ' gray gods,' indefinite evils, are described as ' looking terrible with striped faces.' When subdued, they became yellow jackets.[76]

Arrowsnakes and Rainbow People lived at Striped Mountain, the stripes being represented by rainbows.[77]

The stripes of the figure painting of the Hail and Shooting chants are terrifying to the onlooker but protective to the person on whom they are painted. In the Shooting Chant they represent Day Skies.[78]

In the powerful performances of the Flint Chant for the most serious diseases, the war colors, black and red, are applied in horizontal stripes.[79]

I suggest that the theme of stripes be examined with the symbolism in mind to explain Striped Wind Chant and the associated symbols, which have exorcistic emphasis.

The discussion of colors has shown that each color has an abstract meaning. White is the color of day, of hope, of newness, of change and commencement. The symbol of divinity, white expresses perfect ceremonial control.

Blue is the color of celestial and earthly attainment, of peace, happiness, and success, of vegetable sustenance. Yellow is the symbol of blessing, of generation, of safety, of promise. Black, sinister but protective, is the color of darkness, night, confusion, smoke, omnipresence, of threat, doubt, indefiniteness, wonder, and origin, of finality. Red is the color of danger, warning, and threat, and of protection from those very things; it also represents flesh food and blood. Pink is the color of ' deep sky ' or deep-water motion. Gray is the color of the unpersuadable deities, those known to be against man, of the indefinite and fearsome, and protection against them as well.

In addition to its abstract value, each color has specific connotations, subdivisions of the generalization and related to it. The particular, as well as the general, meanings of color are indicated, often only indirectly for each chant, being determined by other elements with which color functions.

Materials for coloring sand are ground or natural colors. White, red, and yellow are found free in nature on the Navaho reservation in the form of clay and ochers. Black is from soot made by ritualistic burning. All, after being ground, are mixed with ordinary sand to give them enough body to fall evenly through the fingers. Blue, pink, and brown are mixtures.[80]

Chant myths explain the color origins.

Rainboy in the Land-beyond-the-sky was instructed for the Hail Chant: "You will not make the paintings in this form in the future. Instead you will use powdered rock— dark, blue, yellow, white, pink, brown, and red. If we give you the paintings on the stuff we use, they will wear out, so it is better to make them of sand each time anew." [81]

Monster Slayer got the sandpainting colors for the Shooting Chant when he overcame Traveling Rock. When hit with the powerful flint club, the monster fell into four parts, all of which were white. Monster Slayer picked them up and scattered them, saying, "In the future Earth People will use colored rocks." The bone of the monster became white ground rock, its flesh blue, its hair black; its mouth and blood, red; its intestines became the yellow that is now a sandpainting material.[82]

Coloring matter for painting prayersticks and figure painting is of somewhat different character from that mixed with
sand and is often more difficult to obtain. For instance, blue
paint is some form of copper salt, whereas white and black
sands are mixed for the gray-blue of the sandpaintings.
Sparkling rock may be applied to the body, prayersticks, or
bundle properties. Kluckhohn and Wyman point out that
sparkling rock is sometimes specular hematite, sometimes
galena, or even serpentine, a variation of chrysotile.[83]

Black for body paint, like that for sandpainting, is usually
composed of soot from specific herbs or roots. In the Shooting
Chant, corn smut is applied as paint.

Precious Stones

The discussion so far has shown the intimate, almost inseparable, association between color and shells, precious stones,
and other mineral products. For convenience I take up the
stones in the order of their color symbolism.

Whiteshell (yo'lgai) designates the ' white from which beads
are made.' It is one of the many examples in Navaho where
the same word means a part or a whole, the material or
the object manufactured from it. Whiteshell may refer to
the thin, flat, white shell beads greatly treasured by the
Navaho and often incorrectly called wampum by the whites.
Formerly, the beads were made of a seashell, doubtless
imported through trade from the west coast, probably from
the Gulf of California.

According to tłắ·h's creation story, the spirit of whiteshell
was placed inside Moon, which was composed of ice; the
spirit of turquoise was put into Sun, that of abalone into
Black Wind, that of redstone into Yellow Wind.[84] JS, speaking of the Shooting Chant, said Moon's house was whiteshell.

An indispensable requirement of a chant is the basket; at least one is believed to represent whiteshell. All the precious stones are mythical basket materials. Frequently the basket is of one stone with a contrasting rim—whiteshell rimmed with turquoise or the reverse; abalone rimmed with redstone or the reverse, jet with an abalone rim or the reverse. Bowls, though not as common as baskets, may be deific properties. White Body of the fourth world carried a bowl of whiteshell.[85]

A song intoned at the preparation of the War Ceremony rattlestick refers to Child-of-the-water's queue as whiteshell.[86]

Turquoise (do·tłiji·), ' the-particular-one-which-is-blue,' may be the general collective term for all the precious stones, wealth, or mixed offerings. Good fortune is attributed to the stone. A few of the most unusual references to turquoise are as follows:

Sun gave one of his wonderful children a pair of turquoise earstrings to enable him to win at gambling.[87]

The hair of a remarkable girl, desired by many suitors, was covered with images of coyote and birds of different kinds, all of turquoise; and she possessed a huge disk of turquoise.[88]

Four rattles of buffalo hide are important equipment in the Shooting Chant. One explanation says they symbolize Big Snakes, another that they represent Sun's turquoise rattles.[89]

Sun's son smoked a turquoise pipe, as did Frog.[90]

Perhaps the most unusual allusion is that to First Woman, who, in the first world, was intrigued by a distant fire. When she got to it she found a man, who said, "Your fire is rock crystal; mine is turquoise." This identification was cited as a reason why the two should live together.[91]

The Twins' bows and arrows are sometimes said to be of turquoise.

The reference to turquoise as symbolizing green vegetation in Coyote's first model of the world is interesting.[92]

Changing Woman's home had a turquoise door, and four footprints of turquoise led to a turquoise room. Black Sky Man pulled her up with a cane of turquoise and she became a degree younger than she had been when the Sky People came to her. The cane corresponded with one she gave her wandering people with which they struck the desert and brought forth water.[93]

A small but perfect turquoise bead and an olivella shell tied on a string make the bead token of the Shooting and Hail chants (*Bead token*, Concordance B). Sun may be identified with whiteshell or with turquoise.

Abalone (di·tciłi·) is ' the-particular-one-that-is-iridescent, the-one-whose-various-colors-scintillate '; the name probably derives from the stem -tcił, meaning ' tremble.' Abalone is associated with yellow and with Black Wind, whose house, according to JS, was of abalone.

Abalone was offered to Blue Crane to induce him to sing over Holy Man, who had become ill and weak after his many wanderings.[94]

Jet (bá·cdjini·) is the black substance found in large deposits in the Southwest. A soft cannel coal with a structure that lends itself readily to carving, it takes a beautiful polish. Although jet is the jewel representing black, it is mentioned less frequently than the other jewels.

When the domesticated quadrupeds were brought into existence, a basket of jet edged with abalone and one of abalone rimmed with jet were mentioned. Many birds are now black because they ate of the eggs in the jet basket. The jewel symbol of the northern mountain (dibéntsah) is jet.[95]

At the time abalone was offered Blue Heron for his supernatural advice, a piece of jet was offered to a bird called tśih.[96]

When Monster Slayer was knocked out for having drawn the figure of a person on the bull-roarer, Big Fly instructed him to make the offering for restoration by stringing pieces of jet on tassels of grass.[97]

Native *redstone* (tséłtcí˙) contains ferric coloring matter ranging from dull red to dark pink, often streaked with white. Some of it is probably carnelian. Coral, introduced by the Spanish, has become a substitute, even being called redstone. Examples of the role played by redstone have occurred in the discussion of red; others are the following:

After testing his sons, Sun led them to the edge of the world. There they saw sixteen poles extending from earth to sky—four of whiteshell, four of turquoise, four of abalone, and four of redstone. Sun asked them to choose which they would ascend on; Wind whispered that they should choose the red since they had come seeking war.[98]

All jewels are closely associated with Sun's house, which they compose. Opposite it were five mountains—redstone, glittering, abalone, whiteshell, and turquoise—Sun's mountains, all harmless.[99]

The rattles with which Sun tried to destroy his sons are mentioned in the order: turquoise, whiteshell, abalone, redstone.[100]

Yellow Wind's house was of redstone (JS).

Among the canes furnished Earth People by Changing Woman was one of redstone.[101]

It is doubtful that *agate* (no˙lɣíni˙) should be included among the precious stones. If we do, to be consistent we should include the other kinds of ceremonial flint, for agate belongs more properly with them than with precious stones. The following will explain the connection between flints and precious stones:

When Sun was convinced that The Twins were really his children, he placed a small agate man inside the body of

Monster Slayer to identify him with Sun and make him invincible. A miniature man of turquoise became Child-of-the-water's corresponding symbol.[102]

The stones of the sweathouse were of agate when Sun exposed his sons to the heat test; it was expected to destroy them. Although it exploded, the agate did not destroy The Twins because Talking God had dug a small hole into which they crawled, and had covered it with four white shells. When the test was over, the white shells turned into red-stone, abalone, turquoise, and whiteshell.[103]

An agate arrowpoint forms a part of the head bundle of some ceremonies. Fastened to the hair of a patient in the War Ceremony, it represents the flint points that fell from the breast of Big Monster when he was conquered.[104]

Rock Crystal (tséɣá'tíńdí·ni·, ntó·li·, tsésǫ') is usually not mentioned among the precious stones, but has many cere-monial usages. tséɣá'tíńdí·ni· means ' stone-through-which-light-beams'; ntó·li· means ' the-particular-one-which-is-clear, -translucent.' In many rites it symbolizes fire, especially in the symbolical lighting of the prayersticks, which may contain tobacco. tsésǫ', ' rock-star,' may mean glass as well as crystal.

A crystal was put inside the dark cloud in which Scavenger was enveloped to furnish him light.[105]

At creation a rock crystal was put into the mouth of each person so that everything he said would come true, a probable reason why a crystal is part of many pollen bags, especially the personal ones carried for safety; the pollen represents well-being, the crystal the prayer—that is, the word that makes the prayer come true.[106]

The glass cup holding the chant lotion of the Shooting Chant is a substitute for crystal.

Changing Woman had binoculars of rock crystal.[107]

The line of crystal on Coyote's model of the world repre-sented ice, the only association between crystal and ice I have found.[108]

The basket for the emetic in the first War Ceremony was of crystal.[109]

Mixed jewels, the tiny fragments of precious stones accompanying the prayersticks, often indicate that the reed or plant material of which they consist stands for the jewels. Similarly, the feathered wands of the Shooting Chant are substitutes for Sun's jewel arrows, as is the rattlestick of the War Ceremony (Chapter 18). Sun's jewel arrows represent the Sun-Wind combination—turquoise for Sun, whiteshell for Moon, abalone for Black Wind, redstone for Yellow Wind; in the Night Chant, the jewels represent the Day Skies.[110]

When the pot drum was prepared for the War Ceremony, the jewels stood for the ' floor of the drum's home,' into which the sounds were pounded.[111]

CHAPTER 13

COLOR COMBINATIONS

Paired Colors

MEANINGS MAY best be determined in combinations of colors. It has long been assumed that each Southwest tribe has a fixed color pattern for the cardinal directions. I do not know whether this is true of the other tribes, but it certainly is not of the Navaho.

A cursory study of the Shooting Chant sandpaintings showed that different schemes fulfilled various requirements. As more material becomes available, colors are seen to be paired in ways at variance with what is said in Chapter 12. Black and white are one male-female pair in the Shooting Chant, blue and yellow another. In the Bead Chant, however, black and blue are paired as male and female; yellow and white form another pair. Obviously, from this example and others, color is not fixed for male and female combinations. If this question is pursued through the chants for which there are accompanying myths, it becomes apparent that so-called 'chant colors' are not absolute, but that various principles are followed. To discover these principles I studied color references and associations in the literature as well as in my own ritualistic material. The conclusions are suggestive rather than final. The problems posed should be borne in mind by all who collect material so that the color schemes may be confirmed; most of the data now at hand yield only chance conclusions.

Colors have meaning according to their position in a complex, the order being as significant as the color itself. The colors are few, the permutations many. Sex pairing (dominant-secondary) varies with the chant; the pairs are combined in different ways, depending primarily on what they represent. Rules of sequence differ for quadrant, cross, and linear arrangements, and outlining in multiple colors. In addition, color sequences are mentioned in myth and prayer. Color is associated not only with sex but also with cosmic and celestial phenomena, direction, time and seasons, motion, and vegetation, and the various beings who people the different realms.

The simplest combination is pairing. A rather general type is a flat color outlined by a contrasting one, the latter supplementing the former as well as giving a pleasing effect: black is usually outlined in white, white in black, blue in yellow, yellow in blue, and pink in white. Such outlining is common in the Shooting, Wind, Hail, Big Star, Endurance, and Night chants, occasionally even in spite of the color pairing. Yellow Thunder, for instance, though paired with Pink Thunder (outlined in white), may be outlined in blue. Another exception to the common rule is Black Wind outlined in red, though paired with Yellow Wind outlined in white.[1]

In delineations of the precious stones, turquoise (blue) is outlined in white, whiteshell in blue, abalone (yellow) in red, and redstone in yellow.[2]

Color pairing and the combination of pairs depend upon the ideas to be conveyed or the personifications—for example, the Day-Sky cycle, the Sun-Wind, or the jewel sequences. Since only a few colors are combined to indicate a large number of ideas, the same colors appear frequently and, since their position is significant, they sometimes seem to be out of place, but they never are. There is a reason for the position in the sequence, though as yet it cannot always be determined.

In the following scheme the dominant (male) color of the pair is given first; the second (female) is the secondary or weaker member of the pair. The pairing includes combinations not found at all in the sandpaintings to which I have access. They concern simple ritualistic acts or arrangements of a few symbols, or refer to right and left, or up and down.[3]

Color Pair	Significance
w–y	corn, original man
w–var	divinity (TG–X)
b–var	Holy Man–Holy Woman
b–r	danger imminent
u–r (w outline)	danger past (rainbow)
b–w	zigzag lightning
w–b	straight lightning
w–y	sunbeam
u–r	sunray
p–w	serration, threat with light

Sequence in Quadrant Arrangement

Chart III (pages 218–19) continues the pairing and adds more complex associations. Some sequences of four may seem the same, and so they would be were it not for position. Pairs such as w-var or b-r are mentioned for prayersticks, clothes, and some attributes, and do not as a rule enter into a complicated series, but two pairs may be combined in numerous ways. Though it may seem the most complicated, I discuss first the arrangement of the pairs in the quadrants representing the cardinal directions. The examples concern the sandpaintings, since no other part of the ceremonial is so arranged. The directions are considered in two ways. The figures occupying the quadrants may be read in a sunwise direction beginning with east—east, south, west, north—or they may be established by a cross arrangement—east, west, south, north; one method is as common as the other. In determining the significance of the quadrant color combination, it is necessary to know the sex of the color, its opposite in the context, the entire arrangement in the circle, and the basis of the arrangement, whether in the sunwise circle or the cross. In addition, any of the following permutations of male and female colors may be expected:

e	s	we	n
m	f	m	f
f	m	f	m
m	m	f	f
f	f	m	m
m	f	f	m
f	m	m	f

When all these factors—color, sex, arrangement—have been correlated, sequences that seem to be the same may be seen to result from different permutations: w-u-y-b is the circular color sequence of Day Skies and gods, but the former has the sex sequence f-m-f-m, and the latter, m-f-f-m; the similarity is therefore accidental. The circular sequence b-u-w-y, apparently the same for Buffalo and Sky-Earth pictures, is nevertheless different because of the sex of the colors composing them—m-m-f-f in the former, m-f-m-f in the latter. The sequence b-u-w-y occurs also in the picture depicting motion; the colors seem to be arranged in the same sex sequence as in the Snake and Buffalo pictures, but they are not identical, for they indicate the cross rather than the circular sequence.

The sequence *w-u-y-b* is often mentioned in the myths, even if there is no question about the place of the colors in

CHART III

ASSOCIATION OF COLOR WITH OTHER SYMBOLS (SHOOTING CHANT)

Color Pair	Pair Name	Sequence Name (4 elements)	Sequence Association	Color Circuit (e-s-we-n) and sex	Cross Sequence (e-we-s-n)
u-w b-y	Sun-Moon BW-YW	Sun-Wind		u-b-w-y (m-m-f-f)	u-w-b-y (m-f-m-f)
u-w y-r	t-wh ab-re	jewel arrows	chant symbols	u-y-w-r (m-m-f-f)	u-w-y-r (m-f-m-f)
b-w u-y	Night-Dawn Day-Eve-Sky	Skies		w-u-y-b (f-f-m-m)	......
b-w y-u	Snakes Snakes	Snakes		b-u-w-y (m-m-f-f)	b-w-u-y (m-f-m-f)
b-w u-y	z-fl rst-rb	god conveyances		b-u-w-y (m-m-f-f)	b-w-u-y (m-f-m-f)
b-w u-y	Buffalo Buffalo	Buffalo		b-u-w-y (m-m-f-f)	b-w-u-y (m-f-m-f)

Color pair	Subjects	power of realms		
b-u / y-w	Sky-Earth Mt.-Water	Sky-Earth	b-u-w-y	
b-u / y-p	MS-CW RE-ChGr	flint	b-y-u-p (m-f-m-f)	b-u-y-p (m-f-m-f)
b-u / y-p	Deep Water-Deep Sky	Thunders	b-y-u-p (m-f-m-f)	b-u-y-p (m-m-f-f)
b-u / p-y	Deep Sky-Deep Water	Water Monsters	u-p-b-y (m-f-m-f)	u-b-p-y (m-m-f-f)
w-y / b-u	TG-X BG-WSp	Gods	w-y-u-b (m-f-f-m)	w-y-u-b (m-f-m-f)
b-w / u-y	mountains-rocks clouds-water	motion	b-w-u-y (m-f-m-f)	b-u-w-y (m-m-f-f)
b-u / y-p	Sky-Water Sun-Summer	Sky P	b-y-u-p (m-m-f-f)	b-u-y-p (m-m-f-f)
b-u / y-p	Herbs of Emergence Place		b-u-y-p	b-u-y-p
b-r / u-y	Land FrM Water FrM	Fringed Mouths	b-y-u-p	

the quadrants, because it is the one that first occurs to the narrators. I believe it may be called the ' normal ' order, for I find that within each chant the sequence is mentioned automatically in enumerating objects or concepts that seem to have no position in the circle. For instance, the chant sequence of the Hail Chant, b-u-y-w, occurs with unexpected consistency when four or more colors are mentioned. Similarly, w-u-y-b, the sequence of the Shooting Chant, appears when there seems to be no question about the cardinal directions.

The Day-Sky sequence, w-u-y-b, is found in the more general descriptions of origin, such as the emergence myth and other legends of origin and wandering. The Skies, gods, and their equipment, corn, mountains, the hoops representing the motion of the Winds; many items relating to water jars of the Water People, rafts, Ducks, Fish, Grebes, rooms of the deep water regions with moss covers; and the home of Thunders in the vicinity of Winter Thunder's dwelling are all mentioned in the w-u-y-b sequence.

A variation of this sequence is *w-u-y-var*. Variegation, the sum of all colors and occupying the position otherwise given to black, describes corn, corn medicine, and, in the Eagle Chant myth, the home of Monster Slayer, which in this case represents corn as a means of subsistence.

The sequence *w-u-y-r*, representing the jewel sequence in the sex order f-m-m-f read sunwise or in cross arrangement, is used for the skypoles; also in Sun and Moon pictures, for male and female patients in two sand pictures of the Chiracahua Wind Chant.[4]

The most frequent sequence not fully accounted for by the rules of sex and sequence is *b-u-y-w*. The difference between it and the one just discussed is that the colors of the north and east change places. Matthews suggests that the w-u-y-b sequence represents events in lucky or happy places, and b-u-y-w occurrences where there is danger. He goes on to say that this rule is not entirely satisfactory. On the other hand, Sam Day, recording and interpreting for RP, comes to the opposite conclusion: "In paintings presumably of this world black is at the east. The painting of Buffalo's home is beyond this world; hence white is at the east." [5]

Matthews' legends explain chants different from mine, but in none does the color scheme remain constant. Apparently black, the harbinger of danger, as well as protection against it, is placed in that quadrant from which danger is most imminent for the particular event depicted (Chapter 12, *Black*).

In the double sandpainting, for instance, the Ducks in the western section are arranged in the w-u-y-b sequence.[6] Helpers, they bode no ill, but Fish in the southeast, who captured Holy Boy and from whom he had to free himself, are arranged in the order b-u-y-w; there is the same sequence on the mountain at the east. However, in Roman Hubbell's copy of the picture, painted by RP, the color sequence of Ducks, Fish, and mountain is the same, w-u-y-b. The occurrence of the two sequences in the same picture is one of the many examples showing that the sequence is not general even for a chant, and that other reasons must be sought. The details that should be known about these pictures were not collected when they were painted. Probably the one in *Spider Woman* was painted for a male patient; if so, the male color, black, would start the sequence. Perhaps RP had in mind a female patient and started with the female color when he painted the Hubbell picture. This explanation alone does not account for the Duck sequence of the first picture. Certain sequences are well accounted for by the concepts they represent, but at times white and black quite unaccountably change places at the east or north.

When Changing Woman threw colored hoops to ward off the attacks of the monsters, she threw them in the order w-u-y-b, but when she hurled hail and hoops to which flint had been fastened, the order was b-u-y-w. If my theory about danger is correct, the monsters would have come primarily from the north in the first case, from the east in the second.[7]

Another instance that contrasts two versions—more closely related, perhaps, than the two just mentioned—is the contest for the world between Cicada, who represented the emerging people, and the Grebes, the current owners of the world. According to Goddard, the sequence is w-u-y-b, but he notes that since Cicada had already had the two arrows crossed through him, the Grebes did not endanger him. Matthews, on the contrary, has Cicada meet the Grebes, whose colors are black, blue, yellow, white (b-u-y-w), *before* he undergoes the test.[8]

In the material I have analyzed, b-u-y-w occurs more often by actual count than w-u-y-b, although both are frequent. The number is not significant because we do not have all the myths or details of all the Navaho chants. And even if we had, the b-u-y-w sequence would certainly predominate if the reason for transposing black from north to east to give greater protection at the start is valid, for the main purpose of the chant is to overcome and protect from danger. If the episodes of the chant explain original attacks by evils, it is to be expected that the east should frequently be guarded.

Some w-u-y-b and b-u-y-w sequences may be explained by the choice of circular or cross arrangement and the leading sex color. If so, they demonstrate the following permutations, all of which occur:

Circular	Sex	Cross	Sex
b-u-y-w	m-m-f-f	b-y-u-w	m-f-m-f
w-u-y-b	f-m-f-m	w-y-u-b	f-f-m-m

Unfortunately I have never been able to discover what determines the formation or the sex of the lead color. If the lead color depends upon the sex of the patient, the formation and some of the permutations are unexplained. Perhaps like the arrangement of the lines in figure painting, the first color depends upon alternation (Chapter 11).

The sequence b-u-y-w refers to Winds, Whirlwinds, Cactus, Clouds, Hail, Big Flies, to hoops associated with Winds as well as with Stars, and to the mountains of the fourth world (in the Night Chant). It is mentioned for the First Dancers of the Mountain and Night chants and for rocks taken from birds' nests, properties of the Hail Chant.

Where there is no question of the sandpainting position, the sequence may be extended. The colors of the sandpainting are mentioned in the myth of the Hail Chant as b-u-y-w-p-br-r; the gourd rattles carried by the people on the side of Dark Thunder were named in the order b-u-y-w-p-spotted, but those on Winter Thunder's side carried gourd rattles in the order b-u-y-w-striped-var (dotted).[9]

Arranged in the sequence *b-u-y-p* are Sky People—Sky, Sun, Water, and Summer—when each group occurs alone on successive days in the Shooting Chant, and for Snakes in the Male Shooting Chant Evil.

A variation of the b-u-y-p sequence is b-u-y-ser to describe the pistons in Sun's house, the clubs Sun gave The Twins, the home of Monster Slayer, and flint-armored deities (in an invocation).[10]

The sequence *b-y-u-p* represents The Twins in flint armor, Flint Boys acting as hogan posts (in which case the center pole was white), Thunders, Sky People (when all four colors were represented in one picture), the talking prayersticks of the prayerstick branch of the Shooting Chant (when sung for men), and the curing herbs of the Place-of-emergence.

The sequence *b-u-w-y* preserves the sex pairing of the Shooting Chant, but differs from any of the sequences so far mentioned. Buffalo and Snake pictures have it and often the herbs that guard their homes. God conveyances are described in the sequence b-u-w-p, probably not by accident, since Snakes are associated with lightning, and lightnings are two of the god conveyances; moreover, Buffalo have hoop conveyances, which may easily be associated with Snakes.

This sequence is extended to include pink, b-u-w-y-p, when Holy Man uses five herbs to treat Fish after cutting his way out of Fish's belly.[11] Pink in this case represents the zenith.

Pink takes the place of yellow in the picture of the Emergence of the Medicine People, making the sequence b-u-w-p.[12] According to JS, Medicine and Thunder People are so arranged in the Life chants, suggesting that there is a choice when five colors are possible and there are only four places.

In the chants sung for MC and me the order for Snakes was w-y-b-u (f-f-m-m). The female colors may have occupied the first two quadrants, east and south, because we were women, or the rearrangement may have been due to the chanter's sequence in singing the chants (cp. Chapter 11).

In several cases the sequence is *u-b-w-y*, indicating Sun-Wind deities, the closely associated jewel arrow sequences, and the cloud houses of Sun, Moon, Black Wind, and Yellow Wind.

A rearrangement of the jewel sequence is *u-w-y-b*, having the sex pattern m-f-f-m, instead of m-f-m-f, in sunwise circuit. Sun's canes, the entrance to Changing Woman's home, offerings to the corn fetish of the Eagle Chant, and Winds, who dried up the mud of this world when the people first emerged, are described in this sequence.[13]

With red in place of black, the sequence u-w-y-r describes Sun's arrows and their substitutes in the Shooting Chant, the baskets in which Sun, Moon, and Winds were placed when taken down from the sky, the rattles held by the Holy People when they brought down the sun, the Arrow People and their homes, and the order in which Sun applied the pistons to his sons (*Application* . . . [various references], Concordance B).

The sequence *u-y-w-r* is extended in verbal description for the trumpets (pistons) of Sun's house as u-y-w-r with a jet floor; for the canes by means of which Changing Woman was restored to youth and beauty and proceeded into a room made of jet; and for Sun's enumeration of his most valuable horses, rattles, and pollens at the new home he made for Changing Woman. In the center of the jet floor grew a black cornstalk and at its black root there was a jet horse.[14]

Here, as in the Sun-Wind and jewel sequences, red or black may be chosen if there is only one place available, but when five are desirable, all the colors representing jewels are mentioned. The habitat of Dove Man, who helped to bring down Sun, is depicted as having both black and red in the sequence w-b-u-r (yellow is omitted).

There is only one example in which Water Monsters are not dominated by Thunders (sequence b-y-u-p); the sequence seems to be *u-p-b-y*.[15] Since Water Monster and Thunder are closely associated, the transposition of colors east and west and south and north may differentiate creatures of the deep-sky and deep-water realms.

Sequence in Maltese Cross Arrangement

Besides the quadrant arrangement in the sandpaintings there may be a subsidiary arrangement in the form of a Maltese cross, each arm of which occupies the southeast, southwest, northwest, or northeast corner. Sometimes the elements composing them correspond with the major figures of the quadrants; and sometimes, though the elements differ, the colors match those of the four cardinal directions.[16] At other times, however, when elements composing the Maltese and Greek cross differ, there is little explanation for the colors. Two types of design are most common as arms of the Maltese cross: ' medicines ' or herbs, and domesticated plants—corn, beans, squash, tobacco; they are placed in the sunwise sequence—southeast, southwest, northwest, northeast.

Plants accompanying the Arrow People (u-y-w-r) are arranged in the sequence b-u-w-p, and prayersticks made on the days when the double sandpainting was painted were described in this order. In explaining the picture "Emergence of the Medicine People," [17] in which the sequence was the same, RP observed: "The four herbs are of different colors because the disease [he was painting on paper and not for a patient] is due to water. If it was due to Thunder, there would be blue corn, blue bean, black squash, and blue tobacco." The picture belongs to the phase Thunder Lies and suggests that all such details are learned. I do not have enough material to discover the general reasons for one series or another if, as I suppose, they exist.

The sequence b-y-u-w represents corn in the corners between Thunders. Read as a cross arrangement it becomes b-u-y-w, the commonest sequence; thus white corn is beside Pink Thunder. Winter Thunder in the Land-beyond-the-sky makes offerings in the order b-y-u-w.[18]

Corn, bean, squash, tobacco fill corners in the following sequences:

Sequence	Picture of	Chant	Reference
b-u-y-b	Cloud P	Hail	Bush Coll.
	Rain P	Hail	NCWC, p. 188
b-u-b-b	Cloud and Big Fly P	Wind	Bush Coll.
b-b-b-b	Thunders	Shooting	NR, Pl. XXI
u-u-b-u	Snakes	Shooting	MM, Pl. XVI
	Blue Corn P	Shooting	NR, Pl. XXII
	Thunders and Water Monsters	Shooting	NR, Pl. XXXIII
	Arrow P	Shooting	NR, Pl. XXXV
	Flint-armored War Gods	Shooting	MM, Pl. XIX
	Earth	Shooting	NR, Fig. 5
u-u-b-b	Holy Man in power of Thunder	Shooting	MM, Fig. 6
	Crooked Snake P	Shooting	Huckel Coll.
u-u-u-u	Rain P	Water	HCWC, p. 196
	Water Monsters	Water	HCWC, p. 198

Sequence in Linear Arrangement

It is almost certain that in linear arrangement the directional viewpoint of the colors is preserved, but it is equally demonstrated that this viewpoint changes not only from chant to chant but also from picture to picture within a given chant. In Chart IV (pages 228–29) the linear sequence of sandpaintings is from bottom to top—south to north—and, where possible, the direction and color sex are noted. In a few cases descriptions of the position of prayersticks are available; they too are listed.

CHART IV

COLOR AND DIRECTIONAL SEQUENCES, LINEAR ARRANGEMENT

Element	Chant	Color	Sex	Direc-tion	Head Shape
Crooked Snake, and Corn People	Shooting (NR, Pl. IV, XXI)	y	f	we	square
		u	m	s	square
		w	f	e	square
		b	m	n	square
Crooked Snakes	Bead (MM, Pl. II)	w	f	e	
		y	m	we	
		u	f	s	
		b	m	n	
Flint-armored heroes	Shooting (NR, Pl. XVI)	b	m	e	round
		u	f	we	round
		y	m	s	round
		p	f	n	round
Mountain Gods	Mountain (Matthews 1887, Pl. XVIII)	b	m	n	square
		w	?	e	square
		u	f	s	square
		y	f	we	square
Long Bodies	Mountain (Ib., Pl. XVI)	b	m	n	square
		w	m?	e	square
		u	f	s	square
		y	f	we	square
Armored Snakes	Navaho Wind (KW, Fig. 15)	w	f	n	round
Cactus People	Ib., Fig. 16	u	f	s	round
Spiny Cactus People	Ib., Fig. 17	y	m	we	round
Cloud People	Ib., Fig. 18	b	m	e	round

CHART IV—*Continued*

COLOR AND DIRECTIONAL SEQUENCES, LINEAR ARRANGEMENT

Element	Chant	Color	Sex	Direction	Head Shape
Armored Snakes	Navaho Wind (Bush Coll.)	b	m	n	round
		u	f	we	round
		y	m	s	round
		w	f	e	round
Arrows under Holy People	Shooting	u	m		
		w	f		
		var	m		
		r	f		
Buffalo People	Shooting	y	f		
		w	f		
		u	m		
		b	m		
Wind People	Navaho Wind (Bush Coll.)	b	m		
		u	f		
		y	m		
		w	f		
Fish prayersticks	Shooting	w			
Mountain Sheep prayersticks	Night (Matthews 1902, p. 91)	u			
Bee and Coyote prayersticks	Hail	y			
		b			

Sequence in Verbal Order

In dictating the texts of the Shooting and Hail chants, the chanters followed the prescribed order. If the recording is accurate, it gives a clue to color arrangements in addition to the sandpaintings.

Part of Rite	Sequence	Reference
Corn in Turkey lament	w-u-y-var	Matthews 1897, p. 181
Herbs to heal Fish	w-u-b-y-p	Shooting Chant ms.
Medicines on rainbow	w-b-u-spar-y	Ib.
Corn for mush	w-y-u-gray	Ib.
Corn in basket	w-y-u-var	Reichard 1944d, p. 67
Corn for drumstick	w-y-u-gr-str	Shooting Chant ms.
Offering jewels	w-y-u-b-pollen	Matthews 1902, p. 91
Offering to Young Pinyon	w-u-y-b-ashes-u pollen-reed pollen-real pollen	Shooting Chant ms.
Prayer to Big Snakes	w-u-y-b	Ib.
Sand on mountain	w-u-y-b	Ib.
Snakes at home	w-y-u-b	Newcomb-Reichard, Fig. 6
Canes in prayer	b-w-r-p	Haile 1943a, p. 286
Flints in song	b-w-ser(p)-var	Ib., p. 151

The Hail Chant sequence b-u-y-w is mentioned for Clouds, Cloud homes; Cloud, Fog, Lightning, Tadpole, Water, and Moss prayersticks; covers of Changing Woman's cradleboard; doorway covers; pollen food of Snakes; and Wind People with Snakes.[19]

The sequence b-u-y-p is found in invocations to Winds, Thunders, and Water Monsters, prayersticks of Monster Slayer and his brothers, and of Wind; Agate Boys as houseposts (sequence b-u-y-p-w[up]); in the prayer for the journey through the rooms of a black flint house (sequence b-u-y-ser).[20]

An invocation to Cloud houses and to waters has the sequence b-u-y-var.[21]

The sequence b-w-u-y is mentioned for flints blown at Spider Woman by Monster Slayer; superimposed spider webs; hoops made by Holy Man to restore Buffalo; invocation to Pinyon; prayer of Buffalo prayersticks.[22]

Other sequences are found only once; some are extended beyond four elements. A gambler took offerings of jewels and sacred materials—whiteshell, turquoise, abalone, redstone, jet, sparkling rock, blue pollen, pollen, real pollen—to help him win. When he wagered with Talking God, he laid them down in this order, except that he transposed red and yellow.[23]

A mirage-encircling guardian was described as black with white, blue, yellow, and red, the jewel arrow sequence, w-u-y-r, sprinkled on it.[24]

There is often a series of covers or curtains (Concordance B) that vary in sequence. In the Night Chant the gods' sweathouses were covered by Day Skies—black, blue, yellow, white; these were also the cradleboard covers of Changing Woman. Monster Slayer in his babyboard was covered with Darkness, Blue Sky, Blue-evening-light, Yellow-evening-light, Mirage, and Heat, sequence b-u-u-y-var-shining. Curtains in the order Darkness, Daylight, Moon, Sun—that is, in sequence b-w-w-u—hung over the door where Gambler and Talking God gambled.[25]

In introducing a prayer to Snakes, Gray Eyes said, "At the time of the origin of this story these various pollens were shaken down separately and it was decreed that they should not be mixed, but at present they are shaken off any old way and mixed together. On this subject people's minds are not clear. I alone carefully observe this." [26]

In the Hail Chant, color is attached to directions concerning the position of the human body. The ' manos,' equivalent to prayersticks, are crumbled as follows: black in front of the patient, blue at his right, yellow at his back, and white at his left.[27]

Sequence in Outlines

Sequence is important also in outlines around the symbols of places and around or upon certain figures. In the schematic representations the flat or central color, first in the series, is italicized; it is followed by the others, reading from inside out. The most elaborate have a center with four petal-like figures at the cardinal directions. The sequence b-w-y-u-r appears as an outline series at the center of the arrangement in the pictures of the home of the Big Snakes, the Armored Twins, the Arrow People, the Buffalo People (Newcomb-Reichard, Pls. IX, XVII, XXXV; *Navajo Medicine Man*, Pl. XXIV). There is the same sequence around the petal-like figure east of the center in the pictures of Thunders (Newcomb-Reichard, Pl. XXXI) and Buffalo (*Navajo Medicine Man*, Pl. XXIV). In another Buffalo painting the outlines are in this sequence around the element north of the center (*Navajo Medicine Man*, Pl. XXIII). The verbal description of Sky-reaching-rock has the same sequence of outlines with the explanation: black is the mountain itself and the water on the mountain, white is foam on the water; yellow, water pollen; blue-red, the rainbow.

The outline color sequence of the center of *Navajo Medicine Man*, Plate XIV, is, however, y-b-w-u-r. This contrast suggests one reason for the differences frequently encountered: the point of view from which a painting is described must be known; it is often far from obvious or simplistic. The house in Plate XIV is said to have been laid in black to represent water, but what shows is a round design of yellow—standing for real pollen with which the water was covered—with outlines of black, white, blue, and red; there is nothing in the picture to indicate that the center is supposed to be dark.

The center of Newcomb-Reichard, Plate V, appears outlined in the sequence y-w-b-u-r, but is said to be laid in the order b-u-w-y-r.

Lines around the drawing of the newly planned world were described as u-y-b-w-shiny (rock crystal).[28]

Other outline sequences are the following:

Sequence	Direction	Subject of Painting	Reference
u-b-w-y-r	cen	Pollen Boy on Sun	NR, Pl. II, B
	cen	Sun in eclipse	NR, Pl. XI
	cen	Monster Slayer on Sun	NR, Pl. XV
	cen	Feathered Arrow P	MM, Pl. XIII
	s of cen	Buffalo-who-never-dies	MM, Pl. XXIV
u-y-w-b-r	s of cen	Buffalo home	MM, Pl. XXIII
	s of cen	Big Snakes	NR, Pl. VIII
	s of cen	Thunders	NR, Pl. XXXI
w-b-y-u-r	we of cen	Big Snakes	NR, Pl. VIII
	we of cen	Thunders	NR, Pl. XXXI
	we of cen	Buffalo Mountain	MM, Pl. XXIII
	we of cen	Buffalo-who-never-dies	MM, Pl. XXIV
y-u-b-w-r	n of cen	Buffalo	NR, Pl. XXVI
	n of cen	Buffalo and Medicine P	NR, Pl. XXVIII
	n of cen	Thunders	NR, Pl. XXXI
y-u-w-b-r	we of cen	Buffalo home	MM, Pl. XXIII
	n of cen	Big Snake P	NR, Pl. VIII
	n of cen	Buffalo	NR, Pl. XXV
	n of cen	Buffalo	NR, Pl. XXVI
y-b-w-u-r	cen	Snakes at Mountain-fallen-away	MM, Pl. XIV
r-b-w-u-y	cen	Red Snakes at Red Mt.	MM, Pl. XVI

Correspondingly unpredictable are the series of lines made on the bodies of Snakes in some of the sandpaintings:

Plate	Subject	Sequence	Position
NR, IX	Big Snakes	*w*-b-u-y-r *b*-w-u-y-r *y*-u-w-b-r *u*-y-w-b-r	top bottom
NR, VI	Big Snakes	*b*-w-y-u-r *w*-b-y-u-r	n(top) s (bottom)
MM, XV	Crooked Snakes	*w*-b-y-u-r *b*-y-u-r-w *y*-u-w-b-r *u*-y-w-b-r	e we
MM, XIV	Crooked Snakes	*w*-b-y-u-r *b*-w-y-u-r	s
MM, XVI	Crooked Red Snakes	*r*(w)-b-y-u-r *r*(b)-w-y-u-r	s

The above sequences have been taken from their setting to show a particular kind of correspondence. A few duplicates of pictures are available, but, unfortunately, not sufficient information about the circumstances to furnish evidence for the differences. Let us compare two versions of the picture Buffalo-who-never-dies—the version in *Navajo Medicine Man*, Plate XXIV, and one I saw at Rough Rock on November 24, 1938:

Sequence at	*MM, Pl. XXIV*	*Rough Rock Picture*
cen	*b*-w-y-u-r	*u*-y-u-r [29]
e	*b*-w-y-u-r	*b*-w-u-y-r
s	*u*-b-w-y-r	*u*-y-b-w-r
we	*w*-b-y-u-r	*w*-b-y-u-r
n	*y*-b-w-u-r	*y*-u-w-b-r
herbs se to ne	*b*-u-w-y	*b*-u-w-p

This example illustrates the complications of the problems. Both pictures belong to the Fire Dance branch of the Shooting Chant; the one at Rough Rock was made for a male singer. Its function, to restore power to a chanter who made mistakes, may have been the reason for the slight variations. Besides the differences in color, *Navajo Medicine Man*, Plate XXIV, has buffalo houses (horizontal bars) and short rainbows between the center and the major figures of the Holy People; these were missing in the picture at Rough Rock.

Only one generalization emerges from these details: with few exceptions, red or blue-red, the rainbow pair, is on the outside. None of these pictures, except perhaps *Navajo Medicine Man*, Plate XVI, was drawn for the Red Inside phase of the Male Shooting Chant Holy Sun's House branch; if they had been, the sequences would doubtless be different.[30] Obviously, red guards the element with duplicate outlines. The order of the outlines may be a phase of alternation, that is, determined by the relative place of the particular performance in the chanter's sequence. Singers usually insist on having a patient as if the whole ceremony were being performed even when painting or doing only a part of a ceremony for record; doubtless they need a patient to establish a viewpoint for details—of sex, direction, alternation. They cannot think of a chant in terms of a single part; it must be thought of as a whole—even an excerpt includes many kinds of elements.

·   ·   ·

During the course of this analysis I have suggested several reasons for color combinations that occur, and for differences related to the setting and figures in a particular picture, to the colors required by the chant scheme, to the branch or phase of the chant, and even to the sequence of the chanter's singing of chant, branch, and phase. Although it is difficult to account for all these differences, there is enough evidence to show that they are not accidental.

Color sequence differs with the chant in which it occurs, each having its own sequence. If it happens to be the same for more than one chant, it does not necessarily have the same significance in all; indeed, the interpretation may differ somewhat even in the same chant.

Changes of sequence may depend upon the sex of the patient.

The sequences may be read in a sunwise cycle from east to north or in a cross arrangement, east to west, south to north—a matter connected with the sex of both patient and color. The sex of the patient probably dictates the lead color, that is, the one at the east.

Although the symbolism of each chant is dominant and regular, it is by no means universal in a given chant. The sequence may define the deities represented or some symbol of their power, and may take precedence over the chant symbolism, although some adjustment may be made between the two.

The colors of a sequence may signify a choice of colors for a limited number of places chosen from a series containing more units than the places needed. In verbal descriptions all elements may be mentioned.

Sequences represented in different ways, by major figures of the sandpaintings, minor elements of the sandpaintings, paintings of prayersticks, figure painting, and the like, do not necessarily correspond, although their association may be very close.

The sequences may depend upon the position of the chant

sung in the series of four or in the number it chances to be in the chanter's practice (Chapter 19).

Reversal accounts for some color sequences just as it does for other unusual procedures (Chapter 11).

Color Associations

To demonstrate certain ideas of the universe, Chart I was set up to show how dogma synchronizes different types of symbol with the making of the world, especially the placing of the mountains. There is an association between mountains, stones, day skies, jewels, birds, vegetation, sound, body-part of the personified earth, inhabitants, power of motion, special gifts, and physiography. Now that the symbolism of place and position, time and timing, space, direction, sex, dominance, size, alternation, reversal, precious stones, color, and color combinations has been discussed, other associations may be made in schematic form to tell a story. Charts V–XVI (pages 238–40) show several of these associations and illustrate also the complex relationships of the numerous elements.

The color associations of Thunders, Snakes (Chart V), and Sky People (Chart X) are similar. No others, however, are exactly the same; the Sun-Wind and jewel colors are more closely related to one another than to the other groups. Other associations are quite apparent and a few have no explanation.

The directional circuit in which Winter Thunder and Dark Thunder blew smoke (Chart XII) is the reverse of the normal ritualistic scheme—down-up, east-north-west-south—because they were announcing war.

CHART V

ASSOCIATION OF SYMBOLS (SHOOTING CHANT)

Realm	Sex	Color	Sun-Wind Group	Color	Jewel	Thunder	Snake	God Conveyance	Color	Twin Hero	Human Hero
Sky	m	b	Sun	u	t	b	b	zigzag lightning	b	MS	Holy Man
			BW	b	ab	y	y	rainstreamer	y	ChGr	Holy Boy
Earth	f	u	Moon	w	wh	u	u	flash lightning	r	ChW	Holy Woman
			YW	y	re	p	p	rainbow (sunglow)	(var)	RE	Holy Girl

CHART VI

MOUNTAINS AND HERB PEOPLE (SHOOTING CHANT)

Holy Man approached mountain at	Climbed...side of mountain	Sat at...side of mountain	Saw...Herb P
e	n	s	w
we	s	n	y
s	s	—	u
n	n	—	var

CHART VII

BUFFALO HOMES (SHOOTING CHANT)

Homes at	Made of	With...of	Color	Representing
e	Darkness	cen	w	Dawn
s	Blue Sky	upper half	y	Yellow-evening-light
we	Dawn	upper half	b	Darkness
n	Yellow-evening-light	upper half	y	Blue Sky

CHART VIII

ENDLESS SNAKE (MALE SHOOTING CHANT EVIL)

Snake color	Snake guards	Realm color
b	sky	b
u	earth	u
w	mountains	(w)
y	waters	(y)

CHART IX

LINES OF FIGURE PAINTING (SHOOTING CHANT)

Color	Represents
b	zigzag lightning
w	flash lightning
u	sunbeam
y	rainbow

CHART X

SKY PEOPLE (SHOOTING CHANT)

Sky P	Sex	Color	Gave Changing Woman cane of ...
Sky	m	b	t
Sun	m	y	ab
Water	f	u	wh
Summer	f	p	re

CHART XI

TALKING GOD MADE CHANGING WOMAN'S NUBILITY HOGAN
(Haile 1938b, p. 89)

At	Of	With sound of
e	wh	bluebirds
s	t	cornbeetle
we	ab	small, pretty bluebirds
n	j	cornbeetle

CHART XII

WINTER THUNDER AND DARK THUNDER
(Reichard 1944d, p. 45)

Blew smoke in...direction	To
down	Earth
up	Sky
e	Dawn
n	(Night)
s	Blue-horizon-light
we	Yellow-evening-light

CHART XIII

OFFERINGS (SHOOTING CHANT)

Of	Made to
wh	white corn
ab	yellow corn
t	blue corn
j	variegated corn
j	Dark Thunder
ab	Yellow Thunder
t	Blue Thunder
wh	Pink Thunder

CHART XIV

BUFFALO PEOPLE AT THE MOUNTAIN-OF-MOTION
(SHOOTING CHANT)

Color at	Represents
cen	Mountain-of-motion
b	motion of mountains
w	motion of rocks
u	motion of clouds
y	motion of waters

CHART XV

LANDSCAPE
(Sapir-Hoijer, p. 199)

Color	Represents
w	river
b	cottonwoods
u	water
y-green	cottonwoods

CHART XVI

HORSES
(Haile 1943a, p. 287)

Color	Jewel	Kind of Horse
u	t	Sun's
r	re	bay or red-maned
b	j	black
w	wh	white or white-maned
y	ab	roan

CHAPTER 14

NUMBER

Even Numbers

REPETITION IS one of the major devices of Navaho ritual. The attention formerly paid to fourfold repetition has obscured the whole subject of number, since four and multiples of four were selected for emphasis from the vast array of numbers actually found. The analysis of prayers has shown that scarcely any number predominates in Navaho ritual.[1]

Pairing has been mentioned in other connections and twofold repetition is taken for granted (Chapters 10, 13).

The sandpaintings illustrate the progressive use of number; those in the Newcomb-Reichard volume were arranged to illustrate its relative importance. If only one painting of a series is made, either for a test or in a more elaborate rite or chant, it is usually chosen from at least two paintings that differ chiefly in color arrangements, depending on the sex of the patient. Another painting may be chosen from a progressively elaborated series. The Snake series admirably illustrates the rule. Two snakes may be adequate, four is a common choice, eight may be used, and the number may be increased to twelve, sixteen, twenty, and sometimes even forty or fifty-six. Newcomb-Reichard, Plate III, which has twelve figures, may be made with twenty-four. *Navajo Medicine Man*, Plate XV, with fifty-six snakes, is an elaboration of Plate IX, in Newcomb-Reichard, which has forty. Multiplication of elements is believed to strengthen power.

Merely a few of the many possible examples of the use of four and multiples will be given because this phase of number is well-known:

Navaho stars have four points.[2]

The signal for a race is ' 1, 2, 3, 4, go!'[3]

Matthews gives three versions of the number of Earth Pillars; one has four poles at each of the four quarters, one has sixteen, and the third version has thirty-two. In the picture of the People-who-stand-under-the-sky there are six at the south and six at the north.[4]

To announce their presence gods commonly give their call four times, beginning with a faint sound which becomes successively louder and nearer.[5]

Attempts to create new things or to overcome evils are usually unsuccessful three times and successful the fourth.[6]

Mythologically, ritualistically, and often empirically, a request can hardly be refused a fourth time; the very fact of the fourth repetition makes acquiescence compulsory. Refusal the fourth time is serious indeed and rare in the literature.[7]

Four (or a multiple) applies to time reckoning as well as to the designation of space, persons, objects, and actions. The number of days occupied in discussion as well as the number intervening before an assembly or group enterprise takes place is important and depends upon the people as well as on the kind of activity proposed.

When Whiteshell Woman was dying of loneliness, Talking God appeared to her and bade her come to an assembly of the gods four days later.[8]

After the monsters had left only four people in the world, Talking God appeared and bade them meet him at the top of a sacred mountain in twelve days.[9]

Twelve days after being notified, the gods met to perform a ceremony to get back the great shells Gambler refused to give Sun.[10]

The people who desired to travel eastward from the western home of Changing Woman discussed the matter for twelve days, but, once having made a decision, fixed on the fourteenth day as the date of departure.[11]

People allowed considerable time to elapse before they took steps to allay anxiety about one who had disappeared.

The brothers of co, hero of the Night Chant myth, let four nights pass before they began to search for him when he did not return from the hunt.[12]

Twelve days after the Visionary had started making his whirling log, his grandmother began to worry for fear he might leave the family again as he had done once before.[13]

The number of idealized brothers is not the same in all the stories in which they appear. In my text of the Endurance Chant myth there are twelve brothers in addition to the sister, making thirteen in the family. This is understandable since the story and the chant are for driving off evil, a situation that requires odd numbers (see below). In what may be the secular form of the story, Matthews records twelve in the family, including the sister, and refers to ten left after the sister and youngest brother had been lost.[14]

A large and unexplainable even number is the reference to 102 years as the age of man—probably the ideal of a long life span. Matthews was also told that ' seven times old age has killed,' meaning that seven full generations of Navaho had existed up to the time he collected his legends.[15]

Odd Numbers

The use of five elements in the sandpaintings, discussed in *Sandpaintings of the Navajo Shooting Chant*, will not be repeated here. When I wrote in 1937, I had not seen a sandpainting with five major figures. Since then two sandpaintings of the Bead Chant featuring five figures symmetrically arranged have been published.[16]

The number of nights devoted to a rite or ceremony,

whether for blessing or exorcism, is odd. One-night sings are common. I know of only one type lasting an even number of nights, two nights and the intervening day, the second and fourth of the ideal series of four (Chapter 19). Other performances are carried through one, three, five, or nine nights.

The War Ceremony takes three nights. Because it is in the class of evil-chasing, the odd number seems reasonable. Chants sung for five or nine nights may be rationalized on the basis of four. When the more usual five-night form is chosen, each of the first four days is really a unit, for the ritualistic acts are repeated in quite regular order although each day new acts may be added, making the effect cumulative as well as repetitious. The last night is set off by name and by rite as distinct; during this time a summary in song is made of all the preceding acts and symbols. The nine-night form should be thought of as two four-night groupings plus the summary. The chief difference between the five- and nine-night terms is that of relative crowding and elaboration. Emetic and prayerstick offering take up the first four days of the nine-night ceremony; sandpaintings are made on the next four. When the ceremony is to last only five days, all these features are telescoped—emetic, prayerstick offering, and sandpainting being done on the same day. The Night Chant and the Fire Dance branches of other chants must last nine nights. Male Shooting Chant Evil continues five nights and is divided exactly as are the Holy chants: four nights (days) of repeated acts and one night of the song summary. My informants insist that an Evil chant should not be prolonged beyond five nights.

The number five and fivefold repetition must be considered as transitional between good and evil. The rule is that blessing and divinity are represented by even numbers, evil and harm by odd. Nevertheless, five is almost as common as four, although it has a somewhat subsidiary position in the sand-paintings. In the literature, where the full text with all repetitions of prayers, songs, and episodes is available, five-fold repetition is frequent and often five is a ' good ' number.

Remarks about Navaho ceremonies lasting many days refer to the unlimited singing that goes on when a singer or a group of singers performs for a person who seems hopelessly ill. Such singing belongs to the Life chants I have termed ' emergency rites.' It may be continued for days, weeks, even months, but is in some respects outside the pattern of the chant order or charm I am analyzing here. It includes many of the elements prescribed elsewhere, but in a different order. If a person recovers after these extreme ministrations, he is expected to have the ceremony sung over him just as does a person for whom a short test rite has been performed.

The requirement of odd numbers in Evil rites is more con-sistently corroborated by description and in practice than that of even numbers for blessing and holiness. Since odd numbers have never been discussed, I cite several typical cases:

The probable reason for groups of five in the sandpaintings of the Bead Chant is that the major figures are predatory animals.[17]

The Eagle Chant was to begin three days after the cere-monial hut was made. Since the Eagle Chant was to give power in eagle-catching, it belongs to the hunting—that is, Evil—category, as Hill indicates: "The beliefs connected with catching eagles paralleled those current in hunting deer, antelope, and bear." [18]

The war party that attacked Taos was on its way three days, including the journey thither and back. A second trip was proposed five days later, another eleven days after the second, and a fourth nine days after the third. The men sweated for three days in preparing for war.[19]

Monster Slayer gave the people three days to prepare for a raid. Five days intervened before offerings were made again. The warriors met once more after seven days, and a fourth time after nine days had passed.[20]

Hill's account of actual warfare shows that these examples are empirical as well as mythological.

The time between the formation of a war party and its departure must be an uneven number of days, the interval being spent in purification and preparation.[21]

Similarly, an odd number of days intervened between the consultation of the singer and the departure of a hunting party.[22]

When a gambler contested with Talking God for deer, he transformed tiny offerings into a great heap of precious stones. Talking God and Black God gave each of those present fifteen pieces, then thirteen, nine, seven, and five.[23] The reason for the odd numbers, mentioned in descending order, is doubtless the subject of the tale: gambling and hunting (since deer are the wager), both uncertain activities.

Matthews' note regarding the attack of the twelve bears in the Story of Deer Owner is interesting in connection with number. He remarks that the episode is weak and inartistic, even wrong, since there were five devices for killing.[24] According-ing to the rule of odd numbers, five might be expected, since Deer Owner was a wizard and was practicing sorcery on the hero.

Numbers in the myth "Growth of the Navaho Nation," which recounts the wanderings of the people and the origin of clans, are frequently odd.[25]

Once when the Navaho met new people there were twelve, it is true, but instead of being paired, they consisted of five men, three women, one grown girl, one grown boy, and two small children. Another accession was a family of seven adults. Changing Woman gave the people created at her western home five pets and five canes, with which they later struck water from the desert.[26]

I think odd numbers are appropriate here because the people were setting out into uncertain and foreign territory. On the other hand, when Changing Woman's own power, which is firmly, definitely divine, is referred to, the numbers are two and four.[27]

Ceremonial numbers in exorcistic rites (which may occur even in holiness ceremonies) occur according to the rules:

Unraveling is repeated an odd number of times, the number increasing on the successive nights of a chant (*Unraveling*, Concordance C).[28]

The fir garment is usually composed of a specific odd number of knots to be tied at various parts of the body, the numbers increasing on successive nights of a single ceremony (*Plant garment*, Concordance C).

Five hoops recapitulate the were-coyote episode and restoration of Holy Man to divine normality (*Hoop transformation rite*, Concordance C).[29]

After the basket drum had been prepared for Rainboy to eliminate the evil resulting from war, it was turned over and hit five times just before Rainboy was called in.[30]

Some uses of number are difficult, if not impossible, to explain on the basis of the rules for good and evil, since odd and even numbers are combined.

The Twins had brought five hoops back from their second visit to their father, Sun. Changing Woman set up the black hoop so it would roll to the east. Through it she spat a four-cornered black hailstone. She set up a blue hoop at the south and through it spat a six-cornered blue hailstone. At the west the yellow hailstone had eight corners, and at the north the white one had eleven. A shiny hoop, through which four vari-colored flint knives had been cast, was flung to the zenith.[31]

The frequent use of incense in the Holy chants and its infrequency in the Evil form lead me to consider it an element that attracts good. Often it is burned on two coals, but in the Hail Chant myth there were two after the emetic of the first day, three after the sprinkling of the second day, and four after the sprinkling of the third day.[32]

The number of baskets differs greatly and probably does not correspond completely with the chanter's generalization. The Prayerstick branch of the Shooting Chant emphasizes good, yet five baskets were required.

Because they vary so much, no significance can yet be assigned to the number of individual songs in specific rites, combination of songs in groups, or grouping into ceremony. Song lists show that even and odd numbers are common for the songs themselves and repetition within them in Blessing, Holy, and Evil rituals.[33]

First Time

So much importance is attached, in both myth and practice, to beginning an event or to the first time an act takes place as to make initiation a major symbol. The success of a first attack in raiding is an omen of the final outcome, toward which careful ceremonial preparations are directed.

In helping his children overcome the most dangerous and powerful of all the monsters, Sun instructed them: "When you reach the earth, don't do anything. Let me do the first slaying." Consequently, the first blow was struck at Big Monster by lightning, sent by Sun, deafening the enemy, depriving him of sense, and softening him for the later blows of The Twins.[34]

In contributing various elements to the blackening rite of the War Ceremony, Crow instructed: "I myself shall be the first to attack the ghost of the enemy." [35]

After Monster Slayer had restored Sun's blue horse, he instructed: "Suppose that in the future one of you returns from war with booty and the first person meeting you asks for some part of it, you must not deny it to him. Such refusal would mean refusal to part with the enemy." [36]

The import of initial behavior is demonstrated by the ritualistic massage of the pubescent girl, and of The Twins at their first visit to Sun (cp. *Pressing*, Concordance B).

At each of the many sweat-emetic rites I have attended, the first of the series was performed carefully and elaborately, the greatest importance seeming to be attached to it. Succeeding rites were perfunctory, although the third day of the chants, when exorcism was emphasized, was also stressed.

Apparently the first try has power because it signifies the purpose and predicts the outcome. The last of a repeated series is also important because it is culminative; what has been indicated as good has taken place.

Within all these types of symbolism, and so closely connected with them that it can hardly be differentiated, is the aesthetic motive which sometimes manifests itself as a ritualistic rationalization. The notion of multiple selves is a convenient supernatural device for spanning the difficulties of space and necessity. It is an artifice that lends force to the power of repetition and recapitulation, and it is also a means of elaboration, of obtaining balance, symmetry, and contrast especially in plastic representation. Pairing is an illustration of a cultural compulsion. The reason that Whiteshell Woman and Turquoise Woman are doubles for Changing Woman is aesthetic as well as ritualistic. Similarly, although Child-of-the-water is the gentle, pacific, steady foil to the active, impulsive Monster Slayer, the functions of their doubles, Changing Grandchild and Reared-in-the-earth, are hardly discernible except as an artistic device, though the effect of multiplication must not be completely ignored.

CHAPTER 15

PERCEPTUAL SYMBOLS

Light and Seeing

THOUGH THE Navaho are so impressed by color that they have woven it into their entire ritualistic scheme, they seem to regard it as a function of light. In Stevenson's origin myth we are told, "By the time they had reached the fourth world the people had separated light into its several colors." They assigned the colors to the different parts of the sky to be the light manifestations called the Day Skies—Dawn, Blue Sky, Yellow-evening-light, Darkness.[1]

In the upper world the people found only darkness; they had to create the sun, moon, and stars to furnish light. In Matthews' most detailed version, each color lasted an equal interval in the first world; in the second, black and blue lasted longer than white and yellow; in the third, black and blue lasted still longer; and in the fourth, black and blue lasted most of the time. According to tłá·h, although there was neither sun nor moon in the third world (yellow), the mountains gave plenty of light.[2]

Light is an essential of life and protection, whose most outstanding symbol is pollen, tádídí·n (xádídí·n), 'it emits light in all directions, it shines in amongst.' Since light (sunbeams, warmth) is a necessary element of generation, it is not surprising that pollen should be the symbol of fructification, vivification, and the continuity of life and safety. The associations are extended to include glint or sheen as an essential part of an animal, object, or person, a quality repre-

250

sented by pollen. Sheen is distinct from color—Bear had it from a red glow; magpie feathers, though black, have it; water and snakes, whatever their color, may have it. The legs and lower bodies of Buffalo are outlined in yellow to represent their warmth and moisture, which make plants grow and produce pollen.

'Real pollen' is the pollen of the cattail rush and seems to supersede even 'corn pollen,' which is of great ceremonial value.[3] 'Snake pollen' was explained to me by a Shooting Chanter: "They used to collect the scales of Snake's skin, but now they put pollen on, they brush it off, and that is the same as the shine on the snake."

Matthews explains 'water pollen': "During the summer rains, in the Navaho land, a fine yellow powder collects on the surface of pools; it is probably the pollen of pine; but the Navahoes seem to think it is a product of water and call it water pollen."[4] Pollen is the symbol of the water's light, its power of motion and life.

With these interpretations in mind it is less difficult to understand 'blue pollen,' the ground petals of larkspur or other blue flowers, which is pollen only in a functional sense; it represents light.

Animals are killed for ceremonial purposes by smothering in pollen, care being taken not to wound them. The pollen is believed to absorb their 'life.' If they struggle a long time resisting death, it is a sign of strength, which will be communicated to the person for whom the pollen is subsequently sprinkled.

Matthews summarizes the meaning of pollen: "Pollen is the emblem of peace, of happiness, of prosperity, and it is supposed to bring these blessings. When, in the Origin Legend, one of the war gods bids his enemy to put his feet down in pollen he constrains him to peace. When in prayer the devotee says, 'May the trail be in pollen,' he pleads for a happy and peaceful life."[5]

In connection with pollen as the representation of light, distinguished from that associated with color, the relation between pink, shimmer, and white in the atmosphere and yellow in the water should be noted. An unpublished painting in the Huckel Collection, *Buffalo People at the Mountain-of-motion*, represents not the mountains, rocks, clouds, and waters but their *motion*, their life, expressed by color associated with light (cp. Chart XIV, page 240).

Matthews refers to the haze in the air which the Navaho call the pollen of morning and evening sky, an idea probably closely related to the ritualistic acts of The Twins:[6]

Monster Slayer motioned with his hand over Mountain Woman and the glitter of sparkling rock made his face terrifying. Child-of-the-water moved his hand along the surface of Mountain Woman, then touched his face with his hand and it shone frightfully.[7]

The passage refers to 'sparkling rock,' which, paired with red, so frightens evils that they retreat as far as its beams extend.[8]

When Monster Slayer and Child-of-the-water were prepared for the War Ceremony for the first time, the elder made his face terrifying with sparkling medicine; his brother did the same and his face became so light it was impossible to look at it. The words that describe the transformation mean 'flash horror' and 'beam with horror.' Later the explanation is given: "The rubbing with red ocher belongs to Child-of-the-water and the sparkling medicine by means of which your faces strike terror will cause enemy ghosts to fear you."[9]

Flint is of ceremonial importance for several reasons: it reflects light, and when flints are struck together, they make a frightening sound. Flint armor must be thought of as consisting of free pieces that rattle as the wearer moves. Serrated flint has more facets than plain flint, from which light is reflected.

Changing Woman for a long time resisted moving to her new home in the west. At length impersonators of her sons dressed themselves in black, blue, yellow, and serrated flint. As she saw them approaching, she was terrified by the light of their armor. The leader spoke loudly to her and as he spoke his companions stamped the earth, making the flints rattle, scaring her even more. Their attack, undertaken reluctantly as a last resort, finally frightened her into compliance.[10]

When Bat prepared to take the offering to Black God for the restoration of Rainboy, he dressed himself completely in flint. At the ends of his wings were zigzag lightnings, which, with the light of pre-dawn, deprived those beholding him of their courage.[11]

Appearing before the lesser evils—Hunger, Craving-for-meat, Poverty, and Sleep—Monster Slayer looked at them with disgust and they, in their turn, stared at him, for his flint raiment always struck terror into people.[12]

· Flashing light accompanies many of Sun's actions, but is especially emphasized when he appears in his celestial guise to Earth People, and even when he sends a token of his presence.

After Changing Woman had attempted conception with Dripping Water, she suddenly heard a loud noise above her. She looked up and saw a man so light that she could not continue to look at him.[13]

When Sun sent his own symbol of the War Ceremony, a light struck into the center of the room, a sound "so" was heard and there stood the symbol in turquoise! It was the pattern for Earth People, and as soon as they had a good look at it and learned how to imitate it, it disappeared (Chapter 18).[14]

Sun by his light enabled Holy Man to wink once more after he had been shattered by Winter Thunder and his parts had been rearranged for restoration.[15]

Light is a teasing incentive to new adventures which bring new knowledge and ceremonial control, often indicated as a mythological episode in which a person sees a far distant light, searches for it in vain, sets up a sighting device on a forked stick, and is eventually brought or led into the territory of the enticer.

First Woman in the lowest world thus found a mate whose fire was turquoise.[16]

The owner of the pet turkey of the Feather Chant, after planting his garden, saw a light in the distance. It directed him to Deer Owner's home, a visit which eventually gave him control of rare game. Monster Slayer as the hero of the Eagle Chant had a similar experience.[17]

Sunbeam (cáńdí'n) and sunray (cábitłó'l) are mentors, beings who know what is going to happen and guide heroes.

Rock crystal is a symbol of illumination.

When the Eagles had trouble getting Scavenger of the Bead Chant to the sky, Fringed Mouth and Talking God came to prepare him for the journey he was to make. Because it was dark in the cloud in which he was to travel, they gave him a crystal to light his way.[18]

The hero of the Feather Chant was transported by Talking God to a house full of Holy People. The walls were covered with rock crystal, which gave forth a brilliant light. The Stricken Twins of the Night Chant were conducted into a similar dwelling.[19]

Conceptually, light and fire are not completely differentiated, but fire probably symbolizes heat as well as light. The crystal fire owned by First Woman is almost certainly related to the rock crystal that ceremonially lights the prayersticks and tobacco pipe.

The warning prayerstick began to burn when Monster Slayer was in danger.

In the Shooting Chant myth the glow changed the pink of the prayerstick to red. The same incident as recorded by

Matthews has Monster Slayer say to his brother, "If [these prayersticks] take fire from the sunbeam, you may know I am in great danger." Later Child-of-the-water tells him, "About midday the black prayerstick took fire and I was troubled for I knew you were in danger, but when it had burned halfway the fire went out and . . . I thought you were safe again." [20]

The light seems to have shown the danger; no effects of heat, except the change in color, were indicated.[21]

In view of the way light has been woven into ritual, the Navaho words defining phases of light are interesting:

tádídí·n, ' it-shines-in-all-directions, pollen '

cáńdí·n, ' sunbeam '

bitšázdińdí·n, ' a frightening light shone from him '

The following are attributive:

bízdílid, ' polished, glassy, smooth from high polish '

niłxin, ' opaque, greasy '

no·lɣin, ' lustrous like wax '

no·lɣíni·, ' lustrous like agate, agate '

niłtólí, ' somewhat clear '

niłtó·l, ' superficially clear '

niłtó·lí, ' clear all the way through, clean, pure '

nitšílí, ' being somewhat crystalline '

niłtší·l, ' having crystalline structure '

niłtšį·ł, ' glittering ' (in separate particles, as frost)

níłtšįł, ' scintillating ' (as diamond)

To be compared with the last two is nitší·ł, ' healthy, sound.' If these stems are related, we may have to conclude that a person is not healthy or sound unless he has light or glint.

ditcił, ' scintillating varicolored, iridescent ' (as abalone)

disǫs, ' having coppery reflections, pink ' (as star)

yibe·, ' shimmering '

Sound and Hearing

Sound, associated with light, is thought of as issuing from a small orifice—the mouth, for instance—and spreading in a beam which widens like a beam of light from a pinpoint. This perhaps explains why ' talk, discuss, consider in words,' even ' sing,' are words constructed by varying the stem that means ' motion of a round or handy object.' Sound and breath are so closely related that a man is not complete if he lacks either; at the same time, mouth and voice, which produce the word, are also essential (Chapter 3).

The power of Cornbeetle Girl is often indicated by her sound. Her name is included in the series of the small birds whose calls represent happiness, peace, and prosperity. She gave voices to the first people created from corn ears.[22]

Once at an assembly of the gods, Monster Slayer drove Coyote out. Later Talking God and one of the male gods came in; when they opened their mouths to sing, they had no voices. The chant could not be sung until measures had been taken to placate Coyote and induce him to restore the voices.[23]

The loss of hearing is considered a calamity. The hearing of the Stricken Twins was restored when xa·ctčé·'óγan shouted lustily into their ears.[24]

Ordinarily the mentors know everything, even things never expressed by sound, for they can read the thoughts of deity and man. But when First Man instructed The Twins about the monsters, he whispered so low that even the Winds could not hear him.[25]

In the Stephen manuscript the effect of threatening sound on the body is described in a myth fragment about the slaying of the monsters.

The Twins stole up on Burrowing Monster, but a slight noise put him on his guard. Then, as they approached from the south, their noses made a cracking sound. At the west their ears crackled and at the north their flesh pricked—all warnings that they were contemplating wrong.[26]

Sight and hearing are important in divination, which is based upon seeing, listening, and trembling. Of these, listening is at present least popular. Formerly, two men who knew the proper prayer and were regarded as trustworthy were chosen to foretell by listening the outcome of a war raid, apparently after the party had been organized. The magical aids given the diviners included seeing as well as hearing. The war leader rubbed coyote and badger earwax on the ears and under the eyes of the listener to enable him to hear acutely and to see into the future. The men left camp and advanced a short distance toward the enemy country. It was a good omen if they saw horses or sheep, or if they heard the trotting of animals. On the other hand, the cry of the crow, screechowl, hoot owl, wolf, coyote, or other ' man-eating ' animal, the sound of enemy footsteps or conversation, or the moan of an injured person were so unfavorable that the party would turn back. Animal calls were common as war and hunting signals to the Navaho and other Indian tribes.

In the myth describing the attack of the Stricken Twins on Awatobi, the Hopi called their people together by wolf howls.[27]

To the Navaho, sound has forms other than that of a beam, as is evidenced by the explanation of the Thunder figure of the sandpaintings. There is often an arrow at each side of the head, said to represent Thunder's sound; the pink curved featherlike lines at the bottom of the tail are the reverberation.[28]

As is usual with other types of symbolism, sounds attract good and exorcise evil.

The song or call of bluebird, canary, warblers, and corn-beetle at Changing Woman's nubility rite represented the groups of people approaching from all sides—gods who came bearing their gifts for her future welfare.[29]

When Monster Slayer was about to destroy the Frog People, they begged him to let them live, promising, "We shall not be ugly and mean in the future. We shall give our call just as we are doing now, but it will be asking for rain.[30]

Matthews records a rite for bringing rain in which sound is significant:

A singer said that if the Navaho captured a mountain sheep in a dry season they butchered it, cut out and cleaned the paunch. Then they slapped it against a stone. In the summer such an act would bring rain, in the winter, snow.[31]

A fur collar to which a whistle is attached is a ceremonial property of some chant bundles. After a sandpainting of the Shooting Chant has been finished and someone has been sent to call the patient and audience, the chanter puts on the collar and blows the whistle over the painting to signify to the gods that chanter and assistants are ready, that the people and gods should take their places.

The whistle of the Bead Chant also represents preparation, for it was the reed given Scavenger when he was about to be taken to the sky in the dark cloud. It was to supply him with air; every time he breathed, the whistling noise was heard.[32]

Kluckhohn and Wyman record a general explanation of the ceremonial whistle: "Blow sickness off, blow sickness off on all four sides of the sick man, that's what it's for." [33]

Singing in the Flint Chant is accompanied by a hoof rattle and some songs are sung to the rattling of flints.[34]

Coyote visited the Hummingbirds, where there were two beautiful maidens. Their clothing was ornamented with many bone and hoof pendants, which, rattling with every movement, seemed to emphasize the beauty of the garments.[35]

These are some ways in which sounds bring blessings. Sometimes, however, they ward off evil. Each deity, helper, and object has some power expressed by sound. Because of its purpose, primarily to counteract harm done by the monsters but also to control all kinds of enemy ghosts, the War Ceremony has more sound symbolism than any of the other ceremonies for which there are texts.[36]

The underlying explanation is that the harmful sounds of the slain monsters were beaten into the earth and the War Ceremony compensates the earth for the evils left over from prehistoric times. To make it successful, the enemy is sung and beaten into the earth. Beating the pot drum is beating the face of the enemy. With each beat of the stick on the pot drum the minds of enemy ghosts are drawn down toward the earth.[37]

Falsetto, featured in many of the War Ceremony songs— in sway singing, for example—is believed to have power to revive a fainting person. When a war party arrived home, there was sway singing in front of the hogan of every warrior who had taken a scalp.[38]

Even though the sounds of both victor and vanquished may be imitated in recapitulating the attack, care must be taken that the songs do not ' cross.' At the blackening rite one group inside the hogan shouts once in a while and the dancers outside also shout; the two groups should alternate, never call out simultaneously.[39]

As a part of the old-time training to develop strength, boys were taught to clap their hands to their lips as they shouted, as white children ' playing Indian ' do today.[40]

Sound, like taboo and other devices, may seduce a character. xwi'''é·hé, tó· xwi'''é·hé means ' arresting, attractive, seductive, enticing sound.' Girls are distracted from what they are doing by such a sound and, becoming curious, get

acquainted with wonderful men. The function of the capti-
vating noise is the same as that of the teasing fire mentioned
under "Light and Seeing" (above) and may similarly lead
to mating or marriage. In the legend of the War Ceremony,
Bear and Big-snake-man seduced the Corn Maidens with the
attractive sound.[41]

xwi·'é·hé, ' pleasing, arresting,' is applied to The Twins'
song of rejoicing as Changing Woman heard it when they
arrived home carrying the trophy of Big Monster.[42]

Often special sounds are believed to drive out evils: be'-
be'yó is a phrase common to exorcistic rites. Usually the
sound accompanies some motion, like that of brushing.

Each deity sometimes functions through sound and gesture, rather than through articulate language. Monster
Slayer utters his sound, xahą··· xahą···, when he wants to
stay the evil he encounters; Child-of-the-water follows with
his sound, xą xą xą xą. The approach of Talking God is
heralded a long way off by a faint trace of his cry, which
becomes regularly louder as it is repeated nearer and nearer
(Chapter 14). At the fourth cry, Talking God appears. He
explains to co, hero of the Night Chant, "You must tell
[your people] that my voice is ominous, and that if anyone
hears it, something strange will happen to him or to his
people that day." [43]

The application of ceremonial items to the novices at the
Night Chant initiation, accompanied by the characteristic
sounds of the officiating gods, serves to shield the children
from danger that might threaten when they look at sandpaintings.[44]

One or more sounds are significant symbols of every ceremony. They are difficult to reduce to writing, since their
effect depends more upon the manipulation of the breath
than of the speech organs. The sound symbol of the Shooting

Chant is something like blu⋯, articulated with violent and prolonged vibration of the lips and variation in tone approximating that of the bull-roarer. To achieve the effect, it is, of course, necessary to prolong the vowel greatly. JS says the sound ' makes the body holy.'

The corresponding sound symbol of the Hail Chant is bluwe', in which blu- is short and -we' very short, the glottal stop almost a gag. Each syllable of the exorcistic be'be'yó has a very short staccato articulation and a high startling tone. Wyman describes the sound symbol of the Navaho Wind Chant: "hihi'yi, the three syllables represented by the three notes, approximating C below the staff, treble clef, an octave above, the original C; the tempo, a sixteenth note, followed by a note of two beats, a final sixteenth sharply broken off. It is the voice of the wind supernatural, the sound of the wind." [45]

The bull-roarer, called ' thunder speaks,' is said to imitate Thunder's sound. In the Shooting Chant it drives away evil.[46]

To the reflected light, texture, hardness, and strength of flint is added the power of the sound produced when one flint comes in contact with another (ka'j). One of the ritualistic acts of the singer, repeated at intervals, is to rub his hands through flints lying in the ceremonial basket to make them rattle.

To protect The Twins against Crow, the messenger of the monsters, First Man constructed a spiral arrangement of flints which reached the sky. With every light breeze the grind of the flints (kaj) could be heard, and approach to The Twins was impossible.[47]

Flints, as well as persons, must know when to withhold their power—a symbol of negation.

As infants The Twins were a source of great concern. Upon the advice of Rock Crystal and Talking God, they were put on a mirage stone under which flint arrowpoints were arranged, one in each of the four directions. Because of the flints, even though they did not speak, the monsters became aware of unfavorable conditions. Had the flints produced a sound, there would have been no hope for the survival of human beings.[48]

Other effects of sound are the following:

Pursued by Tracking Bear, Monster Slayer climbed a sheer wall. As he did so, he grasped a fruit of the yucca in his left hand and in his right a twig of hard oak. The monster feared the rattle (zai·) of the medicines.[49]

Witch objects shot into the hero of the Big Star Chant were extracted by the screeching of Prairie Hawk and Mountain Lion.[50]

Coyote, trying to overcome Big Monster by cutting his thigh, said, "to· to· to· to·," ostensibly to heal the cut. The formula worked to heal Coyote's thigh but failed when tried on Big Monster. Matthews explains that to· or tóhe means 'stand, stay' and is spoken to ritualistic objects, as in the dance of the standing arcs of the Mountain Chant to make the arcs resume an upright position without support.[51]

Echo is explained as Crushing Rocks' consent to be subjected by Monster Slayer.[52]

The sound of wind passing through the reeds owned by First Man is equivalent to music.[53]

Sound in the body of Cicada made the reed in which the prehuman creatures had taken refuge move.[54]

Odor and Smell

The Navaho conception of smell differs from ours in several respects. xaltcin means 'it has an odor, odor is given out'; xaltcxin, 'it has a strong smell.' Neither word necessarily indicates 'bad odor,' because nothing that is 'natural,' provided by nature, is considered disagreeable. Cabbage and skunk smell strong, perhaps, but not bad. Something is said to smell bad when it it is spoiled (niłtcxon).

Despite the belief that cast-off body material may become dangerous, lack of disgust is remarkable. Women evince no distaste for any of the butchering processes, for instance, and adults make no haste to clean babies, but let them crawl about, soiling things. They pay no attention to a child who smears himself and his vicinity with blood caught from a slaughtered animal or with the contents of entrails.

The role of odor in ritual and myth is, therefore, the more surprising. One of Father Berard's informants told him that the nose is a guide in thinking, the seat of thought.[55] Odor reveals strangers, for although most references explain how disagreeable the gods find the odor of Earth People, the reverse may also be true.

In the darkness The Twins entered an assembly of Earth People and, even though they could not be seen, the people could smell strangers amongst them.[56]

The odor of certain herbs may be pleasant to some deities, offensive to others. Strong-smelling plants, such as the sages, mints, and evergreens, perform the same functions as other ritualistic property—they attract good and disperse evil.

The description of the scene in which the hero of the Feather Chant first saw deer and other rare game includes the following:

The land was filled with deer and covered with beautiful flowers. The air had the odor of pollen and fragrant blossoms. Birds of the most beautiful plumage were flying in the air, or perching on the flowers and building nests in the deer's antlers.[57]

Odor makes chant lotion effective and contributes to the power of emetic, cold and warm infusion (ke·tłoh), and incense.

According to Gray Eyes, the Holy People are afraid of the chant lotion and incense.[58]

When an offering is presented to a deity, he inspects it, then smells it to test its perfection (*Acceptance of offering,* Concordance B).

Food and Taste

Navaho ritual emphasizes color and light rather than sight, sound rather than hearing, odor rather than smell. Not much is made of taste, but food is a major symbol of each chant. Fasting has already been mentioned as a means of purification; feasting, if only on the most ordinary foods, is a great attraction of every ceremony (Introduction). Some of the best recipes are given in the chant mythology.[59]

The idea prevails that special supernatural food imparts its strength to anyone strong enough to consume it.

Talking God and First Man had a discussion about what to feed the wonderful baby who grew up to be Changing Woman. Talking God suggested collected pollens, but First Man said the diet must contain moisture too. He agreed to give it pollen, but said he would add broth of rare game and dew of beautiful flowers. Talking God agreed and gave First Man full charge of the baby.[60]

Changing Woman left her twin infants to the care of Big Bear and Big-snake-man when she went to hunt food. When the mother was home the caretakers fed the children broth made of cottontails and field mice, but, as soon as she left, Bear gave them pollen and mountain dew and Snake fed them earth pollen and dew. Salt Woman stirred the broth with her whole hand, making it very salty. At first the food, being too strong, weakened the babies, but in a short time they thrived on it.[61]

Changing Woman ate whiteshell after she went to live in the west.[62]

When Sun conducted his twin sons to the skyhole through which they were to return to earth, they ate pollen of white and yellow corn, Dawn, Yellow-evening-light, and Sun, all mixed with water.[63]

Food enters into many mythical concepts; for instance, one person may be transformed into another by eating the latter's food, in some cases with no hope of transformation back into the original form. Smoking a man's tobacco may have the same effect; in any case, it is a test of powers. Another mythical concept is the inexhaustible food supply and the representation of much in little (Chapter 7; *Inexhaustible*, Concordance B).

The Eagles were able to change small game, such as rabbits, prairie dogs, and rats, into rare game.

The Hunting Animals, with their power to plant, cultivate, and harvest corn in a few minutes, represent an unlimited food supply.[64]

The Navaho call corn ' life itself,' but that by no means makes them vegetarians. They express their feeling about meat when the mockers of the Racing God twit him: "He is too weak and lazy to hunt. He lives on seeds and never tastes flesh." [65] Later the scoffers learned that racing gave the Racing Gods so much strength that they did not need meat, but possibly their doting grandmother fed them meat privately.

Racing is closely connected with endurance, both being associated with food and abstinence; the pubescent girl races frequently during the period when she continually grinds corn for her ceremonial cake; boys ran for miles as a part of the ancient training, preferably without food and drink, at least with very little. Racers ate ceremonial mush before starting a contest. Coyote explains to Big Monster in the Endurance Chant myth: "One who eats rare game can run fast, but what can one expect of a person who eats worms, grasshoppers, and lizards! No wonder you cannot race." [66]

Supernatural benefits to be derived from attendance at a ceremony may be symbolized by sending food as an invitation. The Meal Sprinklers take food to invite guests, even outsiders, to the Fire Dance and bring back food in token of acceptance. Parched corn has been mentioned as an effective absorptive device (Chapter 7). Cake (sweetened cornbread baked in a pit oven) is a treat of the Girl's Ceremony and the Flint Chant; in both it is an offering to Sun.[67]

Navaho is relatively devoid of words for taste. A general word, xalni· or xalni̜·, probably applies to all the senses, 'there is awareness, it is tasty.' łkan, often translated 'sweet,' should be translated 'pleasing to the taste, savory.'

CHAPTER 16

WORD, FORMULA, AND MYTH

THE NAVAHO cosmogonists were interested in man's culture and institutions no less than in the natural order. Language, perhaps the most intricate phase of culture, is by its nature symbolical, but in addition to the expected linguistic symbolism, there is ritualistic symbolism, like that of color, direction, and number. Speech as one of man's faculties, references in prayer to the 'tip of the speech,' the existence of the word from the very beginning of conceivable time, the requirement that prayer and song be accurately reproduced in spite of stringent restrictions and a strain on the memory—all these are evidences of linguistic awareness I have not found among other so-called primitive peoples; in fact, it is a cognizance almost lacking in our own society— lost rather than undeveloped. The painted symbol of a prayer with its words is further proof of Navaho recognition of the power of the word.[1]

There are references to ' archaic ' words in Navaho myth and ritual, based upon an unfounded assumption. So common have these references become that even the Navaho interpreters glibly speak of archaic words. No work has been done upon which to found an opinion about the relative age of Navaho words. Some of the most common must be very old in view of their relation to remote Athapaskan languages. Nor is it correct to call the expressions ' obsolete '; they are as current as words for water or fire, though the people using them may be fewer. The ritualistic phrases belong to a specialized ceremonial language, a cant, spoken by chanters but not by laymen. The special terms of one chant may differ from those of another; all are not necessarily understood by every singer. In one chant the names of characters may be the lay terms; in another, they may be completely or partly changed. For instance, the ordinary name for ' wolf ' is ' large coyote,' but ceremonially he may be called ' large-one-who-trots-like-a-person,' doubtless a reference to the werewolf. Coyote is often called ' First Scolder ' or ' First Warrior.' Hummingbird, ' animated-one-repeatedly-suspended,' becomes in the Hail Chant ' one-whose-wings-whir.' [2] The ordinary, literal names of the Holy People and their ceremonial names in the Shooting Chant, compared with general usage and other chants, are changed in kind and order. Most commonly the order is Holy Man (diné˙ diɣini˙), Holy Boy ('acki˙ diɣini˙), Holy Woman ('asdzą˙˙ diɣini˙), Holy Girl ('até˙d diɣini˙); in the Shooting Chant, Holy Boy is kiye˙ diɣini˙, Holy Woman is tčiké˙ diɣini˙. Holy Man and Holy Girl have the lay names, and the order in which they are mentioned is Holy Man, Holy Woman, Holy Boy, Holy Girl. This order is emphasized as a primary differentiation between the Male Shooting Chant and the others, particularly the Female Shooting Chant. In the Female Shooting Chant the females come first—Holy Woman, Holy Girl, Holy Man, Holy Boy.

Almost every item of ritualistic value has its own term and derives much of its power from its name, which may differ from chant to chant (*Bundle contents*, Concordance C). I have found nothing in the linguistic pattern that cannot be explained by the grammatical rules; a few variations in vocabulary may be encountered. The situation is comparable to that of English used by persons in ordinary life who have no interest in specialized subjects—science or religion, for instance. The Church has its own vocabulary, rarely under-

stood by the layman, for whom it has little interest; the
Navaho chant lore is the province of the chanters, the lay
Navaho accepts it, and, if he is pinned down to interpret it,
calls it archaic.

War parties had a special language that seems to be a part
of the cant. It is described, but few examples are recorded. I
take the paucity of examples to indicate that informant and
interpreter feared to repeat the exact words, since they were
not engaged in war or protected from its dangers. One illustration is given: "Even if a horse is meant, if it has kicked or
thrown a person, in this changed language [the war language]
it may be called ' merely a life feather,' " [3] a circumlocution
flattering to the horse and signifying its identification with
supernatural speed and lightness.

The following explain the ' war ' or ' altered ' language:

When the warriors entered the enemy's territory, the
leader told the men to use special words for the animals and
booty they hoped to seize. They called the changed language
' war talk, not talking plainly.' The Navaho did not speak
' war talk ' in their own territory because they believed the
enemy would attack if they did. The warriors communicated
in war talk for one to three days of the journey. When the
leader decided that the appropriate time had arrived, the
party lined up in a row facing the enemy's country (cp.
Danger line, Concordance B). At dawn the leader started a
song in which the rest joined. At a certain point in the song
all turned toward their homes and the common language was
resumed. [4]

Turtledove, sent by Monster Slayer to report on the two
old warriors who had attacked Taos, returned with the following message: "The warriors, Turtle and Green Frog, did
not go anywhere unless they spoke a language called 'irrita-
bly they speak.' " This term is explained as a sort of ' twisted
language used by warriors.' Either the word symbol was
slightly changed in the code or a special meaning known only
to fighters was given to the words. Monster Slayer's warband,
advancing on Taos, spoke only in the war language. [5]

The Black Dancers in the war ritual must whisper the war language to one another during their performance,[6] for they represent the Hard Flint Boys, who appeared to Monster Slayer's party on the eve of the attack on Taos.

Similar to the war language is the ritualistic language of the Rain Ceremony, which emphasizes water.

"While in the hogan all conversation had to contain reference to water or to rain. Metaphoric substitution was made. For example, if someone entered, it was said, 'someone is floating.' If that person sat down, he was said 'to have stopped floating.'"[7]

Such circumlocution shows that neither it nor the war language is distinctive; both are variations of the common language for ceremonial purposes, a device of sympathetic magic.

Various quotations have demonstrated the compulsive power of the word. The following examples further illustrate the close identification of person, mind, word, and power and its extension to objects and means:

When the war party was ready to charge, each man talked to his horse: "Be lively; you and I are going into danger, my horse. Be brave when you go to war and nothing will happen; we shall come back safely."[8]

As the war party was about to leave home, the leader instructed the men to spit on their bowstrings and rub them. Then they were told to rub their legs and bodies with their hands and do the same with their arrows. The leader told them that their weapons were like human beings, that they had a mind, that if the warrior was a coward his bow and arrow would be timid. The spitting and rubbing strengthened both men and weapons (cp. Chapter 7).[9]

There are restrictions on as well as requirements for speech: the Stricken Twins got into trouble by disregarding an order for silence; the young man in the whirling log was enjoined to speak only to himself or sing sacred songs; Dark Thunder's party exerted themselves to prevent Winter Thunder from uttering a single devastating word (cp. Chapter 4).[10]

Next to the simple combinations of ritualistically significant sounds (Chapter 15), the simplest linguistic form is the name, usually derived from war. It is conferred by a successful warrior, preferably one old enough to be beyond the possibility of further harm by the uncontrolled evils. In former times and even today among the orthodox, the name was pronounced by its owner only ' if he got into a tight place '; undue repetition wears out its power. A person's name should be his secret possession, something like pollen which he might pit against evil. If he alone knows it, he can gauge the extent of its power; if it is in someone else's possession, he cannot depend on it and it may even be turned against its owner. The secret names of the enemy were among the most important weapons. There are uncounted instances in which mere knowledge of a name and its mention overcame powers.

In the various myths that relate the adventures of The Twins, someone told them the names of the four guardians of Sun's house and, by merely mentioning the names, The Twins gained access to the premises.[11]

Big Fly told Scavenger the names of the eaglets on the ledge where he had been dropped by his enemies, and he was safe because the old eagles addressed him by the eaglets' names.[12]

After Self Teacher had gained the confidence of Deer Owner's daughter (and wife), the girl divulged the names of her father and mother, as well as her own. In his chagrin and grief at seeing his bears overcome, Deer Owner called out their names, thus inexorably forfeiting his power over them.[13]

Attacked by a windstorm, Reared-in-the-mountain overcame it by pronouncing his own name for the first time; later he quieted thunder and lightning with it.[14]

Knowledge of their names greatly assisted Monster Slayer

in overcoming the various monsters, but Sleep reversed the process by mentioning Monster Slayer's name.[15]

Names are often exchanged, one reason being to express cumulative success.

The dominant Twin got his best-known name, na·γé" nei·zγání, ' One-who-repeatedly-slew-monsters,' from his exploits. In childhood and adolescence he was simply called Firstborn. In the introduction to a War Ceremony prayer he is called neidigą́·hí, ' One-starting-out-for-repeated-killings, One-setting-out-for-slaughter.' Father Berard remarks that "this name seems more powerful than the ordinary name. . . . If other means have failed, this invocation is employed in prayer." [16]

Monster Slayer was also called bił najno·ltłi·jí, 'Let-down-on-a-sunbeam,' to commemorate his descent from the sky.[17]

Child-of-the-water, called Secondborn until he had

CHART XVII

TWELVE-WORD FORMULAS

I Hail Chant	II Hail Chant	III Hail Chant [19] War Ceremony
Earth	Earth	Darkness
Sky	Sky	Dawn
Mountain Woman	Mountain Woman	Yellow-evening-light
Water Woman	Water Woman	Sun
Darkness	Darkness	Talking God
Dawn	Changing Woman	xa·ctc'é"óγan
Talking God	Sun	Boy-carrying-single-turquoise
xa·ctc'é"óγan	xa·ctc'é"óγan	Girl-carrying-single-corn-kernel
White Corn	White Corn	White-corn-boy
Yellow Corn	Yellow Corn	Yellow-corn-girl
Pollen Boy	Pollen	Pollen Boy
Cornbeetle Girl	Cornbeetle	Cornbeetle Girl

achieved something, was later called neidiˑgicí, ' One-who-repeatedly-cuts-here-and-there-with-a-knife,' because he took care of the monsters after his brother had killed them, disposing of their bodies and cutting off the trophies.[18]

The formula is a combination of names having tremendous power. It, like the words of the war language, is usually omitted from the texts, probably because its value is not sufficiently realized by recorders. The names included in each formula should be spoken in exact order—none should be added, none repeated, none omitted. Although tłăˑh laid great emphasis on the exactness of the twelve-word formula of the Hail Chant, it is found in his text in three forms. I have discovered three other series of words that seem to indicate such a formula and I give all in Chart XVII so that they may be compared.

CHART XVII—Continued
TWELVE-WORD FORMULAS

IV Twelve-word song [20]	V Holy People in painting [21]	VI Words of prayer [22]
Earth	Earth	Earth
Sky	Sky	Sky
Mountain Woman	Darkness	Sun
Water Woman	Dawn	Moon
Talking God	Yellow-evening-light	Darkness
xaˑctc'éˑ'óɣan	Sun	Dawn
Boy-carrying-single-corn-kernel	Talking God	Talking God
Girl-carrying-single-turquoise	xaˑctc'éˑ'óɣan	xaˑctc'éˑ'óɣan
White-corn-boy	Male Corn	White-corn-boy
Yellow-corn-girl	Female Corn	Yellow-corn-girl
Pollen Boy	Cornbeetle Girl	Pollen Boy
Cornbeetle Girl	Pollen Boy	Cornbeetle Girl
		Restoration-to-youth-boy
		According-to-beauty-girl

The formula of Column I is repeated after the bundle application just before the short singing of the Hail Chant; that of Column II, in which Changing Woman and Sun are substituted for Dawn and Talking God, during the corn-meal sprinkling of the sandpainting; and that of Column III after the restoration of Frog's children. I do not know the reason for the changes.

The series of Column IV is also incorporated in a song, called the ' twelve-word song of blessing,' sung when the War Ceremony rattlestick is deposited, generally for correcting possible mistakes. Father Berard adds the following explanation:

It should be noted that the chief words only are considered for the twelve-word mention. The song is so well-known that the natives recognize it immediately, although there are numerous other songs of twelve words, which are never recognized as such but are designated by other names. Omissions or alterations are not allowed in the twelve-word song.[23]

From these data it would seem that the number twelve is important and that the series are modified for particular occasions. It is likely that words and order, like other symbols, are changed for cause within a single ceremony; unfortunately, the causes have not been ascertained. I believe that the picture *Twelve Holy People* is an illustration of the deities whose names are mentioned in the formula; they are arranged as in Column V.

In what seems to be a song formula of the Flint Chant there are sixteen names, twelve of the usual sort and four of mountains. In a prayer intoned at the cake baking, fourteen words are mentioned (Column VI). The names correspond with the formulas in the kind of deities addressed; they differ in the form, which is song or prayer. A twelve-word song is recorded for the Night Chant. The only sequences that are exactly the same are one of the Hail Chant and the twelve-word song of the War Ceremony (Column III).

The power of the word is as strong for evil as for good, an inverse wish being a curse. One form is name calling; another a malediction similar to ours, "May such and such happen to you!"

The chief who exceeded his powers in punishing adultery was called 'The-red-one,' 'The-changing-one,' 'The-two-faced-one,' 'The-one-with-two-fronts,' and when the horribly deformed creatures resulting from his punishment returned, they taunted the people with these names, and cursed: "One-eyed persons will continue to exist forever! Noseless ones will exist always! We shall accept no prayers and no songs will be ours! Absolutely nothing will move us!" [24]

A group that seems to consist of the same beings came to a Fire Dance held for Big Knee. As the women left the dance circle, they screamed, "May the waters drown you! May the lightning strike you!" [25]

The gambler who was finally overcome by Sun's child was so angry at his defeat that he hurled maledictions at the people: "I will kill you all with lightning! I will send war and disease among you! May fire burn you! May the waters drown you!" [26]

Changing-bear-maiden's brothers were extremely provoked by Coyote and, before they knew he was present, cursed him; when he appeared, they somewhat tempered their language, for they always feared him. Later they got their revenge. Although he was not entitled to it, he insisted on having the fat that grows around the horn of the mountain sheep, the chief hunter's prize, but as he cut it, the Brothers put a curse on it: "Turn to bone! Turn to bone!" [27]

Monster Slayer, much annoyed by two old men who wished to join his war party, shouted at them, "yił tšá·xóckałi·," a common untranslatable Navaho curse. [28]

Formulas and prayers are accorded equal reverence, the same restrictions being placed upon both. Formulas, an elaboration of name power, differ from prayers in having no context. The prayer is a formula in the sense that it functions because of its exactness, completeness, and order. It has content, usually not much disguised by metaphor, and also context, much of it clearly expressed narrative; its main purpose is to identify the person prayed for with the powers addressed. The subject of Navaho prayer is so extensive that I have discussed it in *Prayer: The Compulsive Word.*[29]

Since the myth belonging to a ceremony differs from the lay myth or tale, it seems to be a synthetic symbol of the chant. One, the myth of Blessing, may explain the position of all tribal ceremonies. Still unpublished, it is perhaps the most inclusive. Each chant myth embodies in an interestingly constructed plot a reason for the diverse and intricate items of ritual and, in addition, has a detailed description which explains rite, properties, and behavior, comparing them with the figurative and symbolic text of the narrative proper.

Although the story has several functions, it is not an indispensable part of the chanter's lore. Many chanters today sing before learning the myth, but if they wish to ' be sure ' of their technique and want a secondary guide to the song series to fix the items and events quite thoroughly in mind, they learn the tale and are able to tell it in minute detail.

PART THREE
RITUAL

CHAPTER 17

SONG

SONG, AN indispensable part of ritual, a link between dogma and symbolism, has linguistic, literary, and musical aspects. Although many Navaho songs have been collected, few have been analyzed, the summaries being based on small samples of selected songs.[1] It is doubtless presumptuous to discuss song without discussing music, but since the prospect of the musical analysis is dim, I suggest some problems that should be tackled. Music will certainly be found to be a part of sound symbolism; most likely even its components—melody, rhythm, phrasing, and the like—have an independent function as well as a function related to the whole. The musical patterns are just as systematic and varied as the rest of the ritual; they should be determined and their significance demonstrated.

An obvious question is the relation between language and song. Pitch and quantity are outstanding features of the phonetic system, devices for distinguishing grammatical forms and, therefore, meaning. There are two primary tones, one neutral in value and one relatively higher, and two secondary tones, one rising, one falling, actually combinations of the primary tones. Closely associated with the tonal pattern is quantity, for there are short and long vowels. A half-length is differentiated, but seems to have no phonemic significance. In song linguistic tone and quantity are subordinated to the music.

Songs among the Navaho, as among other Indian tribes,

may be disguised by syllables, which on the surface seem to have no meaning. Furthermore, syllables that have meaning may be separated by syllables whose chief function is to fit the word to the music: that is, words and sentences are lengthened by the addition of syllables, either by insertion or by increment.

The following illustrations may be noted:

Shortening of vowels (they may even be dropped entirely):

(normal) 'ei ye"i·ná 'ei níyá, ' with this life has arrived '
(in song) 'einiya 'eiye-'ina·-h²

Increment:

(normal) dzą· níyá níyá, ' so far it (chant) has arrived '
(song 1st line) dza niya dza niya
(song 2nd line) dza niya dza niya neya

Syllable insertion:

(normal) xa·yáo·ye" xa·yáo·ye", ' one has emerged over the rim '
(song) xa·yao'-wo-ye xa·yao-wo-ye

Distortion:

(normal) xóγé"ê· xóγé"yâ·, ' things are weakening, how terrible '
(song) xoye·h weye'-ta ai···
(normal) 'aya·γá, ' he is going in under '
(song) 'eyo·h

Distortion and dropping of syllables:

(normal) 'aγi'í·yá yah'íyíniyâo, ' in he has come inside upon entering '
(song) na-'aγi'i·ya 'ya'e·niyo
(normal) yah'í·yíníyá 'aya·γá, ' he has come in, he is coming in under '
(song) yah'eniyo 'eyo-h

Navaho is a very breathy language, much being made of h and x; the presence or absence of the aspiration, even its intensity, is one indication of difference in meaning.[3] The h-sound is rarely if ever lost. It may stand before a consonant, for instance, and it may affect a voiced sonant by combining with it to form a surd (for example, h-j > c). h and the glottal stop (') have a place in song sometimes quite different from their function in the language. The Navaho find no difficulty in singing the aspirated sounds; in fact, there are more in song than in speech. Similarly, those of us who do not use the glottal stops might consider it impossible to sing them. Navaho songs, in which the lyrical effect is enhanced by aspiration and glottal stop, show the fallacy of such a conclusion. Other so-called ' difficult ' sounds, such as γ, ł, tł, c, are often not changed, distorted, or omitted.

Much has been made of the meaningless syllables in primitive, particularly North American Indian, songs. AB helped to record, transcribe, and translate the explanation of the song series of the Big Star Chant; his translation differs from all others extant in having a great deal more content. I do not believe the difference is due to the chant materials, for the Big Star Chant belongs to the exorcistic side just as does the War Ceremony, for which there is a reasonably complete set of songs.[4] The song content in both is in many ways quite similar. The translation has greater import, I think, because the Navaho was better able to find his way through the disguising syllables to the essential meaning. Furthermore, AB insists that there are no ' nonsense ' syllables, that all have meaning. Possibly the syllables constitute another kind of symbolism which a full analysis of the songs may prove to exist. Perhaps Father Berard's informant agreed with AB when he said, "The words have no meaning, but the song means, 'Take it, I give it to you.' "[5]

Navaho ritual contains many onomatopoeic elements, which may exist independently without ' word content ' or may be stems, parts of words depending upon grammatical forms. For this reason and because other unusual devices are incorporated in the ritual, it seems quite possible that the nonsense syllables may have a meaning to one who understands the full context of a rite, even if they never became linguistic forms, a possibility all the more likely since the Navaho who suggested it has rarely been wrong in his interpretations, no matter how farfetched they may have sounded at first. Further investigation with other informants and with texts has corroborated rather than refuted his suggestions. Probably few individuals understand the musical-syllabic meanings, even as few understand other types of symbolism, especially the complicated associations. The musical material so far published is unsatisfactory because it refers to tunes or burdens as the ' same ' and ' different.' These words have been shown to be meaningless unless a Navaho definition is given for them. How are the tunes the same? How do they differ, and from what? A rewriting of some of the prayers so that the deviousness of repetition is brought out led to the discovery of intricate rhythmic patterns. A mere glance at the content of some songs shows that they closely parallel the prayers. Although a tedious task, all the songs of a given chant should be recorded if the musical, literary, and ritualistic pattern is to be fully understood. Songs of different chants should be compared as sandpaintings are. I am convinced that certain sets of songs—those of Monster Slayer, Thunder, Talking God, and Dawn, for instance—would show great similarity.

I have said that prayers are harder to learn than songs because of the emotional strain involved.[6] Matthews seemed to think the songs were more difficult to master because of their vast number.[7] He mentions also the requirement that many must be sung without error, indicating that the attitude toward songs and prayers is the same. He further considers the myth a mnemonic device so helpful that a chanter depends on it to remember his songs. I have often heard songs started wrong and corrected simply by a new start as soon as the mistake was realized. tłá·h depended on his songs to recall parts of the Hail Chant myth; he remembered the song though he forgot the plot. Moreover, if a chanter learns the songs though not the myth, he may perform a ceremony; if he knows the myth but not the songs, he is considered incapable of carrying out the chant—he is simply in possession of miscellaneous information.

The conflict between Matthews' opinion and mine is doubtless not serious, for it probably means no more than differences that any two contemporary investigators might find. Emphasis may have changed in the sixty years or more between Matthews' recording and mine. His chanters were almost certainly more rigorous than those of today in their care for ceremonial detail, since the forces making for cultural breakdown had only got started in his day and had not affected a large part of the population.

It is more likely that the differences are due to the materials with which we worked. The Night and Mountain chants should be performed only in the winter; the Shooting, Hail, and Evil chants may be sung any time they are needed. The emergence ritual deals with the most dangerous past, the travail in the lower worlds and the transformation and control of this one, all to be handled with extraordinary circumspection. Once overcome, the monsters should be commemorated, but remembrance, as in the Shooting Chant and War Ceremony, need not be as strongly emphasized as it was the first time (cp. Chapter 14).

More to the point, however, is the suggested reciprocity between various parts of the ritual and what it does for the chanter, his type of mind determining which part of it helps him with another and how. The myth is dramatic and plot may be impressive to some minds. The ritual includes the action, but only implicitly. The songs follow the structure of the ritual much more closely, and the music suggests the organization. One mind relies on plot and action for its cue; another operates better if it can recall what is done. In doing, one sings. Consequently, it is understandable that the myth has lost emphasis while the songs have gained. Ultimately, the ideal of every chanter is to know the chant completely. Each viewpoint helps the others. Some symbols, like song, are indispensable; some, like myth, though desirable, are not absolutely essential.

Origin of Song

The etiology of song is psychologically illuminating. The Navaho are sentimental and eager to express emotion. Isolation has been suggested as a reason for the individualistic character of the Navaho (Introduction). In myth an ever-recurring theme is loneliness. Crying originated in loneliness and from crying came a song.

When Child-of-the-water left Changing Woman, she was overcome with sorrow. She cried and from her crying came a song.[8]

When Child-of-the-water joined his brother, the latter wept for joy at seeing him, but from these tears ' nothing else [that is, no song] flowed.'[9]

I find these peculiarly interesting passages; one indicates a positive development—loneliness to crying to song; the other, a negative statement, very significant since it explains the tear's greeting, an expression of joy, social rather than religious.

Nostalgic crying, brought on by contemplation of natural beauty, is also indicated as an origin of song.

The hero of the Mountain Chant disobeyed his father by going to a forbidden place. From the top of a hill he beheld the beautiful slopes of a mountain. Clouds hung over it; showers of rain fell. As he greeted the land with appreciation he was overcome with loneliness and homesickness and, weeping, he sang a song.[10]

Matthews records a lament for a pet turkey that arose in grief; the translation does not indicate whether it is a song or a prayer.[11]

The Stricken Twins, after an endless journey acknowledged as children of Talking God, were again cast out by the gods. They had to set out on a quest for goods to pay for a curing ceremony. The poor blind one told his lame brother to mount on his back once more. In despair they walked down the canyon, weeping over their mistakes, knowing not where to turn. Without purpose or direction, they cried; at first they uttered meaningless syllables, but after a while they found words to sing. The Holy Ones, hearing a song, inquired of one another, "Why do they sing?" They sent Talking God to bring the children back. The blind boy resisted, but his brother urged that they return and find out what the gods wanted. Arriving where the gods were, they were asked, "What was that you were singing as you went along?"

"We were not singing," they answered. "We were crying."

"Why did you cry?"

"Because you sent us away and we had no place to go."

"What kind of song were you singing?" asked the god. "We certainly heard the words of a song."

Three times the boys insisted that they were merely crying, but when asked the same question the fourth time, the gentler one explained, "We began to cry; we turned our cry into a song. We never knew the song before. My blind brother just made it up as we moved along." Then he sang the song which described their helplessness and despair and included a statement that they would be restored to health. The song impelled the gods to take counsel once more, and they decided never again to turn their children away with no means of saving themselves.[12]

This poignant excerpt shows not only faith in ritualistic aid as a counsel of despair but also the compulsive power of song, which could break even the resistance of the gods, the exact function of Navaho songs today.

The origin of song as a warning or sign given by a protector is suggested by the episode in which The Twins tried to learn who their father was.

Four times the children asked their mother before she answered, "Far away your father lives. Between here and there every conceivable danger lies. So don't think about it any more." They lay still, talking and planning, and soon they heard a song. Their mother scolded them when they accused her of singing it, saying, "Who would give me a song? How could I get a song?"

As the boys persisted in planning a journey to Sun, the younger one heard a song near the door. Then he said, "That must be a young man's song. That will be my song."

He prayed with the song, then both boys heard it, but it was not a young man singing; it was the cover of darkness that protected the youths, a sign that their plan would be successful.[13]

Function and Types of Song

The number of Navaho songs is incalculable. The 576 songs Matthews mentioned as actually sung at performances of the Night Chant he witnessed are the very minimum and do not include those for the various branches or phases of the chant. tłá·h knew 447 for the Hail Chant and had forgotten some. To most rites and chants belong many more songs than are introduced at any one performance. Just as the sandpaintings or prayersticks for a chant are few compared with the number possible, so songs are selected from a large repertoire. Some songs are favorites or required and may be heard often; some are appropriate only under unusual circumstances; occasionally one song and no other will do.

Best known are what Matthews called ' songs of sequence,' a group of songs set up in a definite order that should be preserved and belongs to a rite, ceremony, or chant. Such sets, incompletely recorded though they may be, are complex in structure and function, and furnish the basis for the subsequent discussion of "Content and Structure of Songs" (pages 291ff.).

According to Father Berard, a minimum of 131 songs of sequence is required in the War Ceremony, a relatively small number, supplemented, however, by a very large number of informal or spontaneous songs contributed by the visiting chorus. The Big Star Chant is less often performed and would hardly be considered a major chant, yet we recorded 238 songs of sequence for it.

Matthews, in an early work, "Navaho Gambling Songs," refers to the large number of songs concerned with the moccasin game. One old man said there were four thousand, and another that there was no creature that walked, flew, or crawled in all the world known to the Navaho that had not at least one song in the game and that many had more.[14] The reason is almost certainly that the game originated as a contest for day and night in which all living things participated. The samples recorded are simpler than the chant songs; the words, at least, impressionistically characterize an animal or person. Owl, for instance, repeats: "I do not want the night to end."

Chickenhawk sings of his rival:

The old owl hates me.
I alone bring home many rabbits
That is why he hates me.

Gopher cheated by chewing a hole in the moccasin, thus enabling the guesser to see the stone hidden in it.

Gopher sees where the stone is
Gopher sees where the stone is
Keep striking! Keep striking [the moccasin in which the stone is hidden]!

The account suggests that a charming descriptive narrative drama could be reconstructed on the basis of these songs alone. Their music must differ as much as their literary quality from the long, repetitious chant and rite songs.

After the pilgrimage for collecting waters from the sacred mountains had been accomplished for the Rain Ceremony, the chanter wove the separate events into a song, unfortunately not recorded (*Rain Ceremony*, Concordance C).

The primary function of song is to preserve order, to co-ordinate the ceremonial symbols; a secondary purpose must be enjoyment, if we may judge by the effort exerted by the lay Navaho to attend and participate in the ceremony, for it is unlikely that he knows the deepest significance of the songs.

The example of the song coming from the cover of darkness just cited shows how tangible the Navaho feel the songs are. The song not only came from the cover, it was the cover. Time and again song and a blanket or curtain are identified. A song moving out into the space immediately surrounding an individual—for example, a horseman riding at night or anyone alone and fearful—establishes a zone of protection that gives comfort, for within it is the person who dissipates the evils by the compulsion of sound and words at the same time that he buoys up his own spirit (*Covers*, Concordance B).

Horned Toad Youth sang for Monster Slayer when he attacked the Gray Gods: "The song was set as a cover upon every deed that The Twins performed against the monsters."[15] In the foregoing examples the verb refers to a blanketlike protection; here the verb means something more, like a lid or bottle stopper.

Songs were said to be kept in a paunch and were referred to as casually as cookies in a jar. In line with the song of the living creatures is that of the kernel of dried corn that begged for attention and water.[16]

Song may be a demonstration of inner strength.

Overcome by the Arrow People, the younger Twin said to his brother, "I wonder how strong I am inside; I'll try to speak out," and forthwith he started a song and was able to finish it.[17]

Like blowing, song may cause increase in size. In one version of the emergence myth, when the World Pillars began to sing, the small model of the earth stretched to its present size.[18]

Song has numerous powers, each defined by something in addition to the song itself, and it seems as if the expression of pure joy is subordinated to other functions. Narration, description, and repetition are often compulsive in songs of sequence. Unless a warrior had been killed, rejoicing in the form of gloating and reviling was incorporated in a serenade after the return of a war party. Though enjoyed because of victory, the serenade, like other parts of the War Ceremony, was exorcistic; saying a thing was true made it true.

The importance of song is summarized by the excerpt: "Changing Woman taught songs to her two divine children, admonishing them, 'Do not forget the songs I have taught you. The day you forget them will be the last; there will be no other days.'"[19]

Songs are a form of wealth. Individuals own songs for increase and prosperity, songs belonging to the fetishes of domestic animals and the bundles of the simple domestic rites devoted to family or group welfare.

Hill emphasizes the difference between songs owned and sung by chanters and those ' belonging to the whole group.' "A man should not keep these [the latter] secret because they refer to food and are essential to the life of the people. They should be taught to anyone who asks for them and a man should not have to pay for them." [20]

The commended attitude was displayed when negotiations were made for the dedication of the Gallup stadium. "Will there be any objection to singing the songs of the House Blessing?" the chanter was asked. "No, because they belong to everybody," was the answer.

Poverty is framed in song terms: "I have always been a poor man. I do not own a single song." [21]

Songs, like other forms of wealth, may be exchanged. At an impasse an evil power—Star, Thunder, Snake—says, "My offering, my song, my prayer, I will give in exchange for my life." [22] No one should sing a song unless he can prove ownership, his right to sing it.

Some songs are individualistic. RP composed a song for each of his grandchildren shortly after its birth and, as soon as the child was old enough, taught it the new song. We ought to know if and how such personal songs differ from the ritualistic ones and whether they were a general custom or merely the whim of a doting grandfather. Unfortunately, I did not follow up the matter.

One day, when the lesson at the Hogan School was about birds, RP came in as was his wont. As the name of each bird was written on the blackboard, he quietly sang the bird's song. It was not the imitation of a bird call; indeed, it had little, if any, of such character. As far as I know, such songs have not previously been reported. They may belong to ritual, but I heard them as a spontaneous expression. Perhaps they belong to the moccasin game, played to decide the length of day and night.

Statements about women's singing conflict. Their shyness and aversion to singing in public do not mean that women cannot or do not like to sing at all. They have lovely lullabies and teach other songs to little boys and girls. MA taught such songs to her grandchildren, yet I never heard her sing.

To the Navaho, song is a necessity; it is an inspiration, a hope, a protection and comfort, a guide to one in want of a procedure, a means of transforming frustration into power.

Content and Structure of Songs

Song accompanies all phases of ritual—preparation, use, and disposal of ceremonial items—and is, as well, a summary of the complete performance (Chapter 20; *Vigil*, Concordance C). Much that is treated in prayer is repeated in song, which is nevertheless freer, fuller, more inclusive.

The preparation of the chief symbol of any ceremony is a good example, as the account of the War Ceremony rattle-stick demonstrates. The ten songs have key themes:

In set 1:

    1 ...he is making it for me
    2 ...he has made it for me
    3 ...he has brought it here for me
    4 ...he has placed it in my hand
    5 ...he has put tallow on it for me
    6 ...he has made it red for me

In set 2:

    7 ...he is decorating it for me
    8 ...he has decorated it for me
    9 ...now he is taking it away
    10 ...again everything has become safe.[23]

Songs with these themes are required; a prayer and five other songs of blessing are optional at a War Ceremony performance, but seem culminative, since the singer learns them at the end of his apprenticeship. Probably no performance includes all five and the prayer, selections being made for the particular occasion.

The song content parallels closely that of the prayer. For instance, in prayer Monster Slayer is invoked through the bow symbol marked on the rattlestick; explanations of the various applications to the rattlestick are cited. The songs mention what Monster Slayer is doing, what he has done, what will happen; both prayer and song catalogue the good that will come to the patient.

The second set of War Ceremony songs mentions each relative of the patient who with him expects to benefit from the ritual. The set that goes with the prayer emphasizes motion: [24]

1 Here it stood upright among us when it started to move up repeatedly
2 Here it stood upright among us when he [the patient] started to move about
3 Here it stood upright among us when he arose
4 Here that by means of which he moves about the earth stands upright
5 Here that by means of which he moved about the edge of the earth stands upright

In this set, places, the parts of the rattlestick, the symbolic jewels of which it is made, and the safety of the space around it are mentioned.

It is to be expected that songs belonging to different rites stress different details, not only because of the character of the rites but also because of the symbols that enter into relationship. The ultimate effect is impressionistic because each word includes a great deal that is ritualistically intelligible to the Navaho, if not to the white man.

Songs of exorcistic rites express strong emotion—vengeance, triumph in victory, retribution—elements I have not found in the Holy ceremonies. Neither song nor prayer includes pity, patronage, humility, or gratitude for blessings conferred. Since the Navaho can never be better than he thinks he is, or his lot than he says it is, he alludes to fear, but does not mention it directly. The Blackening songs contrast the apprehension felt in enemy territory with the security of home; characteristically, both ideas are applied to persons:

> Into the ground with [their spirits]
> Everywhere in his own country I wish the enemy may die.

but:

> In all parts of the Navaho country rejoicing, flute-playing, and peace have returned.

and:

> . . . down into the ground with the enemy, down into the ground with him [that is, with his spirit, by means of beating the pot drum].[25]

The songs continue with a vivid description of the slaughter, of the enemy's shortcomings and inability to protect his womenfolk from disgrace—really a curse put into song.

Songs referring to deeds in the Navaho country are ' attractive ' in their content; they identify the patient with success and safety, with long life, with the favorable ritualistic symbols of the blackening as they apply to the Navaho, and they also mention the exorcistic symbols as they apply to the enemy. Whereas the first set of songs curses as it drives out fears, the second mentions the same details with assurance that they are controlled, thus demonstrating the Navaho faith. The evils have been scattered, repelled by the ritualistic machinery (cp. Chapter 11, *Alternation*). The pattern of reviling and the change to satisfaction is similar in the Male Shooting Chant Evil and the Big Star Chant, both of which belong to the Evil side.

A song group of the Big Star Chant, containing eight songs

for the ascent and eight for the descent of the cliff, describes the anger of Spider and Swallow People at Coyote.[26]

Corresponding with the subjects and treatment included in prayer, songs of sequence are mainly descriptive and narrative. The song burdens concerned with the making of the War Ceremony rattlestick illustrate a common narrative feature that is fundamentally linguistic, for it depends upon the tense-aspect system of the verb. In Navaho, verbs of action and motion are differentiated in a rather simple tense system—present, past, and future—and a complicated aspect system—progressive, momentary, customary, inceptive, and cessative.

Often, therefore, the burden of the song has a tense or aspective change to indicate progression from a wish to an accomplishment, a linguistic device related to the symbolism of motion (Chapter 13). Hence, there are songs and prayers, as well as sandpaintings, whose theme is motion. Similarly, too, there is emphasis on place and its description. Several groups of songs having different purposes illustrate these emphases. Generally a song or a song set demonstrates more than one of these points.

Farm songs belong to the entire tribe and are sung for the planting and maturation events rather than for a particular ceremony.[27] The initial song refers to seed planting; it describes the place for planting, the seed, and offerings made to the seed (or perhaps to the earth). The verbs are first in the form ' I wish it to be . . . ' and change later to ' It is becoming . . .' The second song repeats the sentiments of the first, but in the form ' It has become so.'

The songs of the second interval refer to the sprouting of the corn in terms corresponding with those of the first interval. Time is allowed for growth, then song indicates the appearance of tiny blades above the ground, another the fresh yellow-green appearance of the field; another celebrates the normal growth of the corn; a song states that the ' corn loves me' and is therefore doing well under my hand; another, that the leaves are large enough to touch one another when the wind blows; still another, that some plants are large and cast uniform shadows over the field, that red silk has appeared, that pollen has formed. Subsequent songs refer to the harvested ears, emphasizing the crackling sound made when the fully developed stalks are pulled. There are songs to describe the plucking of the ears and the piling of bundles gathered and dumped in the center of the field. The next song describes the extension of the piles of corn—' it increases by spreading'; another summarizes by describing the harvest as a whole. The pattern does not change for the husking, which is again described by sound—' now from my hands it gives forth a sound '—or for the drying, which completes the harvest.

Many song sets from the Night Chant would illustrate the progression, but I choose the scene analyzed by Matthews that concerns the safe entrance to the gods' home called White House in Canyon de Chelley. The sequence is based on a myth relating how Dawn Boy entered the house and returned safely to his home. As he did in ancient times, so now the human incumbent does symbolically, the various stages of the journey and visit being emphasized—an example of identification by recapitulation or commemoration (Chapter 7). Since the only approach to the sacred house was by way of the canyon walls, there was a song for ascending the cliff, one to enter the first doorway (representing the entrance to all connecting rooms), a song for walking around the inside of the house, and one for the visitor preparing to leave. The songs for entrance had power to subdue the fierce guardians —Lightning, Bears, Red-headed Snakes, and Rattlesnakes.

Dawn Boy was taught how to enter the White House; he was to sing the proper songs at the following points: when he got to the place where the White House gods could see him, when he presented offerings to the house owners. In the last song he told who he was, whence he came, and described the gods' home and his own way of entering it.

The prayer was taught to Dawn Boy as he stood on the sacred buckskin (*Prayer on buckskin*, Concordance C).

He sang on his return journey: as he started away from the door, he sang the theme ' with . . . I return'; as he walked four hundred paces, he sang another song; when he crossed a hill, he sang the theme ' with it [power] held in my hand [I move] '; when he was far enough from the White House to see it behind him, yet to begin to think of home, he sang a song quite different from the others, describing the mountain near his home.

Thinking he was still a long way from home, he sang as he ate his lunch, the song having the pattern of the first set with the theme ' now Talking God's food I am about to eat.'

When he had finished eating, he sang the song that now accompanies the administration of pollen with the theme ' xaˑctćé''óɣan's food I have eaten.'

Crossing the valley, he sang the burden ' in safety I walk about.'

When he got to the door of his own home, he sang, ' my home I am approaching.'

After entering, he sang, ' I sit down in my home.'

His relatives begged him to tell the story of his journey, and after they had sung a song at his request, he told of his adventures to prove that he had visited a truly holy place.[28]

Comparable with this series are other song sets, many of them not as thoroughly interwoven into the text or ritual descriptions, at least in the available records.

•   •   •

Two main verb-stems indicate singing: One is -taˑ̀, ' singing, singing and orderly ritual ' and ' having possession of protective lore ':

xatá·l, ' chant, rite, ceremony '

dził xatá·l, ' place where masks are kept ' (lit., ' mountain sacred lore ')

xata·łi·, ' one-who-chants, chanter, medicine man, singer '

'átčá· naxodjita·ł, ' she had power to ward off danger from herself '[29]

'a·dji' nixodjita·ł, ' thus ends one's chanting '

The other stem, -á·ł, is more intimately related to the ' word ' and to speech. It may even be the same stem as that for ' a round or handy object moves,' or a derivative. Apparently both word and song are thought of as ' round things,' a classification that explains how songs may be kept in a paunch or jar. Some of the words based upon this stem are generalized in meaning; others are specific for ritualistic description.

nde·tą́, ' it has been sung through to the end, end of a song '

ndé'ą́, ' he has sung it '

nná·náyide·'á·, ' he is about to start singing another (set of) song(s)'

nxidide·c'á·ł, ' I shall finish singing repeatedly'

xaxidide·c'á·ł, ' I shall start to sing (them) one after another'

xaná·díc'a·, ' I am going to sing again '

di·di xaná·náyidi'a·hígí·, ' another of a series he is about to start singing'

'axóná'ło·l'ą́''i·, ' that which is a song to symbolize (recall, commemorate) the episode'

xóná·'ti'te·stą́, ' the song representing the episode has been sung'

These stems and the words formed from them are interesting in comparison with the noun for ' song,' which has a complicated series of corresponding verb-stems, referring, however, not to singing or song but to holiness, reverence, prayer, and, in the passive voice, to sorcery.

The following are some of the derivative expressions of sin, song: si·ł, ' with (accompanied by) song '; sin bikazí, ' stem (original, basic) songs '; sin bikétłó·l, ' song root, song that suggests another.'

Words indicating groups of songs probably have different specific meanings, although they are sometimes used interchangeably:

sin sidja·', ' songs in a group because they have the same melody '

dabiɣi·n 'axą· dadidja·hgo, ' songs arranged in alternating groups '

sin bina·ńdja·'i·, ' songs belonging to a group because they branch off from a single stem '

sin bą· dahsidja·'i·, ' songs that branch forth from a center '

sin 'ahńti'i·, ' songs-strung-according-to-time, theme songs, songs representative of the set '

sin dahdi·ti' nixodjíta·ł, ' the song series of the chant starts '

sin na·zti'i·, ' songs-strung-here-and-there, songs that represent several phases of the same episode ' (for example, the hiding of Dirty Boy of the Endurance Chant, his sister's missing him, finding him, pulling him out of the fireplace)

sin 'átša· da·zti'i·, ' songs omitted at a particular performance '

sin 'aká·'xa·zti'i·, ' strung-out-barely-touching-the-surface, songs omitted at a particular performance with the expectation of using them at another time; songs for alternative performance '

sin 'ałké·' ńdja·'i·, ' songs of sequence, songs that (must) follow one another '

sin be˙ nixo˙l'ą́, 'concluding songs, songs by means of
which singing comes to an end '

Chapter 18 will explain the relationship between offering,
exchange, and payment, illustrated by names for songs:

sin be˙ na'i˙ṅi˙hi˙, 'songs by means of which trade is carried on.' Such songs are owned individually, sung for success
in acquiring wealth. Like the Farm songs, they do not belong
to ceremonies.

sin be˙ ną́˙ 'i˙ṅi˙hi˙, ' songs of disposal, songs by means of
which sacred objects are disposed of '

The following show variations in the meaning of a single
phrase. The variety of interpretations, common to many
Navaho words, should make us consider that those above
cited may be similarly varied according to their context:

'atła˙ ná˙lγé˙l 1. 'concluding series of songs.' 2. 'last
song of dancers in Night Chant.' 3. ' last song of Girl's
Dance of War Ceremony (falsetto).' 4. ' summary of discussion or decision in ordinary speech '

'atła˙ ná˙lγé˙l be˙ naxaγáh, 'atła˙ ná˙lγé˙l xatá˙l, 'concluding ceremony of chant, concluding rite of a series of rites, a
ceremony made up of rites was required and this is the last '

'atła˙ ná˙lγé˙l sin, ' concluding songs '

'atła˙ ná˙lγé˙l tsodizin, ' concluding prayer '

Probably bitse˙˙ sin, 'tail songs' of the War Ceremony, is
another way of expressing ' concluding,' the same as 'atła˙
ná˙lγé˙l, which is sometimes translated ' tail end of.' [30]

The term 'ałná xo˙ṅił indicates alternation of song groups,
of details within songs, or of sets.[31]

The reality, the tangibility of song is demonstrated by the
verb-stems that picture the objects they predicate:

-dja˙˙ (from -djih) of sidja˙˙ means ' a limited number of
separate objects of a kind exist.' Songs thus referred to are
similar in melody (music).

-n̊ił of xoˑn̊ił (from -n̊ił) ' separable objects, which may or may not be of the same kind, exist or are moved '; 'ałná xoˑn̊ił, ' they (songs) move into space crossing,' that is, ' alternating.'

-ti (from -tih) has several meanings: 1. ' lie (exist) in a line ' (as a taut string or wire). 2. ' lie in a uniformly organized fashion ' (of a well-thought-out argument). The difference between this stem and -'áˑł, ' a round or convenient object lies or moves,' is that the latter refers to each word or sound separately, whereas -tih calls to mind a linear organization of the separate parts.

PRAYERSTICKS

Forms

THE WORD ' prayerstick ' is essential to a discussion of any Southwestern religion. The thing for which it stands occurs in many forms besides the feathered stick from which it takes its name. In Navaho the name is ke·tá·n, which probably means ' place-where-it-is-feathered, place-of-feathering.' Many forms not of sticks with feathers are called ke·tá·n, probably because they serve the purpose of invoking supernatural aid, rather than that they actually look alike. For example, hailstones of meal and herbs and specially selected stones invite some of the Hail Chant deities. On the other hand, many objects not invocatory—bundle items, for instance—are called ke·tá·n. They may represent a good many different things; in some cases they are the chant symbols (explained on page 311).

The leading symbol of the War Ceremony, called 'aγá·ł, 'aγá·łtsi·n, though having an etiology similar to that of the bundle talking prayersticks, is more like a feathered stick than a rattle. It is not used like a rattle, but rather like a flag or standard. Father Berard, relying on the literal translation of its name, has called it ' rattlestick.' The chant symbols of the Shooting Chant are permanent properties of the chanter's bundle (*Bundle contents: SC*, 8 and 9, Concordance C); the rattlestick is made for each performance of the War Ceremony. The bundle talking prayersticks are topped with fluffy feathers; feathers are a part of the rattlestick, but are almost hidden by large twigs and yarn, particularly red yarn.[1]

Another example of ke·táⁿ is the wide board of the Shooting, Hail, Navaho Wind, and Water chants. In practically every respect the wide boards are bundle items as important as the talking prayersticks and comparably significant. The seriousness with which invocatory prayersticks are regarded is attested by the prominent place given their description in the chant myths. Certain parts of the ritual may be left out of the story, but in the major myths no detail is spared concerning the prayersticks; time and again fear is expressed lest the offerings prove unacceptable. One man said, "They are just like a written invitation"—they differ in that the recipient is compelled to accept the invitation if properly proffered.

Matthews and Kluckhohn-Wyman have discussed prayersticks in detail,[2] yet a good deal remains to be learned about them. They are so complicated in their connotations that if we understood fully everything about them, we should know almost all there is about Navaho religion.

Since ke·táⁿ has so many meanings, I use the term ' prayerstick ' to designate symbolical objects having ritualistic value, whether or not they are feathered. The subdivisions of this chapter suggest the points at which prayersticks should be set off from other symbols.

Invocatory Offerings

I call ' invocatory offerings ' the symbols deity refers to as ' my offering ' (ciɣe·l) or ' my featherstick ' (cike·táⁿ), the means by which a god is persuaded. Matthews distinguishes ' cigarettes ' (' reed offerings ' of Kluckhohn-Wyman) and ' wooden kethawns ' (' prayerstick offerings ' of Kluckhohn-Wyman), and says that the latter are usually made less carefully.[3] By ' cigarettes ' he means the invocatory reed offerings, because they may contain tobacco, among numerous other things, and are ritualistically lighted by holding a crystal to the sun. The conceptual difference between the reed and the wooden ke·tá·n is so slight as to be negligible. Those of reeds may contain the complex of offerings within the hollowed internodes; those of solid wood are laid with the offerings around or on them; both kinds may be ceremonially lighted with the crystal. The smeary effect of the paint on the wooden prayersticks—as compared with the smooth application to the reed—has no significance, being due merely to the rougher, less absorbent nature of the material. The correct application of design is stressed, no matter how the finished product looks. I shall discard completely the terms ' cigarette ' and ' wooden kethawn,' calling these composites rather ' invocatory offerings,' ' invocatory prayersticks,' terms that enable me to include a great many things not necessarily composed of reed or wood and sometimes not even feathered. A brief quotation from the chanter's description illustrates the way he regards the ' invitations ':

"A white cloud was laid down. Three [pieces of] reed were brought in. Blue willow was brought in. They were three fingerwidths long and pointed at one end. Sixteen talking prayersticks were made. Eight prayersticks were cut. *Artemisia frigida* was laid beside them and reed across them near the center. Each had eyes and a mouth. There were Cloud prayersticks—Dark Cloud, Blue Cloud, Yellow Cloud, White Cloud. There were others [prayersticks]. The Dark Water, Blue Water, Yellow Water, and White Water prayersticks were merely painted [had no designs].

"Eight down feathers were arranged. Bluebird feathers were laid with them. Four canary feathers were rolled into a ball and pressed into the Cloud prayersticks with a tamper. Down feathers of the long-tailed chat, rolled into a ball, were forced into the Water prayersticks. An owl tail feather was the tamper. The prayersticks were filled with tobacco. They were lighted with a rock crystal held to the sun and the flame was

303

extinguished with water. They were sealed with cattail pollen mixed with water. A down feather was laid on each of the Cloud and Water prayersticks. The prayersticks were laid on the talking prayersticks. The owl tail feather was dipped in water and passes were made with it."[4]

The excerpt describes several invocatory prayersticks of the Hail Chant. Others require jewels, honey, sparkling rock, and corn meal. Anything prescribed for the solid wood pieces is laid beside them, if they have not been hollowed out. A bit of cotton string, said to be from one of the pueblo villages, is laid with soft feathers on Shooting Chant prayersticks. With a turkey beard brush the patient ' paints ' pollen on them from butt to tip, taking care not to allow the light objects to blow out of place by the slightest degree. The Water prayersticks of the Hail Chant were painted all over with earth paints; many of the Shooting Chant prayersticks have designs, some similar to sandpainting elements, but usually simpler, less realistic. As the facets with eyes and mouth indicate, the prayersticks are looked upon as people; they are often said to be ' dressed.' No two chants have the same details; many conform to the general pattern. Kluckhohn and Wyman describe jewel offerings, apparently without prayersticks, and other types may be met with.

I have demonstrated the similarity of figures in different chants and noted the slight variations to indicate the setting —chant, branch, phase, mythological episode, and its significance (Chapters 19, 20); I have suggested that the same sort of resemblances and deviations are a part of song sets to respective deities in different chants. Comparable alterations occur in the prayersticks for similar reasons. To interpret the prayersticks and know which to choose, one must become thoroughly acquainted with the peculiarities and idiosyncrasies of each deity.

Invocatory prayersticks of Sky, Earth, Sun, and Moon
were selected for the last day of both Sun's House and Prayerstick branches of the Shooting Chant; they were also the
offerings of the War Ceremony (in myth) before the war on
Taos and when the warriors started on a second raid.[5] In the
Sun's House branch the sandpainting was the Sky-Earth
picture, in the Prayerstick branch it was the picture of Day
Skies (*Prayersticks used: SC Sun's House branch*, Concordance C). The figure painting, carrying the same symbolism
with additional elements, was made in the 'presence' of
these paintings—that is, of these deities—and the songs and
prayers corresponded. Thus by repetition in varied forms it
was possible to amass a tremendous accumulation of powers.
Although representations of many given powers may often
be combined, the whole will doubtless never be absolutely
identical. In one rite a particular power may be emphasized
by repetition in various guises; in another the same one may
appear only once, possibly in a minor role.

The reason for the selection and the accent may be specified in myth; it is conveyed to the witnesses of the ceremony
by prayers and songs which include honorific names of deities
and the commemorative basis for the ritualistic acts—a
restatement of dogma.

Navaho sentiment generally favors learning and remembering rather than recording in a permanent medium. Yet in
1924 I saw a collection of sample prayersticks near Luka-
chukai. A man, then over seventy, had arranged a prayerstick of each kind for his chant—perhaps thirty or more—
in an unbleached muslin case so that he could refer to them
whenever necessary. He had modeled the collection on that
of an older man, his teacher.[6] At one chant I attended near
Ganado a middle-aged man had paper sketches of the prayersticks. RP referred somewhat slurringly to his dependence on

paper, not to deplore the permanence of the patterns but to ridicule the man's lack of confidence in his memory.

Offering and Reward

I distinguish between offering and reward more for the sake of convenience than because the difference is very significant. By an offering I mean something tendered to compel assent before support is granted. By a reward I mean a material or non-material object given or an effort put forth after aid has been granted. Even the promise of a reward may be an offering, as it was in the case of Monster Slayer who, when he asked Sun's aid in overcoming the monsters, promised the Taos maidens. Originally heroes had few possessions; their ability to ' offer ' depended upon the success of an exploit rather than upon actual possessions. The promise then made the difference between offering and reward chiefly one of time. An offering was presented to a stranger; a reward to a relative whose kinship ties compelled aid. Changing Woman, ' our mother,' sometimes gives upon request. Once when she advised her son (Turquoise Boy), she did so ' expecting offerings from him.' First Man and First Woman must have white corn meal sprinkled to them at night; their offerings must be remembered,[7] not because these gods bring man good but so that they may not render futile the good that may come man's way.

In the Flint Chant are examples of different kinds of offerings: the one to the chanter, the offering of a jewel to a stone that may have injured a person by rolling on him, the offering of ashes bread to the chanter as a reward for singing (that is, a ceremonial rather than a material payment), the offering of a pouch containing tobacco and pipe instead of a prayer-stick to Gila Monster.[8]

Knowledge of what a deity will accept is of prime importance in handling invocatory offerings. An offering may be of the simplest sort; Earth People's greatest original difficulty was to discover its pattern. Since effort, even suffering, were often required to learn the design, the prayerstick is an ' offering '—it is sometimes called a ' sacrifice.' Prayersticks, like other ritualistic property, are a part of the system of payment and exchange. Knowledge of the indispensable songs and prayers that go with the offerings is wealth. When a difficult deity has been overcome by one more powerful, he promises to give his offering, song, and prayer for his life. The three must go together; any one or two are inadequate. Coffee and flour are acquired at the trading post in exchange for something. Offerings are exchanges, tokens to curry deific favor. In Navaho religion no service is gratuitous; it is interchanged, measured, traded, the benefits being reciprocal.

The bead token (Concordance B) is an example of a reward, as is the profit the singer derives from performing any ceremony. The bead token is a symbol of blessings incurred by the patient, a means by which the gods recognize him as ' their child,' a reward for being sung over. A perfect turquoise is the chanter's token of having sung the chant, a recompense for his training and acceptable performance.

Deposit of Offerings

The care with which all offerings are made is paralleled by that with which they are deposited—a demonstration of ritualistic etiquette. Offerings must be found by the deity to whom they are appropriate where he would look for them. Chanters give assistants explicit directions about the place and method of deposit. Since planting prayersticks properly requires trustworthiness and a sense of responsibility, a patient prefers to have a close relative do it for him.[9] Generally, requirements for deposit are specific, depending upon the prayersticks, chant, and other factors. It is said that offerings should not be placed at the north of the ceremonial hogan.[10] Prayersticks of the Holy ceremonies are usually set out somewhere else, but offerings, which in the Evil chants serve the same purpose, should be set at the north, where dangers and evils dwell.

When prayersticks are offered to different deities, each kind may be wrapped in a separate folder—of cornhusk or unbleached muslin—and deposited at designated spots, sometimes a long rite. Or a single wrapper may contain them all; in this case a neutral point, partly fulfilling the requirements for each, is chosen.

In the Shooting Chant, prayerstick offerings may be made to Big Snake, Arrowsnakes, and Blue Lizard at the same time. According to the myth, they should be deposited in the crooked root of a pinyon tree; according to JS, under brush near animal holes. Those of ordinary snake (rattler) should be put under greasewood, those of Arrowsnake at the edge of a hill, those of Blue Lizard near a heap of black rock. One spot could hardly meet all these requirements, but it may be considered representative of them all.

Talking Prayersticks

The 'talking prayerstick' (ke·tá·n yáłtih) is confusing because of the Navaho habit of including different kinds of things under one name. It has been discussed as if it were always the same.[11] The talking prayerstick is doubtless a property necessary to every ceremony, but one that takes on numerous forms in different chants. Much more should be learned about its manifestations.

Many chanters have a pair of talking prayersticks, one male, one female, made of aragonite or wood with eyes and mouth of inlaid jewels, bound together with yarn or twine, decorated with feathers and jewels. A chant property, it furnishes individual protection when carried, makes a prayer come true if held while the prayer is intoned. Dire consequences befell the mythical heroes who forgot to take it with them. The chanters I know all have a pair of talking prayersticks; one pair seems to be enough even though they may know several chants. Rain Singer's and Wind Chanter's were of aragonite; RP's, of the same material, belonged to his bundle of Blessing rites, and was not destroyed at his death.

I think that the indispensable prayerstick—actually a pair made one—is derived from the mythical pair of deities, 'ałké'' na''a·ci·, ' One-who-follows-the-other.' *Navajo Creation Myth* contains more references to this pair than any other account, though they are far from clear.

In the second world 'ałké'' na''a·ci· were created as hermaphrodite twins by be'γotcidí, but, because Black God did not like them, he cut them into small pieces and rearranged their parts with reeds. He then breathed into the body of the male through a reed, and a great sound began in their bodies. Near the mountains of the east, white cotton began to move; in the other directions, blue, yellow, and black cotton moved, rose, and changed into clouds. Black God treated the female the same way and under the clouds that arose vegetation appeared.

In the third world be'γotcidí created the pueblo Indians— Zuni, Hopi, and Taos. To the Taos he gave a male reed, to the Hopi a female reed. Since he and the other gods living with him wanted the Hopi and Navaho to be friends, they gave a female 'ałké· na''a·ci· to the Hopi, a male to the Navaho.[12]

Rain Singer said he got his four aragonite talking prayersticks from a chanter of the third generation of owners; one male prayerstick came from Taos, a female from Oraibi, and a pair, male and female, from Walpi (*Bundle contents: Rain Ceremony*, Concordance C). References other than Wheelwright's suggest that talking prayersticks are the symbol of motion.

Other references in Wheelwright are: ' One ceremony is the story of One-follows-the-other, another is the prayer and song, and another the song only. . . . The spirit of One-follows-the-other is the spirit of life and also the spirit of Wanderer-in-the-dark. . . . be'ɣotcidí in this world took the 'ałké'' na·'a·ci·, motioned toward all creation, and it came to life. . . . After the first man died, be'ɣotcidí reported that he had seen the deceased below in the third world and with him the shadow of the 'ałké'' na·'a·ci·.' [13]

Since there was said to be the special ceremony, and 'ałké'' na·'a·ci· are set apart from the rest of the deities, Wheelwright may be describing the original and all subsequent talking prayersticks.

Rain Singer says that the pair sa'ą na·ɣái and biḱe· xǫ́jǫ́ are the same as 'ałké'' na·'a·ci·.

We ought to know what is meant by male and female in the above references; I suggest that ' hermaphrodite ' may in the context mean a male-female pair, bound together as are today's ' talking prayersticks.' I shall refer to such a pair as a ' personal ' or ' traveler's ' talking prayerstick, since they seem to provide special protection for people in a doubtful position, usually away from home.

. . .

If the ' personal ' talking prayerstick is the general symbol of individual security, the ' bundle ' talking prayersticks represent the confidence inspired by the chant. The Shooting Chant myth accounts for them as the earthly replicas of Sun's original jewel arrows The Twins struggled long and hard to acquire. Sun sent a gleaming turquoise arrow into their midst, left it just long enough for them to memorize its pattern, then withdrew it to the sky, saying the names would serve for the actual arrows. A similar etiology is given for the War Ceremony rattlestick.[14]

There are five talking prayersticks or wands in the Shooting Chant and Mountain Chant bundles, eight in the Hail and Night chants. They are called ndi·á, ' those-which-project-upward,' as are the bundle objects of other chants that can be stuck into the ground. The permanence of the bundle talking prayersticks, the transitoriness of the rattlestick seem to make no difference in their functions. Since these symbols are a major item of many ceremonies, I suggest that they be called the ' master symbol,' that which many ceremonies have in common.

In the Shooting Chant and War Ceremony myths a prayerstick kept at home warned of danger that threatened Monster Slayer abroad. I call this the ' warning prayerstick '; it seems to be a mentor or messenger form of the talking prayerstick, which lighted up when its protégé was in peril. By its brilliance it communicated with its own guardians and those for whose sake it existed. The association between Sun's arrows, bundle talking prayersticks (Matthews' ' plumed wands '), and the mythical warning prayerstick is close and well substantiated: I expect to find some corresponding symbol in other ceremonies, but do not expect its appearance or explanation to be simplistic.

The numerous talking prayersticks mentioned elsewhere are probably duplications and manifestations of the talking prayersticks just described. The chant sung for me had as its ostensible purpose blessing for travel; the Prayerstick branch symbol consisted of eight pairs of so-called ' talking prayersticks,' two pairs of which were stuck upright in the ground floor of the ceremonial hogan in each of the four directions to serve as guards for my safety. They were made especially for the chant and afterward disposed of. The Hail Chant myth, like that of the Shooting Chant, mentions large numbers of talking prayersticks as invocatory offerings. In explanation tłá·h said, "The talking prayersticks are those that have eyes and mouth."

Each of the Sky People in *Navajo Medicine Man*, Plate XXII, holds a talking prayerstick because it represents the departure from Changing Woman as the people set forth upon a journey. In Roman Hubbell's drawing of this picture painted by RP, the prayersticks are exactly as tłá·h drew them for me for the Hail Chant.

Mythological references to talking prayersticks, unfortunately not so described as to designate the kind, have a protective function.

First Man owned prayersticks of whiteshell, turquoise, abalone, and jet, wrapped in unwounded buckskin; these he never laid aside. He carried them when he went to investigate the phenomenon of the cradle on the mountain.[15]

Said Changing Woman to her children, "These talking prayersticks will be with you in your blanketfolds to guide you and to speak to you on your return journey."[16]

As Monster Slayer set off to find the lost tribe of Navaho, he told the people, "Get things ready in four days." By ' things ' he meant the talking prayersticks that had directed the people on their journey.[17]

On the fifth night of the Shooting Chant, Holy Man volunteered to fetch water to moisten the basket that was to serve as a drum. It seemed such a small, casual errand that he did not take his talking prayerstick with him. Water Monster, owner of the spring, drew him down into the water realm and did not release him until powerful gods appeared whose spokesman was the talking prayerstick. Placated, Water Monster explained, "If Holy Man had brought his talking prayerstick with him, this would not have happened."[18]

co had been drawn down by the Winds. Talking God came with his unravelers, which acted like a yo-yo. After they had shown him where the hero was, Talking God restored co's reason by means of the talking prayerstick.[19]

As Holy Man in forbidden territory prepared to skin a mountain sheep he had killed, he laid his arrows aside. Because he was unprotected, he was captured by Thunders.[20] In this episode the arrow and talking prayerstick seem to be associated.

Buffalo arrows were the reward for sparing the Buffalo chief after he was overcome. They are described as the tó bo'oltá, 'bundle talking prayersticks' of the Shooting Chant.[21]

There are at least three kinds of talking prayersticks—one for personal, individual protection, especially when traveling; one a symbol of Sun's jewel arrows, represented as plumed wands (tó bo'oltá) in several chant bundles, and as the temporary rattlestick of the War Ceremony; and one similar to the invocatory prayersticks with the mentor-messenger function. Talking prayersticks should always be carried for the owner's safety no matter how trivial the errand that takes him abroad. No chanter, assistant, or patient should go outside the ceremonial hut without a blanket, lest he leave behind his ' pocket,' including his protective symbols.

CHAPTER 19

CLASSIFICATION OF CEREMONIES

O F THE several classifications of Navaho ceremonies the most inclusive is that of Wyman and Kluckhohn, which is based partly on Father Berard's terminology.[1] My own attempt, far from complete, was arrived at by another method. Instead of starting with the comprehensive view, which assumes that each chanter understands the religion as a whole, I began with the details. Proceeding from the specific to the general, I find myself with a vast number of details—mythological episodes and incidents, rites, color, sound, directional symbols, ritualistic acts, and the like—bound together in a complex organization. Any one of the parts may be slipped from one context to another with ease and with what the Navaho considers complete consistency.

Interpretations always differ and it is to be expected that mine will not agree completely with those cited. None of my Navaho informants concurred in the classification of the ceremonies, each being deeply concerned with the details of his own knowledge but only vaguely or hesitantly with the entire scheme. In other words, generalization is our affair, not that of my Navaho acquaintances. I do not have a single instance in which a Navaho attempt at theoretical summary checked with observed practice, whether it had to do with weaving, farming, or social or ceremonial organization. The situation may be duplicated in our own or any other society because each individual makes his over-all judgments on the basis of his own limited experience, which is rarely representative. Consequently, since in any case Navaho religious organization is confusing, another exposition should have some weight.

Father Berard recorded Gray Eyes' myth of the Male Shooting Chant Holy, I translated it, Wyman and Kluckhohn consulted it for their classification. We were all exposed to the same material, though not equally, since our purposes were different. The differences in our conclusions lie in interpretation—the Navaho interpretation of our queries and our interpretation of their statements. Despite what I have said about generalization, the details of all our materials agree remarkably well.[2] For example, from the time I first analyzed the Shooting Chant myth I considered the following excerpt of prime significance in classification: "But if one should perform all this and use the wrong prayerstick, the patient does not recover and another sing is required. So one after another is tried. Finally, the wise men try out the War Ceremony. If the right chant is happened upon, one is sufficient to cure the patient."

Wyman and Kluckhohn see in it a mere qualification subsidiary to their main argument; consigning it to a note, they remark, "The practice of trying one kind of ceremonial after another in stubborn cases . . . is frequently observed."[3]

There is no difference in data: the Navaho gave his unsolicited opinion; Wyman, Kluckhohn, and I differ about weighting. Since I have frequently encountered in practice exactly what the myth states and since myth is spontaneous, I hold such remarks to be major evidence. To Wyman and Kluckhohn they are secondary, worth merely an incidental note.

My disagreement with Father Berard arises from different, irreconcilable viewpoints about linguistic analysis and translations, and from my experience in the ceremonies. He was not a participant of the 'ways' he records. These two methods, the linguistic and the observational, are interrelated, for the latter permits checking theoretical and folk etymologies by behavior, bringing out the relationship of the particular to the general, and employing a large number of informants and interpreters on a single ritualistic point rather than the spoken opinion of only one.

Based on a consideration of Navaho and English meanings, together with the analysis of Navaho ritual, my terms are somewhat simpler than those of other classifiers. Except for 'chant,' they are as self-explanatory as the English translations warrant. For several reasons I omit 'chantways' and Father Berard's largest category, 'ceremonial.' The latter is such a useful word that the exigencies of writing make me loath to restrict it to a specialized service. I may refer to all performances, whether they last an hour or nine days, as 'ceremonies.' In many cases 'chant' is synonymous with 'ceremony,' although at points they differ. They cannot be distinguished by any one feature or even by a combination of a few; their uniqueness is in the whole.

By a 'rite' I mean the short combinations of ritualistic acts that form a ceremony. For instance, I would call the bath or the offering of prayersticks a rite. I consider each element of one of the shorter complexes a 'ritualistic act.' When I refer to the 'rite of breathing in,' I have in mind a succession of acts—the patient leaves the hogan, holds out his arms, and, with cupped hands, palms up, symbolically draws the sun into his mouth. On the other hand, breathing in, as exemplified by acceptance—for instance, of an offering —may be merely a ritualistic act, not a rite at all.

A chant (xatá·l) cannot be infallibly defined: it is a particular organization that includes many things, not all the same and not always even having the same value. The short and often mixed affairs that last for only a night or a few hours, or that may go on intermittently for days, are more properly a succession of rites or cures. Chapter 6 demonstrates the futility of defining chants by the diseases they purport to cure. Father Berard has picked upon the presence or absence of the rattle as a differentiating feature.[4] The Bead Chant is called yoeʹ xátáʹl, yet no rattle is required for it. The chant is rather a combination of many symbols and the knowledge of what they signify. The information itself, even without the performance, may be referred to as xátáʹl. The heroine of the Endurance Chant was possessed of power that enabled her to ward off evil, such as Coyote's temptation. Her power is referred to by the same verb-stem in ' chant ' and ' chanter ' and seems to mean ' power in the form of a charm to ward off danger' or 'lore that gives power because it is systematic' (cp. Chapter 17). Matthews introduced the word ' chant ' because of the prevalence of song and intoning in the prayers, and since his day the word has taken on a special meaning for Navaho students that we may as well accept. A synonym would be ' a charm ' in the sense of ' any action, process, or thing believed to have (magic) power.'

The problem of defining a chant is in part linguistic. In the chant names, two suffixes, -eʹ and -djí, have been treated as if they had some deep ritualistic symbolism and translated ' side, manner, way.' Literally, -eʹ is added to a word having an inclusive meaning; it may denote ' customs, ways, manners, tradition, mores, culture '; for example, nakaih-eʹ, ' Mexican ways, all the elements included in Mexican culture.' The suffix is relative; it qualifies by setting off Mexican from other customs, Navaho or American, for instance.

With a meaning hardly less restricted, depending on the situation but contrasting different aspects, is the suffix -djí: 'anaʹdjí, ' enemy side,' implies that there is a non-enemy or

317

friendly side. If one compares one phase of Mexican ways with another and the one not mentioned is understood, one may say *silverwork*-djí, ' concerning silverwork,' as against *weaving*-djí, ' concerning weaving.' Similarly, if one contrasts Mexican and Navaho customs, one may say nakai-djí, not nakaih-e·, but one does not properly add -djí if more than one contrasting idea is implied.

-djí, which indicates pairing, explains, therefore, such a chant name as na'aɫoe· baką'djí xótcǫ́'ǫ́djí xatá·l, ' concerning-shooting male-(there is also female) evil-(there is also holy) group-of-charm-symbols.' Since no comprehension of Navaho ceremonials is possible without understanding male and female, Evil and Holy divisions, it seems sufficient to translate the name Male Shooting Chant Evil.

The explanation of the meaning of -e· disposes also of Father Berard's implied question about na·γé''e·; he finds difficulty in the inconsistency that na·γé''e· is a legend of the emergence period but is not necessarily a rite. Doubtless a story ' concerning monsters ' does not have to be assembled in such a way as to be a chant or ceremony, although it may be. Probably it will be found to be closely related to Stephen's emergence legend.[5]

In an attempt to clarify the confusion about an indispensable pair of words—xójǫ́·djí and xótcǫ́'ǫ́djí—I summarize meanings I have heard:

xójǫ́·djí 1. ' Good as opposed to evil, favorable to man as opposed to unfavorable, doubtful.' 2. Derivation of 1. by extension, ' that which attracts or is to be ritualistically attracted ' as opposed to ' that which is to be exorcised.' 3. Of an organized complex, ' various rites based upon the basic myth of instruction,' perhaps even ' organized into ceremony ' (*Vigil*, Concordance C).

xótcǫ́'ǫ́djí 1. ' Evil, bad, that which is to be avoided

unfavorable to man, out of harmony.' 2. Derivation of 1. by extension, ' that which is to be driven away, exorcised.' 3. Of an organized complex, 'instruction, rites, and ceremonies whose main purpose is exorcism.'

xǫ́jǫ́·djí and xǫ́tcǫ́'ǫ́djí have both general and specific meanings whose interrelationship may readily cause misunderstanding. diɣinkeho (diɣinkehdjí) means ' according to that which is holy, that which ritual has changed from neutral (natural) to holy ' (cp. Chapter 7). What is natural is also good (xǫ́jǫ́); therefore xǫ́jǫ́·djí and diɣinkeho are opposed to xǫ́tcǫ́'ǫ́djí. My informants contrasted diɣinkeho with xǫ́tcǫ́'ǫ́djí when referring to organization, but xǫ́jǫ́·djí with xǫ́tcǫ́'ǫ́djí when contrasting good and evil, and details within the ceremonial complex. For instance, they made the main distinctions of Chart XVIII, then contrasted Red Inside phase ('i'·'te·ltci·djí), which is xǫ́tcǫ́'ǫ́djí—that is, exorcistic—with xǫ́jǫ́·djí, which represents the normal, the usual.

Since Navaho ceremonial lore consists of a large number of parts, any one of which is in a sense as important as any other, no ceremony is minor, for if a less elaborate charm is necessary to a cure, it would be wasteful to sing a long, involved chant, like giving a blood transfusion for a slight scratch. The independent as well as the interlocking purpose of every ceremonial item is so vital that to assign one element, or one combination of acts, a greater or higher value than another is like considering a cogwheel more important than any of its cogs.

The explanation of Charts XVIII and XIX is based upon the following dogma as I find it from my analysis of different branches of a single chant, and comparison with available portions of other ceremonies.

Navaho religion, dogma, ritual, and practice must be looked at as an aggregate of diverse ideas, including every possible phase of nature, deity, and supernatural power, of human perception, behavior, emotion, culture, and imagination formulated in myth.

From this congeries, which actually takes all time, space, existence, and sentience for its province, certain elements have been chosen for co-ordinating a single system or order. The selected items may be in one case material, perceptual, and emotional; in another, perceptual or natural only; but whatever they are, they comprise an integrated whole.

All things in the universe, materialistic and abstract, are viewed in terms of their effect on man. If he knows about them and can control them, they are good; if not, they are evil. Some things under only partial control are good when susceptible to that control; otherwise they are bad. Therefore, the fundamental subdivisions—good and evil—which are not absolute, overlap.

The good in all things must be attracted; hence ceremonial control invokes good in Blessing rites or ' chants-according-to-holiness.'

The evil remaining outside ritualistic control must be driven off; hence the ' evil-chasing ceremonies ' with emphasis on exorcism, but from which attraction of good is by no means absent.

Each ceremony is a complex, made up of many kinds of symbols, and is inclusive rather than exclusive, since there is no predictable limit to the items that may be selected.

Each subdivision of a ceremony, which I term ' branch ' or ' phase,' is characterized by features that from our viewpoint are fortuitous and therefore not susceptible to scientific systematization.

Rites, which are further subdivisions of ceremony, may refer to a series of mythological events or dramatize a single episode.

320

Ritualistic acts are the ultimate elements of which the larger divisions are composed. Their significance may sometimes be ascertained, but should not be expected to be the same whenever the act is performed. Each symbol has numerous interpretations, but the more we learn about it, the clearer it becomes that differences are not so much conflicting as associational and therefore, in the Navaho view, harmonious.

The scheme I have determined is as rational as an analysis of rationalization can be. Its simplicity is designed to allow flexibility. Chart XVIII shows how the various forms, branches, and phases of the Shooting Chant—the only one for which we have determining material—are set up.

Doubtless all Navaho ceremonies may be included in the classification; few except the Shooting chants are assigned with confidence. I am least sure in placing the male and female divisions in the same category as ceremony and chant, the reason being that I do not have any actual basis for differentiating male and female chants.[6] RP and all my informants who sang the male chant said, "The female is quite different. If you know one, you do not bother with the other," implying that the other was inferior. Although Female Shooting chanters lived in the Ganado region, the female chant was sung less often than the male, perhaps because of the dominance of the male chant or the superciliousness of its singers.

I was told that the myth is very different from that of the male chant, having to do primarily with the birth and rearing of The Twins. It is primarily on the basis of this information that I put the female and male chants in the same category rather than in subdivisions of the same chant, which they may, of course, turn out to be.[7] I would call them variants if the myth proves to be a more detailed development of some part of the male chant myth, or if the chant includes the same

CHART XVIII

CLASSIFICATION OF CEREMONIES

Rites of instruction
xǫ́jǫ́·djí
    House blessing (T)*
    Girl's adolescence ceremony (T, I)*
    Wedding (T)
    Rain Ceremony (T)
    Rites for subsistence and increase (T)
        Agriculture
        Hunting (related to and derived from other chants)
    Purification rites (T, I)
        Vigil
    Life (emergency) rites (partly xǫ́jǫ́·djí and parts of other chants) (I)
        Flint Chant
        kase·
        Life forms of other chants
            Life Shooting Chant

War Prophylactic: Where-the-two-came-to-their-father (I, T)

Chants According-to-holiness (diɣink'eho) (I)
    Night Chant (winter only)**
    Male Beauty Chant (winter only)**
    Feather Chant
    Bead Chant (winter only)**

Male Shooting Chant:
    Branches:
        Sun's House with phases:
            xǫ́jǫ́·djí
            Red Inside
            Dotted
            Thunder Lies
            Dark-circle-of-branches (Fire Dance, Corral Dance)
        Sandpainting
        Prayerstick
    Hail Chant
    Water Chant
    Wind chants
        Navaho Wind Chant
        Navaho Many Sandpaintings Chant
        Female Wind Chant
Male Mountain Chant
Female Mountain Chant
Eagle Chant (related to Bead Chant)
Female Shooting Chant
Female Beauty Chant
Red Ant Chant (JS says this may be a holy chant)
Hand Trembling Chant

Good (emphasis on transformation from neutral to sanctified, on attraction of good)

CHART XVIII—*Continued*

CLASSIFICATION OF CEREMONIES

Comprehensive

⌈ Prayer chants (sodizin, perhaps part of xǫ́jǫ́ˑdjı́)
  Dark-circle-of-branches, Male Shooting, and Mountain
⌊   chants (perhaps others also)

⌈ Rites of instruction (probably naˑγéˑ'eˑ) (T, I)
    Hunting (T)
    War (T)
    Trade (T)
    Gambling (I)
    Excess (I)
    Traveling which recalls ignorance of underworlds
      (T, I)

  War Ceremony

  Male Shooting Chant Evil
  Female Shooting Chant Evil
  Endurance Chant

Evil (emphasis on   Upward Reaching (this and the preceding may be different
exorcism)   branches of the same chant, xadjíˑnái, xaˑneˑłnéˑheˑ)
  Big Star Chant
  Mountain Chant Evil (probably Male and Female)
  Red Ant Chant
  Hand Trembling Chant Evil
  Wind chants Evil
    Striped Wind Chant
      deˑzla' (1. plan, purpose, intent, usually evil. 2. arrow,
        weapon)
      xaˑcké (Scolding, War)
      Flint

  Chiricahua Wind Chant (Wyman thinks this is indepen-
⌊   dent of the system of Wind Chants above)

---

*T, emphasis on tribal welfare; I, emphasis on individual welfare. Both overlap.
**That is, the full form, a nine-night chant, is sung in winter only, although excerpts, or trial forms, may be sung whenever needed (Wyman-Kluckhohn, pp. 30–31; Kluckhohn-Wyman, p. 106).

ritualistic properties with the same or even different interpretations. I interpret ' different ' as including ' additional.'
Matthews' account is of the Female Mountain Chant, but,
since there is no information about the male chant, there is
no basis upon which I can distinguish the two.

Branch and phase of the Male Shooting Chant Holy are
modifications of the same story and the same general procedure, with emphasis on a different symbolic theme—in one
case the Sun's House; in another, the temporary talking
prayersticks; in another, the prayers; and in still another, the
Dark-circle-of-branches. Each causes some modification of
other details which must be carefully learned and practiced
by the chanter, but not differences of initial pattern or of
myth, variations in interpretation being slight.

Ordinarily red of the rainbow of the sandpaintings is on the
outside, blue on the inside. Transposing the colors in the
paintings and a few other changes constitute a phase, called
' Red Inside ' ('i·'ṫe·ltci·djí).[8] The phase counteracts the
effects of extreme natural danger. Similarly, Dotted and
Thunder Lies phases have slight differences in the songs,
paintings, prayersticks, and prayers, but they drive out evil
effects within the limitations of the Holy chants (Chapters 7, 20).[9]

Certain details of the Male Shooting Chant Holy and the
Hail Chant correspond so closely that one seems, in certain
respects, to be a branch or subdivision of the other. However,
since their myths and interpretation are quite different, and
since each has outstanding features, they must be considered
as distinct.

Under the category ' rites of instruction ' I include ritual
that concerns general knowledge for tribal welfare. There is a
long origin myth with which every chanter should be familiar,
since it includes the fundamental rites for group well-being, a

myth sometimes referred to as a chant, as are also some of the rites based on it. Such rites include the Blessing rite, frequently performed to correct or prevent mistakes, to remove the contamination of contact with the dead; House Blessing, Girl's Adolescence rite, wedding rite, Rain Ceremony, rites of restoration and installation. According to Wheelwright, there was a rite in which One-who-follows-the-other was especially featured. She notes that xǫ́jǫ́·djí is the "most universally understandable of all Navaho ceremonies," that it concerns the blessing of man's trail from life to death.[10]

My informants state that ideally chanters should learn the entire xǫ́jǫ́·djí lore before they take up the study of a particular chant (xatá·l). Gray Eyes, tłǎ·h, RP, and others conformed to this requirement. In enumerating the chants they know, chanters often fail to mention the Blessing instruction, taking it for granted that the singers have mastered the essential background; some whose fundamental knowledge is sketchy list the Blessing rite and recorders put it down as a ' chant.'

On the other hand, some men never become chanters though they specialize in short rites, learning parts of the basic lore, which includes the more simple, sometimes very rare, rites. I predict that when the myth called xǫ́jǫ́·djí with its proper explanation is published in full, a great many of the scattered bits of information now extant, as well as the rites called ' minor ceremonies,' will fall neatly into place within it. The myth of instruction will explain why the great chanters are called upon for ' little sings.' All are part of the chanter's stock-in-trade, which he learned before he came to the more specialized xatá·l. Conservative chanters deplore the ignorance and carelessness of today's youth who tend to neglect the Blessing background.

Of the evil ceremonies there are two kinds: the War

Ceremony ('ana·djí), directed primarily against evil due to ghosts of foreigners, and the Evil form of the chants (xatá·l), which dissipates internal evils, primarily sorcery and local ghosts. I have found exorcism directed more often against intangible and undefined evils, such as unappeasable animals —Coyote, Bear, Ant—than against individuals.[11]

The War Ceremony seems to be in a class by itself. Made up of details quite comparable with those of the other ceremonies, it has additional elements such as the mock battle and give-away; moreover, the entire organization is distinctive. Nevertheless, it fits very well into the general scheme given here.

The Evil chants are held together by similar mythological episodes and rites; the material, though not adequate, indicates that their organization is comparable. There is some reason to consider the Male Shooting Chant Evil a branch of the Holy form. RP, when dictating the story of the sandpaintings to Sam Day, included the episode of Holy Boy marrying Big Snake's daughter and the change into a coyote to explain a sandpainting I saw in the Male Shooting Chant Evil.[12] JS considers the two stories quite different, though the same bundle serves for both, if the chanter knows the Holy as well as the Evil form (cp. Introduction). Whether they are separate chants or parts of one cannot be settled from the evidence in hand, and we must remember that RP tended to draw things together, whereas JS inclines to see each detail for itself.[13]

The Shooting Chant bundles have five bundle arrows, but in no performance I saw was the fifth, the down-feathered arrow, used. RP explained: "This [the fifth] is used in the Evil Chant if the patient has been wounded."[14] Probably a distinction in the diagnosis would make the fifth arrow imperative and cause such modifications as to make it a phase of the Evil chant.

' Emergency ' describes a group of ceremonies whose organization seems more amorphous than the Holy and Evil chants. After considering Wyman's suggestions and reasons (personally communicated), I have accepted his catchphrase 'Life chants' for this group. They are composed of rites similar to those of the better-organized chants; among them some are distinctive and there seems to be freer choice of what must and what may be included. As long as some indispensable rites are performed at intervals, the period during which they are sung may be greatly prolonged and varied, depending upon the patient's condition. JS considers the following, all of which he knows, distinct: Flint (bé·ce·), Shaft (kase·), and Male Flint Life (bé·c bikạ' 'i·ná·djí). Each probably represents a different selection of the available materials. RP considered bé·ce· and kase· the same, but the Male Shooting Chant Life branch different. I have noted Father Berard's failure to distinguish two subdivisions of the Flint Chant; [15] here may lie the difference between bé·ce· and kase·.

The Wyman-Bailey account of the Flint Chant appeared after I had come to these conclusions, and I have since had a long discussion with Wyman.[16] Their approach and data seem to corroborate my previous predictions, although we are still doubtful about the interpretation of Father Berard's versions A and B.

Wyman has recorded that his Upward-reaching-way and my Endurance Chant are based upon three tales.[17] I have listed these as separate chants, for I think that they, too, although they have the same name, may differ somewhat depending upon which of the tales—Emergence, The-return-of-the-two, and Changing-bear-maiden—is the basis of the sing. I have considered also the possibility that all three may prove to be episodes or parts of a single myth, the performances differing according to which is chosen.[18] I have a good detailed text of the Changing-bear-maiden tale, with some explanation of the ritual, but I have not witnessed a performance. The chanter who dictated the text said it was the 'same' as the Big Star Chant which I saw.

My scheme and explanation include the ceremonies for which some comparative material exists. The Night Chant, some of the Wind chants, and, possibly, the Mountain Chant, all of which have numerous subdivisions, belong to the category 'good.' I would not even venture a guess as to their subdivisions, although Matthews indicates that the Night Chant has several and Franc Newcomb has found that the Mountain Chant has branches, possibly phases also.[19]

I hazard several other guesses to be discarded or adopted when and if an analysis based on story, observation, organization, and interpretation becomes available. One is that the story of na·γé·'e·, referred to by Father Berard,[20] is not the story of a chant, but of instructions about the prehistoric monsters, the tale of evil corresponding to the story of man's trail from the lowest to the present world. To some extent Father Berard's material corroborates the guess: the legend (of na·γé·'e·) is a complete unit in itself, but may be one of the origin legends on the assumption that Monster Way furnishes the concluding episodes of the origin legend.[21] The statement is not particularly clear, but should be read with the Emergence myth, which comprises the teachings of xójó·djí, in mind.

At the end of the Night Chant myth the following explanation occurs: "And now [that which] is called Monster Chant, its blessing way had long ago been sung for [the people], they say. When the monsters had been killed,

Horned Toad Boy had sung it for them, they say. 'This [blessing way] will lie on all of [the chants], as far out as the chants extend. At the tip of all of them it will lie, [on] blessing way rites also,' Horned Toad said, they say." [22]

Before interpreting the passage, I would change the translation to read ' monster lore ' for ' Monster Chant,' since the suffix -e˙ may mean 'concerning' and not necessarily 'chant.' The last sentence I would translate: "At the conclusion [summarizing point] of all the chants this one will be. It will be the significant point of them all. It is not xǫ́jǫ́˙djí, that is, it is not Blessing Way, but Monster Way." [23] With these emendations, Blessing Way may properly be understood to belong to monster lore, which should be its opposite, so that any commemoration of the dark past may conclude with blessing. [24] Details of the instruction may, of course, be so organized as to form rites, as they are in the Blessing teachings. I would have supposed that the War Prophylactic Ceremony derived from this material, but Jeff King emphasizes its relation to Blessing Way (probably xǫ́jǫ́˙djí) [25]—an example of classification by emphasis rather than by content.

I should expect the Feather and Eagle chants to be in the Evil division. They may, however, as easily belong to the Holy side, since the Feather Chant has god impersonators and other close affiliations with the Night Chant. In many respects the Eagle Chant resembles the Bead Chant and, since it has no evil-chasing connections, the Eagle Chant may be considered to emphasize good. Both probably owe their position on the good side, as well as the exorcistic emphasis, to the stress on hunting.

My 'comprehensive' category takes care of 'prayer ritual' (sodizin). Some medicine men, instead of learning a complete chant, learn the prayers and prayer songs of as many chants as possible, cutting a cross section, as it were, of the entire

329

ritual. No example has been recorded of this important type of ceremony.

The Dark Circle or Fire Dance branch of any nine-night chant is another kind of cross section. Many chants have Dark Circle symbols and events, hardly apparent in the ordinary performances, but representing the chant whenever a Dark Circle branch is undertaken (see *Red headdress*, Concordance C).

Although some leeway may be allowed for the fact that in Navaho contradiction is more apparent than real, the inconsistencies in the record of the Flint Chant should have been explained. Several times the recorder and his informants say that Flint Chant is in a class by itself, that it is not concerned with ordinary curing, with evil-chasing, with the cutting of invocatory prayersticks, or with the administration of medicine on sandpaintings.[26] On the other hand, Flint Chant is said to be the same as kase˙ and 'i˙ná˙djí (Life Way). JS told me that Flint Way (bé˙ce˙) is a word of the Holy People; Life Way, a word by which the Earth People denote the same thing.

The Male Shooting Chant Holy has a life phase that RP included as follows: "At this point of the story of the Buffalo, a separate chant branches off, called ' the prayer for life.' It is sung in cases of serious injury and the medicines are the same as those Holy Man used when he restored Buffalo-who-never-dies."[27]

Father Berard's informants almost certainly meant that the purpose, emphasis, and function of these chants are the same. An analysis of the text ritual leads to the following suggestions. Apparently the two versions, A and B, the second of which Father Berard more or less scorns, are actually accounts of two forms of the Flint Chant, showing differences at least comparable to branches, if not wider disparity. In version B the offering to Gila Monster is a prayerstick (ke·tá·n); in version A, a tobacco pouch. This one item alone should have been a key to further inquiry and analysis. If it was not enough for a clue, differences in the songs, in the use of the pouch, in the restoration rite, in the act of the Flint or Branch Corral, and in the appearance in version A of pink (disǫs, misleadingly translated ' sparkling ') where version B uniformly has yellow (in prayers and songs, for instance) should have suggested the need for further inquiry.[28]

Instead of following through the meaning of these differences, the recorder says, "Basing our estimate on these merits we have selected version A as the better text for our study of the Flintway." "The introduction of this group [of deities] is somewhat annoying." ". . . minor details and useless repetitions are quite frequent in that version [B]." ". . . he [the informant] apparently loses himself in a sham of repetitions." [29] In view of the Navaho interpretation of ' merit,' and the value the informant as well as the whole culture sets upon repetition, it hardly behooves a recorder to permit himself annoyance at his material or to deplore repetitions. Perhaps the informant is not ideal; to me he seems to have contributed much that the other chanter did not.

Let us discount the apparent prejudice of the recorder against his informant of version B and consider the information in the texts. The Flint Chant, kase·, and 'life branches' of the other chants stress emergencies judged to be more or less imminent, depending upon who is acting for the injured and the diagnostician, if one is consulted. The choice from a wide range of causes will determine the chant, branch, or details of the rites. For instance, a selection may be made from the application of dust from a buffalo track, tapping with the foot in the restoration rite, use of the stretcher, stepping over crossed canes, specially requested prayers and song groups.[30]

The emergency character of the chant is doubtless the main reason for its flexibility and emphasis. The importance of song is demonstrated by the informant's statement that in a serious case one sings even at night and all day, as well as by the interpolation of the vigil songs at intervals if the chant is continued for many days or performed with interruptions. Moreover, chanter and patient should keep awake for five days and nights, fivefold as severe an endurance test as the usual vigil.[31] The Sun painting is so often a part of emergency chant excerpts that it seems to be characteristic. Laid in pollen, it is a part of the Flint Chant.

The relation between the Flint and Male Shooting chants seems close: the same character, Holy Man, is the hero in both; the members of the Holy family have the same names and are mentioned in the same order in both chants; the bundles are so nearly alike that either may be borrowed for the other chant; rites overlap. Many features recall Hail Chant, especially the seduction of the hero by Winter Thunder's wife and his destruction by Winter Thunder. The restoration rites are comparable with the same rites belonging to every chant or ceremony, all being similar in pattern and purpose, differing only in details. The Flint Chant bundle items may *revive* those struck by lightning, but those of the Hail, Water, Navaho Wind, Male Shooting, or Female Shooting chants *remove the effects* of lightning and hail. This differentiation partly explains the significant functional reasons that determine which chant is to be sung. In the myths of both Male Shooting and Hail chants, they, as well as Water, Wind, and Feather chants, are said to be closely related, and mythical episodes account for the relationship; for example, the school of instruction in the Land-beyond-the-sky included novices from all of these chants.[32]

Instead, then, of making the Flint, kase·, and Life chants the same or identical, we should say that they are quite similar, especially in purpose, but that the Flint Chant and perhaps kase· are emergency chants, whereas the Shooting Chants and others have a branch or phase that corresponds with the Flint, this subdivision being expressed by the term ' life.'

The life phase, influenced as it is by the chants to which it belongs, is probably analogous to the ' ways ' described by Hill for hunting.[33] I do not believe that there were separate hunting ceremonies with many names such as he lists—Wolf, Snake, Shooting, and the like—but rather that each hunter abstracted the ' hunting part ' of the chant he knew for the party's protection, just as each chanter carries out the rite of his chant to restore persons and animals to consciousness (*Restoration rite*, Concordance C). In other words, each body of lore provided for specific needs outside the chant organization just as it did for emergencies.

Distinguishing Symbols

The intricacies of ceremonial classification, not the least of which is naming, explain why the scattered accounts of Navaho ceremonies seem inconsistent. Once the classification with its subdivisions is realized, it would be helpful to have a sure sign for placing a performance within the scheme. That, however, is impossible, since we do not know the symbolic value of the various items of any except the Shooting Chant. The layman or uninformed person will be able to spot the determining symbols only if they chance to be prominently displayed. He could not, for instance, determine that the number or words of prayers or songs constitute a branch, or that a repeated performance in which the symbol does not reappear, belongs, say, to the Sun's House or Prayerstick branch. Indeed, an experienced person could classify these chants only by skillful questioning. If we are ever to get a satisfactory classification and differentiation of the ceremonies and their subdivisions, the investigator must not excuse himself from the effort required. Despite the difficulties, much can be learned by intelligent observation and query.

If a performance is the first in a series, the characterizing symbols are likely to be outstanding. The personal or traveling talking prayerstick defined in Chapter 18 will tell little about the chant, but the master or bundle talking prayersticks may be of prime significance. A part of the chanter's bundle property, they can hardly be missed. In such cases they may be called the 'chant' symbols. Generally there is something in addition to the chant symbol to distinguish the chant—the wide boards of the Shooting Chant; wide boards and curved sticks, smooth sticks, ni·cí·h, néji·, and ni·ctci·j of the Hail Chant; the single wide board, curved sticks (crooks), straight and notched snake sticks, and slender sticks of the Navaho Wind Chant. Properties of this sort lie in a basket or on a blanket when not a part of the temporary altar (sandpainting or screen arrangement) or they stand in the sand around a painting.[34] In the War Ceremony the rattlestick (master symbol) is in evidence most of the time; in addition, the 'crowbill' seems to be the 'ceremony' symbol; correspondingly, the 'cranebill' is said to be the 'chief and leading pouch part' of the Flint Chant.[35] The difficulty in differentiating the master and chant symbols is that sometimes they are the same and sometimes both are among many other items, not all of which have the same significance. Chart XIX (page 348) indicates my interpretation of master, chant, branch, and phase symbols, certain for the Shooting and Hail chants, deduced for the others.

In some cases the observer can tell a good deal by the *time* certain rites take place. The first four nights and days of the nine-night Holy chants are primarily days of exorcism, although the prayerstick or offering rites on these days have the preliminary function of invocation. Similarly, the emphasis on the second group of four nights and days and the last night may be devoted to identification with holiness. Since exorcism and invocation are about equally divided on any day of a five-night Holy chant, their differentiation is more difficult. Though the Evil chants last only five nights, the time division within the period and the rites are so different from those of the Holy chants as to be determining.

The branch symbol of the Holy chants will doubtless appear at the beginning of the period calculated to attract good power. In the Sun's House branch the screen is set up on the fifth night; the Dark Circle is indicated by some symbol of the sandpainting of the fifth day and by slight modifications in rites and ritualistic acts. The visitor will hardly be able to detect differences in detail, but he will know by the name, Dark Circle (Fire or Corral Dance), that it is planned for the last night, even if the name of the chant, Mountain or Shooting Chant, is omitted. The uninitiated can tell by the cross in the center of a sandpainting such as those in *Navajo Medicine Man*, Plates XIV, XVI, XVII, and XXIV, that the picture belongs to the Dark Circle branch, but in some pictures there is no cross symbol to represent fire. The novice could help the specialist by finding out the full name of the chant, for the Dark Circle indicates only the subdivision, not the chant itself.

If the Holy chant lasts five nights, the branch symbol will probably be apparent on the first night or day, since in this type of performance, each day is divided between exorcism and attraction instead of four nights being devoted to each. The eight pairs of temporary talking prayersticks for my chant were cut and planted even before the hogan consecration. These symbols might easily be overlooked by a casual visitor, for they are small and stand under the lowest part of the hogan walls. JS's chant symbols were dedicated as branch symbols the first night of the five-night sing; the chant symbol being also the branch symbol, the particular character of the prayerstick branch is the inconspicuous emphasis on song and prayer.

Only information from the Navaho on the manufacture of the prayersticks and of course the name, if ascertained, could determine the phase symbol ' red-inside.' The investigator who knows the significance of the position of red and blue of the rainbows can determine the phase by the sandpaintings of the fifth to eighth days.

The chant or branch symbol may be indicated by its position on the roof or over the doorway. Whereas the Sun's House screen at the back of the hogan guards the ceremonial area at night, the beaded bundle (chant symbol) of the Bead Chant and the temporary arrow of the Big Star Chant lie over the door during the night performances. The swastika property of the Hail Chant seems to have been over the door on some nights, over the smokehole or hanging down into the room from it on some days.

The branch symbol need not appear at the successive repetitions of the chant. The Sun's House screen was absent at the repetitions held for MC because her bead broke; there were no talking prayersticks at the two-night repetition of my chant. In such cases inquiry alone can identify the performance.

Unfortunately no simple, infallible rule of thumb can be

formulated to determine the place of a performance in the ceremonial scheme; all are subject to exceptions and change. No serious investigator should expect casual attendants at the ceremonies to ascertain the classification. He should himself, however, take the trouble to determine the distinguishing symbols of his chant group. General questioning may not always elicit them, because the chanter may consider too many things the ' same ' and he may credit the interrogator with knowing a lot more than he really does. Nevertheless, specific queries in particular situations, to be determined by myth or observation of a performance, will often substantiate the essentials. Proper questions can be formulated only by bearing in mind the Navaho classifications and assumptions and by remembering that the answers themselves may skew the categories and assumptions somewhat in one place and brilliantly corroborate them in others.

CHAPTER 20

ORGANIZATION OF RITUAL

The Chanter's Bundle

WHEREAS THE ethnologist is interested in the classification of ceremonies and the interpretation as a whole,
the singer is engrossed in the details of the chant he knows;
he enlarges the field of his preoccupation only as he obtains
new knowledge. He occupies himself, therefore, with the
elements from among which he has to choose—deities to
invoke with prayersticks, patterns of the prayersticks, songs,
rites, ritualistic acts—and their organization into a ceremony. Properties are as important as songs and prayers;
they are to be found in his bundle, described by Kluckhohn
and Wyman.[1] I record such additional information as I was
able to get under *Bundle contents*, Concordance C.

In my experience the chanter's bundle examined at any
one time does not necessarily include his entire equipment,
but rather that which he happens to select for a performance
(cp. *Rite for removing contamination of the dead*, Concordance C). The properties of the Evil chants are simpler in
certain respects than those of the Holy chants, but there
may be some items of both types included in a bundle on a
particular occasion. The chanter has his full equipment at
home; whenever he is called, he chooses the parts he deems
indispensable. If the people giving the performance decide
to add accessory rites not previously bargained for, he may
send back for more after the chant has begun. In this respect
the bundle is, like most things Navaho, superficially an

unstable aggregate, from which items are chosen and to which others are constantly added.

In case a man knows the Holy and Evil forms of a ceremony, as did RP and JS, the bundles have in common rattle, arrows, bull-roarers, and bows. The chanter gets a set of each for the form he starts with, then adapts the items to the next form he learns—he has ' another sing over them,' adds ' another bead,' or perhaps prayers and songs. JS's bundle properties for the Male Shooting Chant Evil emphasize the Holy side—the first he learned and the one he sings most often—whereas RM's emphasizes the Evil aspect, since he has specialized rather consistently in this form. Property considerations of this sort are probably the chief determinants of the chanter's learning stages.

In the sense that the bundle holds weapons against evil, it may be considered a quiver. But it is much more, for it contains items to attract good as well. Consequently, there is much symbolism pertaining to war in the bundle belonging even to the Holy forms of ceremony. Since they were acquired by The Twins' risking repeated attacks by unknown evils, the bundle talking prayersticks, Sun's arrows, are major items of the Holy chants. Contrasting with but also complementing them are the tiny bows of the Evil side, for which a temporary disproportionately large arrow is made each time the ceremony is performed.

Kluckhohn and Wyman have published an index of ritualistic ideas,[2] many of which I have adopted, changing the catchwords only if they seem inappropriate, insufficiently differentiated, or inadequate. Often my data cover different facets of their subjects, or contain new items. The situation is like that of an archaeologist—in all of his classifications he must leave a place for new finds, and even for subdivisions of those he already has.

Several catchwords refer to bundle properties. ndi"á, 'those-which-stand-up,' have been noted as including bundle talking prayersticks (Chapter 18). When apparently inactive,* they lie with other bundle items in a basket, an arrangement called ' basket layout '; for certain purposes—unraveling, for instance—they lie on a pile of goods; this arrangement is called a ' spread layout.' When they are a part of the mound altar before the door where a sandpainting is in progress, the reference is to ' setout ' or ' setout mound.' When the properties are stuck into the earth around the sandpainting to complete it, the arrangement is called ' setup.' [3] Any of these groupings may be the same in rites performed on successive days, in different rites, or they may vary under the same or different circumstances.

Some bundles are thought to have so much individual power that they are buried with the deceased singer. Others, such as that of the Flint Chant, represent continuous or tribal power, so that when an owner dies, the power he has held in trust survives. The difference between personal and tribal power explains the apparently conflicting statements of Father Berard's informants—that personal medicines should remain the property of the clan and that they should continue to be used for the tribal good, even by a non-clan member.[4] The correctness of each opinion depends more upon the knowledge of the heir than upon the bundle itself. If he is informed about chant details, he may inherit a chant bundle; if he does not possess the requisite tribal lore, he may get it by instruction. On the other hand, the mental and, therefore, religious achievement of the deceased may be so great that his very possessions hold power for which no one wants to be responsible.

---

*Actually no bundle property is ' inactive ' during the ceremony, since its very presence is thought to exert potency.

Allusions to the contrary notwithstanding, I have yet to find a clear case of clan ownership or inheritance of ceremonies or even of information about them, such matters being a factor of Navaho individualism rather than of socialization. I suspect that the remarks about ' clan ' possession are based upon misunderstanding of the words applying to ' clan,' ' group,' ' relative,' some of which sound nearly the same to whites and none of which has been accurately interpreted.

Preparation

Much of the time devoted to any sing is taken up by preparation, which is just as important as the use of the objects, if not more so. Most of the power is not in the item itself, but in what it stands for; it is a product of effort, discrimination, attention, concentration, and care, and therefore is not to be judged by appearance alone. The five-night chant performed for JS to dedicate eight bundle items illustrates not only the materials—from our viewpoint of no value— and acts that give them worth, but also the emotional significance with which they are invested (cp. *Bundle contents: SC*, Concordance C).

Materials must be carefully gathered. After being selected from the proper direction, which must be subsequently ascertainable, parts of a root, bush, or tree must be ritualistically cut, at least symbolically if not completely, with a flint point belonging to the bundle. Care is exercised to preserve the plant and assure its growth, usually by sprinkling pollen on the stump.

Other substances of the most diverse nature are collected. Long hours are spent in arranging them for various rites— prayerstick offerings, hoops, plant garment (Concordance C), and endless other composites. During the manufacture of the

341

properties there is good conversation, information is communicated, and the supervising chanter keeps a critical eye on the least detail as each worker proceeds under his direction.

Whenever a long ceremony involving an old chant symbol is undertaken, some time is allotted to 'refreshing' or 'renewing' it, refurbishing with paint or providing fresh green branches or twigs. The day before the Sun's House screen was set up, it was entirely repainted, the booth on which it was to stand was covered with green branches, the birds were strung on wires so they could be made to fly, the snakes' heads were attached to the booth so they could be moved in and out and from side to side as they protruded from the apertures called their houses.[5] All this preparation was necessary because the screen had not been used for eight years.

The masks of the Night Chant are similarly renewed— they are sung over, live branches form ruffs, new temporary masks are constructed.[6] Unused power dissipates itself; ritualistic effort restores its potency. A chanter should sometimes go through the whole ceremony to revitalize his power.

Sandpaintings, making the hoops for Evil chants, braiding the bandoleers and wristlets for the last day of the Shooting Chant are other examples of time-consuming preparation. Usually the patient should not ' see things being prepared for him,' but after the main work has been accomplished, he often participates in some concluding detail—he ' paints ' the invocatory prayersticks with pollen, holds the strands for the bandoleer-braiding, sprinkles the sandpainting with corn meal. In contrast, the chanter helps with everything done in the chant to review his knowledge until the final touches are put on (Chapter 9).

The family and sponsors are concerned with practical preparations. The chanter requires a designated number of baskets, which may be borrowed or purchased. Someone has to furnish the 'spread layout,' usually new yard goods, most often of unbleached muslin, percale, or calico.

Women exert themselves to provide large quantities of food for the expected guests. Meat, flour, baking powder, salt, coffee, and sugar are the staples. Relatives and debtors of the patient or sponsor are called upon to return favors or pay up debts—one gives a sheep, one a goat; an uncle kills a steer; a cousin sends coffee. If corn, squash, potatoes, watermelons, tomatoes, peaches, prairie-dog, or any other luxuries —anything beyond meat, flour, and coffee is a luxury—are available, so much the better. Before the ceremony is announced, the provision of food is a matter of considerable thought. It is proper to have a large number of guests at a sing, an insult to the family if only a few turn up.

Disposal

Just as important as preparation is the disposal of substances and properties, even of left-over materials. Portions of plants remaining after sorting and bunching for unravelers, neckpieces, hoops, and the like are laid on a blanket, carried out, and discarded according to the chanter's instructions. Remnants should be left where there is little likelihood that they will be touched by domesticated animals. Scattering by wind and rain is 'natural'; the products should be allowed to 'return unmolested to the earth.' When a sandpainting rite is finished, the patient leaves the hogan, the chanter ritualistically knocks down the bundle properties (setup) and gathers them to return to the bundle, the helpers scrape the sand onto a blanket and deposit it outside in a place designated by the singer. If the painting belongs to a Holy chant, all may be emptied in one place without much to-do. If, however, it is a painting of an Evil chant, one portion may be placed under the patient's pillow for the night and another scattered in one or more directions outside, each night farther and farther from the hogan (cp. Chapters 7, 9). After a sweatemetic rite, assistants extinguish the coals left from the fire and carry them out; they deposit the sand basin of the patient outside the hogan, often at the north; the audience follow and dump their sand basins and contents in orderly piles next to the patient's.

The sand of the Hoop Transformation mountains (Concordance C) was deposited a short distance north of the ceremonial hogan in piles corresponding with the respective positions of the mountains it composed. The yucca strips were flung loosely on the piles, the whole giving an effect of studied neglect.

Invocatory objects should be protected until they have attracted the attention of the deities they invoke. Substances nullifying evil power should have freedom to disperse, since dissipation as well as quality is a part of exorcism. Neutral, that is, surplus, remnants have communicated their power to the objects made of them; they should be returned without hindrance to the place of their origin. Plants should not be hurt; good use consists in good treatment.

Rite and Ceremony

The chanter, having determined the aspect of the chant to be sung and selected the properties, must fit all acts, preparations, and dispositions into the time limits of the ceremony fixed by form, branch, and phase. Although Indians never seem to hurry, the singer may feel somewhat rushed, especially if he has been asked to include many accessory rites, or if elaborate sandpaintings have been paid for and there is little assistance. Even though it means working under pressure, a singer takes great satisfaction in being busy, preferring a complicated to a simple performance; he feels flattered at the responsibility devolving upon him. Since all rites appearing in the nine-night chant are included in the five-night, though they may be somewhat abbreviated, the shorter ceremony may be more crowded than the longer one.

Some chanters start the sandpaintings early in the morning, disposing of even elaborate ones by noon. RP was not one of these. If he had a lot to do, he began the sweat-emetic about seven, long after dawn in the summer; if not, he waited until about nine. I note considerable difference among chanters in the timing of the same rites; Kluckhohn and Wyman think that the sweat-emetic should take place just after dawn.[7]

When a singer feels pressed, he may telescope acts or rites. For example, the sounding of the bull-roarer, really a part of the bundle application, becomes in the Prayerstick branch of the Shooting Chant a part of the unraveling rite. The important thing is to get everything in and these things go together; the unraveling and the bull-roarer drive away evil, the application of bundle items resists it. The Hoop Transformation rite of the Male Shooting Chant Evil was performed at the south and north on one day, both being combined with the Prayer on buckskin rite; ordinarily these rites take two days. The whole chant lasted, therefore, four instead of five nights (*Hoop transformation rite, treatment with: SCE*, Concordance C).

I was told that for CF a five-night and two-night performance of the Shooting Chant had been combined into one ceremony, as a substitute for the nine-night form, or perhaps as a single ceremony, instead of two at different times.

On successive nights, during which unraveling and plant garment rites are performed, more time is spent in each rite than on the preceding nights. Such cumulative effect is the Navaho interpretation of climax. Probably no repetition on successive days is exactly like the rites of the preceding days; some details differ, even setting a theme for variation.

Analysis

The most difficult task in analyzing ritualistic material is to sustain a point of view. Too often the investigator is likely to take his from the material he knows best, as if the mere accident of his opportunity to get these rather than other data were a criterion. In stressing the subdivisions of the Shooting Chant I have tried to note many aspects and also to describe comparable performances of similar or differing rites. If an act or property of one seems to be missing, it may be the fault of the observer, or it may be a ritualistic prescription. After numerous repetitions of the same rites, certain lacks may be noted and the cause ascertained. Though we have seen that negation is important, it is usually discovered by chance (Chapter 11). Once, for instance, at a large gathering about the double sandpainting of the Dark Circle branch of the Shooting Chant, an aged white woman wanted to witness the ritual standing up. All activity ceased until she sat down. I had seen dozens of sandpainting treatments, but not until then did I learn that the rites cannot be carried out unless everyone is seated. Up to that time no member of the audience had indicated a desire to stand. For most of the Shooting Chant rites a missing property or act means it was not prescribed; for rites belonging to other ceremonies, I may have missed it, especially when many acts were carried out simultaneously and they belonged to chants whose underlying themes were vague or new to me.

Matthews has presented one analysis of rites and chants, Kluckhohn and Wyman another;[8] both are chronological.

Matthews was interested in the properties, what was done, and why. Kluckhohn and Wyman are interested in behavior and participation—who does what, the relationship of one actor to another. I have experimented with other presentations; none seems wholly satisfactory, chiefly because of the nature of the material and the fact that numerous acts may be carried on simultaneously or have apparently different reasons. For instance, in the nine-night performance of any chant the division of events is relatively clear, the time being almost evenly allotted to exorcism and attraction. On the other hand, in the five-night form all the events are there, but so interwoven that they do not stand out clearly in their contrasting functions.

The chronological order of a chant is of great importance, yet it never indicates to me the actual significance of correlated ritualistic ideas. The differences in branch and phase rites of the same chant emphasize the comparison and avoid unnecessary repetition. I have adopted a system that puts similar things together and, by catchwords alphabetically arranged, I have tried to make them easy to find. The difficulty in this as in any system is to determine what belongs together. I have not been able, for example, to divorce ' treatment on sandpainting ' from the sandpaintings themselves just because it comes under "T" rather than under "S." I have attempted to obviate this difficulty by repeated cross references. Since my fullest information on Evil forms is the Big Star Chant and, on Holy forms, the Sun's House and Prayerstick branches of the Male Shooting Chant Holy, they are my prototypes, but in many cases, because of the alphabetical order, a description of any part may be found after, rather than before, the features I may be discussing at the moment.

Whenever possible, I have summarized the meaning of a

property or rite, but sometimes meaning is so involved that only the entire myth or large parts of it can adequately explain a simple ritualistic act. I find this arrangement more serviceable than any I have tried, but only because such presentations as those of Matthews, Kluckhohn, and Wyman have already been made, and I am far from satisfied with it. Entries cannot always be kept parallel for various reasons— forms change, details are lacking, some rites are much simpler than others. One chanter describes the first order of events and takes the rest for granted, although in actual practice there may be slight differences in repeated performances; another refers to the first and describes the second, third, or last with care. Most informants assume much greater understanding on the part of the white man than is justified; unfortunately, too many investigators share this false premise.

The organization of ritualistic acts, chants, and ceremonies I have seen is indicated by Charts XIX–XXIII and Concordances A, B, and C (Volume II). I do not include the Hail Chant symbols and order of events because I have never seen a Hail Chant performed.

CHART XIX

MALE SHOOTING CHANT HOLY SYMBOLS

Symbol	General	HOLY FORMS			
		SH (9 nights)	DC (9 nights)	SP (5 nights)	P (5 nights)
Master	personal talking prayerstick				
Chant	4 bundle talking prayersticks, 4 wide boards				4 pairs temporary talking prayersticks
Number	4, 5				
Color	b-u-y-w, w-u-y-b				
Sex:					
Male	b-u				
Female	w-y				
Sound	blu···				
Negation					
Branch	Watersnake	SH screen	Dark Circle	sandpaintings, songs, prayers	
Phase			Red Inside Dotted guardian Thunder guardian		

Legend: DC—Dark Circle; P—Prayerstick branch; SH—Sun's House branch; SP—Sandpainting branch.

CHART XX

ORDER OF EVENTS: MALE SHOOTING CHANT HOLY—SUN'S HOUSE AND PRAYERSTICK BRANCHES

	Night 1	Day 1	Night 2	Day 2	Night 3	Day 3	Night 4	Day 4	Night 5	Day 5	Night 6	Day 6	Night 7	Day 7	Night 8	Day 8	Night 9
Branch symbol prepared and placed	P		P		P		P		SH								
Unraveling	P		SH		SH		SH		SH								
Bundle application	SH		P		P		P		SH		SH		SH		SH		
Short singing	P		P		P		P		SH		SH		SH		SH		
Bundle setout	P	SH		SH		SH		SH		SH		SH		SH		SH	
Sweat-emetic		P		P		P		SH									
Prayerstick offerings		SH		SH		SH		P									
Sandpainting		P		P		P		P		SH		SH		SH		SH	
Bath								P								SH	
Figure painting								P								SH	
Vigil									P								SH

Legend: P—Prayerstick branch; SH—Sun's House branch.

CHART XXI

ORDER OF EVENTS: MALE SHOOTING CHANT HOLY—DARK CIRCLE AND SANDPAINTING BRANCHES

	Night 1	Day 1	Night 2	Day 2	Night 3	Day 3	Night 4	Day 4	Night 5	Day 5	Night 6	Day 6	Night 7	Day 7	Night 8	Day 8	Night 9
Branch symbol prepared and placed	SP														DC		
Unraveling			SP		SP		SP				FD		FD		FD		DC
Short singing																	
Bundle setout		SP		SP		SP		SP		DC		DC		DC		DC	
Sweat-emetic		SP		SP		SP				DC		DC		DC			
Sandpainting								SP								DC	
Bath								SP								DC	
Figure painting								SP								DC	
Vigil									SP								
Vigil with Dark Circle																	DC

Legend: DC—Dark Circle branch; FD—Fire Dance rehearsal; SP—Sandpainting branch.

CHART XXII

SYMBOLS OF EVIL FORMS: MALE SHOOTING CHANT EVIL AND BIG STAR CHANT

Symbol	SE	BS
Master	personal talking prayerstick	personal talking prayerstick
Chant	bundle bow, temporary arrow	bundle bow, temporary witch-objects
Number	5–7–9–11	5–7–9–12
Color	b-u-y-w	b-u-y-w
Sex:		
Male	b-u	b-y
Female	w-y	u-w
Sound	be'be'yó	be'be'yó

Legend: SE—Male Shooting Chant Evil; BS—Big Star Chant.

CHART XXIII

ORDER OF EVENTS, EVIL FORMS: MALE SHOOTING CHANT
EVIL AND BIG STAR CHANT

	Night 1	Day 1	Night 2	Day 2	Night 3	Day 3	Night 4	Day 4	Night 5
Unraveling............	SE BS		SE BS		SE BS		SE BS		
Bundle application......	BS		BS		BS		BS		
Plant garment..........	SE BS		SE BS		SE BS		SE BS		
Sweat-emetic...........		SE BS		SE BS		SE BS		SE BS	
Hoop transformation....		SE BS		SE BS		SE BS		SE BS	
Prayer on painting......	BS		BS		BS		BS		
Prayer on buckskin......		SE		SE BS		SE		SE	
Sandpainting...........	BS	SE	BS	SE	BS	SE	BS	SE	SE
Bath..................							SE BS	SE BS	
Over-shooting..........	BS		BS		BS		BS		SE
Blackening............									SE BS
Vigil.................									SE

Legend: SE—Male Shooting Chant Evil; BS—Big Star Chant.

NOTES

INTRODUCTION

1. Because it seems to me to connote more of the intention and historical affiliations, I am using 'War Ceremony' for 'Enemy Way.' The ceremony suggests a relationship to Plains warfare and ritual.
2. By 'Shooting Chant' I refer to Male Shooting Chant Holy. All other subdivisions are written out in full—for example, 'Female Shooting Chant Holy' or 'Male Shooting Chant Evil.'
3. Personal information from Franc J. Newcomb.

CHAPTER 1

(NAVAHO CATEGORIES)

1. Morgan 1936, pp. 12, 17.
2. Reichard, Shooting Chant ms.
3. Kluckhohn-Wyman, p. 19; Goddard, p. 128.
4. Matthews 1902, p. 203.
5. Reichard 1944d, p. 29 and cp. p. 147.
6. Goddard, p. 156.
7. Kluckhohn-Wyman.
8. Wyman-Harris, p. 11; brackets mine, authors' italics omitted.
9. Reichard 1944d, p. 151.
10. Matthews 1897, p. 140. Here and elsewhere I have, insofar as possible, made the Navaho orthography conform with the phonetics of this work.
11. Ib., p. 142.
12. Ib., p. 155; cp. Reichard 1928, Ch. IV.

CHAPTER 2

(WORLD VIEW)

1. Goddard, p. 137; Stephen 1930, p. 103; Reichard 1944d, pp. 91ff.; Wheelwright 1942, pp. 66–7; 1946, pp. 29, 50, 192.

2. Stevenson, p. 275.
3. Matthews 1897, pp. 63–5; Goddard, p. 128.
4. Goddard, p. 137; Wheelwright 1942, pp. 66–7.
5. Matthews 1897, p. 80; cp. Stephen 1930, p. 104.
6. Matthews 1897, p. 80.
7. Matthews 1897, pp. 111, 134; Haile 1938b, p. 101; Reichard, Shooting Chant ms.
8. Matthews 1897, p. 233, 117n
9. Ib., pp. 76, 78.
10. Stephen ms.
11. Sapir-Hoijer, p. 176.
12. Matthews 1897, p. 79; Goddard, pp. 148–9.
13. Matthews 1897, pp. 70, 79, 222, 60n.
14. Goddard, p. 167; Matthews 1897, pp. 149ff.
15. Goddard, p. 175.
16. Matthews 1897, pp. 116, 234, 128, 9n.
17. Matthews 1897, p. 133; Haile 1938b, pp. 179, 255, 102, 3n.
18. Goddard, p. 127; Matthews 1897, p. 70; Newcomb 1940b, p. 51.
19. Matthews 1897, pp. 175–87; Newcomb 1940b, pp. 57–63.
20. Stevenson, p. 279.
21. Reichard 1939, pp. 34–5, Pl. V–VII.
22. Stevenson, p. 278; Matthews 1897, p. 244–5, 207n.
23. Matthews 1902, p. 193.
24. Ib.
25. Stevenson, p. 279.
26. Stephen ms.

CHAPTER 3

(*THE NATURE OF MAN*)

1. Stephen ms.; Matthews 1897, p. 69.
2. Matthews 1897, pp. 104–5, 137, 148; Goddard, p. 168.
3. Matthews 1897, pp. 140, 159.
4. Stephen ms.
5. Goddard, p. 153; Haile 1938b, p. 91; Reichard, Shooting Chant ms; Stephen ms.
6. Presumably warmed by Sun.
7. Haile 1938b, p. 79.
8. Stevenson, p. 277.

9. Reichard 1939, p. 70.
10. Haile 1938b, p. 281, 81n; Reichard 1939, p. 34.
11. Matthews 1897, p. 35 (Navaho names have been translated).
12. I discovered this reference some months after formulating the theory of conception.
13. Goddard, pp. 138-9.
14. Matthews 1897, pp. 71-3, 218, 32-3n; Stephen 1930, pp. 79-100.
15. Reichard 1944b.
16. Hill 1938, p. 111.
17. Reichard 1944b, pp. 51-2.
18. Hill 1938, p. 110.
19. Reichard 1928, Ch. IX. The word in Reichard 1944b, p. 51, should be 'áji' instead of 'aji'.
20. Kluckhohn 1944, pp. 79, 123, 125.
21. Haile 1938b, pp. 25, 49; Hill 1936, p. 18.
22. Matthews 1897, pp. 69, 136-7.
23. Reichard 1944d, pp. 10-1.
24. Haile 1943a, pp. 84, 85.
25. Pollen, Con. B; Pollenpainting, Sandpainting, Con. C; Wheelwright 1942, Set I, 1-4, Set II, 2, Set III, 1-4 and alternates; Oakes-Campbell, p. 37.
26. Hill 1938, p. 106.
27. I knew a woman who was reduced to a mere skeleton with grief at the death of her only daughter. She said she had no reason to live and refused to take part in any activity, yet she was alive some ten years later.
28. Matthews 1897, pp. 77-8; Goddard, pp. 36, 138; Oakes-Campbell, p. 12.
29. Stephen ms.
30. Sapir-Hoijer, pp. 430-3.
31. Wyman-Hill-Ósanai, pp. 32-5; cp. Kluckhohn-Leighton, p. 126.
32. Reichard 1943.
33. Goddard, p. 175 (retranslated).
34. Ib., pp. 64, 65, 152.
35. Haile 1938b, p. 318, 69n (phonetics mine).
36. Wyman-Hill-Ósanai, pp. 11-30.

CHAPTER 4

(PANTHEON: CHARACTERISTICS OF SUPERNATURALS)

1. Matthews 1902, p. 30.
2. Reichard 1939, p. 15; cp. The Twins, Con. A.
3. Haile 1943a, pp. 16, 22; Oakes-Campbell, p. 75.
4. Matthews 1902, pp. 218-9 excerpt.
5. Reichard 1944d, p. 7.
6. Ib., p. 13.
7. Cp. Ch. 9; Reichard 1944d, pp. 37ff.
8. Ib., p. 81.
9. Ib., p. 105.
10. Matthews 1902, p. 212.
11. Matthews 1897, pp. 140, 229, 92n.
12. Ib., pp. 170ff. excerpt.
13. Reichard 1944d, p. 95; cp. pp. 79, 81.
14. Ib., p. 147.
15. Matthews 1902, pp. 212ff.
16. Haile 1938b, pp. 97, 101.

CHAPTER 5

(PANTHEON: TYPES OF SUPERNATURALS)

1. Sapir-Hoijer, pp. 131, 163; Stephen 1930, p. 88; Huckel ms.; Reichard 1944d, p. 27; Haile 1938b, pp. 127, 147.
2. Matthews 1902, pp. 249, 253.
3. Reichard, Endurance Chant ms.
4. Matthews 1902, p. 159; Sapir-Hoijer, pp. 140-1.
5. Reichard 1944d, pp. 133-5; Matthews 1887, pp. 410, 417.
6. Matthews 1897, pp. 81, 224, 71n.
7. Oakes-Campbell.
8. Ib.
9. Matthews 1897, pp. 130-1; Reichard, Shooting Chant ms.
10. Haile 1938b, p. 18.
11. Oakes-Champbell.
12. Wheelwright 1942.
13. Sapir-Hoijer.
14. Wheelwright 1942, Set II, 3.

CHAPTER 6

(*THEORY OF DISEASE*)

1. Hill 1936b, p. 13; Reichard 1928, p. 145.
2. Reichard 1939, p. 80; Newcomb-Reichard, p. 60; cp. Franciscan Fathers 1910, p. 294.
3. Reichard, Endurance Chant ms.
4. Haile 1938b, pp. 193, 255, 108n.
5. Ib.
6. Hill 1936, p. 7.
7. Haile 1938b, p. 137.
8. Matthews 1897, p. 247, 224n (Navaho words omitted).
9. Haile 1943a, pp. 8, 52.
10. Haile 1938b, p. 143.
11. Matthews 1902, p. 214.
12. Haile 1938b, p. 195.
13. Matthews 1902, pp. 166, 236, 258.
14. Ib., p. 236.
15. Ib., pp. 209, 314, 53n.
16. Matthews 1897, pp. 198, 205; Reichard 1939, pp. 28–9.
17. Matthews 1902, p. 211.
18. Wyman 1936b, pp. 240–1.
19. Reichard 1928, p. 149.
20. Kluckhohn-Wyman, p. 175.
21. Hill 1935a; Wyman 1936b, c; Morgan 1931; Tozzer 1909; Newcomb 1938.
22. Morgan 1931, p. 392.
23. Wyman 1936b, p. 238.
24. Ib.
25. Cp. Mulholland, pp. 183–202.
26. Reichard 1939, pp. 7ff.; Newcomb-Reichard, p. 14.
27. Tozzer 1909, p. 308.

CHAPTER 7

(*THEORY OF CURING*)

1. Haile 1938b, pp. 95-7 excerpt.
2. Ib., p. 111 excerpt.

3. Goddard, p. 156, brackets mine.
4. Haile 1938b, p. 81 excerpt.
5. Ib., p. 93 excerpt.
6. Ib., p. 187 excerpt.
7. Haile 1938b, p. 207 excerpt.
8. Ib., p. 191.
9. Matthews 1887, pp. 406, 410; 1897, p. 69.
10. Reichard, Endurance Chant ms.; Big Star Chant ms.
11. Hill 1936, p. 7; Wyman-Harris, p. 57; cp. Kluckhohn-Leighton, p. 155.
12. Matthews 1902, p. 109; Haile 1938b, pp. 46, 201.
13. Matthews 1897, p. 163.
14. Hill 1936, p. 8; Haile 1938b, p. 40.
15. Reichard 1944d, p. 153.
16. Haile 1938b, p. 315; Hill 1936, p. 12.
17. Goddard, p. 151; Newcomb-Reichard, p. 28; Haile 1938b, p. 105.
18. Matthews 1887, p. 401; cp. Haile 1938b, p. 131.
19. Reichard 1944d, p. 135.
20. Reichard 1939, p. 31.
21. Reichard 1944d, p. 135.
22. Matthews 1902, p. 163.
23. Haile 1938b, p. 117.
24. Reichard 1939, pp. 41, 44; Haile 1938b, p. 215.
25. Reichard 1944d, p. 155.
26. Matthews 1887, p. 417 excerpt.
27. Matthews 1902, p. 212 excerpt.
28. Haile 1938b, pp. 145-9 excerpt.
29. Reichard 1944b, pp. 14-5.
30. Matthews 1902, p. 160.
31. Kluckhohn-Wyman, p. 63, 113n.
32. Ib., p. 50.
33. Wyman-Harris, p. 56.
34. Matthews 1887, p. 411.
35. Wyman-Harris, p. 54, brackets mine.

CHAPTER 8

(*ETHICS*)

1. Matthews 1902, pp. 246–56 excerpt.
2. Cp. Matthews 1899, pp. 3, 5.
3. Hill 1943, p. 9.
4. Matthews 1897, p. 108; Reichard, Shooting Chant ms.
5. Goddard, p. 155; Reichard, Shooting Chant ms.
6. Reichard 1944d, pp. 43, 143–5; Haile 1938b, p. 109.
7. Matthews 1897, p. 163.
8. Reichard 1939, pp. 34–5; cp. Oakes-Campbell, p. 24.
9. Haile 1938b, p. 71; Kluckhohn-Wyman, p. 56; Tozzer 1909, p. 317.
10. Haile 1938b, p. 71.
11. Wyman-Bailey 1945, p. 375; cp. Matthews 1902, pp. 185, 197.
12. Matthews 1902, pp. 212ff. excerpt.
13. Reichard 1944d, p. 7; cp. Haile 1943a, p. 56.
14. Reichard 1944d, p. 5; Haile 1943a, p. 56; Newcomb 1940b, pp. 56ff.; Matthews 1897, pp. 175, 191.
15. Reichard, Shooting Chant ms.
16. Matthews 1897, pp. 143–4, 240–1, 183n; cp. Haile 1938b, pp. 79–81.
17. Matthews 1897, p. 187.
18. Reichard, Endurance Chant ms; Matthews 1897, pp. 91–103.
19. Kluckhohn 1944, p. 21.
20. Goddard, p. 128; Matthews 1897, pp. 70–2, 77, 220, 50n.
21. Hill, 1935b.
22. Reichard 1944a.

CHAPTER 9

(*THE NATURE OF SYMBOLISM*)

1. Haile 1938b, p. 317, 52n.
2. Reichard, Endurance Chant ms.
3. Matthews 1897, p. 114; Reichard 1939, p. 44; 1944d, pp. 140–3; Haile 1938b, p. 109.
4. Reichard 1939, Pl. XIII, XV, XIX; Newcomb-Reichard, Pl. XXI, XXVIII, XXX-XXXIV.

5. Matthews 1902, p. 256.
6. Haile 1938b, pp. 199, 201; Hill 1936, p. 12; Goddard, p. 177.
7. Haile 1938b, pp. 157, 254, 87n.
8. Newcomb-Reichard, pp. 29-30; Haile 1938b, p. 111; Matthews 1897, p. 103; Reichard, Endurance Chant ms.
9. Reichard 1934, pp. 203-4.
10. Reichard 1944d, pp. 9, 13, 47, 141; Matthews 1897, pp. 164, 170; 1902, p. 195.
11. Reichard 1934, p. 67.
12. Reichard, Shooting Chant ms.
13. Reichard 1928, p. 115.
14. Goddard, pp. 134-5; Hill 1938, pp. 14-5; Wheelwright 1942, pp. 65-6. The Gregorian-calendar months are only approximate; the Navaho months include half of each; for example, Navaho November actually means the second half of November and the first half of December.
15. Matthews 1892; 1902, pp. 6, 37, 57, 59, 70.
16. Matthews 1902, p. 120.
17. Matthews 1897, pp. 171, 193.
18. Painting in Bush Collection, Columbia University.
19. Haile 1938b, p. 83.
20. Matthews 1897, pp. 147-8.
21. Franciscan Fathers 1910, p. 454.
22. Hill 1938, p. 102.
23. Stephen 1930, p. 92.
24. Reichard 1944d, p. 79.
25. Haile 1938b, p. 169.
26. Ib., p. 239.
27. Reichard 1939, Pl. I.
28. Newcomb-Reichard, Pl. XIII.
29. Oakes-Campbell, Pl. VI, X, p. 39; XIII, p. 40; XIV, p. 41.
30. Newcomb-Reichard, p. 80; Reichard 1939.
31. Reichard, Shooting Chant ms.
32. Ib.
33. Reichard 1944d, p. 61.
34. Ib., pp. 11, 45.
35. Kluckhohn-Wyman, p. 86.
36. Haile 1938b, pp. 267-9.
37. Hill 1936, p. 14; Haile 1938b, p. 272.

CHAPTER 10

(SEX, DOMINANCE, AND SIZE)

1. Reichard 1928, pp. 54–5; Hill 1936, pp. 5, 8.
2. Hill 1938, p. 106.
3. Ib., p. 75; Sapir-Hoijer, p. 207.
4. Haile 1938, pp. 58–9.
5. Stevenson, pp. 235–6.
6. Variation of Reichard 1939, P. XVIII; see Sandpainting: SC Dark Circle branch, Con. C.
7. Haile 1938b, pp. 60, 61, 227.
8. Ib., p. 237.
9. Ib., p. 221.
10. Ib., p. 223.
11. Ib., pp. 73, 223; Reichard 1928, p. 118.
12. Matthews 1902, p. 6; Reichard 1939, p. 78.
13. Matthews 1902, p. 56, Pl. II, D.
14. Ib., p. 93.
15. Reichard 1939, frontispiece, Pl. I, III, XV, XVII, XIX, XXII, XXIV; Newcomb-Reichard, Fig. 4, 20, Pl. IV, V, VII-IX, XIV-XXXV; Wheelwright 1942, Set II, 7.
16. Matthews 1887, 0. 448, Pl. XVII. There are errors in the references of the two pictures, Pl. XVI, XVII; the numbers 'second' and 'third' in the titles of the two plates should be interchanged.
17. Ib., p. 450, Pl. XVI (and note 16 above).
18. Wheelwright 1942, p. 82.
19. Newcomb-Reichard, p. 44; Matthews 1887, p. 450; Oakes-Campbell, p. 38, Pl. IV.

CHAPTER 11

(ALTERNATION, REVERSAL, AND NEGATION)

1. Newcomb-Reichard, p. 61.
2. Huckel ms.
3. Haile 1938b, pp. 30–1.
4. Matthews 1902, p. 100; cp. Haile 1943a, p. 14.

5. Hill 1938, pp. 98-9, brackets mine.
6. Haile 1938b, pp. 161, 239ff.
7. Matthews 1887, pamphlet published and distributed privately by the Bureau of American Ethnology.
8. The following observations fit the Hopi and Zuni audiences, as well as the Navaho.
9. Newcomb-Reichard, p. 28.
10. Reichard 1944d, p. 41.
11. Here the general restriction against eating fish is made specific for the Shooting Chant.
12. Reichard 1944d, pp. 81-3; Matthews 1902, pp. 106, 189.
13. Reichard 1944d, p. 149; Newcomb-Reichard, p. 29.
14. Reichard 1939, p. 34.
15. Reichard 1944d, p. 137; Haile 1943a, p. 154.
16. Reichard 1939, p. 35.
17. Matthews 1902, p. 212.
18. Matthews 1887, p. 410; Reichard 1939, pp. 80-1.
19. Matthews 1887, p. 407.
20. Matthews 1897, p. 185.
21. Ib., p. 137.

CHAPTER 12

(COLOR AND PRECIOUS STONES)

1. Reichard, Shooting Chant ms.; Matthews 1897, p. 137; Goddard, pp. 55-7, 153; cp. Oakes-Campbell, p. 39, Pl. VIII; Hill 1938, p. 72.
2. Newcomb-Reichard, p. 28; Goddard, p. 150; Haile 1938b, p. 87; Newcomb 1940b, p. 54; Reichard 1944d, p. 81; Matthews 1897, p. 184; 1902, p. 262.
3. Reichard 1944d, p. 115.
4. Ib., p. 133. I use 'mask' in its technical sense, a ritualistic face cover worn by god impersonators. This is in contrast to Franc Newcomb and Mary Wheelwright, who generally refer to, facial paintings and do not distinguish paintings and masks.
5. Reichard 1944d, p. 133; Matthews 1902, p. 9.
6. Haile 1938b, p. 197.
7. Ib., p. 101; Reichard 1939, p. 52, Pl. XIV.
8. Huckel ms.; Newcomb-Reichard, Pl. XII.

9. Reichard 1934, p. 194; 1939, Pl. XXII; Newcomb-Reichard, p. 21, Fig. 6.
10. Reichard 1944d, pp. 5, 33; Hill 1938, p. 94, 13n.
11. Reichard 1939, pp. 6–7.
12. Matthews 1902, p. 5.
13. Ib., p. 58.
14. Reichard 1939, p. 52, Pl. XIV.
15. Reichard, Shooting Chant ms.
16. Reichard 1939, Pl. XXII; Newcomb-Reichard, Pl. XIX. There is a mistake in Pl. XIX—black should be at the east, blue at the west.
17. Huckel ms.
18. Matthews 1902, pp. 52, 205; Reichard, Shooting Chant ms.
19. Matthews 1897, p. 127; Haile 1938b, p. 205.
20. Reichard, Shooting Chant ms.
21. Matthews 1902, pp. 128–9, Pl. VII; Newcomb-Reichard, p. 63; Pl. XXIII, XXV, XXVII, XXVIII; Reichard 1939, Pl. XIV, XXIII; 1944d, pp. 137, 139.
22. Reichard 1939, Pl. XX; 1944d, p. 76; Matthews 1902, Pl. VI.
23. Reichard, Shooting Chant ms.
24. Ib.
25. Huckel ms.
26. Reichard, Shooting Chant ms.
27. Ib.
28. Matthews 1887, pp. 400, 401, 459, 464.
29. Reichard 1939, Pl. XV; Huckel ms.
30. Matthews 1897, p. 129.
31. Reichard 1944d, pp. 25–7.
32. Ib., p. 41; Matthews 1897, p. 245, 209n; Goddard, p. 156; Haile 1938b, p. 177.
33. Goddard, p. 156.
34. Ib., p. 136.
35. Newcomb-Reichard, p. 52, Fig. 6; Huckel ms.
36. Reichard 1939, frontispiece, p. 59, Fig. 7.
37. Matthews 1897, pp. 67, 68; 1902, pp. 25–6.
38. Reichard, Shooting Chant ms.
39. Wheelwright 1942, p. 43.
40. Haile 1938b, pp. 113, 123, 137; Matthews 1897, pp. 117, 122.
41. Reichard 1944d, p. 33.
42. Haile 1938b, p. 165.
43. Goddard, pp. 80–1, 159.

44. Wheelwright 1942, p. 109.
45. Reichard 1939, p. 56.
46. Matthews 1897, p. 253, 270n.
47. Newcomb-Reichard, p. 32.
48. Reichard, Shooting Chant ms.
49. Reichard 1939, Pl. XXI.
50. Newcomb-Reichard, p. 43, Pl. XVII.
51. Reichard 1944d, p. 123.
52. Haile 1938b, p. 163.
53. Goddard, p. 163.
54. Kluckhohn 1944, pp. 87-8, 94, 122.
55. Reichard 1939, frontispiece, Fig. 6, 7, 8; Newcomb-Reichard, pp. 47ff., Pl. XXIX-XXXIII.
56. Reichard 1944d, pp. 27, 43-5.
57. Reichard 1939, Pl. XVII-XIX; Newcomb-Reichard, Pl. XVII.
58. Reichard 1939, p. 30, Pl. III, IV.
59. Newcomb-Reichard, Pl. XXXV.
60. Ib., p. 31; Matthews 1897, pp. 92ff., 126-9.
61. Haile 1938b, pp. 123-5.
62. Ib., p. 133.
63. Hill 1938, p. 101.
64. Reichard 1939, Pl. X-XX, XXII; Newcomb-Reichard, Pl. XV, XVI, XXI, XXIV.
65. Ib., p. 35, Fig. 4; Reichard 1939, Pl. XXII.
66. Newcomb-Reichard, Pl. XIV; Reichard 1944d, pp. 77, 115; Matthews 1902, p. 122, Pl. VI.
67. Reichard 1939, Pl. XX, XXIV; Newcomb-Reichard, Pl. XIV, XXVII, XXXIV.
68. Reichard, Shooting Chant ms.
69. Huckel ms.
70. Matthews 1902, pp. 128-9, Pl. VII.
71. Reichard 1939, Pl. V, VII.
72. Reichard, Shooting Chant ms.
73. Reichard 1944d, p. 147.
74. Ib., p. 105.
75. Stephen 1930, p. 102.
76. Haile 1938b, pp. 109, 130-1.
77. Reichard, Shooting Chant ms.; Newcomb-Reichard, Pl. VII.
78. Reichard 1944d, p. 106.
79. Wyman-Bailey 1945, p. 374.
80. Newcomb-Reichard, p. 19.

81. Reichard 1944d, p. 147; cp. Stevenson, p. 278.
82. Newcomb-Reichard, p. 31.
83. Kluckhohn-Wyman, p. 25.
84. Wheelwright 1942, p. 65.
85. Matthews 1897, p. 73.
86. Haile 1938b, p. 314, 14n.
87. Goddard, p. 140.
88. Ib., p. 139.
89. Huckel ms.; Newcomb-Reichard, p. 36.
90. Goddard, p. 142; Reichard 1944d, p. 15.
91. Goddard, p. 127.
92. Ib., p. 136.
93. Newcomb-Reichard, pp. 36, 59; Matthews 1897, p. 151.
94. Reichard, Shooting Chant ms.
95. Goddard, pp. 137, 164, 165.
96. Reichard, Shooting Chant ms.
97. Ib.
98. Matthews 1897, p. 113.
99. Newcomb-Reichard, p. 27.
100. Reichard, Shooting Chant ms.
101. Matthews 1897, pp. 150-3.
102. Reichard, Shooting Chant ms.
103. Newcomb-Reichard, p. 28.
104. Haile 1938b, p. 193.
105. Reichard 1939, p. 29.
106. Wheelwright 1942, p. 107.
107. Ib., p. 114.
108. Goddard, p. 134.
109. Haile 1938b, p. 207.
110. Reichard, Shooting Chant ms.
111. Haile 1938b, p. 265; Kluckhohn-Wyman, p. 29.

CHAPTER 13

(COLOR COMBINATIONS)

1. Reichard 1934, facing p. 194; Newcomb-Reichard, Pl. II., A, C.
2. Ib., Pl. X, XXV; Reichard 1939, Pl. XI, XII.
3. See pp. 745-6.

4. Cp. Kluckhohn-Wyman, pp. 138–9.
5. Matthews 1897, pp. 215–6, 18n; Huckel ms.
6. Reichard 1934, facing p. 194.
7. Matthews 1897, pp. 128–9.
8. Ib., p. 76; Goddard, p. 131.
9. Reichard 1944d, p. 105; cp. p. 204, present work.
10. Haile 1938b, p. 101; Reichard, Endurance Chant ms.
11. Reichard 1934, facing p. 194; Newcomb-Reichard, p. 21, Fig. 3.
12. Reichard 1939, p. 45, Fig. 3.
13. Newcomb 1930, p. 76; Goddard, p. 132.
14. Reichard, Shooting Chant ms.
15. Newcomb-Reichard, Pl. XXII.
16. Ib., Pl. V, VIII, XXIII, XXV, XXVIII, XXX.
17. Reichard 1939, p. 45, Fig. 3, Pl. XII, XIII.
18. Reichard 1944d, p. 43.
19. Matthews 1902, p. 53; Reichard 1944d, p. 59; Goddard, p. 149; Newcomb-Reichard, p. 52, Fig. 6; painting in Bush Collection.
20. Reichard, Shooting Chant ms.
21. Ib.
22. Ib.
23. Goddard, pp. 88–9, 161.
24. Reichard, Shooting Chant ms.
25. Goddard, pp. 149, 162, 163; Matthews 1902, p. 53; Reichard, Shooting Chant ms.
26. Ib.
27. Reichard 1944d, p. 69.
28. Goddard, p. 136.
29. The centers are, perhaps, not comparable, since *Navajo Medicine Man*, Plate XXIV, has the dark center already described and that at Rough Rock had a small blue (perhaps sparkling) center surrounded by a wide yellow band edged with blue and red.
30. At the time MC was sung over I was not aware of the problem.

CHAPTER 14

(*NUMBER*)

1. Reichard 1944b.
2. Stephen 1930, p. 103; Kluckhohn-Wyman, Fig. 23, 24.
3. Reichard 1944d, p. 25.
4. Ib., p. 103; Matthews 1897, pp. 113, 223, 70n; Wheelwright 1946, p. 192.
5. Matthews 1897, p. 104.
6. Ib., pp. 74, 93, 95, 110; Haile 1938b, p. 181.
7. Ib., p. 101; Matthews 1897, p. 184; 1902, pp. 203, 246–56; Wheelwright 1946, p. 46.
8. Matthews 1897, p. 136.
9. Ib., p. 104.
10. Ib., p. 83.
11. Ib., p. 140.
12. Matthews 1902, p. 200.
13. Ib., p. 175.
14. Matthews 1897, pp. 92, 149.
15. Ib., p. 239, 166n; Goddard, p. 135.
16. Reichard 1939, Pl. VI, VII.
17. Ib.
18. Newcomb 1940b, p. 71; Hill 1938, p. 98.
19. Haile 1938, pp. 141, 143.
20. Ib., p. 151.
21. Hill 1936, p. 8.
22. Hill 1938, p. 146.
23. Goddard, pp. 88, 162.
24. Matthews 1897, p. 249, 240n.
25. Ib., pp. 135–59.
26. Ib., pp. 139, 145, 149–50.
27. Cp. ib., p. 148.
28. Haile 1938b, pp. 203, 205, 207; cp. Kluckhohn-Wyman, p. 79.
29. Cp. Wyman-Bailey 1943a, pp. 27–8.
30. Reichard 1944d, p. 95.
31. Matthews 1897, pp. 127–9.
32. Reichard 1944d, pp. 51, 59, 65.
33. Ib., pp. 48–9, 85; Haile 1938b, pp. 195, 217, 225, 259ff.

34. Ib., p. 107; Newcomb-Reichard, p. 29; Matthews 1897, p. 113.
35. Haile 1938b, p. 193.
36. Ib., p. 207.

CHAPTER 15

(*PERCEPTUAL SYMBOLS*)

1. Stevenson, p. 275.
2. Matthews 1897, p. 67; Wheelwright 1942, p. 44.
3. Cp. Dorsey-Kroeber, p. 16.
4. Matthews 1902, p. 42, Pl. II, B; Reichard 1934, p. 194.
5. Matthews 1902, p. 42.
6. Matthews 1897, p. 213, 11n; 1902, p. 42.
7. Haile 1938b, pp. 176, 194; cp. ib. 1943a, p. 46.
8. Cp. Kluckhohn-Wyman, p. 25; Haile 1943a, p. 46.
9. Haile 1938b, p. 194.
10. Newcomb-Reichard, p. 34.
11. Reichard 1944d, p. 39.
12. Reichard, Shooting Chant ms.
13. Ib.
14. Haile 1938b, p. 214.
15. Ib. 1943a, p. 69.
16. Goddard, p. 127.
17. Matthews 1897, pp. 174–5; Newcomb 1940b, p. 55.
18. Reichard 1939, p. 29.
19. Matthews 1897, p. 164; 1902, p. 228.
20. Reichard, Shooting Chant ms.; Matthews 1897, pp. 117, 122.
21. Reichard 1939, p. 30; Newcomb-Reichard, p. 33; Haile 1938b, pp. 113, 123, 137.
22. Matthews 1897, pp. 137, 183; Haile 1938b, p. 83; Newcomb-Reichard, pp. 66–7.
23. Matthews 1902, p. 203.
24. Ib., p. 264; cp. Sapir-Hoijer, p. 245.
25. Haile 1938b, p. 97.
26. Perhaps 'something dangerous.'
27. Hill 1938, p. 109; Matthews 1897, pp. 187, 189, 249, 235n; 1902, p. 251.
28. Reichard 1939, Fig. 6, 7, 8; Shooting Chant ms.; Huckel ms.
29. Haile 1938b, pp. 87, 89.

30. Ib., p. 129.
31. Matthews 1902, pp. 314–5, 62n.
32. Reichard 1939, p. 29.
33. Kluckhohn-Wyman, p. 33.
34. Haile 1943a, p. 3.
35. Matthews 1897, p. 89.
36. If the myth is not recorded in Navaho, there is no way of determining the full use of sound, since the sound words are only roughly translated, if at all, and the sound syllables are not reproduced.
37. Haile 1938b, pp. 169, 170, 215, 272; Reichard 1928, p. 132.
38. Hill 1936, pp. 16–7; cp. Haile 1938, p. 169.
39. Haile 1938b, pp. 234–7.
40. Sapir-Hoijer, p. 285.
41. Haile 1938b, pp. 163–75.
42. Ib., p. 110; cp. pp. 118–21.
43. Reichard 1944d, p. 75; Endurance Chant ms.; Matthews 1902, p. 205.
44. Matthews 1902, p. 117.
45. Kluckhohn-Wyman, p. 127.
46. Reichard, Shooting Chant ms.
47. Haile 1938b, p. 95.
48. Ib., p. 93.
49. Ib., p. 126.
50. Reichard, Big Star Chant ms.
51. Matthews 1897, pp. 93, 227–8, 84n.
52. Haile 1938b, p. 125.
53. Stephen 1930, p. 90.
54. Ib., p. 94.
55. Haile 1938b, p. 250, 3n.
56. Matthews 1897, p. 205; Reichard, Shooting Chant ms.
57. Matthews 1897, p. 185.
58. Reichard, Shooting Chant ms.
59. Reichard 1944d, pp. 19, 81–3; Matthews 1897, p. 183; 1902, pp. 189, 218, 309, 11n; Newcomb 1940b, p. 72.
60. Haile 1938b, p. 85.
61. Newcomb-Reichard, p. 26.
62. Goddard, p. 168.
63. Matthews 1897, p. 233, 119n.
64. Reichard 1939, pp. 30, 34.
65. Matthews 1897, p. 412; Newcomb 1940b, p. 51.

66. Reichard, Endurance Chant ms.
67. Reichard 1939, p. 33; 1944d, pp. 60, 91; Matthews 1887, p. 413; Haile 1943a, pp. 49, 229.

CHAPTER 16

(WORD, FORMULA, AND MYTH)

1. Reichard 1944b, p. 9; 1944d, p. 135; Goddard, pp. 9, 26, 133–4; Wheelwright 1942, Set II, 6.
2. Reichard 1944b, p. 134, line 12.
3. Haile 1938b, p. 238 excerpt; cp. Opler-Hoijer.
4. Hill 1936, p. 12.
5. Haile 1938b, pp. 153–4, 254, 84n excerpt.
6. Ib., p. 239.
7. Hill 1938, p. 74.
8. Hill 1936, p. 12 excerpt.
9. Ib., p. 13.
10. Reichard 1944d, p. 95.
11. Haile 1938b, p. 99; Matthews 1897, p. 110; Newcomb-Reichard, p. 27.
12. Reichard 1939, p. 27.
13. Matthews 1897, pp. 184, 187.
14. Matthews 1887, pp. 404–5.
15. Reichard, Shooting Chant ms.
16. Haile 1938b, p. 256.
17. Reichard, Shooting Chant ms.
18. My translation of this name, as well as of those above, differs from Father Berard's. Mine is based on the analysis of my chant teachers; it fits the grammatical analysis and the context, and was checked by several interpreters I worked with.
19. Reichard 1944d, pp. 87, 101, 135; Haile 1938b, p. 288.
20. Sapir-Hoijer, pp. 257, 523, 225n, order uncertain.
21. Haile 1943a, p. 230; cp. p. 228.
22. Oakes-Campbell, p. 41; Pl. XIII. I have co-ordinated the names with my terminology as nearly as the printed forms allow.
23. Haile 1938b, pp. 288–91.
24. Ib., pp. 78–81.

25. Matthews 1897, p. 144.
26. Ib., p. 86.
27. Ib., pp. 96–7; Reichard, Endurance Chant ms.
28. Haile 1938b, p. 158, line 10; Matthews 1902, pp. 162, 250–5, 311, 28n, 315, 69n.
29. Reichard 1944b.

CHAPTER 17

(SONG)

1. Kluckhohn-Spencer, pp. 50–1.
2. No tones are indicated on the words of the songs, since they are musically, not linguistically, determined.
3. Reichard 1948.
4. Haile 1938b, pp. 258ff.
5. Haile 1943a, p. 293, 69n excerpt.
6. Reichard 1944b, pp. 11–2.
7. Matthews 1894a, p. 185.
8. Newcomb-Reichard, p. 32; Matthews 1897, pp. 148, 171; 1902, pp. 206, 211; Newcomb 1940b, pp. 52–3.
9. Reichard, Shooting Chant ms.
10. Matthews 1887, p. 393.
11. Matthews 1897, p. 181.
12. Matthews 1902, pp. 244–5 excerpt.
13. Newcomb-Reichard, p. 26.
14. Matthews 1889.
15. Haile 1938b, pp. 130–1.
16. Goddard, pp. 90–1, 163; Newcomb-Reichard, p. 38.
17. Reichard, Shooting Chant ms.
18. Goddard, pp. 34, 137.
19. Ib., p. 175.
20. Hill 1938, p. 61 excerpt.
21. Ib., p. 52.
22. Reichard, Big Star Chant ms.
23. Haile 1938b, p. 259, translation mine.
24. Ib., p. 261, translation mine.
25. Ib., p. 272, brackets mine.
26. Reichard, Endurance Chant ms.
27. Hill 1938, pp. 61ff. excerpt.

28. Matthews 1907, pp. 26ff.
29. Reichard, Endurance Chant ms.
30. Haile 1938b, p. 291.
31. Ib., pp. 30–1.

CHAPTER 18

(*PRAYERSTICKS*)

1. Reichard 1928, p. 119; Haile 1938b, pp. 59–60.
2. Matthews 1902, pp. 36ff.; Kluckhohn-Wyman, pp. 88ff.
3. Matthews 1902, p. 39.
4. Reichard 1944d, pp. 58–9; cp. pp. 18–9, 43, 52–3, 65, 73; Wheelwright 1946, pp. 154–60.
5. Haile 1938b, pp. 204–5.
6. Cp. Kluckhohn-Wyman, p. 30, 50n.
7. Reichard, Shooting Chant ms.
8. Haile 1943a, pp. 39, 272, 319, 300n.
9. Kluckhohn-Wyman, pp. 69, 89.
10. Ib.
11. Matthews 1887, p. 452; 1902, p. 313, 50n; Kluckhohn-Wyman, p. 27.
12. Wheelwright 1942, pp. 41–2, 45.
13. Ib., pp. 49, 67–8, 69.
14. Reichard, Shooting Chant ms.; Haile 1938b, p. 215.
15. Ib., p. 83.
16. Reichard, Shooting Chant ms.
17. Ib.
18. Ib.
19. Matthews 1902, pp. 199, 313, 50n.
20. Reichard 1939, pp. 57–8; Shooting Chant ms.
21. Shooting Chant ms.

CHAPTER 19

(*CLASSIFICATION OF CEREMONIES*)

1. Wyman-Kluckhohn; Haile 1938a; 1938b, pp. 9–27.
2. There is one qualification to this statement. The material

from Ramah and Chaco differs considerably from mine, whereas the rest from Mariana Lake through the reservation, even including some from a Tuba City informant, corresponds in detail and, for the most part, in mythological interpretation, the differences being unexplained rather than conflicting.

3. Wyman-Kluckhohn, pp. 30–1, 107n.
4. Haile 1938b, p. 10; 1943a, p. 3.
5. Haile 1938b, p. 15; Stephen 1930.
6. The chant recorded by Kluckhohn (Kluckhohn-Wyman, pp. 155–8) is said to be of Jicarilla Apache derivation. The rites are so similar to those of the Male Shooting Chant in my area as to be non-differentiating, and since there is no myth, there is no interpretation. The fragment of myth given as that of the Female Shooting Chant Evil is quite similar to the main episode of the Male Shooting Chant Evil myth as I recorded it. There is, consequently, no distinction between female and evil. From the account I cannot determine the distinctive symbols upon which my classification has been based.
7. Cp. Wyman-Kluckhohn, p. 24.
8. Father Berard translates the word for this 'angry way' (Haile 1938a). I cannot analyze this on any basis. My own form means 'the phase that involves reddening inside,' an interpretation that corresponds with linguistic and ritualistic forms.
9. Newcomb-Reichard, Pl. XVI, XVII, XX, XXIII, XXV-XXVIII.
10. Wheelwright 1942, pp. 165–6.
11. Cp. Kluckhohn-Leighton, pp. 176-81.
12. Huckel ms.
13. Reichard 1944a.
14. Huckel ms.
15. Reichard 1944c.
16. Wyman-Bailey 1945.
17. Wyman-Bailey 1943a.
18. A cursory reading of a long unpublished myth in Mary Wheelwright's possession seems to corroborate the second alternative.
19. Matthews 1902; personal information from Franc J. Newcomb.
20. Haile 1938b, p. 15.
21. Haile 1943a, p. 34 excerpt.

22. Sapir-Hoijer, p. 257.
23. tá·' aħtso bílátah dasilâ· do· xǫ́jǫ́·djída. There is no way of accounting for the suffix -da in Sapir's translation. It belongs with the negative frame do· . . . -da(h), instead of being taken with dasilá and interpreted as an abbreviation of do·le·ł, 'it will be.' do·, abbreviated from do·le·ł, is common, but I have never found it with the suffix -da. It cannot be -dó· or -dó', 'also,' since Sapir never makes this kind of error in recording, and these suffixes are used only if there is a series of coordinate words.
24. Cp. Ch. 16; Sapir-Hoijer, p. 523, 224n.
25. Oakes-Campbell, p. 56.
26. Haile 1943a, pp. 7, 272.
27. Huckel ms.
28. Haile 1943a, pp. 6, 290, 25n, 292, 44n, 45n, 59n, 294, 90n, 91n, 297, 128n, 306, 37n, 38n, 307, 55n, 56n.
29. Ib., pp. 4, 6, 290, 26n, 307, 56n.
30. Ib., p. 9.
31. Ib., pp. 9, 280.
32. Reichard, Shooting Chant ms.; Wheelwright 1946, p. 5.
33. Hill 1938, pp. 101ff.
34. Reichard 1944d, p. 90; Wheelwright 1946, p. 154, 2A, B; cp. Kluckhohn-Wyman, p. 115, Pl. III, Fig. 5, 6.
35. Haile 1938b, pp. 41, 59-61; 1943a, pp. 22-3.

CHAPTER 20

(*ORGANIZATION OF RITUAL*)

1. Kluckhohn-Wyman, pp. 22-48, 115-6, 159-60.
2. Ib.
3. Ib., pp. 81, 94, 195.
4. Haile 1943a, p. 20.
5. Reichard 1939, pp. 42–4, Fig. 1; Newcomb-Reichard, p. 59, Pl. XIX.
6. Matthew 1902, p. 155.
7. Kluckhohn-Wyman, p. 82.
8. Matthews 1902; Kluckhohn-Wyman.

CONCORDANCES

CONCORDANCE A

CONCORDANCE A is an introductory attempt to characterize the supernatural beings of the animistic Navaho
pantheon, particularly those dealt with in the ceremonies
analyzed in this book; it does not pretend to be complete.
Following most of the names is an abbreviation—a capital
letter or letters—indicating the emphasis placed on the being
in the ritualistic material according to the divisions of the
pantheon as outlined in Chapters 4 and 5. Since few, if any,
of these beings are always in the same category, the letters
indicate merely a tentative preponderance. Comparison with
other chants would doubtless indicate greater homogeneity in
some respects, greater heterogeneity in others. The following
abbreviations are used:

B	Beings somewhere between good and evil
D	Dangers conceived as deities
H	Helpers of deity and man
I	Intermediaries between man and deity
P	Persuadable deities
U	Undependable deities, persuadable only with difficulty
UP	Unpersuadable deities

As the discussion suggests, the animistic nature of the
religion makes it difficult to determine what to enter and
what to omit in a treatment of this kind. For instance, it was
a knotty problem to decide whether Mountains and Worlds
are supernaturals or ideas. Since places are so markedly
ritualistic, they should be included. Worlds are places that
influence the ritual; they have not been found to be personi-

fied and I have placed them in Concordance B. On the other hand, Mountains, since they have 'inner forms,' may be a concept that in some respects parallels our idea of a soul; a person ritualistically fortified has an inner form which gives him invincibility, and Mountains sometimes have other personal qualities. I have, therefore, listed them in Concordance A with Supernatural Beings; they might easily be classified elsewhere.

According-to-beauty (bike xójó·n) (P), see Ch. 3.

Agate Man (H), see *Pollen ball*, Con. B.

'ałké· na·'a·ci· (P), see *First Man, One-follows-the-other*.

Arrowsnake, Racer (tłi·cka·") (U) is said to be a slender snake, six feet long, red and blue on the belly, striped on the back, that moves so fast that when it comes to the edge of a cliff, it flies through space before reaching the ground. The belief that it can actually soar explains why two snakes were able to lift Scavenger after even the Eagles had failed. Sometimes it moves like a measuring worm. Matthews had it identified as *Bascanium flagelliforme* (Reichard 1939, p. 29, Pl. II; Matthews 1897, pp. 200, 250).

Badger (na'actcidi·) (H), not very exactly delineated, is represented as possessing unusually strong power. Since he sprang from the contact of Earth and Sky when the people were in the fourth world, he is a child of Sky. He went back into the hole at the Place-of-emergence.

Badger went among the women when they were separated from the men and made them mad with sexual desire.

Badger is a ' friend ' of Wolf, Mountain Lion, Wildcat, and Bobcat (JS).

Badger's eardrum enables seers to divine by listening (Ch. 6, "Diagnosis"; Matthews 1897, pp. 71, 75–6; Stephen 1930, p. 99; Reichard 1939, p. 16, Pl. VI, VII).

Bat (djabaní, dja"abaní, dja"abań) (H) was a personage in the lower world. JS says he was affiliated with the insects "as a helper; he is the same as Big Fly."

Bat has several functions, usually helpful, besides that of mentor or guardian. In the sandpaintings he (or she) is one of the eastern guardians. A yellow diamond on the body represents a small yellow skin Bat received as a reward for helping the winning side when Gambler was overcome.

Bat Woman rescued Monster Slayer from the ledge where he slew the Cliff Monsters. She appeared with her burden basket fastened with a tumpline only as thick as a grocer's string. After persuading Monster Slayer that it would hold, she carried him down the side of the cliff. He rewarded her with token feathers of the Monster Bird, which eventually turned into all kinds of birds.

Bat helped the Spiders and Swallows to catch Coyote after he got away from the Brothers. As a reward they were given pieces of his skin, which they placed on their backs.

Bat was an important helper of the Hail Chant, in which she served in various capacities. As mentor she rescued Rainboy from the wrath of his family and the villagers who were going to beat him to death.

Bat may have the same relation to Darkness, the pair symbolized for Night, as Wind and Big Fly have to Day. This seems likely, since Big Fly is a feather made to vibrate by Wind, and Bat has a wing hook or a ' vagina wing ' by means of which she clings to rocks and makes an ' embarrassing ' noise.

When the Stricken Twins were going to their father, Bat called to them, but Little Wind told them not to listen. They followed the directions of Little Wind and arrived at a place where Talking God met them and accepted them as his children (Reichard 1939, Pl. IX; Shooting Chant ms.; Endurance Chant ms.; 1944d, p. 3; Newcomb-Reichard, pp. 64–5, Fig. 5, 8; Goddard, p. 143; Haile 1938b, pp. 119, 121; Matthews 1897, p. 121; 1902, p. 242).

Bear (cac) (U) and Big-snake-man are a pair often found together, belief about them being very mixed. In all versions of the visit of The Twins to Sun, Bear, Big Snake, Thunder, and Wind were the guardians of Sun's house; they are stereotyped for houses of other supernaturals as well. Bear and Big Snake, doubtless sent by Sun, were guardians of Changing Woman's first sordid home on the earth. In sandpaintings they seem to be animals, yet at Changing Woman's home act like persons, feeding the children sacred food. The bear and snake were also pets given the people by Changing Woman for protection on their travels (Reichard, Shooting Chant ms.; Goddard, pp. 168, 171, 175–8; Matthews 1897, pp. 149, 151, 153, 155).

The Navaho have what amounts almost to a phobia about bears, so that, despite the mythological references as elements of good, they are to be reckoned with primarily as evils.

Bear is a major power of the Mountain Chant, which includes much bear lore because bears live in the mountains. Many chants have a shock or trance rite. The bear is a being that may bring on the shock and, in the Shooting Chant, the patient is restored on a painting that includes bear tracks and Big Snake. An impersonator of Bear may be the restoring force (Haile 1938b, pp. 157, 175; Reichard 1939, p. 66, Pl. XXI; cp. Haile 1943a, p. 15).

When Secondborn was lost, Bear, who was familiar with all places in the mountains, was chosen to search for him.

After doing much good by protecting people from their enemies, Bear started to cause coughs, fever, and bad luck. The leader of the Navaho performed a ceremony over him and Bear allied himself with evil. He, with his relatives, was assigned to walk at Black Mountain, where there have since been many bears (Reichard, Shooting Chant ms.; Goddard, p. 178).

The details given above seem to refer largely to bears and snakes as a class. They may be personified, however, and Bear Man and Big-snake-man form a pair that appears now and then.

When Monster Slayer was conducting his war party against Taos, two very old men, trembling with weakness and choking with coughing, came into the party's camp. The leader urged them to leave because they represented ' nothing useful,' but they kept coming back. On the last night they said they did not intend to participate in the fight but would like to watch it. After the raid was over, the warriors looked for the scalps of the most desirable victims but could not find them. Upon the second examination, they were found in the ragged bundles of the two old men. Later Monster Slayer, the rest of the warriors, and the old men had an archery contest with the captives, two Taos maidens, as stakes. The old men took their places, trembling and uncertain, but at each try they scored a bull's-eye. Monster Slayer merely looked at them, and did not give them the girls. The two old men turned out to be Bear Man and Big-snake-man.

When the warriors and other people were occupied with ceremony, the two nieces of Corn Man, on whose behalf the raid had been conducted, wound in and out among the dancers, circling around them. When the girls had finished their dance, they moved away from the crowd and went to the water. As they were going back to the dance they were attracted by an arresting sound, a sweet smell, and a light. On a little ridge not far from the dance place they found a campfire in a brush shelter. There lay two handsome men, back to back. Bear was dressed in velvet with pile as thick as plush, Big-snake-man in an embroidered fabric. The girls slept with the strangers, who gave them ceremonial properties as payment. Bear Man gave his girl a life feather; Big Snake's gift was the pulp of the iris.

When the girls woke in the morning, the men were still asleep. The first snored with his mouth wide open. His projecting teeth were old and overlapping, and phlegm was strung like spider webs in his mouth. The man on the other side was also disgusting. His nose was drawn back and mucus bubbled from the corners of his mouth. Both men had reached extreme old age. As the girls ran off, Bear growled and Big Snake rattled.

At sunrise the people stopped dancing and bethought themselves of the girls, whom at first they could not find. Then the leader (presumably Monster Slayer) told the men to cut willow twigs and whip the girls to death. The two old men watched from the top of the hill. When the scourge hit the first girl, it gave out a futile sound as if mush were being slapped (tcog) and, when the second girl was hit, there was a sound like mud slopping (tłic). The victims were standing on the life feather and iris pulp the old men had given them, and the blows were lost in clouds and water. The girls disappeared into the sky, whither they were tracked by Bear and Big Snake. The Mountain Chant originated in the trail taken by Bear, the Beauty Chant in the trail taken by Big-snake-man (Haile 1938b, pp. 157, 175).

Beaver (tca·') (H) is depicted as a well-meaning helper.

Beaver Man and Otter Woman gave their skins to The Twins when Sun tested them by freezing.

Beaver came to Rainboy for some tobacco, then asked, "Why did I come here? What do you need?" After discussion she found out that the gods had not given him the formula for the Hail Chant incense, a part of which was a bit of flesh from Beaver's leg. Incense is feared by Winter Thunder (Reichard, Shooting Chant ms.; 1944d, p. 139).

be'γotcidí, '*One-who-grabs-breasts*,' (P), is a creature of versatile and conflicting characteristics. He is described as the son of Sun, who had ' intercourse with everything in the world.' That is the reason so many monsters were born. According to another version, Sun was put away off so the monsters could not be conceived again, but as the sun rose it touched a flower, which became pregnant and gave birth to be'γotcidí. He was Sun's youngest son, spoiled by his father, who put him in control of many things, such as game and domesticated animals. He was a transvestite and the first pottery maker.

He could move without being seen, and change into different forms at will—into rainbow, wind, sand, water, or anything else. He got his name because he would make himself invisible, then sneak up on young girls to touch their breasts as he shouted "be'go be'go." He also annoyed men who were hunting—just as a hunter was ready to shoot, he would sneak up, grab the man's testicles, and shout. He would behave similarly when a man and woman were engaged in intercourse.

The description agrees with tłă·h's when he said that the details of be'γotcidí's appearance were too 'dirty' to tell the interpreter, his niece, and me. He described be'γotcidí as a blond or red-haired god with blue eyes, dressed like a woman. He was in charge of insects, called them at will, and even sometimes appeared as a worm or insect.

When the Holy Ones, after great difficulty, had prevailed upon Dark Thunder to agree to the restoration of Rainboy and the two war parties had carefully prepared themselves, all the gods who were invited came except be'γotcidí. They started off, each party on a rainbow controlled by Talking God and xa·ctčé·'óγan, and moved toward each other. As Dark Thunder's party passed a placed called Strung-out-under-rocks, they saw a boy lying in the dust. He got up and mockingly threw dust upon the gods. Stopping, they wondered who it was. Then they moved on and looked back and the same thing was repeated. Talking God told them to look ahead and they saw an insect with a yellow head lying on the ground. Talking God said, "Here, fellows, is a worm," whereupon they all gathered round to inspect it. (tłắ·h here omitted the part too vulgar to tell us.)

"Pick it up! Kill it! Don't let it make fun of us!" the gods said. Just as they were about to pick it up, it turned into a man and ran off to the east. The party surrounded him and trapped him at the east, south, west, and north. When they caught him, hornets swarmed from his mouth, June bugs from his ears, and black mud beetles from his nose. Hornets flew into the hair of the gods, whom the insects bit unmercifully. They begged Talking God to do something. Then be'γotcidí drew all the pests back into his mouth and rolled about, laughing as had the decoy boy. He told them what prayersticks, prayers, and songs he wanted. The gods agreed to furnish these, and he said, "When Earth People have sores around the mouth, in the ears, nose, and on the body, I shall be the one to blame."

Then be'γotcidí joined them, but he kept stopping them with his capers; he jumped up and down or lay down in their path. Successively he changed himself into a grasshopper, γósitsiní, γócigici·, tćoc ditłohí, and a cornbeetle. As soon as they would stop he would get up and accompany them as a ' man. '

Matthews recounts several episodes in which be'γotcidí appears:

The defeated Gambler, when shot to the sky by the victor (a son of Sun), came to the home of be'γotcidí, the god who carried the moon. He was very old and dwelt in a long row of stone houses. He took pity on Gambler and made domestic animals for him—sheep, asses, horses, swine, goats, and fowl. He gave him bayeta and other valuable fabrics. He made a new people, the Mexicans, for Gambler to rule over and sent him back to earth to rule far away from his old home, that is, in Mexico. His people were builders and increased in population. They built towns along the Rio Grande somewhat north of Santa Fe, their northernmost limit. When they ceased building, Gambler returned to Mexico and became the god of the Mexicans.

One time be'γotcidí and Sun created the animals: be'γotcidí made antelope, mountain sheep, cow, elk, donkey, jack rabbit, cottontail, prairie dog, woodrat, and many others; Sun created horse, sheep, goat, deer, and mule. Matthews mentions ' identical details ' corresponding with Hill's.

When a Navaho wants a fine horse, he may sing a set of songs to be'γotcidí and describe the kind of horse he wants; he then expects to get it. Stephen notes that The Twins went to ' their father,' be'γotcidí, who gave them horses, identifying him with Sun, an interpretation the description of blondness makes reasonable—he lived high overhead and created the sky with the stars, the earth, and some of its people.

tłǎ·h told me that be'γotcidí had created everything, that he had another name, One-who-made-everything.

In the Wheelwright version of tłǎ·h's creation myth, be'γotcidí is all but identified with the Christian God, an interpretation hardly justified by the above.

The following is abstracted from Wheelwright:

be'γotcidí, whose mother was Sunray and whose father was Sunbeam, was in charge of creation in the lower worlds, in the first of which he created antlike insects, in the second, wasplike insects, as well as a great many other things. In the third world he decreed the separation of the sexes, the final dominance of the men, the punishment of burning in the lower world for ' badness.' First Man ascended to heaven and told the people he would be back in two days. Upon his return he reported on heaven and decreed eternal punishment in hell or happiness in heaven for the people. He created a son, who was short, white-skinned, and had black eyes and black hair. Eventually the god and his son went back to heaven to stay.

According to one of Hill's informants, be'γotcidí made the game animals, but their control was in the hands of Talking God and Black God; according to another informant, be'γotcidí was said to have been more important than the two in control; he was the god of game who taught men the game songs; be'γotcidí taught the stalking ceremony.

Matthews suggests that Moon is identified with be'γotcidí. There is an association between First Man, Sun, be'γotcidí, and possibly Moon (Ch. 5; Matthews 1897, pp. 86–7, 226; 1902, p. 31; 1907, pp. 58–60; Stephen ms.; Reichard 1944a, pp. 16–25; 1944d, p. 47; Wheelwright 1942, pp. 39–41, 47–9, 69; Hill 1938, pp. 99, 123; cp. Wyman 1947).

Big Centipede (UP) is mentioned by Matthews in his subsidiary list of monsters that arose from the blood lost at the birth of the first monsters. Wheelwright describes the creatures as having the form of huge centipedes which, by humping themselves up in the middle, could leap a great distance to bite their victims. The name she gives seems to refer to the praying mantis. The largest could not penetrate the flint armor of Monster Slayer, who killed it and all the smaller ones except two which he bade never to harm anyone. He took the scalp of the largest for a trophy (Matthews 1897, p. 224, n. 71; Wheelwright 1942, p. 95).

Big Fly (dǫ'tsoh) (H), although apparently mythological, has a biological existence. A Tachnid fly of the species *Hystricia pollinosa* Van der Wulp,* it has the habit of lighting on a person's shoulder or chest just in front of the shoulder. It is of major importance in ritual since its powers supersede those of any of the deities for whom it acts. Big Fly is frequently a guardian of the east side of a sandpainting and, in paintings of the Hail and Wind chants, the insect is a major figure, often repeated.

Big Fly found Holy Man when he was captured by Thunder. Big Fly instructed the people about making offerings. Big Fly directed Holy Man after he had been struck by lightning and begged him not to go into dangerous places, explaining, "From now on I will help you. I once carried news

---

*I am indebted to L. C. Wyman for the identification.

to Monster Slayer. That was when the people had no one else to carry the word. Now that they have Dark Wind and Blue Wind as informers, they have delegated me to help you." Monster Slayer insisted upon going to forbidden places to find out what was going on and Big Fly said, "All right! Go ahead, but I will go with you." There was no place he did not know, and he traveled behind Holy Man's ear so he could warn and inform him (Reichard 1939, pp. 61–3, Pl. XII, XIII, XXII; 1944d, p. 37; Shooting Chant ms.; Newcomb-Reichard, p. 39, Pl. XVI, XXI, XXII, XXXI; Haile 1938b, pp. 183–5; Matthews 1902, p. 260).

Big God (xa·ctčé''tsoh) (U), see *Bear, Big-snake-man.*

Big-gray-monster (γé'i·tsoh łbahí) (UP) was overcome by Coyote in the Endurance Chant. There is some reason to believe that a reference to ' gray gods ' or ' gray monsters ' is to evils in general, gray being the color symbol for lack of control and the color feared by evils (Ch. 12, *Gray*).

At a place called Earth-upper-mountain-ridge lived those who devoured the chiefs of the Earth People. Today you can see burnt earth appearing among the rocks where the gray gods used to roast their victims.

In the War Ceremony myth, Monster Slayer encountered Big Gray gods and slew all with his club. Their faces were striped in all colors; they looked fearsome, like yellowjackets, gray bees, bumblebees, and spider ants (Reichard, Shooting Chant ms.; Haile 1938b, p. 131; cp. Wheelwright 1942, p. 99).

Big-lonely-monster (γé'i·tsoh ła'í na·γâi) (UP), see *Big Monster.*

Big Monster (γé'i·tsoh) (UP), the prototype of all monsters, the most feared of all, came ' first ' in all myths. He was in charge of all man-destroying monsters. Sun, who fathered him, wept when requested to kill him, for he loved the monster as an oldest son, though some say Big Monster's father was a rock. He was also called Big-monster-who-travels-alone (γé'i·tsoh ła'í na·γái), and possibly Big Gray Monster is the same (Haile 1938b, pp. 55, 79, 85, 106, 110–1; Matthews 1897, pp. 115–6, 231; Reichard, Shooting Chant ms.; Endurance Chant ms.; cp. Wheelwright 1942, p. 70).

The most consistently emphasized fact about this god is his huge size. He lived at a place called Hot Springs near Mt. Taylor. When The Twins saw him, his face was striped, he had a perfect agate disk on his head, a perfect turquoise around his neck, a perfect whiteshell over his shoulder, and he was armored in flint; the precious stones were later taken by Sun as a reward for helping to overcome the monster. Big Monster had a quiver like a burden basket. He stooped four times to drink from the lake and by the time he was finished it was nearly empty. The Twins were motionless with astonishment at the sight of him, but as he took the last drink, they advanced and he saw their reflection in the water. He raised his head and taunted them as he shot at them. However, they were standing on a rainbow which they could bend and, warned by Wind, they bent it in a direction opposite to that toward which the arrows were aimed so that they escaped four times. Just as the monster was about to draw his fifth bolt, he was hit on the head by lightning, the first shot fired by Sun. The Twins then took their turn and, at the fourth shot, he fell to the ground, unable to get up. The lightning arrows shattered his armor, which later became flint deposits useful to people (Matthews 1897, pp. 115–6; cp. Haile 1938b, pp. 110–1; Wheelwright 1942, pp. 85–6).

In one version The Twins threw Big Monster's head to the east, where it became Cabezon Peak; in another, the lava from the coagulated blood is said to be a spur that runs out from Cabezon Peak.*

Coyote was Big Monster's messenger and seeker of Earth People. After Coyote's report of the existence of The Twins, Big Monster visited Changing Woman in her home. She laid her poker in the ashes when he asked her the first time where the boys were; the second time she picked it up and stirred the ashes with it; the third time she laid it by her side. The fourth time she hit him in the shins with the poker and scolded him, whereupon he bowed his head and wept, signifying that he was to be overcome. Then she chased him out.

This scene is exceedingly interesting in view of the fact that Changing Woman did not have power to look upon the trophies of the conquered monsters or listen to talk about them.

In the Endurance Chant myth, Coyote was required by Changing-bear-maiden to kill Big Monster (called Gray God in Matthews' version). Coyote pretended to have power to make the monster a fast runner, but betrayed him. Only half as tall as the tallest pine tree, he was not as formidable as the creature killed by Monster Slayer. Changing-bear-maiden, to whom Coyote brought the scalp, could not fail to recognize it because it, like all the gods at that time, had long yellow hair (Matthews 1897, pp. 91–3, 234; Haile 1938b, pp. 111, 253, 38n; Newcomb-Reichard, p. 26).

Big-prairie-hawk (ginítsoh, giṅtsoh) (H) helped to scratch through the sky from the fourth to this world (Matthews 1897, p. 75).

Big-snake-man (tⱡi·stso xasti·n) (U) lived with Big God (xa·ctčé·tsoh), who may be a god of thunder or lightning. Both are described as evil. At the smokehole of their house

---

*The Spanish often named places by translating Indian names (*cabezon*, Spanish ' head ').

were two large black rocks between which Big Fly, their guard, lived. These gods had a testy disposition and were not invited when the other gods got together.

When the gods had assembled to divide the spoils brought back by the Stricken Twins, it was specially stipulated that these two should not be invited. However, Big Fly found out about the meeting and its purpose and told his friends. At once Big Snake became angry and said, "Why was I not invited? Let us go over there. Come on!" Big God said, "No, I would do better alone. My mind is better [under control] than yours. I can speak better. I'll go alone and tell the gods what I think of them." Apparently Big Snake allowed him to attend to this affair.

When co had been brought into the gods' 'room of the masks,' a great noise of thunder was heard. It heralded the approach of Big Snake, who, because he had not been invited to the gathering, crawled along the rows of people, once around over their toes, then over their knees, across their chests, and finally, across their mouths. When he settled down in his own place he complained, "Why have you not invited me to this ceremony? This is the way you always treat me. You never let me know when you are having a good time." Monster Slayer, who was officiating, gave him a smoke and attended to other assorted unwelcome guests. When all had been ejected except a carefully selected group, Big Snake was among those remaining. Monster Slayer dealt out medicine to overcome witch power. He gave just a small pinch to each one present. They tied it carefully in little bags or in a corner of a shirt or robe. Big Snake's body was so smooth that he could find no place to stow it. He put it in his mouth and that is the reason he has venom there now.

Reared-within-the-mountain, accompanied by Wind, about to visit a place called Circle-of-red-rocks, found it guarded by two large rattlesnakes which made a rattling sound and threatened to bite, but let the travelers through without harm. Inside they found a bald-headed man, Big Snake, who had a little tuft of hair over each ear. He taught the hero how to make his prayersticks.

Big Snake features in encounters with Deer Owner, who either was Big Snake or had control over him. Deer Owner turned himself into Big Snake, which lay in a tempting ripe yucca fruit, but was overcome by the hero (*Bear, Deer Owner, Snakes;* Newcomb 1940b, p. 61; Sapir-Hoijer, p. 37; Matthews 1887, p. 405; 1897, p. 188; 1902, pp. 202, 257, 261).

Birds enter into various phases of ritual, especially in the manufacture of bundle properties and prayersticks. Many birds were helpers of the Navaho, even in their early pre-human existence. Some are sufficiently characterized to be listed with deities and helpers; many others are more or less taken for granted except as they enter incidentally into ritual. They are closely associated with game and hunting, and with snakes (Matthews 1897, pp. 81, 88, 191, 193, 195; 1902, p. 151).

A systematic study of birds should be made, but until it is, the superficial identifications at my disposal will have to do. In 1942 I took YL, who knew the Shooting Chant, to the Museum of Northern Arizona, where, through the kindness of Edwin McKee, we were able to work for a short while on the bird collections.

YL identified some of the birds most common in the ceremonies. This was an exhilarating experience, for he was from the western part of the reservation, yet he said nothing that conflicted with information I had obtained in the eastern part. However, were we able to test several chanters in this way, their identifications would probably not be in complete agreement. Wyman found differences in his identification of plants and there are local differences in all fields of Navaho teaching.

I showed a copy of Taverner's *Birds of Western Canada*

(abbreviated Tav.) to RP and tłǎ·h, who were much interested and gave a few identifications from plates which I include when they differ from those given by YL. I usually find that Indians are unable to make trustworthy identifications from pictures. However, these two chanters were so graphic-minded and attended to the least detail in sandpaintings, even in copies on paper, so carefully that their identifications may be trusted to a degree. An interesting phase of YL's classification is his calling birds of different genera 'male' and 'female' of the same Navaho category; for example, cowbird is given as the 'female' of Brewer's blackbird. Others are noted in the list.

Bird (gen.)	tsidi·
Blackbird, Brewer	tčagi· (YL says cowbird is female)
Blackbird, red-winged	tčagi·tsoh (RP Tav., Pl. XLVII)
Bluebird, mountain	dóli· (all informants Tav. p. 352)
Bluebird, western	dóli· łtcí" ('red bluebird,' Tav., p. 352)
Bullock oriole	tco·jγá·li·
Canyon wren	tséno·ltčó·ci· nłtcí"
Cedar waxwing	{ tsidi· ya·lti'í / tčíci·cáci·
Chickadee; titmouse	tčíci·be·ji·
Crane	dé·ł
Crow	gâ·gi
Duck, green-winged teal	na·l'e·li·
Eagles and hawks (gen.)	'atsá
Eagle, American	{ tą́·djiłgai (cer. ?) / saig (cer. ?)
Egret, snowy	na·l'e·li· łgai ('white duck')
Finch, common house	tsidi· łbahí ('gray bird')
Finch; green-backed goldfinch	tsidi· łtsŏi ('yellow bird') (RP Tav., p. 318)
Flicker, red-shafted	{ taya· łtci· ('red under wing') / kíya (cer. ? RP Tav., Pl. XXXVII, B)

Flycatcher, vermilion	tsiya·ci łtcí"
Gray titmouse	tćíci·be·ji· (RP ' like cedar wax-wing, only smaller ')
Grouse (extinct)	{ di, dį' { sahya· dê·ya·
Hawk, chicken, sharp-shinned, Cooper's; goshawk	tsiya·ljahí
Hawk, Krider's	'atsá łbahí (' gray hawk ')
Hawk, marsh	{ tćil xa·tagi· { (' one-that-flies- { tćil xa·ta'i· { over-plants ')
Hawk, pigeon, and young of yellow-tailed	dzílí
Hawk, prairie; prairie falcon	giní, giń
Hawk, red-tailed	'atsá łtsoi (' yellow hawk ')
Hawk, rough-legged	'atsá łgai (' white hawk ')
Hawk, western red-tailed	'atsá łtci" (' red hawk ')
Hawk, yellow-tailed	'atsá łkiji· (' spotted hawk ')
Horned lark	djádídlǫ'í, djádícdlǫ'í
Hummingbird	dahi·tįhí
Jay (gen.)	tśáńłání
Jay, Arizona long-crested	djo·gi· (Tav., Pl. XLIV, A, Stellar's jay)
Jay, pinyon	tśání, xa·c'ą'i·
Jay, blue, Woodhouse	tśání dílji·í (RP Tav., Pl. XLIII, B)
Junco, Shufeldt; sparrow	diltćóci·, diltóci·
Killdeer; Wilson's phalarope	tą́bą·xą́sdisi· (' one-that-twists-at-edge-of-water ')
Kingbird	tćiɣí·togi·, tćaɣí·togi (YL says ash-throated flycatcher is female)
Long-tailed chat	dato" no·ɣá·łi·
Magpie	'ą·"ą'i·, 'į·"ą'į·
Meadowlark	tsiya·ɣo·ji·
Mockingbird, western	za· xáłání (' one-that-speaks-lots ')
Mourning dove, western	xasbidi·
Nighthawk, western; bullbat	bi·ji·
Nutcracker, Clarke	bitsi· tcį·cgahí
Nuthatch, black-eared	tsiya· dzo·tihí
Owl, horned	né'écdja" (' ears-along-nose ')

Owl, elf; screechowl   tsidiˑ łdǫ́hí
Owl, pigmy   biníˑ doˑtłij (' blue face '), níkeˑní
Phoebe, black; northern
    violet-green swallow   táctčiciˑjiˑn (' black swallow ')
Phoebe, Say's; thrasher   dibéniˑ'í
Pigeon   xasbidiˑ łbahí (' gray dove ')
Poorwill; screechowl   toˑcdódiˑ, xoˑcdódiˑ
Purple martin; tree swallow   táctčij doˑtłij (' blue swallow ')
Quail, Gambel's   déˑłtání
Raven, black; vulture   gâˑgi nłtcin (' stinking crow ')
Roadrunner; cuckoo   naˑtsédlóziˑ, natsédlojiˑ
Robin, western   djiˑni'í, teˑl xaltcí'í
Rock wren   tsénoˑltčóciˑ łbahí
Rocky Mountain creeper   tsineˑcbíjí
Rocky Mountain nuthatch   tcį́ˑcγą́'iˑ łgai (' white-along-back-of-nose '; YL says red-breasted nuthatch is female)
Rocky Mountain sapsucker; white-rumped shrike; Lewis' woodpecker   né'éjiˑn (' black-nose ') (RP Tav., Pl. XXXVII, A)
Sparrow, desert   yaˑ xaljiˑn (' black-throat ')
Swallow, barn   tátčijiˑ łtcíˑ' (' red swallow ')
Turkey   tąjiˑ
Turkey buzzard; vulture   djeˑcóˑ'
Vireo, plumbeous   teˑl xaltcí'iˑ
White goose   tcį́ˑcłgaihí (' one-that-is-white-along-nose ')
Woodpecker, Mearns'   tsíyiłkałiˑ (YL says white-breasted woodpecker is female)

In the Flint Chant the following associations are made (Haile 1943a, p. 173):

Bird	Associated with
Crane	sky
Red bird	sun
Eagle	mountain
Big hawk	rocks
Bluebird	trees
Hummingbird	plants
Cornbeetle	ground
Heron	water

Black Body (P), see *Black God.*

Black God (xa·ctčé·cjini·) (P) is the Navaho fire god. He represents the being in control of fire and fire making rather than fire itself. He is black in impersonation and sandpainting. Black Body was his counterpart in the fourth world. When the gods came, and tried by gestures to indicate that the people were to be changed into a semblance of the gods, the creatures did not understand. On the fourth day Black Body explained in their own language the plan the gods had in mind. According to the War Ceremony legend, Black God came into being with the earth. The Wheelwright story has him in the first world as the offspring of Fire (male) and Comet (female).

Black Body of the fourth world, who apparently did not differ much, if at all, from Black God, was of great help during the emergence to this world.

As the reed containing the creatures of the fourth world and all their possessions grew, it swayed, and there was fear lest it topple into the water. Black Body blew through the hole at the top and caused a heavy dark cloud to form around the top of the reed to keep it steady. He repeated the maneuver until finally he, as top man, was able to pin it fast to the sky by means of the head feathers he wore (Matthews 1897, pp. 68–9, 75, 246; 1902, pp. 26, 29; Wheelwright 1942, p. 39, Set II, 3; Haile 1938b, p. 185).

In contrast to Sun, Monster Slayer, and Talking God, Black God is phlegmatic. He is sometimes represented as very old; he is quite modest and cannot be tempted with goods, for he uses practically nothing, but he is very exacting about the modest demands he makes. If his advanced age is not mentioned, it is agreed that he is slow-moving and, when he is summoned, considerable time is allowed for him to come from his home, which is far from those of the other gods. Stephen says that Black God lives at the east and brings evil to man; near him Big God and Big Snake live together. Black God rarely accepts invitations, and other gods do not visit him often.

When the Stricken Twins had returned from their raid on Awatobi, the gods arranged a grand assembly and were careful to send their fastest couriers to the Black Gods to tell them to hurry, for they live far away and travel slowly. They stop often to make a fire and lie down before it to rest, then advance a short distance, where they repeat the same thing.

On this occasion they did not arrive until sundown of the fourth day after they had been invited, time enough for all the other Holy Ones to have prepared themselves and to have waited. This delayed approach is symbolized by a whole day's performance in one form of the Night Chant.

The same behavior is recorded in the myth of the War Ceremony, where Black God is depicted as old and helpless. His casual habit of resting as if a war party were not excited and hurried is depicted with great literary skill, for in this case the Navaho themselves manifested the emotions white people feel about delay in a crisis, an attitude quite unusual for them (cp. Child-of-the-water). The pent-up emotions were expressed by the concern of the warriors over Black God's physical comfort; they thought he was lost, that he might freeze, that he could not see well, that he was hungry. The reason for all his delays were ritualistic, as the warriors eventually learned.

His casualness was a demonstration of fearlessness. Nowhere does Black God display spiritual weakness; his physical weakness was a blind to mislead the impulsive. When Big God appeared, everyone fled except The Twins, Talking God, and Black God. Black God alone was unafraid because he controlled fire, a power greater than lightning.

And even as he is fearless, so is he feared, for though he is slow to help, he is quick to anger. When Coyote showed the picture of the sun he had made, Black God said in anger, "gwa···," and tore it up, whereupon Coyote ran off. In certain exploits, however, the two collaborated; Black God aided Coyote in stealing Water Monster's children. Coyote kept entering the assembly of gods for co, although he was told by Monster Slayer to stay out; at length Black God was sent to expel him (Haile 1938b, pp. 184–95; Stephen ms.; Goddard, p. 136; Matthews 1897, pp. 169, 219; 1902, pp. 26–8, 201, 260–1; Reichard 1944d, p. 41; Shooting Chant Evil ms.; Newcomb-Reichard, p. 27).

Various incidents explain the fire rites. The fire drill, a treasured item of the medicine bundle, is Black God's symbol, although the explanations differ. Since he overcame an evil or enemy, its power removes evil.

When the gods began to relent about the Stricken Twins, the Hunchback gods slew a mountain sheep for them; Monster Slayer skinned and butchered it and, with his burning brand, Black God lighted a fire so they could roast it.

The fire made by Changing-bear-maiden, by means of which she sweated out the arrows which the Spider and Swallow People had shot into her, was called Black God's fire and represents his power and her restoration in the Endurance Chant; the meaning is the same for the fire made when Dwarf Boy was sung over.

As Talking God and Wind conducted co on a tour of the gods' homes, Black God laid his firebrand down when they stopped for a rest at Spotted Earth. He did not remember it until arriving at a place some distance away called Where-the-god-sits-up-high. He then asked his companions what to do about it, and Talking God advised, "We may as well leave it. We can use it in the future. Perhaps in the days to come great misfortunes, like war and pestilence, may come to men. Then you can go back to your brand, light four fires from it, one in each cardinal direction, and burn up the world." Black God's fire still exists as a burning coalbank. Thus casually the Navaho gods contemplate world cataclysm.

Black God appears in the chants quite frequently in one form or another. As the head chanter of the Night Chant According-to-collected-waters, his services are of major importance and a large offering is made to him because the largest share of booty taken from Awatobi by the Stricken Twins was given him. He holds a prominent position in the War Ceremony, where his prayerstick is described in detail; he is the leader of the elaborate rites of ' killing the ghost,' 'the blackening,' and the painting of Child-of-the-water and his impersonator. Goddard refers to Black God as originating the body paint of The Twins in Sun's house, a description that agrees with the one given in the War Ceremony, where he is also in charge of the pot drum (Matthews 1902, pp. 27, 209, 242, 260; Reichard, Endurance Chant ms.; Haile 1938b, pp. 185–95, 215, 237; Goddard, p. 156).

In the first world Black God worked with First Man against the four owners of the world, beginning by angrily throwing his fire about, but without much effect. When, however, First Man suggested trying ritual instead of force, he accepted an offering of a tobacco pouch and things improved.

In the second world Black God opposed be'γotcidí, who made some twins over into 'ałké'' na'a·ci·. He closed up the hole from the second world by blowing. In the fourth world Coyote stole fire from Black God. Black God provided the stars, sun, moon, and all the light for the fourth world. He claimed that the Seven Stars were at his feet, knees, hips, back, shoulders, and on his face. Those on his face show in the sandpainting.

Although Black God is depicted as a bachelor, his son is mentioned as a helper in the Night Chant.

Black God, although mentioned less frequently than gods such as xa˙ctčé˙'óγan, stands out clearly as an individualist, fearless and feared, one whose chief duty is to control fire, one who has important ceremonial duties.

Black God is associated with Gila Monster by behavior, offering, and even by the way he accepts his offering (Stephen 1930, pp. 91–3; Wheelwright 1942, pp. 41–3, 54–6, 62, Set II, 3; Matthews 1902, p. 196; Haile 1943a, pp. 66, 172).

Bluebird (dóli˙) (H), a symbol of peace and happiness, is generally beloved by the Navaho, being herald of the dawn and a manifestation of Talking God, who told co, hero of the Night Chant, he would appear among the Navaho as bluebird. His feathers are a requisite of many ceremonial properties (*Prayersticks*, Con. C; Matthews 1902, p. 205).

Blue-horizon-light (naxode˙ctłi˙j) (H) refers to the earth's shadow, which, the Navaho say, is the rise of darkness from the east, a red or rose-colored line that appears just before sunset and gradually rises until it disappears in darkness before it reaches the zenith. It is a manifestation of nature and, in my material, is hardly a deity. However, since it is listed in formula, prayer, and song with the gods and as a member of the Day-Sky group, and since Dawn and Darkness People are defined, it is almost certainly personified.

Bony Bear (cac di˙tṡiní) (UP) seems to be distinct from Tracking Bear and not merely a place name for what was left of the latter. It was a mountain in the form of a reclining bear with yawning jaws which devoured anyone who come near; Wind blew people into its mouth. When Monster Slayer felt Wind dragging him toward it, he forced his flint club between its jaws. An echo was heard, indicating that Bony Bear had been conquered (Haile 1938b, p. 127).

Buffalo ('ayání) (U) are interesting for historical as well as ritualistic reasons. Featured in myth, they are strange and therefore supernatural.

The episode of Holy Man overcoming the Buffalo in the Shooting Chant, though a subsidiary theme, is highly developed. The sandpaintings that recapitulate the encounters with Buffalo are among the most elaborate, and emphasis on such experiences is one of the main points of relationship between the Shooting and Flint chants.

Buffalo-who-never-dies is the chief and four others are named; one male is called Abalone Woman. Buffalo homes, described in myth and depicted in sandpainting, are tepees. Buffalo behave much like Plains Indians. They are said to know how to shoot their arrows along the blood vessels, making exceptionally bloody wounds (*Names*, Con. B; Reichard 1939, pp.68ff., Fig. 9, Pl. XXIII, XXIV; Newcomb-Reichard, Pl. XXIII–XXVIII; Haile 1943a, pp. 81, 187, 208).

Burrowing Monster, Horned Monster (déˑlɣéˑd) (UP) originated as offspring of a daughter of an early chief who abused herself with a fuzzy elk antler. He was thrown into a gully and raised by the winds. Although the round misshapen monster lacked a head, he had four destructive horns with which he dug up the earth. In one version he is described as an enormous gopher. He watched all directions and was such a fast runner that no one could escape him.

Monster Slayer killed him with the aid of Gopher, who was rewarded with bits of the monster's hide. Other rodents were similarly rewarded; their skins were transformed into those

404

they have today, and they in turn contributed properties for future ceremonial aid.

Monster Slayer took the heart for a trophy of the Male Shooting Chant, the horns for the War Ceremony. In both, the paunch full of blood became helpful in conquering Cliff Monster.

In the Wheelwright version, Burrowing Monster was guarded by twelve fierce antelope, which had to be overcome before Monster Slayer could get at the monster itself. The antelope were decoyed by burning torches and finally reduced to a state useful to mankind. The rodents helped just as in the other versions. The trophies taken by the hero were the scalp, neck and leg sinews, horns, and paunch filled with blood. Gopher is said to be a small imitation of Burrowing Monster (Haile 1938b, pp. 77, 113, 116–8; Matthews 1897, pp. 80, 117–8; Reichard, Shooting Chant ms.; Wheelwright 1942, pp. 70, 80, 89).

Bushrat (H), see *Rat*.

Butterfly (ka·lógi·) (U) and various moths are symbols of temptation and foolishness, so despicable that their behavior, ' acting like a moth,' has come to stand for insanity, the punishment for breaking taboos.

The hero of the Mountain Chant acquired the power of the meal sprinklers from the Butterfly People.

Butterfly was a decoy for two girls of the Excess Chant (cp. Ch. 1; *Restriction*, Con. B; Matthews 1887, p. 406; Kluckhohn 1944, p. 104).

Cactus (xoc) (P) is closely related to Wind and Cloud, as indicated by many details, especially the sandpaintings of the Wind Chant, though its character is not clear.

Cactus, mentioned rarely in the Shooting and Hail chants, is only an incidental symbol. When Monster Slayer was injured by the White Weasel People, he was helped by a quartet of Holy People who had transformed themselves into Spiny Cacti.

In the Flint Chant, cactus is associated with flint (Kluck-hohn-Wyman, Fig. 16, 17; many paintings in the Bush Collection; Reichard, Shooting Chant ms.; Haile 1943a, p. 167).

Center-of-the-earth, see *Sky Pillars.*

Changing Grandchild (tsói nádle·hé) (P), counterpart of Child-of-the-water, calmed angry gods.

When at an assembly of the gods the dancers who made the corn grow by magic in the Night Chant took their places to sing, not a sound issued from their throats. Coyote, driven out at the beginning of the ceremony by the gods, had deprived them of their voices. Monster Slayer sent Talking God out to reason quietly with Coyote. When Coyote refused three times to come in, Monster Slayer became angry: "Bring him in if you have to use force. When we did not want him in the hogan, he came; now we want him in the Dark-circle-of-branches, he won't come!"

Changing Grandchild spoke up: "It is no use to be angry with him; angry words and shouting will not influence him. Offer him some gift and perhaps he will come in and help you."

Monster Slayer replied, "You are right. We will do as you say. Let us make him the god of darkness, daylight, male rain, corn and all vegetation, of thunder, and of rainbow." As soon as Coyote heard about the gifts, he consented to enter and restore the dancers' voices (cp. Ch. 1, 16; *Child-of-the-water, Monster Slayer, Reared-in-the-earth, The Twins;* Matthews 1902, p. 203).

Changing Woman ('asdzá· nádle·hé) (P) is the most fascinating of many appealing characters conjured up by the Navaho imagination. Sun is attractive, his character obvious and clear. Changing Woman is Woman with a sphinxlike quality. No matter how much we know about her the total is a great question mark. She is the mystery of reproduction, of life springing from nothing, of the last hope of the world, a riddle perpetually solved and perennially springing up anew, literally expressed in Navaho: ". . . here the one who is named Changing Woman, the one who is named Whiteshell Woman, here her name is pretty close to the [real] names of every one of the girls."

Although Sun and Moon are represented graphically by the figures of their type symbols, Changing Woman is perhaps only verbally described, unless the delineation of the Earth in sandpainting represents her. Her own words seem to be evidence that Changing Woman and Earth are one, and her rejuvenation suggests it: "There will be people, so I cannot remain here and have myself tramped upon." Sun's decree concerning Whiteshell Woman, another name for Changing Woman, also contributes to my opinion: "Whiteshell Woman will go where I live. . . . She will attend to her children and provide their food. Everywhere I go over the earth she will have charge of female rain. I myself will control male rain. She will be in control of vegetation everywhere for the benefit of Earth People."

Mirage Talking God and xa·ctćé''óγan decorated her with all kinds of herbage and flowers wherever they grew.

In sandpainting Earth is set off against Sky, the two making a pair, whereas Changing Woman is really a contrast to Sun. In myth Earth and Sky are primordial, having given rise to Coyote and Badger.

The identification of Changing Woman with Whiteshell Woman is frequently indicated and sometimes they seem to be the same as Turquoise Woman. On the other hand, stories such as that of the Eagle Chant are completely against such an interpretation, for the two ' jewel women ' are the wives of Monster Slayer, a marriage the Navaho would hardly sanction, since the morals of Changing Woman are beyond criticism; nowhere is she remotely connected with incest. The stories of Earth and Sky, of Changing Woman's transformation from corn or whiteshell, and of her supernatural origin as a baby on the sacred mountain tċôʼlʼíʼį must be considered separately and as unrelated until more material shows a connection between them. I therefore describe Whiteshell Woman and Turquoise Woman as individuals, as well as counterparts of Changing Woman (Sapir-Hoijer, p. 295; Reichard, Shooting Chant ms.; Goddard, pp. 156–7; Newcomb-Reichard, Fig. 5, p. 37; Matthews 1897, p. 71; Haile 1943a, p. 16; Newcomb 1940b, pp. 50–77; cp. Kluckhohn-Leighton, p. 150).

One story represents Changing Woman as the first and ideal baby, found under supernatural conditions.

First Man reported to his wife that for four days a dark rain cloud had hovered over tċôʼlʼíʼį, the central sacred mountain; finally, the mountain was covered with rain, an indication that supernatural events were taking place. With song he approached the place and he heard a baby cry. He discovered the baby in a cradle consisting of sky messengers—two short rainbows lay longitudinally under the baby; crosswise at its chest and feet were red sunrays. A curved rainbow arched over the face. Wrapped in a dark cloud, the infant was covered with dark, blue, yellow, and white clouds, held in by side lacings of zigzag lightning with a sunbeam laced through them.

First Man did not know what to do with the baby and took it home to First Woman who, with the aid of Mirage Talking God, reared it.

The eyes of the newly found babe were black as charcoal and there was no blemish (impurity) anywhere on its body. First Man and Talking God agreed that it should be fed on collected pollen moistened with game broth and the dew of beautiful flowers. According to Matthews, Salt Woman said she wanted the child and, presumably, it was given to her. It is thought that since there was no one to nurse it, Sun fed it on pollen. Nourished on such supernatural fare, it grew remarkably fast, developing with miraculous speed.

Changing Woman's adolescence ceremony was the first and most elaborate ever performed, and set a precedent for the future. Ceremonially dressed in whiteshell, the young girl was named—there was an argument about the names Changing Woman and Whiteshell Woman; both were retained—and she was modeled by kneading and pressing; thus she became the most beautiful maiden that ever existed. The entire effort was to make her pleasing to Sun; a cake was baked for his benefit and for him she ran several times to the east. At the appearance of her second menses there was a ceremony at which she raced for Moon's benefit. A rainbow, undoubtedly Sun's messenger, indicating approval of the ceremony, spoke to her: "This is truly Whiteshell Woman" (Goddard, pp. 148ff.; Matthews 1897, p. 230; Haile 1938b, pp. 85–9).

Since from this point on, various tales agree about the essential features of Changing Woman's life and attainment of power, we may pause for a moment to consider a different story of her origin.

The people had been wandering and so many had been devoured by the monsters that only four, an old man and woman and their two children, a young man and woman, were left. They found a small image of a woman fashioned in turquoise. Talking God appeared to the people, bidding them to come to the top of tćôˀlˀįˀį in four days. There they found an assembly of the gods. The Navaho had brought the turquoise image with them, and White Body, the counterpart of Talking God, had one nearly like it made of whiteshell. Talking God and xaˑctćéˀˀóɣan transformed the turquoise image into Changing Woman, the whiteshell image into Whiteshell Woman. At the same time they transformed an ear of white corn into White-corn-boy and an ear of yellow corn into

Yellow-corn-girl. Then the company dispersed, the gods taking the boy and girl with them and leaving Changing Woman and Whiteshell Woman alone on the mountain.

The stories include Changing Woman's attempt to have intercourse by exposing herself to sunlight and water. People did not yet understand sexual relations, but the girl who had just reached puberty in the one case, the two maidens in the other, had sexual desire. After Changing Woman had had intercourse with Sun, First Woman warned her of the danger in going away from home alone. She answered, "I am not entirely without knowledge," indicating that Changing Woman was endowed with supernatural power which did not depend upon instruction. Going to gather seeds, she met the white creature on a white horse with white trappings who turned out to be Sun. He instructed her to meet him in an especially prepared brush shelter. First Man built this for her and Sun visited her four successive nights, after which she became pregnant (Ch. 3; Goddard, p. 153; Haile 1938b, p. 91; Matthews 1897, pp. 105, 231; Reichard, Shooting Chant ms.).

Until the world had been cleared of monsters, Changing Woman's home was at tćô'l'į'į. Numerous references agree that living was hard and required a great deal of labor, subsistence consisting primarily of seeds, berries, and small rodents. The story after the first departure of The Twins concerns Changing Woman slightly. For some time she evidently pursued an ordinary woman's life, keeping the home to which the boys returned to report, to rest, and to get new strength and information about the next adventures.

After they had killed the worst of the monsters, Monster Slayer and Child-of-the-water made a second visit to Sun because there were still numerous lesser evils which had not been overcome. Sun gave them five hoops—black, blue, yel-

low, white, and varicolored—to each of which a large knife of
the same color was attached; in addition, he gave them four
great hailstones colored like the first four hoops, telling them
to ask their mother what to do with them. Changing Woman,
protesting that she had never been visited by Sun but had
seen him only at a great distance, said she would try to do
something with the hoops. By means of the hoops, hailstones,
and knives she caused a fierce storm calculated to find every
evil and danger no matter how well hidden. She said that
now all evil was conquered; when Wind whispered the name
of Old Age into Monster Slayer's ear, she would answer no
question about it, even when asked the fourth time. The
episode led to the tolerance of the powers ' somewhere between good and evil ' (Ch. 5; cp. *Cold, Hunger, Old Age,
Poverty;* Matthews 1897, pp. 130ff.; Reichard, Shooting
Chant ms.).

Although she had borne the children destined to kill the
monsters, which feats made them the chief war gods with
power against all foreign dangers, Changing Woman stood
for peace.

When the gods assembled to consider the war between
Dark Thunder and Winter Thunder, Changing Woman was
the first to enter. As soon as the subject was broached, she
said decisively, "I did not bear these children to go to war,
but to rid the world of monsters." Thereupon Monster Slayer
stood up and said, "I shall not go to war with you. My
mother is not in favor." Child-of-the-water refused to go for
the same reason.

RP explained that the Holy People were children of
Changing Woman in an existence subsequent to the one in
which she bore The Twins (Huckel ms.). JS put it: "Changing
Woman had Monster Slayer and Child-of-the-water for the
monster story (na·γé''e·), Talking God and xa·ctčé''óγan for
the blessing story (xǫ́jǫ́·djí), and the Holy People for the
chants-according-to-holiness (xatá·lkedjí)."

Changing Woman participates in many events, but it is
impossible to get them into temporal sequence; indeed, it is

411

not necessary to do so, since she and her decrees are immortal. A secondary theme, the removal of Changing Woman to the west, is almost as important as the primary.

The Twins had overcome the major obstacles to human life upon the earth, and Sun, in reallocating many of the gods, particularly wanted Changing Woman to live in the west, where he had provided a luxurious dwelling for her. Numerous attempts were made at persuasion, the house being described as unusually beautiful, a duplicate of Sun's house at the east. A horse made of a jewel substance belonged to each of the respective directions; there was a jet horse in the center at the root of a perfect cornstalk, which had twelve ears on each side. On the cornstalk's top sat a black songbird. Food was to consist of pollens, the precious stones, and sacred waters. As a final inducement, eternal youth and the road of perfection (są'ą na·γái bike xójó·n) were offered, but even these did not affect Changing Woman.

The gift of power over rain and vegetation, the enumeration of the most desirable garments and ornaments all failed to move her, as did even the disrespectful words of Monster Slayer's counterpart, Reared-in-the-earth, when he told her she had no sense. When, finally, war power—flashing, rattling flint armor and threatening words—was invoked, she consented.

The leader of the party spoke to her gently and told her that she was frustrating her own plan, for she herself had suggested the assignment of the Holy People to different places. She put up a plaintive plea, although she had actually given in: "Perhaps there is no one there and I may be lonesome." She was assured that the Holy Sky People would often meet at her place, and final directions were given for the removal.

The establishment of Changing Woman in the west is an important feature of the myth of the Male Shooting Chant Holy, more briefly referred to in other versions. In Matthews' version, Sun asks her consent as a reward for his help to The Twins. Her control over her powerful husband and sons is demonstrated by her indignation at the thought that the boys could make a promise for her or that they should think that anything Sun had done would benefit her. In this version Changing Woman described the house she would accept in the west. She wanted it to be on an island reasonably far from shore, so that numerous people would not bother her. She would have the animals for company. Sun granted all requests.

Changing Woman's power over reproduction and birth extends to all that exists on the earth. Becoming lonely in the home in the west, she created new people and directed them how to reach their relatives in the east.

Many of Changing Woman's gifts are rites or ceremonies, not fully enumerated here. Her decrees are kind. She gave man many songs, created the horse, decreed fertility and sterility. She was present at Rainboy's chant, where she made suds for his bath and laid out his clothes, and at another time brought in ceremonial food. Her presence at an assembly of the gods is pointed out with special respect; other gods bow their heads when she comes in.

The simple rite in which the chanter leads the patient onto the sandpainting of the last day of the Shooting Chant represents the perpetual rejuvenation of Changing Woman.

The Eagle Chant story includes an incident of creation. Changing Woman was living on Whirling Mountain, where her five hogans have since become rock. She rubbed epidermis from under her breast and created two women, Whiteshell Woman and Turquoise Woman, who became the wives of Monster Slayer.

RP's Bead Chant story explains that Changing Woman was the mother of five daughters, one of whom was Bead Woman, whose son was Scavenger, hero of the chant.

According to the fragment of a tale noted by Stevenson, the people, upon arriving in this, the upper world, lacked light.

They sent for two women, Changing Woman and Whiteshell Woman, who lived at Ute Mountain. Changing Woman (and here the text reads 'asdzą́·nádle·hé xa·ctčé·"oltohí, ' Changing Woman, the Shooting God ') had white beads in her right breast and turquoise in her left. From these the sun was created, but the people could not raise it far enough from the earth to prevent scorching, until helped by First Man and First Woman, who miraculously appeared.

Another of Stevenson's tales makes Changing Woman and her sister, Whiteshell Woman, the creators of shells. Changing Woman was said to have a beard under her right arm, and Whiteshell Woman a ball under her left, from which they made beads. The Twins had eyes of shell with which they could see far-distant objects (cp. Ch. 3; *Monster Slayer;* Reichard 1939, p. 26; Newcomb-Reichard, pp. 32–4; Matthews 1897, pp. 133, 150; Goddard, pp. 157, 164; Newcomb 1940b; Stevenson, pp. 275, 279; Stephen 1889, p. 135).

Changing-bear-maiden (tčikę́· cac nádle·hé) (U) is the female apotheosis of evil as Changing Woman is of good or as Big Monster is of destruction. She contrasts with her brothers, who are all that is worthy; she forms a pair with Coyote standing solidly on the side of evil. One reference, in a reviling speech of Coyote and, therefore, to be questioned, says she is the daughter of Sun. If so, she might be classed with the Unpersuadable Deities. However, since the Endurance Chant is dedicated to persuading her and she appears in some assemblies of gods, whereas the other monsters do not, she is classed as difficult to persuade.

Her story begins by depicting her as a great beauty, highly desirable, greatly respected and talented, a girl who despises men, one who makes conditions of matrimony so difficult that no man can fulfill them; she is what I have termed a ' decoy maiden.'

414

She exemplified the Navaho model housekeeper and a member of an ideal family, for she did all the work for many brothers, apparently without effort. She kept their home in excellent order—cleanliness is particularly stressed—and saw to it that they had plenty to eat. The Brothers controlled rare game and were good providers; all seemed satisfied and happy with the arrangement.

Into this situation, idyllic though in Navaho terms abnormal, came Coyote, overcome with lust for the girl and with jealousy of The Brothers. He showed himself in his best light and made marriage seem attractive. The girl had been warned against danger in the abstract and had been taught a great deal of lore with which to protect herself, but no one had instructed her about ' the one man.' The description of the seduction of Changing-bear-maiden is a narrative gem. For days the girl met all Coyote's arguments and resisted his blandishments. She practiced all the theory she had been taught, requiring him to kill Big Monster and to undergo death four times at her own hands. Finally, she reached the end of her tests. Soft words and pity made her yield to him and she found out how ' nice it was to have a husband.'

From the moment Coyote was allowed to crawl under the fringe of her robe she was in his power. During their sexual orgies he got control of her own and her brothers' secrets and she also learned something of Coyote's. The tale from here on recounts a conflict between the powers of the two, her recoil from the idealism of her virginal life, and the final conquest of both her own and Coyote's powers by the forces of good, represented primarily by The Youngest Brother. Into a clean, harmonious household entered impurity, filth, and disorder, all characteristic of Coyote; then the horrible potentialities of the beautiful girl began to come out. Her passion for Coyote, opposed by The Brothers, brought about her transformation. She had a long snout, which could break a person's neck. Her canine teeth were long, made of bone awls she had collected from the children of the enemies who had slain her mate. Long, coarse hair grew on her hands, spread to her arms and legs, and finally covered her whole body except her breasts. Her ears grew long and her nails turned into claws. When The Brothers found her thus, they attributed the change to Coyote.

The hero of the Mountain Chant was taken to the home of the Changing-bear-maidens. Two stories high, with four rooms on each story, it has four trees for doors—black spruce at the east, blue spruce at the south, yellow at the west, and white (shining) at the north. In it were four bear creatures, their faces white, their legs and forearms covered with shaggy hair, their hands human, their teeth long and pointed.

Although Navaho ceremonial practice encourages the presence of numerous forces at a chant, particularly on the last night, there are times when certain deities are not welcome. Offerings are grudgingly made to them; they may sometimes be allowed to stay, but at other times they are driven out.

At the ceremony performed over Rainboy, various gods brought in ceremonially prepared food. However, several deities brought in food that was rejected. Among them was Changing-bear-maiden, who brought pinyon nuts. Members of the assembly shouted, ";No! Take them out!" She decreed as she left, "When there are many pinyon nuts, there will be lots of snow and many people will freeze to death." She had contributed pinyon nuts because when she, as the Bear Monster, had been overcome by her youngest brother, he had cut off her breasts and thrown them into a pinyon tree, where they became pinyon nuts.
Conquest of this monster gave the following gifts to man —items that must be expected to differ as references come from different accounts. Her vagina became porcupine (yucca fruit); her breasts, pinyon cones and nuts; her right arm, the Male Shooting Chant; her right leg, the Female Shooting Chant; her left leg, the Male Wind Chant; her left arm, the Mountain Chant; her tongue, cactus; her entrails, snakes.

Driving out guests in cases like those mentioned seems to conflict with the theory which demands harmony of spirit during rituals, but it may also be interpreted as direct expulsion of evil, resembling brushing, ashes blowing, and similar ritualistic practices.

In my material there is no evidence of a relation between Changing-bear-maiden and Tracking Bear, but the informant of Flint Chant, version B, thinks they are the same and it is to be expected that they would be associated (Matthews 1887, p. 407; 1897, pp. 91–102; Reichard, Endurance Chant ms.; 1944d, p. 81; Haile 1943a, pp. 15, 124).

Chickenhawks (H), see *Hummingbirds.*

Child-of-the-water (tóbádjíctcíní) (P), the younger of The Twins, will be discussed here only insofar as his traits differ from those discussed for the two.

When First Man sent his messengers to spy out the newborn humans who had not yet learned to escape them, Child-of-the-water sighted the dangerous crow and Monster Slayer shot it.

Holy Man (that is, Monster Slayer) went to the home of White Weasel, who shot four arrows of turquoise, whiteshell, abalone, and redstone at him so that each pair crossed. He pulled the arrows from the side opposite that which they had entered and Holy Man escaped, losing much blood and stopping at four anthills, at each of which he sang a song. Contrary to his wont, he had not told his brother, Holy Boy (Child-of-the-water) where he was going. Nevertheless, the younger boy followed, but did not enter White Weasel's home; if he had, he too would have been shot. By the time he reached his older brother the latter was unable to proceed; the younger brother carried the older until they came to some Cactus People, who restored him so that he could walk. He was further helped by various people whom they met and the result of this journey was the meeting with the leaders of the Female Shooting Chant, with whom they exchanged some songs and knowledge.

As a young man, Child-of-the-water held a scalp in his hand, causing a black spot to appear, a spot mentioned in a song. Since that time no young man is allowed to hold a scalp or throw ashes upon it, but an old man is selected to do these things in ceremony.

417

Child-of-the-water is the parent of all the waters.

Changing Woman, after the earth had been made safe for humans, talked long and earnestly with her older son and finally dispatched him to the permanent flint home she and his father had prepared for him. She sent the guards of her mountain home, Bear Man and Big-snake-man, to their destined homes, where they would guard the flint house. Then, turning and noticing Child-of-the-water as if she had forgotten him up to this time, she asked him where he wanted to go. She had really hoped that he would stay with her a little longer, even that he might choose to go with her, but he said, "I want to go where my brother went."

Perhaps from habit or to cover her own disappointment, she scolded him: "If you thought this, why did you not say so when your brother started off? Had you spoken, you could have gone with your brother and father when they left in that cloud. Then it would not have been necessary to start all over again."

Recalling the cover of darkness, in which the children had previously been wrapped (either as infants or when hidden in Sun's house), she suggested, "Why not choose Darkness to travel in?" And as Darkness came up, even though it was daytime, she spoke to him: "Darkness, be sure and look after your grandchild." She addressed the same prayer to Moon, Dawn, and Sun. As her baby went out of sight in the darkness, though she had sent the others away quickly without indulging in regrets, Changing Woman wept.

This scene depicts clearly the subordinate place of Child-of-the-water in the universal scheme and his primary place in his mother's heart, a position symbolic of his function as a god and as the baby of the family. And just as in a few telling strokes the passage characterizes the son, it summarizes the mother as woman and mother.

At the risk of anticlimax I cannot resist pointing out that the behavior of Child-of-the-water in remaining silent while Sun waited and the Skies assembled is delightfully and typically Navaho. Had a white person in a situation as heavily charged with emotion asked, "Why didn't you say so?" a Navaho would have answered, "You didn't ask me."

When Secondborn arrived at the new flint home, his brother wept for joy at his coming. When they had done weeping, the older said, "From now on don't go wherever you please [that is, without consideration], but let me do the thinking and let us go together." This sentence, I feel, is the epitome of the character and purpose not only of The Twins but of all pairs in Navaho myth, ceremony, and actuality. One does the thinking, the other goes along; one leads, the other follows, serves, and protects (Reichard, Shooting Chant ms.; Haile 1938b, p. 317, 55n; Stevenson, p. 280).

Chipmunk (xazáitšósi˙) (H)* was a helpful rodent comparable with Rat.

It was customary for him to crawl out to the very end of Burrowing Monster's horn and, when Monster Slayer had supposedly killed him, Chipmunk ran out to be sure he was dead, and reported by his usual sound, tšó˙s tšó˙s tšó˙s tšó˙s. As a reward he was allowed to streak his face and stripe his body with Burrowing Monster's blood.

Chipmunk's function in the Endurance Chant was essentially the same. He told Youngest Brother how to kill Changing-bear-maiden by her own methods, and later hopped about on an oak tree, making his sound to give Youngest Brother the sign that he had found the place where her vital parts were hidden.

Chipmunk fed Rainboy from the inexhaustible yellow bowl, and was rewarded with Measuring Worm's tobacco (Haile 1938b, pp. 115–7, cp. Matthews 1897, p. 118; Reichard 1944d, p. 139; Shooting Chant ms.; Endurance Chant ms.).

Cicada (γó˙ne˙ctèj˙di˙) (H)† has a good deal of power,

---

*Rodents have not been scientifically identified. The translations are colloquial.
†The insects, classified by the Navaho with worms, have not been scientifically identified.

usually expressed in an arrow-crossing contest. He was able
to shove an arrow through each side of his chest, pull it out
on the opposite side, and survive unscathed. He crossed
arrows also from mouth to anus and pulled them through.
The latter proved too hard a test for his enemies and he won
the world from the Grebes. In some versions, the Grebes cut
off parts of his cheeks with their ax. That is why Cicada has
a narrow face. Before he transfixed himself with the arrows
he pushed his vitals into his abdomen, then changed his mind
and pushed them all into his chest; that is why he now has a
big chest (Goddard, p. 131; Matthews 1897, p. 76, 218, 41n).

Cliff Monster, Throwing Monster (tsé nenáxa'li·) (UP), conceived by the self-abuse of a chief's daughter with a feather
quill, was thrown after birth into an alkali bed. He became the
monster He-throws-against-the-rocks, named from his habit
of catching people in his long sharp claws and throwing them
to his children lower down among the rocks. He had a long
beak and large eyes; something like feathers grew on his
shoulders. The male caught his prey, carried it to the highest
ledge of a rock like Shiprock, and threw it down to his wife,
who wore beautiful earstrings. The children waited for their
food below the mother.

Monster Slayer carried the paunch filled with Burrowing
Monster's blood as bait for Cliff Monster. The male, seeing
Monster Slayer traveling with it slung over his shoulder,
swooped down and carried him high, then let him fall to the
nest at the very top of the cliff. Monster Slayer was saved by
a life feather given him by Spider Woman, and the blood
flowing from the broken paunch made the monster think the
boy had been killed. Monster Slayer found himself among
the young, from whom he learned the parents' names. Monster Slayer killed the mother and father monsters, tossing

them down to the children to eat, just as many Earth People had been treated.

The subjection of this monster as recounted in the myth of the Shooting Chant differs in that Monster Slayer did not use the blood bait, for he killed Kicking Monster before Cliff Monster. His helpers were Bear and Snake, and there are ritualistic differences.

The father monster was transformed into Shiprock, which is thought to look like a poised eagle. The young were transformed into the eagles and owls that today furnish many forms of ceremonial property. Monster Slayer took feathers for his trophies. After all these things had happened, he found himself high on a ledge with no way to get down. Bat Woman appeared, carried him down, and was rewarded with a basket of down feathers that subsequently became birds (Reichard, Shooting Chant ms.; Matthews 1897, pp. 80, 119–21, 236, 138n; Haile 1938b, pp. 117–23; Wheelwright 1942, pp. 70, 89–92).

co, hero of a form of the Night Chant (Matthews 1902, pp. 197ff.).

Cold (xaka·z 'asdzą́·) (B) lived at the top of a high mountain where there were no trees and the snow never melted. She was a spare old woman who sat on bare snow, without clothing, food, fire, or shelter. She shivered from head to foot; her teeth chattered; water streamed from her eyes. Snow buntings, her messengers to announce storms, played around her. Her argument for life was: "If you kill me, the weather will always be hot; the land will dry up; the springs will cease to flow; the people will perish. It will be better for your people if you let me live" (Matthews 1897, p. 130; Reichard, Shooting Chant ms.).

Cornbeetle ('ańłtáni˙) (H), the symbol of female generative power, may be represented as male or female comparable with Pollen Boy, with whom she is frequently paired (Reichard 1939, Pl. XII, XIII, XXII; Wheelwright 1942, Pl. Set II, 4).

Coyote (ma'i˙, mą'į˙, 'atsé˙ xacké˙) (U) is a great mischief maker. His ceremonial name, 'atsé˙ xacké˙, may be translated ' First Warrior, First Scolder, the First-to-get-angry, the First-one-to-use-words-for-force.' All refer to anger as an essential of war power. Coyote is the symbol of force with slyness and knavery.

Several origins are given for Coyote. According to one account, the people had not been in the fourth world long when they saw Sky bend down and Earth rise up until for a moment they met. At that moment Coyote and Badger, now considered to be children of Sky, sprang out of Earth at the point of contact. At once Coyote skulked among the people, whereas Badger went down into the hole which led to the lower world. According to another version, Water Coyote, who knows everything about the water and runs on it, and Coyote, who knows everything about the land, were in existence with the First Pair in the lowest world. Still another has First Scolder in the first world, his mother being Sky Maiden.

Coyote is a character well-known to Indian mythology, one with the most diverse qualities of animal and man. He is versatile; many of the adjectives that describe him have a derogatory meaning. If by chance Coyote shows up in a favorable light, there is reason to be on guard, lest he be working up to some betrayal. He is sneaking, skulking, wary, shrewd, tricky, mischievous, provoking, exasperating, contrary, undependable, amusing, disarming, persuasive, flattering, smug, undisciplined, cowardly, foolhardy, obstinate, disloyal, dishonest, licentious, lascivious, amoral, deceptive, sacrilegious, and, in a sense, persistent.

He persists when he wants something, and will not give up until he gets it, as when he tried to seduce Changing-bear-maiden. To pass her tests he killed Big Monster and even allowed himself to be killed four times. He was told to stay away from a place where holy things were being done, but, no matter how carefully the place was guarded, he got in and interfered.

When application and care would be of some help, or obedience to instructions would lead to success, Coyote gives up or deliberately disobeys. When he feathered his arrows, it was with the feathers of ' any old kind ' of bird, including gray (unlucky) birds. Even his skin was ground up by the Bats with earth from ' any old place,' and scattered in every direction. His irresponsibility has been incorporated in myth and ritual. Generally, plants for the chant emetic and other rites are carefully specified and gathered with attention to the direction in which they are plucked. When Coyote collected them, they were whatever he found anywhere he looked. When he sang the concluding songs of the War Ceremony, he danced in a circle and his singing had no order. He chose October for his month; it is the ' mixed-up ' or ' changing ' month, neither summer nor winter. Unable to decide where to place the stars at the time of creation, he hurled them to the sky, thereby creating the Milky Way.

Coyote's position in the assembly of the gods matches his role elsewhere. Theoretically, there are only two choices, the good represented by the south side of the assembly and the evil represented by the north side. Coyote takes his place near the door, so that he may ally himself with either side according to his whim. In gambling he does not bet normally, taking a side and sticking to it, but flatters both sides and changes about during the play, as he thinks one side or the other has the better chance of winning. He usually loses, for his judgment leads him to the flashy side, and in Navaho lore it is the modest side that wins.

He is a liar. Everyone knew him, even though people were sometimes taken in by his disguises. They said of him, "He is an idler and a trickster. Beware of him." He went to Corn Man to learn the conditions that would win his two desirable nieces in marriage, then reported correctly to Monster Slayer what those conditions were, but Coyote was not believed, even when he told the truth, and Mourning Dove was sent to confirm the story.

Coyote was a spy of Burrowing Monster well-known to Changing Woman. As the mate of Changing-bear-maiden and with power superior to hers, he was allied with evil. In his sexual practices he represents excess. The story of the Endurance Chant is in a sense a tale of the human control of sex. It shows the goad which sexual desire imposes on a person like Coyote who, for other ends, has little determination, yet for surfeit will stop at nothing. The story is one of several examples showing Coyote's determination to win the most desirable maidens when apparently insurmountable conditions are imposed on their marriage. In this respect, however, Coyote is not alone in Navaho mythology, for even the most moral of the gods seek and secure such girls. The tale demonstrates how difficult it is for order and control to operate.

Coyote's lasciviousness began in the lower worlds, where desire, incest, and sorcery were uncontrolled. The story of the separation of the sexes does not explain how Coyote, Blue Fox, Yellow Fox, and Badger got over to the side of the women, but it emphasizes their part in license. Badger set the women crazy with desire; he and the others copulated with them constantly and licked them between the legs; that is the reason coyotes and dogs lick each other that way now. There may be a close connection between this myth and the extinct Dog and Coyote ceremonies.

Even death had no power over Coyote. He kept his vital principle in the end of his nose and tail; when the rest of him was destroyed, he pulled himself together and came to life again. Changing-bear-maiden learned from him that he buried his vitals—his heart, lungs, breath, and blood—in the ground, while the rest of him went about on his unholy mission. When she tried the same trick, she was overcome because Chipmunk knew the trick and informed Youngest Brother.

The gods sometimes agreed with Coyote just as Earth People did. Black God seems to have had something to do with the kidnaping of Water Monster's child, according to one version, and there are other indications that Black God and Coyote were sometimes friends. On the other hand, Black God was the only being Coyote feared. It is sometimes difficult to understand why Coyote was put in charge of darkness, daylight, male and female rain, corn and vegetation, thunder and rainbow by Monster Slayer, or why he was given control over dark cloud, dark mist, female rain, and all vegetation by Holy Young Man of Trembling Mountain. One principle of Navaho belief teaches that the greater the danger, the more imperative it is to give a large gift to ward it off. Putting a dangerous person in charge of precious things is quite common to Navaho ritual as a form of control.

A were-coyote episode is common in myth. A person, often a god, is reduced to a pitiable, powerless state when hit with a coyote skin. Only by the efforts—Hoop Transformation—

of the Holy People can the changed one be restored to his normal state.

Coyote prayersticks—white, blue, yellow, black—are mentioned.

Coyote is amusing, but he is also so much feared that most warriors seeing a coyote on the trail would turn back rather than take the chance his appearance portends.

Corn chewed by a coyote should not be eaten as food, but may be used as a medicine. It is given to a child who has become ill because during pregnancy the mother saw a dead dog.

One night when some Navaho from Ft. Sumner were on a Comanche raid, a coyote walked into their camp. They offered prayers and jewels, but bad luck overtook the warriors. Four were killed; the rest were scattered and considered themselves lucky to get back alive (Matthews 1897, pp. 71, 91, 107, 219, 223, 70n; 1902, pp. 203, 229; Goddard pp. 127, 135, 138, 233; Wheelwright 1942, pp. 39, 66; Reichard, Endurance Chant ms.; 1939, p. 31; 1944d, p. 105; Shooting Chant ms.; Male Shooting Chant Evil ms.; Haile 1938b, pp. 149, 199; Stephen 1930, p. 99; Kluckhohn-Wyman, p. 5; Kluckhohn 1944, pp. 14, 21; Wyman-Bailey 1943b, p. 31, 65n; Sapir-Hoijer, p. 211; Hill 1936, p. 14).

Craving-for-meat ('atčą́) (B), see *Sleep.*

Crooked Snake (P) may be a side-winder. It should be drawn with four angles, two on each side, and is directly or indirectly connected with zigzag lightning (Newcomb-Reichard, p. 52, Pl. III, XIII).

Crow (gâ·gí) (U) as a carrion eater, classed with birds of evil propensities, is difficult to persuade. He is important in the myths of the Night Chant and War Ceremony, a ' crowbill ' being a major property of the latter.

Crow gossips if he sees someone covered up early in the morning, spreading the news that the lazy person must be sick.

Before the world was transformed, Red Crow was a messenger of Cliff Monster, reporting to him the existence of human beings (Matthews 1897, p. 107; 1902, p. 159; Haile 1938b, pp. 93, 193; Hill 1938, p. 19; Reichard, Shooting Chant ms.).

Crushing Rocks, Crushing Mountains (tsé 'axé·tšá, dził na·kigoh 'axé·ndiłgoh) (D) were said by Matthews' informant to be real people who could think like men, but were enemies of the pre-Navaho. They were innocent-looking rocks or mountains which, as soon as someone tried to walk between, clapped together and crushed the intruder.

The Twins fooled them by pretending to enter the passage between, then withdrawing four times. Eventually, by means of a ceremonial arrangement of their weapons—clubs, bows, and arrows—The Twins kept the rocks apart long enough to get through. In Matthews' version, they got through with a formula Spider Woman had given them. In the Wheelwright version of creation, Monster Slayer wedged the horns of Burrowing Monster between the rocks, then built a fire under the rocks and, when they were hot, struck them with his club so that the pieces flew in all directions. The burning rock changed to all colors; eventually it became the rock now used in sandpainting (Reichard, Shooting Chant ms.; Matthews 1897, p. 109; Haile 1938b, pp. 97, 125; Wheelwright 1942, pp. 95–6).

Cutting Reeds (lóka·, lóka· digij) (D) grew in a large patch on the way to Sun's house. They had large leaves as sharp as knives that would attack with a sizzling sound anyone who tried to pass through them. Black God once helped The Twins by burning the reeds. The few that survived became materials for prayersticks. In some versions The Twins were able to pass them by reciting Spider Woman's formula or with her gift of life feathers (Reichard, Shooting Chant ms.; Wheelwright 1942, p. 96; Matthews 1897, p. 110; Haile 1938b, p. 99).

Dark Wind (ńłtći diłxił) (P) is the most powerful of the Winds and, paired with Yellow Wind, represents them all. Winds are probably better described in the Wind Chant myths than in those I have analyzed.

Black Wind moves a yellow cloud on an abalone mountain (Huckel ms.).

Darkness (tcaxałxeˑł, tcaˑłxeˑł) (H) is the black sky frequently depicted in sandpaintings of the Shooting Chant. The most effective of the protective covers. Darkness is identified with black to confer invisibility. Darkness covered The Twins as babies and again when Sun's sky wife hid them to protect them from her husband's wrath. Changing Woman would not tell them who their father was or how to get to him, but Darkness, the lowest cover in which they were wrapped, gave them the information in a song.

When Child-of-the-water chose to live permanently with his twin brother, Darkness was called to transport him safely.

Great though he is, Sun cannot penetrate Darkness; hence only Darkness is fleet enough to restore eyes, since they alone can outrun Darkness.

The role of Darkness as a protecting cover may be the same as its function as mentor. Darkness was chosen instead of Wind to search the mind of Gambler ' because he goes wherever he will, yet makes no noise.' For this reason Dark-

ness went into Gambler's house, entered his room, moved
through his body while he slept, searched well his mind, and
returned to report that Gambler was sorry for not having
given some of the valuables he won to Sun. In doing this
Darkness verified the search previously carried on by Wind.

Whirlwind and Flint Boy helped Youngest Brother, concealed under the fireplace, by placing Wind at his right ear
to warn of the approach of danger by day, and Darkness at
his left ear to guard and inform him by night (Reichard,
Shooting Chant ms.; Haile 1943a, p. 135; Matthews 1897,
pp. 83, 101).

Dawn, Dawn People (yikáih, yikáih dine'é) (P) are referred
to incidentally in relation to Sun's sky wife. They are manifestations of the Holy People and there may be a chant in
which they are leading characters.

A group of people killed at Taos were Sun's children. The
two chief ones, girls dressed in spiral strings of jewels, were
called Two-dawns-arrive (Haile 1938b, p. 163; Goddard,
pp. 139–40).

Deer Owner (UP) is included to show associations with
Bear, Snake, Mountain Lion, Rock Crystal, Corn Smut. He
was a sorcerer, his witchcraft power being associated with
incest and wealth. He had his daughter for a wife and he hid
the game animals so he alone could use them. The hero
became acquainted with the daughter and, learning from
her the old man's secrets, was able to release the game for
everybody (Matthews 1897, p. 175; Sapir-Hoijer, pp. 31–7;
Newcomb 1940b, pp. 58ff.; Haile 1938b, pp. 141ff.).

Desire (ńziní) (B), see *Sleep.*

Dog (łé·tcạ·'í, łį·tcạ·'i·) (U) is an animal of bad luck that may spoil anything. The Navaho ascribe to Dog the faults possessed by its relatives, Coyote and Wolf, and despise him because ' he can't take care of himself.' The Mexican hairless seems to have been better thought of. When Rainboy's sister prepared for her ascension, she took with her a Mexican hairless dog.

A small watchdog, tied to a cliff opposite the canyon home of the gods, barked sharply at the Stricken Twins.

Persons to whom dogs are unfriendly cannot foretell events. Those who divined by listening put dog earwax, among other things, into their ears. A rite to drive off the evil power of dogs was a part of the Night and Mountain chants (Hill 1938, p. 75; 1935a, p. 66; Reichard 1944d, p. 155; Matthews 1902, pp. 103, 229; Newcomb 1938, p. 47; Wyman-Kluckhohn, pp. 6, 27; Kluckhohn-Wyman, p. 188).

Dragonflies (táni·l'ái·) (H) were harmful to man until subdued by Holy Man in the contest with White Weasel. They hover over the water which represents the mountain home of the Buffalo and clear water (Reichard, Shooting Chant ms.; 1939, Pl. XXIII, XXIV; Newcomb-Reichard, Pl. XXII, XXV, XXVI, XXVIII–XXXIII).

Eagles ('atsá) (P, H), expert and powerful fliers, are believed to derive from Cliff Monster.

Scavenger of the Bead Chant placed in an eagle's nest by hostile pueblo people, refused to deliver the eaglets to them. He lived with the Eagles for some time, learning about their home and their customs. When the old Eagles came home at night, they took off their downy garments, which opened down the front, revealing human forms in white suits which were never removed.

Eagle feathers were of great value to the Navaho in their ceremonies, but the Eagles of this story shook skin diseases, sores, irritations, and itching on their enemies.

The bald eagle is held to be the ' first ' or ' chief.' In the story of the Eagle Chant, Monster Slayer, learning the details of eagle catching, did not make the chant symbol until he was able, by repeating his experiments, to catch a bald eagle.

Hill's account of eagle catching should be compared with the stories of the Eagle and Bead chants; each record has much to contribute to the others (Reichard, Shooting Chant ms.; 1939, pp. 26–36; Haile 1938b, p. 121; Matthews 1897, pp. 195–208; Newcomb 1940b, pp. 50–97).

Earth (ni') (H) is thought of as the ultimate source of everything and, now that Earth People exist and multiply, as the most important single factor in their existence. Clean sand from the cornpatch and the ritual of agriculture demonstrate the symbolism of origin and subsistence. Disposal of objects in places where they will naturally decompose until they are one with the earth is a more general evidence of the same idea. The earth is identified with Changing Woman, the Earth Mother. The sandpictures, made of earth products, are a complicated form of earth symbolism (Newcomb-Reichard, Fig. 5).

Earth Center, see *Sky Pillars*.

Earth Shadow, see *Blue-horizon-light*.

Earth Woman (naxa'asdzá·n, naxo'osdzá·n, naxo·sdzá·n) (H) is addressed in formulas and prayers, the word probably being another name for Earth or Changing Woman. According to RS, Earth Woman is the same as sa'a na·γái. JS says she is the mother of Changing Woman and that Earth Woman and Sky Man brought about creation by smoking tobacco. Earth Woman's spirit represents growth (Wheelwright 1942, p. 63; Reichard 1944d, pp. 87, 101).

Endless Snake, see *Never-ending-snake*.

Eye Killers (biną·" ye· 'aɣání, biná·" ye· 'aɣání) (UP) were the result of the self-abuse of a chief's daughter with a sour cactus; when born, they were cast away instead of being properly raised by a family. Winds brought them up. They were later found at the place where they were born. The first Eye Killers were twins. Roundish and tapered at one end, they had no limbs or heads, but were provided with depressions somewhat like eyes. They could, however, kill by staring at their victims without winking. As they did so, their rudimentary eyes grew into the eyes of those they were killing. They lived in a conical hogan at the foot of Mt. Taylor. Monster Slayer found them as an old couple with many children. Lightning flashed from their eye sockets. People would try to light a fire to save themselves, but were destroyed before they succeeded. Monster Slayer made a fire with his fire drill and threw into it salt given him by Salt Woman. An explosion threw sparks and salt in every direction, and the monsters were obliged to shut their eyes. The hero was then able to hit them with his flint club and killed all except two, one of which became an elf owl that warns of an approaching enemy, and one a screechowl which makes things beautiful on earth.

According to the Shooting Chant myth, the parents became cacti. Monster Slayer cut off all tips wherever he found them (even though the creatures had no tips!) and made passes with them in all directions, and they became antelope (Haile

1938b, pp. 77, 123; Matthews 1897, pp. 81, 123, 236, 146n; Reichard, Shooting Chant ms.; 1942, p. 94).

Female Gods (xaˑctčéˑ baʼáˑd, γéʼiˑ baʼáˑd) (P) are described by Matthews as female representations of the more familiar gods. The masks and dress of Female Gods differ from those of their male partners. I am not sure whether they are always the same or are modified according to the males with which they are paired. They function only weakly in the chants with which I have dealt most (Matthews 1902, pp. 16–9, Pl. III, D; Curtis, p. 110).

First Man (ʼatsé xastiˑn) *and First Woman* (ʼatséˑ ʼesdzą́ˑ) (U) were transformed from two primordial ears of corn. The gods decreed marriage for them and four days later hermaphrodite twins were born to them. After four more days a normal boy and girl were born, and later other twins until they had five pairs. The first boy and girl mated with each other, as did the members of each succeeding pair; the hermaphrodites alone were barren.

Four days after the last pair of twins was born, First Man and First Woman were taken to the east where the gods dwelt. They were brought back after four days and all their children were taken for a similar sojourn. When they returned, they sometimes wore masks like those Talking God and xaˑctčéˑʼoγan now wear and they prayed for blessings such as man desires. However, in addition to the knowledge of good, they acquired also the secrets of witchcraft, "for," states the myth, "witches always keep such masks with them and marry those too closely related to them."

After their return from the east, the siblings separated and, keeping their unlawful marriages secret, took mates from the Mirage People, had many children who intermarried with the ancient pueblo people and those who had come from underground, and aided in populating the earth. Their immediate descendants made rapid cultural progress. First Man was chief of all people in the fourth world, except the pueblo people who lived there before the Navaho came. He was a great hunter. His wife was very fat and her favorite food was greasy meat. One time, after thoroughly enjoying a hearty meal of fat venison, she wiped her hands on her dress and gave thanks to her vagina. When First Man asked why she did this, she replied that she was only acknowledging the motive for everything that men do. This and her subsequent argument made First Man so furious that he jumped over the fire and remained by himself in silence all night. The next day the men and women agreed to separate (Matthews 1897, pp. 69–73, 218, 32n; cp. Ch. 2 and Stevenson, p. 284).

According to the Goddard version, the First Pair existed in the lowest world, where the perfect corn ears, white for male, yellow for female, came into being with them. The corn was of whiteshell and abalone. The two beings met up with Water Coyote and Coyote, and the group of four stuck together in later times. Because of witchcraft, they left the two lowest worlds, and in the third, First Man decreed marriage and exogamy, the legitimacy of the hermaphrodite's life, and chieftainship. Various cultural advances were made. First Woman angered First Man and all the other chiefs by her unfaithfulness (with Sun, says Matthews) and, because of her offense, the women were separated from the men.

When the men and women eventually came to live together again, and First Man had got the people through to the fourth or upper world, he was accredited with the transformation of the earth, customs, and cultural progress. First Woman tried to lead in sexual matters. For a long time there was no leadership, but rather wrangling and trouble. When, however, Changing Woman was found by First Man, Mirage Talking God decided that the ' mind ' of the baby, Changing Woman, was to be the ruling power.

The First Pair cared for her, calling her ' daughter ' and regulating her life ceremonially. When Changing Woman announced that Sun (whom she did not know) had appeared to her, First Man did exactly as Sun directed, thus co-operating in the conception of The Twins. After they were born, the First Pair helped care for them; First Man made them bird arrows and occasionally gave them advice.

After The Twins had rid the earth of the monsters, First Man and First Woman went to a place at the east beyond Narrow Water.

These accounts indicate that considerable good is to be ascribed to the First Pair, but there is also an underlying suggestion that they may take the bad side instead.

Gray Eyes' myth makes the First Pair wholly bad, for when The Twins, with whose birth they had nothing to do, were young and innocent, First Man and First Woman were allied with Coyote. All were man eaters who lived at Earth Mesa. Crow was their messenger to spy out new humans for their food. After all possible evil had been corrected, the First Pair were assigned a home in the northeast, where evil and danger originate, ' because they are mean (ba'áté).'

The legend of the War Ceremony represents the First Pair as quite the opposite of ' mean,' for First Man is so concerned with the successful outcome of The Twins' adventures that he creates and breathlessly watches the warning prayer-sticks for their safety.

The incidents representing the First Pair working against man almost certainly refer to the undesirable practices of witchcraft the couple learned when they visited the gods at the east. The Stephen version shows some causes of offense, but does not define actual sorcery practices.

First Man and First Woman existed in the first of the three worlds described. By rubbing cuticle from different parts of their bodies they created a man and a woman (called Biting Vagina), then formed Water Monster and Salt Woman. From a small piece of his tongue First Man made a wing, which he placed on his ear. When the wind blew it told him what was to happen. He made also Big Frog and Crane. First Woman created Thunder. After Spider Woman had made ants, the four beings Water Monster, Frog, Salt Woman, and Crane moved to the ends of the world quarters so they would not be annoyed by the ants; their houses were shaped like rainbows and sunrays. When First Man and First Woman looked at these, they prayed for clouds and rain. First Woman sent Thunder to be a guardian for Water Monster, Water Horse to guard Frog's house, Water Sprinkler to guard Salt Woman, and Fish [Turtle?] to guard the bird at the north. Each had a water vessel. When First Man and his wife saw these jars, they were somewhat jealous, but First Man said that if they were wise enough they could have just as many things.

He thereupon went to each creature and borrowed a little water from each of the four directions. He 'planted' the water and raised a spring around which grew five kinds of plants. One was a reed with twelve nodes, from which wind blew, making music because it was a flute. Wind became troublesome; the guards of the four houses could not subdue it and finally gave up the attempt. The First Pair were still praying for something to eat, and when First Man went to look at his spring, he found corn. Water Monster had pumpkins and squash, and Salt Woman beans and cotton. First Woman saw that Frog had watermelons and tobacco and that muskmelons and gourds grew at the north. In the spring First Man also found growing fruit, which Spider Woman changed to whiteshell.

By this time the First Pair had everything, but those living at the edge of the world had no corn. When they asked for it, First Man gave them pollen which grew into small plants, like onions, without ears. Water Monster complained that when First Man had wanted water, he had let him have it and now First Man would not return the favor by furnishing corn seed. Water Monster sent Thunder to strike First Man with lightning, but Horned Toad protected him. Frog sent Water Horse, but Spider Woman spun a web to protect him. Salt Woman sent Water Sprinkler with salt and lightning, but Black God saved First Man.

Then First Man sent Black God against these, his enemies. He went into their houses and broke the water jars so that water ran in all directions, met in the west, and caused a great flood. First Man was not afraid of water. He and his party were able to take symbols of their possessions and float on the water in a large reed. The four enemies sent for help; as a result, Cicada got a bow and two arrows from Water Monster; Black God accepted from Frog a tobacco pouch of water scum beautifully embroidered with beads:

Spider Woman received a nice cotton blanket from Salt Woman; Horned Toad was given a flint shirt and cap. These offerings made them all friendly and First Man let their donors get into his reed. As, with prayer, they bade farewell to their spring, two young men came out of it. First Woman hid them in her blanket.

When the First Pair arrived in the second world, First Man laid down the mountains as they are in this world. He made Talking God, Monster Slayer, and Black God, and placed them on the sacred mountains. He made sky covers for the mountains and fixed day and night. Then the First Pair made people and put chiefs in charge of them. First Man taught Coyote all he knew; the latter quarreled with Wind and carried back lies to First Man.

After the separation and reunion of the sexes, with which the First Pair had nothing to do, and after the people had come up to this world, First Man made sun, moon, and stars as described in the other version (Stephen 1930, pp. 88–104; cp. Stevenson).

There always seems to be some undesignated cause of dissatisfaction that keeps the First Pair in a bad temper regarding man. Perhaps they are only fumbling. They have an inkling of what is good and some desire to bring it about, but because of ignorance, the mixed character of such knowledge as they have, and the absence of harmony, they move back and forth between good and evil in a kind of experiment with the cosmos. For these reasons they belong in the class of Undependable Deities.

According to the myth of the Endurance Chant, First Man and First Woman lived with Sun and Moon. JS says that at the very beginning they lived with Earth Woman, Sky Man, First Boy, and First Girl.

It is certain that much more could be found in Navaho lore, some of which would make clearer the position of the First Pair in the pantheon.

Although the Wheelwright creation story gives the First

Pair merely a minor position in the emergence and transformation of the world, it has the only graphic representation of them published so far. They are shown sitting before their house, in which burns the fire Coyote stole from Black God. First Man has a shirt of various colors; First Woman wears brown, the color of Earth and of Earth People (Goddard, pp. 127, 156; Matthews 1897, p. 217; Reichard, Shooting Chant ms.; Endurance Chant ms.; Haile 1938b, p. 123; Stephen 1930, pp. 86–104; Wheelwright 1942, Set II, 3).

First Pair (U), see *First Man.*

First Warrior ('atsé' xacké') (U), see *Coyote.*

First Woman ('atsé'esdzá') (U), see *First Man.*

Flash Lightning (xatso'olɣał, xatso'lɣał) (H), see *Thunder.*

Forked Lightning (xadjilgic) (H), see *Thunder.*

Fringed Mouth (zaxado·ljăi, zaxa'do·ljăi) (P) is a major character of the Night Chant, whose costume and properties are conceived in great detail. It is, however, difficult to get a clear idea of his function. The name is taken from the mask, which has fringe around the eyes and mouth. There are two kinds of Fringed Mouths, Land Fringed Mouths (tséntci·' zaxado·ltsa') and Water Fringed Mouths (tá·tła·djí zaxado·ljăi). The few references indicate that they are the lifting force of lightning.

When the log containing Self Teacher was stuck at a falls in the San Juan River, the gods labored in vain to release it until the Water Fringed Mouths roped the log with the lightning onto their bodies, and lifted it.

When the log containing the Visionary was stuck in an eddy, the Land and Water Fringed Mouths found out who was responsible and offerings were made to Beaver, Otter, Fish, and Water Coyote to release it.

The Eagles of the Bead Chant found difficulty in lifting the earth boy, Scavenger. When they tried, he spun round so that they were not able to rise. Wind took the news to Land Fringed Mouth, who came with Talking God. The Eagles had wrapped the boy in a dark cloud attached with lightning and rainbow strings. It was dark inside; Talking God and Fringed Mouth put a crystal inside to furnish light and gave him a yellow tube of reed through which to breathe. They placed Fringed Mouth's headdress on Scavenger's head and a reed wand in his hand. The Eagles were able to raise him, so prepared, to the sky (Matthews 1897, pp. 168, 170, 215; 1902, pp. 11ff., 178; Sapir-Hoijer, pp. 157, 505; Curtis, p. 108; Reichard 1939, p. 29).

Frogs, Toads (tċał, tċą́ł) (U) of different kinds are not distinguished.

After his restoration from Winter Thunder's lightning, Rainboy wandered into Frog's cornfield. Frog was hoeing diligently, his back toward the boy. The description of Frog is given in terms of Rainboy's thoughts.

"His eyes are all swollen," thought Rainboy, and at once Frog answered, "Yes, it is funny how swollen my eyes are."

"His Adam's apple puffs in and out strangely," thought Rainboy. "It's funny how baggy I am under my jaw," said Frog.

Frog had a turquoise pipe which he filled with tobacco and lighted by holding to the Sun. He inhaled the smoke and it came out of holes all over his body. "My! He has smoke-holes all over him," thought Rainboy. "That's true! Smoke comes out of all my warts," said Frog.

He invited Rainboy to smoke, but, warned by his mentor, Rainboy refused, thinking, "I wonder what all those rough things on him are." Again Frog answered his thoughts: "Hail-stones, or potatoes, are the things on me, my grandchild."

Frog then challenged Rainboy to a race. Being a chronic gambler, Rainboy could not refuse. He lost and the gods had to restore him with elaborate ceremony. They gave him power to beat Frog in another race.

Frog had the magic stone ax which, when picked up by anyone not its owner, would strike and kill the one who wielded it. This Rainboy was warned not to do even though Frog begged him to use it on him (Reichard 1944d, pp. 15, 27; Matthews 1902, p. 179).

Frog had power over rain (Ch. 1). After contending with Rainboy, Frog was given power to accomplish whatever he wished, in exchange for sending rain whenever Earth People asked for it.

Frog is an uninvited guest at the assembly of the gods. Followed by many unruly grandchildren, who swarmed over the place and wet the floor where the people were sitting, he came in grumbling because he had not been notified. In one of the Hail Chant assemblies, Frog was called by the ceremonial name be˟'ekid na˟γái, ' Lake Traveler.' Surrounded by his grandchildren, he sat down near the basket drum and contributed two songs to the chant.

After the gods had rescued Self Teacher from the Water Monsters, Frog followed the party and told them how to make the prayerstick offerings of Water Monster, Water Horse, Beaver, Otter, Big Fish, and Frog himself (Reichard 1944d, pp. 15, 27–9, 105, 115; Matthews 1897, p. 170; 1902, p. 179).

Gambler, see be'γotcidí, *Sun.*

Gaping Bear (UP), see *Bony Bear.*

Gila Monster (tińlái, xińlái) (P) may be called the god of divination by trembling. He is, therefore, one of the deities invoked to cure harm derived from dealing with hand-trembling.

Gila Monster is prominent in the myth of the Flint Chant.

His offering, attitude, and behavior are so similar to those of Black God that there seems to be a close association between the two and there is some reason to believe that both are associated with Black Star. Gila Monster's protective covering is associated with Flint (Wyman 1936a, pp. 236–46; Kluckhohn-Wyman, pp. 169ff., Fig. 25, 26; Newcomb 1940a, p. 64; Haile 1943a, pp. 62, 66).

Gopher (na'azísí) (H), see *Burrowing Monster, Chipmunk, Pocket Gopher.*

Grasshopper (naxatcagi˙) (H) appears as a weapon of the Stricken Twins furnished by the gods to help destroy the Awatobi gardens. The Navaho know of no defense against a grasshopper plague (Matthews 1902, p. 245; Hill 1938, p. 37).

Gray God (xa˙ctčé˙ łbahí) (P) is specifically envisaged. Though he is not described, his functions are referred to in the Night Chant. With Talking God and Female God he performs the ritual of the circular prayersticks; he participates in the ritual with the Night Chant talisman and he, instead of xa˙ctčé˙'óγan, may administer the medicine. He is one of the begging gods.

He conducted the Stricken Twins on a part of their journey. When they came to the House of Gods, he held up two foxskins; as he pulled them apart, cloud curtains rolled back and the twins entered.

According to Sapir (probably through Father Berard), Gray God, Water Sprinkler, and xa˙ctčé˙'dó˙di˙ are three names for the same deity (Matthews 1902, pp. 69, 94, 126, 130, 238; Sapir-Hoijer, p. 511, 91n).

Ground Squirrel (xazái) (H) was originally all yellow. After Monster Slayer had killed Burrowing Monster, he was weak and faint from smelling the blood and sweat. Ground Squirrel restored him with medicine, whereupon Monster Slayer dipped his hand in the blood and rubbed it over Ground Squirrel's back and face. "After that he was better looking" (Reichard, Shooting Chant ms.).

Hard-flint-people (bé·c ntɫizi·) (P) seem to be a personification of flint and are probably the mythological prototype of the Black Dancers of the War Ceremony. Their noisy behavior was shocking to Monster Slayer, but it was not dangerous because their leader, a woman, had medicine in her quiver which would prevent the enemy from hearing the noise. An unexplained remark doubtless refers to the fearsome flashing of flint—' reddish light shone through her leg tendons.' Flint People were dressed in flint and protected by lightning, sunrays, and rainbows. They had arrows of heat and cold; they stole food from the gardens of the enemy. Monster Slayer had to admit that their power was greater than his (Ch. 12, *Red;* Haile 1938b, pp. 159–62).

Hawk ('atsá) (H), see *Eagles.*

Hermaphrodites, see *First Man.*

Holy Mountains, see *Mountains.*

Horned Monster (dé·lγé·d) (UP), see *Burrowing Monster.*

Horned Toad (na'aⳆó'i· ditĉiji·) (H), see *Armor, Flint,* Con. B.

Hummingbirds (dahi·tɪ̨hí) (H) and Chickenhawks were great hunters who lived together in the same camp.

Hummingbird (biṫa' 'aɣáˑḷi', ' One-whose-wings-whir ')
brought beeweed sauce to Rainboy of the Hail Chant, and
gave him a bead that tinkled like a little bell to wear around
his neck (Matthews 1897, p. 88; Reichard 1944d, p. 135).

Hunchback God (ɣáˑ'ackidiˑ) (P) is possibly so called because of the hump which represents the black bag he carries
on his back, or because he is a deified mountain sheep. Matthews defines him as ' a god of harvest, a god of plenty, a
god of mist.'

Stevenson says the hump is of clouds containing seeds of
all vegetation. Sapir's text has the hump made of rainbow.
While one group of gods was preparing the log for Self
Teacher, another group, consisting of four Hunchback gods
and two xaˑctćéˑˑóɣan—gods of seeds, mists, and cornfields—
was ritualistically preparing the pet turkey.

In all versions of the Night Chant myth, the hero was
lying in ambush for some mountain sheep, but when they
came past him, his fingers froze on the arrow and he could
not shoot. After he failed four times, the sheep threw off
their skins and revealed themselves as gods. According to
Matthews, all were Hunchback gods; Stevenson has them:
Talking God, xaˑctćéˑˑóɣan, one Hunchback, and xa'datciciˑ.
Sapir has Fringed Mouth, Hunchback God, Talking God,
and xaˑctćéˑˑóɣan. They came to the hero to teach him holy
things. They had him take off his clothes and gave him a
sheepskin to hold in his hand. When they blew on him, the
skin slipped onto him and fitted perfectly. They went off as
five mountain sheep.

The mythical description of the Hunchback God is like
that of the impersonator in the dance.

The Stricken Twins, directed by Talking God, had arrived
at a place called Where-the-sheep-trail-comes-out. The cliff

was steeply terraced. The boys heard an attractive voice, that of a Hunchback God, deep in the canyon. The crippled boy reported to his blind brother, "Here comes someone. He has horns on his head and a hump on his back. He bends over like an old man and walks slowly, leaning on a staff." The boys talked to the old man, who had them get on his rainbow; in no time they were on a much lower ledge of the cliff. There was no door, but the figure of a mountain sheep was painted on the smooth rock, and under it was a white spot. The god struck the white spot with his staff and a door opened into an empty room. Its walls were also smooth and on the wall opposite the entrance a ewe was painted; underneath it there was a blue spot. When that spot opened as a door, there was another empty room with a picture of a ram, underneath which was a yellow spot. On the opposite wall of the third chamber, to which the yellow door opened, there was a picture of rain and underneath it a black spot. When the god struck the black spot, a door opened into a room filled with people.

The cripple told his brother this was the most beautiful room they had yet visited. On the east wall, white clouds were painted and above them was a white fog; there were blue clouds and fog on the south wall, yellow on the west, and black on the north wall. On the walls were objects like the heads of Rocky Mountain Sheep which seemed alive. These had the same colors as the clouds and fog in the various directions; the head of a ram was at the east and west; that of a ewe at the south and north. From the male heads zigzag lightning darted; from the female heads, straight lightning. On each wall a large crystal illuminated the room, and with each stone there was a cure for disease. The stone of the east had a cure for blindness, that of the south one for lameness, that of the west one for deafness, and that of the north a medicine for facial paralysis. The boys felt mist and moisture as they stood there.

The gods did not drive the boys away, nor did they cure, but they gave directions by means of which the youths could obtain the wealth necessary to pay for treatment.

When the gods finally relented and helped the Stricken Twins, xaˑctčéˑóɣan said to Hunchback God, "You own all the mountain sheep. Take one over to Bat Rock and leave it there for the boys to kill." A mountain sheep came near the twins and allowed itself to be killed with their poor weapons. In this incident the Hunchback Gods seem to be in charge of the sheep, although they are not necessarily the sheep themselves (Matthews 1897, pp. 166, 245; 1902, pp. 13, 245, 157–66, 235-6, 241; Curtis, p. 104; Stevenson, pp. 278, 283; Sapir-Hoijer, p. 157, 163).

Hunger (ditcin) (B): people so called were found by Monster Slayer when he was looking for evils. Their leader was a big, fat man, though he had nothing more than the little brown cactus to eat. When Monster Slayer threatened him, he said, "If we die, people will not relish their food. They will never know the pleasure of cooking and eating nice things, and they will not enjoy hunting" (Matthews 1897, p. 131; Sapir-Hoijer, p. 129; Wheelwright 1942, p. 99).

Insects (tcoc) (P, U), the fumbling inhabitants of the lower worlds, are often mentioned as helpers. The Navaho do not believe that they are descended from these creatures but that a gradual transformation was brought about with deific aid. When associated with sorcery, insects are difficult to persuade.

be'γotcidí has been described as a deity in charge of various, especially stinging, insects. He played jokes with them on his fellow-gods, but they were his weapons when he was attacked.

The hero of the Bead Chant overcame bees and other stinging insects, thereby furnishing cures for skin diseases (Goddard, p. 127; Reichard 1939, p. 32; 1944d, p. 47: Matthews 1897, pp. 201–2).

Kicking Monster (tsé daxódzi'ɫtaɫiˑ) (UP) lived where two bluffs stood one above the other. At the rim of a narrow passage he sat with his legs doubled up. At the entrance of the passage leading to this place there was fruit of three kinds of cactus to entice people into it. The monster lay on his back, innocently pulling out his whiskers, but as soon as anyone came near, he stretched out his huge leg and kicked the stranger down for his children far below to devour. When Monster Slayer pretended to come, the monster said, "Oh! I was just stretching to get the cramp out of my leg." After Monster Slayer had pretended to pass four times, he struck the monster between the eyes again and again but, although he seemed to be dead, the body did not fall down because the hair had grown fast between the rocks. As soon as the hair was cut, the body of the old male monster fell and was fought over by his children, who waited below to consume it.

Kicking Monster had a wife and children, who, when subdued, became owls. In one version Monster Slayer pursued the smallest, who was very fast, and found him a disgusting dirty boy. Monster Slayer decreed that the boy should be the ancestor of the Paiutes, who would henceforth live a despicable and precarious life. In still another version, one child became a water animal, perhaps Water Horse, and the other became Box Turtle.

The old man's hair became a trophy. In the myth of the War Ceremony, Monster Slayer did not take a trophy, but broadcast seeds of various plants so they would grow in the vicinity where Kicking Monster had been overcome (Reichard, Shooting Chant ms.; Matthews 1897, pp. 122–3; Haile 1938b, p. 125; Wheelwright 1942, pp. 92–3).

Left-handed Thunder (U), see *Thunder.*

Left-handed Wind (U), see *Thunder, Wind.*

Lightning (H), see *Big-snake-man, Thunder.*

Little Wind (H), see *Wind's Child.*

Long Frogs (tčał nne·zí) (U) caused people to sink in a bog and pulled them down into the water. One time when Long Frogs had eaten all the flesh off a Water Monster, Monster Slayer started to burn them, but they begged and promised, "After this we won't be mean if you let us live. We will give our call just as we are doing now, but we shall be calling for rain."

Monster Slayer also encountered Big Toads (tčałtsoh), who promised him, "We shall perform rituals for rain. There will always be dark clouds as there are now."

Long Frog laid the drumstick on the basket drum at Rainboy's Hail Chant, saying, "This is my only song."

When Mourning Dove, in the War Ceremony tale, was sent to find out about two annoying old men, he returned with a story told him by Long Frog and Box Turtle. They had visited some pueblo people and had been hit with a stone ax, which merely glanced off Box Turtle's shell and killed the people wielding it. Later, they had escaped death by fire because Long Frog put it out by urinating; they had escaped boiling in a pot that Turtle had smashed; and finally they had got away when they were tossed into the water. Later these two adventurers won valuable scalps from Monster Slayer in an archery contest (Haile 1938b, pp. 129, 154–7, 165–7; Reichard 1944d, p. 89).

Louse (ya·") (B) was one of the minor evils threatened by Monster Slayer. He begged off, saying, "If you kill me, people will be lonesome. They will have no one to keep them company." Louse was allowed to live (Reichard, Shooting Chant ms.; Sapir-Hoijer, pp. 17, 129; Wheelwright 1942, p. 99).

Male God (xa·ctčé· baką', γé'i· baką') (P) perhaps means ' some male god or other.' He doubtless has different specific aspects and functions in the various ceremonies in which he appears. So far as I know, he is not a part of any of the chants to which the Shooting chants are most closely related.

Male God, paired with Talking God, is a part of a corn-planting rite of the Night Chant, probably another manifestation of Talking God (Matthews 1902, pp. 15–7, 202).

Meadowlark (tsiya·γo·ji·) (U) was a companion of Spider Woman, whom The Twins encountered on their first visit to Sun. She was commissioned by Black God to bring the plants for blackening in the War Ceremony (Reichard, Shooting Chant ms.; Haile 1938b, p. 193).

*Measuring Worm** (γósikidi·) (H), an old man, was passing the Spreading Stream as The Twins contemplated crossing it on their first visit to Sun. He wore a smooth hat with points and whistled as he walked with his arms folded behind his back. He ferried the boys safely across the stream on his long rainbow; they rewarded him with a song.

In the Hail Chant, Measuring Worm's tail had an attachment something like an icepick with which he pierced the ice shield of Winter Thunder's party. Measuring Worm possessed valuable tobacco stolen by Chipmunk, but when he found Chipmunk's tracks, he stuck his tail points into them (presumably to harm Chipmunk) (Reichard, Shooting Chant ms.; 1944d, pp. 34, 139).

Mentor (H), see Ch. 5; *Bat, Big Fly, Darkness, Talking God, Wind's Child.*

Messenger, see Ch. 5; *Mourning Dove, Shooting Star.*

Monster Slayer (na·γé·· ne·zγání) (I) represents impulsive aggression, whereas Child-of-the-water represents reserve,

---

* See footnote on page 419.

448

caution, and thoughtful preparation. Monster Slayer kills for
the future benefit of mankind; Child-of-the-water collects the
trophy and provides for its ritualistic utility.

In some tales of the monster conquest, The Twins go together; in others, Monster Slayer sometimes goes alone while
his brother watches over the warning prayerstick at home.
This prayerstick was made to glow, burn, or turn blood red
when the older hero was in danger and needed help.

After Cliff Monster had been overcome and Monster
Slayer returned home, his brother said to him, "I watched
the prayersticks all the while you were gone. About noon the
black one began to burn and I was troubled because I knew
you were in danger, but after it had burned about halfway,
the fire went out and I was glad, for I thought you were safe
again." His brother answered, "Oh! That must have been at
the time Cliff Monster carried me up and threw me on the
rocks."

In the story of the War Ceremony, First Man watched the
prayerstick which told him of the whereabouts of The Twins.
When they had brought back the trophy of Big Monster, he
gave it the power to burn when they were in danger. Monster
Slayer alone overcame Cliff Monster, and the prayerstick
merely moved a bit while he was gone. When he, again alone,
entered the home of the Eye Killers, the prayerstick was a
little scorched. After hitting Traveling Rock so that chips
flew off, he stepped on a chip with his right foot. His strength
suddenly failed him; he breathed heavily and trembled. Then
the prayerstick at home began to burn and First Man told
Child-of-the-water to go to his aid. The boy shot his zigzag
lightning arrow into the air. In a moment a healing plant
appeared just in front of the older brother. He chewed it and
rubbed himself with it; then a cloud arose and rain cooled
him. The prayerstick once more assumed its ordinary appearance, and Monster Slayer was ready to race with Traveling
Rock (Matthews 1897, pp. 117, 122; Haile 1938b, pp. 113,
123, 135, 137, 155; Reichard, Shooting Chant ms.).

Monster Slayer had led one of the war parties to an attack
on Taos for some valuable beaded scalps, the hair of two

desirable virgins. During the entire journey the party had been disturbed by two very old men, who coughed and looked as though they had no sense and ought to go home. When they turned up at the last night's camp, Monster Slayer even cursed them. Eventually they said they just wanted to look on when the party attacked. After the pueblo had been taken, a search was made for the scalps and no one seemed to have them. In the second search, they fell out of the ragged clothes of the old men. The scalps stood for the girls, and there was an archery contest between the trembling old men and Monster Slayer to decide which should have them for wives. The old men hit the target exactly and the hero's arrow fell beside the mark. He did not acknowledge his failure, but merely gave the old men a mean look.

The Stricken Twins—the blind one carrying his lame brother on his back—went from one place to another, begging the gods to help them. All refused because the children had no offering. They met Monster Slayer, his brother, and Shooting God, who offered them help but did not mention a reward. The Hunchback gods had left a sheep where the Stricken Twins could shoot it (probably with the help of Shooting God) and Monster Slayer skinned it for them and cut off pieces specified by the gods.

When The Twins visited Sun the second time, he said he was willing to help them, but this time he wanted them to return the favor: "I wish you to send your mother to the west that she may make a new home for me." Whereupon Monster Slayer, believing himself equal to any task, replied, "I will do so. I will send her there." Then Child-of-the-water reminded them both: "No, Changing Woman is subject to no one; we cannot make promises for her. She must speak for herself; she is her own mistress. But I shall tell her your wishes and plead for you."

Although it is not directly so stated in Gray Eyes' tale, the duty of rewarding his father is perhaps the reason Monster Slayer tried so hard to get Changing Woman to move.

In the tale of the Eagle Chant, Monster Slayer was domestically inclined and, as an ordinary citizen, seems to have demonstrated little power, at least to help his own malady.

450

Monster Slayer, hero of the legend, took the two ignorant girls, Whiteshell Woman and Turquoise Woman, as wives. They helped him carry out the prescriptions of the Eagle Chant, which, before he learned it, had belonged to a wizard. Monster Slayer, overcome by powers who controlled game, requested many singers to treat him and, despite offers to pay, all refused, giving no reason. At length his three brothers, Child-of-the-water, Reared-in-the-earth, and Changing Grandchild, who had been trailing him, forced the chanters who had denied him aid to give their medicines to Swallow, for he had agreed to sing for Monster Slayer. After he had been cured, the brothers told him to go back to his wives and keep out of trouble.

When Monster Slayer's work, including the subjection of the minor evils, had been completed, Sun sent a conveyance of dark clouds to take him to his new flint home in the sky. The house was provided with food in abundance; there was a comfortable bed with a pillow made of four white lightnings that would prevent bad dreams from coming true (Haile, 1938b, p. 167; Matthews 1897, p. 127; 1902, pp. 232, 242; Newcomb 1940b, pp. 53–70; Reichard, Shooting Chant ms.; 1939, Pl. XVII–XIX; Newcomb-Reichard, Pl. XVI, XVII).

Moon (tłé˙xona'ái) (P) is the weaker of the Sun-Moon pair. Little is known about the person that carries the moon. He is said to be either the maternal uncle (bidá'í) or the father of Sun. In sandpaintings, Moon is usually represented as the orb. The difference between Moon and Sun is primarily one of color—white for the moon and blue for the sun orb. The moon-bearer of the emergence picture is just like the sun-bearer, except that he is white and carries a moon and a cloud (Ch. 4; Reichard, Shooting Chant ms.; Matthews 1897, pp. 75, 80; Newcomb-Reichard, p. 56, Pl. II, XI, XVIII; Wheelwright 1942, Set II, 1).

Moth ('i˙tċ̣ahi˙) (U), see *Butterfly.*

Mountain Sheep (dibéntsah) (H), see *Hunchback God*.

Mountains, though places, are so personalized that I have classified them as deities. They may be included in lists of Holy People mentioned in formula and prayer; they have an ' inner form,' ' something which lies inside ' (bi˙ yi˙sti˙n), and stabilizes them, doubtless a counterpart of the Agate or Turquoise Man which makes a man invincible. When people in the lower worlds were forced by floods to leave, they took special care to bring tokens of the mountains with them. No Navaho conception of the world, whether in the past or the future, is conceivable without the contemporary arrangement of mountains. The mountain symbolism is due no doubt to the belief that they are homes of the gods, associated with hogans.

The outstanding mountains are discussed in Chapter 2, where the difficulty, even impossibility, of determining the precise geography is noted. Here an illustration of conflicting evidence is cited:

The provenience of the ' eastern mountain ' is much discussed by Navaho chanters, but there is no agreement. sisnádjini˙, ' the-particular-one-that-is-black-belted,' is its name. Matthews said it was Abiquiu Peak or the one next to Abiquiu, which may be Pedernal Peak.* Father Berard accepts for the Navaho the mountain identified by the Jicarilla Apache as Blanca Peak in Colorado, and Sapir-Hoijer, doubtless following his lead, also translate sisna˙djiní (their recording) as Blanca Peak. Father Berard's Navaho authorities, convinced that it was the Holy Mountain of the east, collected soil to be ritualistically employed later.

---

*Matthews and others refer to ' Belted Mountain ' as Pelado Peak, not marked with the Spanish name on modern U. S. Geological Survey maps.

On the other hand, when in 1933 the Navaho decided to have the Rain Ceremony performed, the Rain Singer conducted a pilgrimage to Wheeler Peak (sisnádijini·), where they ceremonially collected waters. They explained, however, that "although Wheeler Peak is, as we know, pretty far east, it is the right mountain." From this and other conflicting remarks, we may well exercise caution in accepting any one as ' the right ' mountain. From the Rain Singer's qualification I infer that ' too far east ' indicates Pedernal or Pelado Peak as nearest the mythical location; Blanca Peak seems much too far north. Evidence of men who started out on a ritualistic quest without suggestion from whites is a bit more convincing than that of Navaho taken on a ' scientific ' field trip. I do not by these remarks mean to imply that anyone was insincere—I mean merely to demonstrate that mythical places may be easily rationalized as ' scientifically ' correct, even though one name be assigned to several (Ch. 2; Oakes-Campbell, Pl. I, IV, V, VIII, X–XII; Haile 1938b, pp. 66–7; Sapir-Hoijer, p. 176).

Mourning Dove (xasbidi·) (H), like roadrunner and turkey, is idealized. Mourning Dove was said to report things reliably and to have no equal in speed.

Later, when he was sent to spy on Box Turtle and Long Frog, he brought back an accurate report, since he could understand the special war language. He jerked his head back and forth to imitate the enemy and has retained this, a war habit, to this day.

A pair called Dove Man and Dove Woman aided Monster Slayer and his two wives when he performed his first Eagle Chant (Ch. 16; Haile 1938b, p. 148; Newcomb 1940b, pp. 70ff.).

Needle Cactus (D), see *Cactus, Tearing Cactus.*

Never-ending-snake (t̷i·c do·n̷ihí) (UP) differs from **Big Snake** or represents him in a different guise. He is wholly evil and destroys the mind and consciousness by coiling about and squeezing his victim. He symbolizes the danger of getting into a circle, and only valuable offerings and exorcistic ritual can release a person from his embrace. Never-ending-snake overcame **Bear Man**, **Big-snake-man**, **Black Ants**, and the **Wind People** in the Big Star Chant (Fig. 19, 27, Con. C; Newcomb-Reichard, Pl. XII, XIII; Newcomb 1940b, p. 14).

Old Age (sá, sá̧cdijo·l) (B) was an old woman who walked slowly with the aid of a cane; her back was bent, her hair white, her face deeply wrinkled. According to Sapir, Old-age-lying-in-a-heap was a man, so old he could not move out of his place. He was lying like an animal, curled up, seemingly helpless. However, he was holding his stone ax, which, like **Frog's**, would destroy anyone who took hold of it. When approached, he begged for life, saying, "If you kill me, everything will stand still. There will be no births; young men will not grow older; worthless old people will not die. It is right that people should grow old and die to make place for the young" (Matthews 1897, p. 130; Sapir-Hoijer, pp. 128–31; cp. Wheelwright 1942, p. 99).

One-follows-the-other ('a̷ké· na·'a·ci·) (P) were said to be a divine couple who came together, walking arm in arm. The woman carried two ears of corn, one yellow, one white, in a turquoise vessel. They may be **First Man** and **First Woman**, since both pairs created people from corn. Commonly 'a̷ké· na·'a·ci· means simply that one person walks behind rather than beside another. Father Berard seems not to distinguish the vernacular from the ritualistic usage. In the Hail Chant, Male and Female gods are referred to as

One-follows-the-other, but the text does not mean that this was their name; it merely describes the way they walked. According to Goddard, 'ałké· na·'a·ci· were the two who sought the first person who died. Since the deceased was the first hermaphrodite child, and since First Man and First Woman had the power to wear masks, as these two people did on the journey described, it is quite possible that they are identical with the First Pair (Ch. 18; Matthews 1897, p. 136; Haile 1938b, p. 30; Sapir-Hoijer, pp. 191, 193; Goddard, p. 36; Wheelwright 1942, Set I, 4).

One-who-customarily-sees-the-fish (łó·' nêinê·l'į'į, łó·' náyinê·l'į'į) (P) was the name given to the hero's father-in-law in my version of the Big Star Chant. RM says that the hero is Monster Slayer and that the name refers to the incident of the hero being swallowed by Fish. According to the Shooting Chant, Holy Boy (Child-of-the-water) was drawn into the water by Fish. RM may be thinking of some other version of the tale, of an entirely different tale, or he may associate Holy Boy, Child-of-the-water, and One-who-customarily-sees-the-fish.

A few references seem to point to an association between One-who-customarily-sees-the-fish and the incestuous sorcerer, Deer Owner, of the Eagle and Feather chants. It may even be only a name for him or a similar character, but if there is a name, there is probably a description in some tale or other (Newcomb-Reichard, p. 39, Fig. 3; Reichard 1934, facing p. 194; 1939, Fig. 3).

One-who-grabs-breasts, see be'γotcidí.

Owls (né'écdja·') (H) are not differentiated very carefully in the literature, although they certainly are by the Navaho. According to Matthews, Eye Killers became poorwills (xo·cdódi·), which are said to sleep in the daytime and to come out at night to make things beautiful and the earth happy.

As Talking God left a council of Utes considering the fate of the hero of the Mountain Chant, Poorwill flew through the smokehole, circled around the tent four times, and flew out. Then the Utes began to nod and fell asleep.

Kicking Monster's children became various owls.

níke·ní, which YL identified as pygmy owl, is said to travel along the sides of the canyon.

nike·ní bitsilí, pygmy owl's 'younger brother,' lives in brushy places.

na·ki· do·lγoci· (ceremonial name), 'nighthawk,' lives in gulleys.

tsidi· łdǫhí, ' screechowl ' or ' elf owl,' is found in treetops.

Matthews gives a pretty description of Screechowl (tsidi·-łdǫhí):

Self Teacher met a short man who wore a skin-tight coat that was white on the chest and under the arms, and brown like the skin of a deer elsewhere. The bird does not fly off but sits and looks at a person, moving its head in every direction. It is associated with deer.

Another owl, associated with antelope, was called by the same name, but had a bluish face and skin like an antelope. YL identified the bird as screechowl.

Owls of one kind or another give information and ceremonial properties:

One came to the hero of the Night Chant and told him the formula for incense, which the gods fear.

One covered Rainboy with his (skin as a) blanket; another, on a different night, brought him a cottontail ready to eat, and covered him with his blanket.

An owl traded his medicine, aromatic sumac, with Monster Slayer for four kinds of tobacco. Owl also gave a wing feather for a prayerstick tamper.

Owl was a sorcerer who spirited a child away and taught it his lore. He is depicted as another manifestation of Deer Owner (Matthews 1887, p. 397; 1897, pp. 123, 193, 244n; 1902, pp. 169, 205; Haile 1938b, p. 125; Reichard, Shooting Chant ms.; 1944d, p. 135; Newcomb 1940b, p. 69).

Place-of-emergence, see *Sky Pillars*.

Pocket Gopher (na'azísí) (H) helped at the slaying of Burrowing Monster by digging the four protective tunnels under him.

Gopher lived under Burrowing Monster and, being small, was accustomed to use the fur from over the Monster's heart for her nest. After Burrowing Monster had been killed, Gopher warned Monster Slayer lest he be overcome by the blood, and gave him Gopher medicine, which became the War Ceremony incense. As a reward, she was given the monster's skin. According to Matthews, it was to show people of the future how the monster looked.

Gopher gnawed the roots of the tree for the winning side in the tree-pushing contest (Reichard, Shooting Chant ms.; Haile 1938b, pp. 115-7; Matthews 1897, pp. 84-5, 118).

Pollen Boy (tádídí'n 'acki˙) (P), symbol of the male generative element, is of prime importance in blessing and protective rites. He is paired with Cornbeetle Girl, one of the group, otherwise composed of birds, that brings and accompanies happiness. The names of both occur in all the formulas I have found (Newcomb-Reichard, Fig. 10, Pl. II, B, D, XXI, XXII; Wheelwright 1942, Set II, 4).

Poverty (tȩ́'ȩ́'í, té'é'í) (B) was represented by an old man and an old woman, clad in filthy, ragged garments and having no possessions. They argued with Monster Slayer, saying, "If we did not exist, people would always have to wear the same clothes and would never get anything new. If we live, things will wear out and people will make beautiful new garments; they will have possessions and look nice. Let us live to pull their old clothes to pieces for them."

Poverty will spit and throw dirt on a late riser (Matthews 1897, p. 131; Sapir-Hoijer, p. 131; Reichard, Shooting Chant ms.; Wheelwright 1942, p. 99; Hill 1938, p. 19).

Racer, see *Arrowsnake.*

Racing Gods (t̬á· dza·stí·n, ' He-simply-lies,' and 'acki· nde·sgai, ' Boy-radiating-white-streaks ') (P) are vivid examples of the ' Dirty Boy ' theme. They were treated as inferior creatures to be despised and mocked. The one is described with some detail; the other is said to be like his brother. The office of the meal sprinkler in the Fire Dance is one of great honor. Two are chosen, carefully decorated, and given wands and fawnskin bags containing meal. Since these couriers have to cover a great deal of ground in order to invite people, even strangers, the office requires speed and endurance for which only exceptional persons can qualify. The fullest version of the mythical couriers is in the myth of the Mountain Chant.

When those having charge of the chant sung over Reared-in-the-mountain on the fifth day asked for volunteers to carry out the meal-scattering, no one responded, and even though the young men were coaxed, all refused to go. At night an old woman entered the hogan where the elders were arranging the ceremony and announced, without preliminaries, "I will send my grandson as a meal sprinkler." The people were so astounded that they thought the offer a great joke. The old woman lived near by and whenever anyone visited her hogan, her grandson lay on the ground asleep. He never went out to hunt, and the people concluded he was lazy and worthless. His hair was unkempt, short, and matted; he was dirty, lean, and bent. Because of their low opinion of the boy, the people did not reply to the old woman's offer except with laughter, significant looks, or silence. After the fourth offer, the leader told her to bring in the grandson to show him off. The old woman waited until morning.

When in the morning the boy appeared among the group of singers, he was the ideal Navaho youth. His hair was thick, glossy, and so long that it fell below his knees; his legs were strong and firm; he held his head erect and walked with poise and self-confidence. His brother, no less handsome, came in and sat opposite him. The men in charge were so astonished that, without a word, they began to prepare the youths for the journey.

After careful instructions the boys walked slowly away from the hogan. Those left behind gave way once more to misgivings, saying that the young men would never accomplish their mission. The lads went out of sight just as the sun rose. Those left behind continued to make fun of the runners as, waiting, they played games. About the middle of the afternoon—ordinarily the runners do not return until night—the two couriers were seen returning, one from the north and one from the south. The people said they must have forgotten something and were coming back for it, meaning they had not even got started.

The boys entered, handed their bags to the chanter, and sat down. One pouch contained some corncakes baked in ashes that were still warm, the other some maguey jelly, proving that the couriers had reached their respective destinations, had sprinkled the meal, and received tokens of acceptance from those invited. Not until night did they tell the story of their trip, for they waited until the people who ' had no sense ' had gone out. This time they wore valuable jewelry and embroidered blankets such as the gods once wore but which man no longer sees.

Later in the evening when the guests had all arrived, a chief went among the crowd and found the old grandmother sitting humbly apart. He spoke to her: "Your grandsons have done a great honor to us. . . . Tell me, won't you, how they accomplished this wonderful deed."

The old woman explained, "They are Holy People. For many years my grandson has risen early every morning and run clear around Mt. Taylor time and again before sunrise. That is the reason people have not seen him in the daytime; he has been asleep. At the base of Mt. Taylor are numerous rockpiles, all made by my grandson, who dropped a rock every time he ran around the mountain."

The well-dressed young men, after reporting to the singers, went about the camp visiting and flirting with the wives and sweethearts of those who had mocked, and everywhere the woman fell for their blandishments. There was nothing for the men to do but sulk.

In the myth of the Stricken Twins, the Holy Ones from Red-rock-projects were said to be the best runners and acted as couriers to carry the news of the success of the boys in their attack on Awatobi. The names are not given; these may have been Red Gods (Matthews 1887, pp. 411–5; 1902, pp. 25, 256; Reichard 1944d, pp. 89–93; Haile 1943a, p. 31).

Rainboy (n̓łtsá 'acki˙), hero of the Hail Chant (Reichard 1944d).

Rat, Bushrat, Woodrat (łé'étso) (H) are not accurately differentiated in the myths. Different animals may be meant; the names are rarely given. Matthews identifies what he calls the ' bushrat ' of the Mountain Chant as *Neotoma mexicana*, commonly called ' woodrat.'

According to Sapir's informant, Rat lived in a spiny cactus. He warned the hero of the story against Owl.

The Mountain Chant myth describes Rat as a little old man who was cleaning cactus fruit. He had a sharp nose, small bright eyes, and a little mustache on each side of his upper lip.

Rainboy of the Hail Chant was helped by rats. Rat Man brought in wood, and Rat Woman, wood and a cook pot, in which she made unseasoned gruel.

Later, Rat Woman brought Rainboy various kinds of food, three of which he was warned to refuse. Finally, he ate the fourth kind of food, gruel made of yellow corn meal. She covered him with a squirrelskin blanket. Another time she brought yucca fruit baked with roasted corn, some of which he ate.

After Monster Slayer had killed Burrowing Monster, Yellow Rat, a poor wretch, nothing but skin and bones, was among the rodents who came for a reward (Matthews 1883, p. 384; 1887, p. 400; Sapir-Hoijer, pp. 43ff.; Reichard 1944d, pp. 89, 137, Shooting Chant ms.).

Reared-in-the-earth (łe·ya· ne·yání) (P), another name for Monster Slayer, originated from the afterbirth of the stronger Twin, which was buried in the ground and grew to be a man. Armored in serrated flint (pink), he helped to convince Changing Woman to move to the new home in the west.

In the story of the Eagle Chant, various singers refused to sing for Monster Slayer after he had been overcome by the Game People. Reared-in-the-earth was in the group that violently protested against the refusal of the singers to give their special medicines to Swallow, who finally consented to sing for Monster Slayer (*Changing Woman, The Youngest Brother;* Newcomb-Reichard, p. 34, Pl. XVI, XVII; Reichard 1939, Pl. XVII–XIX; Newcomb 1940b, p. 69).

Reared-in-the-mountain, hero of the Mountain Chant (Matthews 1887, pp. 387ff.).

Red God (xa·ctčé· łtcí·) (P) seems to be a particular manifestation of Racing God.

Red gods were dispatched to find the hero of the Night Chant after he had been gone unduly long.

At their home, Where-red-rock-stands-up, Red gods refused to help the Stricken Twins: "It is not our province to cure. We are the bearers of the whip, the Racing People. It is our duty to punish the runners who lose in the race" (Matthews 1902, pp. 194, 223).

Roadrunner (na·tsédlozi·) (H) is said to have been without fault of any kind (Haile 1938b, p. 193).

Rock Swallows (UP): their destruction is one of Monster Slayer's lesser exploits. The Rock Swallows were so swift in attack that even the hero's lightning arrow could not touch them. At first his flint armor protected him. Meanwhile, the warning prayerstick, guarded at home by Child-of-the-water, began to burn. The younger Twin, accompanied by Cyclone, Hail, and Thunder, hastened to his brother on a white cloud. As the birds swarmed after Monster Slayer like giant bees, all except two were killed by the storm; the survivors became useful to man (Wheelwright 1942, p. 97; cp. Matthews 1897, p. 237, 153n).

Rolling Rock (D), see *Traveling Rock.*

Round Darkness (tcaxaɫxe·ɫ didjoli·) (H) and Round Wind were called by First Man to celebrate The Twins' victory over Big Monster. They sang and danced with much spirit. Round Darkness was said to have been a dwarf (Haile 1938b, pp. 113, 252, 41n).

Round Wind (ńɫtči didjoli·) (H) informed Monster Slayer about the fierceness of Burrowing Monster (Haile 1938b, p. 113).

sa'ą na·γái, tsa'ą na·γái, see Ch. 3, "Destiny."

Salt Woman ('ácį˙ 'asdzą́˙) (P) originated in a lower world when First Man rubbed some skin from under his arm. She is said to live now at a salt lake south of Zuni. When the various creatures of the lower world turned against First Man, Salt Woman gave Water Sprinkler a double handful of salt which was supposed to explode when thrown upon the fire. The salt proved to be harmless because Black God, who had made the fire, had more power than Salt Woman and Water Sprinkler. However, the salt later given by Salt Woman to The Twins exploded with such force that it destroyed the Eye Killers.

According to Gray Eyes, Salt Woman was the sole companion of Changing Woman, her younger sister, before there were people on the earth. Salt Woman prepared rabbit broth, stirring it with her whole hand. Since it was too salty for the baby Twins, Bear Man and Big-snake-man gave them milder food, mountain and flower pollen moistened with dew. After four days the boys had grown so strong that they could eat the broth no matter how salty.

The Shooting Chant story has it that Salt Woman was glad to stay deep in the center of the earth so as to be near her children. There she has her winter home on a male mountain; she spends the summer on a female mountain.

According to tłắ˙h, she went to a place near Crystal, but, since she did not like it there, wandered until she came near Zuni. The Zuni did not like her much, yet they did not want her to leave. Eventually, she went to the salt lake near Zuni, where she told the different Indian tribes to visit her to get salt. They were supposed to dress like gods and sing either her song or that of Changing Woman. If they did, the salt would become liquid so that the people could easily reach it (Stephen 1930, pp. 88, 91–2; Reichard, Shooting Chant ms.; Wheelwright 1942, p. 113; Matthews 1897, pp. 123, 236).

Scavenger (I), hero of the Bead Chant (Reichard 1939, pp. 26ff.; Matthews 1897, pp. 195ff.).

Seething Sands (D), see *Slipping Sands*.

Shiny Wind (H), see *Wind*.

Shooting God (xa·ctčé''oltohí) (P) succeeded in persuading Changing Woman to move to the west when other armored gods had failed.

In the Night Chant, a man wearing a female costume is called Shooting God. According to Stephen's manuscript, Shooting God was a berdache. One lived at each of the sacred mountains with Talking God and xa·ctčé''óγan (Newcomb-Reichard, pp. 34–5, Fig. 4, Pl. XVI; Matthews 1902, pp. 24–5).

Shooting Star (H) was one of Night's messengers (Stevenson, p. 275).

Sky (yá dilxil) (P) is paired with Earth as the origin of all things. It is black, with the chief heavenly bodies depicted on its body, the stars and constellations and their positions differing at various times of the year (Newcomb-Reichard, p. 37).

Sky Pillars (yáya· nzíní) (H), ' Those-who-stand-under-the-sky,' had their origin in the difficulties of getting the sun into the sky. Changing Woman lit a turquoise disk with a crystal (even though up to this time there had been neither light nor heat!) and it became heat incarnate. The heavens were so close to the ' people ' that they could hardly stand upright. When the people looked up, they saw two rainbows crossed. There was so little space between the earth and sky that the heads and feet of the rainbows almost touched the heads of the people. As the people were vainly trying to raise the sun, First Man and First Woman suddenly appeared. The First Pair raised the sun somewhat by means of a sunbeam, a crystal, and a rainbow, but their power gave out before the heat was ameliorated.

Then they made two poles of turquoise and two of whiteshell, and with the four poles the twelve men at each of the four cardinal points raised the sun still higher. Even this was not sufficient to prevent burning, and the men were driven to stretching the earth by blowing, a device that finally succeeded in getting the sun into a place that allows for a satisfactory temperature. Earth's position depends upon the support of the Sky People, assigned their duty by Changing Woman. When The Twins visited Sun, he led them out to the edge of the world where the sky and earth come close together and beyond which there is nothing. Here sixteen poles—four of whiteshell, four of turquoise, four of abalone, and four of redshell—reached from earth to sky. A deep stream flowed between the party and the poles. When asked on which ones they would ascend, The Twins, prompted by Wind, chose the red poles, since they stood for war.

The earth's center (xadjí'nái, ni' ałní'') is a holy place, indicating the Place-of-emergence, which has various geographical locations, none actually fitting the description. The corresponding point in the sky is the Skyhole, the place to which Sun led The Twins when giving them their geography test of the world. It was edged with four smooth, steep, shiny cliffs of the same precious stones as the poles that supported the sky. Sun sat at the west side of the hole, the boys at the east. Even keeping their places would have been impossible, had not Wind blown up through the hole and kept the youths from slipping down through it.

The number of Sky Pillars varies.

One time First Man ground rock and broadcast it; rocks stood up in a line. Then the four People-who-stand-under-the-earth began to sing and, moving away from each other, stretched out the earth.

These supporting people are pictured in a sandpainting of the Hail Chant with the explanation that the twelve people, six males at the north, six females at the south, hold up the earth. Their names are ni' yo·tso, ' Earth-big-whiteshell,' and yáya· nzíní, ' Those-who-stand-under-the-sky.' The same kind of pillars—of reed or precious stones—hold up earth and sky.

The Wheelwright creation story describes the Earth Columns as twelve Big Winds in each direction, explaining that all kinds of winds were sent to support the sky and the stars (Stevenson, pp. 276-7; Matthews 1897, p. 113; Goddard, p. 137; Reichard 1944d, p. 103; Wheelwright 1942, pp. 66-7; 1946, p. 192).

Skypoles, see *Sky Pillars*.

Sleep (bił) (B) was found by Monster Slayer living with Hunger, Craving-for-meat, Poverty, Desire, and Want in the most sordid circumstances. To Monster Slayer's unmitigated shame, Sleep overcame him with a peaceful weapon, his finger (Ch. 5; Reichard, Shooting Chant ms.; Wheelwright 1942, p. 99).

Slipping Sands, Seething Sands (sáiłá·d) (D) were great sand dunes which looked like a range of mountains. Just as a person climbing was about to reach the top, the sand would slide and bury him. Wind himself, according to the Shooting Chant myth, carried The Twins safely across this hazard. In Matthews' version, the sands rose, whirled, and boiled

like water in a pot. The Twins passed them by reciting their
names and a formula given them by Spider Woman. In the
War Ceremony story, The Twins were protected by life
feathers, gifts of Spider Woman (Reichard, Shooting Chant
ms.; Matthews 1897, p. 110; Haile 1938b, pp. 97–9; cp. Oakes-
Campbell, p. 38, Pl. II).

Snakes (tłi·c) (U) dominate the Shooting and Wind chants.
Accounts are conflicting. Snake was one of the pets Changing
Woman gave to her people, but it does not seem to have done
much for them. One account says, "Snake and porcupine
were of no use, but were a bother because they had to be
carried along." They were at last turned loose among the
rocks.

One of Matthews' informants states that when the animals
were people, the birds and snakes built cliff dwellings, and he
asks the rhetorical question, "If they had not had wings, how
could they have reached their houses?" He thus explains why
the snakes were able to help the Eagles and Hawks lift the
boy to the sky in the Bead Chant story.

Snake was a guard at the homes of Sun, Changing Woman,
Thunder, and even of Big-snake-man.

Seeking Kicking Monster, Monster Slayer came to a mountain range where the one called Chuskai rises. Beyond lay
two huge snakes. He walked along the back of one, then
stepped from one to the other and went on. Since that time
the two snakes lie there, having been turned to stone.

Snake was forbidden in the Hail Chant (Ch. 11; Newcomb-
Reichard, Ch. VI; Reichard 1939, pp. 30, 51; 1944d, p. 41;
Kluckhohn-Wyman, Fig. 15, Pl. II, III; Matthews 1897,
pp. 81, 119, 149, 153; 1887, p. 405; Goddard, p. 173).

Spider Woman (na'acdjêi· 'esdzą́·) (U) plays a dual role;
she is sometimes helpful to man and at others a danger so

great that she has to be subdued. She is a symbol of the textile arts, having taught man weaving; she requires woven fabrics as offerings.

When the waters of the first world rose, Spider wove a web that served as a lifesaving raft. In the second world Spider Woman stole Water Monster's baby, capturing it with her web.

The Twins came upon Spider Woman on their way to their father's home the first time. They saw smoke rising from an underground house, to which a ladder with four rungs formed the entrance. There were many seats in the house. Firstborn chose to sit on one of flint, his brother on one of turquoise. In the room sat an old woman, who was very pessimistic about their venture. According to the Shooting Chant myth, when she had been overcome by The Twins, she gave them chant properties—the permanent bundle talking prayer-sticks, sometimes called the 'life feathers.' According to Matthews, she furnished also a formula that would quiet the anger of enemies.

Spider Woman was instrumental in fixing the flint and turquoise ' men ' within The Twins to make them invincible.

Scavenger of Matthews' Bead Chant encountered a Spider Woman who had a big mouth with uneven, protruding, widely separated teeth and claws like a bear's. She told him that her ' life hoops ' needed new feathers; these he procured for her from his friends, the Eagles. She said she would use them to adorn her walls. In exchange she gave him a black cane and medicine with which to fight Bees and Tumble-weeds.

In RP's Bead Chant legend, Spider Woman captured Scavenger, who was escaping from the great rain he had brought on by opening the Eagles' little blue water jars. Black God saved him. The Spider People were said to be the wealthiest of the pueblo people.

The Spider People helped the Swallows to trap Coyote after he had disobeyed the Twelve Brothers in hunting. As a reward they received pieces of his skin, which they laid on their backs, where they may still be seen.

In the Flint Chant myth, Spider Woman helped the hero through a test by stringing webs from one flint to another. With the aid of Crane's sound, dó·d, he was able to walk over the flints without injury (Stephen 1930, pp. 94, 100; Matthews 1897, pp. 109, 201–3, 232, 109n; Reichard, Shooting Chant ms.; 1939, pp. 31–4; Endurance Chant ms.; Haile 1943a, p. 117).

Spotted Thunder (U), see *Thunder.*

Spotted Wind (U), see *Thunder, Wind.*

Spreading Stream (tótšózí, tséko·*) (D) was ' as narrow as the string with which the trader ties up sugar,' but whenever anyone tried to cross it, it spread so wide that the person was destroyed.

The Twins, arriving at Spreading Stream, found their rainbow too short to span it. Measuring Worm carried them across on his long rainbow; they rewarded him with a song (Reichard, Shooting Chant ms.; cp. Haile 1938b, p. 97; Wheelwright 1942, p. 96).

Squeaking God (P), see *Whistling God.*

Stalking Antelope (UP) were among the monsters to be overcome, two females who killed women, two males who killed men. Monster Slayer found Coyote trying to subdue them with a torch made of yucca strips tied to his tail. Having lighted it, he drove the antelope toward Monster Slayer, who shot them with his lightning arrow. He plucked a hair from each tail, one from the region of the heart, one from the tip of the ear, and one from each nose. Monster Slayer threw the hairs to the ground, transforming them to

---

*This word, the name given by Father Berard and Miss Wheelwright, refers to the bottom of the arroyo, hence, its contents or stream.

deer—a buck, a doe, and two fawns (Reichard, Shooting Chant ms.; Wheelwright 1942, pp. 70, 88).

Stars (sǫ') (U) are feared by the Navaho. Big Stars figure in the Big Star and Hand Trembling chants, both Evil. Perhaps, being closely associated with First Man and Coyote, stars were never brought under dependable control. When First Man was planning the sky, he intended to arrange the stars deliberately and carefully. He had placed a few constellations nicely when Coyote passed by, pulled out some hairs, and blew them up to the sky, where they became red stars. Coyote then gathered up the rest of the stars and, by blowing, sent them up to the sky, where they now shine in the indeterminate clusters of the Milky Way (*Darkness;* Reichard, Big Star Chant ms.; Goddard, pp. 137–8; cp. Tozzer 1908, pp. 28–32; Haile 1938b, pp. 67–8).

Stricken Twins (I), see *The Stricken Twins, Child-of-the-water, Monster Slayer, The Twins.*

Striped Wind (H), see *Wind.*

Sucking God (P), see *Whistling God.*

Sun (djóxona''ái) (P), the deity, is to be differentiated from sun, a light which he carries. Usually, especially in the Shooting Chant, Sun is designated by the orb that gives life to the world. In one drypainting a person is drawn.

Sun is portrayed by numerous references to his ritualistic functions, specific details about his appearance, life, social relationships, and temperament. His symbol is a blue disk with eyes and mouth; it sometimes has horns. Surrounding the disk are colored lines that represent powers rather than persons, as do other appendages such as rain streamers, lightnings, and feathers. Sun is said to be a large person, having a huge foot, known because he left tracks when he visited Changing Woman.

In the Stephen version of creation, Sun and another young man arose in the first world. Both were carried by First Woman to the uppermost world, where the more powerful became Sun, the weaker, Moon. According to Matthews, two men, one old and gray-haired, one young, appeared when the people had given up hope of escaping from the fourth world, and created the reed through which they were delivered.

After the sun and moon had been made in the fifth world, as a great honor they were given to these men to carry, as they had endeared themselves to the people. Nevertheless, Sun and Moon exacted human lives as a reward for moving far enough away from the earth not to burn things on it.

Two contrasting impressions of Sun are developed, one held by the young women he seduced, one indicated by his behavior at home when confronted by his sky wife and those who claimed to be his children. To women he was so handsome that they dared not look at him; they bowed their heads in shame at their own inferiority. He appeared to Changing Woman suspended some two feet above the ground on a white horse with a white bridle. His clothing and moccasins were all white.

He did not ask women for what he wanted, he told them what to do, and, where the details are described, as they are for Changing Woman, guardians were only too glad to arrange for a romantic mating with Sun.

When, however, the results of these meetings, Sun's children, appeared in his home, a different side of the love story, one more familiar to Earth People, comes out. He had a permanent, acknowledged wife who was fat and jealous, and many children. Knowing that The Twins were hidden in his house, that things were not going too smoothly, he entered with blustering bravado and sometimes brought evil with him, causing an eclipse on earth. When accused by his wife of philandering, he simply did not answer.

Apparently so many children claimed him as their father that only the severest tests could prove their legitimacy.

The Twins' visit brings out details of Sun's powers. His house with its furnishings is described. Two Winds, Thunders, a pair of Snakes, and a pair of Bears guarded it. The house was of the pueblo type, white at the east, blue at the south, yellow at the west, and black at the north. In one version it is represented as a pueblo house made of turquoise standing on the shore of the great ocean; in another, it was said to be of whiteshell. Stephen describes rooms giving off from the central room as showrooms for Sun's wealth: at the south a room opened to exhibit his flocks; at the west were stores of blankets and at the north farms and corn.

Impressive features of the house were pistonlike devices made of barbed flints, which Father Berard translates ' trumpets '; the narrator said they were something like phonograph horns. The objects are mentioned in numerous myths, but details differ: Gray Eyes has the ' trumpets ' of precious stones—turquoise at the east, abalone at the south, whiteshell at the west, redstone at the north—and JS describes the houses of Sun, Moon, Black Wind, and Yellow Wind as of the same materials in the same order. On the other hand, JS says the ' trumpets ' are of flint in sunwise circuit sequence: black, blue, white, yellow, and variegated at the center. RP's description of the colors was black, blue, yellow, white, whereas Slim Curley mentioned black, blue, yellow, and pink (serrated); Matthews' and Curtis' informants say the pistons are of jewels—whiteshell, turquoise, abalone, and jet.

In most versions, The Twins were hurled against the spikes; in RP's, they were put into the machine to be ground to bits. In all cases they escaped, thereby proving they were Sun's children.

At each side of the house, and composed of the same substances, were twelve rattles, which sounded and gave forth lightning to warn of Sun's arrival. On the walls were many pegs, upon which hung clothing and weapons; on a special peg the sun was hung every night when Sun returned home.

One of Sun's cherished possessions, frequently pictured in the sandpaintings, is his tobacco pouch. It is painted blue, with blue tapering flaps, a white border of porcupine quills, and fringe of fawnhooves. The tubular pipe and the pipe cleaner, kept in the pouch, are of turquoise. A black spot at the narrow end of the pipe represents tobacco; a streak of white at the wide end represents a smoke; a rock crystal lights the pipe.

Sun had a large number of other weapons, among them lightning arrows and flint clubs and armor which The Twins obtained and adapted to ceremonial purposes with the consent and instruction of their father.

Sun's wife, who kept his permanent home for him in the east, is identified as Dawn Woman or Whiteshell Woman. She was jealous of Changing Woman and nagged her husband about his behavior when he was away from home. Nevertheless, she protected the children of the other women from her husband's wrath. In Gray Eyes' version she harped on the time and care Sun bestowed upon the boys once he had proved them his own. She even suggested that he drive them out with a club, but Sun rebuked her severely and said that ' holy things were taking place.' When he wanted the Earth Twins to restore the Sky son from the bite of Watersnake, Sun apologized to them: "My wife sometimes uses poor sense when she gets to talking."

The Sky wife and Changing Woman probably represent

the same woman in different guises. The affair with Changing Woman was permanent, since, after persuading her to move to the perfect house in the west, Sun visited her nearly every day.

The famous gamblers were Sun's children. One had won two valuable shells from the people of Blue House, a pueblo. Sun tried to get Gambler to give up the shells, but he refused until Sun provided another young man (the son of xa·ctčé'-'óγan) with the power to beat him.

Sun was vulnerable before his children. After The Twins had proved that he was their father, he pleaded with them: "My children, be careful not to ask too much of me. If I offer certain things to you, be satisfied. Do not ask me for more that I can grant."

Nevertheless, the boys, prompted by their mentor, refused everything he mentioned and asked for his most precious weapons, which they needed to kill the monsters. When they had blurted out their demand, Sun, overwhelmed by their power, bowed his head and wept. Eventually recovering himself, he explained: ". . . he [Big Monster] was your older brother. Above all others I loved him. Be sure you let me make the first move; then I shall not regret it."

Sun was even the father of Navaho enemies. Two of his pueblo daughters were called Two-dawns-arrive. Their clothing consisted of four spirally arranged layers of jewels. They were killed by the war party led by Monster Slayer and, when Sun realized this, he rose red and trembling with sorrow and anger. When, however, the jewels were offered to him, he calmed down and steadied himself (*Changing Woman, The Twins;* Stephen ms.; 1930, p. 93; Haile 1938b, pp. 91, 94, 99, 101, 105, 107; Goddard, pp. 135, 140, 142, 154; Matthews 1902, p. 213; 1897, pp. 74, 80, 83, 111, 132, 223, 239; Reichard,

Shooting Chant ms.; 1939, Pl. XVI–XIX; Newcomb-Reichard, p. 29, Pl. XVII, XX; Stevenson 1886, pp. 279–80).

Superior God (xa·ctčé· 'ayói) (P) is mischievous and only incidentally helpful. In one myth he seems to be identified with the Visionary of the Night Chant.

His offerings are described. He made a device to hinder the progress of the whirling log of the Night Chant, pretended to be friends of the Holy Ones concerned with its progress, but did not help them.

In two myths of the Night Chant, Superior God kidnaped co, the hero.

Superior God, accompanied by Talking God, met the Stricken Twins at a crater in the vicinity of Mt. Taylor and told them that anyone trespassing on the territory of Superior Gods would be whipped and would never again return to his own people (Matthews 1902, pp. 162, 181, 204, 237).

Swallows (táctčiji·) (U) are often introduced into a tale and seem to have great power, but are not thoroughly described. They helped the Spiders overcome Coyote. As a reward they got pieces of his skin, which they laid as ornaments on their wings (Reichard, Endurance Chant ms.).

Syphilis People (tcatčoc, tcétčoc dine'é) (UP) had pretty decoy women belonging to Deer Owner's family, who tempted Monster Slayer. When Monster Slayer and Deer Owner went hunting together, the deer changed to flies. Eventually, the old man turned the flies into deer. Sunbeam told Monster Slayer not to eat the meat lest he become a sorcerer. Monster Slayer accused the Syphilis People of being the vilest of venereal diseases. He was about to burn them up when they pleaded for their lives. They said that people who

475

catch these diseases have no sense anyhow, that telling and teaching the people does no good, but for this reason, they, not the Syphilis People, should be punished. They concluded, "Therefore we shall be the last resort of painful instruction. If we become extinct, the major monsters which you have already killed will come into being again." Monster Slayer thought their reasoning good and permitted them to live (Haile 1938b, pp. 131–5).

Talking God (xaˑctćéˑłtihí, xaˑctćé'éłtihí, xaˑctćé"edlí, γé'iˑ bitcei) (P) in myth frequently communicates with Earth People in words in spite of the injunction that a man impersonating him must use only gestures. To speak while wearing his mask is tantamount to suicide. As grandfather of the gods, Talking God is the tutelary of the Night Chant. He has control of dawn and the eastern sky, of rare game and corn. He gave corn to the ignorant girls of the Eagle Chant.

Talking God had a counterpart called White Body in the third world. According to one myth, Talking God was the son of Changing Woman. He was transformed from white corn, which she placed at the top of a mountain where fogs meet.

Talking God, one of the great gods, acts as a mentor, often directing mythical characters, warning them, or telling them the answers to test questions which they would not otherwise have known.

He is the only god I have found with a sense of compassion. When the gods of the White House asked Talking God why he pleaded for the Stricken Twins, he answered, "Because they are pitiable. One is blind and carries the one who cannot walk. They are poor, hungry, and helpless. It makes me sad to look at them. Someone should take pity on them. I pity all the people on the earth."

Though he has charge of many of the most valuable of earth's treasures, Talking God is modest. He acknowledges the superiority of other powers, apparently without exerting force.

His leadership is outstanding. The ordinary mode of travel is on a rainbow or sunbeam which he furnishes. He stands at the helm, so to speak; Earth People, and often the other gods, take their places behind him while xa·ctċé''óγan, his frequent companion, brings up the rear. He is acknowledged leader of the gods in the dances of the Night Chant. Though mild, he is firm, as in warning First Woman, when she threatened to bring harm to man, "You must not talk [make threats]. If you do, we will know about it." He meant that if she did he and xa·ctċé''óγan would come to man's aid. When the Eagles protecting Scavenger of the Bead Chant myth discovered he had been shot by Turkey Buzzard and Black Eagle, they said, "Talking God will never forgive us if anything happens to him and he does not return to earth."

Talking God is characterized by playfulness. He looks funny; his sound is amusing, as are his motions and actions. He may tease a person whom he actually plans to help.

The youthful hero of the Mountain Chant myth, escaping from the Utes, who had taken him captive, had come to a canyon with high, steep walls and could see no way of crossing. At daylight he saw a tall spruce tree and was thinking of climbing down it when Talking God appeared. The young man stretched out his hand to grasp it when it swayed in the opposite direction. Then Talking God looped it with a rope of lightning and drew it close to the cliff. Talking God met the Navaho at the base of the cliff and told him to go to his dwelling, but the bottom of the canyon was so rough they could not traverse it. The god blew a strong breath and at once a great white rainbow spanned the canyon. The Navaho tried to step on it, but it was soft and his feet went right through it. Talking God stood beside him and laughed.

477

Finally, after he had sufficiently enjoyed the sport, he blew
another strong breath, the rainbow hardened, and together
they crossed the canyon on it.
The god then showed the youth a small hole which he said
was the entrance to his house. The noise made by the Ute
pursuers terrified the boy because he thought he would be
grabbed at any moment. He made desperate attempts to
enter Talking God's cave home, but Talking God clapped
his hands and roared with laughter. He blew a breath and the
hole became large enough for the two to enter together.

Talking God teased the adults when The Twins were born.
He took Firstborn aside and washed him. As he did so, he
laughed and pretended he was cutting the baby in slices. The
gods challenged The Twins when four days old to a race
around a mountain. When the boys weakened, the gods beat
them with twigs of mountain mahogany. Talking God won
this race and promised to try the boys again in four days.
This time the boys won and scourged the gods. Talking God
and xa·ctčé·'óɣan laughed and clapped their hands to show
their satisfaction.

Talking God had coiled strings that, when thrown, un-
coiled and rewound, returning to his hand like a yo-yo. As the
Visionary of the Night Chant was walking along in the company of the Hunchback Gods, he suddenly disappeared.
When the gods failed to find him, they appealed to Talking
God, who brought six magic strings, each wound loosely in
a separate ball. He threw the white one to the east and it
returned, then the blue to the south, the yellow to the west,
and the black to the north, and each returned. He threw the
spotted string down and the end stuck, showing that the
Navaho was in the earth, a captive of the Winds. Another
time when the same youth disappeared from an assembly of
the gods, all five strings returned to Talking God; he then
threw his second blue string up; it stuck at the zenith and
they knew the boy had been taken to the sky.

The tale of the Stricken Twins is a moving account of
Talking God's family relationships and the effect of kinship
on the other gods.

478

When he coaxed the mother of the Stricken Twins to marry him, he induced her to keep his fatherhood a secret by telling her, "You need tell no one about it and I also promise not to tell. Such is the custom of my people [the gods]. We marry in secret and tell no one."

As the Stricken Twins, offspring of this mating, wandered from the home of one god to another begging for aid, Talking God did not admit that they were his sons. Had he done so, the gods would have helped them. Nevertheless, he watched over them, seeing to it that a few bits of supernatural food came their way, and giving broad hints to the gods about their relationship: "These children may even be your relatives."

Talking God is generally addressed as 'maternal grandfather' and he calls Earth People 'my daughter's children'; to give Monster Slayer and Child-of-the-water the assurance of full kinship privileges, he called them 'my son's children' as well. Corn Girl is mentioned as his daughter.

The versatility of Talking God's power is demonstrated by his interest in Changing Woman and The Twins when they were infants, his officiating at Changing Woman's nubility ceremony, his frequent aid to The Twins and other heroes throughout their career, his composition of songs, his gifts of jewels and prayers to the mountains.

There are various kinds of Talking gods, which may be duplicates—Whiteshell Talking God, White Wind Talking God, Rock Crystal Talking God, Mirage Talking God.

Various homes of Talking God are described, places where other gods lived with him. At one the walls of the house in the rock were of brilliantly glittering rock crystal. Another, of four rooms, was at the base of a high cliff and had a very small entrance. Another, over a large spring, was of corn pollen with a ceiling supported by four white spruce trees. The door was of daylight. Within the house rainbows were

479

stretched in every direction, making it gleam with their bright colors.

Red God is another name for Talking God, or there is, perhaps, a Red God group of Talking Gods.

xa·ctćé''edlí is another name for Talking God. It means God-turned-back-from-fright (tłá·h) (Matthews 1887, pp. 106, 140, 397–9; 1897, pp. 68–9, 82, 86, 105–6, 163–4; 1902, pp. 9–10, 190, 193, 199, 204, 222–3, 231; Newcomb 1940b, pp. 51, 55, 73; Goddard, pp. 149–53, 156, 162; Hill 1938, pp. 19, 99; Stevenson, p. 277; Haile 1938b, pp. 83, 85, 89, 93, 123, 163; Reichard 1939, p. 31; Sapir-Hoijer, pp. 171, 183, 193).

Tearing Cactus, Needle Cactus (xoc détsahi·) (D) was much like the Cutting Reeds. When a person tried to pass through them, they ran their needlelike points into him. The Twins got through them safely with the aid of their life feathers and the formula given them by Spider Woman (Haile 1938b, p. 97; Matthews 1897, p. 110; cp. Wheelwright 1942, p. 97).

The Brothers (diné na·kitšâ·da) (P), ' the twelve people,' are idealized individuals who control rare game and game lore. According to Matthews, there were eleven, who lived with and provided well for their only sister; according to my version, there were twelve. Both stories concern The Youngest Brother more than the others; the life of the older ones is suggested rather than revealed. One was named Reared-in-the-earth by the Holy Ones because they had hidden him in the earth to spy upon his sister. This name, which was given also to a counterpart of Monster Slayer for other reasons, suggests that The Brothers may be duplicates of The Twins. There is reason to conclude that all are children of Sun and Changing Woman.

In my version of the myth, The Brothers fear Coyote; in Matthews' version, they openly flaunt him. Although they were destroyed in the contest with Coyote, Changing Woman restored them; their remark puts them in the class of intermediaries: "We do not visit the people, but we stand on the mountains and watch them."

The twelve snakes on each side of the center of the Grinding Snakes' painting are said to represent the Twelve Brothers, as are twelve Medicine People on each side of the Hole-of-emergence in an unpublished painting (Matthews 1897, pp. 92–9, 103, 149, 226; Reichard, Endurance Chant ms.; 1939, Pl. XV; Newcomb-Reichard, Pl. IX; Huckel ms.).

The Stricken Twins (I) are heroes of the Night Chant, sons of Talking God and an Earth Maiden. They represent The Twins in a form the opposite of that in the myth of creation and of the Shooting Chant. Instead of being helped by merely appealing to the gods, they were refused help again and again. Originally poor, they were made helpless; one became lame, the other, blind. They had no powers at all, but they had perseverance. Their struggles and persistence eventually gave Earth People the Night Chant (Matthews 1902, pp. 212–68).

The Twelve Brothers (P), see *The Brothers, The Youngest Brother.*

The Twins (I), children of Sun, were born that men might live. They may be put into any category of supernatural personages except the evil ones. The attributes that appear most often and characterize them best show them as intermediaries between god and man; yet they are major deities appearing with Talking God and xa·ctćé''óγan, and indeed, in some respects more powerful than Sun, for they challenge his pet creations and he ' bows his head before them.' Although they possess tremendous power—that of their respected mother, Changing Woman, that of their dynamic father, and the combined powers of all Earth and Sky creatures, deific and humble, even the power of the subdued evils—they walk with men and are sometimes called ' Earth People.' They belong, therefore, in every realm; they are the personification of all conceivable power of the universe.

There is disagreement concerning their parentage, strange as it may seem, on their mother's side, for the Navaho seem not to doubt that these wonderful boys were fathered by Sun. The various stories agree that Monster Slayer, at least, was the ' real ' child of Changing Woman and in many tales they are Twins. Others make Child-of-the-water the son of Changing Woman's sister, Whiteshell Woman, or perhaps another. Kinship terms of the divine genealogies do not settle the question, since both boys, even in the myths that make them twin sons of Changing Woman, call her ' mother ' or ' maternal grandmother.' If the weaker twin was not the direct, he was the collateral son of Changing Woman, and he looks to her for her powers as if she were his ' real ' mother. The mother's sister feels that her sister's child is as close as her own and addresses it by the same kin-terms; of primary interest is the close clanship.

The Twins have many names, among them Reared-in-the-earth and Changing Grandchild; these, as well as other names, indicate manifestations of Monster Slayer and Child-of-the-water somewhat different from the usual ones. For example, Monster Slayer is expected to be warlike; Reared-in-the-earth is his threatening manifestation, a bully; Holy Man and Holy Boy are nearer Earth People than are The Twins.

I had come to the conclusion that the theory of multiple

selves, although not quite proved, was justified, when I found
in RP's story, dictated to Sam Day in 1924, the statements:
"Holy Man is the same as Monster Slayer; Holy Boy is the
same as Child-of-the-water" and "Changing Woman was the
mother of Holy Man, Holy Woman, Holy Boy, Holy Girl,
and Monster Slayer was her son in an earlier existence."
Firstborn and Secondborn, Gray Eyes' first names for the
boys, are called Holy Man and Holy Boy by RP. In a long
discussion tłá·h said, "Changing Woman and Whiteshell
Woman are two names for the same person. Monster Slayer,
Reared-in-the-earth, and Came-down-on-a-sunbeam (bił
najno·ltłijí) are three names for the same person. The younger
boy was called Child-of-the-water, Changing Grandchild
(tsói nádle·hé*), and One-cuts-around-it (nêidigicí). The
afterbirths of the two children were buried in the ground. They
did not die, but grew supernaturally. Since the afterbirth of
Firstborn was a part of him, how could it be anyone else?
He was called Reared-in-the-earth because he grew underground. The second afterbirth became Changing Grandchild"
(Ch. 4).

Other names are obvious or explained by mythological
events. Dress and characterization, as well as name, denote
the manifestation. Compare, for instance, Monster Slayer in
Sun's House, The Twins in Armor, and Holy Man and Holy
Boy.

Soon after they were born the gods made cradles for The
Twins similar to the one in which their mother had been
found.

As The Twins grew miraculously, Talking God made them
bows and arrows; when very young they became acquainted
with the methods of the monsters' spies. Events led to adventures which included escaping dangers on their way to Sun's

*There is disagreement about the translation of this word and I have accepted
the one most commonly used, since the authority for it is as good as any.

house, passing tests given them by Sun, and proof that they were indeed his children. Assured of Sun's aid, they systematically conquered one monster after another. They made a second visit to Sun—this is the theme of an unrecorded chant myth, perhaps that of the Wind Chant—and, as a result, overcame numerous minor evils. When this work was done, The Twins did all they could to persuade Changing Woman to move to the west and finally succeeded. They eventually went to live at Where-the-rivers-flow-together (tó'óxe·dlî'ni'), whither people used to go to offer prayers to them.

Even a summary of the scenes in the life of The Twins would be unduly long, for the narration covers many pages in the literature. Each episode has some function in the ceremonies; many illustrations have been given throughout this work (Reichard 1939, pp. 15, 38, Pl. X, XVIII, XIX, XXIV; Huckel ms.; Haile 1943a, p. 34; Matthews 1897, pp. 105, 112, 134; Pl. IV, VII; Goddard, p. 156; Newcomb-Reichard, p. 46, Pl. XIV–XXVII, XXXIV).

The Youngest Brother (I) is the hero of the Endurance Chant, the humble one become great. He is called náke·ctcą'í, ' Disgusting Eyes ' or ' He-has-matter-in-his-eyes,' a name Matthews says is general for the youngest boy of a family. He says also that the youngest brother is the choice for a chanter since the Navaho believe his mind and memory are best, a remark not corroborated by mythical ideal or practice. The Youngest Brother is also called 'acki·tcil, ' Dwarf Boy,' a name that contrasts his unfavorable appearance with the greatness of his final achievement.

He was left in a hole in the ground to spy on his sister, Changing-bear-maiden, and Coyote. He learned their lore and witchcraft secrets, which they exchanged while indulging in sexual excess. After Coyote had been killed and the sister finally discovered the little boy, she insisted on delousing him as a mark of affection. As she was doing this, Dwarf

Boy, by watching her shadow, discovered that she was rapidly becoming a bear. By means of her knowledge, acquired while he was hidden, he eventually overcame her.

The text of the Flint Chant says that Changing-bear-maiden's Youngest Brother was Monster Slayer; the recorder says it cannot be. And in a note, Reared-in-the-earth is said to be her youngest brother. These are doubtless merely different names for the same person—The Youngest Brother is a manifestation of Monster Slayer (Reichard, Endurance Chant ms.; Matthews 1902, pp. 170, 312; Haile 1943a, pp. 127, 295, 98n; 310, 108n).

Throwing Monster (tsé nenáxa·li·) (UP), see *Cliff Monster.*

Thunder ('i·ṅi') (U), an evil placated only with difficulty, is graphically represented as a kind of bird. When Reared-in-the-mountain visited Thunder, he found a man almost completely bald, with only a little tuft of hair above each ear.

In many Indian languages one word stands for both 'thunder' and 'lightning,' but the Navaho distinguish them: 'i·ṅi' is 'thunder, that-which-moans-indefinitely,' a form emphasizing sound, whereas the words for 'lightning' stress light and form. 'atsinltłic is 'zigzag lightning,' xadjilgic 'forked lightning,' and xatso'olγa·ł 'flash or straight lightning.'

Lightning is prominent in the Shooting Chant, which counteracts the effects of things that move with lightning speed, often in a zigzag fashion—lightning, arrows, and snakes. The contest between Dark Thunder and Winter Thunder is one of the main themes of the Hail Chant, and Winter Thunder is an important character of the Flint Chant.

According to Stephen, Thunder was created in the first world by First Woman from a bit of her scalp skin. He was later sent naked to guard the home of Water Monster at the east, where he was given a garment and hat, both of feathers, representing forked-lightning armor.

Gray Eyes' myth describes Left-handed Thunder, Winter Thunder, Spotted Thunder, Left-handed Wind, and Spotted Wind as ' powerful ' or supernatural, whereas the others are called ' Earth People.' JS says Winter Thunder is not represented in sandpainting because "he is a mean one; to draw him would bring trouble" (cp. Ch. 6).

A singer of the Rain Ceremony should not be paid with animals because, if he were, lightning might strike them. The Thunder People, who accompany rains, are boys just like the Navaho; they get careless and shoot animals and people.

Thunders have power to find things. Because Yellow Thunder knew every inch of space in the clouds, he was sent to hunt for Holy Boy, who had disappeared when he was seized by Fish.

When the brothers of the Visionary, seeking him, lost his trail at the river where he had entered the whirling log, they said, "Only the Thunder People, only those who dwell above in the clouds, know where our brother has sunk beneath the river." Thunder People then began to signal by means of lightning and, when they had located the boy, drove a rainbow stake into the river to show the gods where to look for him (Newcomb-Reichard, pp. 21, 39, 61-2, Pl. XXIX, XXXIII; Reichard 1939, frontispiece, Fig. 6, 7, 8; Matthews 1887, p. 405; 1902, p. 175; Stephen 1930, pp. 88-9; Hill 1938, p. 74).

Toads (U), see *Frogs, Long Frogs.*

Tracking Bear (cac na'aɫka·hi) (UP), a monster from whom there was no escape, was born because a chief's daughter abused herself with a smooth stone and a piece of leg sinew. He lived in a cave in the mountains.

Monster Slayer, pursued by Tracking Bear, was protected by the rattle of a slim-leaved yucca fruit held in his left hand and some twigs of hard oak in his right. He shot the monster, cut off its claws and large canine teeth, and took the gall and windpipe as trophies. In one version, the nipples became pinyon nuts, half of a piece of fat cut from around the tail ran off as a bear, the other half came toward him as a porcupine. In another version, Monster Slayer cut the head in three pieces: one became the broad-leaved yucca, one the narrow-leaved yucca, and one the mescal. People are now forbidden to eat bear, though they may eat porcupine.

Twelve Tracking Bears helped Deer Owner, the sorcerer. Self Teacher of the Night Chant killed them all.

The relationship between Tracking Bear and Changing-bear-maiden is not clear; they seem to be distinctive. On his way to kill Tracking Bear, Monster Slayer met the Maiden and on the way back he killed, then restored her. The transformations of the Endurance Chant have a certain similarity to those of Tracking Bear. Some results of throwing away Changing-bear-maiden's body-parts are not mentioned in Matthews' version of the tale (Haile 1938b, pp. 77, 127; Matthews 1897, pp. 124–5, 189; Wheelwright 1942, p. 98; Reichard, Endurance Chant ms.).

Traveling Rock (tsé na·γái) (UP) had as another name ' The-one-having-no-speed ' ('ádin djá·dgo). If he saw a person in the distance he would start in pursuit. If the person stood still, Traveling Rock would pass him, then return and roll over him, cutting him to death. As Monster Slayer circled this creature, planning how to attack it, Coyote came up and offered to help. He struck the monster with a heavy rock. Then Monster Slayer clubbed Traveling Rock four times. Pieces flew off it in every direction and became various kinds of rocks, now ground for sandpainting pigments. The bone became white rock; the flesh, blue pigment; the hair, black coloring matter; the mouth and blood, red pigment; the intestines, yellow ocher. All parts of the creature's body that had moisture—urine, tears, mucus, and perspiration—became wet spots caused by moisture oozing from rocks.

According to Matthews, Traveling Rock lived in a lake and escaped Monster Slayer three times by rolling into the water. The fourth time he appeared under the water gleaming like fire and surrendered. He promised Monster Slayer to cause rivers to flow; he became Water Monster.

Because he stepped on the chips that flew off Traveling Rock, Monster Slayer was in such great danger that the warning prayerstick left with First Man began to burn. As his strength failed and he breathed with difficulty, his twin brother caused a plant to spring up near him and rain to fall upon him, whereupon he revived (Reichard, Shooting Chant ms.; Matthews 1897, p. 125; Haile 1938b, p. 138).

Turkey (tąji·) (H) is featured in the emergence of the people from the fourth to this world. He was the last to take refuge in the reed, and when he gobbled it was a sign to the people that he was in imminent danger of drowning. The waves washed the end of his tail; consequently, today his tail feathers are marked with white.

To Turkey is accredited the gift of seed for domesticated plants, including corn, although corn existed in the earliest conceivable world. In the Night and Feather chants, Turkey is associated with the hero and theme of the whirling log.

The boy of the story, repudiated by his family, tried to make a conveyance out of a log so he could journey by water. He did not succeed, but the gods came to his aid. His niece had a pet turkey which the gods told him to take along. Later, when he was all alone and nearly dying of homesickness, the turkey was his great comfort. It dropped seeds of corn, pumpkin, watermelon, muskmelon. and beans from its wings, and taught him agriculture.

Through Turkey the association of game (hunting) and agriculture is emphasized, for actually Turkey's owner exchanged his knowledge of agriculture with that of the sorcerer, Deer Owner, and obtained the game animals for the Navaho. Turkey is treated in the literature as whites treat a remarkable dog. He is a pet who understands, remains faithful, comforts his master in hours of loneliness, and eventually leaves him with precious knowledge. The hero of the Feather Chant apotheosizes his pet in a beautiful lament.

Turkey made his master's long dangerous journey comfortable, covering him with a wing at night to protect him from cold (Matthews 1897, pp. 164ff., 172, 181, 218, 38n; 1902, pp. 171ff., 186; Sapir-Hoijer, p. 29).

Turkey Buzzard (dje·có") (U) is allied with Crow, Magpie, and other carrion-eating birds. Monster Slayer succeeded in overcoming Turkey Buzzard, who offered his feathers as the soot for the War Ceremony blackening (Ch. 4; Haile 1938b, pp. 95–7, 193).

Turquoise Boy (do·tłiji· 'acki·) (P) appears in a curious description by Sandoval:

In the third world, at the east side of the eastern mountain, lived Turquoise Boy, with twelve male companions and the Mirage People. After First Man had decreed many things about this third world, including the months and seasons, he said to Turquoise Boy, "Step inside the sun and put the reed flute with twelve holes under your shirt. Let the Mirage People step inside with you to keep you invisible to Earth People." Turquoise Boy agreed and said that whenever he passed by he should be recompensed by the death of a person. Whiteshell Boy was put into the moon for the same purpose.

There is perhaps some connection between this happening and the gift of the agate or turquoise ' man ' Sun gave The

489

Twins, represented by the pollen ball in the Shooting Chant (*Pollen ball*, Con. B; Goddard, pp. 128, 135).

Turquoise Woman (P), see *Whiteshell Woman.*

Twelve Brothers (P), see *The Brothers.*

Visionary, hero of a form of the Night Chant (Matthews 1902, pp. 159ff.).

Want (la·na·) (B), see *Sleep.*

Water Horse (té·lį·) (U), depicted in sandpainting and occasionally referred to in myth, was said to be Water Monster's pet; the name means literally ' deep-water-pet.' He was the guardian of Water Monster's home.

When The Twins were about to visit Hanging Cloud, the assembly which was to consider the matter of originating chants was announced by Water Monster and Water Horse, and was held at their home (Newcomb-Reichard p. 62, Pl. XXIX, XXXIII; Matthews 1897, p. 168; Reichard, Shooting Chant ms.).

Water Monster (té·xo·łtsó·di·) (U) is said to look much like an otter with fine fur, but has horns like a buffalo. The young look something like buffalo calves, but have spots of all colors, yellow hands, and a generally strange appearance. In sandpaintings Water Monster resembles Thunder, but has an elongated body. Monster Slayer transformed parts of the subdued Traveling Rock into Water Monster, who promised to keep mountain springs open and rivers flowing.

Water Monster was a character of the lower worlds.

Spider Woman stole Water Monster's child in the second world and it has been lost to this day.

Water Monster kept following the people to get back his child. The people made Spider give it back and Water Monster returned to the world below.

Water Monster is everybody's friend.

After the separated men and women agreed to live together again, a woman and her two daughters were left behind. The men promised to fetch them the next morning, but the women were so eager they jumped into the water. The mother drowned and the daughters were seized by Water Monsters. The people, aided by White Body (Talking God) and Blue Body (Water Sprinkler), went under the waters to the home of Water Monster. Coyote sneaked along. The monster refused to return the girls and Coyote stole two of his children, concealing them under his robe. He thereby caused the floods that drove people out of the fourth world.

Water Monster represented a large group of Water People who grabbed Self Teacher as he traveled in the whirling log. He defied Water Sprinkler, who came after the youth, but gave up to Black God when he set fire to the waters. An incident of the War Ceremony, in which Coyote and Owl sing, represents the conquest of Water Monster by Monster Slayer. In another version, Monster Slayer, attacked on his way to Sun's home, overcame Water Monster with a prayer. When I first wrote of sandpaintings I called this creature Water Ox, because I thought the horns distinguished him from Water Horse. The name was unfortunate, for horns do not characterize, but symbolize, power. The name means ' One-who-grabs-in-deep-water ' (Newcomb-Reichard, p. 62; Matthews 1897, pp. 73–7, 168–70, 212, 8n; 232, 110n; Wheelwright 1942, p. 55; Stephen 1930, pp. 100–1; Goddard, p. 131; Haile 1938b, pp. 127–8).

Water Sprinkler (tó niṅili·, tó neinili·) (P) often accompanies Black God, but he appears too with Talking God. Water Sprinkler, said to be the ' same ' as Blue Body of the fourth world, is the rain bringer and water-carrier of the gods. The jar of collected waters is his symbol in story and sandpainting, though, curiously enough, he does not carry it in the masked impersonations. He controls rain and waters. He causes rain by sprinkling the collected waters in his jar in the four directions. He can separate and walk through deep or underground waters.

In the Night Chant, he is impersonated as a clown. His clothing is of inferior quality because he 'might get wet.' He is usually out of step with the other dancers. He gets in their way, peers about while the others concentrate on song and steps, moves away to inspect little things among the audience, or sits on the ground with his hands clasped around his knees and rocks his body to and fro. Sometimes he dances with the group, concentrating so seriously that he does not notice they have left the dance place; then discovering that he is alone, he runs after them as fast as he can go. Sometimes he carries the skin of a small animal which he drops and pretends not to notice. Suddenly he hunts everywhere for it in great agitation, although it lies in plain sight. When, after much tomfoolery, he finds it, he jumps on it as if trying to kill. At length he lifts it like a heavy burden and carries it away on his back. He is said to act like this because he is pleased with what is being done in the ceremony.

One of Water Sprinkler's duties, besides separating deep waters, is to extinguish fire made by Black God; in addition, he is often sent to investigate things in the water. He went to see what stopped the whirling log at an eddy and found a dam, but could not find the people who had made it. When the Fringed Mouths discovered it had been the Flat Tails, he helped to negotiate with them. When the log stopped again, Water Sprinkler found the people who had made the dam.

Water Sprinkler taught the Visionary of the Night Chant how to prepare and preserve the products of his garden.

Nearly all the gods officiate in some capacity at the bath rite of novices. At one of Rainboy's baths, numerous gods participated: the yucca roots had been pounded on one side and they were supposed to stand upright. Water Sprinkler volunteered to hold them up. Changing Woman made suds while Talking God sang, Water Sprinkler poured water into the basket, and Changing Woman removed the yucca roots.

Water Sprinkler lived at Big Willow, a long distance from Talking God's home in the canyon, but when anything happened that concerned them both, they met for consultation in between (Matthews 1897, pp. 68, 166, 168, 170; 1902, pp. 29, 175, 178, 180, 189–92, 208; Curtis, p. 106; Reichard 1939, p. 31; 1944d, p. 79).

Water Woman (tó 'asdzá·n) (P) lives in the water and presides over all small tributaries. Rain is her child (Stephen ms.).

Water's Child (tó biyájí) (H) is said by Father Berard to be spring water and by Matthews to be the splash of rain falling into a quiet pool (Haile 1938b, p. 254, 98n; Matthews 1902, p. 311, 22n).

Whipping God (P), see *Red God*.

Whirlwind (niyol) (U) is a common phenomenon in the Navaho country. If a person sees one coming toward him, he may rush toward it and say "s-s-su!" (the Navaho equivalent of "Scat!") and the whirlwind will turn in the opposite direction and subside.

Whirlwind and Flint Boy helped Youngest Brother when he was hidden in the fireplace, watching Changing-bear-maiden and Coyote. They made tunnels for him to hide in, gave him weapons and the monitors, Wind and Darkness (Matthews 1897, p. 101).

Whistling God, Sucking God, Squeaking God (xa·ctčé·-'idiłtṣǫ·si·) (U) is quite well described by Matthews. He gets his name from the sucking noise which the Navaho compare with that of a mouse. He has a black face and dwells in a cave in which there is a white rainbow; he is considered 'bad.'

He joined Superior God in hindering the progress of the whirling log.

Whistling Gods released the cave trap which had caught the Stricken Twins. These gods moved very fast and carried a four-stranded yucca whip. One of them told the Stricken Twins that every one who came to their house, even the gods, must be whipped; naturally they had few visitors.

Offerings are described for Whistling God.

There are some hints that Whistling God may be related to Wind (Sapir-Hoijer, pp. 177, 185, 224–7, 511, 93n; Matthews 1902, pp. 181, 215, 236).

White Body (P), see *Talking God.*

White Goose (tcį·cłgaihí) (P) was an important and respected (feared) member of Winter Thunder's party in the Hail Chant. When the party had been brought under control and Rainboy was observing his period of restriction after the ceremony, White Goose brought him a dish of food made of parched corn and pinyon nuts, and spread over him the blanket of Old Age (Reichard 1944d, p. 135).

Whiteshell Boy (P), see *Turquoise Boy.*

Whiteshell Woman ('asdzą́· yo·łgai) (P) and Turquoise Woman have been considered in the characterization of Changing Woman. There can be no doubt that in some situations the three names stand for the same individual (tłă·h and JS say they are the same). However, in some cases Whiteshell Woman seems to be distinct.

According to Stevenson's fragment of the story of The Twins, Whiteshell Woman was the sister of Changing Woman, who The Twins believed was their mother, although she was really their mother's sister. When they journeyed to the east, they found the house of Sun's wife, which is of whiteshell. It is impossible to tell whether this wife was the same woman who, living on the earth, advised them to go to Sun, or whether there are more than one of a kind. However this may be, she was angry at Sun when he returned at night, and questioned him about his behavior on earth, an attitude stereotyped for Sun's sky wife.

After the creation from the stone images, Whiteshell Woman lived with Changing Woman (who, because she was created at the same time, was her sister) on Whirling Mountain, and was the mother of the younger 'Twin,' Child-of-the-water. Whiteshell Woman figured in the life of the children only in a minor capacity. One day, after the children had been discovered and Big Monster had been deceived by Changing Woman, Whiteshell Woman went to the top of a hill to look about and saw a number of monsters hurrying in the direction of their home. She reported to her sister, who raised such a storm that the monsters had to turn back. When Changing Woman was ready to depart for the west, Whiteshell Woman chose to go to La Plata Mountain. For five days she wandered about, consumed with loneliness, until Talking God and the other gods took pity upon her and created more people from corn. Perhaps to indicate that this is a secondary or subsidiary creation, the text continues: "No songs were sung and no prayers were uttered during the rites, which were all performed in one day."

Whiteshell Woman took the young man and woman to her hogan, which has since become a little hill. She married Corn Boy to Heat Girl and Corn Girl to Mirage Boy, who started new lines of descent. Their story helps to explain the origin of the Navaho clans. Sometime later Talking God came to Whiteshell Woman and spoke secretly to her. She slept with a little girl who was her favorite. After the second visit of Talking God, she said to the child, "I am going to leave you. The gods of tséγi' have sent for me, but I shall not forget your people. I shall often come to watch over them and be near them. Tell them this when they waken."

The next morning the people looked for her in vain. They believed she had gone to tséγi' where she stayed for a time before she went to La Plata Mountain to dwell forever in the house of whiteshell that had been prepared for her. The little girl had a dream in which Whiteshell Woman came to her and said, "My grandchild, I am going to La Plata to dwell. I would take you with me for I love you, were it not that your parents would mourn for you. But look always for me in the gentle rain when it comes near your dwelling, for I will be in it."

In the Eagle Chant, Whiteshell Woman is the sister of Turquoise Woman, both created by Changing Woman from epidermis rubbed from under her breast. Theirs, like the story of all these primordial women, is a tale of wandering and hiding to escape monsters, of a quest for food meagerly rewarded, and of incredible loneliness. Eventually Talking God and xa·ctčé·'óγan gave them corn. Monster Slayer visited their camp and taught them the use of game, eventually taking them to his home as his wives. He showed them how to cleanse themselves ritualistically and gave them beautiful clothes. He provided them with long hair and eyebrows, bright eyes, and smiling mouths.

The rivals of the wives were Corn Maidens, wily pueblo girls who were really a decoy to entice Monster Slayer into the home of wizards who had control of the game and knew the secrets of eagle catching. When he had overcome these old men and learned their powers, he returned to his Navaho wives, the girls of the mountain. Later, they all started forth on interminable wanderings to place eagles in the Navaho country and to make the Eagle Chant a success by repeatedly performing it. As a part of it, these women were instrumental in originating the rites of building the ceremonial hogan. They finally went to one of the sacred mountains and Monster Slayer went to his old home.

The Corn Maidens, who with their urban pueblo tricks won Monster Slayer away from Whiteshell Woman and Tur-

quoise Woman, looked exactly like them, and it was only by
their bold manners that they could be distinguished from
the Navaho girls. Here, then, is an instance of subidentifi-
cation: Changing Woman made two girls who were close
models of herself and they were for a long time superseded by
two other girls sent by Deer Owner who were their replicas
(Stevenson, p. 279; Matthews 1897, pp. 105, 108, 135-6, 139,
Newcomb 1940b).

Wind (n̊łtči) (H), the fourth guardian of Sun's house, is a
character with many traits. The reed of emergence from the
second to the third world had four holes, each guarded by a
different-colored Wind. Wind represents the flute and other
wind instruments.

One of Wind's functions is to give life (motion). Little
Winds, crossing inside the newly made bodies, enabled the
Navaho to stand up, and body hair to grow out of their pores.
The Winds conducted co to the homes of various gods where
he was accepted. Then one of the Wind People said to him,
"Henceforth you will be one of the gods. You have breathed
them in. They will be in the ends of your toes, in the ends of
your fingers, and all through your body."

Wind, as the preceding paragraph suggests, may be personified. The appearance of Wind People is mentioned incidentally in the Hail Chant: "All the Wind People looked
exactly alike with their curly hair hanging down." An odd-
looking headdress in a painting (Bush Collection) represents
Wind's curly hair. The sandpainting of Reared-in-the-mountain's visit to Snakes' home depicts Wind, said by Matthews
to be a γé'i·, who conducted the hero thither. The picture is
simple, without distinguishing features. Wind People had a
home with four rooms deep in the ground where Reared-in-
the-mountain hid during a fierce hailstorm.

Wyman illustrates four Wind People in a sandpainting;
since they are armored with flint, the picture does not show

the typical Wind features. The only distinguishing characteristic is the lightning on their bodies. Without the Wind Chant
story it is impossible to read the symbols.

In contrast to his destructive or mischievous characteristic, Wind is said to be without fault. Winds performed
many beneficial functions.

After Cicada had won the earth from the birds, Winds
dried up the earth, then stretched it by pulling the mountains away from its center so that Sun was far enough away
to make the temperature bearable. Left-handed Wind, aided
by Striped, Spotted, and Shiny Winds, was the leader of this
group.

Spotted and Pink Winds lived Beyond-the-sky.

After Holy Boy had been destroyed by Bears, the Wind
People, helped by the ants, restored him.

Even Gambler's guardians despised him. They petitioned
Wind to blow hard so as to give them an excuse for not keeping watch when he was in danger, and thus Wind helped
defeat him. Among other things, Wind won two pretty wives
from his opponent.

Wind has lifting or supporting power. When the gods,
carrying the whirling log containing Self Teacher, began to
fag and threatened to let go, the Winds helped so that they
were able to convey it to the river.

When Sun took The Twins to the skyhole where he paused
to test them on the geography of the world, they would have
slipped down had not Winds blown up through the hole and
assisted them to hold on.

Sometimes the Winds drew people into their home. They
pulled co down into their dwelling and deprived him of his
reason. After Talking God had restored him, one of the Winds
took him to visit the gods who lived in tséγi', an event that
showed no ill will.

Winds dragged people into the mouth of Bony Bear.

As mentors Big Fly and Wind are closely related. Dark and Blue Winds were sometimes substituted for Big Fly. For this reason it seems reasonable to differentiate the Wind mentors from the Wind gods or people.

The Youngest Brother was given Wind at his right ear to warn him of the approach of danger by day, Darkness at his left ear to warn him of danger by night.

When the Navaho were wandering from the west, some people who had seemed friendly to them followed to attack them. A great wind arose and warned their pet bear so that he scared off the intruders.

Wind cautioned a hero against eating the food of people who wished him ill lest he be transformed and never see his relatives again.

Wind conducted Reared-in-the-mountain to the homes of Big-snake-man, Thunder, and the other potentially dangerous gods.

As a reporter, Wind is paired with Darkness, but the latter is perhaps a shade more powerful because he can travel without making a noise. Both—Darkness, who was sent, and Wind, who went voluntarily—searched well the mind and body of Gambler in order to learn his attitude about giving up the precious stones to Sun. They both discovered and reported back that he was telling the truth when he said he was sorry he had refused to do so.

Wind, like Big Fly, reports without considering whether news will have good or bad effects. Wind children heard Corn Man enumerate the qualifications required of the man who could marry his niece and reported them to Coyote.

Wind gods are connected with Whistling God; perhaps he is another manifestation of Wind (Stephen 1930, p. 101; Goddard, p. 147; Matthews 1887, pp. 402, 405, Pl. XV; 1897, pp. 83, 85, 101, 113, 151, 166, 223; Reichard 1944d, pp. 104–5, 151; Shooting Chant ms.; Kluckhohn-Wyman, Fig. 15; Huckel ms.; Sapir-Hoijer, pp. 147, 177; Haile 1938b, pp. 79, 127, 147).

Wind's Child (ńłtči biyájí) (H) advised Rainboy when he raced with Frog.

First Man, First Woman, Salt Woman, and Coyote lived at Rumbling Mountain, where Wind's Child and Sunbeam kept them informed about happenings in the world.

Wind's Child carried news of the killing of Water Monster to the Owl People, who feared the monster.

When the Corn Maidens came of age, their brother announced the conditions of their marriage to various spirits: whoever was to have them must avenge the death of their relatives in the earlier slaughter by the Taos Indians. The Wind children who played about the fireplace had first reported the eligibility of the girls and now announced the qualifications of their prospective husbands (Reichard 1944d, p. 27; Haile 1938b, pp. 83, 127, 147).

Winter Thunder ('i·ni' djiłgai) (U) is the jealous husband, his wife the decoy woman, in Rainboy's life and that of Holy Boy, hero of the Flint Chant.

The wife lived in a white house—presumably a description of Winter Thunder's home—at the middle of which a rainbow was strung. The door had a rainbow border. Inside hung another rainbow, and there was forked lightning like a blanket with a pattern of fire. There were numerous turquoise and whiteshell ornaments. The woman's white face, dark eyes, and subtle smile attracted Rainboy. When he, overcome with shame at his poverty, tried to leave, she drew him back four times—with a flash lightning, a rainstreamer, a forked lightning, and a rainbow. The rainbows referred to here are the so-called ' white rainbows ' reflected from snow crystals.

Winter Thunder, seeing all that was going on from the top of La Plata Mountain, where he was hidden by a white cloud, sent a fierce hailstorm and lightning; as a result Rainboy was completely destroyed. The news was taken to the other Thunders, of whom Dark Thunder was chief. Blue, Yellow, White, Spotted, and Pink Thunders belonged to the faction, as did Big Dark, Big Blue, Big Yellow, and Big White Whirlwinds, and Dark, Blue, Yellow, and White Winds. During the council meeting, when it was decided to restore Rainboy, Spotted Thunder and Pink Thunder said nothing. When they were asked to agree, they grudgingly said, "All right!"

Rainboy got into one scrape after another, and each time was restored by a group of gods at a great ceremony. Dark Thunder led a war party against Winter Thunder, and there was a long struggle before Winter Thunder consented to help Rainboy. Even after he had promised, Winter Thunder had to be watched carefully to prevent him from nullifying the chant.

Winter Thunder represents all thunder. In the Flint Chant, it is summer thunder, in the Hail Chant, the thunder which accompanies hail and destruction, hence properly belonging to winter. White Thunder, appearing in summer, represents evil. In the Shooting Chant, thunder is pictured as Dark Thunder.

According to Matthews, Winter Thunder was the owner of the northern quadrant of the first world (Ch. 2, 4; Reichard 1939, p. 58 and frontispiece; 1944d, pp. 27, 43–5; Haile 1938b, pp. 83, 127; 1943a, pp. 24, 52, 56, 289, 3n; Matthews 1897, p. 64).

Wolf (mą'į·tsoh, ma'i·tsoh, na·tłé·tsoh) (U) is a contrast to Coyote in that he is considered dependable. He is the leader of the hunting animals.

Wolf, as a chief of the second world, behaved very much like First Man. He quarreled with his wife about sex matters and brought about the separation of the sexes.

In the Flint Chant, Wolf represents different animals: Dark Wolf represents Bear; White Wolf, Wolf himself;

Yellow Wolf, Mountain Lion; Pink Wolf represents all those mentioned as well as Otter (Newcomb-Reichard, p. 64, Fig. 3; Reichard 1939, p. 33, Pl. V–VII; Stephen 1930, p. 97; Haile 1943a, p. 54).

Woodbeetle (tsį 'ayą́hi˙) (H) was among the insects mentioned in the Hail Chant, a member of the warring party who carried a jar of hot water, from which zigzag lightnings darted in four directions (Reichard 1944d, pp. 34–5).

Woodpecker (tsįyikałi˙) (H) helped the people from the third to the fourth world by pecking through the sky.

Later he hid in a ball of mud, ' loaded ' for the contest with Gambler, and was rewarded with a whiteshell.

In the vast Navaho mythology, woodpecker is not much in evidence, though he is ubiquitous in Apache myth as the ' carpenter ' bird (Goddard, pp. 131, 143; Opler 1940).

Woodrat (H), see *Rat*.

World Pillars, see *Sky Pillars*.

xa˙ctčé˙'óɣan, xa˙ctčé'ôɣan (P) is an untranslatable name of the weaker companion of the pair dominated by Talking God. Matthews translates it ' House God,' and strangely, his translation has been followed by all his successors except Goddard. Sandoval from Shiprock, who worked with Goddard, thought the misconception very amusing. tłǎ˙h, who was from Newcomb, thought the translation ridiculous, but was more annoyed than amused by it. The informants at Ganado agreed in not attaching a meaning to the name.

xa˙ctčé˙'óɣan is minutely described by Matthews. What

has been said of Talking God to the effect that symbols are emphasized, not exclusive, holds for his companion as well. xa·ctčé''óγan is represented as having charge of farm songs and is the god of evening or sunset.

Two origins are given for him: Yellow Body stood for xa·ctčé''óγan in the third world; he is said to have been created by Whiteshell Woman from a yellow corn ear.

As the gods flocked around the Visionary marveling at his turkey, he explained every symbol of its body. When he finished, the youth said to xa·ctčé''óγan, "That is the way my pet turkey is dressed. Tell me now, how is your pet turkey dressed?" The god answered, "I have no pet turkey. Things that belong to the water are mine."

Water Boy is said to be the son of xa·ctčé''óγan. The young man pitted against the sometime successful Gambler, the one who finally overcame him, was the son of xa·ctčé''-'óγan, whose name is not given; he was a young married man who had no children.

The god xa·ctčé''óγan is mentioned as often as Talking God, usually as his companion. xa·ctčé''óγan helped the Visionary by negotiating with the Water People, who impeded the whirling log; he blew upon the rainbow on which the Visionary moved his crops to start it. xa·ctčé''óγan was severe to the Stricken Twins until they had obtained the treasures of Awatobi; later, he was prominent in the ceremony for their treatment.

xa·ctčé''óγan is concerned with fees: Sun told his son by Rough Woman, groomed to beat Gambler, to get the stakes for betting from xa·ctčé''óγan. After everything had been prepared and the young man was ready to start off, the god asked about his fee. When it was promised, xa·ctčé''óγan advised the party to wait yet another day in order to make the mind of Gambler 'forked,' that is, to keep him from

503

concentrating on his games; an additional fee was paid for this information.

When Monster Slayer caught his first eagle, he gave twelve choice tail feathers to Talking God and twelve tail feathers of the second eagle to xa·ctćé·''óγan; these may now be seen in their headdresses and as rays of the rising and setting sun.

According to Stephen, xa·ctćé·''óγan lives with Talking God inside La Plata Mountain; both guard the game animals.

When the gods took co, hero of the Night Chant, on a round of visits to the gods, they came to the home of one of the xa·ctćé·''óγan (one of these gods was in the party but the house was not his). It was made of blue sky. On top of it grew four spruce trees: at the east, a white one with a pigeon on its tip; at the south a blue spruce with a bluebird; at the west, a yellow spruce with a pygmy owl; and at the north, a black spruce with a yellow-shouldered blackbird.

During their wanderings the Stricken Twins, with the connivance of Talking God, came into an assembly led by the xa·ctćé·''óγan at Broad Rock. The house was among the rocks; on its front there was a rainbow of two colors; as soon as the boys touched the rock, it flew open and they entered an empty chamber. On the opposite wall they saw an arched door of three rainbow colors, which also flew open. They continued through three rooms, each of which had one more color in the arch of the secret door, until they entered the fourth door, over which was a rainbow of five colors. The door itself was covered with beautiful rock crystals glittering like stars. When they entered the fourth room, they were confronted with so many Holy People that the lame boy was abashed and hung his head (Matthews 1897, pp. 68, 82–3, 225; 1902, pp. 10, 16, 179, 192, 208, 218, 263, 316, Pl. III, B, VI; Stevenson, p. 227; Goddard, pp. 142–3; Newcomb 1940b, pp. 63, 73; Stephen ms.).

xa·ctćé·dó·dí (P) is said to be another name for Water Sprinkler and Gray God.

When the Stricken Twins approached the gods' home, their dog barked. xa·ctćé·''óγan, sent by Talking God to investigate, led the twins in.

xactčé·dó·dí had a blue face and a quiver of puma skin, and accompanied Monster Slayer and Child-of-the-water in a rite.

When the Stricken Twins returned with the treasures of Awatobi, xa·ctčé·dó·dí accompanied xa·ctčé·'óγan as he went to meet them.

xa·ctčé·dó·dí helped Water Sprinkler to get sand for a sandpainting.

Possibly xa·ctčé·dó·dí is identified with Crane (Sapir-Hoijer, p. 511, 91n; Matthews 1902, pp. 230, 232, 256, 263; cp. Haile 1943a, p. 22).

xa·dactcici· (P), associated with yucca, appears in some forms of the Night Chant. His home·is called Narrow-yucca-spreads; he carries a yucca plant on his back and a whip of yucca fiber in his hand. Whipping with yucca, believed to relieve lumbago or headache, is his only power.

xa·dactcici· conducted the Stricken Twins into one of the homes of the gods.

One of the mountain sheep that turned into gods became xa·dactcici· (Matthews 1897, p. 251, 266n; 1902, pp. 14–5, 233; Stevenson, p. 283).

Yellow-evening-light (naxatsoi, naxotsoi, naxa'atsoi) (H) is the last of the western sunset glow; it is coupled with Blue-horizon-light, the earth's shadow.

Yellow Thunder (H), see *Thunder.*

Yellow Wind (ńłtči łtsoi) (P), see *Wind.*

Zigzag Lightning (H), see *Thunder.*

CONCORDANCE B

CONCORDANCE B deals with ideas relevant to the ceremonies, including the mythological concepts that purport to explain them. It is far from exhaustive, the items listed being those related to the chants with which I have had most experience—Male Shooting Chant Holy and Evil, Hail, Endurance, Big Star. The concordance parallels to some extent those of Kluckhohn and Wyman, and two of Father Berard Haile—one of the Enemy Way, one of the Flint Chant. I have tried to make the entries comparable, either by using the same catchwords, including theirs with mine when they differ, or by cross references. It is not to be expected that any two works will coincide, since the materials and, particularly, the viewpoints differ; besides, I have had the advantage of the work of the authors mentioned, whereas they were pioneering.

I make no apology for the oddity of the titles or for their apparent incongruity—properties, ritualistic acts, mythological themes, motives, and plots (ax, decoy fire, inexhaustible), socio-psychological attitudes (ceremonial indifference, compulsion, peace), geography (travel, lower worlds). The titles are self-determining. The discussion shows that the Navaho religion is functional, and that it has become so through association of ideas, some of which are here explained.

Acceptance of offering is as ritualistic as the construction of the offerings. Usually the offering is laid on the foot of the one to whom it is made; until this time the god maintains ceremonial unconcern. If, however, the offering is correct in every particular he deigns to look at it, carries it up one side of his body and down the other. He then smells it, inspects it, and breathes in from it—acts indicating that he accepts. Different deities varied this ritual slightly.

Black God sat upright, humming a tune and tapping his toe when the people came with the tobacco pouch. They put it on his left toe; he picked it up, carried it up his left side, across his forehead, and down his right side, where he rested it on his right toe. He stared at the person presenting it, then at the offering. He looked at it, smelled it, reached into the pouch, took out the prayerstick and inspected it more carefully, took out the turquoise pipe and the tobacco, and, by smoking, accepted.

The gods of the Hail Chant sought the approval of their followers. Frog called in Frog Girl, Frog Boy, and all his relatives and friends. When they approved by blowing frog medicine over the offering, Frog breathed in from it to indicate his favor.

Bat placed his offering on Winter Thunder's lap. Winter Thunder did not touch it, but merely looked at it, until his retinue had smelled and approved it; then he breathed in from it.

When Black Thunder and Winter Thunder presented prayersticks to each other, each indicated acceptance by breathing in from the offering and pressing it to his heart (Reichard 1939, p. 31; 1944d, pp. 21, 41, 45, 53; Haile 1938b, pp. 185, 227).

Agate, see *Bead token, Pollen ball.*

'álí'l, ' power; special, extraordinary power,' is well explained by Father Berard. Briefly, it is supernatural power beyond that which is ordinarily displayed. Generally 'álí'l is a part of the unusual Fire Dance or Dark Circle branch of a chant. One of my informants (JSS) says, "When a sing fails to cure, it is because 'álíˑl was left out; to get well you have to have it. But it also means those who dance in the Dark Circle performance."

'álíˑl is the cause of disease symptoms in the myth of the Shooting Chant: "In the stomach of Firstborn was the power [be'élíˑl] of Thunder and Water People. That's the reason his appetite was poor. In his heart was the power of Wind, Crystal, and Mirage People that impaired his [Firstborn's] sight and hearing" (Ch. 15; Haile 1943a, pp. 13, 162; Reichard, Shooting Chant ms.).

Ambush, a shelter formed by two trees or shrubs whose branches intermingle, is a setting repeatedly occurring in myth, giving the explanation for various ritualistic properties —emetic frames, hoops, pokers, prayersticks, wood samples.

A hero, hoping to shoot a mountain sheep or other animal he did not recognize as a god, lay behind the ' ambush trees,' but when the animal appeared, was numb until it had passed. The animal deity, revealing himself, taught the hero ceremonial lore.

In the were-coyote episodes, the intertwined trees become a shelter for the forlorn hero, bewitched into a coyote.

Hoops of the Night Chant are made of the ambush woods, which appear again in the pit-baking, associated with the ' wood samples ' of the sweat-emetic (Matthews 1902, pp. 96, 162, 259; Sapir-Hoijer, pp. 155, 235; Haile 1943a, p. 57; Reichard, Shooting Chant Evil ms.).

Application of corn meal after the bath is an act of the bath rite. After the patient has washed his body and shampooed his hair in yucca suds with the attendant ceremony, he applies corn meal—white for male, yellow for female—to his body, clothes, and valuables, particularly his jewelry. There is some reason to conclude that the application of corn meal after the bath symbolizes the donning of new, clean (white or variegated) clothes (Ch. 12).

Application of corn meal to sandpaintings is done as soon as the sandpainting is finished, first by the chanter, then by the patient, following the chanter's direction. The details of such corn-meal sprinkling are very specific—few have been recorded (Reichard 1944d, pp. 93, 99, 109).

Application of pollen is perhaps the most general form of application, being the formal, as well as the lay, means of asking for blessing. When a person wants to pray, he takes a pinch from his pollen sack, touches a bit to his lips, throws a little up to Sun (and Sky), and puts a little on the top of his head either with or without mumbled words, a shortened form of the full rite that may be performed by the chanter who applies the pollen to the essential body-parts at a particular word in the song accompanying the ritualistic act.

The forms of pollen application are too numerous to mention. Various kinds of pollen are a part of the foam prepared for the bath. Application differs in detail in almost every rite, although a general plan is east to west and back, south to north and back, and around, done with one or numerous pollens, even with other medicines.

Pollen application varies from the simplest act to painting in pollen, as on the emetic of the War Ceremony, and on buckskin of the Rain Ceremony (cp. *Application to body-parts*, Con. B; *Pollen paintings: Rain Ceremony*, Con. C; Reichard 1944d, p. 11; Wheelwright 1942, Plates; Oakes-Campbell, Plates; Kluckhohn-Leighton, pp. 150–1).

Application of sandpainting brings about identification of the patient with the deities figured. The sand from different parts of the sandpainting figures—feet, chest, head, arms—is applied to the corresponding parts of the patient's body. Often the chanter wets his hands with lotion or sacred water before placing them on the sand so that more of it will adhere (Reichard 1944d, pp. 93, 97, 99, 105).

Application to body-parts includes touching any ceremonial item to the patient's body in a stereotyped manner. Pollen, for example, may be smeared over the lower jaw, the chanter carrying the substance from left to right from in front of one of the patient's ears to the other and passing it between the lower lip and chin. This form of application is called xaya·dá·" na'idzoh, ' under-the-edge someone-is-marked.'

Pollen and other substances, bundle properties of all kinds, are touched or pressed to the following body-parts: soles of feet, legs, knees, palms of hands (hands held out, palms up, in front of patient), arms, chest, shoulders, back, jaw, mouth, and top of the head. It is said that enemy ghosts often remain at these points; their presence was shown by the rough spots on the body-parts of the War Ceremony patient. The application begins on the right and follows at the left side of the patient or is reversed, depending on whether the rite is attractive or exorcistic; it is usually accompanied by song, the points being touched at a particular word of the song (Kluck-hohn-Wyman, pp. 29, 57, 62; Matthews 1887, p. 404; Haile 1938b, p. 195; Reichard 1944d, pp. 23, 87, 91, 95).

Armor of various kinds is mentioned, the most common being flint, protection even against lightning.

Gila Monster of the Flint Chant had flint armor of the same colors as The Twins and their duplicates—black, blue, yellow, pink. Cattail armor was made for Rainboy by the gods so that he could withstand Frog's weapons. The armor of the Thunder People was of different layers, the innermost of cattail fibers, on top of it layers of colored flint.

Navaho warriors probably wore rawhide armor. Cicada wore it as a protection from Turtle's lightning and arrows.

Turtleshell armor was offered to and refused by First Man in the lower worlds; it was accepted by Horned Toad, who had flint armor also. Turtleshell, flint, and scales are doubtless associated (Reichard 1939, Pl. XVII-XIX; 1944d, pp. 23, 31, 38, 39; Haile 1938b, p. 155; 1943a, p. 133; Newcomb-Reichard, Pl. XV-XVII; Stephen 1930, pp. 91-3).

Armor, feather, see *Feathers.*

Arms spread by Talking God and xaˑctċéˑ'óγan stopped the fight between Black Thunder and Winter Thunder.

Winter Thunder stood up and spread his arms after he had accepted the prayerstick. All the people imitated him because they were pleased (Reichard 1944d, pp. 35, 45).

Arms waved by Water Sprinkler, who carried nothing when the gods moved Visionary and his harvest, kept the rainbow conveyance moving (Matthews 1902, p. 195).

Arrow, evil (deˑzla') designates the weapon that enters a person's body and harms him, leaving bad after-effects even after he has ostensibly got rid of a disease; it may be removed by sweating and emetic.

Arrows are described for the Flint Chant bundle corresponding to those of the Shooting Chant, but in the Flint they are not used with the bow; both arrows and bow should be taken out of the Shooting Chant bundle if it is to be substituted for that of the Flint Chant. The arrow is a part of the Life branch of the Female Shooting Chant.

Today small arrows are shot into the carcass of a coyote

511

which has been shot or trapped to be traded with singers of
Evil chants (Reichard, Shooting Chant ms.; Endurance
Chant ms.; 1944d, pp. 51, 57; Sapir-Hoijer, p. 95; Wyman
1936a, p. 637; Kluckhohn-Wyman, p. 24; Haile 1943a,
pp. 14, 58, 105).

Arrow poison includes so much that is ritualistic that it is
difficult to determine which part, if any, is drug and which is
ritualistic. According to Hill, arrow poison was of three
kinds: (1) black paint with rattlesnake blood or the stings
of insects; (2) a rattlesnake killed on a rock, the juice of a
roasted yucca leaf, and soot of *Yucca baccata;* (3) soot of
lightning-struck wood mixed with yucca-leaf juice. The
bundle attached to the quiver gave the arrows (and possibly
the bows) added power.

Wyman's formula is: deer blood, *Phacelia cremulata*, and
Rhus toxicodendron (presumably reduced to soot), combined
with the soot from lightning-struck wood. Presumably formulas for arrow poison differed as much as those for emetic and
other mixtures (Hill 1936, p. 10; Wyman-Harris, p. 70).

Arrows (ka``) as supernatural weapons are constantly
emphasized, as is to be expected, in the Shooting Chant,
which has for its theme ' things that move in a swift, squirm-
ing fashion '; it is a chant in which lightning, snakes, and
arrows are closely indentified. "The arrow made for The
Twins is the symbol of the Shooting Chant.... This chant is
the story of the contest with the Arrow People," explains the
chanter. Although these are statements made about the Male
Shooting Chant Holy, the arrows are chant symbols of the
Evil form also, for the list of bundle items shows that the
' arrows ' belong to both; they may differ slightly in appearance, but their significance is the same.

The myth and sandpaintings show the concept of the Ar-

512

row People and their power. After each night's performance
the temporary arrows of the Big Star Chant are laid over
the door of the ceremonial lodge, where they remain until
morning.

It is believed that lightning will not strike a person who
carries an arrow.

When The Twins were mere babies, their mother had a
prevision of the earth as it should exist after man had gained
control. Talking God gave the children an arrow to protect
them as they played. They saw messengers of the monsters
in every direction. After they decided to go to their father,
they returned the arrow to Talking God. They went as far as
Spider Woman's house with the direct protection of Talking
God and from her they got two bows and arrows which were
henceforth to protect them; these weapons are represented
in the bundle.

In the story of the War Ceremony, First Man made The
Twins a bow of cedar and arrows with owl feathers, but after
the children had described the monster's messengers, he took
back the toy arrows and gave them carefully made ones with
lightning on the shaft.

He then set up a complicated arrangement of arrows.
Arrowpoints placed at each of the cardinal directions were
arranged in a spiral that reached toward the sky. Every time
a slight breeze blew, a terrifying grinding sound was heard
and approach was impossible. It repelled Buzzard's arrows,
fletched with his own wing feathers, and when he was dying,
the arrows were directed to restore Buzzard; arrows are now
held in the hand during prayer.

An Oraibi warrior feathered an arrow with Cliff Monster's
feathers and tried in vain to shoot it over a Navaho war
party. Had he succeeded, the Oraibi would have won.

Association of arrows with the magic conveyances—zigzag
and flash lightning, sunray, and rainbow—is well established
both in myth and ritual.

Monster Slayer killed Big Monster and Tracking Bear with
the zigzag lightning.

513

The People, preparing for war against the Taos people, were instructed to mark their arrows with lightning symbols.

When The Twins had conquered all the man-eating monsters, they wrapped the lightning, sunray, and rainbow arrows, the flint clubs, and armor in a rainbow and returned them to Sun, keeping one sunray as a means of travel. Sun gave them substitutes of mountain mahogany on which the lightning symbols were drawn—the substitutes have the same power as the original supernatural weapons (see also *Flint;* Reichard, Shooting Chant ms.; 1939, Pl. XI-XIII; Newcomb-Reichard, Pl. XXXV; Haile 1938b, pp. 95-7, 111, 127, 139, 151; 1943a, p. 273; Hill 1936, p. 5).

Arrow-crossing is a mythical episode. I am not sure that any ritualistic act represents it, although it is likely that the crossed quill feathers in the headbands of The Twin impersonators of the Overshooting rite may stand for it.

When two powers meet, each shows his strength by sticking arrows into his body, one from each side of the chest, and pulling them out at the opposite side. The opponent counter-demonstrates by pushing one arrow through his mouth and extracting it from his anus, and by repeating the act from anus to mouth.

Cicada and a water bird had such a contest to get possession of one of the worlds, usually this one.

Holy Man was nearly bested in an arrow-crossing encounter with White Weasel.

In the Mountain Chant myth, the father directed his son to shoot into a deer pluck hung on a mountain mahogany tree and draw the arrow clear through the pluck. He then told the boy that hereafter he need only shoot into such a tree without the pluck and he would be successful in the hunt.

The sorcerer called White Hair of the Eagle Chant myth demonstrated his evil power to Monster Slayer by crossing arrows in his body.

The Winds crossed inside the body of Holy Man of the Flint Chant to aid in his restoration (Goddard, p. 131;

Matthews 1887, p. 391; 1897, p. 76; Stephen 1930, pp. 92, 102; Wheelwright 1942, p. 51; Newcomb 1940b, p. 64; Haile 1943a, p. 68; cp. Reichard 1944d, pp. 117, 121, 132).

Arrow-swallowing is a rite representative of some mythological episode enacted in the Fire Dance. Possibly it is related to arrow-crossing, but it is not explained as a part of the Shooting Chant in any form or myth I have encountered (Matthews 1887, p. 409; Reichard 1944d, pp. 117, 119, 127; Shooting Chant ms.).

Ashes (łe·ctči·) protect man against undefined, unknown, suspected evils and confer immunity upon the person or vicinity where they are found. Consequently, they are common in the exorcistic rites and chants.

When taken out before sunrise, ashes are equivalent to pollen; that is, they scatter the evils of the night. Contrariwise, throwing out ashes in the daytime is an insult to Sun; spilling them makes a trail for Poverty, who is avoided by the Holy People.

The exorcistic function of ashes and the idea that ' evil must be driven off as far as possible ' are noted in the myth of the War Ceremony: the proper site for the ceremonial hogan must have enough open space to allow ashes to be strewn on the enemy, that is, the scalp, at a safe distance.*

Meadowlark sat in front of the ash pile and with her left hand took ashes to the scalps that were to be ' killed,' that is, rendered harmless. Now in the War Ceremony the ashes-strewer places the scalp in the midst of the dancers, sprinkles ashes on and around it four times. Just before the next to last song is started he deposits the scalp some distance away.

---

*The opinion "ordinary wood ashes are worthless in themselves" (Haile 1938b, p. 32) is in error, since ashes have great ritualistic value.

Before each rite of the Male Shooting Chant Evil, ashes are gathered from four directions around the fire and taken out of the hogan.

Stress laid upon sitting in the ashes when sulking and quarreling may seem to mean mortification of the person one is trying to impress, but there seems also to be the idea that the one who resorts to ashes is trying to drive away the evil of discord.

When the people of Awatobi would not give the Stricken Twins a place to sleep, they spent the night on a pile of ashes outside the houses. This choice of a sleeping place was a threat to the Awatobi people, later carried out.

The more directly magical properties of ashes are exemplified by methods of driving cutworms, classed with indefinite evils, from the cornfields.

Ashes were mixed with water and the mixture poured at the base of the plants.

A few cutworms were gathered from a field and put into hot ashes to drive the remaining worms from the field. If any survived, they would dry up as had those taken for the symbol.

Protective properties of ashes are demonstrated by rites or ritualistic acts.

Changing Woman stuck a poker into the ashes, then hit Big Monster with it to drive him off. Here the strength of the poker and its power as the danger line are joined with the exorcistic power of the ashes.

After The Twins had survived the tobacco-smoking test, Sun spat upon the ashes left in the pipe, and rubbed them on the boys' feet, as he molded their bodies. Here ashes power is combined with tobacco power, smoke, and rubbing. The purpose of the whole is the recognition of power. There is a similar episode in the Mountain Chant myth.

Ashes helped to overcome Eye Killers. Monster Slayer threw salt into the fire; it crackled and sputtered, flinging embers and ashes into Eye Killers' eye sockets. The salt was the dynamite, so to speak. The embers would destroy the eyes; the ashes would drive off the creatures forever (cp. *Ceremonial indifference;* Hill 1938, pp. 19, 59; Haile 1938b, pp. 32, 105, 123, 197, 201, 219, 233, 237; Matthews 1887, p. 404; 1902, p. 248; Reichard, Shooting Chant ms.).

Ashes blowing ('í·dilyoł), common in exorcistic rites, combines the significance of ashes and blowing which transforms evil into good or moves evil to a distance.

The patient in the Shooting Chant blows ashes from a feather just before inhaling incense, an act that ends the bundle application each night.

In the Evil chants, on the other hand, blowing and ashes blowing are frequently repeated. In the Big Star Chant, the patient blows ashes from the bull-roarer; the audience, from feathers. Ashes to be blown are put first near the butt of the object held, the second and third times successively nearer the tip, the fourth time at the very tip. The rite represents approaching immunity, dispersion of evil.

Ashes may be put on the feather with the rib downward, although for one repetition in the prayer the rib should be toward the blower (cp. Kluckhohn-Wyman, p. 73).

Ashes-strewer, see *Black God,* Con. A; *Ashes,* Con. B.

Associations have been suggested as the key to the Navaho system of symbolism; for instance, associations between various aspects of deity—First Man, be'γotcidí, Talking God, xa·ctčé''óγan, Winds, Coyote, and Black God as manifestations of Sun; First Woman, Sun's Sky wife (Dawn Woman), and Earth as manifestations of Changing Woman (Ch. 5). Though they may often seem to be peculiar, these associations are by no means ' free,' but are held together in a stipulated pattern which only the details that compose it can explain.

The following list shows some of the elements and their combinations, not always the same. If we had all the pieces of the Navaho ceremonial puzzle, we could doubtless understand why a relation is posited, whereas now too many myths are unrecorded or too sketchily recorded to be definitive. Notes are not appended at this point; as a rule they may be found under the same title in the concordances; many have been included in the discussion there.

abalone
yellow corn

'aĺké˙ na"a˙ci˙
sa'a na˙γái
Twins
Talking God
xa˙ctc'é"óγan

ambush woods
emetic frames
pokers

arrow
Wind
Cicada
arrow-crossing
life

arrow-crossing
power
possession
life

aspen
white
summer
pink

bandoleer
Burrowing Monster's colon
encirclement protection

Bat
Darkness
wing feather
Big Fly

Bear
Reared-in-the-mountain
Meal Sprinklers
Meal Sprinklers' trail
Racing Gods

Big Fly
feather
Wind
skin at tip of tongue
speech

Big Monster's blood
blood of all monsters
Reared-in-the-earth

black
Darkness
Black Wind
yellow squash

Black God
Gila Monster

Black God
Black Star
Darkness

Blue Snake
Blue Thunder
straight (flash) lightning
blue flint

bluebird communication
prayerstick

bluebirds and cornbeetles
gods talking

breath
Wind
Whirlwind
whorls
down motion

buckskin
life
song
protection
cover

bull-roarer
lightning
snakes
pokers
danger line
hoops

Burrowing Monster
Gopher

cane
digging stick
arrow
water

cloud water
fog
moss

corn
Changing Woman
whiteshell
snakes

cotton
motion
clouds

dawn
freedom
rejuvenation
life

Deer Owner
Big-snake-man
Never-ending-snake
Big God
Tracking Bear

down feather
breeze
motion
life feather
unraveler
hoop
deliverance

Earth
Moon
Blue Thunder
Child-of-the-water
Blue Snake
Straight Lightning
whiteshell
Holy Woman

Earth
Yellow Wind
Pink Thunder
Reared-in-the-earth
Pink Snake
rainbow
redshell
sunglow
Holy Girl

519

⌈ emetic frame hoops
| snakes
| hoops of Hoop Transformation rite
| Stars
⌊ Snakes

⌈ feather cloak
⌊ yellow lightning

⌈ flies
| deer
| Syphilis People
| evil
| fever and venereal diseases
| prevention of Big Monster's revival
| instruction of Earth People
| monsters' ghosts
| enemy ghosts
| Monster Slayer's bow and Child-of-
| the-water's queue
⌊ life

⌈ flint
| oak
⌊ oak sprigs

⌈ Frog
| hail
| potatoes
⌊ dumplings

⌈ insects
| sores
| be'ɣotcidí
| Montezuma
⌊ Gray Gods

⌈ lower worlds
| sorcery
| lack of control
| incest
| grave robbery
| bisexualism
⌊ wealth

⌈ Old Age
| ax
⌊ Frog

⌈ One-who-customarily-sees-the-fish
| Monster Slayer
⌊ Dwarf-boy's-father-in-law

⌈ perspiration
| fear
| danger
⌊ illness from enemy breath

⌈ prayerstick
| life feather
⌊ unraveler

⌈ pursuit by Owls
⌊ pursuit by Utes

⌈ Rainboy
| racer (snake)
| Frog
| Racing Gods
⌊ Meal Sprinklers

⌈ red willow
| Sun
⌊ yellow

⌈ red willow
| water
⌊ blue

⌈ Red Wind
⌊ squash tendri

⌈ Sky
| Night
⌊ Black God

⌈ Sky
| Black Wind
| Yellow Thunder
| Changing Grandchild
| Yellow Snake
| rainstreamer
| abalone
⌊ Holy Boy

520

Sky
Sun
Black Thunder
Monster Slayer
Black Snake
zigzag lightning
turquoise
Holy Man

Sky Pillars
Winds
Place-of-emergence

smoke
cloud
rain
acceptance
breathing in

Snake
Thunder
Wind
Arrow

spiderweb
unraveler
down feather

spiderweb
nerves and veins
marrow
conveyances

talking prayerstick
'ałké˙ na''a˙ci˙
warning prayerstick
Sun's arrows
mentor

talking prayerstick
unraveler
circular prayersticks

Thunder
Buffalo
Water Monster

Traveling Rock
Water Monster

Twelve Brothers
World Pillars
Snakes

Water Sprinkler
Gray God
xa˙ctc'é˙dó˙dí
Spider
Crane

wind
hail
storm
flint
armor
Gila Monster
divination
cincture rite

yellow
Yellow-evening-light
Yellow Wind
black squash

yellow bowl
mush in rock crystal basket
inexhaustible vessel

Yellow Snake
Yellow Thunder
sunray
yellow flint

Yellow Thunder
power to find lost person
divination
Gila Monster

521

Ax (tsénił), which destroyed anyone who took hold of it, other than the owner, was possessed by Frog, Gambler, and Old Age. It seems that this magic ax was changed into Monster Slayer's club. The references may point to a connection between Frog (Toad), Gambler, Old Age, and The Twins' club (Reichard 1944d, p. 27; Haile 1938b, p. 153; Goddard, p. 146; Sapir-Hoijer, p. 129).

Basket (tša") has already been extensively treated. There are, however, certain points that have not been stressed; one concerns the number of baskets necessary to a ceremony— the discussions often imply that there is only one (Ch. 14). A part of the agreement between chanter and sponsor is the provision of the baskets, as important as the payment to the singer. When the chant is over, some baskets are presented to the chanter or some other participant in the ceremony; borrowed baskets are returned to the owner, who may be the chanter or almost anyone who can provide them. Certain taboos, some very strict, attach to the basket. Nowadays it has become an article of trade, procurable at a trading post. Baskets so bought may be considered neutral, having no restrictions and no evil attached to them; the ceremony gives them blessing value.

Because of the ' drawing power ' of the earth, sacred objects should not touch the ground; consequently, ceremonial properties—War Ceremony rattlestick, prayersticks, hoops, bundle equipment—must be placed on or in something; it is often a basket, especially for assembled bundle equipment.

I had to provide five baskets for the Shooting Chant Prayerstick branch. I paid for four and borrowed one from RP, the chanter. One was used for the layout of branch symbol prayersticks during their preparation and for the subsequent bundle equipment layout, one for the emetic, one for the drum, one for the bath, and one for the ceremonial mush. After the bath the chanter put his bundle layout in the basket that had been used for the bath. Every ceremony undoubtedly has similar requirements; some have more, some fewer.

The basket represents jewels and therefore the potentiality of wealth, with its provision for proper offerings. Baskets are often thought of as consisting of one of the precious stones, rimmed with a contrasting jewel (Ch. 12); such baskets are prescribed for the Hail Chant. In addition, one of Heat and one of Mirage (aragonite) are required. The War Ceremony emetic was prepared and the unseasoned mush was served in a rock-crystal basket. Since the mush was inexhaustible, there is a relation between the rock-crystal basket and the yellow bowl.

The Flint Chant baskets represent jewels; the plants put into them ceremonially became meat which, with other plants eaten by rare game, became gruel (Kluckhohn-Wyman, pp. 44, 60; Matthews 1894b, pp. 202–8; 1897, p. 211, 5n; Haile 1938b, pp. 33, 105, 207, 243; 1943a, pp. 15, 184, 190; Goddard, pp. 142, 164; Reichard 1944d, p. 49; Shooting Chant ms.; Tschopik, pp. 257–62).

Basket drum was described by Matthews and Kluckhohn-Wyman (Matthews 1894b; 1902, pp. 59–63, 163, 165; Kluckhohn-Wyman, p. 44; Haile 1938b, pp. 33, 243).

Bath, see Ch. 7; *Bath*, Con. C; and cp. Kluckhohn-Wyman, pp. 89–92; Matthews 1897, p. 69; 1902, pp. 99–103, 211; Haile 1943a, pp. 15, 219, 279, 282; Goddard, pp. 129, 150, 175; Newcomb 1940b, p. 54; Hill 1938, pp. 81–2; Wheelwright 1942, p. 83; Reichard 1944d, pp. 13, 79–81; Shooting Chant ms.

Bath corn meal, see *Application of corn meal after the bath*.

Bead token (yo'' didjo'li') is my catchword for Father Berard's 'recognition mark' and Kluckhohn-Wyman's 'token.' I should prefer the term 'chant token' for this symbol, but Kluckhohn-Wyman have adopted that for the 'head-feather bundle,' an item of the chanter's bundle. These, I think, should be distinguished. The bundle is a piece of property corresponding with bundle prayersticks, brush, bull-roarer, etc.; the bead token is a permanent symbol in the patient's possession to signify that he has been favored by the gods of a given chant, that he is under their protection, that his power is equal to theirs. The token has recognitive significance in identifying the patient as a 'child' to the deities themselves; another major purpose is to warn off less powerful supernaturals who may be expected to fear those powers which have been persuaded.

The Shooting Chant token, which made it safe for me to deal with the Hail Chant also, is a tiny, perfect turquoise tied with a small olivella shell. At Ganado and Newcomb the token is the same for men and women, prescribed by other chanters as well as by RP.

In a sense the token becomes the patient's 'life,' since that which happens to the token happens also to its owner. Some five years after MC had first been sung over, her token broke, exposing her to danger, a threat which could be counteracted by a series of four repetitions of the chant.

After RP had sung the Shooting Chant for me, he explained the token: "You don't need to be afraid of lightning or snakes any more. They won't hurt you. Don't kill a snake, though. If you see one, just leave it alone. Go the other way—leave it alone. And if you are in a bad storm with wind, thunder, and lightning, just take the bead in your hand, shake it at the storm, and tell it to stop and it won't hurt you."

Subsequent inquiry indicated that the ' telling ' could be done in Navaho or English. It was not in the form of a prayer; it need have no words.

When the bead is removed from the scalplock on the last day of ceremonial observance, it is tied to some part of the patient's person or wearing apparel—the hair or hairstring, the hat, belt, purse, or necklace; the owner feels more comfortable if he has it with him, especially when traveling or undertaking an uncertain activity.

The bead token of the Hall Chant is agate. To judge by the mythical description of the Blackening, a corresponding symbol was a part of the War Ceremony: an agate was placed on the patient's chest, a sack of gopher dust on his back; the agate seems not to have been given to the patient (Ch. 12; *Figure painting*, Con. C; Kluckhohn-Wyman, pp. 38–9; Haile 1938b, pp. 62, 93; Reichard 1944d, p. 103).

Black Dancers (dja·cjiní, tca·cjiní), who may put on an accessory act in the War Ceremony, are included in the myth. Their act is an example of reversal: they perform daring, shocking stunts, apparently scoffing at the most sacred decrees. A few additional points may be added to the extant descriptions: mixed with the mud with which the Black Dancers are smeared is ' dung of every kind available.' "Those weak in body or mind, though not actually sick, may be caught, dressed, and thrown, if arrangements have been made by their people." The informant (AB) was so treated as a small child. "Besides strengthening those treated, the Black Dancers' performance brings rain" (Haile 1938b, pp. 34–5, 231, 234–41; Reichard 1928, pp. 132–3).

Blanket, see *Covers*.

Blowing is a ritualistic act that has various results. Blowing increases size or quantity. Blowing on the large reed made it grow until it reached the sky. The world was stretched by blowing to keep the sun from burning the people. An entrance too small was enlarged by blowing; as soon as those allowed had entered, it reassumed its usual small size. Similarly, rooms too small for those entering were enlarged by blowing. A small rainbow was enlarged when Talking God blew on it. When Gambler came home, he put four ears of corn into empty bins, and blew on them; all the bins filled up.

Blowing causes motion, speed, and growth, and may also make a thing steady or permanent. Perhaps the steadying effect must be achieved by blowing chewed herbs: The rainbow on which the Stricken Twins traveled moved when blown on by Talking God. Evil influences, gathered under the reversed basket (drum) by the beating, were caused to move out of the smokehole by blowing after the basket was turned upright. Spider Woman, by blowing, caused the ' invincible man ' to move into and remain in The Twins' bodies. First Man chewed an herb and blew it four times on the sun in his map of the world, sending it to the sky, which then began to move. By blowing, the entrance to the lower worlds was closed.

Blowing makes skins fit persons for whom they were not designed, sometimes permanently, sometimes temporarily. Blowing causes transformation, closely related to fitting and permanence: Blowing caused a monster's blood to congeal. Blowing by be'γotcidí changed water animals into rocks. Blowing caused the stars to move from the plan made on the earth to their permanent place in the sky. Pluck of game hung in a tree was shot; the arrow was pulled through it. When the arrangement was blown upon, it turned into game.

Blowing may bring or dissipate a storm: Changing Woman,

by spitting hail through hoops, throwing flints, and blowing, caused all to disappear into the sky and by this means prevented a storm. When Wind blew mud balls, a great hailstorm arose. When there was a bad storm with terrific lightning, the hero of the Night Chant sang his Thunder songs and blew in the four directions, whereupon the storm passed.

The following ritual was performed if a hailstorm threatened: A man put into his mouth some sacred clay, salt, and the first hailstones that hit the field. He then blew the mixture to the four directions and the hail was expected to turn to rain (*Pollen ball*, Con. B; Stevenson, p. 276; Matthews 1887, pp. 391, 399, 400, 403, 409; 1897, pp. 129, 175, 232, 109n; 1902, pp. 186, 206, 246, 263; Wheelwright 1942, pp. 41, 43, 54, 79, 80, 86; Sapir-Hoijer, p. 43; Goddard, pp. 130, 133, 136, 138, 161; Haile 1938b, pp. 89, 117; Stephen 1930, p. 101; Reichard 1944d, p. 135; Hill 1938, p. 61).

Bow symbol is a bundle item often depicted in sandpainting and elsewhere. It is drawn with chant lotion on the body painting of Monster Slayer's impersonators, and on the bullroarer before it is twirled.

Monster Slayer explained the symbol as he raised his left foot toward the people: "This act represents the means I used to overcome the monsters. In days to come you shall remember the one whose name is Bow-whose-string-extends-on-oneside" ('ałtį˙ γa˙'ozti'). The bow symbolizes the death of the monsters whose ghosts have left death or weakness behind. The ghosts of any enemy may be the same as the ghosts of the monsters. The bowstring entices the enemy to his death and is therefore a decoration of the victor (Haile 1938b, pp. 37, 59, 179, 256, 123n, 315, 27n; 1943a, p. 44; Reichard 1928, p. 118; Matthews 1897, p. 24; 1902, pp. 21, 23).

Bowed head means, for one thing, acknowledgment of superior power.

When The Twins asked Sun for power to overcome Big Monster, he bowed his head, holding it in his hands, and remained speechless for some time. When he raised his head, there were tears in his eyes.

Sun's behavior signified his resignation, acceding to the request for aid to man, for until then he had worked primarily on the side of evil.

The tales imply that all creatures and powers bowed before Changing Woman.

When Changing Woman came into the assembly of the gods, each one bowed his head.

The sacred mountains bowed to the people returning from a visit, presumably to acknowledge the power of ' their mother,' Changing Woman.

Many powers bowed to acknowledge The Twins' power, and also to indicate fear, an emotion not a part of the respect paid to Changing Woman.

The gods assembled for the Hail Chant house blessing, and, as Talking God and xaˑctċé˝óɣan stood ready to sing, the audience was told to bow their heads and place their hands, palms up, on their knees as The Twins entered and blessed the hogan; the people were thus to receive the gods' power.

Talking God was overcome by Monster Slayer when he gave the symbol called 'acmé'iˑ and its explanation to the War Ceremony. Talking God, his head bowed low, moved off toward the east.

Frog bowed his head after he had accepted the offering for Rainboy's restoration.

There seems to be a slight variation of head bowing in the case of sorcerers, who, when defeated, hung their heads between their knees in surrender.

The bowed head is also a sign of relative humility or respect, a meaning differing not in kind but in degree, according to the status of the two persons meeting. A girl confronted by a strange man, for instance, bowed her head and rubbed her feet together; the behavior indicated that the girl had been properly reared.

Novices bowed their heads before the gods; the Stricken Twin who could see was so overcome by the beauty of Talking God and the Holy People that he lowered his head.

Rainboy hung his head, apparently in doubt, as he hesitated to accept the power of Spotted Thunder (Reichard, Shooting Chant ms.; 1944d, pp. 13, 23, 31, 53, 147; Haile 1938b, pp. 107, 163; Wheelwright 1942, pp. 118–9; Matthews 1897, p. 187; 1902, pp. 213, 217, 218).

Breathing in ('ájí yidjij) is a ritualistic act: the patient faces the power, usually Sun, stretches out his hands, palms up, pulls or draws the power into himself by cupping his hands and sucking; the motions are repeated four times. One informant (AB) compared this act to a kiss, signifying acceptance of all that has been done for the patient and willingness to carry out all ceremonial requirements (Reichard, Shooting Chant ms.; 1944d, pp. 13, 43, 59, 85, 109; Haile 1938b, pp. 213, 245).

Brushing ('akí· na'ałxa·ł, 'akí· díní·yó·d) is an act of some of the Holy chants occurring after the patient and audience have been cleansed by sweating and emesis and the hogan has been cleared of the embers of the ceremonial fire and the emetic sand basins. The chanter dips the eagle tail-feather brush into the chant lotion, taps the end near his hand so that it falls like rain upon the participants, and, as he utters his chant sound, moves around the house from the back to the door as if brushing out invisible objects. More vigorous is the brushing act in the Evil chants with the sound be'be'yó and without lotion (cp. Kluckhohn-Wyman, p. 72).

Buckskin (bį˙tso łgai do˙kakehi˙) taken from a deer killed with pollen—that is, without wounding—is an important ceremonial article. Actually, the goods laid down at certain points in the ritual—unraveling, body painting, sandpainting—are substitutes for the buckskin. They stand for it, but only rarely does the pile of goods ('aya˙ sika˙d) include a real buckskin. It is said that in the old days such goods consisted largely, perhaps exclusively, of buckskin (yódí).

On the other hand, even today a buckskin must be furnished for the rite of Prayer on buckskin. With few exceptions, the only deerskins now available are purchased from traders and are from animals that have been shot. After the rite the buckskin becomes the chanter's property in the Male Shooting Chant Evil and the Big Star and Endurance chants.

Mythologically buckskin is an emblem of life; ritualistically it is a life symbol: Creation, really transformation, was accomplished by laying corn, precious stones, or both between buckskins. Restoration is brought about in much the same way—the properties and procedure are almost identical for transformation from inanimate to animate and for restoration from unconsciousness or death to life.

Bits of Rainboy's body were assembled on one buckskin and another was laid over the parts. A rite with buckskin, described in the Bead Chant myth, transformed feathers into animals whose skins have since been a chant property. Two buckskins figured in the preparation of seed for planting, the rite signifying life and transformation.

Rites in which the patient stands on a buckskin are described for the visit of Dawn Boy to the home of the gods and his return to his own home, and for the two children abducted by the gods so they could visit Changing Woman.

Buckskin must be worn over the shoulders by the person depositing the Rain Ceremony prayerstick (cp. *Prayer on buckskin:* Con. C; Matthews 1897, pp. 104–5, 137, 214, 12n; 1902, p. 115; 1907, pp. 28, 34; Haile 1938b, p. 71; Kluckhohn-Wyman, p. 172; Reichard 1939, p. 32; 1944d, p. 9; Hill 1938, pp. 71, 86; Wheelwright 1942, p. 124.

Bull-roarer (tsin diñi), representing different but related powers—Thunder in the Shooting, Snake in the Big Star Chant—drives off evil.

Summarizing the rites, Monster Slayer says, "The first thing they did was to carry out the bull-roarer in order to drive evil out of the house."

The act of erasing sandpainting guards or sweat-emetic fire paintings with the bull-roarer indicates that the evils are gone, the guardians no longer needed (Kluckhohn-Wyman, pp. 33–4; Reichard, Shooting Chant ms.).

Cake ('ałka·n, 'ałką'd) is a ceremonial mark of respect to Sun in the Girl's Adolescence ceremony, the Flint Chant, and the Feather Chant. It is not mentioned in any of the Shooting Chant material (Reichard 1934, pp. 104ff.; Haile 1943a, pp. 49, 229).

Cane (gic) seems to be a symbol of ritualistic power; perhaps that is the reason why at the coming of the whites it became an emblem of government.

Changing Woman gave her people canes by means of which they got water from the desert; at the places where the people struck the canes into the ground certain clans originated. Spider Woman gave Scavenger a long black cane with which he gathered tumbleweeds to burn.

Canes are not much in evidence in the chants I describe, but they form a part of the Wind Chant bundles. In the Shooting Chant, one of the tests given The Twins by Sun was to walk on the tips of four upright jewel canes. They were able to do so with the aid of the life feathers given them by Spider Woman. The unraveling rite is the current representation of this episode.

Deer Owner's daughter, conducting Self Teacher to the home of rare game, opened the entrance to the game reserve in a subterranean world with a turquoise cane or wand (Matthews 1897, pp. 152–3, 185, 201; Goddard, p. 169; Haile 1943a, p. 19; Kluckhohn-Wyman, pp. 115–6, Fig. 4; Reichard, Shooting Chant ms.).

Cattail (te'ł), see *Armor*.

Ceremonial approach to a new place or experience is done in four stages symbolized by the various approaches to a house, the leading onto a sandpainting, and other ritualistic acts. Between each act there is a pause for singing.

Big Monster appeared over the eastern mountain so that only his head was seen; over the southern mountain his head and chest showed; over the western mountain he could be seen as far as his waist; finally, at the north he could be seen as far down as his knees. He then appeared fully and went to the lake to drink.

In the same way First Man approached the summit of the mountain where the wonderful baby lay: he ascended the four sides of the same mountain, showing himself a little more as he approached from each side.

When Self Teacher crawled into his whirling log to test it, he first put his head in nearly as far as his chest. The second time he went nearly to his waist, the third time almost to his knees, and finally, all the way to his feet. The first three times he started in, Talking God called him out; the last time, he stayed in (Matthews 1897, pp. 114, 162; Haile 1938b, p. 83).

Ceremonial coup-counting is one of numerous elements in Navaho ceremony that point to Plains influence. A suggestion of coup-counting appears in names; the importance of an initial act may be a reflection of the same idea.

When the War Ceremony was first organized and the killing of Burrowing Monster was to be commemorated, Chipmunk said, "Since I was the first to reach Burrowing Monster after he was killed, I have medicine."

The details of procuring and decorating the rattlestick remind one of the center pole rite of the Sun Dance, although counting coup on it is not mentioned.

The first person to arrive running at a slain deer was entitled to its hide (Reichard 1928, p. 106; Haile 1938b, pp. 177, 223; Sapir-Hoijer, p. 323).

Ceremonial indifference is signified by the gods in the same way as anger by a sulking husband.

Black God sat upright and hummed as he tapped his toe, and Gila Monster assumed the same position.

Unconcern may also be a means of attraction. When the Corn Maidens of the War Ceremony story saw the handsome men, they asked for a smoke, but the men paid no attention. At the second request, the men raised their heads and looked at each other. The third time, Bear told Snake to prepare a smoke, and the fourth time, Snake told Bear to do it; they then accepted the girls as mates for the night (Haile 1938b, 171, 185; 1943a, p. 62).

Ceremonial language is too pretentious for inclusion in this work, for it involves first the careful presentation of the ordinary language; it is impossible to judge what is extraordinary

533

when we do not even know what is ordinary. Here I shall give a short list of common and ceremonial words to illustrate the most obvious types of the pattern. Reference is to the ceremony in which each example occurs, since the same idea may be expressed by different words in different chants (Ch. 16).

English	Common word	Ceremonial word	Meaning
American	belagána	tł'ohya·gai	White-streak-under-grass (War Ceremony)
Cattail	te'l	bita'í ła	Many Feathers (HC)
Chiricahua Apache	tciji	lók'a·" nídi·gai	Vertical-white-streak-reed (War Ceremony)
		lók'a·" xagai	White-reed-place (War Ceremony)
Corn	na·dá"	diɣin bina·dá"	Holy Corn (HC)
Cotton	tł'ó'l (rope)	tł'ó'ózó'l	fluffed grass
Elkhorn	djé·h bide"	djéhtoh	(Flint Chant)
Hail	níló	'áló	(Hail Chant)
Mexican	nakaih	tséjin sinil	Black-rocks-lie
		dził ná·ɣisi·	Spinning Mt. (War Ceremony)
Mountain (mythical)	dziłnáxodili·	dziłnádjódili·	(Hail Chant)
Pretty	njóní	'ayá·c	(especially of birds)
Squash	na'aɣízí	'abéckaní	(Hail Chant)
Tall reed	te'l ní·ɣizí	bikaz ntsá·z	enlarging stalk (HC)
Ute	no·da'á	dziłgai	White mountain
		xojdí·lid	Smoking place
Wolf	ma'i·tsoh	na·tł'é·tsoh	Big-he-trots-like-a-person

Chant lotion (ke·tłoh) has several functions. The Male Shooting Chant lotion contains the same ingredients as the emetic, ground and mixed by a group of singers who divide the dried mixture and keep it as bundle property. The chanter's supply contains dried herbs in case the season or place in which the chant is held is unsuitable for collecting the fresh plants. The bulk of the lotion and emetic is composed, when possible, of fresh plants to which the small quantities from the dried supply may be added.

The lotion and emetic of the first day of the Hail Chant, made by those in charge of the Shooting Chant, were of dodgeweed to which a mixture of hail and ice rolled in corn meal was added. On the second day hoarfrost was another ingredient.

Black God's fagot was extinguished with the Night Chant lotion (Kluckhohn-Wyman, p. 51; Reichard 1944d, pp. 51, 57, 87, 99, 105–7; Matthews 1902, p. 28).

Chant token, see *Bead token.*

Charcoal, see *Soot.*

Chewing and spraying is a common ritualistic act. The chanter chews a dry substance, sometimes with water, sometimes without, then sprays the result over the patient or some particular part of his body.

In explaining the chewed herbs sprayed over the War Ceremony patient, Black God told the people it was Chipmunk's medicine. It commemorates Chipmunk's help after Monster Slayer killed Burrowing Monster.

An allusion indicates that chewing and spraying may have aided the Winds to hold up the world at its creation. They were directed by be'γotcidí to chew roots and herbs and blow them in various directions.

Scavenger of the Bead Chant, instructed by Spider Woman, chewed and spat dodgeweed juice at the insects trying to sting him (Haile 1938b, pp. 38, 179, 195; Wheelwright 1942, p. 67; Matthews 1897, pp. 202–3).

Circle (bạ·s) has been discussed as a division of space to be avoided by the layman and regulated ceremonially. Here a few examples are given:

Encircling a man's house may cause his death.

When First Man was making the earth, he put guardians first in one, then in two, three, and finally, four concentric circles around himself and his work. Coyote broke through each circle in turn, demonstrating that his power was greater than First Man's.

The Dark-circle-of-branches, symbol of the Fire Dance branch of some chants, is the most elaborate ritualistic form of the circle. When the rite was performed for co of the Night Chant, the Dark Circle had four openings instead of one. The one made for the first Mountain Chant had power because of its size and the large number of participants; even though it was six miles in diameter, it was crowded.

At Sun's direction, temporary circular shades were made of branches where he met Changing Woman. Similar shades with slight variations of detail were camps of warriors, hunters, and anyone away from home. The shade may have been a circle of protection in strange or doubtful country. In the War Ceremony myth, a large crowd of people rushed up to Black God's camp and piled up pebbles in a circle so as to make a kind of fort.

The circle was part of a rite to destroy cutworms. Four worms were collected, impaled, and turned inside out over twigs of the slender sunflower. Then the cutworms were taken to a cliff ruin kiva, where they were stuck into the earth flush with the ground, and covered with a potsherd. Four circles were drawn around the arrangement with an arrow-point and it was left. The worms within the circles would have to disintegrate since they belong to the dead—they were inside out, they were buried in a place of the dead, and covered with an object that had belonged to the dead; the four circles left no way for tčî·ndi· to get out.

The same ends were sought in restoring a field struck by lightning. A chanter deposited offerings at the base of a stalk that had been struck, sang songs, and prayed to lightning. Then with the bull-roarer he drew a circle around three or four plants near the first one (cp. Ch. 6; *Hoop transformation rite, Prayer on buckskin:* Con. C; Newcomb 1940a, pp. 23, 25, 51; Franciscan Fathers 1910, p. 294; Sapir-Hoijer, p. 83; Matthews 1887, p. 414; 1902, p. 202; Haile 1938b, pp. 91, 157, 163, 171, 191; Goddard, pp. 153–4; Hill 1936, p. 12; 1938, pp. 59–60).

Clothes are of great significance in myth and ritual. The representation of characters in sandpaintings and on prayersticks is referred to as ' dressing.' It is clear from the material and the behavior of the chanter and his assistants that rough directions serve for the sandpaintings, since each element from the Navaho viewpoint is realistic and easily understood. Directions about the prayersticks are, by contrast, meticulous, oft repeated and rechecked because their decoration is largely symbolical, not at all apparent.

Dressing Changing Woman in white and whiteshell indicates a change from profane to divine.

After the monsters had been subdued, The Twins heard a song that told them to put on their ordinary clothes to receive Sun.

When Holy Man visited Thunder's and Big Snake's homes, he saw their clothes hanging on the wall of the room.

Even though the prayersticks of Pollen Boy and Cornbeetle Girl are painted in self-color, the myth has a detailed description of their face painting and moccasins.

For comparative purposes it should be noted that mythical descriptions of ideal clothes are Plainslike (Ch. 7; *Eagles,* Con. A; Newcomb-Reichard, Ch. VI; Matthews 1897, pp. 131, 184, 191; 1902, p. 262; Reichard, Shooting Chant ms.; 1944d, pp. 77, 91; Haile 1938b, pp. 87, 105, 213; Goddard, p. 150; Sapir-Hoijer, p. 161).

Clouds (kos) figure in almost every field of ritual. In the Hail and Wind chants they are related to Storm, Wind, and

Cactus, portrayed in the sandpaintings. Generally, clouds are desirable because they bring rain, but they must be ritualistically controlled. A curb mentioned by Hill for the Rain Ceremony illustrates control and reversed power. Female rain and white clouds are referred to in the prayer only if it is exorcistic or for witchcraft, since such references bring hail and damage to crops.

Clouds, considered as People, are depicted as the major figures in sandpaintings, such as those of the Wind and Hail chants; in any sandpainting, all the unfilled background may be filled in with black wavy lines, symbols of clouds (Kluck-hohn-Wyman, Fig. 18, p. 94; Wheelwright 1942, p. 42; 1946, p. 94).

Club (xał) was one of Sun's gifts to The Twins. It may be a manifestation of the 'killing ax,' and is an item of some bundles. Frequently depicted in the paintings of the flint-armored boys, it serves many purposes besides clubbing.

It was stuck between the 'closing rocks' and, along with elkhorn, now a property of the War Ceremony, it overcame them. Big Bear was rendered harmless when the club was wedged in his mouth.

By hitting with it Monster Slayer overcame the Big Gray Gods (insects) and made Traveling Rock useful to man (Haile 1938b, pp. 125, 127, 131, 137; Reichard 1939, Pl. X, XVII-XIX; Newcomb-Reichard, p. 48, Pl. XV-XVII).

Coals (tsi'd) are an intimate part of the incensing rite. Each ceremony has a specified number of coals; they must be carefully extinguished with lotion or water and disposed of; they are treated in the same way as the sweat-emetic embers. Two coals from a flaming fire are prescribed for the Male Shooting Chant Holy and Evil, Big Star, and Endurance chants; in the Hail Chant myth two, three, four, and five are required for successive rites; one is mentioned for the Mountain Chant (*Incense;* Reichard, Male Shooting Chant Holy and Evil ms.; Endurance Chant ms.; Big Star Chant ms.; 1944d, pp. 59, 65, 73, 95, 97; Matthews 1887, p. 421).

Collected substances (... na῾ctcí῾n), such as soil, water, pollen, belong to the bundle or may be assembled especially for a ceremony. They may appear insignificant to the casual onlooker; the chanter sprinkles a pinch here, pours a few drops there quite unobtrusively. Each represents, however, great effort on the part of someone, usually the chanter himself. Such substances are tokens of the power embodied in everything for which they stand, often being collected from widely scattered geographical localities (Wyman-Harris, p. 67; Goddard, pp. 130, 137; Matthews 1897, p. 223, 67n; Reichard 1944d, p. 81; Shooting Chant ms.; Haile 1938b, p. 85).

Collected tallows, see *Tallows.*

Collected waters, see *Waters, collected.*

Compulsion has been noted as a ritualistic method of approaching the gods—an offering correct in every respect must be accepted.

Black God had been prevailed upon to assist in the War Ceremony; he told the messengers who brought an acceptable offering, "Had I refused to perform, the monsters' ghosts would have been again devouring you, more so than they had been doing before. . . . Why should I keep it [knowledge of ceremony] to myself without letting others know what I intend to do?" (Haile 1938b, pp. 185, 187; 1943a, pp. 109, 111, 271, 309, 91n, 96n).

Conveyance, see *Hoops, Rainbow, Sunbeam.*

Cooking utensils prescribed for ceremonial use are another example of ritualistic thoroughness. We have already noted the prominence of the basket and the restrictions about food. An old-fashioned straight-necked cooking jar or pot, sometimes provided by the chanter, is the proper receptacle for cooking on the coals in the ceremonial hogan. In one text it is specified that the pot have no bulge. This pot probably represents the small yellow bowl, the inexhaustible food supply of the gods.

Special stirring sticks and the ladle for the ceremonial mush are designated (Reichard, 1944d, pp. 89, 103, 137; Haile 1938b, pp. 105, 191; cp. Newcomb 1940a, pp. 71-2).

Corn (na·dá̜"), in myth and ritual at least, is reaffirmed as belonging to the Navaho from time immemorial and there is probably no rite or ceremony in which corn does not function in some form or other. The feeling about corn is expressed: "Corn is more than human, it is divine; it was connected with the highest ethical ideals."

When Talking God gave corn to the lonely sisters of the Eagle Chant legend, he directed that they should never give it away. "Because," he explained, "there is no better thing in the world, for it is the gift of life." Later, when through ritualistic instruction their lot had improved, he said again, "Corn is your symbol of fertility and life."

Of the many representative references that might be given, a few follow: Hill 1938, pp. 20-95; Newcomb 1940b, pp. 51, 71, 73, 76; Matthews 1897, pp. 137, 140, 183; 1902, pp. 27, 29, 106, 187-93; Haile 1938b, pp. 87, 191, 231; 1943a, pp. 162, 313, 174n; Reichard 1939, pp. 27, 30, 34, Pl. IV-VII; 1944d, pp. 19, 81, 91, 113, 135; Shooting Chant ms.; Sapir-Hoijer, p. 31; Goddard, p. 174; Wheelwright 1942, p. 122, Set I, 1-4; II, 2; III, 1-4.

Corn meal (na·dá̜·ká·n) is one of the commonest forms of corn in ceremony. It is coarsely ground, white for a man, yellow for a woman, mixed if there is a patient of each sex. Sometimes it must be ground by a virgin or at some particular place or time in the ritual cycle. It is invariably used for the hogan blessing, for sandpainting sprinkling, and as a drier after the bath in all the rites I have seen, Evil as well as Holy. Often it serves as a substitute for pollen, since corn meal is plentiful and pollen is scarce. It usually denotes the same thing, life and success along the road, exemplified by footprints laid in corn meal.

With Big Fly's help, people overcome by Spider Man heaped corn pollen and white corn meal on Spider Man until he could no longer move. Big Fly took some of these substances for future rituals.

The corn-meal drier of the Night Chant bath was said to stand for the patient's body and blood (Haile 1938b, pp. 180–3; Sapir-Hoijer, p. 251).

Corn smut (dá'átca·n, ' corn excrement ') was the paint for the black hail spots of the Shooting Chant figure painting.

Hill describes cooked corn smut as a food. The eater applied some to his feet with the formula, "We are going to have much rain and large crops, but hail will not ruin the crops."

Corn smut was a part of the Feather Chant blackening.

Cornsmut Man was one of the Eagle Chant characters; he blackened himself with corn smut before starting to catch eagles (Hill 1938, p. 46; Newcomb 1940b, pp. 63, 65).

Corral Dance, see *Dark-circle-of-branches*.

Cotton (na·ką') is required for many invocatory offerings and some unravelers. Pueblo-grown cotton was formerly traded to the Navaho, but now thin cotton string or strands raveled from cotton cloth, retwisted, are more common.

Cotton with feathers constitutes a conveyance; the Holy People guide the rainbow with cotton, feathers direct it. Even Spindle had an invocatory offering (*Unraveling*, Con. C; Sapir-Hoijer, pp. 165, 185, 508, 64n).

Cotton fabric (na'aką') is valued for offerings and payment. Unbleached muslin and yard goods of all kinds, especially cotton prints, calico, and percale, make up the ' spread.'

Cotton is associated with spiderweb and cotton cloth with weaving, taught to the Navaho by Spider Woman; cloth and weaving are therefore her manifestations.

A cotton blanket, offered by Salt Woman to First Man, was refused; offered to Spider Woman, it was accepted.

Water Monster offered a cotton fabric to Coyote for the return of his children and with it Coyote said he would make clouds, rain, and vegetation (Franciscan Fathers, p. 222; Stephen 1930, p. 93; Goddard, p. 131).

Covers, blankets serving also as curtains, are indispensable to the Navaho.

Covers of the Skies were placed over and under Changing Woman and The Twins when they were babies. The Twins were hidden in similar covers to protect them from their father's wrath.

When heroes wandered alone they were often protected at night by a cover furnished by a deity.

Various covers—of Darkness, Dark Water, and dark, blue, yellow, and white clouds—were laid down for Rainboy's rites by their respective owners.

After the Fire Dance, Rainboy was left alone for four nights. The first night a large dark owl covered him with her wing. The next night White-nosed Duck covered him with the blanket of Old Age. The third night White Owl covered him, and the fourth night Rat Woman laid a squirrel skin over him.

Although the Stricken Twins seemed the most miserable of creatures, Talking God, their father, laid a cover of Darkness over them at night.

The curtains of the sweathouse and hogan doors, no matter how tattered or shabby they may appear, stand for deific qualities; they must be of a particular number and hung in a required order for each ceremony.

During the creation people were sent to Owl for a sweathouse curtain. He let them choose from those he had—white, blue, yellow, black, and flashing—and they chose the flashing one (Haile 1938b, p. 101; Reichard 1944d, pp. 23, 135, 137; Matthews 1902, pp. 216, 246; Wheelwright 1942, pp. 42, 57).

Cradleboards ('awé·tšá·l) of the supernaturals—Changing Woman, Monster Slayer, Child-of-the-water—were prototypes of the modern baby carrier. The lengthwise boards and footrests were of sunbeam or sunglow; the arch over the head of rainbow, the lacings of zigzag, flash, or forked lightning; the children were wrapped in clouds and covered with Skies— Darkness, Dawn, Blue Sky, Yellow-evening-light, Sunbeam. A rainstreamer was the fringe of the top cover; there were carrying straps of sunbeam, pillows of Mirage and Heat (tłǎ·h; Matthews 1897, pp. 106, 231; Haile 1938b, pp. 85, 91; Goddard, p. 149; Wheelwright 1942, p. 74).

Cross arrangement and even the cross as a design element are frequently encountered. A red cross, representing a fire, is a sandpainting indication that the picture belongs to a Fire

543

Dance branch, although not all pictures in this branch have it. The parts of the cross may have specific meanings; for instance, the black and blue cross in the center of *Navajo Medicine Man*, Plate XXII, represents wood, and the red cross in the center stands for the fire.

Little crosses of pollen or corn meal are a protection for the hands and knees of the patient when kneeling in the bath rite and when drinking the emetic.

A yellow cross on the shoulders of the Shooting Chant patient represents Big Fly's home.

After the original performance of the Shooting Chant was over, Holy Man was taken to the young pinyon tree. Before intoning the prayer, the chanter ' made footprints of pollen for the patient, but for himself only a cross.'

A cross may represent a person's gait, a journey, stars, or a 'spirit' (Newcomb-Reichard, p. 75, Pl. V; Reichard 1939, Pl. XIV, XVI, XVII; Shooting Chant ms.; Sapir-Hoijer, p. 251; Wheelwright 1942, Set I, 3; III, 4; Oakes-Campbell, pp. 38, 39, 41).

Cup of any kind may be the container for the chant lotion, according to JS, but the infusion specific must be administered from a turtle shell or abalone cup.

A small cup, providing an inexhaustible water supply, was sometimes furnished by the gods (cp. Kluckhohn-Wyman, p. 51).

Curtains, see *Covers*.

Cutting (taogic) is a release of evil; the most elaborate rite is the cutting of the plant garment. Made of knots, the garment represents tied-in power; cutting the knots signifies freeing the patient and destroying the evil.

A song of the Big Star Chant refers to the cutting of the garment as the cutting up of the monsters.

The withes for the Big Star Chant hoops should be cut at right angles (a male cut) for stomach trouble and loss of blood; diagonally (a female cut), for head trouble.

The ritualistic cutting of yucca for the Night Chant is explicit, as it is for the Flint Chant (Reichard, Big Star Chant ms.; Matthews 1902, p. 211; Haile 1943a, p. 54).

Dancing of all kinds is ritualistic; when accompanied by the proper sounds and behavior, it may indicate gloating; in forms such as the Fire Dance, it represents respect and honor to the deities of the many chants.

The Utes, who captured a Navaho, held a big celebration and danced around him; the old women whistled for joy at his capture.

In the Night, Feather, and Mountain chants, dancing is a major feature, a form of symbolism characteristic of the chant (*Dark-circle-of-branches;* Matthews 1887, p. 395; Reichard 1944d, pp. 116–35).

Danger line, line of protection ('atčą́˙ xo˙dzoh) may prove to be one of the most important concepts in the understanding of American Indian war patterns. Dr. Parsons suggests in a brilliant deduction that the reason for Estevan's death was his daring to ' cross the line ' which until then had doubtless been sacrosanct, for it is to be inferred that other Indians, who believed as the Zuni did, felt the same way and did not cross.

The idea is corroborated for the Navaho by Hill's explicit account of the war procedure and by other references. The line was composed of a zigzag and a flash lightning, a sunray and rainbow, designs that would prevent the enemy from overtaking the war party. The statement may even mean that the line would prevent the enemy from crossing into Navaho territory. An understanding of this idea makes clear the belief that evils dare not cross the pokers, since we know that the pokers stand not only for snakes but also for the supernatural conveyances.

Other elements that designate the line are meal sprinkling, flints, yucca, and mountains. On the other hand, pollen and meal sprinkling have blessing value in that they make the road safe for the traveler as long as he stays on the right side. The interpretation discloses the fundamental reasons for the elaborate preparations and procedure of hunting, war, and trading expeditions, which by their very nature cause men to cross the line.

Literary and ritualistic references confirm the interpretation: The hoops of the Big Star Chant, called sǫ'bą·s, 'star hoops,' are believed to furnish transportation, but when laid down one upon the other they are called 'atčą́· xo·dzoh, ' obstructing lines or marks '; a zigzag and a flash lightning are crossed upon the hoops. In the flat position they do not lose their travel power, but rather restrict territory to a manageable space, a zone of safety, while the riders enter into otherwise dangerous country.

Evil spirits cannot cross the mountains or flints of the Hand Trembling Chant, which represent the trail of life.

Blood formed the line after the killing of Big Monster and Changing-bear-maiden.

The danger line explains the ritualistic facing in two directions, toward and away from the enemy country, in the War

Ceremony. The enemy was ' talked out ' in prayer and a line was drawn against him in the valley.*

The following illustrate the zone rather than the line of protection:

The singer of the Rain Ceremony drew a line in his mind around the territory where he wanted rain. During the Rain Ceremony no one should step over the poker (actual, non-ritualistic) that lay by the fire. Holy People followed those who came into the house. If an Earth Person stepped over the poker, he blocked the passage to the Holy People. In other words, passing the poker would lead them into the fire. Furthermore, the poker should not at this time have its point toward the fire (its normal position). Hill says the reason is that there is too much chance of stepping over it.

If a poker lay in a vertical position east of the fire, the chances of stepping over it were as great no matter which way it was pointed. Another explanation is that the poker ordinarily should point toward the fire so that evils entering the door be attracted toward the fire, but at the time of the Rain Ceremony only good should enter and nothing should be done to cause it to detour (Parsons 1939, p. 363; Hill 1936, p. 16; 1938, pp. 75, 88; Kluckhohn-Wyman, p. 177; Matthews 1897, pp. 103, 116; Reichard, Endurance Chant ms.; Haile 1938b, pp. 45-6, 111, 157, 254, 87n).

Dark-circle-of-branches, Fire Dance, Corral Dance ('ił nás-djin) is a spectacular last- (ninth-) night performance of some chants to which other chants send their specialties ('álí'l). It is a part of the Shooting Chant; the Hail and Bead chants,

---

*Father Berard's translation, ' for ' instead of ' against ' him, is due to failure to distinguish the context of the bipolar post-positions (cp. Reichard 1944d, p. ix).

tho ugh their myths describe it in detail, forbid the Dark Cir cle events. Apparently custom has changed the restrictio ns and requirements of this branch of the chants.

The Fire Dance branch initiates novices and renews, confirms, and corrects a chanter's power. Since it agrees with the sandpainting branch in being primarily attractive of good, one may readily understand why the Evil ceremonies do not have it.

Some chants have their symbol in the Fire Dance. The red feather headdress, representing sunglow, and a dance with lightnings decorated with feathers are the symbols of the Shooting Chant in the Fire Dance complex (Ch. 11; Haile 1943a, pp. 13, 21, 25, 44; Matthews 1887, pp. 432ff.; Reichard 1939, pp. 35–6; 1944d, pp. 113ff.; Newcomb 1940b, p. 72).

Decoy fire, a plot motivation of various mythical episodes, seems to set up a relationship between sex, incest, and sorcery. Someone sees a beckoning fire at a great distance. He sets up a forked stick as an indicator so he can find the place in the daytime; his device leads to the discovery of new people, sometimes the household group of a sorcerer who has taken his daughter as a wife. The hero frees the daughter from her incestuous union and overcomes the sorcerer, sometimes obtaining the gift of rare game.

A fire decoy led Monster Slayer to the homes of the people who were neither good nor bad but in between (Ch. 5; Matthews 1897, pp. 138, 174; Newcomb 1940b, p. 55; Goddard, p. 127; Sapir-Hoijer, pp. 29ff.; Wheelwright 1942, p. 98).

Decoy woman entices a man to new acquaintance and often to mating. She is attractive; she has magic power from which only the gods can save the hero. Such women were

Changing-bear-maiden, Winter Thunder's w:fe, the daughter
and wife of Deer Owner, the pueblo Corn Maiden seducers of
Monster Slayer (Reichard, Endurance Chant ms.; 1944d,
pp. 5ff.; Haile 1943a, p. 56; Matthews 1897, pp. 174ff.;
Newcomb 1940b, pp. 55ff.).

Decoys are stereotyped in Navaho myth and ritual. Gods
entice heroes from their normal surroundings to teach them
holy things. The conflict of a hero with Deer Owner, the
arch-sorcerer, includes several decoys.

Game caught by a decoy, whether set by an evil or a helpful
being, eventually redounds to the profit of future Navaho,
since the episode results in ritual control: The eagle decoy set
the myths of the Bead and Big Star chants in action.
Changing-bear-maiden exploited an older sister's love for her
little brother—the privilege of combing his hair—to his
undoing, but he, with the supernatural decoy of a shadow,
thwarted her effort.

Sound is a common decoy (Ch. 15; Goddard, p. 162;
Matthews 1897, pp. 174ff., 195; Haile 1938b, p. 171; Newcomb 1940b, pp. 57ff., 65; Wheelwright 1942, p. 98; Reichard
1939, pp. 26ff.; 1944d, pp. 5–7; Big Star Chant ms.; Endurance Chant ms.).

Deer and rare game (dini') are symbolical of hunting power
and methods—stalking, killing and butchering, propitiation
of the animal spirit, and restrictions. Though hunting is almost
extinct, having been supplanted by pastoral pursuits, it still
occupies a major position in the ritualistic pattern (Hill 1938,
pp. 96ff.; Goddard, p. 162; Matthews 1887, pp. 391–2; 1897,
pp. 70, 154; Newcomb 1940b, p. 59; Reichard, Shooting
Chant ms.).

Disposal is illustrated by the following specific requirements (cp. Ch. 20; Kluckhohn-Wyman, p. 68):

Property disposed of	Place of disposal
Cattail garment	in lake (HC)
Dark-circle-of-branches	turned into rock (HC)
Drumstick	untied and placed outside house (HC)
Emetic coals and sand basins	at north some distance from hogan (SC, SCE, BS)
Hoops of Buckskin rite	at north (SCE)
Invocatory prayersticks:	
Arrowsnake	at edge of hill (SC)
Blue Lizard	near heap of black rock (SC)
Buffalo	on flat ground (SC)
Holy Man	on hilltop (SC)
Snake	under greasewood (SC)
Big Snake	in crooked pinyon root (SC), under brush near a hole (JS)
Tadpole	in lake (HC)
Rattlestick	see Haile 1938b, p. 245
Sand of painting	under shade of young pinyon (SC); on successive days farther and farther from hogan (Endurance Chant)
Sky-reaching-rock	see *Disposal of Sky-reaching-rock*, Con. C.
Yucca of bandoleer, necklace, and wristlets	inside cedar tree or bush with pollen strewn below and on top (Haile 1938b, p. 243)

Dreams have much to do with disease and curing. Legend occasionally includes dreams as a means of supernatural communication.

Whiteshell Woman appeared in a dream to the little girl she loved and explained why she had left home.

After Reared-in-the-mountain had had his Earth family purified and had stayed with them a while, he became accustomed to their odor, but he dreamed that the gods were begging him to return to them.

Dreams are related to belief in sympathetic magic and in reversal: Dreams of deer or of killing rare game are good.

Monster Slayer dreamed he was picked up by Throwing Monster, and told his mother about the dream. He took it to mean that he would succeed in subduing the creature.

Dreams during a ritualized activity are exceptionally potent, hence the rigidity and number of restrictions at such times: the interpretation of dreams during a Rain Ceremony was related to it. Dreams of rain, corn, or flowers were good; dreams of drought were bad (cp. Ch. 11, 15; *Whiteshell Woman*, Con. A; Morgan 1931, 1936; for Lincoln, see Kluckhohn-Spencer, p. 54; Hill 1936, p. 13; 1938, pp. 43, 50; Matthews 1887, pp. 390, 417; 1897, p. 139; Reichard, Shooting Chant ms.).

Dress, see Ch. 15; *Clothes*.

Drum as we usually think of it, a permanent percussion instrument, probably does not exist among the Navaho; their drum is improvised, a basket or a pot covered with a skin. The probable reason is that since noises are believed to drive away evil, it is dangerous to keep a drum. The basket is reversed and pounded on as a rhythmic accompaniment. According to the Night Chant myth, evil influences are gathered under the basket that serves as a drum, and once they have been confined into a controlled space, they are released and blown out the smokehole.

Since the pot drum is feared, it is constructed, used, and disposed of with special care.

The ghost of the Ancient People was killed by beating the pot drum, for when the Navaho beat it, they beat the face of the enemy (Matthews 1894b, p. 203; Reichard 1928, p. 132; 1944d, pp. 94–9; Shooting Chant ms.; Kluckhohn-Wyman, pp. 44, 59ff.; Tozzer 1909, pp. 337ff.).

Drumstick directions are given in the chant myths, for the drumstick, like the drum, is an improvised object, made each time it is needed (Matthews 1894b, pp. 202–8; 1902, pp. 59–63; Kluckhohn-Wyman, p. 44; Reichard 1944d, p. 85; Shooting Chant ms.; Haile 1938b, p. 44).

Dust token, a small quantity of soil, may be placed in the patient's moccasins during a rite or ceremony. In the Shooting Chant figure painting rite, the soil is taken from the sandpainting; it represents Gopher's aid in restoring Monster Slayer after the latter had overcome Burrowing Monster; it has the same meaning in the War Ceremony.

A little pouch containing a forked lightning, rain streamer, zigzag lightning, flash lightning, rainbow, and sunray was attached to the Hail Chant head bundle. These conveyances could be put into the sack by the Holy People, but now chanters substitute small quantities of soil from the sacred mountains for the same purpose.

When I asked MC about the bead token of the Night and Mountain chants, she said, "No, no bead, just the dirt in the moccasins"; from this remark it would appear that in these chants the dust is correlated with the bead token.

Dust from the tracks surrounding a wounded buffalo is a bundle substance of the Flint Chant, a means of identification with Buffalo. Its application seems to be a rite, possibly of restoration (Ch. 7; Haile 1938b, pp. 50, 193; 1943a, p. 18; Reichard 1928, p. 126; Shooting Chant ms.; 1944d, p. 103; Goddard, p. 130).

Error, see *Mistakes.*

Excess, see *Overdoing.*

Feathers are a ubiquitous requirement. Live feathers (xiná bitšos), usually of down, are from a live bird, caught and smothered with pollen. The longer the bird struggles, the more potent are its parts in ceremony. The feathers represent strength, speed and motion, deliverance; the pollen exposed to them stands for light and life, that is, the sheen of the feathers.

The power of feathers, especially of eagle down, originated in the conquest of Cliff Monster and the subsequent origin of birds.

Feathers that are not live are not necessarily dead; they are not from a bird ritualistically strangled, but may have dropped from a bird in flight.

Spider Woman gave life feathers to The Twins on their first trip to Sun; they are represented by the unravelers of the Shooting and Big Star chants, and combine Spider and Bird powers. The first feather, kept distinct among the unraveling strings, has more power than the others. It is tied to the first hoop or ring of the Big Star set as a charm against enemies.

Whenever a transformation was about to take place, feathers were laid between buckskins.

In an early world First Man took cuticle from his scalp, laid it on the ground, and it became Thunder with wings. At one time First Man sent Thunder, naked, to the home of Water Monster, who gave him a feather cloak, the ' same as forked lightning.'

Eagle feathers were sewed around the edge of the warrior's shield to aid his cause.

Eagles preparing for battle donned their feathers; others painted themselves. The feathers were inadequate against an attack of stinging insects that flew between the feathers and stung the skin.

Birds are closely associated with the Skies; the Dawn rays are Talking God's headdress feathers. Curiously, too, Dawn,

Day Sky, Evening Light, and Darkness are thought of as feathers, but they have birds to represent them as well.

The small brightly colored birds and their feather tokens stand for beauty and happiness.

Turkey feathers are commonly a part of traveling and bundle talking prayersticks and of other properties of Evil as well as Holy chants (Huckel ms.; Stephen 1930, pp. 88–9; Matthews 1897, pp. 109, 202; Haile 1938b, pp. 96, 101, 103, 193, 255, 108n; 1943a, p. 187; Hill 1936, p. 11; Reichard, 1939, p. 43; Newcomb-Reichard, p. 58, Pl. XVIII; Oakes-Campbell, p. 38, Pl. III).

Feinting, see *Passes.*

Fire (kǫ') is the symbol of annihilation among the Navaho as among most tribes believing in magic; it is said to burn evil. Fire enters into practically every ceremony with many variations, from the simplest restrictions to the Fire Dance with its varied displays of control—the Fire Dance itself, washing the hands in burning pitch, exposure to intense heat.

Sweating removes evils, conceived as arrows and witch objects, from the body; the fire into which they fall irrevocably destroys them. A woman subjected to the sweat-emetic rite was much disturbed because she could not remove her turquoise earrings; she made the best of things by wrapping them in rags.

Throwing pollen into the fire is an act of sacrilege; to annihilate pollen is to destroy hope.

Fire is more powerful than rock, for Traveling Rock, a monster, was overcome by fire, even after Monster Slayer's flint club had failed to annoy him. Reared-in-the-mountain encountered a fire made of pebbles in the home of the Bears.

Fire could burn the waters, as Black God demonstrated to

Water Sprinkler and others; burning is a symbol of the universal struggle between fire and water. Water Sprinkler could divide the waters and get to Water Monster, but he could not influence the ruler of the water realms once he got there. Black God, on the contrary, could not get to Water Monster's dwelling with his own power, but once there, he overcame the chief. Water is the antidote to fire; it soothes and calms, counteracts the fear inspired by fire, and represents escape.

The sweat-emetic rite includes many fire symbols—ceremonial kindling, fire jumping, fortitude in enduring heat, pokers as protective lines—but in the Night Chant Collected Waters branch an entire day's ritual is devoted to the kindling alone; in the Eagle Chant, to judge by the myth, similar emphasis is placed on burning incense. Ordinarily, the coals of the sweat-emetic fire are completely extinguished with water or the emetic, but the Hail Chant prescribes that some coals should be left to glow.

Fire and flame are ritualistically distinguished. When a sandpainting is prepared for the Sandpainting branch of the Shooting Chant there should be no flame at the fire. If necessary the hogan may be warmed by embers, but the fire should be kept relatively dormant (Hill 1938, pp. 98, 99; Reichard, Shooting Chant ms.; Shooting Chant Evil ms.; 1939, p. 31; 1944d, p. 73; Matthews 1887, p. 404; 1897, p. 169; 1902, pp. 28, 50ff., 75-6, 172, 209; Haile 1938b, p. 129; 1943a, p. 25; Newcomb 1940b, pp. 71-2; Kluckhohn-Wyman, p. 85).

Fire Dance, see *Dark-circle-of-branches.*

Fire Decoy, see *Decoy fire.*

Fire jumping (kǫ' bitis dacdi˙lɣo') is an act of purification; in the sweat-emetic rite it symbolizes purging the patient of

introduced evils—arrows, witch objects, and the like. In the
Evil chants participants must get as close to the fire as they
can, since exorcism is emphasized and fire is one of its chief
agents (Kluckhohn-Wyman, pp. 86–7; Goddard, p. 151;
Reichard 1944d, pp. 71–3).

Flame, see *Fire.*

Flash lightning, see *Thunder,* Con. A.

Flint (bé·c) armor was impervious to lightning arrows
unless they were accompanied by other supernatural weapons.
When Sun gave his children the arrows, clubs, and other
weapons, he clothed them in flint.

Flint has power because of its hardness, the sound of the
pieces rattling against one another, and the flashes of light
from its facets, flashes that represent lightning and pre-dawn
in the Hail Chant myth. In the Flint Chant, Flint stands for
the restoration of bones and strength.

Flint originated when the monsters' hides disintegrated.
From Big Monster, for example, flints ' leaked away ' after
he was attacked.

Flint exploded when heated; Sun tried to kill The Twins
by heating agate stones for the sweathouse fire. Flint was a
threat when, in the Flint Chant, it was said, "Winter Thunder may make you walk on flints."

Sun's piston was of flint; sound, light, color, and hardness
exerted squeezing power.

Flint was Horned Toad's protection against lightning;
turtle shell could be substituted for flint—thick scales of any
kind are doubtless associated with it (Reichard 1939, Pl.
XVII-XIX; 1944d, pp. 38–9; Shooting Chant ms.; Newcomb-
Reichard, Pl. XV-XVII; Haile 1938b, pp. 31–2, 111; 1943a,
pp. 2, 14, 25, 29, 40, 116, 305, 27n; Stephen 1930, p. 91).

Flint arrowpoints (bé·sisṭogi), numerous in the exorcistic ceremonies, seem to be considered separately from their function as part of an arrow; that is, they are knives rather than penetrating weapons. The discussion of sound, light, and color has brought out three ways in which their symbolism is worded and they, like arrows and armor, frighten.

Flint arrowpoints are required to cut vegetation and may be an offering to the plant cut; their role in cutting knots in the plant garment rite is release (*Cutting;* Kluckhohn-Wyman, pp. 34–5; Hill 1938, pp. 96–7).

Flute (sǫ́·s, tsisǫ́·s, ndilnih) is not, as far as I know, a property of the chants with which I am most concerned in this work, but it is referred to in the creation myth and in the Eagle Chant story. The whistle probably takes its place in the Shooting, Hail, and Bead chants (Goddard, p. 135; Newcomb 1940b, p. 54; Haile 1938b, p. 48; 1943a, p. 27).

Food as a symbol of plenty indicated the success of a ceremony, strength, endurance, and transformation. Creatures in myth provide food, sometimes to give, sometimes to deprive of power. Some characters, though having many powers, suffer for want of a particular food. Ceremonies require certain foods, forbid others.

Scavenger of the Bead Chant did not eat when the birds were trying to get him to the sky because had he done so, even lightning could not have lifted him. The Eagles had plenty of their own food, but they fed him corn from the packets they carried, and gave him water from the reeds packed in their tails.

Food provided for the warrior impersonators of a War Ceremony and for the singers of the tail songs represents food given to Black God.

The fat around the base of the mountain sheep horns was valued for sausage and belonged to the man who brought down the sheep. Even a person as powerful as the oldest Brother became resentful when Coyote insisted on having the choice fat, and made it hard and corrugated (Ch. 15; Reichard 1939, p. 35; 1944d, pp. 19, 80–3, 88–91, 103, 113, 135–9; Shooting Chant ms.; Endurance Chant ms.; Haile 1938b, pp. 85, 87, 131, 191, 231, 233; 1943a, p. 229; Matthews 1887, pp. 388–9, 394, 412; 1897, pp. 72, 96, 153, 182–3, 198, 233, 119n; 1902, pp. 106, 168, 189, 203, 204, 213, 218–9, 224–5, 309, 11n; Hill 1938, p. 8; Goddard, p. 168; Newcomb 1940b, p. 72; Sapir-Hoijer, p. 79).

Footprints are a common symbol, especially of pollen and sandpaintings, where they represent the road of life, or the trail of safety.

When a girl and boy were spirited away from the mythological cornfield, the people made four footprints of white corn outside the house and four footprints and handprints of corn pollen inside the house and prayed for the return of the children.

This is one of two references to handprints I have found, the other being a note that people prayed with their hands pressed into handprint impressions in a rock.

Footprints lead onto sandpaintings as in those of the Shock and Prayer on buckskin rites of the Evil ceremonies.

One of the few descriptions of Sun's physical features is a reference to giant footprints (Wheelwright 1942, p. 122 and paintings; Goddard, pp. 154, 174; Newcomb 1940b, p. 56; Kluckhohn-Wyman, p. 172; Reichard 1944d, p. 113; Matthews 1887, p. 164; 1897, p. 108; 1902, pp. 164, 181; Haile 1938b, p. 125; Oakes-Campbell, pp. 38, 39).

Forked lightning, see *Thunder,* Con. A.

Forked stick, see *Decoy fire, Decoy woman, Decoys; First Man,* Con. A.

Fumigant, see *Incense.*

Game, rare, see *Deer and rare game.*

Gopher dust, see *Dust token.*

Gourd rattles accompany the singing of the Hail, Endurance, and Big Star chants and the Shooting Chant Evil. There is doubtless some connection between the rattle and the species of wild gourd sometimes placed in a hogan to protect it from lightning. Gourds seem to be associated with stars (Reichard 1944d, p. 105; Endurance Chant ms.; Big Star Chant ms.; Hill 1938, p. 60; Tozzer 1908).

Guardians are often mentioned for supernatural dwellings, but it is possible that all guardians are the same—Bear, Thunder, Wind, and Snake, the guards of Sun's and Changing Woman's homes, in the sky, on earth, and in the west.

The creation tale includes the following variations: guards of Sun's house—Thunders, Water Monster, Big Snake, Mountain Lion; guards of Changing Woman's house—Hail, Thunder, Lightning, Rain, Water Monster; guards of the White House home of the gods—Lightnings, Bears, Red-headed Snake, Rattlesnakes. All were blinded when Wind, helper of the hero, blew dust in their eyes.

Most sandpaintings have an encircling guardian and two small guardians of the eastern opening. Some chanters, as RP and JS, almost always paint the small ones, others omit them. So far I have found no good reason for the difference. The chanter generally erases the small eastern guardians before the treatment on the painting begins because ' they must not see the healing ceremony ' (Newcomb-Reichard, pp. 64, 76; Reichard, Shooting Chant ms.; Wheelwright 1942, p. 81; Matthews 1907, p. 26; Huckel ms.).

Hand clapping is mentioned several times in the myths in such a way that it seems to be ritualistic; I have never seen it. The song leader of the War Ceremony claps his hands as an accompaniment of four songs.

When The Twins, being trained by Talking God and xa·ctćé''óɣan, beat the gods in a race, the latter showed their pleasure by laughing and clapping their hands.

Talking God clapped his hands as he laughed with glee when the hero of the Mountain Chant tried to get into a hole too small for him. At another time he bade his companions go ahead of him as they approached his house. They refused and, after the fourth time, he clapped his hands, uttered his call, and led them in.

In the Flint Chant, Talking God clapped his hands as a sign of hope (Haile 1938b, p. 243; 1943a, p. 59; Matthews 1887, pp. 399, 410; 1897, p. 106).

Hand on heart is a mythological and perhaps ritualistic way of accepting an offering.

When Sun was ready to put the agate man inside Monster Slayer, he first closed his eyes and placed his hand on his own heart.

In restoring Rainboy, Talking God put one hand over Rainboy's heart and the other at his back. This act had the same meaning as placing the agate man inside Monster Slayer (*Acceptance of offering;* Reichard, Shooting Chant ms.; 1944d, p. 11).

560

Hand over mouth is a gesture ascribed to Talking God and Water Sprinkler. When a Navaho woman is embarrassed or surprised, she puts her hand over her mouth. I have never seen a man do so. Talking God seems to make the gesture ritualistic.

When the Visionary of the Night Chant had been snatched from directly under the noses of the gods by Superior God, Talking God searched the sky for his grandchild, asking everyone he met if they had seen him. As they disclaimed knowledge of the boy's whereabouts, Talking God put his hand over his mouth and smiled. He meant that he knew they were lying, and soon after he found the boy where he lay hidden in a corner. The gesture showed superior knowledge, absence of gullibility, or perhaps surprise.

One day the Stricken Twins were awakened by their father's call. When he came to them, he clapped his hands and put his hand over his mouth—"as if he were surprised," Matthews adds. The interpretation may be correct, but I think it means also, "As if he intended to do something surprising."

The text and translation of the Goddard story which includes the gesture seem to justify my interpretation. When Mirage Talking God came to First Man and First Woman as he was showing her the baby found on the mountain top, Talking God put his hand over his mouth, then clapped his hands and said, "Something wonderful is happening, my grandchildren."

Clapping the hand over the mouth while shouting and bathing in snow is recommended for boys' training to make them strong. Whooping with hand clapping accompanies the naming rite in the War Ceremony (Reichard 1938, p. 39; Matthews 1902, pp. 167, 175, 231, 239, 314, 61n; Sapir-Hoijer, pp. 105, 285, 297; Goddard, p. 60).

Handprints, see *Footprints.*

Haste in performing ritual may be due to fear. When Matthews recorded the creation myth, his informant, contrary to his usual demeanor, seemed under great tension. He hurried the narration and was impatient at interruptions, even for eating. After he had finished the tale, the chanter explained that both he and Matthews were in danger as long as their minds remained in the lower worlds, but as soon as they arrived in this world, they could take their time.

The haste of the Shooting Chanter in certain rites—aspersing of sweat-emetic rite, application of unraveler—may have been due to a similar cause (Matthews 1888, p. 150).

Head feather bundle is a bundle item called by Kluckhohn and Wyman ' chant token,' a name I consider misleading, since it does not differ markedly from other bundle items. Called ' enemy down feather,' the head feather bundle of the Hail Chant was composed of magpie, roadrunner, and red duck tail feathers, and wing feathers of eagle, turkey, bluebird, and green-winged finch. To its bottom was tied a little pouch containing dust from the sacred mountains; the pouch is equivalent to the chant token of the Night and Mountain chants. But in the Hail Chant a piece of agate tied with the bundle during the sing is kept by the patient as his token. Hence it must be that the pouch of the Hail Chant is a part of the head feather bundle retained by the chanter.

The name of the head feather bundle and other features— the way it is tied, for example—suggest that it refers to a scalp protecting the patient from foreign enemies.

The War Ceremony bundle, containing roadrunner's tail sprinkled with pollen shaken from a goshawk, represents Cliff Monster's feathers, plucked by Monster Slayer as a trophy to preserve for future ceremonies.

A head feather bundle of owl and eagle feathers, to which

abalone and whiteshell were tied, was worn attached to the warrior's cap in actual warfare. Probably something like or corresponding to the head feather bundle is an indispensable item of all ceremonies and bundles (*Bundle contents: SC*, item 16, Con. C; Kluckhohn-Wyman, pp. 37–8; Reichard 1944d, p. 103; Haile 1938b, pp. 62, 121, 193, 319, 74n; 1943a, pp. 27–8 [Headplume]; Hill 1936, p. 8).

Head-bowing, see *Bowed head.*

Head lifting, a ritualistic act of the Girl's Adolescent Ceremony, may be explained by a reference in the creation myth. The girl lifts little children by their heads. Changing Woman, after her puberty ceremony was over, lifted the attendants present by their heads to thank them for their gifts. Another reference indicates that the slight stretching is thought to make children grow tall (Curtis, p. 124; Wheelwright 1942, p. 77).

Heat, see *Fire.*

Homes (xo·γan) have been mentioned as characterizing deity. Several good descriptions of the Navaho home are available. The following notes concern concepts centering about the home (and house) and the house blessing.

The houseposts, according to the Shooting Chant myth, were originally of agate arranged in the flint-armor colors, black at the east, blue at the west, yellow at the south, pink at the north, and white at the top or central portion. It was decreed that in the future the posts should be of oak instead of agate. Today the oak sprigs of the house blessing represent the posts.

In the Eagle Chant myth, the description of the first house

prescribes cleansing and song. The construction of the house
was simultaneous with the making of the eagle trap; both
were done with ritualistic care (Mindeleff, pp. 475–517;
Reichard 1944d, pp. 3, 5, 17, 51; Shooting Chant ms.; Matthews 1887, pp. 399, 400, 407, 408; 1897, pp. 161, 164, 168,
185, 204; 1902, pp. 47, 168, 192, 206, 210, 230; Newcomb
1940b, pp. 54, 57, 58–60).

Hoops and rings (tsįbą's, sǫ'bą's) play a large part in ceremony, especially emphasized in exorcistic forms. Provided
with a life feather, hoops symbolize a swift, easy, magical
means of travel; they are closely identified with Winds, Stars,
Hail (perhaps when accompanied with flint), Buffalo, and
Snakes.

The little rings on the bundle talking prayersticks of the
Shooting Chant are conveyances, as are the feathered hoops
carried by Buffalo.

The hoops that appear so frequently in the Big Star Chant
represent Stars, as the name sǫ'bą's, ' star hoops,' suggests.
The party that went to rescue the Big Star Chant hero, who
had become a coyote, encountered difficulties in handling
their hoops. They thought the hoops would travel if rolled in
the cardinal directions, but Talking God had to show the
people that the hoops had to be laid flat and turned a ritualistic number of times. The incident is illustrated by the
accessory Prayer on buckskin rite of the Shooting Chant
Evil and by a similar rite of the Night Chant.

Hoop rites commemorate retransformation from a coyote
to the hero's deific self (*Circle, Danger line,* Con. B; *Hoop
transformation rite, Prayer on buckskin,* Con. C; Reichard,
Shooting Chant Evil ms.; 1939, pp. 31, 69–73, Pl. XXIII;
1944d, p. 31; Newcomb-Reichard, p. 64, Pl. XXVIII; Matthews 1897, pp. 84, 109, 127, 128; 1902, pp. 68, 96, 259).

Horns are an evidence of power. Sun may be depicted as a disk with a face, feathers, lightning, and rain, but he is considered more powerful if he has horns; the same is true of Moon, Dark Wind and Yellow Wind, Water Monster, Water Horse, Sky, and Earth. Snakes of the Wind chants are horned; those of the Shooting Chant are not. Possibly horns represent shine, glint, or control of lightning (Newcomb-Reichard, pp. 57–8, Fig. 5, Pl. XXVIII, XXIX, XXXII, XXXIII; Reichard 1939, pp. 43, 48, 63; Wheelwright 1942, pp. 63, 65, 66).

House blessing (xo·γan yilzį́·h, xo·γan da'atłic) is an initial rite of all ceremonies. It consists of laying new oak sprigs in the hogan (or shade) walls at the cardinal directions, sprinkling the places with corn meal, and singing. The blessing of a new home is more elaborate, being a rite or ceremony in itself, a part of the general Blessing complex. The songs and prayers, addressed to Sky, Earth, and Rain, are necessary to happiness in the new home. Four songs are required, twelve may be sung; two prayers are the minimum, six may be chanted.

The mountains, inhabited by Talking God and xa·ctčé·- 'óγan, were the first homes; after the Blessing rites, they became hogans—the foregoing are JS's notes of summary, given me when he presided at the dedication of the new stadium at Gallup (Kluckhohn-Wyman, pp. 76–7; Goddard, p. 151; Reichard 1944d, p. 51; Haile 1937).

Incense (yadidiṅił), called ' fumigant ' by Kluckhohn and Wyman, is prepared from a specific formula and kept in the chanter's bundle. A synthetic symbol, it purifies the patient, drives away disease, and immunizes him from dangers that might arise from the very powers he has invoked. Incensing is a conclusive act of various rites—in a sense, a benediction, but it is also a prophylactic. "It is what the Holy People fear," says the helper who communicates the formula to the hero.

In myth, after the Holy People have sung over the hero and retired, a helper—Beaver for the Hail Chant, Owl for the Night Chant, Gopher for the War Ceremony—instructs the patient and offers the unique part of the formula for the hero's future aid.

Since incense is common in Holy rites, rare in Evil, it seems to be a force for attracting good. In the Flint Chant, it is the conclusive act of a little rite to correct evil ensuing from sexual excess; it symbolizes renewed strength.

Apparently in the Eagle Chant, incense-burning is incorporated in the firemaking rite that specifies burning yucca and bluebird and canary feathers, often a part of the incense formula.

The incense formula of the Shooting Chant is ' willow as a foundation,' white, blue, and gray corn, head feathers of bluebird, canary, and robin, all ground together. That of the Hail Chant includes down feathers of bluebird, western bluebird, red-winged blackbird, canary, Bullock oriole, Arizona jay, cedar waxwing, gray titmouse, long-tailed chat, hummingbird, and an unidentified bird (dziłγá· nakehé). White corn meal is also mentioned, but I do not know whether it alone formed the incense or was combined with the feathers (*Coals*, Con. B; Kluckhohn-Wyman, pp. 49–50; Reichard, Shooting Chant ms.; 1944d, pp. 59, 65, 73, 95, 139; Matthews 1887, p. 42; 1897, p. 177; 1902, pp. 44, 169; Sapir-Hoijer, p. 229; Haile 1938b, p. 115; 1943a, pp. 18, 280; Newcomb 1940b, pp. 71–2).

Inexhaustible food, water, tobacco supply is frequently referred to in myth. A supernatural being offers a tiny

566

receptacle, often a yellow food bowl, or a tiny water cup. The recipient takes all he can, never succeeds in emptying it. The owner, with one mouthful or one sweep of the fingers, exhausts the contents and returns the utensils to his pouch. The mush-eating rite demonstrates the inexhaustible theme; one should eat a lot so that one will always have plenty (cp. *Corn, Mush;* Matthews 1897, pp. 165, 199; 1902, pp. 168, 186, 204, 216, 243; Haile 1938b, pp. 105, 133).

Inner form, see *Pollen ball.*

Intertwining trees, see *Ambush.*

Jumping or *jumping over* is probably only a slight variant of the stepping over act; both signify transformation or restoration.

The gods, having secured a token quantity of precious stones, arranged them between buckskins; then they jumped over the whole and it turned into five large jewel baskets (cp. *Fire jumping;* Matthews 1902, p. 165).

Kneading, see *Mush, Pollen ball, Pressing.*

Knots symbolize the circle of frustration. Consequently they occur often in exorcistic rites. Four cincture rites are described in the myth of the Hail Chant, having taken place on four successive days. The Twins cut Rainboy free with flint knives. Patients undergoing the Plant Garment rites of the Evil chants are released by flints wielded by impersonators of The Twins. Cutting every knot demonstrates the freeing of the patient and control of the evils that tied him in (cp. *Cutting, Flint; Plant garment,* Con. C; Kluckhohn-Wyman, pp. 102–3; Reichard 1944d, pp. 52–5, 60–3, 66–9, 74–5).

Lifting with bundle properties is an act in which the chanter leads the patient onto the sandpainting. The chanter closes his hand over half a bundle item—bull-roarer, for instance—and holds it out to the patient, who grasps it, is raised, and is led to his place on the painting; often there are stops at points between the patient's seat and the goal, during which songs are sung.

Lotion (ke·tłoh), see Kluckhohn-Wyman, p. 51.

Lower worlds as the place of origin of the pre-human creatures who antedated the Navaho are discussed in Chapter 2. Here the derivations and occurrences in each world according to the different versions are abstracted from the myths, an attempt being made to keep the descriptions parallel—character of the world, kind of people encountered, advances toward human traits and customs.

The *first* world was red, small, and barren. Since there was an ocean in each direction, it must have been like an island.

It was inhabited by black insectlike creatures; among them was Bat. First Man, First Woman, and Black God were there. From cuticle a man and a woman, Water Monster, Salt Woman, Thunder, Big Frog, Crane, and a mentor were created. Water Monster was the chief of the eastern ocean, Crane (Blue Heron) of the southern, Frog of the western, and Winter Thunder of the northern ocean. These people moved to the edges of the world because, although the First Pair had made Cicada, Ants, and Horned Toads for food, they became intolerable to their creators.

The four chiefs had seeds, corn, pumpkin, squash, watermelon, tobacco, beans, cotton, muskmelon, gourd—all desired by the people living in the center of the world. The situation gave rise to a bitter struggle that ended in the flooding of the world. In one myth the people moved in circles to the sky, which they found smooth and hard; just before they finally gave up hope of getting through, Swallow showed them a hole through the sky leading to his home in the east. In another myth the chief who had sent the flood gave offerings to First Man, who allowed all to escape in a reed that grew from the water to the sky of the second world. Two young men appeared from a spring, were hidden by First Woman under her arm, and later, in the third world, became sun and moon bearers.

In the Wheelwright version, Coyote and Salt Woman, as well as the gods and the black insects mentioned by Matthews, existed; be'γotcidí was in charge of creation. He made the principal mountains, on which he planted vegetation. Black God set the world afire as a result of a quarrel with be'γotcidí because he also wanted to exert authority. be'γotcidí had the people escape through a reed to the world above, leaving the first world burning below (Matthews 1897, pp. 63–4; Stephen 1930, p. 88; Goddard, p. 127; Wheelwright 1942, pp. 39–41).

The *second* world was blue, dry, and cheerless. Because it was overcrowded, the people bewitched one another. It was inhabited by Swallows and other blue birds. All who came into the second world from the first had legs, feet, bodies, heads, and wings like (corresponding with) those of the second world's people. They understood one another's language and solicited friendship by using kin terms. According to Goddard, First Man, First Woman, Water Coyote, and Coyote appeared in the second world. According to Stephen, First Man made Talking God, xaˑctčéˑˀóγan, Monster Slayer, and Black God, and placed them on the four main mountains, which were oriented as they had been in the world below. The gods had charge of the game that roamed the mountains.

The accounts of the second world feature light and color. The people of the first world found in the second world sun, moon, and the four colors, black, white, blue and yellow. From the colors First Man made day and night. When white and yellow met in the center there was day; when blue and black met there was night. Coyote came into being at the east from the contact of white and yellow light and Yellow Fox sprang from the yellow light at the west. Similarly, from the meeting of blue and black, Blue Fox originated at the south, Badger at the north.

First Man started a ceremony to which he invited strangers. They came, made friends, and taught the new people agriculture. The First Pair created twelve people, who became pueblo Indians. First Man planted the seed he had brought from below, and all kinds of people (animals) joined his group.

According to Matthews, the use of kinship terms succeeded in placating the people of the second world for twenty-three days, but again the intruders took the wives of the natives and were driven out. A second version gives First Woman's intercourse with Sun as the cause of their expulsion.

The Stephen version stresses instruction in evil (which became witchcraft) in the second world, including the separation of the sexes and the subsequent birth of the monsters. As the men were getting the women back across the river that separated them, Water Monster stole one of the children and Spider Woman hid it from him; he therefore sent a flood to destroy all the people.

Though the reasons for the departure are different in detail, they are similar in kind. Again the people came to the sky and were unable to find a passage through. Wind with a white face showed them a way through at the south; apparently these people flew up to the next world. According to Stephen, Cicada contested with the birds living in the third world and won the land; four people went through the hole and made arroyos and canyons so that the waters could run off. Then Winds dried the land, and the people, setting up long ladders in their reed, climbed to the third world.

The Wheelwright version continues its account with be'γotcidí as creator in the second world. He made the wasp-like insects and twin males and females, each pair called One-who-follows-the-other. be'γotcidí destroyed then restored them. He also created cotton, which ' became motion and sound,' clouds, and vegetation. Black God continued to quarrel with be'γotcidí and, when the latter would not let the people move to the mountains to enjoy the flowers, Black God burned the waters and the people moved up once more through the large reed to a third world (Matthews 1897, pp. 65–6, 216–7; Goddard, p. 128; Stephen 1930, pp. 95ff.; Wheelwright 1942, pp. 41–3).

The *third* world was yellow and barren, but had a river flowing through it toward the east. It was measured by sending couriers in all four directions; they reached land's end and returned to report in one day. Mountains had the same position they have in this world.

The people of the third world—grasshoppers, yellow ants, red ants, and black ants with red heads—were at first friendly to the newcomers. At the eastern side of the eastern mountain, Turquoise Boy lived with twelve male companions and Mirage People, who owned large reeds. At the west, White-shell Woman lived with twelve female companions and Heat People, owners of twelve female reeds. In the third world First Man appointed five chiefs—Big Snake, Bear, Wolf, Panther, and Otter.

Corn and agriculture are described for the third world. Turkey, who owned gray corn and lived at Gray Mountain, is introduced. White corn, created with First Man, was planted by him; First Woman planted her yellow corn, and Turquoise Boy planted his blue corn. Then First Man called Turkey, who danced and dropped gray corn, spotted beans, and seeds of watermelon and muskmelon from his wings.

In the third world, First Man established marriage and clan exogamy, and decreed that there should be transvestites.

Matthews says that the separation of the sexes, caused by First Woman's unfaithfulness to First Man, took place in the third world. Many lives were lost and First Woman blamed the misfortune on her husband's bad leadership. When she took over, a flood came up, caused by Water Monster, whose children Coyote had lassoed with a rainbow and kidnaped. First Man saved the people by causing a reed to grow from the top of the eastern mountain to the sky; by blowing he enlarged it so that the people could get into it. Woodpecker pecked a hole in the sky, through which Water Monster appeared to claim his children. Here a trade was made: Coyote gave back one child and kept the skin of the other (who did not necessarily die) to produce rain and vegetation. The Wheelwright version agrees substantially with this account.

According to Matthews' version A, the newcomers were ousted from the third world for abusing the hospitality of the residents. Red Wind showed them the passage, made by Whirlwind and twisted like a tendril, through the smooth hard sky. Matthews' version B has the people escape from the flood of the third world in a reed.

The third world was the last, according to Stephen. Here the Pueblos built their houses, the Navaho built hogans, and presumably their life on this earth began.

The Wheelwright version places the elements of the Goddard and Stephen versions in the third world—the Navaho living in peace with the Zuni, Hopi, and Taos pueblos; the separation of the sexes; the theft of Water Monster's child; the flood and escape through the reed. Before the quarrel the people acquired clothes, methods of hunting, the institution of marriage, a language, and some ceremonies. There was no sun or moon, but the mountains gave plenty of light (Matthews 1897, pp. 66–7; Goddard, pp. 128–31; Stephen 1930, p. 102; Wheelwright 1942, pp. 43–51).

The *fourth* world resembled the others but was larger; the couriers took four days to return from their survey of it. By the time the people reached the fourth world many materials, techniques, customs, and institutions were known, since they they had been accumulating for a long time.

In Matthews' legend, the events of the fourth world that had occurred in the previous worlds of the other versions were: the appearance of Coyote and Badger where the sky colors met, the separation of the sexes, the theft of Water Monster's children, the flood, and the escape through the reed to the fifth world.

The people, now of many kinds, encountered the ancient pueblo people and, strangely enough, created First Man and First Woman from corn which they produced.

The Goddard version contains many of the details already mentioned for the fourth and lower worlds and adds a detailed account of First Man's model of the earth and the seasons. In contrast Coyote spoiled plans for the future, such as the model of the moon and the pattern of the stars. In the Wheelwright version, be'γotcidí found Talking God, owner of the new world, friendly to the strangers. According to this version, the fourth is our world.

In various accounts there are brief references to two men who rose from a spring at some place or other in the upward journey; these were later chosen by the people to act as Sun and Moon, that is, the orb bearers (Matthews 1897, pp. 67–8; Goddard, pp. 131ff.; Wheelwright 1942, pp. 51–6).

Massage, see *Pollen ball, Pressing.*

Medicine sprinkling is much like pollen sprinkling. For instance, in the Flint Chant the first line sprinkled over the medicine in the turtle shell represents the messenger who called the singer; the second, the singer coming to the patient; the third, the administration of the medicine; the fourth, the patient returning to his place (Haile 1943a, p. 32).

Mistakes are, of course, usually inadvertent and may be corrected. There is a prayer to correct unremarked errors or omissions. Careful reporting is a provision to avoid harm that might result from blundering.

When the singer of the Rain Ceremony returned from depositing the prayerstick, he gave an accurate account of all that had happened during the time he was alone: he admitted hesitancy in reciting the prayers and acknowledged his mistakes. Similarly, the war leader reported to his men the exact details, favorable and unfavorable, about his performance of the private ritual. Mythical heroes upon their return often spent an entire night narrating their doings while away from home.

Chanters doubtless resort to divers means to undo or revise slight deviations from the rule: at one sing a chanter suddenly discovered, after the patient had left the sandpainting, that he had forgotten the chant lotion, which should have been administered while the patient was on the sandpainting, whereupon he surreptitiously applied it to himself.

One time prayersticks, correctly made, had been placed in

the wrong order—b-u-b-u-y-u, instead of b-u-u-b-y-u. The chanter did not notice the mistake until after the whistling, whereupon, much annoyed, he ordered them changed.

It is to be expected that chanters, under the strain of the protracted ceremonies, should at times show signs of fatigue. One singer I observed seemed to let down a bit on the sixth day of a nine-night chant. He made little errors, but immediately caught himself up and corrected them. Another chanter, on the fourth day of a five-night performance, started the wrong prayer, stopped himself, and started over again. During the day he seemed less sure than usual about the ceremonial order. The following day, in both cases, the chanters were as alert as usual.

I have emphasized the confidence and finish with which RP and tłắ·h practiced their profession. Although not as learned, JS is exacting and composed under the most trying circumstances. Other chanters I have seen excel at certain points and are less accurate at others. One, for instance, was very sure about songs and ritualistic order, but made many mistakes in a common sandpainting and in the figure painting that were not corrected. Another chanter told me they were errors, but he had not called them to the attention of the presiding chanter; perhaps there was so much wrong that expostulation would have meant discontinuing the performance.

Chanters do not by any means always agree and one time I saw two men actually quarrel. Arrangements had been made to have two chanters come into town to lay some sandpaintings and to record prayers and songs. They brought a singer of lesser reputation as a helper. The older men had frequently recorded for whites; he had not. When he discovered that they intended to recite the prayers without a patient, he made a great fuss. They talked and talked; finally they thought the matter had been satisfactorily explained and worked again on the paintings. Soon, however, one of the seniors said he could not continue because the younger man was spoiling the painting, purposely making mistakes. The two older men quickly decided to send him home; they could not put up with his arguments and they would not have him ruin their work.

The following are expressions of effects that might ensue from ritualistic errors: "If a chanter makes a little mistake, the patient won't get well and something might happen to the chanter too. The leaders are very careful to have the feathers of prayersticks tied and placed so they do not turn back or blow in the wrong direction." "If they make a mistake the gods will say, 'Let him come here and talk with us.' Then he will die and go to Thunder." "Mistakes will make people go crazy or become crippled," said a chanter, and the teachings of the Night Chant corroborate the belief (cp. Ch. 1; Hill 1936, p. 14; 1938, p. 95; Huckel ms.; Matthews 1902, p. 211; Sapir-Hoijer, p. 309; Haile 1943a, pp. 33–4).

Modeling, see *Pressing*.

Mush is required at most ceremonies. The most common kind is ta·ńil, ' meal is placed in water '; it is made of coarsely ground blue corn, dropped into boiling water and boiled until quite thick. Ashes from juniper wood are added as leaven. "Without ashes the mush would be just like tortillas without baking powder," said RP. ta·ńil was eaten for a regular meal (not ritualistically) during the Sun's House branch of the Shooting Chant.

gad 'ádin, ' no cedar, unseasoned mush,' is a thick gruel like that described above, but with no flavoring of any kind, especially no salt or ashes. It is eaten at the end of the treatment on the sandpainting of the last day of the Shooting Chant; each mouthful of mush is followed by a drink of water.

Winter Thunder provided unseasoned mush for Rainboy; seasoning of beeweed greens was served with it. Rat Woman served it to the Racing Gods, and Changing Woman gave it for another rite of the Hail Chant; it was eaten also at the Prayer on buckskin rite.

Unseasoned mush in a rock-crystal basket was offered to The Twins by Dawn Girl on their first visit to Sun. The boys were urged to eat more and more, but could not empty the basket because it turned out to be the inexhaustible food supply. "A patient should eat lots and no mush should be left in the basket."

tó'i· yiṅil, ' dropped into water,' is described as thin gruel, originally prepared for Black God and now given to the stick-receiver of the War Ceremony to induce him to carry out his part carefully (Reichard 1944d, pp. 83, 89, 103, 113; Kluckhohn-Wyman, p. 100; Haile 1938b, pp. 105, 191, 203).

Names are full of power, ritualistic items of tremendous value. A few examples are cited. The different names for the same person should be noted—all names belong to the specialized ceremonial language (Ch. 16; Reichard 1928, pp. 96–107; Haile 1938b, pp. 55–6; 1943a, p. 34–5).

Big Fly	ts'e·k'idicjí·n	
Big-snake-man Monster Slayer Dwarf Boy	ło· nêi·ne·l'í"	One-who-customarily-sees-the-fish
Bow	'ałti· γa'o·ti'	Bow-whose-string-extends-away-from
Buffalo chief	di·tcili· 'asdzá·n	Abalone Woman
Buffalo chief's wife	násídídí·n	
Buffalo male	de·γádjíl'ái	Horned Chief
Buffalo female	biyájí łtsoi	His-yellow-little-one
Buffalo name of blue rattle (SC)	{ yá bił nídidáhi· { noxodacdjini· biká"gi	One-who-looms-on-the-horizon

CONCORDANCE B

Child-of-the-water	'aké'dé'' tóbádjíctcíní cá' bitł'ó'l na'ti' nêi'digicí neidi'gicí xatsi'zis xayi'znilí tsói nádle'hé	Next (Secondborn) Child-of-the-water Let-down-on-a-sunray He-who-cuts-around-it He-who-gazes-on-enemy One-who-arranges-scalps Changing Grandchild
Child-of-the- water's cradle	tó do'tł'ij	Blue Water
Dwarf, Youngest Brother	'ack'i'tcil nák'e'ctca''	Dwarf Boy There-is-matter- in-the-eyes
Female God	na'dá'' ła'í nêiyo''á'li' 'até'd do'tł'iji' ła'í náyo''á'li' 'até'd	Girl-who-carries- single-corn-kernel Girl-who-carries- single-turquoise
Frog	tcał diɣoli' be'ek'id na'ɣái	Rough Frog One-who-wanders- about-lake
Hummingbird	tc'iké' nazi'li'	Maiden-who-goes- about-rattling
Hogan, ceremonial	xo'ɣan na'ts'o'di'	Hogan-that-stretches- in-all-directions
Male God	do'tł'iji' ła'í nêiyo''á'li' 'acki' tc'ína'dá'' ła'í náyo''á'li' 'acki'	Boy-who-carries- single-turquoise Boy-who-carries- single-corn-kernel
Monster Slayer	'ala'dji' djil'íni' na'ɣé'' nei'zɣání bił na'jnoltł'iji' łe'ya' ne'yání na'ɣé'' neidi'gáhí	Firstborn One-who-slays- monsters-here-and-there One-who-descended- on-zigzag-lightning Reared-in-the-earth One-who-repeatedly- kills-monsters
Monster Slayer's cradleboard	tó diłxił	Dark Water
Scavenger	naxodidáhí	One-who-goes- about-foraging
Self Teacher	'áxodizá'li'	One-who-moves-featherlike

578

Offering circuit, see *Acceptance of offering.*

Overdoing is to be avoided in all activities. The happy medium is to be sought, so that even in ritual there are curbs. One often gets the impression that it is impossible for the Navaho to have enough rain, yet moderation is required even in the performance of the Rain Ceremony. The prayerstick should be deposited on a pile of drift rubbish at least four fingerwidths but never more than eighteen inches high. The size of the drift pile regulates the amount of rain to be expected; too much would be courting bad luck.

In the Night Chant, Water Sprinkler throws rain up so that it will help the people, but rainmaking is done outside the chant—that is, in the Rain Ceremony—because the chanters do not want it to rain all the time during the Night Chant performance (*Restriction, Withholding;* Haile 1938b, pp. 78–81; 1943a, pp. 44, 223, 247; Reichard 1934, pp. 79–93; 1944d, p. 27; Hill 1938, p. 88; Matthews 1902, pp. 180, 312, 41n; Franciscan Fathers 1910, p. 294).

Painting with white clay, see *White clay.*

Paralysis of hero, see *Ambush.*

Participation has been stressed as an indispensable part of ritual. In some acts or rites power is concentrated in the behavior of the chanter, assistants, and patient; in others, everyone present must participate—in the sweat-emetic, ashes blowing, prayer with pollen, holding sacred objects during prayer, and application of yucca suds in the Rain Ceremony (if there is no patient). Proper audience participation helps the patient and the entire tribe; even attendance at a ceremony is a part of the sustaining effort (Introduction; Hill 1938, p. 81).

Passes, feints, are a large part of the chanter's stock-in-trade; some are made with the hands only, some with properties—for instance, arm-waving, arm-spreading, and hand-pointing to the cardinal directions. Brushing and the ceremonial lighting of prayersticks with a crystal are examples of passes made with sacred objects. The marking of the bull-roarer with the chant lotion is a pass. Some thrusts attract good, others are exorcistic; usually they may be understood in connection with the ritualistic context, but perhaps even then only if mythical details are known (Haile 1943a, p. 223; Goddard, p. 177).

Peace meant merely absence or end of war, not an ideal for which other values should be yielded. Navaho culture is built on the premise that war is necessary, that nothing esteemed can be achieved without it. "Before this [the union of separate groups] the Navaho had been a weak and peaceable tribe," relates the myth. The saga of The Twins is a succession of warlike deeds; Changing Woman's opposition to their going to war in the Hail Chant is an unusual and notable incident; it doubtless furnishes contrast and completeness.

Peace overtures show Navaho understanding of neighboring cultures worked out according to the enemies' values. After a fight the Navaho smoked the peace pipe with the Utes, embraced, and exchanged gifts—all symbols that trust had been established.

The Navaho delegate for peace entered a Hopi village singing. If he was received, a date was set for a conference; smoke signals announced his safe arrival and the possibility of a get-together. The delegates of each party, who were peace, not war chiefs, made cigarettes ' in their own way.' The Navaho filled a cornhusk wrapping with mountain tobacco to which harmless insects were added to ' make the

Hopi friendly.' The insects doubtless symbolize the siege of Awatobi by the Stricken Twins with their destructive worm and grasshopper (Ch. 6; cp. *Smoke, Tobacco smoking;* Matthews 1897, pp. 113, 127, 145; Reichard 1944d, p. 31; Hill 1936, p. 19).

Perfect corn ear (do·xono·tíni·h), often required for ritualistic purposes, is a short ear with all kernels in even rows and completely covering the end so that no part of the cob is visible.

Pine, single-budded, see *Overshooting rite: SCE,* Con. C.

Pistons, see Ch. 4; *Sun,* Con. A.

Pokers (xone·cgic, xonicgic, konicgic) are symbols of the danger line in the sweat-emetic rite. On the first night of the Big Star Chant, helpers were sent to gather the pokers and emetic herbs with the instructions: "Get the pokers from a tree that has been struck by lightning, if it has straight branches; if not, take them from trees near it. Offer to the tree three jewels, sparkling rock, blue pollen, and pollen tied in a small piece of cloth. As you sprinkle pollen, repeat a prayer. Take a poker from each direction and remember from which it was cut."

The Hail Chant pokers represent forked lightning, rain-streamer, and zigzag and straight lightning, symbols that prevent the enemy (evil) from crossing. In the Shooting Chant the pokers lie beside the conveyance symbols, strewn in sand. All lie near ashes and are applied to the body after poking in ashes, thus indicating an exorcistic function.

A poker was given the boy raised by Owl to serve as a compass to his mother's home (*Danger line;* Kluckhohn-

Wyman, p. 86; Reichard, Shooting Chant ms.; 1944d, p. 51; Sapir-Hoijer, p. 49).

Pollen (tádídí'n, xádídí'n) has been discussed in several of its aspects—composition, representation of glint or 'light life,' application. Here some additional notes explain the complexity of its symbolism.

Pollen clears the trail so that a person may walk safely. It opened the way for the Holy People of the Rain Ceremony. Pollen sprinkling on mush often symbolizes people and travel: In the Hail Chant myth, Winter Thunder marked the mush twelve times with pollen for good attendance at the ceremony. On the mush of the War Ceremony, the pollen represents a means of travel for patient and audience, and the guidance of the patient's life. Pollen on the bath foam of the Night Chant stands for the patient's life and thoughts; on the bath foam of the Flint Chant, for the mind and gait of the one-sung-over, the Sun's course, the messenger to the singer, the singer, and the medicine he administers.

Pollen increases the power of the person to whom it is applied or administered; it is commemorative since it represents control (Ch. 15; *Feathers, Mush, Pollen ball,* Con. B; *Pollen paintings,* Con. C; Hill 1935a, pp. 66–7; 1938, pp. 37, 86; Reichard 1944b, p. 13; Matthews 1897, p. 213, 11n; 1902, pp. 41–2, 251; Haile 1938b, p. 213; 1943a, pp. 36, 219, 282; Sapir-Hoijer, p. 251).

Pollen ball administration is one of the rites of the sandpainting treatment on the last day of the Sun's House and Prayerstick branches; it was not a part of the Sandpainting branch of the Shooting Chant. The pollen ball is a synthetic symbol, something like a large pill, an inch and a half in diameter, consisting of a number of dry ingredients and coated with pollen. Fish blood is a part of the pollen ball of the Shooting Chant, named do·tⁱiji·, ' turquoise.' RP got the fish for mine at Ganado Dam: he cut the fish open with a bundle flint, took a bit of the blood, sprinkled the fish with pollen, and returned it to ' live ' in the water. There were many other medicines in the ball.

The pollen-ball administration is associated with mush eating and pressing with bundle properties of the last (fifth or ninth) day's ritual. Mythical references explain the property and the rites.

After Sun had tested The Twins and consented to help them, he shaped a miniature man of agate and one of turquoise. As he gave Monster Slayer the pollen ball, Sun placed the agate man in his son for a heart; as he fed mush to his son, he outlined the position of the agate man inside Monster Slayer's body—"The mush you ate from the east side of the basket stands inside you as the man's legs, that from the west is his head, that from the north his left hand, that from the south his right hand, that from the center his heart. When I said, 'He eats the pollen of Restoration-to-youth and Trail-of-well-being,' I meant that his mind would be standing within you. When I said, 'He eats the dew of Dark Cloud, Restoration, and Well-being,' I referred to the intestines of the man inside you. Nothing is missing; complete he stands inside you."

Sun then identified Monster Slayer with himself and the agate man by pressing different parts of his body to corresponding parts of his son's body. When the identification rite was finished, Sun told why he had performed it: "Although the flint armor will protect you against existing monsters, the man I put inside you will make you invincible to any evil you may encounter in the future." Sun placed in Child-of-the-water a turquoise man with the same ritual and meaning.

Not only is it important that a ' turquoise ' be an internal symbol of indomitability, but it must at all times be kept upright—the reason for pressing with bundle items. One of Kluckhohn-Wyman's informants explains that the pollen ball stays in one place within the patient's body like a spirit, a comment that agrees with the Shooting Chant myth (*Mush, Pressing;* Reichard, Shooting Chant ms.; Matthews 1897, pp. 232, 109n; Kluckhohn-Wyman, p. 53 and cp. p. 101; Haile 1943a, p. 31).

Pollen sprinkling, see *Application of pollen, Pollen.*

Pot drum, see *Drum.*

Pressing is a common procedure, meaning identification by absorption. Kneading or modeling should be included with pressing. It is assumed that until a person has been made holy, he is not an image of the power he seeks to control, but after such a power takes him in hand, kneading, pressing, or massage will make him resemble the Holy People. Because Changing Woman was molded when she became mature, there is now a massaging rite in the Girl's Adolescence Ceremony. The Twins were shaped by their counterparts in the sky. Pressing of the plumed wands to the Stricken Twins by the two daughters of Broad Rock xa·ctčé''óγan made them acceptable to the gods; Reared-in-the-mountain was molded into holy likeness by Butterfly (Goddard, p. 15; Reichard, Shooting Chant ms.; Haile 1938b, p. 105; Matthews 1897, p. 409; 1902, p. 262; Sapir-Hoijer, pp. 287, 291; Kluckhohn-Wyman, pp. 62-3).

Pressing to heart, see *Acceptance of offering.*

Protective line, see *Danger line.*

Punishment ('até'él'į) is generally meted out by supernaturals for offenses against them; if imposed by human beings, it is explained as necessary for success with the gods. An offended power summons a hero by saying, "Bring him to me so I can punish him," yet when the culprit is brought, he is instructed, his chastisement being ritualistic discipline, ending in a contribution to future ceremony.

Some punishments, however, seem to be final decrees of fate that explain what happened to individuals.

Gambler was punished by being shot to the sky by Wind, as he said, "You have bet yourself and lost. You are my slave. You are not a god, for my power has prevailed against yours." Buzzard was punished for his voracity by disintegration.

Punishment for the excesses committed during the separation of the sexes was the birth of the monsters, but Stephen reports more specific retribution—men who copulated with the deer does were struck by lightning and burst open, those who copulated with the antelope does were killed by rattlesnake bites, and those who copulated with mountain sheep were killed by bears (*Overdoing, Whipping;* Leighton-Kluckhohn, p. 52ff.; Matthews 1897, p. 86; Reichard 1939, p. 60; Endurance Chant ms.; Newcomb 1940b, p. 68; Haile 1938b, p. 95; Stephen 1930, p. 99).

Queue (tsí·γé·ł) represents Child-of-the-water as the bow represents Monster Slayer (*Bow symbol;* Haile 1938b, pp. 59, 179, 315, 27n).

Racing is a rite that seems to symbolize strength and fortitude, qualities that please the gods.

Changing Woman ran at the Adolescence Ceremony and ended the race by jumping over the fire. According to the myth of the War Ceremony, she ran the race ' because of, at the instigation of Sun ' and at the time of her second menses because of Moon.

Rainboy of the Hail Chant lost his life in a race with Frog and later with supernatural aid won Frog's life.

One of the Racing Gods, exemplary youths, was challenged to run an impossible race—around the base of Mt. Taylor—for the Navaho; his brother was to run for the visiting tribes. The older Racer won the high stakes put up by the Navaho. At a second try—to run around all the foothills of the San Mateo range—the Navaho bet only half as much as they had won on the first race and lost; the younger brother won the stakes for the visitors. The strangers regretted their net loss, but one of their wise men spoke comfortingly: "You have done well, for had you lost the second race you would have lost with it the rain, the sunshine, and all that makes life glad" (Goddard, p. 151; Haile 1938b, pp. 86–9; Reichard 1944d, pp. 15–7, 23; Matthews 1887, pp. 415–7).

Rainbow (ná·'tśí'lid) has numerous functions, all interrelated. It serves as an encircling guardian of the sandpainting: when it has only bunches of feathers at the ends it may be a garland, or it may be female instead of male (tłá·h); when it has a head and feet it represents the goddess. According to Matthews, the rainbow has five colors—presumably red, yellow, green, blue, and white—each representing a goddess. Rainbows are covered with feathers, which give them their colors.

The design consisting of red and blue stripes separated by and outlined with white (sometimes incorrectly called ' sundog ') differs from ' sunray ' (cábitłó·l), which is red and blue without white. Small rainbow designs are often painted at the ankle and wrist joints of supernaturals; they symbolize lightness and ease in moving and handling things. Such designs are especially important for the left side, since it is ' naturally ' stiff and awkward and needs more protection than the right.

Rainbows on a metate stand for the power of the hands in grinding. Rainbows in a sandpainting are a prayer. They are protective; gods often stand on them and they may be given to a hero to keep him safe.

Some rainbows are short or stubby; the one Talking God gave The Twins to keep was only a fingerlength long. An arched or bent rainbow about eight paces long was their means of travel for long distances; it could be folded and carried in a pouch or blanket fold, but through supernatural power became long enough for any purpose.

Coyote lassoed Water Monster's children with a rainbow. The gods helping the Visionary to transport his garden produce wrapped it in clouds and bound the parcels with rainbows.

" It is unlucky to point at a rainbow with any digit except the thumb. If you point with a finger you will get a felon " (Matthews 1887, pp. 399, 446, 449; 1902, pp. 194–5, 231, 246, 309, 60n; Reichard, Endurance Chant ms.; 1939, Pl. XV-XX, XXII-XXIV; Newcomb-Reichard, Pl. IV, VII-IX, XVIII, XX, XXIV-V, XXXI-XXXIII; Goddard, p. 130; Wheelwright 1942, Set II, 6).

Rare game, see *Deer and rare game.*

Rattle, see *Gourd rattles*, Con. B; *Bundle contents*, Con. C.

Rawhide, see *Armor.*

Red headdress, see *Sunglow*, Con. B; *Bundle contents*, Con. C.

Red ocher is Child-of-the-water's impersonation symbol. It is rubbed on the hair, as well as on the body. Ghosts are afraid of red ocher (Haile 1938b, pp. 177, 197, 318, 71n; 1943a, pp. 39, 40, 53, 96, 97).

Reddening, see *Red ocher*, Con. B; *Body painting*, Con. C; cp. Haile 1943a, p. 40.

Refusal has been woven into ritual. The most obvious is non-acceptance of an offering either because it is not the proper thing or it is not modest or appropriate enough. An offering refused by one power may be accepted by another. A second type is refusal to sing for one who requests help. The Stricken Twins were turned down by god after god because they had no valuables to pay for treatment and could not demand it because they did not know who their father was. Monster Slayer was refused by many singers of the Eagle Chant; the reason is undiscernible. When, after long journeying, Swallow undertook to sing for him, Monster Slayer's brothers forced each singer to contribute his power (Reichard 1939, p. 31; 1944d, pp. 135-7; Big Star Chant ms.; Matthews 1897, p. 219, 49n; 1902, pp. 219, 222–4, 228, 231, 232, 234, 240; Newcomb 1940b, pp. 68ff.; Stephen 1930, p. 93; Haile 1938b, p. 183; Hill 1936, p. 14).

Restriction (xastį, xasti', 'atŝá de'ṫah), if properly treated, would require a discussion far too complex for this account. Franc Newcomb started a collection of taboos, but included only some general ones and some very specific and localized. Most of those I have collected apply to ritual, a field Mrs. Newcomb hardly touched; few of her items and mine overlap.

I mention the subject here primarily to point out that such discussions as exist are either unassimilated bodies of data without reference to function or position in the ceremonial and daily life, or they are too simplistic to bring out the full significance of restriction. For instance, avoidance of the dead is mentioned in practically every article on the Navaho; few people know that members of one clan can bury the dead with impunity, even without undergoing the customary purification rites afterward.

The restriction on eating fish is general. Yet additional pressure is put upon one who has eaten the pollen ball containing fish blood; if he should eat a water animal, he would swell up, sicken, and die.

Similarly, one who eats the mixed stew that contains liver, kidneys, heart, tripe, and other internal organs of rare game (now sheep) is enjoined not to eat entrails. Since most Navaho do not, even under modern conditions, have occasion to eat fish and almost all eat the internal organs of animals, the restrictions, their ostensible reasons, and the degree to which they are observed are very uneven; they cannot be the result of the same reasoning.

The Navaho say, "Ghosts cause people to break taboos by telling them to do the opposite of what has been decreed," and their correction for breaking rules is participation in a ceremony.

Kluckhohn and Wyman summarize some ritualistic restrictions and the adverse effects that ensue if they are not observed (Newcomb 1940a; Haile 1938b, pp. 62, 187; Sapir-Hoijer, p. 309; Kluckhohn-Wyman, pp. 19, 54). The following is a partial list of restrictions relating to: coyote, Hill 1936, p. 4; crops, handling and preparation of food, Matthews 1902, pp. 189, 193; Hill 1938, p. 55; deities, Goddard, p. 153; eating, Matthews 1897, pp. 187–8, 212, 5n; Hill 1938, pp. 47, 55; Sapir-Hoijer, p. 287; origins, Haile 1938b, p. 121; Matthews 1887, pp. 390–3; 1897, pp. 75, 190; Newcomb 1940b, p. 73; rites and ceremonies, Reichard 1939, pp. 30, 35; Matthews 1897, p. 212; 1902, p. 240; Sapir-Hoijer, p. 181; Haile 1938b, pp. 40, 62, 229, 234–9; 1943a, pp. 9, 20–1, 29–30, 50, 270, 280, 284; Hill 1938, p. 89; Newcomb 1940b, p. 73; sex, menstruation, pregnancy, birth, Goddard, pp. 130, 155,

163; Stevenson, p. 235; Newcomb 1940b, p. 74; Hill 1936, pp. 8–9; Sapir-Hoijer, pp. 207, 309; Haile 1943a, p. 269; war, Hill 1936, pp. 6–14.

Restriction on looking has been set off from other restrictions because it recurs so frequently, signifying that supernatural power is about to be demonstrated. Someone is told not to look; if he obeys, he benefits; if he does not, he may be punished. Sometimes the restriction is imposed when the power is attractive; again, it may be enjoined with exorcistic intent.

The restriction on looking backward is explained for the war scout. After starting off with the leader's quiver, he informed the leader of everything, but he was not supposed to look back for fear he might see something unlucky which would mean defeat.

There is probably a close connection between the taboo when it concerns other dangerous activities—carrying the dead, for example, to the place of burial.

The Stricken Twins were told not to look at the house of the gods lest they be tempted to touch the rainbows over them; touching rainbows might have given them felons.

At Rock Pinnacle the Stricken Twins were told to keep their heads down so they could not see what was going on, or they would be whipped.

An arched rainbow would move if the persons on it kept their eyes shut. When Coyote was requested not to look, he did so and the rainbow moved in jerks.

Bat Woman asked Monster Slayer not to look as she carried him down the cliff in her burden basket. When he peeped, she dropped suddenly.

Observance of the taboo sometimes led to transformation.

Talking God told the hero of the Mountain Chant to close his eyes as he took the very last and most difficult step to the summit of a little hill. He obeyed and the hill became a mountain.

Self Teacher was told by Deer Owner not to climb a hill lest the deer see him. The hero, prompted by Little Wind, broke the taboo and encountered fierce bears, which he overcame.

Monster Slayer was told to turn his back to Deer Owner and not to look. He disobeyed and saw the sorcerer step over flies and transform them to deer.

The Stricken Twins made the Awatobi people promise not to look when they called off the rat and worm so they would no longer eat the crops (Hill 1936, p. 13; Reichard 1928, p. 142; Endurance Chant ms.; Franciscan Fathers 1910, p. 454; Matthews 1887, p. 402; 1897, pp. 121, 164, 186; 1902, pp. 176, 177, 230, 231, 236, 246, 247, 249; Haile 1938b, pp. 121, 133).

Restrictions on patient of Shooting Chant continue for the duration of the chant and four nights after. Sex continence is required, the patient being under constant surveillance. He, as well as the chanter and an assistant, should sleep in the ceremonial hogan. When I was the one-sung-over, instruction and ritualistic prescription were inextricably combined. I had a house within calling distance of the Navaho family and I customarily slept outside where I could be seen. I was, therefore, allowed to sleep there during the first nights of of the chant; either I was trusted or the Navaho were watched—I suspect that an unobtrusive guard was put on all of us.

For four days after the end of the singing the patient should refrain from certain activities. Fire and water are to be avoided after the Shooting Chant. One should not wash oneself, or start or tend a fire. Persons in the dangerously holy state are fed by others who have had the chant or a related one sung over them, for contact with eating utensils

591

should be avoided. Feeding and tending a person during the period of restriction is a labor of love somewhat comparable to the care of a convalescent who has had a contagious but immunizing disease.

I was not informed about the restrictions directly or all at once; rather they were suggested from time to time. At the very beginning of the sing I was told not to go to the north and not to comb my hair. The fifth day after the Prayerstick branch had started, RP said I could travel in the car, to Ganado, for instance (he was planning to go to Ganado!). I said I would not go anywhere with figure painting which was to remain undisturbed for four days and he agreed: "It is a good thing because after all Ganado is toward the north and there is a cemetery there. It is like old times to observe the restrictions in full." He then hunted up his horse and rode to Ganado. I was told not to eat fish because I had eaten the pollen ball containing fish blood. I was not to kill a snake because of the snakes painted on my feet, nor was I to kick. I was told not to throw water out of the door, but to go outside to pour it.

It rained during the two-night repetition of the Prayerstick branch of the Shooting Chant; until then I had not known about the restrictions against fire. I was cold and started to make a fire. Immediately a brother-in-law who had been the chanter's assistant came to my house and asked if I was cooking. I said no, I was cold. Then he told me that I should not handle fire or water and he made a fire for me. I was also told that eating hot foods or drinking hot liquids was dangerous.

Irked by the restrictions, particularly those against washing and hair combing, I argued with RP that H, a young visitor, had told me that her mother had observed only two nights of restriction. At once he advanced arguments to show

how ill-advised the woman had been: Wasn't H's mother bitten by a snake soon after the chant? Her family had had to have the chant repeated for her. They had considered asking RP to sing it, but finally decided on the chanter who had sung the first time—and shortly after even he had been bitten by a snake! An additional reason for the failure of the chant was that the people where H lived did not make sandpaintings correctly. RP considered vital the differences between some of the paintings in Newcomb-Reichard and those in *Navajo Medicine Man.*

After RP had sung over T's wife, she had started to cook the very day her chant was over; this is the reason she never got well.*

For the Sun's House branch Red Inside phase, restrictions were more stringent than for the Prayerstick branch. The patients were not allowed to sleep in the sun's presence; consequently their vigil lasted for nearly twenty-four hours beginning with the ninth night; they were not to sleep until sunset of the ninth day. Every morning they were wakened at dawn. I was allowed to go to sleep as early as three P.M. of the sixth day and whenever I wanted to thereafter; MC and AD had been ill, I had not.

At dawn of the fifth day after the last night of the chant, the chanter takes the patient to a young pinyon, upon which the necklace (bandoleer) and wristlets are hung. When the patient returns he bathes and shampoos his hair in yucca suds, dresses in clean clothes, ties his bead to his hairstring, and resumes his normal life (cp. Kluckhohn-Wyman, pp. 18–20).

Rings, see *Hoops*.

---

*Note that at another time RP had said that the woman was ill because of mistakes made by the chanter (p. 96).

Rockpiles (wayside altars) may sometimes be seen in isolated parts of the Navaho country. It is customary for passing travelers to add a rock to a rock heap and utter a prayer.

In the War Ceremony story, man-eating quadrupeds contested with man-eating flying creatures by piling up river boulders as they passed through a gap. The rocks left over from these piles became the prayer rockpiles of today; each rock represented a ghost overcome. Although these rocks were said to be river boulders, there is reason to believe that they are associated with flint (Reichard 1944b, p. 17; Haile 1938b, pp. 72–3, 97, 188–9; 1943a, p. 53; Matthews 1887, p. 415; Curtis folio, Pl. 30).

Rocks, all that remains of the monsters, have commemorative value, sometimes in the form of flint. Stones that have been struck by lightning, that bears have turned over, and upon which snake-shaped lichen grows are prescribed for the sweathouse fire of the War Ceremony.

Tiny smooth stones carried to the ground surface by ants are witch weapons of the Shooting Chant Evil.

Four small stones, gathered from the vicinity of Wren's nest, were a part of the Hail Chant unraveling (Haile 1938b, p. 203; 1943a, p. 235; Reichard 1944d, p. 69).

Rubbing is a ritualistic act related to pressing. Formerly it was customary for people to rub their legs after the evening meal with a prayer: "May they [legs] be lively; may I be healthy."

Legs were rubbed with corn smut to cause plentiful crops.

After Reared-in-the-mountain had knocked out the bears by giving them Ute tobacco, he resuscitated them by rubbing with the tobacco ash (Hill 1938, pp. 19, 46: Matthews 1887, p. 404).

Sacred water, see *Waters, collected.*

Safety zone, see *Circle, Danger line, Hoops.*

Saliva, see *Spitting.*

Salt ('ácį') in food is supposed to furnish strength, perhaps against dangers, since it is not added to ceremonial mush whose purpose is identification. The Twins were fed on salty food by Salt Woman; she gave them salt as a weapon against Eye Killers. Apparently it had not attained its power in the first world, for when Water Sprinkler threw the salt given him by Salt Woman, it did no harm. The mush of the War Ceremony was salted to give power to the performers.

Salt Woman contributed salt from the lake near Zuni to the Hail Chant lotion, and later offered salt as a food gift (Stephen 1930, p. 92; Haile 1938b, pp. 63, 191; Reichard 1944b, pp. 73, 83; Hill 1940a).

Scalp (tsi·ziz), the theme of the War Ceremony, has prominent associations also among the symbols of the Shooting, Hail, and Endurance chants, being related to the trophies collected from the monsters and war, and to Coyote's fulfilling Changing-bear-maiden's requirement to obtain Big Monster's scalp. The correspondence between myth, ritual, and recorded war procedure is remarkable; it corroborates many of the conclusions of this work.

Despite the phobia of the dead, mythology represents the Navaho as scalp-takers. According to Hill, scalps were taken from both male and female enemies by anyone except a woman or a boy on his first war raid—the individuals whose spirits were weak. Some warriors took only a small piece of skin; others preserved the whole scalp including the ears. Other parts of the body, such as the Achilles' tendon or the neck sinew, as well as the foetus of a pregnant woman, were collected for ceremonial purposes and witchcraft; they were

595

requisites of sorcery formulas. Although formerly only the scalp would do in the War Ceremony, now any part of a dead enemy—bone, hair, even a piece of clothing—may represent the scalp. These possessions are the enemy's bitcxin and a token is sufficient to cause an outsider's undoing.

Mythological references confirm the fact that the cedar branch of the rattlestick stands for the warrior's trophy, often tied to a piece of cedar or laid in a juniper tree.

When the singing over the scalp-taking was finished, the trophies were hidden among rocks where no rain could touch them until they were needed for the War Ceremony; enemy ghosts adhered to them but had to be guarded to prevent escape (Haile 1938b, pp. 30, 63–4, 149, 155, 162–9; Reichard, Endurance Chant ms.; Shooting Chant ms.; Hill 1936, pp. 6, 15, 17; Goddard, p. 177; Matthews 1897, p. 93).

Sex symbolism was explained in Chapter 10. The following are some pairs to which dominance and secondary qualities are assigned:

Male	*Female*
Animals: antelope	deer (Feather Chant)
Birds:	
Bluebird feathers	canary feathers (BS, SC)
Black vulture	turkey vulture (YL)
Brewer blackbird	cowbird (YL)
Mearns' woodpecker	white-breasted woodpecker (YL)
Rocky Mt. nuthatch	red-breasted nuthatch (YL)
Colors:	
Black (Sky)	blue (Earth) (Matthews 1902, p. 57; Newcomb-Reichard, Fig. 5)
Black	blue (WC, BeC)
Black	white (SC, HC)
Blue	yellow (SC, HC)
Blue (Sun, turquoise)	white (Moon, whiteshell)
White	yellow (corn, WC, BeC)
Cuts of shrub stems:	
Right-angled	diagonal (BS)

Male	Female
Deities:	
Black God (b)	Water Sprinkler (u) (NC)
Holy Boy (b)	Holy Girl (var) (SC, HC)
Holy Man (b)	Holy Woman (var) (SC, HC)
Monster Slayer	Child-of-the-water
Sun (u)	Changing Woman (w)
Sun (u)	Moon (w)
Talking God (w)	xa·ctc'é·'óɣan (y)
Directions:	
North (b)	south (u)
Natural phenomena:	
Cloud	mist
Hard rain with wind and lightning	light rain
Rain	pool, body of water
Sky (b)	Earth (u)
Zigzag lightning	flash lightning
Sunbeam	sunray
Plants:	
Coarse sunflower	slender sunflower
Juniperus pachyphloeu	*Juniperus scopulorum*
Mountain mahogany	cliffrose
Pinyon	juniper
tsélkani·	k'ic di·tsói (BS)
Hard oak	mountain mahogany (FW)
Rivers:	
San Juan	Rio Grande
Seasons:	
Winter	summer (SC)
Stones:	
Flint of head feather bundle	lightning-struck oak (SCE)
Striped aragonite	white aragonite

Shaping, see *Pressing*.

Shock (xode·tɫá·d), see *Restoration*, Con. C.

Shoulder bands, see *Bundle contents*, Con. C.

Shoulder straps, see *Bundle contents*, Con. C.

Single-budded pine, see *Overshooting rite: SCE*, Con. C.

Sky-reaching-rock, see *Disposal of Sky-reaching-rock,* Con. C.

Smallness, see *Blowing, Token.*

Smile ('adloh) indicates deific approval of ritualistic acts properly performed.

Sun smiled when Dark Thunder rubbed chant lotion on Rainboy's hair as he sang the words ' Sun's hair.'
The Racing Gods smiled at each other when they met after completing their run carrying invitations to the Fire Dance.
be'γotcidí smiled as he created the animals.

Decoy women seduced young men with a sly, tantalizing smile (Reichard 1944d, pp. 5, 87, 93; Wheelwright 1942, pp. 41, 44, 102; Matthews 1897, p. 175).

Smoke is associated with creation, clouds, war, power, and purification. According to JS, Earth Woman and Sky Man smoked to bring about creation: "The de'nalγé prayers were called 'way on top' because they gave off smoke for creation and good health."

When Rainboy first raced with Frog, the latter threw down a dark cloud so that Rainboy could not see where he was going; when it cleared, he found himself running in the wrong direction. Heat laid a smokescreen of Darkness to help a war party. The origin of the smoke is not explained in any of the cases cited (*Darkness, Frogs, Winter Thunder,* Con. A; *Incense,* Con. B; Reichard 1944d, pp. 23–5; Goddard, p. 176).

Soil token, see *Dust token.*

Soot (te·c), though called ' charcoal ' by others, seems a better name, since it is the fine powdered residue of burning. The following are explanations of soot: Spots made of ritualistically burned soot protect against dangers. The temples are blackened because they are the seat of ghosts. Black spots are put on the palms of Child-of-the-water's impersonators because he held the dangerous monsters' scalps. Collected soot (ṭe·cígí· and 'aĺtade·dlí·c) represents, in the War Ceremony, vegetation and dark mist for the women and dark cloud for the men.

Soot is applied to the jaw in the War Ceremony (*Blackening*, Con. C; Kluckhohn-Wyman, pp. 55, 169, 239; Haile 1938b, pp. 169, 177, 237; 1943a, p. 52).

Sparkling rock, see Ch. 15; Kluckhohn-Wyman, p. 25; Haile 1938b, pp. 197, 280; 1943a, pp. 98, 308, 68n.

Spiral shape or motion stands for escape from the circle of frustration or prevention from entering it; it is a form of the danger line. Crow and Turkey Buzzard could not get near The Twins because of flints arranged in a spiral; Coiled Snakes are one of its forms.

The systematic method of covering ground in a search is in a spiral. Sun, looking for The Twins, hidden by his sky wife, moved in an enlarging spiral from the center of the room. Changing-bear-maiden, hunting her Youngest Brother, concealed under the fireplace, started at the outer edge of the hogan and moved in a diminishing spiral toward the center (Haile 1938b, pp. 95, 101; Reichard, Endurance Chant ms.; Newcomb-Reichard, Pl. XII, XIII).

Spitting as a ritualistic act seems to have the function of identification.

When a warrior bade his wife farewell, he spat into her hand and mixed pollen with the saliva. She preserved the pollen in a little bundle, which she held as she prayed for his safety.

A war leader had his companions rub spittle over their legs, bodies, and weapons. The spittle and the rubbing strengthened the warriors and their arms.

When RP arranged the four pokers of mountain mahogany around the sweat-emetic fire, he spat upon the poker, then stuck its end into the fire and laid it at the left of the sandpainting snake. After all four were in place, he spat in the four directions and around.

After the smoking test, Sun rubbed his children with tobacco ashes mixed with saliva.

Changing Woman brought on a terrific storm by spitting hailstones through hoops (Hill 1936, pp. 12–3; Haile 1938b, p. 105; Matthews 1897, pp. 128, 202–3; 1902, p. 308, 7n).

Spread ('aya· sika·d) serves two purposes: it keeps persons and properties from contact with the ground, and is a reward for assistance. Of the rites I have seen, sweat-emetic and the first part of the bath have no blanket or spread. The spread may be of various materials. Formerly it may have been of skins; now it is of yard goods or, on rare occasions, of buckskin or buffalo hide (yódí). The greater the value of the goods, the better for the chant. On the ' soft goods ' tobacco, silver money, and jewelry may be laid. The material must be of the best, since it represents gifts to the gods such as the Stricken Twins got from the people of Awatobi. In the house of the gods the Stricken Twins were seated on patterned fabrics, a form of ideal spread.

The patient or his sponsor provides the spread, but guests may add to it; it is often divided among assistants or singers at the end of a rite (*Buckskin, Covers;* Matthews 1902, pp. 243, 246ff.; Haile 1943a, pp. 44, 52).

Stepping on a property is to be distinguished from ' stepping over.' It is dangerous to step on some properties, helpful to step on others.

Monster Slayer fainted when he stepped on the bull-roarer

on which he had drawn a man, and again when he stepped on a chip left after Traveling Rock had been subdued. Gambler shot up to the sky when he stepped on a bow given him by his father, Sun. The hero of the Mountain Chant was given two white lightnings to stand on, that is, to enable him to do something extraordinary.

The style of the war shield incorporated ritualistic and practical protection. It had a crease in the middle so it could be opened and closed by stepping on it (Reichard, Shooting Chant ms.; Haile 1938b, p. 137; Matthews 1887, p. 406; Franciscan Fathers 1910, p. 317).

Stepping over accomplishes restoration, transformation, and increase; it is invariably an act of the Restoration rite. Related to the rite is the restriction that one should never ' step over another person's legs ' unless he is a joking relative. Stepping over in the Restoration rite of the Flint Chant represented Gila Monster's ' pouch ' (bundle) as well as Gila Monster's cutting up his own body and scattering the fragments in imitation of what Winter Thunder had done to Holy Man.

After cactus and yucca are collected for the bath, the plants should be stepped over—an act to restore them to normal. When the gods stepped over those killed in the struggle between Youngest Brother and Changing-bear-maiden, they all came to life. Stepping over a particular arrangement of corn caused it to change into people. Stepping over flies transformed them to deer. Stepping over a small mysterious bundle to the accompaniment of Monster Slayer's flute transformed the contents into beautiful clothes for his new wives.

When Gambler stepped over a token quantity of precious stones four times, they became a big heap; stepping over a

601

bit of tobacco in an offering prayerstick caused it to be greatly augmented (Haile 1938b, p. 133; 1943a, pp. 7, 43, 46–8, 69, 290, 27n; Reichard, Endurance Chant ms.; Matthews 1897, p. 69; Newcomb 1940b, p. 54; Goddard, pp. 147, 162; Kluckhohn-Wyman, p. 90).

Stirring is a ritualistic act preceding the administration of the infusion specific; it may be done with the aspergill, the bull-roarer, a bundle property, or the finger. The singer stirs the infusion, tastes it, sprays it, either over the sacred properties, over the patient, or over both. In the War Ceremony, the infusion specific was sprayed over the unraveler herbs after they had been laid aside (*Salt Woman*, Con. A; Haile 1938b, p. 213).

Stones, see *Rocks*.

Stretching signified promise of aid and success after prayersticks had been accepted by Winter Thunder and Dark Thunder in the Hail Chant. All the people in attendance stretched themselves as they said, "Everything will be all right!" (Reichard 1944d, p. 53.)

Substitution was discussed in Chapter 7. A short list of substitutions selected from the texts follows:

Article substituted	For
Bundle talking prayersticks and wide boards	Sun's jewel weapons (SC)
Imitation beads	dancing beads (Bead Chant)
Imitation sorcerer's bundle	real bundle (Haile 1938b, pp. 143, 145)
Medicine and flints	cranebill (Haile 1943a, p. 275)
Motions	actual bath ritual for one too weak to go through with it (Haile 1943a, p. 279)
Rattlestick	Sun's arrow, Black God's prayerstick (Haile 1938b, p. 199)
Sandpainting	painting on cloud (Matthews 1902, p. 165)
Soil from sacred mountains	lightning, rainbow, sunray, sunstreamer (HC)

Sunbeam and *sunray* are partners acting as mentor, protection, and conveyance. Most translations do not differentiate them. After much discussion with informants, who do not agree, I have translated cádídí'n as ' sunbeam,' the light ray from a cloud with the sun behind it, and cábitłó'l as 'sunray,' the alternating dark rays between the light beams. The former is generally yellow and white in sandpainting; the latter is red and blue.

Sunbeam and sunray formed field glasses through which Monster Slayer could see long distances.

The pattern for the War Ceremony rattlestick was originally brought to Earth People by Sunbeam and Sunray (Haile 1938b, pp. 205, 215; Stephen 1930, p. 89).

Sunglow (cábitła· djiłtci") is represented by a red headdress. Many of the Shooting Chant paintings show figures wearing this headdress. It is one of the chanter's bundle properties, worn by his representative in the Fire Dance.

In the origin story it is said that Cicada offered sunglow to birds of the second world for the right to enter it. The birds put it on their wings and were so pleased that they gave permission.

A red bonnet was worn by Scavenger of the Bead Chant. It had been given Sun as a trophy of a pueblo chief's daughter (Stephen 1930, p. 94; Reichard 1939, p. 28; Newcomb-Reichard, p. 48).

Sunray (cábitłó'l), see *Sunbeam*.

Swastika is a favorite Navaho design, probably because the whirling log (tsił no'oli·) is a theme of the Night and Feather chants. The chant symbol of the Hail Chant is a cross to the ends of which down feathers are fastened, giving it a swastikalike effect. It (tónáxabił) is the protective device of Winter Thunder's and Frog's home; according to Wheelwright, it is Thunder's whirling seat. When angry, Winter and Dark Thunder twirled their seats; when the gods were good-tempered, the seats became rainbows (Matthews 1897, pp. 62ff.; 1902, p. 172, Pl. 6; Goddard, p. 161; Stevenson, p. 278; Reichard 1944d, pp. 17, 41, 90-1, 145; Wheelwright 1946, pp. 12, 47, 154, Pl. 2A, B).

Tallows (tłah na·ctcí·n), a property of many ceremonies, are a means of applying body paint. Tallow is ceremonially collected and should contain token quantities of fat from the rare game and hunting animals.

To provide collected tallows Monster Slayer made a pass with his hand along the mountain tops, then rubbed mixed tallow of the rare game over his own body.

Tallow will make the body moist, even if it is gray, that is, feverish from an enemy ghost; collected tallow was rubbed on the surface of Earth Woman at the first performance of the War Ceremony to produce moisture on earth.

Tallow mixtures have different formulas for various chants, tallow being required in large quantities in the exorcistic rites in which body painting is a common procedure. Generally the bulk is of sheep tallow, to which token quantities of 'sacred' tallow are added (Haile 1938b, pp. 70, 177, 195, 237; 1943a, pp. 50-1; Reichard, Shooting Chant Evil ms.; Endurance Chant ms.; Big Star Chant ms.).

Tests prove strength and power, and determine auguries, as in war. The following selected references illustrate the wide range of tests:

Clothes test, Matthews 1897, p. 180; 1902, p. 168; Corn Maidens, Newcomb 1940b, p. 56; fatherhood, Matthews

1902, p. 240; food, Matthews 1897, p. 178; geography, Matthews 1897, p. 114; Reichard, Shooting Chant ms.; 1944d, pp. 142–5; Haile 1938b, p. 109; 1943a, pp. 169, 179; identification, Sapir-Hoijer, p. 217; Reichard, Shooting Chant ms.; race, Reichard 1944d, pp. 15–7, 23; smoking, Matthews 1897, pp. 112, 176, 178; Haile 1938b, p. 107; Newcomb 1940b, pp. 58ff., 69; Reichard 1944d, p. 137; Shooting Chant ms.; song, Matthews 1902, p. 169; The Twins, Haile 1938b, pp. 101–3; Reichard, Shooting Chant ms.; Stephen ms.; augury, Hill 1936, p. 14; and cp. Haile 1938b, p. 183).

The Day, see *Vigil*, Con. C.

The Night, see *Vigil*, Con. C.

Throwing down an object is a demonstration of superior power I have so far found only in the Hail Chant.

Black God threw down his fire violently to intimidate Winter Thunder. Rainboy, by casting down his cattail hat with great force, caused Frog to lose the race. Frog threw his man-killing ax at people, asking them to hit him with it, but Rainboy was saved from picking it up by Little Wind (Reichard 1944d, pp. 24–7, 41).

Tobacco ash, see *Rubbing*.

Tobacco pouch is a ceremonial property often depicted in sandpainting—a possession of Sun and Moon. A tobacco pouch with pipe and tobacco, instead of a prayerstick, is Black God's and Gila Monster's offering.

First Man in the first world refused Water Horse's pouch of green water scum, but Black God accepted it.

Deer Owner, encountered by Self Teacher, had a tobacco pouch with Sun and Moon figures on it; on his large pipe there were drawings of rare game (Newcomb-Reichard, pp. 57–8, Fig. 5, 8, 9; Reichard, Shooting Chant ms.; Haile 1943a, pp. 62, 63; Stephen 1930, p. 93).

Tobacco smoking is as indispensable in Navaho ritual as in daily life, tobacco being an ever-welcome gift or contribution. A Navaho finds it hard to refuse a request to one bearing smokes.

Names of tobacco are sometimes a part of the ceremonial language; again they are botanically specific. Tobacco given to Beaver in the Hail Chant myth was called na·ke·naxahí and consisted of a mixture of wide-leaved and narrow-leaved tobaccos and of one called na·ke'elgai. Some mixtures are said to be actually poisonous; they would account for the fainting of those exposed to the smoking tests, though innocuous compounds may be supernaturally stunning.

Tobacco seeds were among the gifts given by the pet turkey to Visionary of the Night Chant.

Smoking meant peace to the Navaho, as to the Plains Indians, and it also meant an attempt to bring success in war. The first evening a war party was out, a pipe was lighted and passed sunwise around the group. When peace delegates met, the first pipe was prepared by the tribe suing for peace; the first puff was taken by the 'enemy,' then all smoked, and the two groups embraced and exchanged gifts. The Navaho say they used a tubular pipe, whereas the Ute used a pipe with such a long stem that it rested on the smoker's toe.

Smoking the ceremonial pipe by the group is not emphasized in the ceremonies I witnessed, but RM said that in the Rain Ceremony, a tribal affair, the pipe was passed around to be puffed by everyone present. RP said the tobacco pouch of the sandpaintings symbolized peace.

Though I have never heard of ' eating ' tobacco among the Navaho—a common phrase among other Indian tribes, particularly of northern North America—as a smoke it is classed with food and considered equally refreshing.

After the gods had fed Self Teacher and given him to drink from the inexhaustible cup, he smoked as the gods examined his offerings.

When Rainboy was a frog he could eat Frog's food with impunity, but he was warned against smoking lest he never resume his proper form.

Smoking transformed Snake and Bear, the ugly old men of the Beauty Chant, into handsome young men.

The tobacco of Big Snake and Bear, like their odor (and perhaps this was actually the odor of the tobacco), was so attractive that it seduced the two Corn Maidens of the War Ceremony.

Beaver came to Rainboy for tobacco, and throughout the Hail Chant tobacco seems to be closely associated with Frog; Frog is associated with rain, rain with clouds and mists, and clouds with smoke (*Black God*, Con. A; *Incense*, Con. B; Wyman-Harris, pp. 26, 45; Matthews 1887, p. 404; 1897, pp. 112, 165, 176, 247, 218n, 223n; 1902, pp. 179, 187; Newcomb 1940b, p. 58; Haile 1938b, pp. 105, 171; Hill 1936, pp. 7, 19; Reichard 1944d, pp. 19, 137; Shooting Chant ms.; Huckel ms.; Curtis, p. 108).

Tracks, see *Footprints*.

Transformation, see Ch. 2, 7; *Food, Smoke, Stepping over, Tests, Tobacco smoking*, Con. B; *Hoop transformation rite*, Con. C.

Travel is a part of many myths and is included in prayers (Haile 1938b, p. 139; Newcomb 1940b, pp. 52, 69, 70, 74;

Matthews 1887, pp. 417ff.; 1902, pp. 178, 207, 216ff.; Sapir-Hoijer, pp. 178, 207; Reichard 1944b, pp. 26–7).

Trumpets, see *Sun,* Con. A.

Turtleback armor, see *Armor.*

Tying, see *Cutting, Knots,* Con. B; *Plant garment,* Con. C.

Unconcern, see *Ceremonial indifference.*

Unseasoned mush, see *Mush.*

Unwounded buckskin, see Haile 1938b, p. 7.

Vital parts of a person depend on his powers. If speed is protection—as it was for Rainboy, Frog, and Big Monster—the soles of the feet, the hip joint, the shoulder blades, and the occipital point are vital.

Coyote and, in imitation, Changing-bear-maiden hid their vital parts—pluck, breath, blood, and entrails—in the ground; their persons could not be harmed unless these parts were destroyed. Coyote kept his vital principle at the end of his nose and tail; his uncanny sound, preserved in the same places, is a part of his power (Reichard 1944d, pp. 14–7; Shooting Chant ms.; Endurance Chant ms.; Matthews 1897, p. 91; Haile 1943a, p. 22).

Vulnerable points, see *Vital parts.*

Warning prayerstick, see Ch. 18; *Monster Slayer, Rock Swallows, Traveling Rock,* Con. A.

Water sprinkling, see *Water Sprinkler,* Con. A.

Water throwing is a ritualistic act of the last day of the Shooting and Hail chants. After the figure painting and sandpainting application are finished, the patient is told to throw some water out the door of the ceremonial hogan " so that he may enjoy rain and long life " (JS) (cp. Wheelwright 1946, p. 52).

Waters, collected (tó 'ała na·ctcí·n) from many places, are an important element of the Rain Ceremony and others. Waters are of specific kinds: Matthews defines collected water as water of all kinds—spring water, hail water, snow water, and water from the four world quarters. In the first world water was collected from each cardinal direction. The water token of the War Ceremony was collected after a rain or snow from pools and stone depressions (Matthews 1897, p. 223, 67n; 1902, p. 45; Stephen 1930, p. 90; Haile 1938b, pp. 254, 98n).

Were-coyote, see *Hoop transformation rite*, Con. C.

Whipping is a ceremonial act that stresses fortitude, strength, and purification, rather than punishment as we understand it.

When The Twins were only four days old, Talking God and Water Sprinkler raced with them and beat them with twigs of mountain mahogany when they lost. The Twins, after practicing for four days more, won and scourged the gods, who were greatly pleased.

The god who carries the yucca plant in the Night Chant whips people with its leaf fibers to cure disease.

Corn Man's nieces were whipped for spending the night with Bear and Big-snake-man, but the lashes were unfelt because the girls were protected by the cattail and feather given them by their suitors.

609

Rainboy was to be beaten to death by the people of his father's settlement because of his addiction to gambling; he was saved by Bat.

The Utes had decided to whip Reared-in-the-mountain to death, but he was saved by divine intervention.

The initiation rite of the Night Chant is the ceremonial model for whipping. Moderation is the rule for boys; girls are not beaten but are pressed with corn-ear bundles. Many Navaho beat their children, as they seem to have done in the past, but those I know consider whipping a poor form of discipline. The mythological cases indicate that whipping is ceremonially correct but that the gods disapprove of overdoing (Matthews 1887, p. 297; 1897, pp. 106, 116–20, 133, 252, 266n; Kluckhohn–Leighton, pp. 145-6; Haile 1938b, pp. 172–5; Reichard 1944d, p. 3; Dyk, pp. 6–7, 9–10; cp. Simmons, p. 84).

Whirling log, see *Swastika.*

White clay (dle'c) was identified as montmorillonite in the Ganado region; other clays are used for whitening in other parts of the reservation, depending on the available deposits. Kluckhohn and Wyman found argillaceous sandstone (na'-saládle'c) as the whitening medium in the regions where they worked.

Whitening or painting with white clay ('adle'c) is a part of many ceremonies—figure painting, prayersticks, sandpaintings (Kluckhohn-Wyman, p. 72; Haile 1938b, pp. 177, 197, 201, 213; Matthews 1897, Pl. IV, VII).

Whitening, see *White clay.*

Witch objects ('axidaxacgąj) may be distinct from arrows (also used by witches). In the Big Star Chant, they were smooth colored stones about the size of a pinyon nut. The chanter gave his assistants who were to collect the objects the following directions: "The four stones you choose must be lying there naturally, black at the east, blue at the south, yellow at the west, and white at the north. Choose all of them before you start to pick up any. Don't start to pick up any if you see, say, two or three, but be sure to locate four, then pick them up in proper order" (cp. Kluckhohn 1944, p. 20).

Withholding, see Chapter 11; *Incense, Substitution;* and cp. Haile 1938b, pp. 107, 139, 193; Goddard, p. 149; Hill 1938, p. 75; Reichard 1944d, p. 149).

Wood samples (tsintšósí) are symbols of the sweat-emetic rite, representing all fire wood. The wood is sometimes the same as that of emetic frames, pokers, hoops, and other properties.

Wood samples of the Shooting Chant sweat-emetic represent the trees against which Bear rubbed himself when Holy Man was seized by Thunder—aspen at the east, spruce at the south, red willow at the west, and chokecherry at the north (these were the materials and directional sequences of the emetic frames also).

The wood samples of the first day's fire of the Hail Chant were oak for Dark Thunder's side and hard scruboak for Winter Thunder's. On the second day, Douglas fir represented both sides; on the third day, Dark Thunder's people brought juniper, Winter Thunder's pinyon; and on the last day, Dark Thunder brought pinyon and juniper, and Winter Thunder, spruce, *Juniperus sibirica*, gray willow, and blue willow.

On successive days Visionary of the Night Chant, burning down a tree from which to make his whirling log, made his fire of cottonwood, pinyon, juniper, and spruce; according

611

to Matthews, the woods for the fire to heat stones for the sweatbath were pinyon and juniper only.

All warriors participated in the fire making of the War Ceremony, each being instructed to fetch wood wherever he could find it. They stacked it on a pile of rocks in preparation for Black God's performance to drive off ghosts.

The fire-making ceremony that takes the place of the sweat-emetic rite in the Flint Chant has as wood samples cedar, pinyon, oak, scruboak, and various other woods (Kluckhohn-Wyman, p. 83; Matthews 1902, pp. 52, 172; Reichard 1944d, pp. 51, 57, 63, 71, 115; Haile 1938b, pp. 151, 169, 191; 1943a, p. 236).

Wristlets, see *Bundle contents*, Con. C.

Yellow bowl, see *Inexhaustible, Mush.*

Yucca (tsá'ászi') is the favorite among wild as corn is among domesticated plants. Before it became scarce, yucca was valued for food, cordage, and soap. Even now it is a part of various rites. The name means ' it-is-the-main-fibrous-one.' Some of the Navaho names may be ceremonial variations: Wyman and Harris have identified only two—tsá'ászi', *Yucca baccata*, and tsá'ászi'tšó·z, *Yucca glauca*. I have tsá'ászi' nte'lí and tsá'ászí' ntsa·hígí' also for *Yucca baccata*, and in addition, tsá'ászi' bide'', ' horned yucca '; tsá'ászi' bitse''í, ' tailed yucca '; γé'i· bitsá'ászi', ' god yucca.' *Yucca baccata* is preferred for bath and shampoo; failing this, others may be used, but the Navaho say they ' itch like everything.'

Suds were made from all four in Changing Woman's and Rainboy's bath rites. Leaves of all four were a part of the Shooting Chant Evil Transformation rite; they represent the protective line.

Braided yucca fibers of the War Ceremony represent the arrow and clubs with which Monster Slayer slew the monsters. The shoulder straps of braided yucca made by Black God represent Burrowing Monster's colon filled with blood that Monster Slayer slung over his shoulder as bait for Cliff Monster (Wyman-Harris, p. 21, Nos. 67–8; Matthews 1897, pp. 102, 231, 101n; 1902, p. 310, 11n; Haile 1938b, p. 193; 1943a, pp. 54–5, 225, 237–9, 278; Sapir-Hoijer, p. 239; Reichard 1944d, pp. 76–7).

Zone of protection, see *Danger line*.

CONCORDANCE C

Application of bundle (A)

Application of bundle, identification (A).

Application of bundle: SC Prayerstick branch.

Application of bundle: SC Sun's House branch Red Inside phase.

Application of bundle, layout: SC Prayerstick branch.

Application of bundle, meaning of (A, E).

Application of paint, *see* Overshooting.

Application, of unravelers.

Bandoleer and wristlets, disposal of: SC Prayerstick branch.

Bandoleer and wristlets, d posal of: SC Sun's House branch.

Basket layout: BS.

Bath (E)

Bath: BS.

Bath: Feather Chant.

Bath: SC Prayerstick and Sun's House branches and repetitions.

Bath: meaning of (E).

Bead Chant, excerpt.

Blackening (E)

Blackening, preparation for: BS and SCE.

Blackening rite: BS.

Blackening rite: preceding purification of deceased chanter's bundle.

Blackening (E)—*continued*
    Blackening rite: War Ceremony.
    Blackening rite, meaning of (E).
Body painting (A)
    Body painting: Feather Chant.
Bull-roarer, preparation of: SC
    Bull-roarer, whirling of: SC.
Bundle contents: BS
    Bundle contents: Flint Chant.
    Bundle contents: Rain Ceremony.
    Bundle contents: SC.
    Bundle contents: SCE.
    Bundle contents, procurement of: SC.
Dedication of new bundle prayersticks (A).
Deposit of offerings.
Disposal of bandoleer and wristlets.
Disposal of Sky-reaching-rock: SC Sun's House branch.
Distinguishing symbols.
Emetic.
Emetic formula.
Emetic frames.
Feather Chant.
Figure painting: SC.
Flint Chant, excerpt.
Girl's Adolescence Ceremony (A).
Hoop transformation rite (E)
    Hoop transformation rite, hoops; preparation of: BS.
    Hoop transformation rite, preparation of: BS.
    Hoop transformation rite, treatment with: BS.
    Hoop transformation rite, preparation of: SCE.
    Hoop transformation rite, treatment with: SCE.
    Hoop transformation rite, meaning of (E).
Invocatory offerings.

Master symbol.

Mixed stew.

No sleep.

Offerings.

Overshooting rite: BS

    Overshooting rite: SCE.

Plant garment (E)

    Plant garment, preparation of: BS.

    Plant garment (spruce), preparation of: SCE.

    Plant garment, tying and cutting of: BS.

    Plant garment, tying and cutting of: SCE.

    Plant garment: Unknown Chant.

    Plant garment, meaning of (E).

Plants, collection of: SCE.

Pollen paintings: Rain Ceremony

    Pollen paintings, rites on: Rain Ceremony.

Prayer on buckskin: BS

    Prayer on buckskin: SCE.

Prayer to Young Pinyon.

Prayersticks, preparation and invocation of: SC

    Prayersticks, temporary talking: SC Prayerstick branch.

    Prayersticks used: SC Prayerstick branch.

    Prayersticks used: SC Sun's House branch.

Rain Ceremony.

Restoration (E)

    Restoration rite: HC.

    Restoration rite: SC.

Rite for releasing sheep from lightning contamination (E).

Rite for removing contamination of the dead (E).

Rite to control snow.

Rite to undo harm caused by camping on trail to old deer
    impound.

Rites, combined.

Sandpainting: Bead Chant, excerpt

Sandpainting setup: Bead Chant, excerpt.

Sandpainting, treatment on: Bead Chant, excerpt.

Sandpainting: BS.

Sandpainting, treatment on: BS.

Sandpainting: Feather Chant.

Sandpainting setup: Feather Chant.

Sandpainting, treatment on: Feather Chant.

Sandpainting: SC Dark Circle branch.

Sandpainting, treatment on: SC Dark Circle branch.

Sandpainting: SC Prayerstick branch.

Sandpainting setup: SC Prayerstick branch.

Sandpainting, treatment on: SC Prayerstick branch.

Sandpainting: SC Sandpainting branch.

Sandpainting setup: SC Sandpainting branch.

Sandpainting, treatment on: SC Sandpainting branch.

Sandpainting: SC Sun's House branch Red Inside phase.

Sandpainting setup: SC Sun's House branch Red Inside phase.

Sandpainting, treatment on: SC Sun's House branch Red Inside phase.

Sandpainting: SCE.

Sandpainting, treatment on: SCE.

Sandpainting setout mound: SC Prayerstick branch

Sandpainting setout mound: SC Sun's House branch Red Inside phase.

Sandpainting setout mound, meaning of (A).

Shock rite.

Short singing.

Sweat-emetic (E)

Sweat-emetic, emetic formula: BS and Endurance Chant.

Sweat-emetic, emetic formula: SC Prayerstick and Sun's House branches.

Sweat-emetic (E)—*continued*

Sweat-emetic, emetic frames.

Sweat-emetic, emetic frames: SC Prayerstick and Sun's House branches.

Sweat-emetic, emetic sandpaintings: SC.

Sweat-emetic, fire.

Sweat-emetic, fire sandpaintings: SC Prayerstick branch.

Sweat-emetic, fire sandpaintings: SC Sun's House branch.

Sweat-emetic, order of events: BS.

Sweat-emetic, order of events: SC Prayerstick branch.

Sweat-emetic, order of events: SC Sun's House branch Red Inside phase.

Sweat-emetic, pokers: SC.

Sweat-emetic, preparation of: SC Sun's House branch Red Inside phase.

Sweat-emetic: SCE.

Sweat-emetic rite, meaning of (E).

Talking prayersticks, bundle; dedication of: SC Sandpainting branch.

Unraveling (E)

Unraveling, preparation of unravelers: BS.

Unraveling, preparation of unravelers: HC.

Unraveling, preparation of unravelers: SC.

Unraveling, preparation of unravelers: SCE.

Unraveling, preparation of unravelers: War Ceremony.

Unraveling, unravelers; application of: BS.

Unraveling, unravelers; application of: SC Prayerstick branch and two-night repetition.

Unraveling, unravelers; application of: SC Sun's House branch Red Inside phase.

Unraveling, meaning of (E).

Vigil; The Day, The Night

Vigil: Blessing rite 1.

Vigil; The Day, The Night—*continued*
  Vigil: Blessing rite 2.
  Vigil: Feather Chant.
  Vigil: SC.
Wildrose circle: SC Sun's House branch Red Inside phase.

. . .

Application of bundle (A). The bundle items are specific for each chant, the selection differing somewhat for phase, sex of patient, or night of performance. The rite differs from the application of unraveler bundles in that it includes the large bundle items, even the otter collar; they were applied with crossing, as were the unraveler strings. The bundle application was part of three forms of the performance, all remarkably similar: in the Sun's House branch on nights 5, 6, 7, and 8; in the five-night Prayerstick branch on nights 1, 2, 3, and 4; and in the two-night repetition on night 1.

Application of bundle, identification (A). Hastily and in an excited manner, the chanter pressed a wide board to each of the patient's body-parts, first pressing hard, then touching the part of his own body to the wide board and to the corresponding part of the patient: the Skyhole wide board to the head, the Dawn wide board to the shoulders, the Sun wide board to the palms, the Moon wide board to the soles (Fig. 3). In the Prayerstick branch the order of application was reversed, beginning with the soles of the feet and ending with the head.

Application of bundle: SC Prayerstick branch. The rite was the same as that for the Sun's House branch, except that the bull-roarer was applied after each application of the bundle items.

Application of bundle: SC Sun's House branch Red Inside phase.

Patient marched around fire to position on spread.

Meal sprinkling—e, we, s, n, and around, over men at south of hogan, over women at north.

Preparation of bull-roarer (related to and sometimes a part of unraveler layout).

Chanter twirled bull-roarer.

Application of bull-roarer with crossing and sound blu ˙ ˙ ˙.

Application of chant lotion as in unraveling.

Application of bundle to patient with crossing, sound blu ˙ ˙ ˙.

Identification of chanter, patient, and bundle.

Whistling.

Incensing: two coals.

Application of bundle, layout: SC Prayerstick branch. Figure 3 shows the layout of the bundle properties.

Application of bundle, meaning of (A, E). The rite is both sanctifying and exorcistic. It carries the patient over from evil-dispersing by means of the bull-roarer, the sweeping away of the bundle application with sound, lotion drinking, and infusion drinking, to identification with the synthetic power of the bundle, identification of deity, chanter as intermediary, and patient.

· · ·

Application of paint, see Overshooting.

Application, of unravelers, see Application, Con. B; *Unraveling,* Con. C.

· · ·

Bandoleer and wristlets, disposal of: SC Prayerstick branch. About 9 o'clock on the morning after the chant was concluded, the chanter instructed the assistant how to arrange

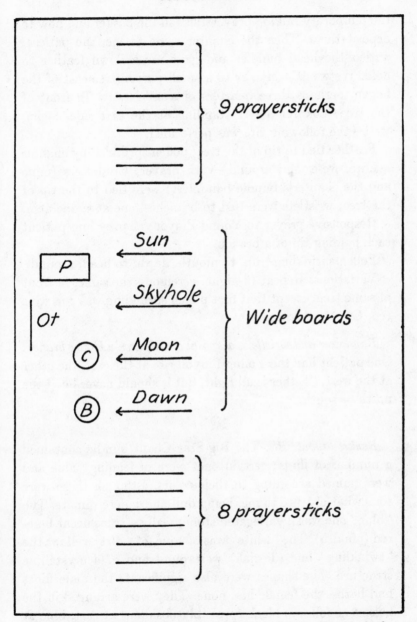

Fig. 3. Bundle layout: Shooting Chant. P—patient; Ot—otterskin collar with whistle;
C—cup of chant lotion; B—basket with bull-roarers standing tip up at west

the temporary talking prayersticks in the basket and how to deposit them. Then the chanter came to me, the patient, untied the head bundle, and gave me a down feather to hold. We went in my car to a small pinyon tree east of the hogan, perhaps three quarters of a mile away. In front of the tree—chanter and I standing at the east side, facing west—the following rite was performed:

Feather tied to tip of the tree; pollen sprinkled by chanter —e-we, we-e, and around—with prayer; bandoleers (mine and the chanter's bundle bandoleer) were tied to the tip of the tree; wristlets were tied to branches, one at s, one at n.

Responsive prayer to Young Pinyon; chanter and patient each holding tip of a branch.

Pollen sprinkling—up, to mouth, down, to head, around.

Variations: Repeat (2-night) ceremony the same, in front of same tree, except that first pollen sprinkling was s-n, we-e (cp. Ch. 11, *Alternation*).

Bandoleer and wristlets, disposal of: SC Sun's House branch. One patient had the Young Pinyon rite at the east, the other at the west. "Either is all right, but it should never be at the north or south."

. . .

Basket layout: BS. The Big Star Chant bundle contained a number of flints; certain ones were of leading value and were named according to their colors, although these were somewhat obscure to me, being dull and indeterminate. The ' blue ' one was a variegated stone, really a translucent blue-red (pinkish). The ' white ' was opaque, of a dirty yellow; the ' twinkling ' one (de'cjah) was round and of a crystalline structure. The shapes were also significant; the male flints had barbs, the female had none. They were arranged in the basket as follows: black (probably obsidian) at east, blue at south, yellow at west, white at north, and twinkling in the center. The rest of the bundle equipment was arranged on the flints; bows, arrows, and bull-roarer were most prominent (Kluckhohn-Wyman, p. 44, Fig. 4).

. . .

Bath (tá'ágis) (E) as described by Kluckhohn-Wyman (pp. 89–90) is so similar to mine that variations only will be noted.

Bath: BS. The bath platform was on the same spot as the corn-meal hogan of the Hoop Transformation rite. The three plants—dodgeweed, *Artemisia frigida*, and grama grass— were the same as those tied to the hoops of the same day. Dodgeweed was placed in all four directions, grama grass at the south over it, and *Artemisia frigida* at the north. The ritualistic acts were:

Preparation and whirling of bull-roarer.

Sprinkling of foam with real pollen—e-we, n-s, and around.

Pollen crosses made for patient's knees and hands.

Bath: Feather Chant. The bath rite was performed at 3:30 P.M. *after* the last sandpainting was finished.

Bath: SC Prayerstick and Sun's House branches and repetitions. The plants for the sand platform were spruce, *Artemisia frigida*, and rock sage. The grama grass and dodgeweed of the unraveling are said to be ' burning ' plants; for the bath only the ' cooling ' herbs are appropriate. The remark is interesting because the five are thought of together and it explains the plants' functions.

Suds design: five kinds of pollen—green, one undetermined, blue, yellow, white—applied n-s, s-n, we-e, e-we, and around.

Suds application: by chanter to all ceremonial body-parts of women patients.

Bath, meaning of (E). RM said that the bath represents the restoration of the children kidnaped from the garden by the

623

Wind People after jewels—jet, turquoise, whiteshell, and abalone—had been offered. It transforms a person from evil or neutral to holy. The mound of earth, upon which the basket for water and suds is placed, commemorates the visit of the two children to Changing Woman's home, where they witnessed her rejuvenation. The emergence story notes that grass at the place where the children washed will be plentiful and will provide riches.

The bath originated in the fourth world to change the then existing creatures into godlike forms.

The careful details of the bath in every ritual myth indicate its importance. In most ceremonies the patient must take the bath; others may take it if they wish, but in the Rain Ceremony it is obligatory for all participants (Matthews 1887, p. 40; 1897, pp. 69, 73; 1902, pp. 190, 211, 310, 17n; Goddard, pp. 150, 174–5; Wheelwright 1942, p. 83; Newcomb 1940b, p. 54; Reichard 1944d, p. 77; Shooting Chant ms.; Hill 1938, pp. 81–2; Haile 1943a, pp. 219, 279, 282).

. . .

Bead Chant, excerpt. L, a young man, complained of extreme distress in his stomach and a two-day performance of the Bead Chant, sung by RP, was tried as a test. I saw the treatment on the sandpainting like that in *Navajo Medicine Man*, Pl. I. It was held in the summer (Aug. 30); if L recovered, the full nine-day performance was to be held the following winter, after he had undergone the War Ceremony. He survived the latter, but died before the full Bead Chant performance could be given (cp. *Sandpainting setup: Bead Chant, excerpt* and *Sandpainting, treatment on: Bead Chant, excerpt*).

. . .

Blackening ('ante·c) (E) is a rite with almost exclusively exorcistic purposes, hence, emphasized in Evil forms; sometimes, as in the War Ceremony and the Removal of contamination of the dead, it plays a major role (Haile 1938b, p. 32).

Blackening, preparation for: BS and SCE. A large amount of soot, obtained by burning the five chant herbs—dodgeweed, grama grass, spruce, rock sage, and *Artemisia frigida*—was laid on a blanket (or buckskin) in front of the bundle layout. Five flints were placed in the chant lotion dish as they had been arranged in the basket on the first night (cp. *Basket layout: BS*), and water was poured in from five directions—e, s, we, n, and above; the dish was set on the blanket in front of the other bundle properties.

An assistant worked bundle tallow into a soft mass. It was then divided, each portion to be colored—white, black, and red; sparkling rock was provided, but not worked into the tallow. When colored, the tallow balls were laid at the southeast corner of the blanket.

Blackening rite: BS (10:30 P.M. to 12:45 A.M.).
Assistant took ashes outside—from e, s, we, and n of fire.
Female patient undressed.
Bull-roarer was sounded outside by assistant at n, we, s, e (anti-sunwise); bull-roarer applied to patient; bull-roarer string moistened in chant lotion; bull-roarer sounded again as before, then returned to chanter, who wound it and returned it to bundle layout.
Brushing bundle equipment with ashes and long brushing over it to accompaniment of long song; brushing of patient's head (with strong pressure), accompanied by another part of same song; brushing of ashes over layout to smokehole, off patient to smokehole.
Application to patient of flints lying in chant lotion; application and drinking of chant lotion by audience; sprinkling of chant lotion on audience.

Flints returned by assistant to layout; chanter put them back in basket.

Application of black salve to patient, a lot on chin and scalplock; audience applied it to their faces; application of white tallow to entire body of patient; audience applied it to their limbs.

Patient stepped on blanket containing soot and, with the help of the assistant, painted herself thoroughly with it; women in audience applied some to themselves and the children.

Application of red salve to patient's face, especially to cheeks and forehead; spotting of patient's face with lightning-struck sparkling rock; spotting of patient's limbs and body with white salve.

Soil from gopher hole put in patient's moccasins.

Bandoleer put on patient's left shoulder and under right arm; bandoleer put on patient's right shoulder and under left arm; wristlets (like a string) tied on patient.

Patient's hair unbound and rubbed with dry red ocher.

Passes made by chanter with head feather bundle—e, s, we, n, and up.

Head bundle tied to patient's scalplock by chanter; beads and jewelry, including silver belt, put on by patient.

Patient put on moccasins and sat on her bedroll until songs were finished.

Blackening rite: preceding purification of deceased chanter's bundle (9:40 to 10:40 P.M.). This rite was sponsored by RP's daughter some three months after his death; the bundle belonged to the general Blessing part of his knowledge and, at his death, was not disposed of but inherited by MC, who was the patient because she was to ' stand for ' the bundle.

The rite differed from the Big Star Chant blackening in the following respects:

Chanter held bull-roarer in left hand and hit it with brush at patient's body parts, head to foot.

The audience were all given quill feathers, the patient held the bull-roarer; in front of each a little pile of ashes was placed. At signals given by chanter, as he sang vehemently, a pinch of ashes was blown up from the feather (or bull-roarer), a new pinch having been placed on it four times, each nearer the tip.

Tallow applied to patient and audience: the old women woke the little children, to whom they applied the tallow. Sparkling rock and lightning-struck rock were not shared by the audience.

Flint tied to patient's scalplock.

Chant lotion chewed and blown over all by assistant.

Patient went outside.

Disposal of soot and ashes by assistant.

Patient re-entered hogan.

Five-minute intermission followed by Blessing rite (see *Vigil.*

Blackening rite: War Ceremony, see Sapir-Hoijer, pp. 265, 271; Haile 1938b, pp. 35, 169, 177, 191–7, 205, 233–5, 239, 318, 70n.

Blackening rite, meaning of (E). The following are explanations of the blackening rite:

Monster Slayer blackened himself so evils would fear him (RM).

The Holy People gave blackening to Earth People to protect them from evil spirits (RM).

The white spots of the Big Star Chant represent stars (RM).

Blackening makes the patient invisible to evils which exert their greatest power at night.

Enemy ghosts fear the soot; therefore, it will drive them away.

Blackening is the evil part of the War Ceremony and represents all roaming enemy spirits.

Blackening helps a person to reach old age.

Blackening was done with corn smut in the Feather and Eagle chants (Haile 1943a, p. 292, 61n; Hill 1938, p. 46; Newcomb 1940b, p. 63).

. . .

Body painting ('aki na'adzoh) (A) has been differentiated from figure painting, and described for the Navaho and Chiricahua Wind chants by Kluckhohn and Wyman. The Shooting, Hail, Wind, and Eagle chants have intricate figure paintings. The exorcistic ceremonies—War, Evil forms, and perhaps others—have body painting. Figure painting includes many symbols of the chant to which it belongs, whereas body painting represents impersonation, chiefly of the masked gods and The Twins. As usual, there is overlapping, for the Eagle Chant seems to have both.

Warriors painted their bodies in a fashion somewhat different from the ritualistic paintings, apparently selecting excerpts of the chant figure paintings—snakes, bear tracks, or human hands were depicted with red ocher, white clay, blue paint, or soot. The marks were to make the warrior feared, as was the animal represented.

Mythological people were painted, while traveling, with lightning on their legs; corn on their breasts and backs; a rainbow on chests and shoulder blades; their faces white.

The Meal Sprinklers of the Shooting Chant Fire Dance had the figure painting on their bodies when they announced the Fire Dance to their neighbors (*Figure painting;* Kluck-hohn-Wyman, pp. 96–7, 125, 150, Fig. 22; Haile 1943a, pp. 223, 230, 283; Hill 1938, p. 14; Wheelwright 1942, p. 121; cp. Reichard 1944a, p. 106).

Body painting: Feather Chant. There was no body or figure painting as a part of the sandpainting treatment, but after the bath the patients were smeared on the body, neck, and face with white paint, over the corn-meal drier. Brown spots were painted on the temples, and below them spots of sparkling rock; the usual yellow pollen streak was drawn across the lower jaw from ear to ear.

. . .

Bull-roarer, preparation of: SC. Bull-roarer corresponding with sex of patient or patients taken from basket layout; bull-roarer marked with pollen in form of bow; bull-roarer set outside basket with tip resting on basket: in Sun's House branch, at south; in Prayerstick branch, at west (the difference may be due to alternation rather than to a branch requirement).

Bull-roarer string soaked in chant lotion, which had been sprinkled with blue pollen; this act was accompanied by many songs.

Bull-roarer, whirling of: SC. Bull-roarer was taken outside by chanter, whirled six times at east, brought in, and applied by making passes in a cross at ceremonial body parts with sound blu ˙ ˙ ˙; same act repeated at we, s, and n, then from north, returned counter clockwise; bull-roarer was then returned to basket layout.

. . .

Bundle contents: BS. The items of the Big Star Chant bundle are numbered correlatively with those of the Male

629

Shooting Chant Holy (see *Bundle contents: SC*) where they have the same function; for example, BS 1 means an item of the Big Star Chant corresponding with item 1 of the Shooting Chant. It is much the same, but may have a few different details which, when known, I have noted. Absence of remarks does not necessarily mean complete identity, but, more likely, that I do not know the difference.

BS 2–6. Arrows like 2–6 with slight differences: 3 is named 'aḱi·cdi·tsói in the Big Star Chant.

BS 7. 2 bows, male and female.

BS 11a. 2 bandoleers (as in SC), male and female.

b. 2 wristlets.

BS 12. 1 quill feather brush (as in SC).

BS 13. 2 bull-roarers, male and female.

BS 15. 1 fire drill (as in SC).

BS 16. 2 head feather bundles, male and female.

BS 17. 4 buffalo hide rattles (as in SC).

BS 18. numerous unraveling strings.

BS 22. 1 shield.

BS 23. Arrowpoints, many of flint; 2 special to cut plant garment, 5 special to represent stars.

BS 2–6. *Arrows.* Two of these are mentioned by name: the pointed tail-feathered arrow is called tse· de·sťá·n, the yellow pointed arrow 'aḱi·cdi·tsói. Their points and attachments differentiate them from those of the Shooting Chant. Four are of hard oak to which eagle feathers (and almost certainly numerous other things) are tied with unwounded buckskin. Combined with fresh properties, they are a part of the Overshooting rite.

BS 7. *Bows* have two robin tail feathers at the center; three olivella shells along the string, represented by white dots in the sandpaintings. The male bow is dark, the female blue.

BS 13. *Bull-roarers* of the Big Star bundle lack the abalone shell of the Male Shooting Chant Holy. They represent Snake, whereas those of the Shooting Chant Evil stand for Thunder.

BS 16. *Head feather bundles* of the Big Star Chant are the same as those of the War Ceremony: five tail feathers of unwounded roadrunner are tied on with unwounded buckskin. The end of each feather is sprinkled with live pollen collected from each of the animals who aided in overcoming the monsters—goshawk, blue lizard, horned toad, and roadrunner. A live eagle feather and other feathers compose the rest of the bundle.

BS 18. *Unraveling strings* are of wild cotton, when it is available. RM's were of sheep wool, because he could not get the rarer article. The string was 3-ply, made in the usual way by a simple cat's-cradle (Reichard 1936, p. 208).

BS 22. *Shield* (gą·ga xa·zdje·') is of twisted buckskin made from the pants of a captured Ute, with shells of the olivella type, but larger and varied in size and markings; one flint is tied to the shield. RM paid one hundred dollars for the shield for his bundle.

Bundle contents: Flint Chant, see Haile 1943a, pp. 36–7, 39, 148, 232.

Bundle contents: Rain Ceremony. The bundle equipment I saw used for the pollen paintings of the Rain Ceremony included:

4 aragonite prayersticks, one male from Taos; one female from Oraibi; a pair from Walpi, the male having an inlaid turquoise, the female having no jewel.

5 plumed arrows named: For-bear-it-moved-fast, male and female; For-horned-toad-it-moved-fast; For-coyote-it-moved-fast, male and female.

"These five stand for one, the model sent from the sky as

631

a pattern for humans to go by. It was taken back to the sky as soon as pollen had been put on it. It was named For-thunder-it-moved-down-fast." (I consider these the master symbols.)

1 slate bull-roarer.

2 flint points, one red and white; one yellow. Both are called ' flash lightning ' and are used to scoop up soil from the sacred mountains.

2 flint points, one black (male), one white (female) (held by the one-sung-over during prayer).

1 small basket called Dawn Mountain and many down feathers to be tied to it (the basket represents the eastern holy mountain).

1 so-called ' smooth-horned-toad.'

2 crystals, male and female. These were flashed over the pollen paintings as the first act.

1 tubular pipe with a whiteshell bead set in the mouthpiece, and tobacco from everywhere.

Varied herbs from Gray Mountain in a sack with a red flint point from Taos Mountain (Wheeler Peak), called 'Bear-is-shot-with-it' (cac bił 'ółto·h). "Everything is afraid of this medicine."

Bundle contents: SC. The bundle items are numbered to correspond with those of other chants. Items 1–10 are listed and described in this order because the chanter (JS) regarded it as the relative order of their power. The sequence from 11 on has no significance.

1. 1 pair talking prayersticks for praying (ke·łá·n yáłti).
2. 1 male eagle tail-feathered arrow ('atse· be'está·n).
3. 1 female tail-feathered arrow (tse·gic di·tsói ba'á·di·).
4. 1 eagle down-feathered arrow ('atšos ka·").
5. 1 male feathered arrow (gis yistá·n).

6. 1 female red-feathered arrow (ɫaɫtci· ka·").
7. 2 bows ('aɫtį·), male and female.
8. 4 bundle talking prayersticks (tó bo'oltą́).
9. 4 wide boards (tsinte·l).
10. 2 aspergills, male and female ('axe·' bidá· ditį).
11. a. 2 bandoleers, male and female (dahna'iɣizí).
    b. 2 wristlets.
12. 1 quill feather brush (nditį).
13. 2 bull-roarers, male and female (tćétćil bo'osn̈i·).
14. 2 collars.
15. 1 fire drill (ɣo·ɫką·").
16. 2 head feather bundles, male and female (na·ɣé·tšos).
17. 4 buffalo (or cow-) hide rattles ('akaɫ 'aɣá·ɫ).
18. numerous unraveling strings (ɣoltá·d).
19. varied equipment (see Kluckhohn-Wyman, pp. 28ff.).
20. 1 tubular blackstone pipe (náɫostse').
21. Sun's House screen (djóxona·"ái bikin) (for Sun's House branch).
22. red feather headdress (for Dark Circle branch).

1. *Talking prayerstick* of blue willow (kai do·ɫij) from ' a long distance away.' "Some chanters make theirs of aragonite." The female has a facet to indicate the face, the male has none. Tied to it are: 2 live eagle feathers, 1 turkey breast feather, 1 piece of white cotton, 1 turquoise bead.

2. *Male eagle tail-feathered arrow* of large reed (lóka·tsoh) ' from the east.' It had the following attachments: 3 stiff eagle tail feathers and 3 eagle down feathers tied at each side, many bluebird feathers amongst the other feathers, many jewels—olivella, whiteshell, jet—tied on with cotton string, buffalo and deer sinew wound underneath the feathers where they do not show. Inside the arrow there are various medicines, soil, and plants from the mountains.

633

This arrow is used for male patients. Its jewel name is Turquoise Arrow; it is white in sandpaintings. "The eagle down represents the six sacred mountains."

3. *Female tail-feathered arrow* differs from 2 in the follow ing respects: it is made of big reed from the San Francisco Peaks; has eagle feathers as has 1 but canary feathers instead of bluebird; many olivella shells, and one large whiteshell. Its jewel name is Abalone Arrow (di·tcili· ka·").

4. *Eagle down arrow* has only one name, no sex, and is used for a male or female patient in the Evil ceremony (or exorcistic phases) when the patient has been wounded by shooting (Huckel ms., parenthetical comment mine). The jewels—olivella and whiteshell beads—differ from 2.

5. *Male feathered arrow* is used for a female patient and differs from 2 as follows: it is made of mountain mahogany with medicine placed inside; it has whiteshell beads, one large piece of whiteshell, and olivella shells. Its jewel name is Whiteshell Arrow (yo·łgai ka·"); another name for it is bó'ósni·.

6. *Female red-feathered arrow* is for female patients. It is like 5 except: it is solid with no medicine inside; the bottom is spatulate and not wound with sinew; the jewels are white-shell beads and redstone. Its jewel name is Redstone Arrow (tséłtci·" ka·"); another name is bó'osni·.

7. *Male bow* ('ałtį· diłxił, ' Dark Bow ') is of tséłkani· with strings of wolf sinew; it is colored black. Bluebird feathers and one robin tail feather are tied at the center; both ends are wound with buffalo and deer sinew.

Female bow ('ałtį· tséłkani·) is of the same material as 7, which gives it its name. Other differences are: color yellow; canary feathers are tied at the center and ends, and a robin tail feather at center is tied with mountain lion tail sinew.

8. *Bundle talking prayersticks* of lightning-struck *Quercus*

undulata (tcétċil ntłizi˙). One piece, much longer than the finished object for which it was to be used, was collected from each of the four cardinal directions, each carefully noted. JS marked them in pencil with initials of the directions. Each had a small ring attached to it. They were trimmed down with pocket knives and a small ax, then carefully shaved and polished. During the entire time they were being worked on they were oriented with the tips to the east and kept as nearly in the color order b-w-u-y (cross formation of chant colors) as possible with four men working on them. All materials were laid on a thick pile of goods on top of a buckskin ('aya˙ sika˙d). All were smeared first with *Sphæralcea coccinea*, var. elata ('aze˙ ntłini˙), then with white clay (dle˙c). They were then painted with mineral colors mixed with juice squeezed from the roasted leaves of *Yucca baccata* (tsá'ászi' nte˙l).

The colors were black, white, blue, and yellow, black and blue being male, white and yellow female. Facets were cut at the top of all, male as well as female; the eyes and mouth of each were of the contrasting color. The colors were hardly discernible after the wrappings had been put on, but the prayersticks could be distinguished by the hoops and jewels. The pointed bases were left white.

Twenty-four or more turkey feathers and four or five eagle down feathers were tied to each stick by careful winding of a specially twisted woolen string. The winding began one hand from the bottom and, after it had been continued for about one and half or two inches, a down feather was tied to the end of the string. Toward the top a little hoop was caught firmly into the winding by two laps of the string. Care was taken to have the crossing of the hoops on top, that is, outside. A jewel bead of characterizing color was tied to each—

635

jet to the black, whiteshell to the white, turquoise to the blue, and redshell to the yellow.

9. *Wide boards* (Fig. 4) were made for JS at the same time as the talking prayersticks. They were of lightning-struck wild cottonwood collected east of Mt. Taylor. In addition to preserving the direction at which they were cut, the top (biká") and bottom (biɣi') were marked to indicate the way the wood grew. Each piece was cut and shaved to size and shape. Holes were bored at the upper corners with a brace and bit, of which the chanter-patient was very proud; all the assistants admired it too. It was not particularly efficient; much coaxing was required to get the tool into action since the holes were to be very near the edge. Since there was nothing to hold the boards in place, the bit slipped and broke, but the job was finished with the broken bit. The boards were shaved and polished like the talking prayersticks; the same plant juice and white clay were smeared over them.

A hole was cut out of the center of the board called the Skyhole, made of the wood collected from the south. Before the hole was cut, it was outlined with pollen and singing was started. At this moment it became holy. The painting, as in Fig. 4, was done with the same materials used for the talking prayersticks. When the painting was finished, an eagle down feather was tied at each corner and each knot was sprinkled with pollen (cp. Kluckhohn-Wyman, pp. 26–7).

10. *Aspergills* (in Flint Chant called tó bikésta') are named by Kluckhohn-Wyman ' medicine stoppers,' perhaps because of Father Berard's literal translation. The aspergill is laid over the cup containing the infusion specific. The chanter tastes the medicine from the butt of the aspergill; with its feathered top he sprinkles the infusion over the sandpainting and touches the parts of the sandpainting figures and corresponding parts of the patient's body.

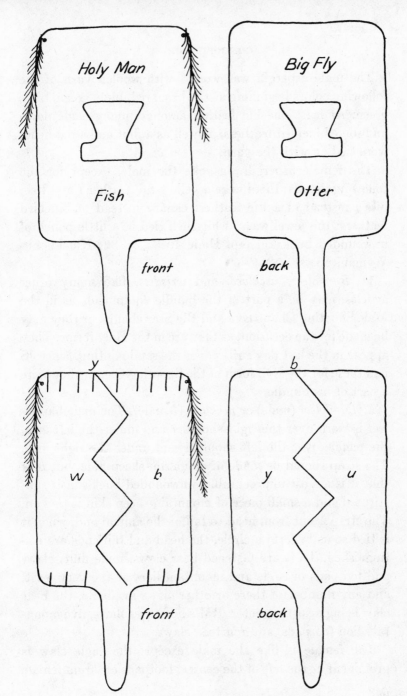

Fig. 4. Wide boards: Shooting Chant

The male aspergill was wound with woolen yarn of the following colors beginning at the base: red, blue, green, blue, green. At least one life feather amongst many eagle down and some bluebird feathers, as well as a flint and a red bead, were tied on with the yarn.

The female aspergill was like the male, except for the following details: there were a yellow tail feather ('atse'ltsoi bita') instead of a life feather; canary instead of bluebird feathers; the jewel was a whiteshell tied in a little pouch of unwounded buckskin (cp. Haile 1943a, p. 32; Kluckhohn-Wyman, pp. 31, 52).

11. *Bandoleer, necklace,* and *wristlets,* like many other articles, may be a part of the bundle equipment, as in the Male Shooting Chant Evil and Big Star chants, or they may be made for the occasion, as they are in the Holy forms. They appear in the last day's rites over the sandpainting. Since JS had these for the Evil form of the Shooting Chant, they were a part of his bundle.

a. *Bandoleer* (male) or *necklace* (female). The male bandoleer is worn over the right shoulder and under the left arm, the female over the left shoulder and under the right arm. The strap should be made of mountain-sheep hide, but now that it is almost unprocurable, unwounded buckskin is substituted and a small piece of mountain-sheep skin is tied on. The strap is cut from head to tail of the animal and, when it is tied so as to form a circle, the head and tail ends are distinguished. To it are fastened bear claws, male flint, claws and footpads of eagle and mountain lion, at the very least, and any number of these or other claws available, the bear claw being near the center. RM's had three flints, five mountain lion footpads, and fourteen claws.

The female is like the male except: the eagle claw is prominent at the left of the center; footpads are from female animals; flints are ' female.' RM's had two female flints and fifteen female claws.

A female patient wears this bundle item around her neck like a necklace.

b. *Wristlets* are, like the bandoleers, of buckskin cord or strap. One of RM's had sixteen wildcat claws; the other, eight mountain lion claws.

12. *Brush*, in the Male Shooting Chant Holy, serves the same purposes as in the other branches. In the Holy chant the chanter asperses the chant lotion with the brush after the sweat-emetic, showering blessings; it cools fever and refreshes. In the Evil forms, the brush disperses evils as, for instance, in ashes blowing (cp. Kluckhohn-Wyman, pp. 35, 37, 73).

13. *Bull-roarer*. The male, which represents a man, is of hard oak, into which three turquoise beads are set with pitch to indicate a face. On the back, which has a ridge, there is an inset of abalone to indicate the man's brain. The string is of mountain-sheep hide.

The female bull-roarer is the same, except that there is no ridge at the back.

14. *Collars with whistles* (tšitšǫs), the male of beaver (tca·''), the female of otter (tą́bą·xastí·n, tą́bą·stí·n), represent the help given The Twins by these animals when Sun tested them by freezing. The foundation of the collar is the skin, to which ribbon fringe and the whistle are fastened.

According to JS, the whistle shows that patient and chanter are ready for the Holy People, and drives off evil. For these reasons, it is blown just as the audience is to be invited to the sandpainting rite. In the myth, the whistle represents Holy Man's mind as he journeys; consequently, the fringe is held so as to touch the patient's head when the whistle is blown.

639

According to the Hail Chant myth, the whistle (tcoγá) is the ' same ' as that of the Shooting Chant; it is used by the Meal Sprinklers. Matthews' picture of a meal sprinkler, wearing a beaverskin collar, looks much like that of the Shooting Chant; it is explained: "This [the collar] will be a means of recognition for you" (Matthews 1887, pp. 424–5).

15. *Fire drill.* The fireboard is made of *Nolina microcarpa* (xogicí), a slow-burning flower stalk, collected in ' Apache country.' There are three fire sticks of oak, one longer than the others, to which a small piece of yucca fiber is tied (cp. Kluckhohn-Wyman, p. 40).

16. *Head feather bundles, male and female* have the following feathers:

Ceremonial name	Common name	English
'ayá·c do·tł'ij	dóli·	bluebird
'ayá·c łtsói	tsidi· łtsói	green-backed finch
'ayá·c bite'l xaltcí"	dji·ni'í	robin
'ayá·c tco·jγá·li·	tco·jγá·li·	Bullock oriole
táctcoj do·tł'ij	táctcoj do·tł'ij	purple martin
'anłtáni·	'anłtáni·	cornbeetle
taji·	taji·	turkey
'atsá	'atsá	eagle
xiná bita dé'l	dé'l	crane live feathers
'ayá·c 'axano·γá·l	dahi·tíhí	hummingbird

The hummingbird feather was tied on last; all strings are of unwounded buckskin.

The female bundle differs from the male in having canary, instead of bluebird, feathers and a whiteshell bead instead of turquoise.

17. *Hide rattles.* Four buffalo hide or cowhide rattles are a complete set. If buffalo is not available, cowhide may be substituted and a buffalo token—the tail, for instance—is added. The tail gives life, the hair, power, to the rattle. The feathers at each corner must be from a live wild (not captive) eagle; they also give the rattle life. On the broad side of the male rattle there is a zigzag lightning; on the broad side of the female, a flash lightning; on the seam, a red-blue symbol of sunglow. The lightning gives the rattle strength and protection. Jewels inside are jet, whiteshell, turquoise, and abalone, one kind in each. The rattles, therefore, have jewel names and are said to belong to the Holy People: jet to Holy Man, whiteshell to Holy Woman, turquoise to Holy Boy, and abalone to Holy Girl.

The cotton string by which the feathers are tied came originally from one of the Hopi mesas; it represents the rattle's earstring and gives it strength and power.

The core of the wrapped handle, wide part at the bottom, is made of lightning-struck *Quercus undulata*. The handle is bound with beaver and deer skin and porcupine quills; the buffalo tail is fastened to the handle.

The chanter's strength depends upon the number of his rattles. RM had only three—he lacked the abalone rattle—but used them and a gourd rattle, which belongs to a lesser ceremony. After a man has procured four rattles he uses them for every sing, whether they are required or not. RM got the buffalo tails from other chanters, two of whom were his teachers.

According to RM, there were originally five rattles, but the one of redshell came from a turquoise matrix, and belongs to the Holy People; there are only four for Earth People. RM got one rattle after each chant he learned in the following order: Big Star, Endurance, Female Mountain Chant. After learning the Male Shooting Chant Evil, his next choice, he will have a complete set of four. "Maybe when I am very old I will have them all," he said hopefully.

tłǎ·h said that the rattles contain dry yellow seeds of the thunder plant ('aze'' tċił tċił).

18. *Unraveling strings* consist of wool or cotton and are tied with one or more live feathers. One with a live eagle feather, cut straight across the rib (a male cut), is the first, ' head or chief ' unraveler; the last has a turkey down feather; the others, plucked eagle feathers.

Chanters have a varied number of the unraveling strings. JS has only twenty-four (of sheep's wool), because he does not take more than two patients at a time. The strings, the same for Holy and Evil forms, are dedicated by a ceremony.

The unravelers represent, among other things, the life feather given The Twins by Spider Woman.

20. *Pipe.* RP's bundle contained a tubular blackstone pipe, which he valued very highly. He said it came from a ruin, but he did not tell me how he got it. He smoked the sheep and corral with it in the Rite for releasing sheep from lightning contamination.

21. *Sun's House screen* should be a bundle property, but if it is lacking, a sandpainting may be substituted. The screen is of withes laid close together and painted in various colors, as illustrated in Newcomb-Reichard, Plate XIX. The snakes are carved and painted, and so arranged that they may be pulled in and out of the holes at the bottom of the screen. Elaborate preparations mark the erection of this symbol. The screen is set up like a booth, over the top fresh spruce boughs are carefully arranged, and carved birds are strung with wires to the hogan ceiling. During the treatment on the sandpaintings the birds are made to fly and sing, and thè snakes to move in and out of their ' houses ' (Reichard 1934, Ch. XXIII; 1939, pp. 42–4, Fig. 1; Shooting Chant ms.; cp. Matthews 1902, p. 196).

22. *Red feather headdress* is an elaborate folding affair.

When worn by two special dancers, who represent the Male Shooting Chant Holy in the Fire Dance, it looks exactly like the painted headdress of the sandpainting figures (Reichard 1939, Pl. XII-XVI; *Sunglow*, Con. B).

Bundle contents: SCE. Items 1–18 are the same for Holy and Evil forms except:
8, 9, 10, and 14 are not used in the Evil form.
SCE 13. JS has two male bull-roarers, instead of one male and one female.
SCE 16. 2 head feather bundles are different.
SCE 23. Many flint arrowpoints (bé·cistogi·).
16. *Head feather bundles, male and female.* The male bundle is composed of the following: male roadrunner's tail feather, which has a white tip, is tied with a piece of unwounded buckskin; there are many live eagle feathers tied with a white cotton string, to which a flint point is fastened.

The female bundle differs from the male: roadrunner feather has no white tip; there are canary, instead of bluebird, feathers; a little sack of lightning-struck rock, instead of a flint, is fastened to the bundle.

Bundle contents, procurement of: SC. JS got his bundle properties in the following ways:

He bought talking prayerstick 1 from a dying chanter and had a chant performed to protect himself. He uses them only for praying.

He bought 2–7 from a chanter; they were dedicated by a performance of the chant. 8 and 9 were made and dedicated by the performance described as the Sandpainting branch of the Male Shooting Chant. JS bought 14, the male beaver collar, from one xasti·n 'asá·l'in. JS had three whistles, two of which he made himself. I gave him a fine otterskin, bought

643

for the purpose from a New York furrier. JS intended to make two collars of it, one for himself, one to trade.

. . .

Dedication of new bundle prayersticks (A), see *Talking prayersticks, bundle; dedication of: SC Sandpainting branch.*

Deposit of offerings (A), see Ch. 18, 20.

Disposal of bandoleer and wristlets, see *Bandoleer and wristlets, disposal of.*

Disposal of Sky-reaching-rock: SC Sun's House branch. On the tenth day after the beginning of the Sun's House branch —that is, the day after the necklace was disposed of—the assistant and patients took the clay of Sky-reaching-rock, a part of the double sandpainting of the sixth day, far away to a canyon east of the place where the chant was held. It was deposited there in a spot very hard to find.

Distinguishing symbols, see Ch. 20.

Emetic, see *Sweat-emetic.*

Emetic formula, see *Sweat-emetic, emetic formula.*

Emetic frames, see *Sweat-emetic, emetic frames.*

Feather Chant ('atso·se·) was a nine-night ceremony at which I saw three elaborate, unusual, beautifully made sand-paintings, the treatment, and the vigil. It was started on September 7 of a warm season; there had been no frost. The date is important because masked dancers played a major role.

There were five patients: S and X, males; U, a male co-patient; and the female co-patients, BMW and TA. BMW was so ill that on day 7 an emergency painting was laid for her a few yards south of the ceremonial hogan, the treatment for her making a subsidiary rite not directly connected with the Feather Chant but, as we shall see, affecting it. On this day she was slightly better than on day 6; she said that she had not been aware of anything that had happened on the day before.

The Sun painting, made in her behalf, was similar to one of the figures in Newcomb-Reichard, Figure 8. A white stripe was drawn in corn meal across the patient's forehead; a yellow band across her chin; between the two, her face was painted red; large white dots were described on her arms. In the evening, she was blackened; the next morning, her son, who worked some 28 miles away, took her to the Agency hospital. The emergency rite was conducted simultaneously with the treatment on the sandpainting going on inside the hogan. Another woman was substituted for BMW, so that there were still five patients, as there were when the chant was started.

Figure painting ('akina'adzoh): *SC*. Designs are carefully drawn, as contrasted with the application of a solid color to the entire body common in some chants (Fig. 5, over). The pattern is for Sun's House and Prayerstick branches and repetitions of both, all patients being female. The painting ritual corresponded closely with that described by Kluckhohn-Wyman.

Between the breasts, a blue sun was made with the bundle crystal; at the center of the back, a white moon was similarly applied. From one of these circles to the other, lines of the color combination, y-u-w-b (black outside), were drawn

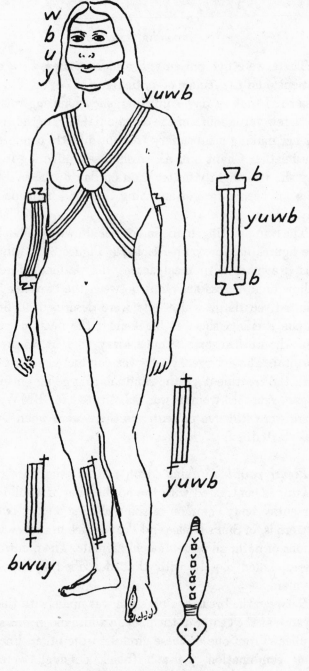

Fig. 5. Figure painting: Shooting Chant

down the front and around the waist, then up over the shoulders so that they met correspondingly at the back.

On each arm, passing the inside of the elbow, with one end on the upper, one on the forearm, there was a black cloud design edged in white at each end; the cloud designs were connected by stripes as described above, the stripes being symmetrical with black outside.

On the shins, stripes were arranged in the same order, but on the right the white one was extended and crossed at the bottom; the yellow was extended and crossed at the top (the female colors were crossed). On the left shin, the yellow extended and crossed at the bottom, the white at the top.

On the right foot, a white Big Snake with black outline was painted, the head on the big toe, the tongue and fangs underneath; the Snake's body had a ' snake's house ' and deer-hoof markings on the instep. On the left foot, there was a similar yellow Big Snake with blue outline.

All lines were straight; had the patient been a man, they would have been drawn with four angles.

Spotting: the chanter dipped two fingers in white clay and daubed double spots over the whole body; then repeated the spotting with a mixture of corn smut and water; he returned what was left of the mixture to his bundle.

Red salve was applied under the patient's jaw (audience participation).

Two small parts of the patient's forelock were separated and smeared with white clay.

Face striping: wide stripes of blue were drawn across the nose and cheeks, white across the forehead, black across the eyes, yellow across the chin.

Variations: In a two-night repeat performance of Sun's House Red Inside, in both five- and two-night performances of the Prayerstick branch and in the Sandpainting branch, colors were in reverse order, b-w-u-y, with yellow outside. On the right leg, yellow (outside) was crossed at the top, white (inside) at the bottom. On the left, white (inside) was crossed at the bottom; yellow (outside) at the top. These variations are explained by alternation (Ch. 11).

Face: when I had the five-night performance, RP asked me if I wanted stripes or spots. I said stripes. He said I must remember and I could have spots the next time. I forgot; he forgot to ask me, and I had stripes both times.

Repeat of Sun's House branch (two-night): On the face were a red background with yellow and white stripes—usual for sandpainting faces of Shooting Chant—no blue or white stripes, but white dots in pairs, representing hail. (This was the alternation I forgot.)

In the Sandpainting branch the variations were chiefly those of sex, the one-sung-over being male. Instead of smooth lines on body and legs, there were zigzag lines with four angles. Those on the legs had crosses as follows: on the right leg, blue was crossed at the bottom, black at the top; on the left, black was crossed at the bottom, blue at the top (male colors were crossed).

Snakes on the instep were angled, instead of smooth; black on the left, blue on the right.

The two forelocks, when separated, were smeared with soot from burnt rock sage. The black stripe for the face was made with the same soot, applied with the sound blu·˙·.

Stripes on the face were made in the following order: blue, white, yellow, black. Several spots were made on the face with sparkling rock (cp. Kluckhohn-Wyman, pp. 96–7; New-comb-Reichard, pp. 52–4).

Flint Chant, excerpt: An emergency rite was sung for MA, who had cutting pains in her lungs the day after undergoing

the interrupted War Ceremony (Ch. 6). The following acts
were performed:

Part I (3 to 4 P.M.):

Long singing with accompaniment of fawn-hoof rattle.
Movement in sunwise and anti-sunwise directions. The
southwest quadrant was left open, entered once by chanter
and patient; all others were restricted from entering it.
The sound bl-bl-bl-bl was made after every set of songs,
but not over patient.

Restrictions: Anyone was allowed to enter the shade during the singing, but no one was allowed to go out.

The bath had the following variations: Pollen was sprinkled
on the bath foam in the order, r-u-b-w-y, in the directions—
e-we, we-e, s-n, n-s, and around the sand platform. There
were pollen crosses on which the patient was to put her
hands and to kneel. The patient, after circling the fire in
sunwise direction, stepped carefully over these crosses.

Part II (4:20 to 5:10 P.M.): Administration of infusion
specific.

Part III (7:50 P.M. to 1:10 A.M.):

Singing.

Administration of infusion specific.

Blowing of infusion specific at patient's sides by chanter
(cp. Kluckhohn-Wyman, 51–2; Wyman-Bailey 1945, p. 356;
Haile 1943a).

Girl's Adolescence Ceremony (A), see Franciscan Fathers
1910, p. 446ff.; Reichard 1928, p. 135; 1934, p. 100; Matthews
1897, p. 134; Haile 1938b, p. 87; Wyman-Bailey 1943a, pp.
3–12.

⋅ ⋅ ⋅

Hoop transformation rite (E) is a major part of the Big Star,
Male Shooting Evil, and Endurance chants, perhaps of all

Evil forms of the chants. An arrangement of mountains, sandpainting, and hoops is set up outside the ceremonial hogan; a corn-meal trail connects all its parts from the outermost hoop to the painting inside the hogan.

Hoop transformation rite, hoops; preparation of: BS. Withes of the chosen woods were collected with care. The hoops were of four colors; one was called ' shiny, twinkling ' (de·cjah). All represent stars. The associations are as follows:

Direction	Color	Sex	Wood	Painted with	Jewel
e	b	m	oak	coal from fire / soot from plants	jet
s	u	f	hard oak	white clay and soot	t
we	y	m	coyote corn	yellow ocher	ab
n	w	f	juniper	white clay	wh
cen	tw	—	wildrose	unpainted	re (?)

The black and yellow withes, being male, should be cut straight across; the blue and white, being female, should be cut diagonally. On the other hand, slanting cuts are for head trouble and, since the patient, a girl, had had stomach trouble and loss of blood (meningitis), the cuts were all made straight across. The knife of an assistant slipped and made a slight scratch on one withe and the chanter made him fetch another.

Paint was smeared on with the hands. Three or four bunches of the plants used for the unraveling rite, except spruce, were tied to each withe at regular intervals. The ends were crossed—care being taken to keep the butt end toward the worker—the tip end underneath, and tied with the unraveling strings in a slipknot, so that the feather hung down at the left on the side opposite the worker. The wildrose hoop was a little longer than the others because of the thorns.

Each wood has a color; only one color appears each day, all four hoops of a kind being painted the same color; the wildrose hoop was the same every day. The wood required

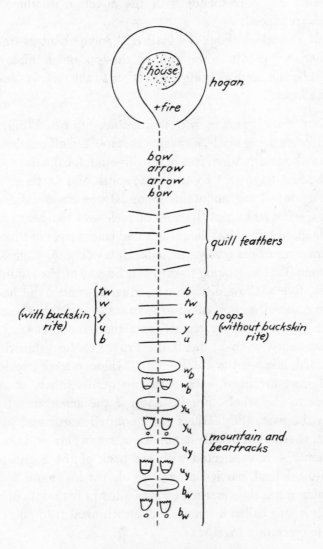

Fig. 6. Hoop transformation: Big Star Chant

for each day corresponds with the direction in which the hoops are placed.

RM remarked about the feather, "Some chanters tie the feather so it points to the right at the top, but I think that would be the same as tying the feather to the feet, instead of to the head."

Hoop transformation rite, preparation of: BS. While the hoops were being made, a space was smoothed off outside the hogan about a hundred feet in the direction for the day—east on the first day, west on the next; south and north on succeeding days. Four mountains (mounds) were made of different colors, a few feet apart. In front of each were two bear tracks of the mountain color; mountains and tracks were outlined in contrasting colors (shown as subscripts) (Fig. 6, page 651). In front (that is, looking toward the hogan) of the mountain series, five shallow ditches were dug, in which the hoops, when finished, were planted so as to stand upright. The color order for an ordinary chant, from the outside toward the hogan, is u-y-w-tw-b; but if the Prayer on buckskin rite is included, it is b-u-y-w-tw. In front of these, piles of uncolored sand were arranged, each with two quill feathers at right angles to the whole. For instance, if the arrangement was from the east, the feathers were pointed north and south. Next, there were bundle items—bow, arrow, arrow, bow. All elements were connected with the back of the hogan by a corn-meal trail, carried around as shown in Figure 6. The circular space thus marked off was filled in with dots of corn meal; it was called a ' house.' The corn-meal trail holds the whole ceremony together.

Hoop transformation rite, treatment with: BS.

Day 1. The patient, wearing a piece of unbleached muslin over her shoulders and holding as many as possible of her valued possessions, sat within the corn-meal circle in the hogan, waiting until everything was ready. Then the chanter led the procession to the place of the bundle layout; the patient followed him and the audience followed her—all blanketed and carrying the things they valued most: clothes, small grips, even a baby. At the far end of the hoop arrangement the patient pulled the unbleached muslin over her head, and placed her feet on the bear tracks, then bent over and passed through the hoops; the chanter stood beside the hoop farthest from the hogan. As the patient passed through the black hoop, the chanter pulled the muslin off her head; when she went through the blue hoop, he pulled it off as far as her neck; as she came under the yellow hoop, the muslin was pulled below her shoulders; when she passed through the white hoop, it fell to her waist; and, as she went through the thorny hoop, it fell off completely.

Day 2. As on day 1 with the following variations: The hoops and mountains were at the south. The hoops were of hard oak, painted black with soot from burnt herbs (the herbs were not available on day 1; a ground coal from the fire was substituted). There were five bunches of herbs on each hoop.

The hoops, one on top of the other, were moved from east to west over the fire, accompanied Monster Slayer's sound xą̆' xą̆' xą̆' xą̆', and from south to north with the sound xanêiní.

Day 3. Arrangement at the west was yellow with hoops of coyote corn (*Forestiera neomexicana* 218).*

Day 4. Arrangement at the north was of white juniper hoops; the colors were reversed, w-y-u-b-tw, because ' it was at the north.' There were only three plants—little dodge-

---

*Numbers after Latin names refer to Wyman-Harris, pp. 17–34.

weed, *Artemisia frigida*, and grama grass—among the five bunches tied to each hoop.

Passes were made by the chanter with all the hoops lying flat—e, s, we, n, around fire, and up; then hoops were laid on the blanket in the same order as on day 2.

Yellow corn meal was sprinkled from south of the mountains, around to the west and south of the hogan, and inside (interpreted as sunwise because the viewpoint was from the inside of the hogan, that is, as if it had been started there).

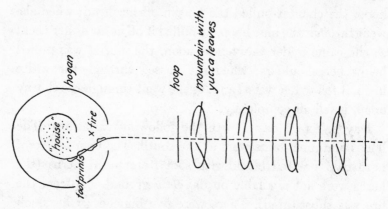

Fig. 7. Hoop transformation: Male Shooting Chant Evil

Bull-roarer was whizzed at north during the entire treatment.

Steps in the procession: both feet on bear tracks, left foot between, right foot first on right bear track, and so on.

Unraveling as patient passed through each hoop; later, the strings were applied crossed to patient as she sat inside the corn-meal circle.

Bull-roarer whirled in front of the hogan and applied crossed to the patient's ceremonial body-parts.

Pollen sprinkling.

Long song and prayer from Blessing rite—'to end with good.'

Hoop transformation rite, preparation of: SCE (Fig. 7). This rite differed from the same rite of the Big Star Chant in the following particulars: Whereas in the Big Star Chant the mountains and bear tracks were of different colors on each day at the respective directions, in this they were all of the same color at any one direction. The hoops were placed in front of the mountains so that mountains and hoops alternated. The spiny hoop is called ditłohí, 'fuzzy.' On each of the mountains, instead of quill feathers, yucca leaves were crossed, a pair each of: *Yucca baccata, Yucca glauca,* 'god yucca,' and 'big yucca's horn.' Leaves of the same yuccas were crossed on the mountains, which were a part of the Never-ending-snake sandpainting (see *Sandpainting: SCE*).

Hoop transformation rite, treatment with: SCE.

Day 1. At the east were four white hoops of aspen, one of wildrose; the mountains were white.

Day 2. At the west were four yellow hoops of red willow and one of wildrose; mountains were yellow.

The feather head bundle was tied to the patient's head before he was led out to the hoops; an assistant carried his clothes.

The audience, led by the patient, stood at the west end of the mountains; the chanter near the thorny hoop, that is, at the east. The chanter blew through the hoops.

Singing by the chanter, accompanied by hide rattle.

Chanter passed through the hoops, e-we, to meet patient.

Singing by chanter.

Patient and audience went through the hoops as fast as possible, taking care not to knock down hoops—to do so would bring bad luck. Patient and audience went into hogan, while mountain-hoop arrangement was dismantled by assistants. Hoops were taken into hogan to be used for Prayer on buckskin.

Day 3. Mountains and hoops were at south and north on this day, two days' performance having been put into one. Willow hoops at the south were blue; red willow hoops at the north were black. The blue hoops, representing Yellow Snake People, were held facing Black Wind of the sandpainting in the hogan. Another hoop had two pairs of yellow rings near each end, the one nearest the tip being left open. All hoops had facets. With an unraveler bunches of spruce and a bluebird feather were tied to the blue hoop near the painted rings. Bunches of dodgeweed, grama grass, rock sage, spruce, and juniper were tied to the spiny hoop.

Hoops of red willow, representing Black Snake People, were painted black with blue faces, yellow eyes and mouth; they were marked with zigzag lightnings, and held facing a yellow horned Wind figure of the sandpainting. A turkey feather was tied to each with an unraveler. The spiny hoop was the same as that of the blue set.

The telescoping of two days in one caused the following order of treatment:

Treatment as on day 1, but with blue hoops.

Audience went into hogan.

Treatment as on day 1, but with black hoops.

Audience went into hogan for Prayer on buckskin.

Hoop transformation rite, meaning of (E). Most of the Evil chant myths have an episode relating how the hero was transformed by Coyote into a mangy coyote, because Coyote, coveting the hero's wife, hit him with a coyote skin. The rite represents the change back to normal.

In the Big Star Chant, the transformation rite, in addition, recapitulates the struggles of the hero's relatives and deific protectors to reach the Stars by whom he had been taught; the hoops, therefore, represent conveyances and stars.

Participants carry their valuables so they ' will carry good things throughout their lives ' (Reichard, Shooting Chant Evil ms.; Huckel ms.; cp. Wyman-Bailey 1943b, pp. 27ff.).

. . .

Invocatory offerings, see Ch. 18.

Master symbol, see Ch. 18.

Mixed stew ('aɫtaˑ naˑbéˑj) seems to me a better term than ' mixed decoction,' as Kluckhohn-Wyman have it, for it contains much solid substance—internal organs and flesh. It was a part of the Sun's House branch performance, essentially as described by Kluckhohn-Wyman, though doubtless the ingredients differed somewhat. The patient eats after the chanter, then anyone who wishes may eat of the stew; it should be entirely consumed. Like the bowl of mush, the stewpot is placed at the west; the participants group themselves around it, facing east as they eat (Kluckhohn-Wyman, pp. 54–5).

No sleep, see *Vigil*.

Offerings, see Ch. 18.

. . .

Overshooting rite: BS includes extensive preparations, one of which is the dressing of the shooters. They receive careful instructions, undress, and are painted to represent the War Gods. By impersonating these gods they expose themselves to great danger; consequently, they do the patient a favor.

657

Because their responsibilities are so onerous, they may bear a close relationship to the patient. The rite becomes more complicated as night succeeds night, the first being the simplest, the last the most elaborate.

Night 1. Black is rubbed on the shooters' cheeks, across the lower jaw from ear to ear, and across the trunk where the bandoleers are to hang.

The shooters squatted behind the witch objects, which were a part of the blanket layout, each holding a tiny bundle in the left hand, and one of the bundle arrows in the right. Monster Slayer's impersonator held the male eagle tail-feathered arrow; Child-of-the-water's, the female. They remained there during a long singing.

The shooters went outside and shot witch objects in all directions, according to instructions, then returned.

Administration of chant lotion by the chant, audience participating.

Arrows, the chant symbols, were placed over the door by the chanter and left there all night.

Night 2 (8:30 to 9:55 P.M.). Chant lotion was prepared with five flints in it; the bull-roarer was placed so that its string soaked in the lotion.

Shooters undressed, applied ashes and black salve to their bodies. A bundle bandoleer was put over each shoulder; each shooter put a wristlet on the other's left wrist; each tied a head feather on the other's scalplock. These had to be tied firmly; it would be dangerous if they came off during the performance.

Meanwhile bunches were laid out on the blanket, one of spruce at the north, one of juniper twigs at the south. Sitting behind these herbs, the shooters made three cuts with flints through two wide yucca leaves, then rubbed their hands and the yucca leaves with red ocher.

Feathers lay on each side of the blanket to form the layout, bows and bundle arrows in front of them. Bunches of dodge-weed and grama grass were exchanged for the spruce and juniper. The shooters cut each twig very small with flints, one of which was red and had previously been tied to the bunch of herbs. Bundle arrows were stuck into the bunch of herbs and held, as were the arrows of night 1, during the singing.

The shooters shouted loudly, "baih baih baih baih 'ayó," and the light was put out. There was only a kerosene lantern and at no time could the procedure be seen clearly.

Then the shooters stood over the patient, one in front of, one behind her, holding the arrows over the bows during the singing; they shouted, "be' be' be' be' yó," during the intervals between songs.

The shooters threw the arrows down on the floor and retrieved them, then repeated the act, standing first at the right, then at the left of the patient. They advanced and repeated the acts at different points of the hogan, finally, at the north of the fire, and out the door where the shouting was repeated.

While the shooters were outside, the chant lotion was placed before the patient; the Monster Slayer impersonator, upon his return inside, made a bow symbol with chant lotion on the female bull-roarer.

The bull-roarer was taken out and whirled around the hogan; it was brought back in, applied to the patient with crossing at feet, hands, front, back, shoulders, and head.

Repetition of bull-roarer preparation, twirling, and application to Child-of-the-water.

One warrior sat at the door while the other administered chant lotion to patient and audience. Warrior and patient were bathed with it; all was used.

659

Ashes blowing: the patient blew from the bull-roarer, the audience from feathers held so that the rib was toward the person holding the feather. Shooters went out with a handful of ashes.

Night 4. Repetition of night 2 with exceptions and additions:

Clean little piles of ashes were made at the north and south of the fire; they were later used when the shooters dressed as gods.

The layout had bows, four arrows, and oak, hardoak, *Artemisia frigida*, and grama grass.

The preparation of the arrows took a very long time, during which the impersonators were not allowed to speak.

Overshooting rite: SCE was performed on the fifth or last night, the only time a sandpainting was made. The latter was finished before the beginning of the Overshooting rite, which may be considered as the treatment on the sandpainting.

Long preparation of arrows included fastening the one-budded pine to one of the bundle arrows, the *Juniperus sibirica* to the other, and dressing of the Warrior impersonators.

The impersonators held bundle bows under the brush quill feathers in a loose bunch and trembled as a song was sung; the bows were held over the feathers during the first part of the singing, under the feathers as the singing continued.

The shooters ripped yucca leaves with a wildcat claw from the bandoleer, and rubbed them with sparkling rock.

Headbands were made of yucca strips and two quill feathers; two yucca blades were crossed over the shooters' foreheads. Everything was carefully checked and rechecked by the chanter.

The shooters were dressed as in the Big Star Overshooting rite.

The patient sat on the figure of Holy Man in the center of the Never-ending-snake sandpainting, holding the bull-roarer, while the Warriors shot over him, the audience, and the hogan, with the sound be· be· be· yó; the act was repeated at different positions on the painting so as to include all the directions.

Arrows were taken out and the light extinguished (there was no fire); as the audience sat in complete darkness, the sound be· be· be· yó could be heard receding into the distance.

The shooters returned; the lamp was lighted; the painting was removed, except for the central figure of Holy Man; a spread was placed over the figure; the patient undressed and sat on it for the chant lotion administration.

After a short intermission, the Blackening took place, as in the Big Star Chant. After the chanter had taken the spread, the patient took his place on his bedclothing, which had been spread over the sandpainting figure.

The night was spent in the Vigil.

. . .

Plant garment (E). The rite of tying a person in a wrapping of string and plants, then cutting it to pieces, is characteristic of the Evil chants, but not restricted to them; it is, for instance, a rite of the Night Chant. I may sometimes refer to this rite as ' tying and cutting,' naming it from its most outstanding ritualistic acts. It, like other rites, requires long and arduous preparation. After the garment has been tied on, the patient can hardly be seen (Matthews 1902, p. 82ff.; Kluckhohn-Wyman, p. 102).

Plant garment, preparation of: BS. A large quantity of the plants was secured. They were the same as those for unraveling—small dodgeweed, spruce, rock sage, grama grass, and *Artemisia frigida*. A number of bunches were then made by separating the twigs; all five plants should be included in each bunch, but once in a while one may be missing, although all are represented in the whole. While the helpers were arranging the bunches, the chanter prepared yucca strings by splitting the fibrous leaves with one of the wildcat claws from the bandoleer or wristlet.

Then the strings with herbs were prepared, a special one with a given number of bunches for each part of the body. The number for the waist and head should be the same as the number of unravelers on the same night. Before tying, the strings were rubbed with red ocher because ghosts fear it. Two feathers from the brush were tied to the head string so that they would cross just above the forehead.

In the Big Star Chant the numbers were as follows:

Night	Ankle and wrist	Shin and forearm	Thigh and upper arm	Waist	Each way across chest	Each way across back	Neck, front and back	Head
1	3	4	5	5	7	7	5	5
2	3	4	7	7	7	7	7	7
3	3	4	9	9	7	7	9	9
4	3	4	12	12	7	7	12	12

Plant garment (spruce), preparation of: SCE. Spruce only was used in the Male Shooting Chant Evil. The straps to which it was fastened were in straight bands on nights 1 and 3, and were tied in spirals on nights 2 and 4.

The spiral sunrise winding was started at the small toe of the left foot and the large toe of the right foot. The pieces spiraled on the arms ended at the left thumb and right small finger, respectively.

Four of the brush quill feathers were fastened in a cross on the patient's forehead the fourth night. The number of spruce branches tied on the bands varied as follows:

Night	Ankle and wrist	Shin and forearm	Thigh and upper arm	Waist	Each way across chest	Each way across back	Neck, front and back	Head
1	3	4	5	7	7	7	7	5
2	3	4	5	7	7	7	7	7
3	3	4	5	7	7	7	7	9
4	3	4	5	7	7	7	7	11

Plant garment, tying and cutting of: BS. The rite is named from the cutting (tao'gic); it follows the Overshooting rite, the shooters being the main actors in both. The strings were put on from left to right; if they were in pairs, the pairs were arranged from right to left; all were tied at the back. After the garment had been put on the patient, the following acts took place:

Shooters feinted at cutting in the order: front, right, back, left; shooters cut with an unhafted flint point the entire garment, laying the pieces cut off on a blanket on which the patient sat—a long, tedious job.

After all the strings were cut, the patient cut two knots.

The shooters held the pieces with knots over the patient's head, and let pieces of fiber touch her head as they fell; the shooters carefully inspected all pieces to be sure no knots were left.

Application of the spruce to patient.

Rough brushing of ashes with the spruce on the patient's head, at the east and west—the chanter actually pounded the brush on the head; violent brushing of audience by shooters; brushing around patient to smokehole by each shooter; then the patient stood and was brushed once more.

Disposal of garment fragments and ashes.

Plant garment, tying and cutting of: SCE. The ritualistic acts were similar to those of the Big Star Chant with some variations:

Motioning away with rattle after knots had been cut.

Brushing six times with ashes taken from the four directions around the fire; ashes blowing by patient and audience.

Pollen administration.

After cutting, a long litany, the patient holding three bundle arrows, each member of the audience holding a bundle item.

Pollen administration.

Night 4. Jewels were taken out with the ashes at the beginning of the rite.

The litany was the longest on this night (cp. Reichard 1944d, pp. 58–93).

Plant garment: Unknown Chant. I saw this rite before I knew anything about the Evil forms of the chant and did not know what to look or ask for. It was called xótcǫ́'ǫdjí, but it has not been my experience, as it has Dr. Wyman's, that this term necessarily means xańe'łné·he·, Endurance Chant. I have heard it used for the chant that later turned out to be Big Star. The chant may have been either the Upward Reaching or the Endurance Chant—I believe they are different. However, it was not the one described by Wyman and Bailey for night 3; the tentlike plant garment I saw was a part of the night 5 rite. It may have been a part of Female Shooting Chant Evil or of the Mountain Chant Evil. I was told that the shooters had put on the plant garment the night before I saw it; perhaps it was a part of the impersonators' costume.

The shooters had yucca bands around the ankles, below the knees, around the waist, and on the upper arms; the bandoleers and wristlets had shells (instead of or in addition to claws?).

Overshooting preceded tying and cutting.

The garment, prepared before the rite began, was tied in the form of a tent; it was simply unfolded and set over the patient.

Application of bundle items to the two female patients— they were crossed at the ritualistic body-parts.

The shooters took each item given them by the chanter out of the hogan before using it.

Bull-roarers were taken out but not whirled.

Chant lotion contained smooth pebbles, which were returned to the chanter after the lotion had been drunk by the audience; shooters bathed with lotion outside the hogan.

Short singing (cp. Wyman-Bailey 1943a, p. 5).

Plant garment, meaning of (E). In the plant garment rite, the knots indicate frustration, the cutting indicates release. There are differences in materials, both for the strings and plants, variations in tying on, and the like. Although the rite is exorcistic, it is not a part of the War Ceremony where it might be expected—there is a flint arrangement in myth that would suggest it. On the other hand, it is described in full detail for the Hail and Night chants, which are Holy, not Evil. Matthews was correct in his assumption that the garment represents the bonds of disease and the cutting freedom from these bonds. JS says for the Male Shooting Chant Evil, "The knots show Holy Man captured by ghosts; cutting the knots gets him free." He also says that Traveling Rock gave the garment to Holy Man in exchange for life.

The plant garment (cattail) also symbolizes armor for Rainboy of the Hail Chant. According to the myth, Rainboy was tied up on four successive days, after the prayersticks had been offered; the first day the plant was *Artemisia frigida;* the second, dodgeweed; the third, spruce and *Juniperus sibirica;* on the fourth day, *Artemisia frigida,* dodgeweed, rock sage, and grama grass represented Monster Slayer; horned yucca, Child-of-the-water. The herbs were used together on the last night.

The herb garment of the Endurance Chant should be prepared while the sun is abroad; the tying and cutting should be done before the sandpainting songs are sung. In the Endurance Chant the tying and cutting stand for the severing of Coyote's and Changing-bear-maiden's bodies and freeing the patient from their power (Matthews 1902, pp. 84, 259; Reichard 1944d, pp. 53–5, 61–3, 67–9, 75; Endurance Chant ms.).

• • •

Plants, collection of: SCE. The single-budded pine and *Juniperus sibirica* obtained in the episode described in Chapter 8, were made into arrows for the Overshooting rite on the last night. The spruce, which does not grow near White Sands where the chant was held, was collected before the ceremony began. On the second day I took the chief assistant, an elderly man so experienced and adept that he almost acted as the chanter, to a place twelve miles south of White Sands where he got all four kinds of yucca near the road. Yucca is a chant theme; yuccas are a part of the unraveling; they are crossed on the Hoop transformation mountains and on those of the Never-ending-snake sandpainting of the fourth night; four pieces of wide-leaved yucca were a part of the bath platform.

• • •

Pollen paintings: Rain Ceremony were made on unbleached muslin, a substitute for buckskin, of pollen and pollenlike

666

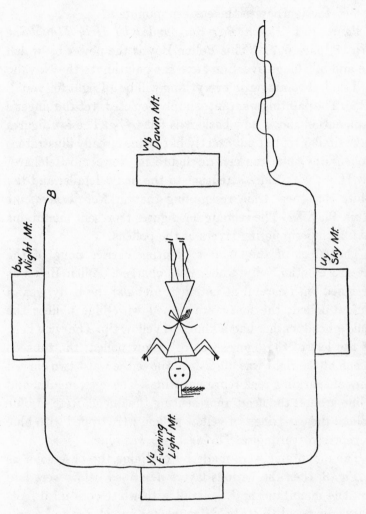

Fig. 8. Pollen painting, Pollen Boy: Rain Ceremony

Wb
Dawn Mt.

B

bw
Night Mt.

Uy
Sky Mt.

Yu
Evening Light Mt.

substances. Blue pollen was of flower petals from Wheeler Peak, since the part of the ceremony here described concerned the journey to the eastern mountain.

Painting 1. *Pollen Boy Surrounded by Holy Mountains* (Fig. 8, page 667). "This Pollen Boy is the power by which we and all things live. Sun gave the painting to the Navaho and said, 'From now on everything will be all right for you' " (RS). The painting was quite simply depicted, yet the singer's explanation shows how basic it is felt to be. The few figures were similar to, but not exactly like, some already illustrated: Pollen Boy, like the central figure in Newcomb-Reichard, Pl. II, B, with more attention to the body details; and the white corn-meal trail, resembling that in *Navajo Medicine Man*, Pl. XXI. The rectangular figures represent mountains laid by superimposing layers of the pollens.

The effect of the modest painting carries none of the intense emotion with which it is charged. Pollen Boy was designed with careful attention to details: the body was of yellow pollen; the feet were tipped with blue pollen; the yellow head feather had a blue and yellow tip. The wide belt, at the left of the figure, was of yellow pollen; the tobacco pouch at the right was blue. Just above the waist two curved lines of sparkling rock represent wings. The eyes, mouth, and a line around the head, representing the queue, were of blue pollen; the earstrings, of yellow pollen, were tipped with blue to represent turquoise. The necklace was blue.

The mountains were made by outlining the base color as in Fig. 8, then the various layers described below were laid on. The mountains and the trail with white corn-meal footprints represent the tribe's struggle for knowledge and man's individual walk through life. "If anyone should step on the mountains, it would mean the end of his walk" (RS). B represents a small basket belonging to the singer's bundle,

668

placed at the end of the trail—another representation of a mountain. The mountain symbolism is as follows:

Direction	Mountain	Representing	Home of	Substance	Representing
e	sisnádjini˙	Dawn	xa˙ctc'é''óɣan	spar u pollen y pollen	storm and freezing vegetation life, glint, holiness
s	tsodził	Blue Sky	Talking God	u pollen w corn meal spar y pollen	w flowers
we	dok'o'oslí˙d	Yellow-evening-light	Talking God	y pollen w corn meal spar u pollen y pollen	
n	dibéntsa	Darkness	xa˙ctc'é''óɣan	spar corn pollen u pollen y pollen	

Painting 2. *Cornbeetle Girl Surrounded by Holy Mountains,* a companion picture of painting 1, has Cornbeetle Girl in the center and the mountains in the four directions. No trail was drawn because "people have already entered with the first picture and the trail is understood to be there."

Cornbeetle Girl has a square head and a body like that of painting 1; the mountains have the same names; they represent the same Skies and homes of the same gods.

Their composition and symbolism are as follows:

Direction	Color	Substance	Representing
e	w	w corn meal	dawn
		4 or 5 horizontal lines of spar	black clouds
		5 horizontal b lines	?
		4 horizontal y lines	water
		u vertical lines over all	flowers

669

Direction	Color	Substance	Representing
s	u	4 or 5 horizontal w lines	clouds
		4 horizontal y lines	clouds
		spar	vegetation and jewels
we	y	5 horizontal spar lines	clouds
		y surface	rain
		u surface	flowers
n	b	5 w lines	clouds
		y surface	rain
		u surface	flowers

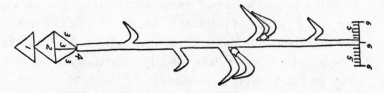

Fig. 9. Pollen painting, Male and Female White Corn: Rain Ceremony

Painting 3. *White Male Corn* (Fig. 9, upper) consisted of a large white cornstalk; it would be yellow if the one-sung-over were female.

The three lines *a* in yellow pollen represent the corn roots; they are yellow because "the pollen has fallen down from the tips of the ears to the root tips." The space *b*, representing a large cornfield, was outlined but only sparsely filled in.

"When the White Corn paintings are drawn, singers make pouches for their bundles. On the fourth day of the Rain

Ceremony, the sing is devoted entirely to making pouches for the People. The pouches are filled with pollen and jewels, and buried on top of the mountains" (RS).

Painting 4. *White Female Corn* (Fig. 9, lower) was in white —the information about it is not conflicting, the representations being of White Male and Female Corn, but the drawing in white or yellow depending upon the patient's sex; hence, there may be *yellow* paintings of *white* corn.

The meaning of the lines is as follows:

1 the triangle is the cornpatch.
2 the triangle is the cornpatch boundary.
3 the three lines are the corn roots.
4 w stalk and leaves with y center.
5 the small lines underneath the horizontal lines are y.
6 the 3 lines above the horizontal lines are w; they represent the female corn tassel.

Pollen paintings, rites on: Rain Ceremony.

Painting 1. The ritualistic acts were:

Basket (B in Fig. 8) was given yellow and blue outlines and was sprinkled with three crosses, yellow and blue, to represent thought.

Prayer, as the sponsor stood on the trail.

Footprints erased.

Pollen administration to sponsor and audience; pollen sprinkled on painting with prayer for riches, sponsor holding bundle equipment.

Tobacco smoked by sponsor—e, s, we, n, at basket, and at Pollen Boy (audience participation).

Sponsor erased Pollen Boy with his feet, walked to the north, and sat down.

Pollen application to sponsor's body by singer, who held bundle prayersticks.

671

Painting erased with bundle prayersticks; all the pollens were piled in the center of the cloth.

Painting 2. The mountains were covered as follows:

Direction	Colors	Representing
e	w	corn
	4 or 5 layers spar	4 or 5 b clouds
	4 layers b and y	
	alternating	water
	u horizontal	vegetation
s	u	mountain
	w	5 w clouds
	4 alternating	
	layers y and w	4 clouds
	spar	vegetation and jewels
we	y	
	spar	5 clouds
	y	rain
	u	flowers
n	b	4 or 5 clouds
	w	5 clouds
	y	rain
	u	flowers

The rite was the same as for painting 1. The first song was for gathering clouds, the second to start rain.

• • •

Prayer on buckskin: BS, an accessory rite, is a continuation of the Hoop transformation rite; each affects the details of the other. A buckskin is placed within the corn-meal circle in the hogan, and on it a painting of Pollen Boy and Corn-beetle Girl is made. The corn-meal trail ends a short distance east of the hogan; another starts at the feet of the figures and extends out the door and around the hogan, with an opening at the doorway (Fig. 6, page 651).

Prayer on buckskin: SCE.

Day 2. A sandpainting, *Horned Moon,* with a red outline (Newcomb-Reichard, Pl. XVII), was made inside the hogan;

four human footprints of white corn meal led up to the figure; a trail from the hoop-mountain arrangement outside led up to the first footprint. The ritualistic acts were:

A buckskin was laid on the sandpainting after the Hoop transformation rite; the audience waited outside until the hoop arrangement had been dismantled.

The hoops were laid flat—the thorny one on the bottom, the white, yellow, blue, and black on it—and brought into the hogan; the chanter moved the pile of hoops e-we, we-e, s-n, n-s, and laid them on the buckskin.

The patient, holding three bundle items, walked on the footprints to the place enclosed by the hoops and sat down.

Footprints were erased by the assistant.

Long responsive prayer, each member of the audience holding a bundle property. (A year-old baby got one of the plumed arrows and waved it about, putting itself in jeopardy. The chanter, noting this, quietly traded with the baby for a flint arrowpoint.)

Pollen administration: the audience moved to the south side of the hogan while five men held the hoops upright at the north; pollen administration to hoops sunwise by each member of the audience; then the hoops were held by five women so that the men could administer pollen.

Hoops disposed of at north of hogan.

Day 4. The painting was *Black Horned Wind* (Newcomb-Reichard, Pl. XVIII) with a red outline. The rite was like that of day 2, with the addition of two very long prayers, the patient sitting inside the hoops on the sandpainting (cp. *Hoop transformation rite*).

. . .

Prayer to Young Pinyon, see *Bandoleer and wristlets, disposal of*: SC *Prayerstick branch*; cp. *Restrictions on patient of Shooting Chant,* Con. B.

Prayersticks, preparation and invocation of: SC. Variations in the prayerstick offerings of the Shooting Chant are few and slight; the whole process compares favorably with the accounts already published. The materials were: a plug of bluebird down feathers; jewels; 4 feathers of green-backed finch, 2 from the tail, 1 from each wing; 3 bluebird tail feathers; 1 eagle down feather; 1 turkey down feather; 1 turkey beard hair for pollen brushing—turkey beard hairs are kept in a little case made of turkey leg bone in a sack in the chanter's bundle.

The prayerstick preparation and the rite of invocation are so intimately related as to be one; the patient, by performing certain acts, aids in the preparation. After the chanter's assistants had cut and painted the reed sticks and laid them with their offerings, the patient was called in and the following acts were performed:

Patient dipped the turkey beard in water and pollen, then brushed it over the prayersticks, taking care not to cause the eagle and turkey down feathers to blow out of place—pointing away from her.

Chanter dipped turkey beard in white substance and brushed the same way.

Jewels and tobacco were put into the reeds; then the bluebird feather plug was inserted by the assistant and pushed in with the owl quill feather tamper.

The reeds were sealed with pollen moistened with water by the assistant; the prayersticks were lighted by the patient, who held a crystal to the smokehole (sun) and made a pass down to the prayersticks; she brushed them once more away from herself.

Chanter blew the whistle over the offerings, put the turquoise reward to his mouth and head, made a pass with it over the offerings, and put it into his pocket.

Water, which I had brought from the Hudson River, was poured into a little hole made in the floor at the west side of the hogan (Sun's House branch). It represents the water through which Holy Boy was pulled by Big Fish.

Assistants disposed of remnants.

Pollen sprinkling from bottom to top of offerings and patient by chanter.

Offering applied by assistants to patients with sound blu˙ ˙ ˙ blu˙ ˙ ˙.

Litany with patient holding offerings in left hand (Prayerstick branch).

Disposal of offerings by assistants, according to chanter's directions (Ch. 18).

Prayersticks, temporary talking: SC Prayerstick branch. A little before sunset of the first night I was called to the ceremonial hogan. Sixteen (eight pairs of) reed prayersticks had been made. Since I was the patient, I did not see the preparation. Prayersticks were (Fig. 10, over): 4 black with white zigzag lightnings, 4 blue with yellow outlines, 4 yellow with blue outlines, 4 pink with black stripes. Each had a facet at the top, on which eyes and mouth were painted. Medicines were put in their cavities—I know only that spruce was one—then they were tied together in pairs with cornhusks and two pairs were placed at each direction in a basket in circular formation, b-y-u-p, a Thunder sequence.

At the time the prayersticks were being finished the emetic was made ready, and the remnants disposed of; the sandpainting mound was made four steps east of the hogan door in line with the fire and the basket layout. Coarse white meal had been put in the basket.

As patient, I went through the following acts:

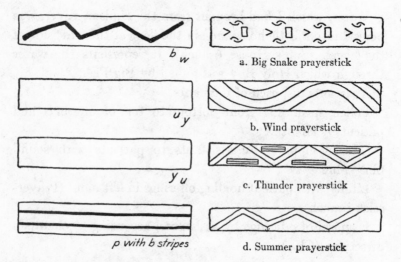

Fig. 10. Temporary talking prayersticks: Shooting Chant Prayerstick branch

Fig. 11. Prayersticks: Shooting Chant Prayerstick branch

Pollen administration to patient as she held basket of prayersticks.

Patient led to south side of the door, where she stooped with the chanter, who stuck two pairs of talking prayersticks into the ground, the patient touching them as he did so; the prayersticks were sprinkled with corn meal twice by chanter and patient. The talking prayersticks were stuck into the ground underneath the sprigs of scruboak laid on the rafters at the Hogan Blessing rite.

Prayer by chanter.

The same rite was repeated at the west with blue prayersticks, at the south with the yellow, and at the north with the pink.

Prayer as the patient sat on a blanket at the west, holding the basket.

Pollen administration to patient, foot to head, some eaten.

For the duration of the chant the prayersticks stood guard

at the cardinal directions. On the morning of the sixth day (morning after Vigil), they were once more laid in the basket, this time by the assistant, who disposed of them according to the chanter's directions.

Prayersticks used: SC Prayerstick branch:

Day 1. 4 Big Snake prayersticks—b, w, u, y, outlined in contrasting colors—four fingerwidths long,* were marked with Snake's house, deer-hoof, and moon phases in the corresponding outline colors as in Figure 11, a (cp. *Crooked Snake* sandpainting, Newcomb-Reichard, Pl. IV and pp. 52–4; the sandpainting was used later on the same day).

Day 2. 2 Wind prayersticks—one black, one blue, with contrasting colors—three fingerwidths long, marked as in Figure 11, b. The four scalloped lines represent white and yellow suntracks.

4 Thunder prayersticks—one black, marked with white as in Figure 11, c; one white marked with black as in Figure 11, c; one plain yellow outlined in blue; one plain pink outlined in black—four fingerwidths long. The marks represent lightning and rainbows. "Winds and Thunders always go together" (*Thunder* sandpainting, Newcomb-Reichard, Pl. XXX, was used later on the same day).

Day 3. 4 Summer prayersticks—two black with white zigzag lightnings, two variegated—four fingerwidths long (Fig. 11, d). They were arranged from south to north— variegated, lightning-marked, variegated, lightning-marked (*Holy People* sandpainting, Newcomb-Reichard, Pl. XIV, on same day).

Day 4. 4 prayersticks, four or five fingerwidths long,

---

*The length is measured by placing the closed fingers of the right hand at right angles over the closed fingers of the left, so as to make the length of the left forefinger as great as the width of the designated number of fingers of the right.

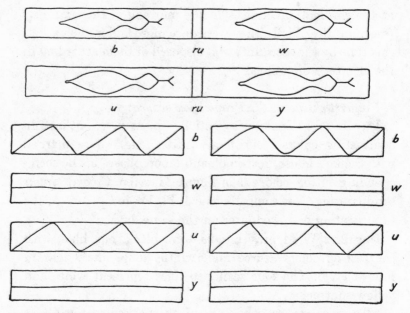

Fig. 12. Arrowsnake and Blue Lizard prayersticks: Shooting Chant Sun's House branch

marked with designs like those on the wide boards (Fig. 4), but much simplified, as follows: 1. Sky with black ground and white markings of stars; 2. Earth, white with blue corn; 3. Sun, blue with rays; 4. Moon, white (*Day Skies* sandpainting, Newcomb-Reichard, Fig. 9, used on this day).

Prayersticks used: SC Sun's House branch.

Day 1. 2 Big Snake prayersticks, six fingerwidths long (double); marked as in Figure 12. 8 prayersticks, three fingerwidths long, colored as indicated in Figure 12—four were offerings to Arrowsnakes, four to Blue Lizard (*Many Snakes* sandpainting, Newcomb-Reichard, Pl. III, used on day 5).

Day 2. 3 plain Arrowsnake and Blue Lizard prayersticks —pink, blue, and black—three fingerwidths long.

4 Wind prayersticks, six fingerwidths long, each with two colors—p-y, y-u, p-y, u-b—equivalent to eight.

3 Water Monster prayersticks—one plain yellow, one plain blue, one black marked with white lines as in Figure 13. The markings on the black prayerstick represent Water Monster's tail. These prayersticks were arranged from south to north: three prayersticks, p-u-b; p-y Wind, y-u Wind, p-y Wind, u-b Wind, y Water Monster, u Water Monster, marked Water Monster (*Double* sandpainting, Reichard 1934, p. 194, used on day 6).

Fig. 13. Water Monster prayerstick: Shooting Chant Sun's House branch

Day 3. 2 prayersticks, three fingerwidths long, 2 six fingerwidths long. All were said to be Fish prayersticks; all were marked elaborately—I failed to get the details, except that two were variegated (*Buffalo* sandpainting, *Navajo Medicine Man*, Pl. XXIV, used on day 7).

Day 4. 4 prayersticks, three fingerwidths long, with background colors, b-u-u-b, the first blue one had Sun on it.

2 tiny prayersticks (about one and three-quarters inches long), one blue, one yellow. They were arranged from south to north as follows: small blue, small yellow, large black, blue, black, blue, but when the chanter was whistling over them, he noted with chagrin that the order was wrong and rearranged them in the order: small blue, small yellow, large black, blue, blue, black. The larger prayersticks were offerings to Sky, Sun, Earth, and Moon (*Sky-Earth* sandpainting, Newcomb-Reichard, Fig. 5 on day 8).

· · ·

Rain Ceremony. I am greatly indebted to Roman Hubbell for a description of the journey, which was a part of the Rain

Ceremony, said ' not to be xatá·l, but the beginning of all things desirable—clouds, rain, fertility, and happiness of every kind. It is xǫ́jǫ́·djí ' (Ch. 19).

Journeys to the sacred mountains for water tokens (' collected waters ') were undertaken after a succession of three dry, unfavorable seasons. The party went by automobile as far as Taos, where they met with the pueblo officials for permission to go to the sacred lake by the usual route—a climb of fourteen miles. After talking until after midnight, the Taos men came to the decision that it would be better if the Navaho did not go; in fact, they would see to it that they did not. They had guards around the lake, sacred to them as well as to the Navaho.

The Navaho party left the conference, but not for home. Hubbell knew a way to drive around the foot of the mountain (sisnádjini·). The route meant a climb of thirty, instead of fourteen, miles; it had to be made at night and now, as with a war party, without discovery. When the party got to a place impassable with the car, they undressed and climbed in ceremonial fashion. The leaders made the way safe with pollen and prayer. They warned Hubbell that he must not falter; the trip was all or nothing. He thought he had the stamina called for.

They had not gone more than two thirds of the way, however, when he gave out; he could not take another step and lay down. The Navaho were quite prepared for the emergency. They laid him on a blanket, head toward the east, and prayed over him, stepping up to him as in the Restoration rite. He regained his strength, got up, and climbed; he did not even feel tired.

When the party came near the lake, two Navaho crawled up on their bellies like warriors and collected the water, undetected by the Taos guards. The water was taken back to the reservation, where it was sung over. In less than a week there was a hard rain.

"After the rain singers make the pilgrimage to the mountains for water, they get lots of livestock." Rain Singer, who led the party, had nothing when he started for Wheeler Peak; two years later he had eight herders caring for his flock (cp. Hill 1938, pp. 71, 95).

. . .

Restoration (E) is a rite of every ceremony; it restores to normal a person who has been shocked or frightened into unconsciousness (xode·tłá·d). "This rite may be used in any kind of sing, if the people pay for it." It may be an emergency measure, as it was when the sheep were struck by lightning. I did not see the rite performed at that time—it is too dangerous for anyone but the singer. However, there is an account of it in Gray Eyes' myth, and another in the Hail Chant myth.

Although related, the Restoration and the Shock rites should be differentiated. The first is performed at a crisis; the second may be prepared for—it includes a sandpainting and an impersonator.

Holy Man, though restored by the Male Shooting Chant Evil, did not regain his full strength because Coyote had been killed; there could not be vigor or health until such a wrong had been righted. Punishment, which leaves the transgressor worse off than when he started, rebounds on the one who administers it; ceremonial procedure can prevent it.

The restoration symbol looks something like a crank; in the Shooting Chant it represents a straight lightning. It sticks up over the back of an animal figure to indicate that it has become immune to certain dangers and fears (Matthews 1902, p. 28; Sapir-Hoijer, pp. 159, 233; Haile 1943a, pp. 15,

681

46, 50; Reichard 1939, p. 66, Pl. XXI, XXIII, XXIV; Shooting Chant Evil ms.; cp. Wyman-Bailey 1946b—the authors call the rite a 'Repairing Ceremony' and treat it and the Shock rite together, somewhat differently from this description).

Restoration rite: HC (from mythical description) (Fig. 14). The numbers correspond with the acts summarized below;

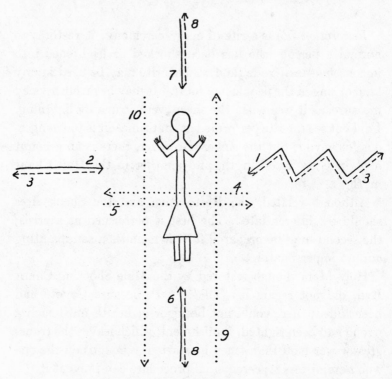

Fig. 14. Ritualistic acts of Restoration rite: Hail Chant

the lines indicate the laying of a symbol: broken lines, erasure; dotted lines, stepping. Patient is laid with his head to the north. The directions are:

1 Make a zigzag lightning—with pollen, corn meal, or the like—from the east toward the patient.
2 Make a straight lightning from the west.
3 Erase 1 and 2 with the foot, away from patient.
4 Step over patient from east to west.
5 Step over patient from west to east.
6 Mark straight line (sunray) toward patient at south.
7 Mark straight line (sunray) toward patient at north.
8 Erase 6 and 7 with foot, away from patient.
9 Step from south to north.
10 Step from north to south.
11 Body massage at ceremonial parts.
12 Incensing (Reichard 1944d, pp. 9–11; cp. Matthews 1902, pp. 182, 190; Stevenson, p. 283; Newcomb 1940b, p. 58).

Restoration rite: SC (mythical description). When Holy Man and Holy Boy described the Sun's House painting to the women, Holy Girl went into a fit. Holy Man then instituted the Restoration rite, which is believed to revive men or animals struck by lightning. Holy Man laid the girl with her head toward the north. The directions are as follows (Fig. 15, over):

1 Mark two crossed zigzag lightnings in the sand with the tail-feathered arrow from the east, toward patient.
2 Erase 1 with foot, away from patient.
3 Make two straight lightnings crossed at the west, toward patient.
4 Erase 3 with foot, away from patient.
5 Make drawing 1 at south, toward patient.
6 Erase 5, away from patient.
7 Make drawing 3 at north, toward patient.
8 Erase 7, away from patient.

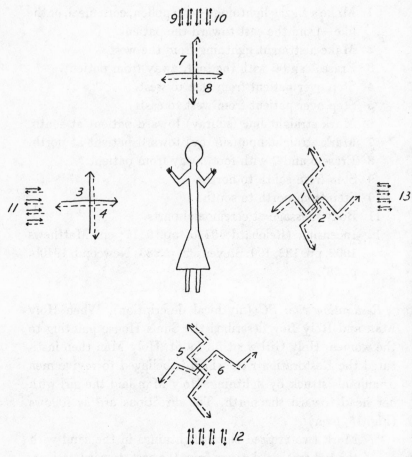

Fig. 15. Ritualistic acts of Restoration rite: Shooting Chant

9 Make four small straight lines at north, toward patient.
10 Erase 9, away from patient.
11 Repeat 9 and 10 at west.
12 Repeat 9 and 10 at south.
13 Repeat 9 and 10 at east (note anti-sunwise circuit).
14 Press patient at ceremonial parts.
15 Incensing: 2 coals.

After the rite had been performed, Holy Girl was strong enough to hear the details of the sandpainting.

. . .

Rite for releasing sheep from lightning contamination (E). Nine sheep were killed by lightning. RP arrived at the scene two hours later, and performed the Restoration rite. The rest of the sheep (300–400) were isolated in a new corral and were not allowed to eat until after the purification ceremony the next day. The events were:

Day 1. Prayer in the hogan.

Rite at the scene of the disaster, RP's oldest daughter helping him as sponsor for the sheep.

Rite at the corral (3 P.M.): a trail from the corral to the place where the sheep had been struck, east of the hogan, was kept open—no one was allowed to walk there. The chanter, followed by the sponsor, carrying the bundle layout in a basket, moved to the corral entrance, where he paused and sang.

Sprinkling of sheep with herbal medicine. (Some sheep broke out of the corral; the herd girls were reprimanded for chasing them back anti-sunwise.)

Singing at corral entrance.

Long litany, the chanter and sponsor standing at the west of the corral.

At the corral entrance the sponsor removed her blanket, then entered the corral and put medicine from a pouch into the mouths and along the backs of certain sheep (about ten), caught and held by assistant.

The trail was opened and the sheep driven out; they were allowed to eat for the first time since the lightning had struck (after about twenty-four hours).

I was told that a little sing was held at night; about 11 P.M.

I heard the old man praying aloud at the corral (Reichard 1934, pp. 84–9).

Day 2 (about 12:15 p.m.). Medicine was mixed in a basket (token), then in a tub.

Litany as on day 1.

Medicine administration by sponsor to sheep, three times in the mouth, once across the head. To a few she gave black powder from a pouch; the rest were bathed from the tub by the herders. During the whole time there was uninterrupted singing.

The chanter fetched his blackstone tubular pipe and a burning corncob from the hogan.

An assistant, after instructions, smoked up to Sun and to the four directions; medicine was sprinkled over the sheep from a dipper; every one had to be touched while the smoking was going on; the pipe, almost burned out by this time, was smoked by the sponsor.

Day 3. The herders treated the sheep with medicine. There was no ceremony; the chanter was not even present.

The rite was to be followed by a Vigil in four days, but for various reasons it was put off and I left before it was held.

Rite for removing contamination of the dead (E) was called a Blessing rite (xǫ́jǫ́·djí); it was performed to purify the deceased RP's bundle to make its ownership safe for his heir, MC, his daughter, who acted as sponsor and was, therefore, the one-sung-over (patient).

The bundle had the properties of the Life chants. It contained: a large number of flints varying in size, from a five-inch club of smooth yellow stone (Monster Slayer's) to a tiny redstone arrowpoint; the black tubular pipe used in the rite to restore the sheep from lightning contamination; a tiny pouch that had belonged to RP's wife's mother, who had got it from her maternal grandfather; and a number of small objects.

Everything at this rite was done in a leisurely manner with many pauses for rest; time was allowed for the buckskin to dry after it had been washed in yucca suds; there were a few songs during the work. The spirit was one of pride and pleasure, such as white men display in showing a cherished collection, yet there was an attitude of reverence—the reverence of order. Though there was sadness, there was also satisfaction in doing the right thing, in handling these treasures, so descriptive of the man who had owned them and so expressive of his interests. There was good talk, joking, and smoking.

Night 1. Blackening; disposal of blackening properties.

Beginning of xǫ́jǫ́·djí: The sponsor, blackened, sat on a blanket; the chanter laid out the bundle contents, untied all the pouches, then laid out all the bundle properties to match, piece by piece, as nearly as possible, those of his own bundle.

The chanter ground all stone pieces slightly on another stone; an assistant ground a special flint point at the ritualistic body-parts of the sponsor.

Long litany, the sponsor holding the prayer bundle talking prayersticks; the chanter holding the bull-roarer and a sack of pollen; each member of the audience holding a flint point.

Pollen administration, audience participation.

Day 1. The sponsor was wakened at pre-dawn—there was no rite.

Bath (8:45 A.M.): basket opening was at the west; the basket platform had dry medicines and pollen crosses; foam was sprinkled with pollen. The bath was done thoroughly. When the yucca suds gave out, MC sent for a washcloth and a cake of Woodbury's soap, which she applied diligently until all the soot of the previous night's blackening was removed. Drying with yellow corn meal, afterward emptied south of

687

the back hogan center, and later used for purifying the bundle equipment.

Long prayer, the sponsor holding pollen sacks, the chanter a special pollen pouch.

Breathing in four times from sacks by sponsor.

Unwrapping of all bundle parts (10:20 A.M.). Present were: chanter, sponsor, her husband as assistant, and I.

All pouches and strings were washed in yucca suds, dried in yellow corn meal, and kneaded until pliable. The contents were preserved with great care because it is very dangerous to lose any; sparkling rock from the northern mountain was handled with special reverence.

New strings were twisted of raveled unbleached muslin for the bundle containing the aragonite talking prayersticks. This bundle contained also a number of small buckskin pouches, three of which were wound with string threaded with whiteshell and turquoise beads; the old beads were strung on the new strings. Each bundle was tied in its particular way and secured, some with square knots, others by turning the end under (Fig. 2).

Brief intermission for dinner (11:30 A.M.).

Disposal (1:15 P.M.): Sheep fetishes were laid in a basket— always to be kept by the family; the basket was set at the north side of the hogan; the chanter's bundle equipment was placed in the basket that had been used for the bath and contained some of the yellow corn meal left after drying the bundle wrappings; the basket was placed south of the sponsor's basket and left until after the night's Vigil. Leftover corn meal was spread on the floor at the west. Old strings and a partly worked fossilized shell were thrown out.

Night 2. Vigil.

Rite to control snow, see Matthews 1902, pp. 312, 41n.

Rite to undo harm caused by camping on trail to old deer impound (E). A woman and her six-month-old baby were treated together.

The rites were held outside the hogan with much twirling of bull-roarer and brushing, while the audience marched toward a shade, symbol of the impound.

Blackening.

Application of bull-roarer to patient with a sound uh····-uh-uh-uh····.

Circuit: sunwise, then anti-sunwise, leaving eastern quadrant open.

Days subsequent to rite: patient left the blackening and face paint on for two days, but had no other restrictions.

Rites, combined, with no name as a whole, were performed for the year-old male child of an educated Navaho who worked for the Government. The white doctor had told her that the child was suffering from an obstruction of the bowels and that nothing could be done for it. The mother and father brought the child to White Sands, where they left him in charge of a female relative, whom I shall call MH. They put MC in complete charge, and understood that both the baby and the nurse, MH, were to be treated; then they left. The boy was the chief patient, the nurse the co-patient, so that her care would not harm him and his treatment would not affect her.

The child was an unusually well-developed, jolly baby, who looked and acted as if nothing whatever ailed him. He submitted to the ceremonial requirements with the utmost patience and good temper, almost nonchalance. He even endured the figure painting with hardly a protest.

In a Hand Trembling rite it had been determined that

Male Shooting Chant Evil was indicated as a cure—the first part of the chant here described was from that chant.

Sandpainting 1. The first rite was a sandpainting (Fig. 16): two pairs of crossed snakes—a black and a white, a blue and a yellow. Each snake had a red dot above the tail to represent the anus.

The painting was started at 4 P.M. and finished at 5:30 on Sunday, November 13, 1938. The treatment lasted an hour and was almost exactly like that on a sandpainting of the Shooting Chant Holy. The baby was set on the tail of the black-white snake pair and sat a long time by himself. When he got tired, his nurse sat on the snakes, holding him; she gave him a bottle. The ritualistic acts were:

Sprinkling the painting with white corn meal.

Administration of chant lotion to baby.

Long singing.

Administration of infusion specific to baby and nurse.

Fumigant: 2 coals (at 6:30 P.M.).

There was no audience participation for any act.

Sandpainting 2 (started at 7:30 P.M. Sunday), *Moon in Eclipse* (Newcomb-Reichard, Pl. XI, with Pollen Boy on a white moon), had merely a red line around the moon, no arrows, rattles, or travel hoops. Guardian circle had the white snake inside, black outside. Each snake had snake's house, one deer hoof, and curved marks, which JS says are Snake's gait. The eastern guardians were black Big Snake at the south pointing north, blue Big Snake at the north pointing south; the encircling snakes had a red dot above the tail.

The acts were exactly as in the first rite. The eastern guardians were erased before the administration of infusion specific.

Sandpainting 3 (finished at 11 A.M. Monday), *Sun in Eclipse* (Newcomb-Reichard, Pl. XI), had zigzag rains darting from

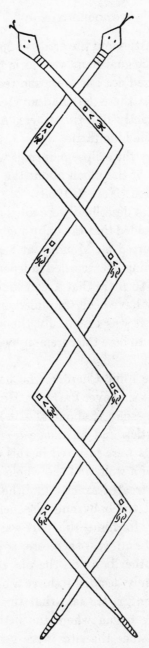

Fig. 16. Rites, combined, sandpainting 1

the blue sun, the rattles and the arrows in jewel sequence, but no travel hoops. The guardians were as in the picture, except that they had the red dot and were spotted with contrasting colors—JS said that these dots had no meaning.

The rite was exactly like the others. All three paintings were erased with the hide rattle.

No one knew why the eclipse paintings were chosen. There was a total eclipse of the moon about the time of the Hand Trembling divination (Nov. 7, 1938).

Probably the rites described were all the diviner had prescribed, but MC decided that the baby ought to be blackened. The blackening started on Monday at 8 P.M. I have many accounts of blackening, all recorded independently at various times. They differ so little that I conclude that this rite is very stable. It may have been simplified and shortened a bit for this baby, but it was essentially the same as the other times I saw it. "Up to here the ceremony was the Evil form," said the chanter.

On Tuesday, the Flint Chanter who had sung over MA (Ch. 6) was asked to sing over the baby. He came on Tuesday night, and on Wednesday at about 11 A.M. made a small blue invocatory prayerstick and an image of specially collected clay. Jewel offerings were inserted in this clay; it was fashioned in the form of a wolf, and the whole was painted blue; these objects were treated exactly like the usual invocatory offerings. MH held the baby and also held the objects as she spoke the litany for him—this part was said to be a part of the Night Chant and was, therefore, xǫ́jǫ́·djí.

By this time another baby on the place, EM, contracted a bad cold. The family decided to have a blackening for her, calling in a third singer. He said that this little girl should not be in the same hogan where the little boy was being treated. However, since the rites were being held in EW's

692

mother's hogan and since her mother did not pay much attention to any recommendation, things continued as they had started.

On Thursday the Flint Chanter made a cactus symbol much like the one described by Kluckhohn, but without hoops. It was not an invocatory prayerstick, but may have been a chant symbol, for it was later applied to the patient. This rite may have been from the Chiricahua Wind Chant.

At one o'clock (Thursday) the bath was given to the baby boy—the little girl was now only a whining member of the audience. After a brief pause, the ceremony continued with the figure painting, like that in Kluckhohn-Wyman, Figure 22, but with zigzag, instead of smooth, lines (the patient was male). The male Wind figure was black on the baby's chest, blue on his back, whereas the female was yellow in front, yellow in back. The nurse also was painted. The black and white lines were carried down the left arm, ending in an arrow at the palm; the blue and yellow lines down the right arm into the palm. (The same lines described by Kluckhohn ended at the middle of the forearm.)

The treatment included the following: soil from the medicine bundle was put into the shoes of baby and nurse, and directions were given that the baby should keep them on. The tokens—turquoise for the baby, turquoise and abalone for the nurse—were tied. The cactus prayerstick was applied with the sound ei'yi'ya, ei'yi'ya; there was incensing with 2 coals; pollen sprinkling and breathing in of Sun.

Although the baby was more docile than could possibly be expected of a child of his age, it was difficult to paint the intricate figures on him, and occasionally it seemed expedient to hold his arm or leg. MC and I were allowed to do this, because we were the only ones present who had bead tokens. It made no difference what kind of

bead a person had, but he must have submitted to a chant
that entitled him to such a token—these, said MC, would be
any of the Holy Shooting or Wind chants (cp. Kluckhohn-
Wyman, pp. 148–9).

The baby recovered. Four years later I was told that he
had grown normally, never having been sick since the treatment.

. . .

Sandpainting: Bead Chant, excerpt, see *Bead Chant, excerpt*.
The painting was that in *Navajo Medicine Man*, Plate I,
sketched in Figure 17 (insert).

Sandpainting setup: Bead Chant, excerpt. The setup is
shown in Figure 17; the explanation is as follows:

aa 2 braided headbands, each with two feathers crossed,
were perched on two feathered sticks; each stick had four
marks where branches had been cut off; one had a tip of blue,
the other, of yellow feathers (male and female).

b an elaborately beaded property with many polished
shells—some of abalone—and ends of fur or feathers lay on
an abalone shell, very highly polished inside and out. The
shell was filled with medicine (lotion or infusion?). *b* is the
chant symbol (Reichard 1939, p. 34).

c an ordinary sauce dish containing medicine.

Sandpainting, treatment on: Bead Chant, excerpt. Many acts
were performed simultaneously. I note some, but I am not
sure of the exact order, nor am I convinced that I have
them all:

A bowl of thin gruel was passed to the chanter, who ate
four handfuls and rubbed some on his face and neck; each
member of the audience tasted the mush; the last one, a
little girl, had to eat all that was left.

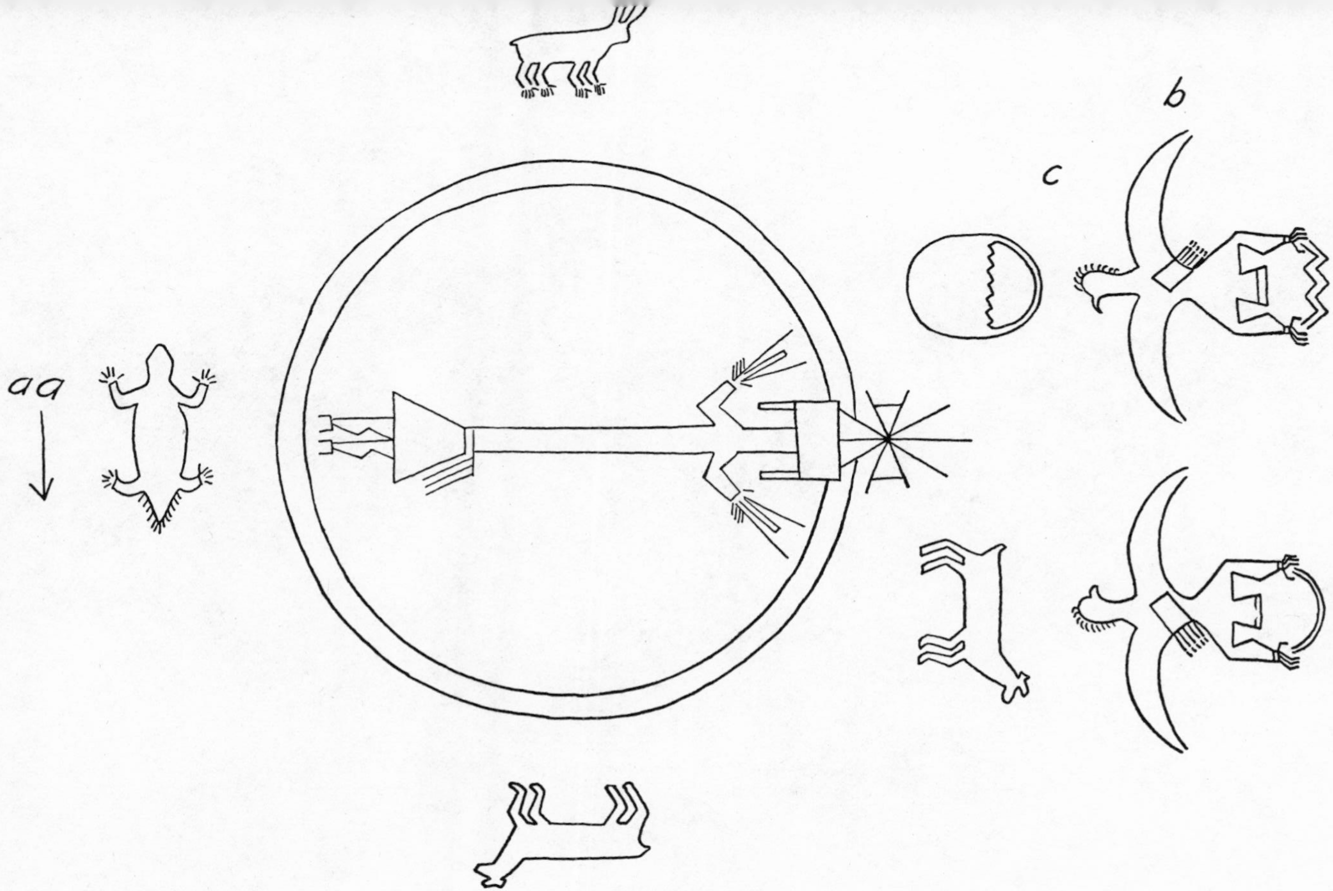

Fig. 17. Sandpainting: Bead Chant excerpt

Corn-meal sprinkling of painting by patient.

The chanter put on one headband, the patient the other; chanter sang and made passes with *b* (the headband is worn by various sandpainting figures, Reichard 1939, Pl. I, III, V-IX).

Patient sat on painting along center figure; headbands were laid at his feet.

Sand application to patient's body-parts with twisting motion from patient toward smokehole with each application.

The end of *b* was dipped in red powder and administered to patient four times; sand from the heads and feet of all figures applied to patient's body-parts.

Medicine in abalone bowl drunk by chanter and patient; that in sauce dish drunk by patient, who applied it to his body.

Chanter brushed patient's head and shoulders, with sound be' be', then brushed toward the smokehole, blowing a small whistle.

As patient inhaled incense, the chanter touched the tip of the brush to four sides of the fireplace and brushed over the patient.

Throughout the treatment the chanter stepped at the south side of the picture only.

According to the myth, the property *b* seems to be the chant symbol, representing valuable beads taken by the hero from his enemies. The feathered sticks may be prayersticks or aspergills; they are shown in the hands of the sandpainting figures. The whistle is the reed given to the hero as a means of breathing on his journey to the Sky. Many of the acts are exorcistic, although the Bead Chant is a Holy form.

Sandpainting: BS. The workers usually started the paintings after the Overshooting rite was finished. However, a painting of night 4, the most elaborate, was started just after sundown (at 6:30 P.M.) and the Unraveling, Plant garment, and Overshooting rites were all performed as it lay in the hogan. The painting was made by inadequate light, yet it was as well done as many good paintings I have seen done by daylight, much better than some. The first paintings were reasonably simple, and although there was plenty of help, it took two and a half hours or longer to lay them.

The treatment on the paintings differed from that on the Male Shooting Chant Holy paintings in that there was much less singing; the prayer was said with the patient on the painting (absorption and defense against evil); the elements were largely exorcistic; and the patient slept on some of the sand; the rest was kept at the back of the hogan. The person who woke first in the morning took it out and placed it somewhere at the east; the next day the sand was taken farther in the same direction and on each succeeding day it was taken still farther. The retention of part of the sand demonstrates absorption in reciprocal directions: the patient absorbs good from it; the painting absorbs the evil that was in the patient; the sand is dispersed—evil is dissipated.

Night 1. *Big Black Star* painting: The center was a large four-pointed Black Star, like that of Figure 18, with rays of every color, except black. The Star People were like the figures of Figure 19; each carried a bow in the left hand; an arrow lay at the right side. Their colors in circular arrangement were b(m)-u(f)-y(m)-w(f) with contrasting outlines; they had zigzag lightnings on arms and legs; a white line across the forehead represents bath suds. Above each figure was a small circle, with opening toward the center, of matching color and outline—a mountain home of the Star; there were no guardians.

Nights 2 (10:05 P.M. to 12:05 A.M.) and 4 (6:30 to 9:30 P.M.).

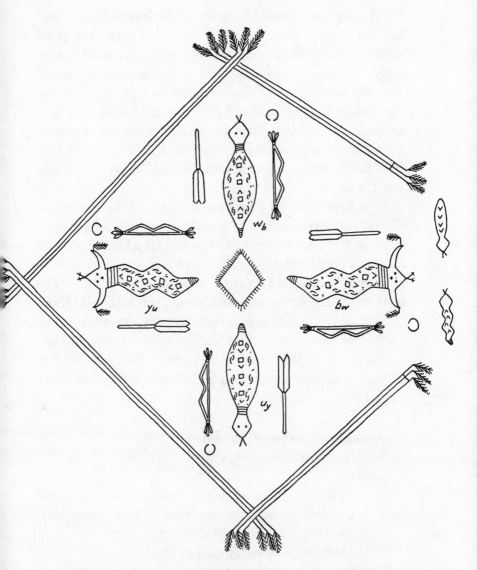

Fig. 18. Big Snakes with Crossed Rainbow Guardians: Big Star Chant, nights 2 and 4

Big Snakes with Crossed Rainbow Guardians painting (Fig. 18): On night 2 the center Star was blue with rays of all colors, except blue; on night 4, blue with rays of all colors, except white—otherwise the two paintings were the same. The Big Snakes had the same colors and positions as the Star People of night 1; they held bows and arrows. The four crossed rainbows that form the circular guardian represent a male rainbow by means of which the hero was transported from Earth to Sky, where he met the Star People, who taught him the chant.

"The figures are all Star People, but only the center one shines." "Snakes and Stars are the same." "The red spot between the neck and eyes of the male Snakes [b, y] is to show the dread with which the figure is regarded by all who look upon it. All evils should have this red spot." "The feathers on the horns represent power and motion" (RM).

Night 3. *Never-ending-snake* painting (Fig. 19, insert): The center was a Big Yellow Star. Figures and arrangement were the same as in the painting of night 1, but with Never-ending-snake as the encircling guardian and two blue bears as eastern guards.

Sandpainting, treatment on: BS.

Night 1. *Big Star* painting:

Singing.

Patient (female) sat on center of painting, with feet extending over the black figure at the east; she held bows and arrows.

Ashes blowing (audience participation).

Short litany with ashes blowing at intervals.

Sand disposal: a small pile was put under the patient's bed, the rest at the back of hogan.

Night 2. *Big Snakes with Crossed Rainbow Guardians*, Blue

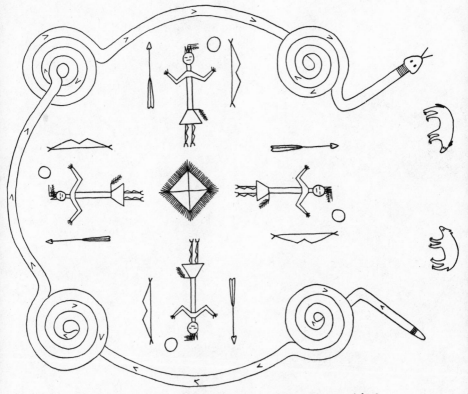

Fig. 19. Never-ending-snake sandpainting: Big Star Chant, night 3

Star center: Patient entered hogan; each member of audience provided with a quill feather from brush.

Patient sat on center, holding bow and arrow.

Litany, patient and chanter each holding a bull-roarer.

At end of first group of songs, blowing without ashes, audience participation; at end of second and third groups, ashes blowing; at end of fourth group of songs, flints passed around audience four times; at end of song groups five, six, and seven, ashes blowing.

Application of bull-roarer, bows, and arrows to patient.

Pollen administration; sand disposal as on night 1.

Night 3. *Never-ending-snake* painting with Yellow Star center: I did not see the treatment on this night.

Night 4 (11:30 to 11:50). *Big Snakes with Crossed Rainbows*, Big White Star center: The painting was made before the unraveling because "the chanters and the people were tired and wanted to get through."

Audience were given flints and brush quill feathers.

Patient, holding bow and arrows, sat on Big White Star.

Litany with chanter holding bull-roarer, patient and audience holding flint points.

At the end of first, second, and third song groups, audience blew along the feathers, moving them upward; at the end of fourth group, audience blew along feathers, moving them upward and around; after fifth group, no ritualistic act; after sixth group, blowing upward once; at the end of seventh group, blowing upward and around four times.

Application of bows and arrows to patient.

Pollen administration.

Sandpainting: Feather Chant. Figures 20 (over), 21 (insert), and 22 (on page 702) are sketches of the sandpaintings of days 6, 7, and 8 of a nine-night Feather Chant. They omit some

699

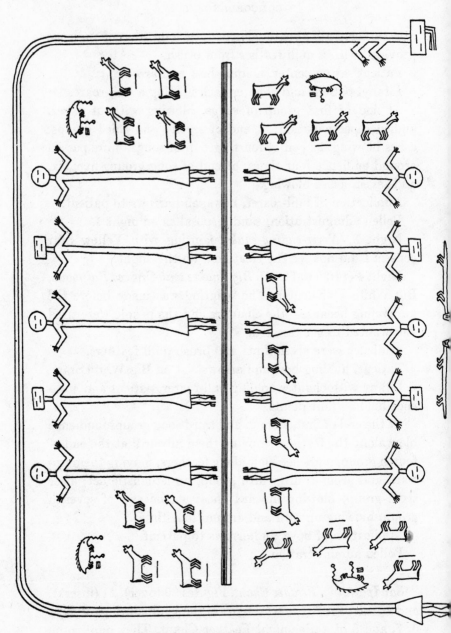

Fig. 20. Sandpainting: Feather Chant, day 6

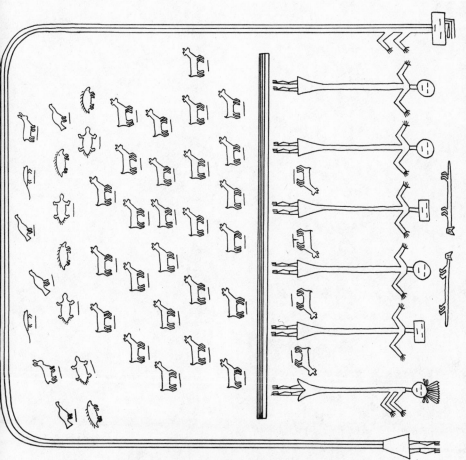

Fig. 21. Sandpainting: Feather Chant, day 7

details, but suggest what a collector might look for. All the pictures had animals as a theme. That of day 6 (Fig. 20) had five deities standing on each side of a central black bar, extending from north to south, with narrow outlines, y-w-u-r, at the west. Talking God and Water Sprinkler lead the lines at the east and west sides of the bar; they are the southernmost figures. At each corner small units composed of running animals—antelope, deer, porcupine—form a pattern which, with the center bar, makes a whirling log. (I was not told the symbolism of these pictures, but from Matthews' tale of the Feather Chant, I think the pictures represent the incident of the whirling log that the gods helped the hero to make, and guided to the confluence of two great rivers. The whirling log story runs into the origin of corn and the release of the game animals with the help of the hero's pet turkey.)

The painting of day 7 (Fig. 21) has six deities in line east of the center bar; the entire field at the west is filled with animals, so arranged that they seem to be running fast from southwest to northwest. The effect of motion was very well carried out and when the painting, about twenty feet in diameter, was finished, the chanter complimented the workers on their success at getting the effect. The animals are: antelope, deer, porcupine, turkey, rat, prairie dog, rabbit. All except the porcupine had a pollen line underneath. When I came in, I was told to sprinkle a line of pollen underneath any animal that had none; this should be done by every person entering the hogan.

In the picture of day 8 (Fig. 22) six deities stand at the east side, the animals at the west, but the bar is at the northeast; above it four buffalo, b-u-y-w, run eastward. This painting, like the other two, has a rainbow encircling guardian and two small wildcats at the east. I was not allowed to stay in the hogan very long, because the men were to fix the masks

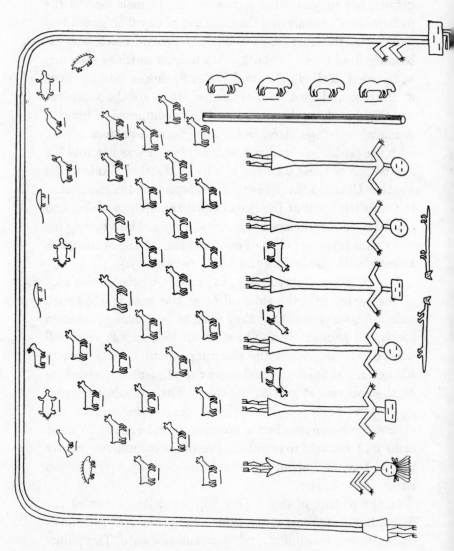

Fig. 22. Sandpainting: Feather Chant, day 8

for the dancers. After the painting was finished, many small animal images were made of corn meal and placed on the yellow line underneath the corresponding animal. Others like them were prayed over and deposited quite far away, treated, in fact, like offering prayersticks (Matthews 1897, p. 160ff.; cp. Haile 1947a).

Sandpainting setup: Feather Chant. Twelve talking prayersticks, called tóbo'oltá, were placed at regular intervals around the painting from southeast to northeast.

Sandpainting, treatment on: Feather Chant. The outstanding feature of the treatment was the clowning of Talking God and Gray God impersonators.

Day 6. 3 songs; entrance of two gods; Talking God with his foot erased the mountain lion eastern guardians.

Medicine administration by gods, with much clowning.

Sandpainting application by gods with calls and foolish behavior: Chanter gave a bunch of feathers to Talking God; Gray God wanted some and, after much to-do, got only one feather; Talking God took the bunch of feathers in his hand, patient S took hold of it and was pulled up; Gray God pulled X up with his feather; the other patients got up by themselves.

Talking God erased the painting with the feather head bundle before the audience went out.

As the audience sat outside, the gods clowned inside, then went off, and later returned unmasked. The two patients, wearing blankets, had entered the hogan carrying baskets of corn meal; they came out soon after.

Day 7. The treatment was similar to that of day 6, but the clowning was more exaggerated. Gray God pretended he had to lift the logs of the hogan ceiling to get the incense powder, then made much business of putting them back just right.

(These acts may have represented the gods' effort to transport the log or to float it when it was stuck.)

Day 8. The treatment was like that of the preceding days, the clowning longer and sillier.

Medicine and sand administration.

The corn-meal images were given to the patients; then the audience moved to the sandpainting and grabbed an image, or a piece of one, and ate it.

Incense inhaled (cp. Matthews 1897, p. 160ff.).

Sandpainting: SC Dark Circle branch.

Day 6. *Double* sandpainting (see *Sandpainting: SC Sun's House branch Red Inside phase*, day 6) differed from the published picture (Reichard 1934, facing p. 194) in the following details: there were two encircling guardians, one for each picture—a rainbow guardian for the southern picture; a zigzag lightning with white outside for the northern. Small rainbow around Sky-reaching-rock (at west) had red inside, blue outside; all other blue-red combinations had red outside.

Day 7. *Buffalo-who-never-dies* painting (*Sandpainting: SC Sun's House branch Red Inside phase*, day 7) was the picture in *Navajo Medicine Man*, Plate XXIV, with the following variations: center was blue, sprinkled with sparkling rock; Holy People all wore otterskin collars; there were pink, instead of white, herbs at the east; red of the small rainbows was inside; the encircling garland was a mirage garland.

Day 8. *Flint-armored Arrow People* painting (Fig. 23, insert) resembles that in *Navajo Medicine Man*, Plate XVII, quite closely, but is quite definitely a different painting.

Sandpainting, treatment on: SC Dark Circle branch.

Day 6. The treatment was simple, most of it singing by two large and energetic choruses; chant lotion administration; sand application; infusion specific administration.

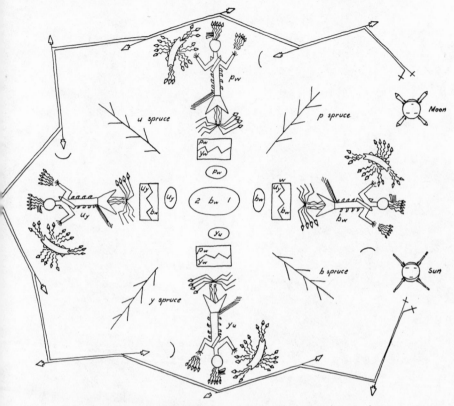

Fig. 23. Flint-armored Arrow People: Shooting Chant Dark Circle branch, day 8

Sandpainting: SC Prayerstick branch.

Day 1. *Crooked Snakes*, Newcomb-Reichard, Plate IV, with the following variations: Snake colors, south to north, b-w-u-y (reverse of the one illustrated); Snakes had yellow tongues.

Day 2. *Thunders*, Newcomb-Reichard, Plate XXX, with the following variations: A cup of water was sunk at the center and covered with black; all ovals around the center had a black ground with white dragonflies; instead of b-y-u-p medicines, there were blue corn, blue bean, black squash, and blue tobacco.

Day 3. *Holy People*, Newcomb-Reichard, Plate XIV.

Day 4 and day 1 of Sun's House branch 2-night repetition. *Day Skies*, Newcomb-Reichard, Figure 9 (p. 58).

Sandpainting setup: SC Prayerstick branch.

Days 1 and 2. Setup the same as for Sun's House branch, day 5, except that there was no screen.

Day 3. Setup as for days 1 and 2, except that there was no bull-roarer.

Day 4. Setup as for day 8, Sun's House branch, except that there was no bull-roarer.

Sandpainting, treatment on: SC Prayerstick branch.

Day 1. *Crooked Snakes* painting: sprinkling of painting with corn meal: over each Snake and around on rainbow guardian and on two eastern snake guards.

Painting sprinkled with chant lotion from aspergill.

Patient undressed and sat on White Snake.

Sand application: chanter spat on his hands and applied them to body-parts of Snakes and to corresponding parts of patient.

Chanter, holding infusion specific, erased eastern guards with his foot; infusion drinking.

Chant lotion applied by bathing.

Incensing: 2 coals.

Patient went outside and breathed in sun; bundle setup kicked down by chanter; disposal of sand.

Day 2. *Thunders* painting: variations in treatment were: meal sprinkling by patient, e-we and back, s-n and back; repeated and sprinkled around.

Chant lotion sprinkling with aspergill from cup and center cup.

Patient sat on Blue Thunder at west where aspergill had been lying; drank infusion specific;* sand applied twice.

Application of chant lotion* from cup and center cup by bathing; very little was drunk, the remainder was thrown out of doors.

Incense inhaled.

Day 3. *Holy People* painting (Newcomb-Reichard, Pl. XIV) with the following variations: there were headdresses and feathers on the heads of the Holy People; the dresses of females had only four colors, black, white, blue, and yellow; there were rainbow edges at the top of waist pouches; many bunches of feathers on armstrings and small white crosses where they joined and at the ends; black and white lightnings extended from the feet of the males; there were rainbows under the feet of females; the eastern guards were: black Big Fly at south, white Big Fly at north, facing each other.

Day 4. *Day Skies* painting with the following variations: Mountain Goat at east had no lifeline; Maltese cross was of blue corn, blue bean, black squash, blue tobacco; corn had five leaves, two ears and a blackbird with yellow on its tip; rainbow encircling guardian touched the Skies; it had four bunches of five feathers each, those of the two ends being at

---

*The infusion and chant lotion tasted different from those of the previous days.

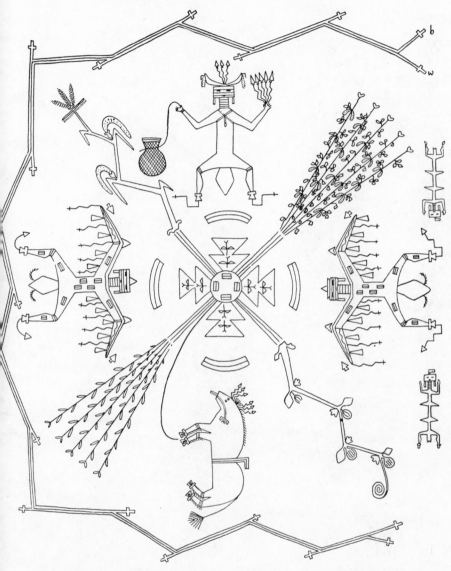

Fig. 24. Thunders and Water Monsters: Shooting Chant Sandpainting branch

the eastern end of the rainbow of the blue and black Skies; Bat guardian at north faced west; Sun's pouch guardian had Sun at top, pipe at bottom, no pipe cleaner. Each figure was sprinkled with pollen at the foot joint.

Sandpainting: SC Sandpainting branch. Many features correspond with those of the Prayerstick branch, the chief difference being the absence of most exorcistic elements.

Day 1. *Crooked Snakes* like day 1 of Prayerstick branch with the following variations: red dots on center blue feather of five; white dots on red feathers at each end of bunch; marks on Snakes: deer hoof only, on arms, legs, and body, with point toward head. Position of Snakes (south to north) —Black Snake on zigzag lightning, White Snake on sunray, Blue Snake on flash lightning, Yellow Snake on sunbeam. Black and Blue Snakes held white-yellow bows in left hand, arrows in right; White and Yellow Snakes held yellow-white bows in left hand and wands in right.

Day 2. *Thunders and Water Monsters* painting (Fig. 24, insert): at the center a blue glass bowl was placed; water was poured into it from the four directions and from above; it was covered with chant lotion herbs, black sand, and four rainbows; then it was sunk into the floor, surrounded by white and yellow outlines, and sprinkled with pollen. The double-tiered clouds at the center correspond in color with the major figures. The Maltese cross is composed of black squash, blue tobacco, blue corn, blue bean.

The figures are: Black Thunder at the east, Blue Thunder at the west, Pink Water Horse at the south, and Yellow Water Monster at the north. The Thunders' black tails have no rain symbols; they are outlined in w-y-u-r-br; Yellow Water Monster's tail is outlined in w-u-b-r. The trail from Water Horse's feet to the center is white.

Day 3. *Holy People* painting: treatment as on day 2 except: patient sat on Holy Man; sand was applied with hands dampened in chant lotion; there was whistling over patient; singing was longer than on preceding days, when it was longer than in any of the other branches.

Day 4. *Day Skies* painting: the treatment differed from that of the Prayerstick branch in the following details: sand and pollen from the feet of the sandpainting figures was put in the patient's moccasins; the patient was led onto the painting with the male bull-roarer; the cord of the bead token was rubbed with colored pigment—black, white, yellow, and blue; when it was tied on, the chanter pressed it very hard with his hands; the pollen ball was placed with the Sky and Sun wide boards; the identification of chanter and patient with the wide boards was at the feet and hands only. After the identification, the chanter put on the bandoleer and necklaces, and put the jewelry in his pocket. The bandoleers were put over the left, then over the right, shoulder, instead of around the neck; as for females, the wristlets were put on, right first, then left.

Identification with wide boards crossed, Sky at the head, Sun at the feet, Moon at the knees, Dawn at the shoulders.

Whistling over patient.

Identification with all upright bundle properties.

Incensing: 2 coals.

The patient was raised with the black and blue bundle talking prayersticks and led, step by step, outside; a cup of water was thrown ahead of him; outside, he breathed in the sun.

Sandpainting was erased with whistling and removed; a blanket was spread and mush bowl was placed; mush was eaten first by patient, then by audience.

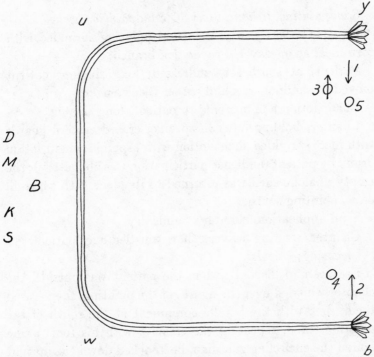

Fig. 25. Sandpainting setup: Shooting Chant Sandpainting branch

Sandpainting setup: SC Sandpainting branch, as in Figure 25 with the following explanation:

D   Dawn wide board.

K   Skyhole wide board.

M   Moon wide board.

S   Sun wide board.

B   bull-roarer set to stand against the Skyhole wide board (K) as the chanter walked onto the painting.

1   pile of soft bundle items, pointing south.

2   same as 1, but pointing north.

3   chant lotion in abalone shell, aspergill pointing north laid on the shell.

4, 5 extra cups of chant lotion and infusion specific.

Sandpainting, treatment on: SC *Sandpainting branch.*

Day 1. *Crooked Snakes* painting: painting sprinkled with corn meal as on day 1, Prayerstick branch.

Patient, at southeast, undressed; long singing; patient moved to sandpainting and sat on Black Snake.

Chant lotion administered to patient; long singing.

Chanter, holding infusion specific, erased eastern guards with foot; sprinkled chant lotion with aspergill; chant lotion drunk by patient (audience participation was obligatory); the empty abalone shell was returned to its place with aspergill on it, pointing south.

Sand application, chanter's hands dry.

Chanter, wearing beaver collar, whistled over patient.

Incensing: 2 coals.

Erasure and disposal: when the patient was outside, the chanter whistled over the figures of the painting, then erased them, first with the bundle equipment at the south of the painting, then, repeating the erasure, with his foot; as he erased the encircling guardian, he knocked down the upright properties with his foot, then gathered them up; a little sand was taken outside; most of it was brushed to the west of the hogan, where it was left.

Day 2. *Thunders* painting: the treatment was like that on day 1 with the following variations: the patient sat on Black Thunder; aspersing was done with the chant lotion and the contents of the center bowl; the aspergill was touched lightly to the body-parts of all painting figures, including plants; there was no whistling over the patient.

Sandpainting: SC *Sun's House branch Red Inside phase.*

Day 5. *Blue Corn and Snakes* painting (Newcomb-Reichard, Pl. III) with the following variations: there was a black horizontal bar between the cloud from which the corn

710

springs and the encircling guardian, a rainbow which had red inside, blue outside.

Day 6. *Double* painting: there is some information additional to that of Reichard 1934, facing page 194: on the mountain at the north on the east side of the picture were two specially cut branches of *Juniperus sibirica*, collected some 135 miles northeast of White Sands. The helper cut them with a bundle flint, then sprinkled the cut with pollen. The branches had a double-cross arrangement where the twigs opposed each other; at the bottom of each there was a knot of blue cloth. After cutting these branches, the assistant laid them in blue cloth, keeping the tips toward the north. During the entire return trip he carried the cloth on his lap.

The center of the picture at the south was very high; called Sky-reaching-rock, it was shaped of carefully collected and prepared clay in a bluntly truncated cone; a turtle shell with the aspergill rested on it.

All rainbows had red inside; the encircling rainbow goddess had bunches of five feathers at the southwest and northwest corners; except for the turtle shell and aspergill, the setup was the same as on day 5; two choruses, one at the north, one at the south, sang alternately.

Day 7. *Holy Man Kills Buffalo-who-never-dies* (*Navajo Medicine Man*, Pl. XXIV) with red inside; setup as on day 5.

Day 8. *Sky and Earth* (Newcomb-Reichard, Fig. 5) had no encircling guardian.

Sandpainting setup: SC Sun's House branch Red Inside phase. The Sun's House screen, with spruce boughs, moving snakes, and birds, was at the west for all painting of this branch. The beaver collar (male) hung over the south end of the screen and the otter collar (female) over the north. Note that this position corresponds with the position on the setout mound of the male and female bundle properties and with the position of men and women in the ceremonial hogan. In front of the screen, and leaning against it, were the wide boards and the bull-roarer, Figure 26, explained as follows:

D   Dawn wide board.

K   Skyhole wide board.

M   Moon wide board.

S   Sun wide board.

B   Bull-roarer leaning against screen.

b
w
u } bundle talking prayersticks (tó bo'oltá).
y

1   turtle shell with infusion specific.

2   cup with chant lotion.

3   aspergill.

4, 5 places where female patients sat

The dots indicate the position of snake figures.

Days 5, 6, 7. Setup as described above.

Day 8. The wide boards were in the same position, but the reverse, instead of the face, was outside; in addition, there were: a basket of ceremonial mush in front of the wide boards; an extra pan of chant lotion at the northeast (for audience participation); aspergill and bundle arrows lay over the turtle shell; bundle items not previously included lay at the southeast corner; pollen balls lay on Sky's and Earth's mouths.

Sandpainting, treatment on: SC Sun's House branch Red Inside phase.

Day 5. *Blue Corn and Snakes* sandpainting: patients entered and sprinkled painting with corn meal; undressed

712

and walked down the cornstalk to sit on the head of the Snakes; all acts were done rapidly and in close succession.

Administration of chant lotion: applied to the chest and carried back and around the body at the front and back, diagonally across the chest and back, around the waist at

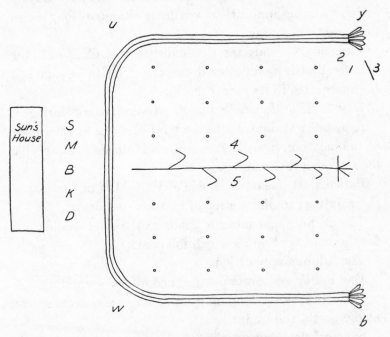

Fig. 26. Sandpainting setup: Shooting Chant Sun's House branch Red Inside phase

left toward the back, at right from front to back, then over arms, legs, feet, and head (a representation of figure painting).

Sand application: on this and on the three following days the chanter ran about on the painting with a kind of prancing step as he gathered the sand; he erased the snake guards with his foot.

Administration of infusion specific.

Incensing: 2 coals.

Patients left sandpainting and hogan; breathed in the sun. Sandpainting erased and disposed of.

Day 6. *Double* painting: patients entered hogan, sprinkled corn meal, infusion specific, and chant lotion over painting; took their places on the feet of Holy Man and Holy Boy.

Sandpainting application to patients with many long songs, no haste.

Incensing: 2 coals (as the audience was filing out, the chanter hastily administered the chant lotion, which had been forgotten in its proper place).

Day 7. *Holy Man Kills Buffalo-who-never-dies* painting: Aspergill was dipped into the bowl of water at the center of the painting, into chant lotion, and into infusion specific for aspersing the painting.

Patients sat one on each side of Holy Man at the east of the painting; administration of infusion specific.

The chanter spat into his hands so the sand would stick for the sand application which followed.

Chant lotion application.

Day 8. *Sky and Earth* painting: corn-meal sprinkling.

Patients entered, took up position on an elaborate spread at the north, and undressed.

Sand application to patients.

Figure painting.

Patients put on their jewelry; chanter put necklaces, to which wristlets were fastened, around his neck.

Infusion specific sprinkled on painting (audience participation).

Sand from painting placed in patients' moccasins.

Patient was led onto painting by grasping bull-roarer, co-patient following; one sat at the center of Sky, the other at the center of Earth.

Bead tokens were tied to the right forelocks; * pollen ball administered with water; * application of Sun and Moon wide boards to patients' chests and backs; necklaces put on patients with sudden jerky motions of the chanter; head bundles were tied to the left forelocks with the sticks hanging down over the patients' eyes.

Infusion specific administered; bundle applied.

Identification of chanter and patients with Moon wide board at head, Sun board at feet, Skyhole board at hands and shoulders, Dawn board at chest and back.

Incensing: 2 coals.

Painting erased, accompanied by whistling.

Sandpainting: SCE. The paintings were made in connection with the Prayer on buckskin and Hoop transformation rites. The hoop-mountain arrangement may be considered as a sandpainting in itself, or a continuation of the painting made inside the hogan.

The paintings inside the hogan were the separate elements, one each day, of the center of the Skies painting, Newcomb-Reichard, Plate XVIII; on the third day, only the Black Wind was painted to represent Black Wind and Yellow Wind, because two days' performance were done in one; Sun, Moon, and Black Wind had horns and a red line completely around them.

Night 5. *Never-ending-snake* sandpainting (Fig. 27, insert): on each mountain two yucca leaves were crossed, the kind at each direction corresponding with that used on the mountains of the same direction in the Hoop transformation rite.

---

*With each of these acts the chanter made passes up, down, and out to the east side of the hogan.

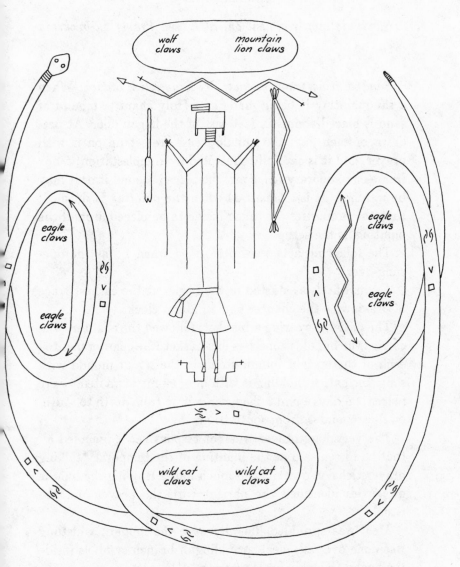

Fig. 27. Never-ending-snake: Shooting Chant Evil, night 5

Sandpainting, treatment on, SCE, see *Prayer on buckskin rite.*

. . .

Sandpainting setout mound: SC Prayerstick branch. When a sandpainting is being made in a Holy chant, a mound of sand is placed about six feet east of the hogan door. At pre-dawn of each day, the bundle items are set up on it with prayer, and it is carefully protected from molestation; a box frame or temporary fence may be placed around it or it may be watched. It is dismantled when the painting is finished; then the properties are taken inside to be placed around the painting as the setup.

The following acts were performed when I was the one-sung-over:

A small fire was started in the hogan at the earliest trace of pre-dawn—the chanter had an alarm clock.

The patient, wearing a blanket, followed the chanter, who carried the bundle properties in a basket; the chanter planted each of the upright bundle items in the setout mound with song, the patient holding it with him; twenty-two items were placed; on days 1 and 3 they were set up from north to south, on days 2 and 4, from south to north.

The very long prayer was not responsive; it included all that had been said at the planting of the temporary talking prayersticks on night 1, and much more. Holding the bundle properties identified the patient with the prayer and the ritual.

Meal was sprinkled liberally over the mound; whistling was done over all; meal sprinkling of branch symbols inside the hogan (Kluckhohn-Wyman, p. 81).

Sandpainting setout mound: SC Sun's House branch Red Inside phase. At dawn of day 5 the patients, facing east, took

716

their places in front of the screen; the birds were set to flying and singing, the snakes to moving in and out of their houses. Then the chanter went outside and set up the bundle properties on the mound—chanters may differ about this rite. The properties were set up in the following order: standing north to south: y-u-Dawn-Moon-Skyhole-Sun-w-b (color initials stand for bundle talking prayersticks); lying with points toward the south: otter collar, male eagle tail-feathered arrow, male feathered wand, black bow, male aspergill, male head bundle, and prayer talking prayerstick; lying with points toward the north: corresponding female properties (cp. Kluckhohn-Wyman, pp. 81–2).

Sandpainting setout mound, meaning of (A). I summarize here the meanings I got, and, with emendations in brackets, the meanings given by Kluckhohn-Wyman: The patient represents Talking God (that is, the dawn); the meal stands for the dawn. The setout involves "recognitive [chant in progress], protective [protecting hogan from intrusion], ingratiatory [attracting the supernaturals], and symbolic [bundle prayersticks symbolize gods] motives" (Kluckhohn-Wyman, p. 81).

. . .

Shock rite (xode·tłá·d) (E) is an accessory rite, which purports to induce and correct symptoms due to the contemplation of supernatural things too strong for the patient. The Shooting Chant shock is induced by a Bear impersonator, who represents the dangers and sufferings encountered by Holy Man, and is intended to eliminate fear and inspire confidence.

In the Big Star Chant myth, Never-ending-snake stunned the hero, so that the prayers, songs, and other powers of the supernaturals would become a part of the chant. Shock rites are described for the Mountain and Night chants. It is likely that the rite is a part of many chants.

The fit or seizure for which it is indicated renders the victim unconscious; it is also a sign that the correct cure has been chosen for the patient's ills. The Shock rite differs considerably from the Restoration rite (Reichard 1939, p. 66, Pl. XXI; Big Star ms.; Shooting Chant ms.; Huckel ms.; Matthews 1887, p. 423; 1902, pp. 115–6, 182, 263, Pl. II, D; cp. Wyman-Bailey 1946b, pp. 332–7).

Short singing of the Shooting Chant is accompanied by rattles and drumming on the reversed basket. It is a part of the patient's identification with the chant. In both Sun's House and Prayerstick branches, the patient, sitting at the south side of the hogan, holds two bundle talking prayersticks in the left hand; with them he beats time to the singing; thus he indicates that he is paying attention. Short singing is a part of Sun's House branch on nights 5, 6, 7, and 8, and of Prayerstick branch on nights 1, 2, 3, and 4, occurring in both cases after the bundle application. It is followed by ashes blowing and incensing with two coals (cp. Kluckhohn-Wyman, pp. 80–1; Haile 1943a, p. 283).

• • •

Sweat-emetic (E). The main acts of the long, complicated Sweat-emetic rite are set forth by Kluckhohn-Wyman. I have not encountered the prescription for even numbering (of times a person must participate in this rite) which they mention. Many individuals took part in it only once. The chief requirement of the Holy and Evil Shooting chants and of the Big Star Chant is that everyone present in the hogan during its performance *must* participate in every act.

Preparations were begun early in the day, although the rite did not start until 8 or 9 A.M. Kluckhohn and Wyman say that there is hearty eating before it starts. In the chants I attended the patients were not allowed to eat; the participants preferred not to. I have been a part of this rite many times. The ritualistic acts are numerous; it seems to me that the following are distinctive. I have given acts and properties names somewhat different from those of Kluckhohn-Wyman, chiefly because they require more particular specification. I once used the term 'prayer paintings,' one I now discard—all sand and pollen paintings are prayer paintings and the term has no meaning. At the sweat-emetic rite three types of paintings should be distinguished: paintings around the fire (sometimes with pokers); a painting under the emetic; and paintings to indicate the patient's position while drinking the emetic—places upon which to rest his hands and knees. Painting under the emetic basket and those orienting the patient really form a unit, but I separate them in order to indicate their variations (Kluckhohn-Wyman, p. 82).

Sweat-emetic, emetic formula: BS and Endurance Chant. Herbs for the emetic and the chant lotion and the sticks for pokers were gathered at the same time. They should be collected in the vicinity of a tree struck by lightning. The following are desirable if available, otherwise, ' any kind will do '—juniper, pinyon, pine, spruce, chokecherry, *Ceanothus Fendleri* 101* (tčí·dá·''), *Tetradymia canescans* 122 (tčį·di· tčil), *Pseudocymopterus montanus*, cp. 127 (tčóltci·n), *Stanleya pinnatifida* or *Sisymbrium linearifolium* 86 (tṣą̀bį·h), and ' that-which-smells-like-rat-urine ' (łé'étsoh bilijí xaltcini·). Others used by RM were: an odorous plant (xaltciní tčil)

---

*The numbers are those in Wyman-Harris, pp. 17–34.

(probably generic), and cliffrose ('awé'' tšá·l) (cp. Kluckhohn-Wyman, pp. 122, 162).

Sweat-emetic, emetic formula: SC Prayerstick and Sun's House branches. The emetic contained the following: spruce, *Monarda pectinata* 48 ('aze'' ndo·łe·jí, in flower), thunder plant ('i·ṅi' tċil), *Parryella filifolia* 237 (natša· 'íł'į), *Pentstemon trichander* 133 (dahi·tįhídą·'', one flower, a few stems and leaves), *Ranunculus micropetalus* 96 (tċałdą·'', roots and plants with seeds), ' small hard wood ' (tcétċilyájí, root and plant), *Berula erecta, Ranunculus cymbalaria* 268 (táká·'' dahi·kał, root and plant in flower), *Pseudocymopterus montanus* 127 (tċóltcin, root and plant); three plants added from the chanter's dried supply—two unidentified (dinąs and ni'kéhí dináka·d) and juniper; red willow, ' Monster Slayer's emetic ' (na·γé'' nei·zγání bi'iłkó·h, small amount of dried root), odorous sunflower, *Verbesina encelioides* 241 (ndi·γilí nłtcin); ' matured watermelon ' (łé·tċí·yá·n yiłą'í); bat corn (dja·bańdą·''), root of two unidentified plants; stem and bark of an unidentified plant, from dried supply; montmorillonite (dle·c); ground rock (tséká·n).

Sweat-emetic, emetic frames are specific for a chant. Such a frame is called a hoop by Kluckhohn and Wyman, but the hoop is only one of the forms in which it occurs. The emetic frame is prepared with care; it is placed over or under the basket containing the emetic, and the patient drinks through it; in some cases, he vomits through it. According to Kluckhohn-Wyman, it acts as "a one-way valve, preventing any ejected material from returning to the patient"—an excellent explanation (Reichard 1944d, pp. 50–1, 56–7, 64–5, 71; cp. Kluckhohn-Wyman, p. 84).

Sweat-emetic, emetic frames: SC Prayerstick and Sun's House branches. Four hoops for each patient were made of different materials and colors to represent Snakes; the hoops had facets to indicate faces. Contrasting colored rings were painted on the hoops at regular intervals; those near the place where the hoops were tied were left open. The hoops were tied with *Yucca glauca* fibers, which were loosened when the frames were placed around the emetic basins, so that on day 1 they lay as in Figure 28, a; on day 2 they were laid

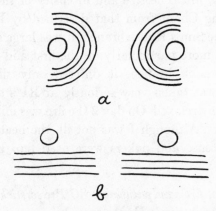

Fig. 28. Emetic frames: Shooting Chant Sun's House branch Red Inside phase

straight (north to south) in front of the sand basins (Fig. 28, b). The following scheme indicates the details:

Day	Material	Ground color	Rings
1	aspen, *Populus tremuloides* 275 (ɫiˑs ɫbahí)	w	b
2	red willow (k'aí ɫtcí")	y	u
3	spruce (tc'óh)	u	y
4	chokecherry, *Prunus melanocarpus* (didzé)	b	w

Sweat-emetic, emetic sandpaintings: SC, on which the basket, full of the emetic, stood, were the cloudlike elements in New-comb-Reichard, Plate XIX (there is a mistake in the orientation of this picture; it should be corrected as in the following scheme). In the sweat-emetic only one quadrant of the picture was painted; it represents the gods from one direction, and on successive days, the cross sequence:

Day	Direction	Color	Name of element
1	east	b	Sky People
2	west	u	Water People
3	south	y	Sun People
4	north	p	Summer People

Sweat-emetic, fire. The size and intensity of the fire differ in the Shooting Chant from that described by Kluckhohn-Wyman. In the Sun's House branch, it was large and intense all four times, more particularly on the first and third days. In the Prayerstick branch, it differed only slightly—the sweat-emetic was taken very seriously at RP's and restrictions were rarely relaxed. On day 2 the fire was mildest; there were no pokers. Although I was not ill, the heat on days 3 and 4 was intense and pokers were used (cp. Kluckhohn-Wyman, p. 84).

Sweat-emetic, fire sandpaintings: SC Prayerstick branch.
Days 1, 3. As in Sun's House branch.
Days 2, 4. As in Sun's House branch, except that the arrow points were not outlined in red (cp. Reichard 1944d, pp. 51, 71; Haile 1938b, p. 231).

Sweat-emetic, fire sandpaintings: SC Sun's House branch. Although there is much repetition of the simple elements placed around the sweat fire, there is probably always some difference in detail. The following were a part of the Sun's House branch: Day 1. Big Snakes, like those at the corners in Newcomb-Reichard, Plate VIII, in the circular color order, b-u-w-y (the marks on the Snakes were different from those on day 3).

Day 2. Conveyance symbols as in Figure 29, with points of all figures outlined in red.

Day 3. *Crooked Snakes,* each like the corner snakes in Newcomb-Reichard, Plate V, in circular color sequence, b-w-u-y.

Day 4. Arrows like those of day 2 were said to have been

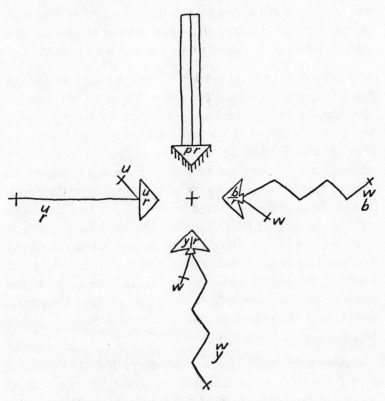

Fig. 29. Sweat-emetic fire sandpainting: Shooting Chant Sun's House branch Red Inside phase

used. I did not see them, but, since the paintings of the Prayerstick branch were the same on days 2 and 4, they were probably the same in this branch also (cp. Haile 1943a, pp. 24, 207).

Sweat-emetic, order of events: BS. There were no wood samples; ' any old kind of wood would do.' Otherwise, the acts were much like those of Sun's House branch with the following variations: Fire jumping was by chanter and two assistants, not by patient or audience, e-we and back, s-n and back (in Sun's House branch there was no fire jumping). On day 2 all participants of the rite jumped as near the hot coals as possible, e-s, s-we, we-n, n-e, and back each time.

Sweat-emetic, order of events: SC Prayerstick branch. Like Sun's House branch except: on days 1 and 4 there was fire jumping, by chanter and assistants ne-sw and back, se-nw and back; on day 2 sw-ne and back, se-nw and back. The chanter added ashes on the poker to the contents of the patient's sand basin; assistants brought ashes to the members of the audience, who sprinkled them over their own basins. The audience marched around the fire four times and outside the hogan; they deposited the sand-basin contents north of the hogan. Outside, the patient sat south of the sandpainting mound, facing west, and the other women sat south of the hogan, while the assistants cleared the hogan of all properties, except the embers and pokers. After their re-entrance, the same acts were performed as in Sun's House branch.

Sweat-emetic, order of events: SC Sun's House branch Red Inside phase. This description is the prototype for all others in this work: preparation of fire, paintings, pokers, emetic basket, and frames; the emetic bowl was set to boil on the coals; sand for the basins was brought in, the emetic frames were placed on the patients' basins, after the hoops had been untied—the openings of MC's were at the south, those of AD's at the north.

Fire procession (entrance): the leader—first person—entered, passed sunwise around the fire, placing the right foot over the eastern sandpainting and poker, then paused for a song; next, the left foot was placed over the painting and poker at the south, and so alternating until all had passed around the fire to the north, the procession pausing at each direction while a song was sung. From the north the audience took their places, men at the south, women at the north.

Poker application: the chanter first poked the poker in the fire, then applied it to himself, especially to his legs and ankles, then to the patients; he took the pokers in the order e-we-s-n; those members of the audience who wished to applied the pokers to themselves, often applying only two pokers—perhaps those of the individual's sex; CF was very thorough about this act.

Dry emetic was put into emetic baskets and the audience's porcelain basins; hot liquid was added, then cold water so as to fill the basin; the chanter sprinkled two kinds of pollen over each vessel; then strained off the remaining particles of medicine on the surface with the unbound end of a hair brush.

Fire procession took place when the fire was hottest; all participants repeated fire procession without pausing.

Emetic: the patients led the drinking at a particular word of a song; emetic was applied to the body; emesis.

Bull-roarer was sounded outside six times; it was brought in and applied to patients.

Wood samples of cedar from the north woodpile were placed e-we on the fire, those from the south pile were placed s-n.

Procession from the hogan, led by the assistants, who took out the patients' sand basins and contents; on day 2 they were deposited in line, west of the hogan—first the patients' basins, then those of the audience, one by one.

The audience stayed outside while the assistants removed the sandpaintings, leaving the pokers in position.

The audience re-entered and sat near the patients at the west and southwest; assistants separated the hot coals with the pokers, extinguished the fire, and removed all remnants to a designated place, north by east of the hogan, near the sand-basin disposal.

Aspersing with chant lotion, shaken from the feather brush, e-we-s-n-up-down and over all, with speed, vigor, and excited singing.

Incensing: 2 coals.

Patients got dressed outside of hogan (cp. Kluckhohn-Wyman, p. 86).

Sweat-emetic pokers: SC. My information about pokers and their function differs somewhat from that given by Kluckhohn-Wyman. The pokers of day 1 were of mountain mahogany; they were laid at the left of each fire sandpainting.

The pokers represent Changing Woman's weapon when she drove off Big Monster, who visited her, attempting to find her baby Twins. She hit him on the shins—the reason the poker application is emphasized at ankles and leg parts. The application purports to cure leg pains (cp. Kluckhohn-Wyman, p. 84).

Sweat-emetic, preparation: SC Sun's House branch Red Inside phase. The hogan was cleared of everything, except the materials to be used in the rite—participants sit on blankets for most rites; in this, they sat on the bare floor.

A bark torch was waved e-we, s-n, and around; on day 1 fire was made with the drill; hoops, for the emetic frames; small fire sandpaintings were laid and pokers placed beside them; emetic and patients' positional paintings were made.

Sweat-emetic: SCE. The fire sandpaintings were: Black Crooked Snake at the east, Blue Crooked Snake at the south, Yellow Crooked Snake at the west, and White Crooked Snake at the north, all with markings exactly as in the Holy form. The emetic frame was a sand rainbow around the basin; for hands and knees, small sand rainbows—all these symbols were said to have been the same for the four days.

The ritualistic acts were like those of the Holy chant, except that fire was emphasized; the fire was larger and lasted longer in the Evil chant. When it was kindled with the drill, a little lightning-struck rock was put on the fireboard—a ceremonial material which facilitated kindling. The men were required to jump over the fire and the women to walk as close as possible; at the end of the rite, ashes were blown from the pokers just before the fire was removed. Incensing with two coals.

Sweat-emetic rite, meaning of (E). The essential purpose is purification, to rid the body of evils which may have intruded. Particular evils and the way they have attacked the patient are noted in the chant myth. The rite differs from the sweathouse rite, pit-sweating, and other purificatory fire rites, more in its ritualistic makeup than in meaning. In the Shooting Chant Holy, it represents Sun's test of The Twins by sweating and their delivery by Talking God, yet the episode gave the chant a negative prescription, for it was decreed that Earth People should not imitate the sweathouse purification because, if something evil should happen, there would be nothing to counteract it. Therefore, they should have only a fire, they should not use hot stones.

Generally it is assumed that evil is shot into people, that sweating will cause arrows and witch objects to fall out of the flesh, that vomiting will drive evils from the body interior.

As the people of the Hail Chant moved about the fire, they shook arrows out of themselves into the fire, where they were consumed.

The Shooting Chant emetic frames represent trees against which Bear rubbed his back after Holy Man was taken by the Thunders.

Changing-bear-maiden was shot full of arrows by the Spider and Swallow People; she originated the sweat-emetic rite by her own power. Holy Man was overcome by Coyote so that he became a despicable, mangy coyote; the evil power was partly eradicated by the sweat-emetic rite. When a Navaho shoots a coyote—a rare occurrence—he may shoot the carcass full of arrows. Parts may then become equipment of exorcistic rites.

In the land of the Star People, the hero of the Big Star Chant was shot with witch objects, extracted by the sweat-emetic rite. The War Ceremony emetic—there is no sweating —is said to remove enemy evil, especially that of dead enemies (Reichard 1944d, pp. 51, 56–7; Shooting Chant ms.; Endurance Chant ms.; Kluckhohn-Wyman, p. 24; Haile 1938b, p. 209).

. . .

Talking prayersticks, bundle; dedication of: SC Sandpainting branch. The day before the Sandpainting branch was started, the prayersticks and wide boards were dedicated in a short rite: when finished, the properties were placed in a basket, each new one on top of the corresponding one belonging to the presiding chanter. JS, wearing a blanket, held the basket, with which he beat time to the songs, accompanied by two rattles in the hands of the chanter and an assistant. Then JS motioned with the basket, e-we-s-n-up; then he set it down. JS applied pollen to the mouths of all the figures on the wide boards and of the talking prayersticks; then twice from butt to tip of each property (audience participation).

Litany (45 minutes), JS holding the basket of bundle items, the chanter holding a pollen pouch; JS breathed in from the basket and contents four times; pollen prayer by all present (see *Bundle contents, procurement of: SC*).

. . .

Unraveling (E) is a complicated procedure, felt to be of great importance as a releasing process. The rite consists of pressing of specific unraveler bundles to the patient. The pressing with bundle equipment was more forceful each night than on the preceding night; in fact, it sometimes made the patients wince—once I thought my neck had been dislocated. The pressure on the head and legs was especially strong in the chant for MC and AD because they had headache and their legs ached. The bull-roarer, seemingly a part of Prayerstick branch unraveling, appears on nights 5–8 of the Sun's House unraveling (cp. Kluckhohn-Wyman, pp. 77–81).

Unraveling, preparation of unravelers: BS. The herbs of the Big Star unraveling rites, for tying up the patient, and for the Hoop transformation rite, are the same as those of the Male Shooting Chant Holy unraveling, except that the dodgeweed is of the small variety. In the Big Star Chant they are tied with the unraveling strings and one brush quill feather. There are no bundle properties corresponding with bundle items 8 and 9 (see *Bundle contents*).

The numbers are 5, 7, 9, 12 on successive nights. The five plants that compose the bundles are: red grass, *Sorghastrum nutans* 299 (tłoh łtcí"), little dodgeweed, *Gutierrezia sarothrae* 113 (tċil dilγé·siyájí), *Artemisia frigida* 279 (tóka·ł), spruce, rock sage, *Artemisia Wrightii* 75 (tsé'éji·) (cp. Kluckhohn-Wyman, Fig. 7).

Unraveling, preparation of unravelers: HC (from mythical description). There is no mention of unraveling for night 1, it being doubtless taken for granted. Unraveler bundles consisted of different properties on different nights: night 2, 11 bundles—6 on Winter Thunder's side, 5 on Dark Thunder's —were made of: *Artemisia frigida*, 1 unraveling string, 1 bundle talking prayerstick; night 3, *Juniperus sibirica* (tćóh de'niní), 1 unraveling string, 1 rainstreamer (god's form, Earth People's symbol is not mentioned).

Unraveling, preparation of unravelers: SC. Each bundle is made by tying an unraveler in a slipknot with a bunch containing a sprig of each of the plants and one of the chant symbols. The number of the symbols differs from night to night, as does their position on the layout; the composition of the unravelers may vary also with the number of the patients and their relative position in the chant—patient, co-patient, or participant in small rites. One set for MC, the patient, had two wide boards and the black and white talking prayersticks; the other, for AD, the co-patient, had only the Thunder wide board and the blue and yellow bundle talking prayersticks. The plants were: grama grass, *Bouteloua gracilis* 300 (tłoh na'astasi'), dodgeweed, *Artemisia frigida*, spruce, rock sage.

Unraveling, preparation of unravelers: SCE. The plants, numbers, and bundle items differed from night to night. The numbers were 5, 7, 9, 11 on successive nights. The composition of unravelers was as follows: night 1, blue bundle arrow, red bundle arrow, *Yucca baccata*, *Yucca glauca* (tsá'ászi' ntśó·z), god's yucca (γé'i· bitśá'ászi'), yucca's horn (tśá'ászi' bide"), juniper (gad), pinyon (tca'oł), spruce, 5 unraveler strings, 1 eagle quill feather, laid on top of all the rest; night 2 as on night 1, but with 7 strings; night 3, bundle items and plants as on night 1 with 9 unraveling strings and rock sage, grama grass, dodgeweed; night 4 as on night 3, but with 11 strings.

Unraveling, preparation of unravelers: War Ceremony. There were 5 (or 3) unraveling strings of *Yucca glauca* fiber; 13 plants are mentioned for the War Ceremony, but it is not clear whether they are for unraveling, emetic, or chant lotion, or for all (Reichard 1928, p. 124; Haile 1938b, p. 207).

Unraveling, unravelers; application of: BS. The rite was very similar to that of Shooting Chant Holy. Unravelers were applied, crossed, and pulled out: at the feet, knees, chest, back, and at the top of the head. Acts much exaggerated in the Evil forms and included only perfunctorily in the Holy forms were brushing and the use of ashes.

After unravelers had been applied to the patient, the chanter dipped the brush in ashes, brushed the patient vigorously from head to foot, and made passes toward the smokehole, then brushed far around the patient through the entire hogan, at times even out the door. On night 4 unraveling took place after the sandpainting was on the floor; it was done hastily but thoroughly, lasting only ten minutes.

Unraveling, unravelers; application of: SC Prayerstick branch and two-night repetition, as for the Sun's House branch, except that unraveler bundles were applied with a great rush, almost a swooping motion.

Unraveling, unravelers; application of: SC Sun's House branch Red Inside phase. The patients undressed and circled the fire from their place at the northwest to the west, where they sat on the layout.

Chant lotion was mixed in the cup; infusion specific, in the turtle shell; chant lotion was tasted by the chanter, then blown (called 'spitting' by Kluckhohn-Wyman) over patients with sound symbol.

Unravelers were gently pulled along the patient's body-parts; the strings were crossed and the knots pulled out: at the soles, palms, chest, and head.

Chant lotion was blown, touched to the patient's chest, back, arms, and over her face; bow design was made with chant lotion at the front and back of the patient's limbs; chant lotion tasted by patients, who rubbed it downward over their bodies.

The same acts were repeated with the infusion specific; it was then tasted by the patients and blown by the chanter, who drank all that remained.

Ashes were blown from a brush feather by the chanter and patients with the sound blu· · ·.

Incensing: 2 coals.

The following variations took place on successive nights: nights 2 and 3 (and probably 4), same as night 1, except that the second bundle application took place after the unraveler herbs had been taken out and the strings returned to the basket; night 2, before incensing, the otter collar was held so that all the fringes touched the patient's head while the whistle was blown; night 3, whistling was after incense inhaling (cp. Kluckhohn-Wyman, p. 79).

Unraveling, meaning of (E). Unraveling in the Holy Shooting chants and in the Big Star Chant represents the delivery of The Twins from danger; they were able to walk on the talking prayersticks because of the life feathers given them by Spider Woman, symbolized by the feathers of the unraveling strings.

In the War Ceremony unraveling songs are the same as those sung by Changing Woman when her sons returned safely with Big Monster's trophy; they are called 'the songs with-which-he-customarily-returned.' Unraveling also commemorates the episode of Monster Slayer's securing a horse for Sun, a war motive.

In the Hail Chant, approximately half the unravelers were assigned to Dark Thunder, half to Winter Thunder, who were at war with each other. The unravelers of the Endurance Chant represent the transformed and no longer dangerous Changing-bear-maiden. The rite refers to monsters, enemies, and other evils. Odd numbers, the use of plants, often strong-smelling, and of the bull-roarer, brushing, ashes, and blackening are exorcistic. The absence of unraveling in the Sand-painting bra ch. is further evidence of the evil-dispersing purpose.

Kluckhohn-Wyman explain unraveling: "The theory of the practice is that pain and evil influences are tied within or upon the patient's body and this ceremony unties or releases them, transferring them to the herbs that are later disposed [sic]." They say that unraveling is never practiced in the "Fighting or Angry Way [Red Inside phase] rituals"; we have seen that they were a part of the Sun's House branch Red Inside phase (Ch. 14; Reichard, Shooting Chant ms.; Big Star Chant ms.; Haile 1938b, pp. 205, 207, 239, 270–1; Wyman 1936a; Kluckhohn-Wyman, pp. 79, 80).

. . .

Vigil, The Day, The Night (bidjí) (A). The Night is called ' The Day ' at White Sands; it refers to the last day of the ceremony, particularly the last night, the vigil. In the Holy chants, there is little action, the entire night being devoted to singing, which, to judge by the interest taken in it and the vigor with which it is carried out, is of the greatest importance to the participants. The first and last song groups seem to have the same function, if not the same content, as the short singing (cp. Introduction; Kluckhohn-Wyman, p. 103; Sapir-Hoijer, p. 32).

Vigil: Blessing rite 1 (xǫ́jǫ́ˑdjí, doˑʼiˑɣáˑc). I have been present at several so-called Blessing rites, no two of which were alike. The first was sung for MC's son, a boy of about seventeen, who ʻ didn't feel very good.' The outstanding feature, the rite symbol, was a small piece of unbleached muslin, which had a black thread tied in one corner. It was laid out on a blanket and sprinkled with four pollen crosses from south to north. MC said the family would always have to keep this cloth for the boy. She had once had this sing; her cloth lay under the basket layout.

Night 1. The patient went around the fire and sat on the two central marks of the cloth during the singing.

Litany: The patient stood on the two crosses at the south; the chanter, beside him, on the two at the north; the patient held two pouches in each hand, the chanter, a pollen pouch; after the prayer, the patient motioned four times in a sunwise circuit and in front of his forehead; he breathed in from the sacks, turning toward the east and pulling the sacks in toward himself four times; pollen administration (audience participation); the patient went outside and returned.

Day 1. Bath; all members of the family washed their hair informally, not in the ceremonial hogan; the patient went through the usual bath rite.

Vigil: Blessing rite 2 was privately sung at an isolated place some forty miles from the patient's home, for a man who lives like a white man; it was said to be ʻ just for good luck.' The short singing took about an hour and a quarter. During this time a group of thirteen songs, another of ten, then one song, summarizing all the others, were sung without intermission.

After a short pause, the singing continued with short rest periods until dawn.

Vigil: Feather Chant. About 10 P.M. of night 9 Talking God and Gray God, masked, started their act inside the hogan. They had prepared mixed stew in the afternoon; now they put it in a Hopi pottery bowl. Talking God burlesqued pollen sprinkling from four directions and the center; he was followed by Gray God, pouring water with a gourd out of an old Apache pitch-coated jar, which had been covered with Douglas fir branches; a fire of sage fuel was kindled in the same silly fashion.

The gods, each holding a pair of bundle talking prayersticks, danced for a very long time. At long intervals the impersonators turned their backs to the women and lifted their masks to cool off. After the long dance, they sat down with the chorus and took off the masks, holding them in front of themselves. Dancing for long periods alternated with pauses for rest all night.

Vigil: SC. The time division was about the same for Sun's House and Prayerstick branches: The period of Sun's House branch was from about 9:30 P.M. (August 1) to 5 A.M.; that of Prayerstick branch, from 11 P.M. (September 12) to 6 A.M. Although there may be some relaxation of the vigil rules in some ceremonies at White Sands, the chanters were very strict about restricting dozing in the presence of Sun's House screen during the vigil.*

The patient, holding two bundle talking prayersticks, with which she beat time, sat at the south side of the hogan during the short singing, which lasted from 45 to 75 minutes; people

---

*This does not include the intermissions in ritual during the nights when Sun's House stands guard at the back of the hogan, but is not ' alive '—that is, it does not have the birds and snakes moving.

were enjoined against leaving the hogan during this period, though anyone might enter.

After the short singing, the patient went outside to show herself to the gods—if anyone else should go out, the deities might make a mistake and favor the wrong person.

At intervals in the long singing, the patient walked around the fire, then returned; between the short and the long singing, she sat at the patient's usual place at the west, but returned to the place at the south for the last set of songs, again beating time with the talking prayersticks; when the mixed stew was included, she even held the prayersticks while she ate. After the last song, pollen was eaten by the patient; then she followed an assistant, who carried a basket of corn meal, around the fire four times and went outside, where she breathed in the rising sun four times (cp. Kluckhohn-Wyman, pp. 103–5).

·   ·   ·

Wildrose circle: SC Sun's House branch Red Inside phase. Before the mixed stew was placed on the fire, a wildrose circle, about four feet in diameter, was buried around the fireplace; this was dug up and disposed of after the stew had been eaten.

LIST OF CONCORDANCE TOPICS

Breathing in, Con. B.
Brushing, Con. B.
Buckskin, Con. B.
Buffalo, Con. A.
Bull-roarer, Con. B, C.
Bundle contents, Con. C.
Burrowing Monster, Horned Monster, Con. A.
Bushrat, *see* Rat, Con. A.
Butterfly, Con. A.

Cactus, Con. A.
Cake, Con. B.
Cane, Con. B.
Cattail, *see* Armor, Con. B.
Center-of-the-earth, *see* Sky Pillars, Con. A.
Ceremonial approach, Con. B.
Ceremonial coup-counting, Con. B.
Ceremonial indifference, Con. B.
Ceremonial language, Con. B.
Changing Grandchild, Con. A.
Changing Woman, Con. A.
Changing-bear-maiden, Con. A.
Chant lotion, Con. B.
Chant token, *see* Bead token, Con. B.
Charcoal, *see* Soot, Con. B.
Chewing and spraying, Con. B.
Chickenhawks, *see* Hummingbirds, Con. A.
Child-of-the-water, Con. A.
Chipmunk, Con. A.
Cicada, Con. A.
Circle, Con. B.
Cliff Monster, Throwing Monster, Con. A.
Clothes, Con. B.
Clouds, Con. B.
Club, Con. B.
co, Con. A.
Coals, Con. B.
Cold, Con. A.
Collected substances, Con. B.
Collected tallows, *see* Tallows, Con. B.
Collected waters, *see* Waters, collected, Con. B.

Compulsion, Con. B.
Conveyance, *see* Lightning, Con. A; Hoops, Rainbow, Sunbeam, Con. B.
Cooking utensils, Con. B.
Corn, Con. B.
Cornbeetle, Con. A.
Corn meal, Con. B.
Corn smut, Con. B.
Corral Dance, *see* Dark-circle-of-branches, Con. B.
Cotton, Con. B.
Cotton fabric, Con. B.
Covers, Con. B.
Coyote, Con. A.
Cradleboards, Con. B.
Craving-for-meat, *see* Sleep, Con. A.
Crooked Snake, Con. A.
Cross, Con. B.
Crow, Con. A.
Crushing Mountains, *see* Crushing Rocks, Con. A.
Crushing Rocks, Crushing Mountains, Con. A.
Cup, Con. B.
Curtains, *see* Covers, Con. B.
Cutting, Con. B.
Cutting Reeds, Con. A.

Dancing, Con. B.
Danger line, Con. B.
Dark-circle-of-branches, Con. B.
Dark Wind, Con. A.
Darkness, Con. A.
Dawn, Dawn People, Con. A.
Decoy fire, Con. B.
Decoy woman, Con. B.
Decoys, Con. B.
Dedication of new bundle prayer-sticks, Con. C.
Deer and rare game, Con. B.
Deer Owner, Con. A.
Deposit of offerings, Con. C.
Desire, *see* Sleep, Con. A.
Disposal, Con. B.

Hoops and rings, Con. B.
Hoop transformation rite, Con. C.
Horned Monster, *see* Burrowing Monster, Con. A.
Horned Toad, *see* Armor, Flint, Con. B.
Horns, Con. B.
House blessing, Con. B.
Hummingbirds, Con. A.
Hunchback God, Con. A.
Hunger, Con. A.

Incense, Con. B.
Inexhaustible, Con. B.
Inner form, *see* Pollen ball, Con. B.
Insects, Con. A.
Intertwining trees, *see* Ambush, Con. B.
Invocatory offerings, Con. C.

Jumping, jumping over, Con. B.

Kicking Monster, Con. A.
Kneading, *see* Mush, Pollen ball, Pressing, Con. B.
Knots, Con. B.

Left-handed Thunder, *see* Thunder, Con. A.
Left-handed Wind, *see* Thunder, Wind, Con. A.
Lifting with bundle properties, Con. B.
Lightning, *see* Big God, Big-snakeman, Thunder, Con. A.
Little Wind, *see* Wind's Child, Con. A.
Long Frogs, Con. A.
Lotion, Con. B.
Louse, Con. A.
Lower worlds, Con. B.

Male God, Con. A.
Massage, *see* Pollen ball, Pressing, Con. B.
Master symbol, *see* Ch. 18.
Meadowlark, Con. A.
Measuring Worm, Con. A.

Medicine sprinkling, Con. B.
Mentor, *see* Ch. 5.
Messenger, *see* Ch. 5.
Mistakes, Con. B.
Mixed stew, Con. C.
Modeling, *see* Pressing, Con. B.
Monster Slayer, Con. A.
Moon, Con. A.
Moth, *see* Butterfly, Con. A.
Mountain Sheep, *see* Hunchback God, Con. A.
Mountains, Con. A.
Mourning Dove, Con. A.
Mush, Con. B.

Names, Con. B.
Needle Cactus, *see* Cactus, Tearing Cactus, Con. A.
Never-ending-snake, Con. A.
No sleep, *see* Vigil, Con. C.

Offering circuit, *see* Acceptance of offering, Con. B.
Offerings, *see* Ch. 18.
Old Age, Con. A.
One-follows-the-other, Con. A.
One-who-customarily-sees-the-fish, Con. A.
One-who-grabs-breasts, *see* be'γotcidí, Con. A.
Overdoing, Con. B.
Overshooting rite, Con. C.
Owls, Con. A.

Painting with white clay, *see* White clay, Con. B.
Paralysis of hero, *see* Ambush, Con. B.
Participation, Con. B.
Passes, Con. B.
Peace, Con. B.
Perfect cornear, Con. B.
Pine, single-budded, *see* Overshooting rite: SCE, Con. C.
Pistons, *see* Ch. 4; Sun, Con. A.
Place-of-emergence, *see* Sky Pillars, Con. A.

Plant garment, Con. C.
Plants, collection of, Con. C.
Pocket Gopher, Con. A.
Pokers, Con. B.
Pollen, Con. B.
Pollen ball, Con. B.
Pollen Boy, Con. A.
Pollen paintings, Con. C.
Pollen sprinkling, see Application of pollen, Pollen, Con. B.
Pot Drum, see Drum, Con. B.
Poverty, Con. A.
Prayer on buckskin, Con. C.
Prayer to Young Pinyon, Con. C.
Prayersticks, Con. C.
Pressing, Con. B.
Pressing to heart, see Acceptance of offering, Con. B.
Protective line, see Danger line, Con. B.
Punishment, Con. B.

Queue, Con. B.

Racer, see Arrowsnake, Con. B.
Racing, Con. B.
Racing Gods, Con. A.
Rain Ceremony, Con. C.
Rainbow, Con. B.
Rainboy, Con. A.
Rare game, see Deer and rare game, Con. B.
Rat, Bushrat, Woodrat, Con. A.
Rattle, see Gourd rattles, Con. B; Bundle contents, Con. C.
Rawhide, see Armor, Con. B.
Reared-in-the-earth, Con. A.
Reared-in-the-mountain, Con. A.
Red God, Con. A.
Red headdress, see Sunglow, Con. B; Bundle contents, Con. C.
Red ocher, Con. B.
Reddening, Con. B.
Refusal, Con. B.
Restoration, Con. C.
Restriction, Con. B.

Restriction on looking, Con. B.
Restrictions on patient of Shooting Chant, Con. B.
Rings, see Hoops and rings, Con. B.
Rite for releasing sheep from lightning contamination, Con. C.
Rite for removing contamination of the dead, Con. C.
Rite to control snow, Con. C.
Rite to undo harm caused by camping on trail to old deer impound, Con. C.
Rites, combined, Con. C.
Roadrunner, Con. A.
Rock Swallows, Con. A.
Rockpiles, Con. B.
Rocks, Con. B.
Rolling Rock, see Traveling Rock, Con. A.
Rolling Stone, see Traveling Rock, Con. A.
Round Darkness, Con. A.
Round Wind, Con. A.
Rubbing, Con. B.

sa'ą na·γái, see Ch. 3, "Destiny."
Sacred water, see Waters, collected, Con. B.
Safety zone, see Circle, Danger line, Hoops and rings, Con. B.
Saliva, see Spitting, Con. B.
Salt, Con. B.
Salt Woman, Con. A.
Sandpainting, Con. C.
Sandpainting setout mound, Con. C.
Scalp, Con. B.
Scavenger, Con. A.
Seething Sands, see Slipping Sands, Con. A.
Sex symbolism, Con. B.
Shaping, see Pressing, Con. B.
Shiny Wind, see Wind, Con. A.
Shock, see Restoration, Con. C.
Shock rite, Con. C.
Shooting God, Con. A.
Shooting Star, Con. A.
Short singing, Con. C.

Unconcern, *see* Ceremonial indifference, Con. B.
Unraveling, Con. C.
Unseasoned mush, *see* Mush, Con. B.
Unwounded buckskin, Con. B.

Vigil, The Day, The Night, Con. C.
Visionary, Con. A.
Vital parts, Con. B.
Vulnerable points, *see* Vital parts, Con. B.

Want, *see* Sleep, Con. A.
Warning prayerstick, Con. B.
Water Horse, Con. A.
Water Monster, Con. A.
Water Sprinkler, Con. A.
Water sprinkling, *see* Water Sprinkler, Con. A.
Water throwing, Con. B.
Water Woman, Con. A.
Water's Child, Con. A.
Waters, collected, Con. B.
Were-coyote, *see* Hoop transformation rite, Con. C.
Whipping, Con. B.
Whipping God, *see* Red God, Con. A.
Whirling log, *see* Swastika, Con. B.
Whirlwind, Con. A.
Whistling God, Con. A.
White Body, *see* Talking God, Con. A.
White clay, Con. B.
White Goose, Con. A.

Whitening, *see* White clay, Con. B.
Whiteshell Boy, *see* Turquoise Boy, Con. A.
Whiteshell Woman, Con. A.
Wildrose circle, Con. C.
Wind, Con. A.
Wind's Child, Con. A.
Winter Thunder, Con. A.
Witch objects, Con. B.
Withholding, Con. B.
Wolf, Con. A.
Wood samples, Con. B.
Woodbeetle, Con. A.
Woodpecker, Con. A.
Woodrat, *see* Rat, Con. A.
World Pillars, *see* Sky Pillars, Con. A.
Wristlets, *see* Bundle contents, Con. C.

xa·ctc'é·"óγan, Con. A.
xa·ctc'é·dó·dí, Con. A.
xa·dactcici·, Con. A.

Yellow bowl, *see* Inexhaustible, Mush, Con. B.
Yellow Thunder, *see* Thunder, Con. A.
Yellow Wind, *see* Wind, Con. A.
Yellow-evening-light, Con. A.
Yucca, Con. B.

Zigzag lightning, *see* Thunder, Con. A.
Zone of protection, *see* Danger line, Con. B.

743

ABBREVIATIONS

The following is a key to the abbreviations in the schematic analysis in the text:

ab	abalone.	FW	Flintway (Flint
b	black (dark).		Chant).
BeC	Bead Chant.	gr	gray.
BG	Black God.	HC	Hail Chant.
br	brown.	HCWC	Wheelwright 1946
BS	Big Star Chant.		(*Hail Chant and*
Bush Coll.	Bush Collection,		*Water Chant*).
	Columbia	j	jet.
	University.	KW	Kluckhohn-
BW	Black Wind.		Wyman.
cen	center.	Leg	Matthews 1897
ChGr	Changing Grand-		(*Navaho Legends*).
	child.	m	male.
ChW	Child-of-the-	MC	Mountain Chant.
	water.	MM	Reichard 1939
Coy	Coyote.		(*Navaho Medicine*
e	east.		*Man*).
eve	Yellow-evening-	MS	Monster Slayer.
	light.	mt	mountain.
f	female.	MW	Male Wind
fl	flash lightning.		Chant.
FrM	Fringed Mouth	n	north.
	God.	NC	Night Chant.

ne	northeast.	se	southeast.
NR	Newcomb-Reich-	ser	serrated.
	ard (*Sandpaint-*	spar	sparkling, spar-
	ings of the Navajo		kling rock.
	Shooting Chant).	sr	sunglow.
nw	northwest.	str	striped.
NWC	Navaho Wind	sw	southwest.
	Chant.	t	turquoise.
P	pink.	TG	Talking God.
r	red.	tw	twinkling.
rb	rainbow.	u	blue.
re	redstone.	var	variegated.
RE	Reared-in-the-	w	white
	earth.	we	west
rst	rainstreamer.	WC	Wind Chant.
s	south.	wh	whiteshell.
sb	sunbeam.	WSp	Water Sprinkler.
SC	Male Shooting	y	yellow.
	Chant Holy.	YW	Yellow Wind.
SCE	Male Shooting	X	xa·ctčé·'óɣan.
	Chant Evil.	z	zigzag lightning.

BIBLIOGRAPHY

BIBLIOGRAPHY

Two spellings are customary, the Spanish ' Navajo ' and the English ' Navaho.' Since the literature is extensive and diverse and the spelling largely a matter of taste, there is no way to make the spelling uniform.

Adahooniligii	*Adahooniligii, The Navaho Language Monthly.* Window Rock, Arizona.
Adair, John	*The Navajo and Pueblo Silversmiths.* University of Oklahoma Press. Norman, Oklahoma. 1945.
Bitanny	Bitanny, Adolph Dodge. *Medical Dictionary, English to Navajo.* Medical Division, Navajo Service. Window Rock, Arizona (mimeographed).
Cannon	Cannon, Walter B. " 'Voodoo' Death." *American Anthropologist,* Vol. 44, pp. 169–81. 1942.
Curtis	Curtis, E. S. *The North American Indian.* Cambridge University Press. 1907.
Dorsey-Kroeber	Dorsey, G. A. and Kroeber, A. L. *Traditions of the Arapaho. Field Museum Anthropological Series* 81. 1903.
Dyk	Dyk, Walter. *Son of Old Man Hat.* Harcourt, Brace and Co. New York. 1938.

Franciscan Fathers 1910   Franciscan Fathers. *An Ethnologic Dictionary of the Navaho Language.* St. Michaels, Arizona. 1910, reprinted 1929.

Franciscan Fathers 1912   Franciscan Fathers. *A Vocabulary of the Navaho Language.* St. Michaels, Arizona. 1912.

Goddard   Goddard, P. E. *Navajo Texts. Anthropological Papers of the American Museum of Natural History,* Vol. 34. 1933.

Haile 1934   Haile, Father Berard. "Religious Concepts of the Navaho Indians." *Proceedings of the Tenth Annual Meeting of the American Catholic Philosophical Association.* The Catholic University of America, Washington, D.C. 1934.

Haile 1937   Haile, Father Berard. *Some Cultural Aspects of the Navajo Hogan.* 1937 (mimeographed).

Haile 1938a   Haile, Father Berard. "Navaho Chantways and Ceremonials." *American Anthropologist,* Vol. 40, pp. 639–52. 1938.

Haile 1938b   Haile, Father Berard. *Origin Legend of the Navaho Enemy Way. Yale University Publications in Anthropology,* No. 17. 1938.

Haile 1943a   Haile, Father Berard. *Origin Legend of the Navaho Flintway. University of Chicago Publications in Anthropology.* 1943.

Haile 1943b — Haile, Father Berard. "Reichard's Chant of Waning Endurance." *American Anthropologist*, Vol. 45, pp. 306–11. 1943.

Haile 1947a — Haile, Father Berard. *Navaho Sacrificial Figurines.* The University of Chicago Press. 1947. (Published too late for its material to be incorporated in this book.)

Haile 1947b — Haile, Father Berard. *Prayer Stick Cutting.* The University of Chicago Press. 1947. (Published too late for its material to be incorporated in this book.)

Hill 1935a — Hill, W. W. "The Hand Trembling Ceremony of the Navaho." *El Palacio*, Vol. 38, pp. 65–8. 1935.

Hill 1935b — Hill, W. W. "The Status of the Hermaphrodite and Transvestite in Navaho Culture." *American Anthropologist*, Vol. 37, pp. 273–9. 1935.

Hill 1936 — Hill, W. W. *Navaho Warfare. Yale University Publications in Anthropology*, No. 5. 1936.

Hill 1938 — Hill, W. W. *The Agricultural and Hunting Methods of the Navaho Indians. Yale University Publications in Anthropology*, No. 18. 1938.

Hill 1940a — Hill, W. W. "Navajo Salt Gathering." *University of New Mexico Bulletin* 349, pp. 1–25. 1940.

Hill 1940b

Hill, W. W. "Some Navaho Culture Changes During Two Centuries." *Smithsonian Miscellaneous Collections* 100, pp. 395–415. 1940.

Hill 1943

Hill, W. W. *Navaho Humor. General Series in Anthropology* 9. 1943.

Hill-Hill

Hill, W. W., and Hill, Dorothy W. "Navaho Coyote Tales and Their Position in the Southern Athabaskan Group." *Journal of American Folk-Lore*, Vol. 58, pp. 317–43. 1945.

Huckel ms.

Huckel Collection, manuscript describing sandpaintings by Miguelito (RP).

Kluckhohn 1944

Kluckhohn, Clyde. *Navaho Witchcraft. Papers of the Peabody Museum*, Harvard University, Vol. 22. 1944.

Kluckhohn 1945

Kluckhohn, Clyde. "A Navaho Personal Document with a Brief Paretian Analysis." *Southwestern Journal of Anthropology*, Vol. 1, pp. 260–83. 1945.

Kluckhohn-Leighton

Kluckhohn, Clyde, and Leighton, Dorothea. *The Navaho.* Harvard University Press, 1946.

Kluckhohn-Spencer

Kluckhohn, Clyde and Spencer, Katherine. *A Bibliography of the Navaho Indians.* J. J. Augustin, New York. 1940.

Kluckhohn-Wyman

Kluckhohn, Clyde, and Wyman, Leland C. *An Introduction to Nav-*

aho Chant Practice. Memoirs of the American Anthropological Association 53. 1940.

Leighton-Kluckhohn — Leighton, Dorothea and Kluckhohn, Clyde. *Children of the People.* Harvard University Press. 1947.

Lincoln — Lincoln, Jackson S. *The Dream in Primitive Cultures.* London. 1935.

Matthews 1883 — Matthews, Washington. "The Origin of the Utes. A Navaho Myth." *American Antiquarian*, Vol. 7, pp. 271-4. 1883.

Matthews 1886 — Matthews, Washington. "Navajo Names for Plants." *American Naturalist*, Vol. 20, pp. 767-77. 1886.

Matthews 1887 — Matthews, Washington. "The Mountain Chant." *Annual Report of the Bureau of American Ethnology*, Vol. 5, pp. 385-467. 1887.

Matthews 1888 — Matthews, Washington. "The Prayer of a Navajo Shaman." *American Anthropologist*, o.s., Vol. 1, pp. 149-70. 1888.

Matthews 1889 — Matthews, Washington. "Navajo Gambling Songs." *American Anthropologist*, o.s., Vol. 2, pp. 1-19. 1889.

Matthews 1892 — Matthews, Washington. "A Study in Butts and Tips." *American Anthropologist*, o.s., Vol. 5, pp. 345-50. 1892.

Matthews 1894a   Matthews, Washington. "Songs of Sequence of the Navajos." *Journal of American Folk-Lore*, Vol. 7, pp. 185–94. 1894.

Matthews 1894b   Matthews, Washington. "The Basket Drum." *American Anthropologist*, o.s., Vol. 7, pp. 202–8. 1894.

Matthews 1897   Matthews, Washington. *Navaho Legends. Memoirs of the American Folk-Lore Society*, Vol. 5. 1897.

Matthews 1899   Matthews, Washington. "The Study of Ethics among the Lower Races." *Journal of American Folk-Lore*, Vol. 12, pp. 1–9. 1899.

Matthews 1901   Matthews, Washington. "The Treatment of Ailing Gods." *Journal of American Folk-Lore*, Vol. 14, pp. 20–3. 1901.

Matthews 1902   Matthews, Washington. *The Night Chant. Memoirs of the American Museum of Natural History*, Vol. 6, 1902.

Matthews 1907   Matthews, Washington. "Navaho Myths, Prayers and Songs." *University of California Publications in American Archaeology and Ethnology*, Vol. 5, pp. 21–63. 1907.

Mindeleff   Mindeleff, Cosmos. "Navaho Houses." *Annual Report of the Bureau of American Ethnology*, Vol. 17, pp. 469–517. 1902.

Morgan 1931   Morgan, William. "Navaho Treatment of Sickness: Diagnosticians." *American Anthropologist*, Vol. 33, pp. 390–402. 1931.

Morgan 1932   Morgan, William. "Navaho Dreams." *American Anthropologist*, Vol. 34, pp. 390–405. 1932.

Morgan 1936   Morgan, William. *Human Wolves Among the Navaho. Yale University Publications in Anthropology* 11. 1936.

Mulholland   Mulholland, John. *Quicker than the Eye*. The Bobbs-Merrill Co. Indianapolis. 1932.

Newcomb 1938   Newcomb, Franc J. "The Navajo Listening Rite." *El Palacio* 45, pp. 46–9. 1938.

Newcomb 1940a   Newcomb, Franc J. *Navajo Omens and Taboos*. The Rydal Press. Santa Fe. 1940.

Newcomb 1940b   Newcomb, Franc J. "Origin Legend of the Navajo Eagle Chant." *Journal of American Folk-Lore*, Vol. 53, pp. 50–77. 1940.

Newcomb-Reichard   Newcomb, Franc J., and Reichard, Gladys A. *Sandpaintings of the Navajo Shooting Chant*. J. J. Augustin. New York. 1937.

Oakes-Campbell   Oakes, Maud, and Campbell, Joseph. *Where the Two Came to Their Father*. The Bollingen Series I. Pantheon Books Inc. New York. 1943.

Opler	Opler, Morris E. *Myths and Tales of the Jicarilla Apache Indians. Memoirs of the American Folk-Lore Society*, Vol. 31. New York. 1938.
Opler-Hoijer	Opler, Morris E., and Hoijer, Harry. "The Raid and Warpath Language of the Chiricahua Apache." *American Anthropologist*, Vol. 42, pp. 617–34. 1940.
Parsons 1923	Parsons, Elsie Clews. "Navaho Folktales." *Journal of American Folk-Lore*, Vol. 36, pp. 368–75. 1923.
Parsons 1939	Parsons, Elsie Clews. *Pueblo Indian Religion*. University of Chicago Press. 1939.
Reichard 1928	Reichard, Gladys A. *Social Life of the Navajo Indians. Columbia University Contributions to Anthropology*, Vol. 7. 1928.
Reichard 1934	Reichard, Gladys A. *Spider Woman*. Macmillan Co. New York. 1934.
Reichard 1936	Reichard, Gladys A. *Navajo Shepherd and Weaver*. J. J. Augustin. New York. 1936.
Reichard 1938	Reichard, Gladys A. *Dezba, Woman of the Desert*. J. J. Augustin. New York. 1938.
Reichard 1939	Reichard, Gladys A. *Navajo Medicine Man*. J. J. Augustin. New York. 1939.

Reichard 1942   Reichard, Gladys A. "Two Navaho Chant Words." *American Anthropologist*, Vol. 44, pp. 421–4. 1942.

Reichard 1943   Reichard, Gladys A. "Human Nature as Conceived by the Navajo Indians." *The Review of Religion*, Vol. 7, pp. 354–60. 1943.

Reichard 1944a   Reichard, Gladys A. "Individualism and Mythological Style." *Journal of American Folk-Lore*, Vol. 57, pp. 16–25. 1944.

Reichard 1944b   Reichard, Gladys A. *Prayer: The Compulsive Word. Monographs of the American Ethnological Society*, Vol. 7. 1944.

Reichard 1944c   Reichard, Gladys A. Review of Father Berard Haile, *Origin Legend of the Navaho Flintway. The Review of Religion*, Vol. 8, pp. 384–6. 1944.

Reichard 1944d   Reichard, Gladys A. *The Story of the Navajo Hail Chant*. Privately lithoprinted by the author, Barnard College. New York. 1944.

Reichard 1945a   Reichard, Gladys A. "Distinctive Features of Navaho Religion." *Southwestern Journal of Anthropology*, Vol. 1, pp. 199–220. 1945.

Reichard 1945b   Reichard, Gladys A. "Linguistic Diversity Among the Navaho Indians." *International Journal of American Linguistics*, Vol. 11, pp. 156–68. 1945.

Reichard 1948 — Reichard, Gladys A. "Significance of Aspiration in Navaho." *International Journal of American Linguistics*, Vol. 14, pp. 15–9. 1948.

Reichard — Reichard, Gladys A. *The Story of the Big Star Chant*. Text manuscript.

Reichard — Reichard, Gladys A. *The Story of the Male Shooting Chant Evil*. Text manuscript.

Reichard — Reichard, Gladys A. *The Story of the Male Shooting Chant Holy, by Gray Eyes*. Text manuscript.

Reichard — Reichard, Gladys A. *The Story of the Endurance Chant*. Text manuscript.

Sapir-Hoijer — Sapir, Edward, and Hoijer, Harry. *Navaho Texts*. Linguistic Society of America. Iowa City. 1942.

Simmons — Simmons, Leo. *Sun Chief, The Autobiography of a Hopi Indian*. Yale University Press. 1942.

Stephen 1889 — Stephen, Alexander M. "The Navajo Shoemaker." *Proceedings of the U. S. National Museum for 1888*, Vol. 11, pp. 131–6. 1889.

Stephen 1893 — Stephen, Alexander M. "The Navajo." *American Anthropologist*, o.s., Vol. 6, pp. 345–62. 1893.

Stephen 1930 — Stephen, Alexander M. "Navajo Origin Legend." *Journal of American Folk-Lore*, Vol. 43, pp. 88–104. 1930.

Stephen 1936	Stephen, A. M. *Hopi Journal of Alexander M. Stephen.* Edited by E. C. Parsons. *Columbia University Contributions to Anthropology,* Vol. 23. 1936.
Stephen ms.	Stephen, Alexander M. Manuscript.
Stevenson	Stevenson, James. "Ceremonial of Hasjelti Dailjis." *Annual Report of the Bureau of American Ethnology,* Vol. 8, pp. 229–85. 1886.
Taverner	Taverner, P. A. *Birds of Western Canada. Canada Department of Mines, Museum Bulletin* No. 41, Biological Series, No. 10. 1926.
Tozzer 1902	Tozzer, Alfred M. "A Navajo Sand Picture of the Rain Gods and its Attendant Ceremony." *Proceedings of the International Congress of Americanists,* 13th Session, New York, pp. 147–56. 1902.
Tozzer 1908	Tozzer, Alfred M. "A Note on Star-Lore among the Navajos." *Journal of American Folk-Lore,* Vol. 21, pp. 28–32. 1908.
Tozzer 1909	Tozzer, Alfred M. "Notes on Religious Ceremonials of the Navaho." *Peabody Anniversary Volume,* pp. 299–343. 1909.
Tschopik	Tschopik, Harry, Jr. "Taboo as a Possible Factor Involved in the Obsolescence of Navaho Pottery and Basketry." *American Anthropologist,* Vol. 40, pp. 257–62. 1938.

Wheelwright 1942   Wheelright, Mary C. *Navajo Creation Myth.* Museum of Navajo Ceremonial Art. Santa Fe, New Mexico. 1942.

Wheelwright 1946   Wheelwright, Mary C. *Hail Chant and Water Chant.* Museum of Navajo Ceremonial Art. Santa Fe, New Mexico. 1946.

Wyman 1936a   Wyman, Leland C. "The Female Shooting Chant: A Minor Navaho Ceremony." *American Anthropologist,* Vol. 38, pp. 634–53. 1936.

Wyman 1936b   Wyman, Leland C. "Navaho Diagnosticians." *American Anthropologist,* Vol. 38, pp. 236–46. 1936.

Wyman 1936c   Wyman, Leland C. "Origin Legend of Navaho Divinatory Rites." *Journal of American Folk-Lore,* Vol. 49, pp. 134–42. 1936.

Wyman 1939   Wyman, Leland C. Review of Walter Dyk, *Son of Old Man Hat. American Anthropologist,* Vol. 41, pp. 309–10. 1939.

Wyman 1947   Wyman, Leland C. Review of Mary C. Wheelwright, *Hail Chant and Water Chant. American Anthropologist,* Vol. 49, pp. 633–7. 1947.

Wyman-Bailey 1943a   Wyman, Leland C., and Bailey, Flora L. "Navaho Girl's Puberty Rite." *New Mexico Anthropologist,* Vol. 6, pp. 2–12. 1943.

Wyman-Bailey 1943b   Wyman, Leland C., and Bailey, Flora L. "Navaho Upward-Reaching Way." *University of New Mexico Bulletin* 389, pp. 1–47. 1943.

Wyman-Bailey 1945   Wyman, Leland C., and Bailey, Flora L. "Idea and Action Patterns in Navaho Flintway." *Southwestern Journal of Anthropology*, Vol. 1, pp. 356–77. 1945.

Wyman-Bailey 1946a   Wyman, Leland C., and Bailey, Flora L. "Navaho Striped Windway, An Injury-Way Chant." *Southwestern Journal of Anthropology*, Vol. 2, pp. 213–38. 1946.

Wyman-Bailey 1946b   Wyman, Leland C., and Bailey, Flora L. "Two Examples of Navaho Physiotherapy." *American Anthropologist*, Vol. 46, pp. 329–37. 1946.

Wyman-Harris   Wyman, Leland C., and Harris, S. K. "Navajo Indian Medical Ethnobotany." *University of New Mexico Bulletin* 366. 1941.

Wyman-Hill-Ósanai   Wyman, L. C., Hill, W. W., and Ósanai, I. *Navajo Eschatology. University of New Mexico Bulletin* 377. 1942.

Wyman-Kluckhohn   Wyman, Leland C., and Kluckhohn, Clyde. *Navaho Classification of Their Song Ceremonials. Memoirs of the American Anthropological Association* 50. 1938.

Young-Morgan   Young, Robert W., and Morgan, William. *The Navaho Language.* Education Division, U. S. Indian Service. Phoenix, Arizona. 1943.

INDEX

A

Abalone, 14, 194, 201, 204, 208, 209, 210, 211, 255, 312, 428, 544, 634
Abalone Woman, 194, 404
Ability, 34
Abiquiu Peak, 452
Absorption, 113, 584, 696
Acceptance of offering, 264, 316, 506, 529
Accessory rites, 127, 338, 344, 672
Accident, 11, 84
Accomplishment, xlii, 39
According-to-beauty, 382
According-to-beauty-girl, 273
According-to-perfection, 47
Accumulation, 305
Achievement, 45
Acute indigestion, 98
Adjustment, 34
Adolescence, 37, 38, 272, 322; see also Girl's Adolescence Ceremony
Adultery, 106, 137, 138, 139, 275
Afterbirth, 461, 483
Afterlife, 41, 42, 43, 45
After-image, 100

Agate, 33, 211, 212, 255, 392, 452, 489, 525, 556, 560, 562, 583; see also Bead token, Pollen ball
Agate boys, 230
Age, xlv, 40; see also Old age
Agriculture, 68, 78, 148, 322, 431, 489, 570; see also Harvest, Planting
'álí'l, 507
Altar, xxxv, 334
Alternation, 180, 181, 223, 235, 237, 293, 299, 629, 648
Ambush, 443, 508
Analogy, 7, 11, 13, 91, 121
Anatomy, 32
Ancestors, 16
Ancient pueblo people, 15, 159
Anger, 79, 195, 401, 422, 468, 474, 532
Antagonism, 40
Animals, 11, 23, 24, 48, 49, 66, 76, 77, 142, 143, 151, 185, 200, 205, 251, 257, 265, 269, 343, 387, 388, 413, 460, 486, 701, 703
Ant, 326, 435, 454, 498, 568, 571, 594
Ant Chant, Red, 122
Ant People, 109

BIOGRAPHICAL NOTE

Gladys Armanda Reichard was born in 1893 in Bangor, Pennsylvania, the daughter of a Quaker physician. She was graduated from Swarthmore College and in 1925 earned the Ph.D. at Columbia University, where she was a student of Franz Boas. In 1926–27, she engaged in postdoctoral study at the University of Hamburg (Germany). From 1923, Dr. Reichard was a member of the faculty of Barnard College (Columbia); she became a full professor in 1951. The Morrison Prize in natural sciences was awarded her in 1932 by the New York Academy of Sciences for her studies in Melanesian art, begun at Hamburg, and the Chicago Folklore Prize in 1948 for her work on Coeur d'Alene Indian mythology. Her publications included *Melanesian Design* (2 vols., 1933), *Spider Woman: A Story of Navajo Weavers and Chanters* (1934), *Sandpaintings of the Navajo Shooting Chant* (with Franc J. Newcomb, 1937), *Dezba, Woman of the Desert* (1938), *Navajo Medicine Man* (1939), *Prayer: The Compulsive Word* (1944), *An Analysis of Coeur d'Alene Indian Myths* (1947), and *Navaho Grammar* (1951), as well as numerous articles in learned journals.

During more than twenty-five years, Gladys Reichard spent frequent long periods of research and study among the Navaho Indians on their reservation in Arizona. She elected to work in the more difficult and remote parts of the Navaho country, learning the complex language fluently and living in the Indian homes and encampments. She mastered the art of Navaho weaving during four summers spent living as "daughter" of an Indian family, and she participated as observer, patient, and finally assistant in many curing ceremonies.

Gladys Reichard died July 25, 1955, at Flagstaff, where she was engaged in research at the Museum of Northern Arizona.

MYTHOS

The Princeton/Bollingen Series in World Mythology

Joseph Campbell
THE HERO WITH A THOUSAND FACES

Henry Corbin
AVICENNA AND THE VISIONARY RECITAL

Joseph Henderson and Maud Oakes
THE WISDOM OF THE SERPENT

Erich Neumann
AMOR AND PSYCHE

Otto Rank, Lord Raglan, Alan Dundes
IN QUEST OF THE HERO

Gladys Reichard
NAVAHO RELIGION